Second Edition

Philosophical Reflections on Mind, Matter and God

Arranged by J. Christopher Maloney

Excerpts taken from
From Plato to Derrida, Third Edition
by Forrest E. Baird and Walter Kaufmann

PEARSON

Custom
Publishing

Cover Art: *Wander Above the Sea of Clouds,* by Caspar David Friedrich, 1818, courtesy of the Bridgeman Art Library.

Excerpts taken from:

From Plato to Derrida, Third Edition
by Forrest E. Baird and Walter Kaufmann
Copyright © 2000, 1997 by Prentice-Hall, Inc.
A Pearson Education Company
Upper Saddle River, New Jersey 07458

This special edition published in cooperation with Pearson Custom Publishing.

Printed in the United States of America

10 9 8 7 6 5

Please visit our web site at *www.pearsoncustom.com*

ISBN 0–536–74620-6

BA 998011

JW/KG

PEARSON CUSTOM PUBLISHING
75 Arlington Street, Suite 300, Boston, MA 02116
A Pearson Education Company

✦ Contents ✦

Preface

There is no better introduction to philosophy than to read some of the great philosophers. But few books are more difficult to read than Aristotle's *Metaphysics* or Spinoza's *Ethics*. Even works that are less puzzling are sometimes like snippets of a conversation that you overhear on entering a room: What is said is clear, only you cannot be sure you have got the point because you do not know just what has gone before. A slight point may be crucial to refute some earlier suggestion, and a seemingly pointless remark may contain a barbed allusion. As a result of this difficulty, some students of philosophy cry out for a simple summary of the "central doctrines" of the great philosophers. Yet carving up great books to excerpt essential doctrines is one of the greatest sins against the spirit of philosophy. If the reading of a whole Platonic dialogue leaves one more doubtful and less sure of oneself than the perusal of a brief summary, so much the better. It is part of the point of philosophy to make us a little less sure about things. After all, Socrates himself insisted that what distinguished him from other persons was not that he knew all, or even most, answers but rather that he realized his ignorance.

Still, one need not despair of joining this ongoing conversation. In the first place, you can get in near the beginning of this conversation by starting with Plato and moving on from there. Given that they are over two thousand years old, his early dialogues are surprisingly easy to follow. The later Platonic dialogues, Aristotle, and much which follows will be more difficult, but by that point you will have some idea of what the conversation is about.

Secondly, the structure of this book is designed to make this conversation accessible. There are section introductions and introductions to the individual philosophers. These latter introductions are divided into three sections: (1) biographical (a glimpse of the life), (2) philosophical (a resume of the philosopher's thought), and

(3) bibliographical (suggestions for further reading). To give a sense of the development of ideas, there are short representative passages from some of the less important, but transitional, thinkers. To make all the works more readable, most footnotes treating textual matters (variant readings, etc.) have been omitted and all Greek words have been transliterated and put in angle brackets. My goal throughout this volume is to be unobtrusive and allow you to hear, and perhaps join in, the ongoing conversation that is Western philosophy.

This third edition now includes eight selections from twentieth-century thinkers as well as an introduction to Continental and Anglo-American philosophy. I have also added brief selections from the Renaissance thinker Pico della Mirandola and the early modern Blaise Pascal. To make room for these additional texts, I have made a number of small changes. John Scotus Eriugena, John Duns Scotus, Nicholas Cusanas, and Francis Bacon have been deleted. The partial selections from Plato's *Parmenides,* Leibniz's *Theodicy,* Hegel's *Reason in History,* and Mill's *On Liberty* have also been cut as have small portions of a number of other texts. In several cases, I have substituted texts that seem more representative of the thinker such as more material from the *Summa Theologica* in place of Thomas Aquinas's *The Principles of Nature* and additional sections of Nietzsche's *The Twilight of the Idols* in place of the previous selection from *The Genealogy of Morals.* Throughout the editing of this edition, I have tried to follow the same three principles I used in the individual volumes of the *Philosophic Classics* series: (1) to use complete works or, where more appropriate, complete sections of works (2) in clear translations (3) of texts central to the thinker's philosophy or widely accepted as part of the "canon." Those who use this volume in a one-term introduction to philosophy, history of philosophy, or history of intellectual thought course will find more material here than can easily fit a normal semester. But this embarrassment of riches gives teachers some choice and, for those who offer the same course year after year, an opportunity to change the menu.

* * *

I would like to thank the many people who assisted me in this volume, including the library staff of Whitworth College, especially Hans Bynagle, Gail Fielding, and Jeanette Langston; my colleagues, F. Dale Bruner, who made helpful suggestions on all the introductions, Barbara Filo, who helped make selections for the artwork, and Corliss Slack and John Yoder, who provided historical context; Stephen Davis, Claremont McKenna College; Jerry H. Gill, The College of St. Rose; Rex Hollowell, Spokane Falls Community College; Arthur F. Holmes, Wheaton College; Stanley Obitts, Westmont College; Wayne Pomerleau, Gonzaga University; Timothy A. Robinson, The College of St. Benedict; Glenn Ross, Franklin & Marshall College; and Charles Young, The Claremont Graduate School, who each read some of the introductions and gave helpful advice; Edward Beach, University of Wisconsin, Eau Claire, and John Justice, Randolph-Macon Women's College who graciously called my attention to errors in the previous edition; my secretary, Michelle Seefried; my production editor, Bruce Hobart; my acquisitions editor, Karita France of Prentice Hall; and my former acquisitions editors, Angela Stone and Ted Bolen. I would also like to acknowledge the following reviewers: James W. Allard, Montana State University; David Apolloni, Augsburg College; Robert C. Bennett, El Centro College; Herbert L. Carson, Ferris State University; Mary T. Clark, Manhattanville College; Sandra S. Edwards, University of Arkansas; Steven M. Emmanuel, Virginia Wesleyan College; David Griesedieck, University of Missouri, Saint Louis; Helen S. Lang, Trinity College;

Scott MacDonald, University of Iowa; Angel Medina, Georgia State University; Eric Palmer, Allegheny College; Katherine Rogers, University of Delaware; Gregory Schultz, Wisconsin Lutheran College; Stephen Scott, Eastern Washington University; Daniel C. Shartin, Worcester State College; Walter G. Scott, Oklahoma State University; Howard N. Tuttle, University of New Mexico; Richard J. Van Iten, Iowa State University; Donald Phillip Verene, Emory University; Sarah Worth, Allegheny College; and Wilhelm S. Wurzer, Duquesne University.

I am especially thankful to my wife, Joy Lynn Fulton Baird, and to our children, Whitney Jaye, Sydney Tev, and Soren David, who have supported me throughout this enterprise.

Finally, I would like to thank my dear friend and mentor, Jack B. Rogers, to whom this volume is dedicated.

Forrest E. Baird
Professor of Philosophy
Whitworth College
Spokane, WA 99251
fbaird@whitworth.edu

Philosophers in This Volume

400 B.C.	200 B.C.	0	A.D. 200	400	600	800	1000

Plato
    Aristotle
    Epicurus
        Epictetus
          Plotinus
            Augustine
              Boethius
                Anselm

Other Important Figures

Socrates
  Pyrrho   Sextus Empiricus
  Alexander the Great   Porphyry
  Zeno of Citium   Pseudo-Dionysius Areopagite
  Cleanthes   Mohammed
    Julius Caesar   Charlemagne
    Lucretius   Avicenna
      Philo of Alexandria
      Jesus
      Paul
        Justin Martyr
        Marcus Aurelius
          Ptolemy (astronomer)
          Clement of Alexandria
          Tertullian
          Origen

A Sampling of Major Events

Death of Socrates
    Punic Wars and rise of Roman Empire
      Wall of China built
          Jerusalem Temple destroyed
         Furthest extent of the Roman Empire
              Council of Nicea
              Roman Empire divided
              Fall of Rome
                 Schools of philosophy in Athens
                 closed by Justinian
                     Muslim conquest
                     of Northern Africa
                     and Spain
                       Peak of Mayan
                       civilization in Central
                       America

400 B.C.	200 B.C.	0	A.D. 200	400	600	800	1000

1200	1400	1600	1800	2000

Moses Maimonides
Thomas Aquinas
William of Ockham
Pico della Mirandola
Thomas Hobbes
René Descartes
Blaise Pascal
Baruch Spinoza
John Locke
Gottfried Leibniz
George Berkeley
David Hume
Immanuel Kant
G.W.F. Hegel
John Stuart Mill
Søren Kierkegaard
Karl Marx
Friedrich Nietzsche
Edmund Husserl
Bertrand Russell
Martin Heidegger
Ludwig Wittgenstein
Jean-Paul Sartre
Willard Van
Orman Quine
A. J. Ayer
Jacques
Derrida

Peter Abelard
Hildegard of Bingen
Averroës
Zhu Xi (Chu Hsi)
Genghis Khan
Francis of Assisi
Bonaventure
Dante Alighieri
Catherine of Siena
Leonardo da Vinci
Martin Luther
John Calvin
Galileo
Shakespeare
Rembrandt
Louis XIV
Isaac Newton
J. S. Bach
Voltaire
Thomas Reid
J. W. Goethe
Mozart
Mary
Wollstonecraft
Napoleon Bonaparte
Beethoven
Simon Bolivar
Queen Victoria
John Dewey
Henri Bergson
George Santayana
Mahatma Gandhi
G. E. Moore
Martin Buber
Jacques Martin
Adolf Hitler
Gilbert Ryle
Simone
de Beauvoir
Michel Foucault

Paris University founded
Magna Carta
Bubonic Plague
Ming Dynasty in China
Gutenberg invents moveable-
type printing
Columbus sails to America
Luther begins Protestant Reformation
English defeat Spanish Armada
Charles I executed
English "Glorious Revolution"
Declaration
of Independence
French Revolution
Chaka founds Zulu Empire
American Civil War
Wright brothers
invent airplane
World War I
Russian
Revolution
World War II
Korean
War
Vietnam
War
First men
on the
moon

1200	1400	1600	1800	2000

ANCIENT GREEK PHILOSOPHY

———◀◦▶———

Something unusual happened in Greece and in the Greek colonies of the Aegean Sea some twenty-five hundred years ago. Whereas the previous great cultures of the Mediterranean had used mythological stories of the gods to explain the operations of the world and of the self, some of the Greeks began to discover new ways of explaining these phenomena. Instead of reading their ideas into, or out of, ancient scriptures or poems, they began to use reason, contemplation, and sensory observation to make sense of reality.

The story as we know it began with the Greeks living on the coast of Asia Minor (present-day Turkey). Colonists there, such as Thales, tried to find the one common element in the diversity of nature. Subsequent thinkers, such as Anaximenes, sought not only to find this one common element, but also to find the process by which one form changes into another. Other thinkers, such as Pythagoras, turned to the nature of form itself rather than the basic stuff that takes on a particular form.

With Socrates, the pursuit of knowledge turned inward as he sought not to understand the world, but himself. His call to "know thyself," together with his uncompromising search for truth, inspired generations of thinkers. With the writings of Plato and Aristotle, ancient Greek thought reached its zenith. These giants of human thought developed all-embracing systems that explained both the nature of the universe and the humans who inhabit it.

All these lovers of wisdom, or *philosophers*, came to different conclusions and often spoke disrespectfully of one another. Some held the universe to be one single entity, whereas others insisted that it must be made of many parts. Some believed that human knowledge was capable of understanding virtually

1

everything about the world and the self, whereas others thought that it was not possible to have any knowledge at all. But despite all their differences, there is a thread of continuity, a continuing focus among them: the *human* attempt to understand the world and the self, using *human* reason. This fact distinguishes these philosophers from the great minds that preceded them.

The philosophers of ancient Greece have fascinated thinking persons for centuries, and their writings have been one of the key influences on the development of Western civilization. The works of Plato and Aristotle, especially, have defined the questions and suggested many of the answers for subsequent generations. As the great Greek statesman Pericles sagely predicted, "Future ages will wonder at us, as the present age wonders at us now."

* * *

For a comprehensive, yet readable, work on Greek philosophy, see W.K.C. Guthrie's authoritative *The History of Greek Philosophy,* six volumes. (Cambridge: Cambridge University Press, 1962–1981). W.T. Jones, *The Classical Mind* (New York: Harcourt, Brace & World, 1969); Frederick Copleston, *A History of Philosophy: Volume I, Greece & Rome* (Garden City, NY: Doubleday, 1962); Friedo Ricken, *Philosophy of the Ancients,* translated by Eric Watkins (Notre Dame, IN: University of Notre Dame Press, 1991); J.V. Luce, *An Introduction to Greek Philosophy* (New York: Thames and Hudson, 1992); C.C.W. Taylor, ed., *Routledge History of Philosophy, Volume 1: From the Beginning to Plato* (London: Routledge, 1997); and David Furley, ed., *Routledge History of Philosophy, Volume 2: Aristotle to Augustine* (London: Routledge, 1997) provide basic introductions. Julie K. Ward, ed., *Feminism and Ancient Philosophy* (London: Routledge, 1996) provides a feminist critique while Robert S. Brumbaugh, *The Philosophers of Greece* (Albany, NY: SUNY Press, 1981) is an accessible introduction with pictures, charts, and maps.

SOCRATES
470–399 B.C.

PLATO
428/7–348/7 B.C.

Socrates has fascinated and inspired men and women for over two thousand years. All five of the major "schools" of ancient Greece (Academics, Peripatetics, Epicureans, Stoics, and Cynics) were influenced by his thought. Some of the early Christian thinkers, such as Justin Martyr, considered him a "proto-Christian," while others, such as St. Augustine (who rejected this view) still expressed deep admiration for Socrates' ethical life. More recently, existentialists have found in Socrates' admonition "know thyself" an encapsulation of their thought, and opponents of unjust laws have seen in Socrates' trial a blueprint for civil disobedience. In short, Socrates is one of the most admired men who ever lived.

The Athens into which Socrates was born in 470 B.C. was a city still living in the flush of its epic victory over the Persians, and it was bursting with new ideas. The playwrights Euripides and Sophocles were young boys, and Pericles, the great Athenian democrat, was still a young man. The Parthenon's foundation was laid when Socrates was twenty-two, and its construction was completed fifteen years later.

Socrates was the son of Sophroniscus, a sculptor, and of Phaenarete, a midwife. As a boy, Socrates received a classical Greek education in music, gymnastics, and grammar (or the study of language), and he decided early on to become a sculptor like his father. Tradition says he was a gifted artist who fashioned impressively simple statues of the Graces. He married a woman named Xanthippe, and together they had three children. He took an early interest in the developing science of the Milesians, and then he served for a time in the army.

When he was a middle-aged man, Socrates' friend, Chaerephon, asked the oracle at Delphi "if there was anyone wiser than Socrates." For once the mysterious oracle gave an unambiguous answer: "None." When Socrates heard of the incident, he was confused. He knew that he was not a wise man. So he set out to find a wiser man as "an excuse for going back and cross-examining the oracle." Socrates later described the method and results of his mission:

> So I examined this man—there's no need for me to mention his name, let's just say he was a politician—and the result of my examination . . . and of my conversations with him, was this. I decided that although the man seemed to many people, and above all to himself, to be wise, in reality he was not wise. I tried to demonstrate to him that he thought he was wise, but actually was not, and as a result I made an enemy of him, and of many of those present. To myself, as I left him, I reflected, "Here is *one* man less wise than I. In all probability neither of us knows anything worth knowing; but he *thinks* he knows when he doesn't, whereas I, given that I don't in fact know, am at least *aware* I don't know. Apparently, therefore, I am wiser than him in just this one small detail, that when I don't know something, I don't *think* I know it either." From him I went to another man, one of those who seemed wiser than the first. I came to exactly the same conclusion, and made an enemy of him and of many others besides. (*Apology* 21c)

As Socrates continued his mission by interviewing the politicians, poets, and artisans of Athens, young men followed along. They enjoyed seeing the authority figures humiliated by Socrates' intense questioning. Those in authority, however, were not amused. Athens was no longer the powerful, self-confident city of 470 B.C., the year of Socrates' birth. An exhausting succession of wars with Sparta (the Peloponnesian Wars) and an enervating series of political debacles had left the city narrow in vision and suspicious of new ideas and of dissent. In 399 B.C., Meletus and Anytus brought an indictment of "impiety and corrupting the youth" against Socrates. As recorded in the *Apology,* the Athenian assembly found him guilty by a vote of 280 to 220 and sentenced him to death. His noble death is described incomparably in the closing pages of the *Phaedo* by Plato.

Socrates wrote nothing, and our knowledge of his thought comes exclusively from the report of others. The playwright Aristophanes (455–375 B.C.) satirized Socrates in his comedy *The Clouds.* His caricature of Socrates as a cheat and charlatan was apparently so damaging that Socrates felt compelled to offer a rebuttal before the Athenian assembly (see the *Apology,* following). The military general Xenophon (ca. 430–350 B.C.) honored his friend Socrates in his *Apology of Socrates,* his *Symposium,* and, later, in his *Memorabilia* ("Recollections of Socrates"). In an effort to defend his dead friend's memory, Xenophon's writings illumine Socrates' life and character. Though born fifteen years after the death of Socrates, Aristotle (384–322 B.C.) left many fascinating allusions to Socrates in his philosophic works, as did several later Greek philosophers. But the primary source of our knowledge of Socrates comes from one of those young men who followed him: Plato.

*   *   *

Plato was probably born in 428/7 B.C. He had two older brothers, Adeimantus and Glaucon, who appear in Plato's *Republic,* and a sister, Potone. Though he may have known Socrates since childhood, Plato was probably nearer twenty when he came under the intellectual spell of Socrates. The death of Socrates made an enormous impression on Plato and contributed to his call to bear witness to posterity of "the best, . . . the wisest and most just" person that he knew (*Phaedo,* 118). Though Plato was from a distinguished family and might have followed his relatives into politics, he chose philosophy.

Following Socrates' execution, the twenty-eight-year-old Plato left Athens and traveled for a time. He is reported to have visited Egypt and Cyrene—though some scholars doubt this. During this time he wrote his early dialogues on Socrates' life and teachings. He also visited Italy and Sicily, where he became the friend of Dion, a relative of Dionysius, the tyrant of Syracuse, Sicily.

On returning to Athens from Sicily, Plato founded a school, which came to be called the Academy. One might say it was the world's first university, and it endured as a center of higher learning for nearly one thousand years, until the Roman emperor Justinian closed it in A.D. 529. Except for two later trips to Sicily, where he unsuccessfully sought to institute his political theories, Plato spent the rest of his life at the Athenian Academy. Among his students was Aristotle. Plato died at eighty in 348/7 B.C.

Plato's influence was best described by the twentieth-century philosopher Alfred North Whitehead when he said, "The safest general characterization of the European philosophical tradition is that it consists of a series of footnotes to Plato."

*   *   *

It is difficult to separate the ideas of Plato from those of his teacher, Socrates. In virtually all of Plato's dialogues, Socrates is the main character, and it is possible that in the early dialogues Plato is recording his teacher's actual words. But in the later dialogues, "Socrates" gives Plato's views—views that, in some cases, in fact, the historical Socrates denied.

The first four dialogues presented in this text describe the trial and death of Socrates and are arranged in narrative order. The first, the *Euthyphro,* takes place as Socrates has just learned of the indictment against him. He strikes up a conversation with a "theologian" so sure of his piety that he is prosecuting his own father for murder. The dialogue moves on, unsuccessfully, to define piety. Along the way, Socrates asks a question that has vexed philosophers and theologians for centuries: Is something good because the gods say it is, or do the gods say it is good because it is? This dialogue is given in the F.J. Church translation.

The next dialogue, the *Apology,* is generally regarded as one of Plato's first, and as eminently faithful to what Socrates said at his trial on charges of impiety and corruption of youth. The speech was delivered in public and heard by a large audience; Plato has Socrates mention that Plato was present; and there is no need to doubt the historical veracity of the speech, at least in essentials. There are two breaks in the narrative: one after Socrates' defense (during which the Athenians vote "guilty") and one after Socrates proposes an alternative to the death penalty (during which the Athenians decide on death). This dialogue includes Socrates' famous characterization of his mission and purpose in life.

In the *Crito,* Plato has Crito visit Socrates in prison to assure him that his escape from Athens has been well prepared and to persuade him to consent to leave. Socrates argues that one has an obligation to obey the state even when it orders one to suffer wrong. That Socrates, in fact, refused to leave is certain; that he used the arguments Plato ascribes to him is less certain. In any case, anyone who has read the *Apology* will agree that after his speech Socrates could not well escape. For this series, both the *Apology* and the *Crito* are given in translations by Tom Griffith.

The moving account of Socrates' death is given at the end of the *Phaedo,* the last of our group of dialogues. There is common agreement that this dialogue was written much later than the other three and that the earlier part of the dialogue, with its Platonic doctrine of Forms and immortality, uses "Socrates" as a vehicle for Plato's own ideas. Once again, the translation is that of F.J. Church.

Like the *Phaedo,* the *Meno* and the *Republic* were written during Plato's "middle period," when he had returned from Sicily to Athens and had established the Academy. The *Meno* gives a fine and faithful picture of Socrates practicing the art of dialogue; it also marks the point at which Plato moves beyond his master. This dialogue answers the question, "Can virtue be taught?," and treats the issues of knowledge and belief. The *Meno* is given in W.K.C. Guthrie's authoritative translation.

There are few books in Western civilization that have had the impact of Plato's *Republic*—aside from the Bible, perhaps none. Like the Bible, there are also few books whose interpretation and evaluation have differed so widely. Apparently it is a description of Plato's ideal society: a utopian vision of the just state, possible only if philosophers were kings. But some (see the following suggested readings) claim that its purpose is not to give a model of the ideal state, but to show the impossibility of such a state and to convince aspiring philosophers to shun politics. Evaluations of the *Republic* have also varied widely: from the criticisms of Karl Popper, who denounced the *Republic* as totalitarian, to the admiration of more traditional interpreters, such as Gregory Vlastos and Francis MacDonald Cornford (whose translation is used here).

Given the importance of this work and the diversity of opinions concerning its point and value, it was extremely difficult to decide which sections of the *Republic* to include in this series. I chose to include the discussion of justice from Book II, the descriptions of the guardians and of the "noble lie" from Book III, the discussions of the virtues and the soul in Book IV, the presentations of the guardians' qualities and life-styles in Book V, and the key sections on knowledge (including the analogy of the line and the myth of the cave) from the end of Book VI and the beginning of Book VII. I admit that space constraints have forced me to exclude important sections. Ideally, the selections chosen will whet the student's appetite to read the rest of this classic. The marginal page numbers are those of all scholarly editions, Greek, English, German, or French.

* * *

For studies of Socrates, see the classic A.E. Taylor, *Socrates: The Man and His Thought* (London: Methuen, 1933); the second half of Volume III of W.K.C. Guthrie, *The History of Greek Philosophy* (Cambridge: Cambridge University Press, 1969); Hugh H. Benson, *Essays on the Philosophy of Socrates* (Oxford: Oxford University Press, 1992); and Thomas C. Brickhouse and Nicholas D. Smith, *Plato's Socrates* (Oxford: Oxford University Press, 1994). For collections of essays, see Gregory Vlastos, ed., *The Philosophy of Socrates* (Garden City, NY: Doubleday, 1971); Hugh H. Benson, ed., *Essays on the Philosophy of Socrates* (Oxford: Oxford University Press, 1992); Terence Irwin, ed., *Socrates and His Contemporaries* (Hamden, CT: Garland Publishing, 1995); and the multi-volume William J. Prior, ed., *Socrates* (Oxford: Routledge, 1996). For discussions of the similarities and differences between the historical Socrates and the "Socrates" of the Platonic dialogues, see Gregory Vlastos, *Socrates: Ironist and Moral Philosopher* (Ithaca, NY: Cornell University Press, 1991), especially Chapters 2 and 3, and Thomas C. Brickhouse and Nicholas D. Smith, *Plato's Socrates* (Oxford: Oxford University Press, 1994).

Books about Plato are legion. Once again the work of W.K.C. Guthrie is sensible, comprehensive, yet readable. See Volumes IV and V of his *The History of Greek Philosophy* (Cambridge: Cambridge University Press, 1975 and 1978). Paul Shorey, *What Plato Said* (Chicago: Chicago University Press, 1933), and G.M.A. Grube, *Plato's Thought* (London: Methuen, 1935) are classic treatments of Plato, while Robert Brumbaugh, *Plato for a Modern Age* (New York: Macmillan, 1964), I.M. Crombie, *An Examination of Plato's Doctrines,* two volumes (New York: Humanities Press, 1963–1969), R.M. Hare, *Plato* (Oxford: Oxford University Press, 1982), and David J. Melling, *Understanding Plato* (Oxford: Oxford University Press, 1987) are more recent studies. For collections of essays, see Gregory Vlastos, ed., *Plato: A Collection of Critical Essays,* two volumes (Garden City, NY: Doubleday, 1971); Richard Kraut, ed., *The Cambridge Companion to Plato* (Cambridge: Cambridge University Press, 1991); Nancy Tuana, ed., *Feminist Interpretations of Plato* (College Park, PA: Pennsylvania State University Press, 1994); Terence Irwin, ed., *Plato's Ethics* and *Plato's Metaphysics and Epistemology* (both Hamden, CT: Garland Publishing, 1995); and Gregory Vlastos, ed., *Studies in Greek Philosophy, Volume II: Socrates, Plato, and Their Tradition* (Princeton, NJ: Princeton University Press, 1995). Jane M. Day, ed., *Plato's Meno in Focus* (Oxford: Routledge, 1994) and Robert G. Turnbull, *The Parmenides and Plato's Late Philosophy* (Toronto: University of Toronto Press, 1998) give insights on their respective dialogues. For further reading on the *Republic,* see Nicholas P. White, *A Companion to Plato's Republic* (Indianapolis, IN: Hackett, 1979); Julia Annas, *An Introduction to Plato's Republic* (Oxford: Clarendon Press, 1981); Nickolas Pappas, *Routledge Guidebook to Plato and the Republic* (Oxford: Routledge, 1995); Daryl Rice, *A Guide to Plato's Republic* (Oxford: Oxford University Press, 1997) and Richard Kraut, ed., *Plato's Republic: Critical Essays* (Lanham, MD: Rowan & Littlefield, 1997). Terence Irwin, *Plato's Ethics* (Oxford: Oxford University Press, 1995) examines several dialogues while thoroughly exploring Plato's ethical thought. Finally, for unusual interpretations of Plato and his work, see Werner Jaeger, *Paideia,* Vols. II and III, translated by Gilbert Highet (New York: Oxford University Press, 1939–1943); Karl R. Popper, *The Open Society and Its Enemies; Volume I: The Spell of Plato* (Princeton, NJ: Princeton University Press, 1962); and Allan Bloom's interpretive essay in Plato, *Republic,* translated by Allan Bloom (New York: Basic Books, 1968).

APOLOGY

Well, I don't know what effect the prosecution has had on you, men of Athens. As far 17
as I'm concerned, they made me all but forget the position I am in, they spoke so plau-
sibly. And yet, to all intents and purposes, there was not a word of truth in what they
said.

Of their many lies, one in particular filled me with amazement. They said you
should be careful to avoid being led astray by my "skill in speaking." They were not in
the least embarrassed at the prospect of being immediately proved wrong by my actual
performance, when it becomes clear that I am not in the least skilled in speaking. That b
was what I found the most shameless thing about their behaviour—unless of course
they call "skilled in speaking" someone who merely speaks the truth. If *that's* what
they mean, then I would agree that I am in a different class from them as an orator.

As I say, they have told you little or nothing that was true, whereas from me you
will hear the whole truth—certainly not a piece of polished rhetoric like theirs, men of
Athens, with its words and phrases so cleverly arranged. No, the speech you are going c
to hear from me will use everyday language, arranged in a straightforward way—after
all, I have confidence in the justice of what I have to say—so I hope no-one is expecting anything different. And I shall tell the truth, because it wouldn't be appropriate to
appear before you at my age making up stories like a schoolboy.

However, there is one important request and concession I am going to ask of
you, men of Athens. If you hear me making my defence in the same language I generally use in the city, among people doing business—where many of you have heard
me—and elsewhere, do not be surprised on that account, or start interrupting. The reason for it is this. This is the first time I have ever appeared in court, though I am now
seventy years of age. The kind of speaking practised here is, quite simply, foreign to d
me. Imagine I really were a foreigner; you wouldn't hold it against me, presumably, if
I spoke in the dialect and manner in which I had been brought up. In the same way 18
now, I make this request—justified, in my view—that you pay no attention to the manner in which I speak, be it inferior or superior. Please consider one point only, and
focus your attention on that. Is there any justice in what I have to say, or not? That,
after all, is the function of a member of the jury; the speaker's task is to tell the truth.

First of all, then, men of Athens, I am entitled to defend myself against the earliest false accusations made against me, and against my earliest accusers; after that
against the more recent falsehoods, and my present accusers. After all, there have been
many people, over the years, making accusations about me to you, and speaking not a
word of truth. I fear them more than I fear Anytus and his supporters, dangerous b
though they are as well. But the earlier ones are more dangerous, gentlemen. They took
you in hand from childhood, for the most part, and tried to win you over, making accusations every bit as false as these today; they told you there was this man Socrates, an
intellectual, a thinker about the heavens, an expert on everything under the earth, a
man who could make the weaker argument the stronger.

These people, men of Athens, the ones who have saddled me with this reputation, are my most dangerous accusers, because those who listen to them think that stu- c
dents of these subjects do not recognise the gods. What's more, there are a great many

of these accusers, and they have been accusing me for a long time now. And thirdly, they were speaking to you at the age when you were most likely to believe them, when many of you were children and adolescents. Quite simply, they were prosecuting in an uncontested case, since there was no-one there to answer their charges.

d   What is particularly unfair is that I cannot even know, or tell you, their names—unless maybe one of them is a writer of comedies. But all those who tried to influence you, out of spite and malice, together with those who were trying to influence others because they were genuinely convinced themselves—all these accusers are very hard to deal with. It is not possible to call any of them as a witness here, or cross-examine them; I just have to make my defence like someone shadow-boxing, and conduct my cross-examination with no-one there to answer.

e   So I hope you will accept my claim that I have two sets of accusers—the ones who have just now brought this case against me, and the ones from way back, the ones I have been telling you about. Please believe also that I must make my defence against this second set first; after all, you heard their accusations at an earlier age, and on many more occasions, than you heard the later ones.

19   Very well. I must make my defence, men of Athens, and try to remove from your minds, in the very brief time available, the prejudice which you have so long held. I hope that is how things will turn out, provided it really *is* the best outcome for you and for me, and that I shall achieve something by my defence. But I think it is difficult, and I am well aware of the magnitude of the task. Still, let it turn out as god wills, I must obey the law, and make my defence.

b   Let us go back to the beginning, then, and see what the accusation is which has created this prejudice against me—the prejudice which Meletus was presumably counting on when he brought this case against me. What exactly did the originators of this prejudice say? We ought really to read out a sworn statement from them, just like the prosecution's. "Socrates is guilty of being a busybody. He enquires into things under the earth and in the heavens, and makes the weaker argument the stronger, and

c he teaches these same things to other people." That's roughly how it goes. You saw it for yourselves in Aristophanes' comedy; you saw a Socrates there, swinging round and round, claiming he was walking on air, and spouting a whole lot of other drivel on subjects about which I make not the slightest claim to knowledge. Not that I have anything against knowledge of this kind, if anyone is an expert on such subjects; I hope Meletus will never bring enough cases against me to reduce me to that. No, it's just that I myself have no share in such knowledge.

    Once again, I can call most of you as witnesses. I'm sure you can make the posi-

d tion clear to one another, and explain, those of you who have ever heard me talking—and a lot of you come in that category. Tell one another then, if any of you has ever heard me breathe so much as a word on such topics. That will help you to see that the rest of what is generally said about me has as little foundation.

    No, there is no truth in these stories. And if anyone has told you that I undertake

e to educate people, or that I make money out of it, there is equally little truth in that either. Mind you, if anyone *can* educate people—as Gorgias from Leontini can, or Prodicus from Ceos, or Hippias from Elis—then that seems to me to be a fine thing. Any of these men, gentlemen, can go to any city and persuade the young men, who are at liberty to spend their time, free of charge, with whichever of their fellow-citizens they

20 choose, to abandon the company of those fellow-citizens and spend time with him instead—and pay money to do so, *and* be grateful into the bargain.

    Come to that, there is even one of them here, a wise man from Paros. I found out he was living in Athens when I ran into Callias, the son of Hipponicus, the man who has paid more money to these teachers than everyone else put together. I asked him— you know he has two sons—"Callias," I said, "if your sons were colts or calves, we b would be able to find and employ someone to look after them, someone who would turn them into outstanding examples of their particular species; and this person would be a trainer or farmer of some kind. But they aren't colts or calves; they are men. Whom do you propose to find to look after them? Who is an expert in this kind of excellence—the excellence of a human being and a citizen? I imagine, since you have sons, you must have thought about this question. Is there someone," I asked him, "or not?"

"There certainly is," he said.

"Who is he?" I said. "Where is he from? What does he charge?"

"Evenus," he said. "He is from Paros, Socrates, and he charges 500 drachmas."

I took my hat off to Evenus, if he really did have this ability, and yet taught for so reasonable a fee. I wouldn't. I'd start giving myself airs, and become extremely c choosy, if I had this kind of knowledge. But I don't have it, men of Athens.

I can imagine one of you interrupting me, and saying, "That's all very well, Socrates; but what *do* you do? Where have all these prejudices against you come from? I take it all this gossip and rumour about you is not the result of your behaving just like anyone else. You must be doing *something* out of the ordinary. Tell us what it is, so we can avoid jumping to conclusions about you." This seems to me to be a valid point, so d I'll try and explain to you what it is that has given me my reputation and created the prejudice against me. Give me a hearing. It may seem to some of you that I am not being serious, but I promise you, every word I say will be the truth.

I have gained this reputation, men of Athens, as a direct result of a kind of wisdom. What sort of wisdom? The sort we might perhaps call human wisdom. In fact, if we are talking about this kind of wisdom, I probably *am* wise. The men I mentioned e just now may well be wise with some more-than-human wisdom; I don't know how else to describe it. It's not a wisdom *I* know anything about. Anyone who says I do is lying, and trying to increase the prejudice against me.

Please do not interrupt me, men of Athens, even if you find what I say a little bit boastful. The claim I'm about to make is not *my* claim; I shall appeal to a reliable authority. I shall call the god at Delphi to give evidence to you about my wisdom; he can tell you if I really do possess any, and what it is like.

You remember Chaerephon, I imagine. He was a friend of mine, from an early age, and a friend of most of you. He shared your recent exile, and returned from exile 21 with you. You know what Chaerephon was like, how impetuous he was when he set about something. And sure enough, he went to Delphi one day, and went so far as to put this question to the oracle—I repeat, please do not interrupt, gentlemen—he asked if there was anyone wiser than me; and the priestess of Apollo replied that there was no-one wiser. His brother here will give evidence to you about this, since Chaerephon himself is dead.

Let me remind you of my reason for telling you this. I am trying to show you the b origin of the prejudice against me. When I heard the priestess's reply, my reaction was this: "What on earth is the god saying? What is his hidden meaning? I'm well aware that I have no wisdom, great or small. So what can he mean by saying that I am so wise? He can't be lying; he's not allowed to." I spent a long time wondering what he could mean. Finally, with great reluctance, I decided to verify his claim. What I did was this: I approached one of those who seemed to be wise, thinking that there, if anywhere, I could prove the reply wrong, and say quite clearly to the oracle, "This man is c wiser than I am, whereas you said that I was the wisest."

So I examined this man—there's no need for me to mention his name, let's just say he was a politician—and the result of my examination, men of Athens, and of my conversations with him, was this. I decided that although the man seemed to many people, and above all to himself, to be wise, in reality he was not wise. I tried to demonstrate to him that he thought he was wise, but actually was not, and as a result I

d   made an enemy of him, and of many of those present. To myself, as I left him, I reflected: "Here is *one* man less wise than I. In all probability neither of us knows anything worth knowing; but he *thinks* he knows when he doesn't, whereas I, given that I don't in fact know, am at least *aware* I don't know. Apparently, therefore, I am wiser than him in just this one small detail, that when I don't know something, I don't *think* I know it either." From him I went to another man, one of those who seemed wiser than

e   the first. I came to exactly the same conclusion, and made an enemy of him and of many others besides.

After that I began approaching people in a systematic way. I could see, with regret and alarm, that I was making enemies, yet I thought it was essential to take the god seriously. So on I had to go, in my enquiry into the meaning of the oracle, to

22   everyone who seemed to have any knowledge. And I swear to you, men of Athens— after all, I am bound to tell you the truth—what I found was this. Those with the highest reputations seemed to me to be pretty nearly the most useless, if I was trying to find out the meaning of what the god had said, whereas others, who appeared of less account, were a much better bet when it came to thinking sensibly.

I can best give an account of my quest by likening it to a set of labours—and all, as it turned out, to satisfy myself of the accuracy of the oracle. After the politicians I

b   went to the writers—writers of plays, and songs, and the rest of them. That would be an open-and-shut case, I thought. I should easily show myself up as less wise than them. So I took to reading their works, the ones which struck me as showing the greatest skill in composition, and asking them what they meant; I hoped to learn from them.

Well, I'm embarrassed to tell you the truth, gentlemen; but I must tell you. Practically anyone present could have given a better account than they did of the works

c   they had themselves written. As a result, I quickly came to a decision about the writers too, in their turn. I realised that their achievements are not the result of wisdom, but of natural talent and inspiration, like fortune-tellers and clairvoyants, who also say many striking things, but have no idea at all of the meaning of what they say. Writers, I felt, were clearly in the same position. Moreover, I could see that their works encouraged them to think that they were the wisest of men in other areas where they were not wise. So I left them too feeling that I had got the better of them, in the same way as I had got the better of the politicians.

Finally I went to the craftsmen. I was well aware that I knew virtually nothing,

d   and confident that I would find much fine knowledge in them. Nor was I disappointed. They *did* know things which I didn't know; in this respect they were wiser than I was. However, our good friends the skilled workmen seemed also to me, men of Athens, to have the same failing as the writers. Each one, because of his skill in practising his

e   craft, thought himself extremely wise in other matters of importance as well; and this presumptuousness of theirs seemed to me to obscure the wisdom they did have. So I asked myself, on behalf of the oracle, whether I should accept being the way I was— without any of their wisdom, or any of their foolishness—or whether I ought to possess both the qualities they possessed. The answer I gave myself and the oracle was that it was best for me to remain as I was.

This survey, men of Athens, has aroused much hostility against me, of the most

23   damaging and serious kind. The result has been a great deal of prejudice, and in partic-

ular, this description of me as being "wise." That is because the people who were present on such occasions think that I am an expert myself on those subjects in which I demolish the claims of others. The truth probably is, gentlemen, that in reality god is wise, and that what he means by his reply to Chaerephon is that human wisdom is of little or no value. When he refers to the man here before you—to Socrates—and goes out of his way to use my name, he is probably using me as an example, as if he were b saying "That man is the wisest among you, mortals, who realises, as Socrates does, that he doesn't really amount to much when it comes to wisdom."

That's why, to this day, I go round investigating and enquiring, as the god would have me do, if I think anyone—Athenian or foreigner—is wise. And when I find he is not, then, in support of the god, I demonstrate that he is not wise. My preoccupation with this task has left me no time worth speaking of to take any part in public life or family life. Instead I live in extreme poverty as a result of my service to the god.

Another problem is that young people follow me—the ones with the most time at c their disposal, the sons of the rich—of their own free will; they love listening to people being cross-examined. They often imitate me themselves, and have a go at cross-examining others. Nor do I imagine they have any difficulty in finding people who think they know something, when in fact they know little or nothing. The result is that the victims of their cross-examination are angry with me, rather than themselves; they say Socrates is some sort of criminal, and that he has a bad influence on the young. d When you ask them what I do and what I teach that makes me a criminal, they can't answer; they don't know. But since they don't want to lose face, they come out with the standard accusations made against all philosophers, the stuff about "things in heaven and things under the earth," and "not recognising the gods" and "making the weaker argument stronger." The truth, I think, they would refuse to admit, which is that they have been shown up as pretenders to knowledge who really know nothing. Since, therefore, they are ambitious and energetic, and there are a lot of them, and e since they speak forcibly and persuasively about me, they have been filling your ears for some time now, and most vigorously, with their attacks on me.

That is what Meletus relied on when he brought this charge against me, with Anytus and Lycon—Meletus feeling offended as one of the poets, Anytus as one of the craftsmen and politicians, Lycon as one of the orators. The result, as I said at the beginning, is that it would surprise me if I were able to remove from your minds, in so short a time, a prejudice which has grown so strong. This is the truth, I assure you, men of 24 Athens. I speak with absolutely no concealment or reservation. I'm pretty sure it's this way of speaking which makes me unpopular. My unpopularity is the proof that I am speaking the truth, that this *is* the prejudice against me, and these *are* the reasons for it. You can enquire into these matters—now or later—and you will find them to be so. b

So much for the accusations made by my first group of accusers. I hope you'll find what I've said a satisfactory defence against them. Now let me try and defend myself against Meletus, that excellent patriot (as he claims) and my more recent accusers. Let's treat them as a separate prosecution, and consider in its turn the charge brought by them. It runs something like this: it says that Socrates is guilty of being a bad influence on the young, and of not recognising the gods whom the state recognises, but practising a new religion of the supernatural.

That's what the charge consists of. Let's examine this charge point by point. He c says I am guilty of having a bad influence on the young. But *I* claim, men of Athens, that Meletus is guilty of playing games with what is deadly serious; he is too quick to bring people to trial, pretending to be serious and care about things to which he has never given a moment's thought. That this is the truth, I will try to prove to you as d   well. Come now, Meletus, tell me this. I take it you regard the well-being of the young as of the utmost importance?

MELETUS: I do.

SOCRATES: In that case, please tell these people who it is who is a good influence on the young. Obviously you must know, since you're so concerned about it. You've tracked down, so you say, the man who is a bad influence—me—and are bringing me here before these people and accusing me. So come on, tell them who is a good influence; point out to them who it is.

You see, Meletus? You are silent; you have nothing to say. Don't you think that's a disgrace, and a sufficient proof of what I am saying—that you haven't given it any thought? Tell us, my friend, who is a good influence?

e   MELETUS: The laws.

SOCRATES: Brilliant! But that's not what I'm asking. The question is what *man*—who will of course start off with just this knowledge, the laws.

MELETUS: These men, Socrates, the members of the jury.

SOCRATES: Really, Meletus? These men are capable of educating the young and being a good influence on them?

MELETUS: They certainly are.

SOCRATES: All of them? Or are some capable, and others not?

MELETUS: All of them.

25   SOCRATES: How remarkably fortunate—no shortage of benefactors there, then. What about the spectators in court? Do they have a good influence, or not?

MELETUS: Yes, they do, as well.

SOCRATES: What about the members of the council?

MELETUS: Yes, the members of the council also.

SOCRATES: But surely, Meletus, the people in the assembly—the citizens meeting *as* the assembly—surely they don't have a bad influence on the young? Don't they too—all of them—have a good influence?

MELETUS: Yes, they do too.

SOCRATES: Apart from me, then, the entire population of Athens, as it appears, makes the young into upright citizens. I alone am a bad influence. Is that what you mean?

MELETUS: Yes, that's exactly what I mean.

b   SOCRATES: That's certainly a great misfortune to charge me with. Answer me this, though: do you think the situation is the same with horses as well? Do the people who are good for them make up the entire population, and is there just one person who has a harmful effect on them? Isn't it the exact opposite? Isn't there just one person, or very few people—trainers—capable of doing them any good? Don't most people, if they spend time with horses, or have anything to do with them, have a harmful effect on them? Isn't that the situation, Meletus, both with horses and with all other living creatures?

It certainly is, whether you and Anytus deny it or admit it. After all, it would be a piece of great good fortune for the young, if only one person has a bad influence on them, and everyone else has a good influence. No, Meletus. You show quite clearly

c   that you have never cared in the slightest for the young; you reveal your own lack of interest quite plainly, since you've never given a moment's thought to the things you're prosecuting me for.

Another point. Tell us honestly, Meletus, is it better to live with good fellow-citizens, or with bad? Answer, can't you? It's not a difficult question. Isn't it true that bad citizens do some harm to those who are their neighbours at any particular time, while good citizens do some good?

MELETUS: Yes, of course.

SOCRATES: That being so, does anyone choose to be harmed by those close to him rather than be helped by them? Answer, there's a good fellow. Besides, the law re-   d quires you to answer. Is there anyone who chooses to be harmed?

MELETUS: No, of course not.

SOCRATES: Well, then. You bring me to court for being a bad influence on the young, and making them worse people. Are you saying I do this deliberately, or without realising it?

MELETUS: Deliberately, I'm sure of it.

SOCRATES: Really, Meletus? How odd. Are you, at your age, so much wiser than me at mine? Are *you* aware that bad people generally have a harmful effect on those they come into contact with, and that good people have a good effect? And have *I*   e reached such a height of stupidity as not even to realise that if I make one of my neighbours a worse man, I'm likely to come to some harm at his hands? And is the result that I deliberately do such great damage as you describe? On this point I don't believe you, Meletus; and nor, I think, does anyone else. No. Either I'm not a bad influence on the young, or if I do have a bad influence, I do so without realising it. Either way you are   26 wrong. And if I have a bad influence without realising it, it's not our custom to bring people here to court for errors of this sort, but to take them on one side, and instruct them privately, pointing out their mistakes. Obviously, if I'm taught, I shall stop doing what I don't at the moment realise I *am* doing. But you avoided spending time with me and instructing me; you refused to do it. Instead you bring me here to court, where it is our custom to bring those who need punishment, not those who need to learn.

I needn't go on, men of Athens. It must now be clear, as I've said, that Meletus has never given the slightest thought to these matters. All the same, Meletus, tell us this: *in what way* do you claim I'm a bad influence on the young? Isn't it obvious I do   b it in the way described in the charge you've brought against me—by teaching them not to recognise the gods the city recognises, but to practise this new religion of the supernatural instead? Isn't that your claim, that it's by teaching them these things that I have a bad influence?

MELETUS: Yes, that certainly is exactly what I claim.

SOCRATES: Well then, Meletus, in the name of these gods we are now talking about, make yourself a little clearer, both to me and to these gentlemen here, since *I* at   c least cannot understand you. Do you mean I teach them to accept that there are *some* gods—not the gods the state accepts, but other gods? In that case I myself must also accept that there are gods, so I am not a complete atheist, and am not guilty on that count. Is this what you charge me with, accepting other gods? Or are you saying that I don't myself recognise any gods at all, and that I teach the same beliefs to others?

MELETUS: Yes, that's what I am saying. You don't recognise any gods at all.

SOCRATES: Meletus, you are beyond belief. What can possess you to say that?   d Don't I accept that the sun and moon are gods, in the same way as everyone else does?

MELETUS: Good heavens, no, men of the jury. He says the sun is a stone, and the moon is made of earth.

SOCRATES: Is it Anaxagoras you think you're accusing, my dear Meletus? Do you have such contempt for these men here? Do you think them so illiterate as to be unaware that the works of Anaxagoras of Clazomenae are stuffed full of speculations of that sort? And do the young really learn these things from me, when there are often

books on sale, for a drachma at the very most, in the Orchestra, in the Agora? They can
e   laugh at Socrates if he claims these views as his own—especially such eccentric views.
However, as god is your witness, is that your view of me? Do I not accept the existence of any god at all?

MELETUS: No, in god's name, no god at all.

SOCRATES: What you say is unbelievable, Meletus—even, I think to yourself.
This man here, men of Athens, strikes me as an arrogant lout; his prosecution of me is
prompted entirely by arrogance, loutishness, and youth. It's as if he were setting a trick
27   question, to test me: "Will Socrates the wise realise that I'm playing with words and
contradicting myself, or will I deceive him and the others who hear it?" He certainly
seems to me to contradict himself, in his accusation. He might as well say "Socrates is
guilty of not recognising the gods, but recognising the gods instead." And that is not a
serious proposition.

Please join me, gentlemen, in examining the reasons why I think this is what his
accusation amounts to. You, Meletus, answer us. And you *(to the jurymen),* as I asked
b   you at the beginning, remember not to interrupt me if I construct my argument in my
usual way.

Is there anyone in the world, Meletus, who accepts the existence of human activity, but not of human beings? He must answer, gentlemen. Don't allow him to keep
making all these interruptions. Is there anyone who denies horses, but accepts equine
activity? Or denies the existence of flute-players, but accepts flute-playing? No, my
very good friend, there isn't. If you refuse to answer, then I'll say it—to you and
everyone else present here. But do answer my next question: is there anyone who ac-
c   cepts the activity of the supernatural, but denies supernatural beings?

MELETUS: No, there isn't.

SOCRATES: How kind of you—forced to answer, against your will, by these people here. Very well, then. You claim that I practise and teach a religion of the supernatural—whether of a new or conventional kind—so I do at least, on your own admission,
accept the existence of the supernatural. You even swore to it, on oath, in your indictment. But if I accept the supernatural, it follows, I take it, that I must necessarily admit
the existence of supernatural beings, must I not? I must; I take your silence for agree-
d   ment. And don't we regard supernatural beings as either gods or the children of gods?
Yes or no?

MELETUS: We certainly do.

SOCRATES: In that case, if I accept supernatural beings—as you admit—and if supernatural beings are gods of some sort, then you can see what I mean when I say that
you are setting trick questions, and playing with words, claiming first that I do *not* believe in gods, and then again claiming that I *do* believe in gods, since I do believe in
supernatural beings. If, on the other hand, supernatural beings are some form of illegit-
imate children of gods—born of nymphs or of some of the other mothers they are said
to be born from—who on earth could believe that there are children of gods, but no
gods? It would be as absurd as saying you believed there were such things as mules,
e   the offspring of horses and donkeys, but didn't believe there were horses and donkeys.

No, Meletus, the only possible explanation for your bringing this accusation
against me is that you wanted to test us—or that you didn't have any genuine offence
to charge me with. There's no conceivable way you could persuade anyone in the
28   world with a grain of intelligence that belief in the supernatural and the divine does not
imply belief in supernatural beings, divine beings and heroes.

So much for that, men of Athens. I don't think it takes much of a defence to
show that in the terms of Meletus' indictment I am not guilty. What I have said so far

should be enough. There remains what I said in the earlier part of my speech, that there is strong and widespread hostility towards me. Be in no doubt that this is true. It is this which will convict me, if it does convict me—not Meletus, not Anytus, but the prejudice and malice of the many. What has convicted many other good men before me will, I think, convict me too. There's no danger of its stopping at me.

b

That being so, you might ask "Well, Socrates, aren't you ashamed of living a life which has resulted in your now being on trial for your life?" I would answer you, quite justifiably, "You are wrong, sir, if you think that a man who is worth anything at all should take into account the chances of life and death. No, the only thing he should think about, when he acts, is whether he is acting rightly or wrongly, and whether this is the behaviour of a good man or a bad man. After all, if we accept your argument, those of the demigods who died at Troy would have been sorry creatures—and none more so than Achilles, the son of Thetis. Compared with the threat of dishonour, he regarded danger as of no importance at all. When he was eager to kill Hector, his mother, who was a goddess, said something like this to him, I imagine: 'My son, if you avenge the death of your friend Patroclus, and kill Hector, you will yourself be killed, since death awaits you immediately after Hector.' When Achilles heard this, he gave no thought to death or danger; what he feared much more was living as a coward, and not avenging his friends. 'Let me die immediately,' he said, 'after making the wrong-doer pay the penalty, rather than remain here by the curved ships, a laughing-stock, like a clod of earth.' You don't imagine *he* gave any thought to death or danger."

c

d

That's the way of things, men of Athens, it really is. Where a man takes up his position—in the belief that it is the best position—or is told to take up a position by his commanding officer, there he should stay, in my view, regardless of danger. He should not take death into account, or anything else apart from dishonour. As for me, when the commanders whom you chose to command me told me to take up position at Potidaea and Amphipolis and Delium, on those occasions I stayed where they posted me, just like anyone else, and risked death. Would it not have been very illogical of me, when *god* deployed me, as I thought and believed, to live my life as a philosopher, examining myself and others, then to be afraid of death—or anything else at all—and abandon my post?

e

It would indeed be illogical, and in that case you would certainly be completely justified in bringing me to court for not accepting the existence of the gods, since I disobey their oracle, and am afraid of death, and think I am wise when I am not. After all, the fear of death is just that, gentlemen—thinking one is wise when one is not—since it's a claim to know what one doesn't know. For all anyone knows, death may in fact be the best thing in the world that can happen to a man; yet men fear it as if they had certain knowledge that it is the greatest of all evils. This is without doubt the most reprehensible folly—the folly of thinking one knows what one does not know.

29

b

As for me, gentlemen, perhaps here too I *am* different from most people, in this one particular; and if I did claim to be in any way wiser than anyone else, it would be in this, that lacking any certain knowledge of what happens after death, I am also aware that I have no knowledge. But that it is evil and shameful to do wrong, and disobey one's superiors, divine or human, that I *do* know. Compared therefore with the evils which I know to be evils, I shall never fear, or try to avoid, what for all I know may turn out to be good.

Suppose you now acquit me, rejecting Anytus' argument that either this case should not have been brought in the first place, or, since it *had* been brought, that it was out of the question not to put me to death. He told you that if I got away with it, your sons would all start putting Socrates' teachings into practice, and be totally over-

c

whelmed by my bad influence. And suppose your response were to say to me: "Socrates, on this occasion we will not do what Anytus wants. We acquit you—on this condition, however, that you give up spending your time in this enquiry, and give up the search for wisdom. If you are caught doing it again, you will be put to death."

d   Even if, then, to repeat, you were to acquit me on these conditions, I would say to you, "Men of Athens, I have the highest regard and affection for you, but I will obey god rather than you. While I have breath and strength, I will not give up the search for wisdom. I will carry on nagging at you, and pointing out your errors to those of you I meet from day to day. I shall say, in my usual way, 'My very good sir, you are a citizen of Athens, a city which is the greatest and most renowned for wisdom and power. Aren't you ashamed to care about money, and how to make as much of it as possible, and about reputation and public recognition, whereas for wisdom and truth, and mak-

e   ing your soul as good as it can possibly be, you do not care, and give no thought to these things at all?' And if any of you objects, and says he does care, I shall not just let him go, or walk away and leave him. No, I shall question him, cross-examine him, try to prove him wrong. And if I find he has not achieved a state of excellence, but still

30   claims he has, then I shall accuse him of undervaluing what is most important, and paying too much attention to what is less important.

"That is what I shall do for anyone I meet, young or old, foreigner or citizen— but especially for my fellow-citizens, since you are more closely related to me. That is what god tells me to do, I promise you, and I believe that this service of mine to god is the most valuable asset you in this city have ever yet possessed. I spend my whole time going round trying to persuade both the young and old among you not to spend your

b   time or energy in caring about your bodies or about money, but rather in making your souls as good as possible. I tell you, 'Money cannot create a good soul, but a good soul can turn money—and everything else in private life and public life—into a good thing for men.' If saying things like this is a bad influence on the young, then things like this must be harmful. But if anyone claims I say anything different from this, he is wrong. With that in mind, Athenians," I would say, "either do what Anytus wants, or don't do it; either acquit me, or don't, knowing that I will not behave differently even if I am to be put to death a thousand times over."

c   Don't interrupt, men of Athens. Please stick to what I asked you to do, which was not to interrupt what I say, but to give me a hearing. It will be in your interest, I think, to hear me. I have some more things to say which you could object to quite violently. Please don't, however.

I have just described the kind of man I am. Take my word for it, if you put me to death, you will harm yourselves more than you will harm me. As for me, no harm can

d   come to me from Meletus or Anytus, who *cannot* injure me, since I do not think god ever allows a better man to be injured by a worse. Yes, I know he might put me to death, possibly, or send me into exile, or deprive me of citizen rights. And perhaps *he* regards these as great evils—as I suppose others may too. However, *I* do not. I regard it as a much greater evil to act as he is acting now, attempting to put a man to death unjustly.

It follows, men of Athens, that in this trial I am not by any means defending myself, as you might think. No, I am defending you. I don't want you to fail to recognise

e   god's gift to you, and find me guilty. If you put me to death, you will not easily find another like me. I have, almost literally, settled on the city at god's command. It's as if the city, to use a slightly absurd simile, were a horse—a large horse, high-mettled, but which because of its size is somewhat sluggish, and needs to be stung into action by some kind of horsefly. I think god has caused me to settle on the city as this horsefly, the sort that never stops, all day long, coming to rest on every part of you, stinging each one of you into action, and persuading and criticising each one of you. 31

Another like me will not easily come your way, gentlemen, so if you take my advice you will spare me. You may very likely get annoyed with me, as people do when they are dozing and somebody wakes them up. And you might then swat me, as Anytus wants you to, and kill me, quite easily. Then you could spend the rest of your lives asleep, unless god cared enough for you to send you someone else.

To convince yourselves that someone like me really is a gift from god to the city, b look at things this way. Behaviour like mine does not seem to be natural. I have completely neglected my own affairs, and allowed my family to be neglected, all these years, while I devoted myself to looking after your interests—approaching each one of you individually, like a father or elder brother, and trying to persuade you to consider the good of your soul.

If I made anything out of it, and charged a fee for this advice, there'd be some sense in my doing it. As it is, you can see for yourselves that although the prosecution accused me, in their unscrupulous way, of everything under the sun, there was one point on which they were not so unscrupulous as to produce any evidence. They didn't c claim that I ever made any money, or asked for any. I can produce convincing evidence, I think, that I am telling the truth—namely my poverty.

It may perhaps seem odd that in my private life I go round giving people advice like this, and interfering, without having the courage, in public life, to come forward before you, the people, and give advice on matters of public interest. The reason for this is what you have often heard me talking about, in all sorts of places, the kind of divine or supernatural sign that comes to me. This must have been what Meletus was d making fun of when he wrote out the charge against me. It started when I was a child, a kind of voice which comes to me, and when it comes, always stops me doing what I'm just about to do; it never tells me what I *should* do. It's this which opposes my taking part in politics, and rightly opposes it, in my opinion. You can be sure, men of Athens, that if I had tried, at any time in the past, to go into politics, I would have been dead long ago, and been no use at all either to you or to myself.

Please don't be annoyed with me for speaking the truth. There is no-one in the e world who can get away with deliberately opposing you—or any other popular assembly—or trying to put a stop to all the unjust and unlawful things which are done in pol- 32 itics; it is essential that the true fighter for justice, if he is to survive even for a short time, should remain a private individual, and not go into public life.

I shall give you compelling evidence for this—not words, but what you value, actions. Listen to things which have actually happened to me, and you will realise that I would never obey anyone if it was wrong to do so, simply through fear of dying. No, I would refuse to obey, even if it meant my death. What I am going to say now is the kind of boasting you often hear in the lawcourts; but it is true, for all that. b

I have never, men of Athens, held any public office in the city, apart from being a member of the Council. It turned out that our tribe, Antiochis, formed the standing committee when you decided, by a resolution of the Council, to put on trial collectively the ten generals who failed to pick up the survivors from the sea battle. This was unconstitutional, as you afterwards all decided. On that occasion I was the only member of the standing committee to argue against you. I told you not to act unconstitutionally, and voted against you. The politicians were all set to bring an immediate action against me, and have me arrested on the spot, and you were encouraging them to do so, c and shouting your approval, but still I thought I ought to take my chance on the side of law and justice, rather than side with you, through fear of imprisonment or death, when you were proposing to act unjustly.

That was when the city was still a democracy. When the oligarchy came to power, the junta in its turn sent for me, with four others, and gave me the task of bring-
d ing Leon of Salamis from his home in Salamis to the Council chamber, so he could be put to death. They often gave orders of this kind, to all sorts of people; they wanted to implicate as many people as possible in their crimes. Again I demonstrated—by what I did this time, rather than what I said—that my fear of death was, if you will pardon my saying so, negligible; what I was afraid of, more than anything, was acting without re-gard for justice or religion. I was not intimidated by the junta's power—great though it was—into acting unjustly. When we left the Council chamber, the other four went off to Salamis and fetched Leon, but I left, and went home. I might perhaps have been put
e to death for that, if their power hadn't soon after been brought to an end. Of these events any number of people will give evidence to you.

Do you think I would have survived all these years if I had taken part in public life, and played the part a good man should play, supporting what was just, and attach-ing the highest importance to it, as is right? Don't you believe it, men of Athens. Nor would anyone else in the world have survived. As for me, it will be clear that, through-out my life, if I have done anything at all in public life, my character is as I have de-scribed—and in private life the same. I was never at any time prepared to tolerate in-
33 justice in anyone at all—certainly not in any of the people my critics say were my pupils.

I have never been anyone's teacher. Equally, I never said no to anyone, young or old, who wanted to listen to me talking and pursuing my quest. Nor do I talk if I am paid, and not talk if I am not paid. I make myself available to rich and poor alike, so
b they can question me and listen, if anyone feels like it, to what I say in reply. And if any of these people turns out well or badly, I cannot legitimately be held responsible; I neither promised any knowledge, ever, to any of them, nor did I teach them. If anyone ever claims to have learnt or heard anything from me privately, beyond what anyone else learnt or heard, I can assure you he is lying.

c Why then do some people like spending so much of their time with me? You have heard the answer to that, men of Athens; I have told you the whole truth. They like hearing the cross-examination of those who think they are wise when they are not. After all, it is quite entertaining. For me, as I say, this is a task imposed by god, through prophecies and dreams and in every way in which divine destiny has ever im-posed any task on a man.

All this is the truth, men of Athens, and easily tested. If I really am a bad influ-
d ence on some of the young, and have been a bad influence on others in the past, and if some of them, as they have grown older, have realised that I gave them bad advice at some point when they were young, they ought to come forward now, I'd have thought, to accuse me and punish me. And if they weren't prepared to do so themselves, some of the members of their families—fathers, brothers, or other close relatives—ought
e now to remember, if those close to them came to some harm at my hands, and want to punish me. Certainly I can see plenty of them here today—Crito there, for a start, my contemporary and fellow-demesman, the father of Critobulus, who's here too. Then there's Lysanias from the deme of Sphettos, the father of Aeschines here; or indeed Antiphon over there, from Cephisus, the father of Epigenes.

Then there are the ones whose brothers have spent their time in my company:
34 Nicostratus the son of Theozotides, the brother of Theodotus—Theodotus of course is

dead, so he couldn't have put any pressure on his brother; and I can see Paralius, the son of Demodocus, whose brother was Theages. Then there's Adeimantus I can see, the son of Ariston, whose brother is Plato here; or Aiantodorus, whose brother Apollodorus is present also.

There are plenty more I could name for you. Ideally, Meletus would have called some of them himself to give evidence during his speech. However, in case he forgot at the time, let him call them now—I give up my place to him—and let him say if he has any evidence of that kind.

It's the exact opposite, gentlemen. You'll find they're all on my side—although I'm a bad influence, although I harm their relatives, as Meletus and Anytus claim. I can   b see why the actual victims of my influence might have some reason to be on my side; but those who have not been influenced, the older generation, their relatives, what reason do they have for being on my side, other than the correct and valid reason that they know Meletus is lying, and I am telling the truth?

Well, there we are, gentlemen. That, and perhaps a bit more along the same lines, is roughly what I might have to say in my defence. There may possibly be those among   c you who find it irritating, when you remember your own experience; you may, in a trial less important than this one, have begged and pleaded with the jury, with many tears, bringing your own children, and many others among your family and friends, up here to arouse as much sympathy as possible; whereas I refuse to do any of these things—even though I am, as it probably seems to you, in the greatest danger of all.

Thoughts like this could make some of you feel a little antagonistic towards me.   d For just this reason, you might get angry, and let anger influence your vote. If any of you does feel like this—I am sure you don't, but if you did—I think I might fairly say to you: "Of course I too have a family, my good friend. I do not come, in Homer's famous words, 'from oak or rock.' No, I was born of men, so I do have a family, and sons, men of Athens, three of them. One is not quite grown-up, the other two still boys. All the same, I am not going to bring any of them up here and beg you to acquit me."

Why will I not do any of these things? Not out of obstinacy, men of Athens, nor   e out of contempt for you. And whether or not I am untroubled by the thought of death is beside the point. No, it's a question of what is fitting—for me, for you, and for the whole city. I don't think it's right for me to do any of these things, at my age and with the reputation I have. It may be justified or unjustified, but there's a prevailing belief   35 that Socrates is in some way different from other people.

If those of you who seem to be outstanding in wisdom or courage, or any other quality, were to behave like this, it would be deplorable. Yet this is just the way I *have* seen men behaving when they are brought to trial. They may seem to be men of some distinction, but still they act in the most extraordinary way; they seem to think it will be a terrible disaster for them if they are put to death—as if they'd be immortal if you didn't put them to death. I think they bring disgrace on the city. A visitor to our country might imagine that in Athens people of outstanding character, those whom the Athenians themselves single out from among themselves for positions of office and   b other distinctions—that these men are no better than women.

Such behaviour, men of Athens, is not right for those of you with any kind of reputation at all; and if we who are on trial behave like that, you should not let us get away with it. You should make one thing absolutely clear, which is that you are much more ready to convict a defendant who stages one of these hysterical scenes, and makes our city an object of ridicule, than a defendant who behaves with decorum.

Quite apart from what is fitting, gentlemen, I think there is no justice, either, in begging favours from the jury, or being acquitted by begging; justice requires instruc-   c tion and persuasion. The juryman does not sit there for the purpose of handing out justice as a favour; he sits there to decide what justice is. He has not taken an oath to do a favour to anyone he takes a fancy to, but rather to reach a verdict in accordance with the laws. So *we* should not encourage in you the habit of breaking your oath, nor should *you* allow the habit to develop. If we did, we should neither of us be showing any respect for the gods.

d   Do not ask me, therefore, men of Athens, to conduct myself towards you in a way which I regard as contrary to right, justice and religion—least of all, surely, when I am being accused of impiety by Meletus here. After all, if I did persuade you and coerce you, by my begging, despite your oath, then clearly I *would* be teaching you to deny the existence of the gods; my whole defence would simply amount to accusing myself of not recognising the gods. And that is far from being the case. I do recognise them, men of Athens, as none of my accusers does, and I entrust to you and to god the task of reaching a verdict in my case in whatever way will be best both for me and for you.

*   *   *

e   If I am not upset, men of Athens, at what has just happened—your finding me guilty— there are a number of reasons. In particular, the result was not unexpected; in fact, I'm
36   surprised by the final number of votes on either side. Personally, I was expecting a large margin, not a narrow one; as it is, if only thirty votes had gone the other way, apparently I would have been acquitted. Indeed, on Meletus' charge, as I see it, I *have* been acquitted, even as things are. And not just acquitted; it's clear to anyone that if Anytus had not come forward, with Lycon, to accuse me, Meletus would have incurred
b   a fine of a thousand drachmas for not receiving twenty percent of the votes.

So the man proposes the death penalty for me. Very well. What counter-proposal am I to make to you, men of Athens? What I deserve, obviously. And what is that? What do I deserve to suffer or pay, for . . . for what? For not keeping quiet all through my life, for neglecting the things most people devote their lives to: business, family life, holding office—as general, or as leader of the assembly, or in some other capacity—or the alliances and factions which occur in political life. I thought, quite hon-
c   estly, that my sense of right and wrong would not allow me to survive in politics; so I did not pursue a course in which I should have been no use either to you or to myself, but rather one in which I could give help to each one of you privately—the greatest help possible, as I claim. That is the direction I took. I tried to persuade each of you not to give any thought at all to his own affairs until he had first given some thought to himself, and tried to make himself as good and wise as possible; not to give any thought to the affairs of the city without first giving some thought to the city itself; and to observe the same priorities in other areas as well.

d   What then do I deserve for behaving like this? Something good, men of Athens, if I am really supposed to make a proposal in accordance with what I deserve. And what's more, a good of a kind which is some use to me. What then *is* of use to a poor man, your benefactor, who needs free time in which to advise you? There can't be anything more useful to a man of this sort, men of Athens, than to be given free meals at the public expense; this is much more use to him than it is to any Olympic victor among you, if one of you wins the horse race, or the two-horse or four-horse chariot
e   race. The Olympic winner makes you *seem* to be happy; I make you really happy. He doesn't need the food; I do need it. So if I must propose a penalty based on justice, on
37   what I deserve, then that's what I propose—free meals at the public expense.

22

Here again, I suppose, in the same sort of way as when I was talking about appeals to pity and pleas for mercy, you may think I speak as I do out of sheer obstinacy. But it's not obstinacy, men of Athens; it's like this. I myself am convinced that I don't knowingly do wrong to anyone in the world, but I can't persuade you of that; we haven't had enough time to talk to one another. Mind you, if it were the custom here, as it is in other places, to decide cases involving the death penalty over several days rather than in one day, I believe you would have been persuaded. As it is, it was not b easy in a short time to overcome the strong prejudice against me.

But if I am convinced that I don't do wrong to anyone else, I am certainly not going to do wrong to myself, or speak against myself—saying I deserve something bad, and proposing some such penalty for myself. Why should I? Through fear of undergoing the penalty Meletus proposes, when I claim not to know whether it is good or bad? Should I, in preference to that, choose one of the things I know perfectly well to be bad, and propose that as a penalty?

Imprisonment? What is the point of living in prison, and being the slave of those c in the prison service at any particular time? A fine? And be imprisoned until I pay? That's the same as the first suggestion, since I haven't any money to pay a fine. Should I propose exile? I suppose you might accept that. But I'd have to be very devoted to life, men of Athens, to lose the power of rational thought so completely, and not be able to work out what would happen. If you, my fellow-citizens, couldn't stand my talk and my conversation, if you found them too boring and irritating, which is why you d now want to be rid of them, will people in some other country find it any easier to put up with them? Don't you believe it, men of Athens.

A fine life I should lead in exile, a man of my age—moving and being driven from city to city. I've no doubt that wherever I go, the young will listen to me, the way they do here. If I tell them to go away, they will send me into exile of their own accord, bringing pressure to bear on their elders; if I don't tell them to go away, their fathers e and relatives will exile me, out of concern for them.

I can imagine someone saying, "How about keeping your mouth shut, Socrates, and leading a quiet life? Can't you please go into exile, and live like that?" Of all things, this is the hardest point on which to convince some of you. If I say that it is disobeying god, and that for this reason I can't lead a quiet life, you won't believe me— 38 you'll think I'm using that as an excuse. If on the other hand I say that really the greatest good in a man's life is this, to be each day discussing human excellence and the other subjects you hear me talking about, examining myself and other people, and that the unexamined life isn't worth living—if I say this, you will believe me even less.

All the same, the situation is as I describe it, gentlemen—hard though it is to b convince you. Equally, for myself, I can't get used to the idea that I deserve anything bad. If I had any money, I would propose as large a fine as I could afford; that wouldn't do me any harm. As it is, I have no money, unless you are willing to have me propose an amount I *could* afford. I suppose I could pay you something like a hundred drachmas of silver, if you like. So that is the amount I propose.

Plato here, men of Athens—and Crito and Critobulus and Apollodorus—tell me to propose a penalty of three thousand drachmas; they say they guarantee it. I propose that amount, therefore, and they will offer full security to you for the money.

* * *

For just a small gain in time, men of Athens, you will now have the reputation and re- c sponsibility, among those who want to criticise the city, of having put to death

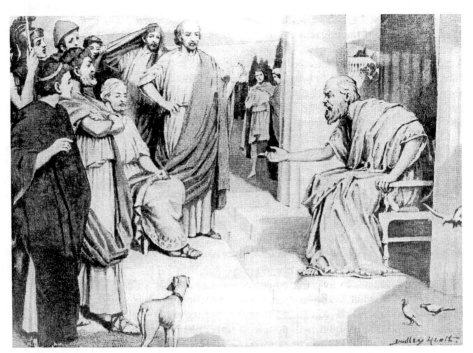

Despite refuting his accusers (as recorded in the *Apology*), Socrates was found guilty of impiety toward the gods and of corrupting the youth. He was sentenced to die by drinking the poison hemlock. (*Corbis-Bettmann*)

Socrates, that wise man—they will *say* I am wise, the people who want to blame you, even though I am not. If you'd waited a little, you could have had what you wanted without lifting a finger. You can see what age I am—far advanced in years, and close to death.

I say that not to all of you, but to those who voted for the death penalty. And I have something else to say to the same people. You may think, men of Athens, that I have lost my case through inability to make the kind of speech I *could* have used to persuade you, had I thought it right to do and say absolutely anything to secure my acquittal. Far from it. I have lost my case, not for want of a speech, but for want of effrontery and shamelessness, for refusing to make to you the kind of speech you most enjoy listening to. You'd like to have heard me lamenting and bewailing, and doing and saying all sorts of other things which are beneath my dignity, in my opinion—the kind of things you've grown used to hearing from other people.

I did not think it right, when I was speaking, to demean myself through fear of danger, nor do I now regret conducting my defence in the way I did. I had much rather defend myself like this, and be put to death, than behave in the way I have described, and go on living. Neither in the courts, nor in time of war, is it right—either for me or for anyone else—to devote one's efforts simply to avoiding death at all costs.

In battle it is often clear that death can be escaped, by dropping your weapons and throwing yourself on the mercy of your pursuers—and in any kind of danger there are all sorts of other devices for avoiding death, if you can bring yourself not to mind what you do or say. There's no difficulty in *that,* gentlemen, in escaping death. What is much harder is avoiding wickedness, since wickedness runs faster than death. So now, not surprisingly, I, who am old and slow, have been overtaken by the slower of the two. My accusers, being swift and keen, have been overtaken by the faster, by wickedness. Now I am departing, to pay the penalty of death inflicted by you. But they have already incurred the penalty, inflicted by truth, for wickedness and injustice. I accept my sentence, as they do theirs. I suppose that's probably how it was bound to turn out—and I have no complaints.

Having dealt with that, I now wish to make you a prophecy, those of you who voted for my condemnation. I am at that point where people are most inclined to make prophecies—which is when they are just about to die. To you gentlemen who have put me to death, I say that retribution will come to you, directly after my death—retribution far worse, god knows, than the death penalty which you have inflicted on me.

You have acted as you have today in the belief that you will avoid having to submit your lives to examination, but you will find the outcome is just the opposite; that is my prediction. There will be more people now to examine you—the ones I have so far been keeping in check without your realising it. They will be harder to deal with, being so much younger, and you will be more troubled by them. If you think that by putting men to death you can stop people criticising you for not living your lives in the right way, you are miscalculating badly. As a way of escape, this is neither effective nor creditable; the best and simplest way lies not in weeding out other people, but in making oneself as good a person as possible.

That is my prophecy to you who voted for my condemnation, and now I am prepared to let you go. To those who voted for my acquittal I'd like to make a few remarks about what has just happened, while the magistrates get on with the formalities, and it is not yet time for me to go where I must go to die. Please keep me company, gentlemen, for this little time; there's no reason why we shouldn't talk to one another while it is permitted. I regard you as my friends, and so to you I am prepared to explain the significance of today's outcome.

Gentlemen of the jury—since you I properly *can* call jurymen—a remarkable thing has happened to me. The prophetic voice I have got so used to, my supernatural voice, has always in the past been at my elbow, opposing me even in matters of little importance, if I was about to take a false step. You can see for yourselves the situation I'm now in. You might think—and this is how it is generally regarded—it was the ultimate misfortune. Yet the sign from god did not oppose my leaving home this morning, nor my appearance here in court, nor was there any point in my speech when it stopped me saying what I was just about to say.

Often in the past, when I have been talking, the sign has stopped me in full flow; this time it has not opposed me at any stage in the whole proceedings—either in what I have done or in what I have said. What do I take to be the reason for this? I'll tell you. The chances are that what has happened to me here is a good thing, and that it is impossible for those of us who think death is an evil to understand it correctly. I have strong evidence for this. The sign I know so well would unquestionably have opposed me, if things had not been going to turn out all right for me.

There is another reason for being confident that death is a good thing. Look at it like this. Death is one of two things; either it is like the dead person being nothing at all, and having no consciousness of anything at all; or, as we are told, it is actually some sort of change, a journey of the soul from this place to somewhere different. Suppose it is a total absence of consciousness—like sleep, when the sleeper isn't even dreaming. Then death would be a marvellous bonus. At least, I certainly think that if a

b

c

d

e

40

b

c

d

man had to choose the night on which he slept so soundly that he did not even dream, and if he had to compare all the other nights and days of his life with that night, if he had to think carefully about it, and then say how many days and nights he had spent in his life that were better and more enjoyable than that night—I think that not just a pri-

e vate individual, but even the great king of Persia could count these dreamless nights on the fingers of one hand compared with the other days and nights. If death is something like that, I call it a bonus. After all, the whole of time, seen in this way, seems no longer than a single night.

If, on the other hand, death is a kind of journey from here to somewhere different, and what we're told about all the dead being there is true, what greater good could

41 there be than that, gentlemen of the jury? Imagine arriving in the other world, getting away from the people here who claim to be judges, and finding real judges, the ones who are said to decide cases there—Minos, Rhadamanthys, Aeacus, Triptolemus, and others of the demigods who acted with justice in their own lives. Wouldn't that be a worthwhile journey?

Or again, what would any of you give to join Orpheus and Musaeus, Hesiod and Homer? Personally, I am quite prepared to die many times over, if these stories are

b true. For me at least, time spent there would be wonderful—I'd keep meeting people like Palamedes, or Aias the son of Telamon, or any other of the ancients who died as a result of an unjust verdict; I could compare my own experience with theirs. That would be entertaining, I imagine. Best of all, I could spend my time questioning and examining people there, just as I do people here, to find out which of them is wise, and which thinks he is wise but isn't.

What would you give, men of the jury, to interview the man who led the great

c expedition to Troy—or Odysseus, or Sisyphus, or thousands of others one could mention, men and women? It would be an unimaginable pleasure to talk to them there, to enjoy their company, and question them. They certainly can't put you to death there for asking questions. They are better off than us in many ways—and not least because they are now immune to death for the rest of time, if what we are told is true.

You too, men of the jury, must not be apprehensive about death. You must regard one thing at least as certain—that no harm can come to a good man either in his life or after his death; what happens to him is not a matter of indifference to the gods.

d Nor has my present situation arisen purely by chance; it is clear to me that it was better for me to die now and be released from my task. That's why my sign didn't at any point dissuade me, and why I am not in the least angry with those who voted against me, or with my accusers. Admittedly that wasn't their reason for voting against me, and accusing me; they thought they were doing me some harm. We *can* blame them for that.

However, I do have one request to make. It concerns my sons. When they grow

e up, gentlemen, get your own back on them, if you think they are more interested in money—or in anything else—than in goodness, by annoying them in exactly the same way as I annoyed you. If they think they amount to something when they don't, then criticise them, as I criticised you. Tell them they are not giving any thought to the things that matter, and that they think they amount to something when they are worth

42 nothing. If you do this, I shall myself have been fairly treated by you—and so will my sons.

I must stop. It is time for us to go—me to my death, you to your lives. Which of us goes to the better fate, only god knows.

CRITO

SOCRATES: What are you doing here at this time, Crito? Isn't it still early?

CRITO: Yes, it is.

SOCRATES: How early, exactly?

CRITO: It's not yet started to get light.

SOCRATES: I'm surprised the warder didn't refuse to answer your knock.

CRITO: He's become something of a friend of mine, Socrates, what with my coming here so often. Besides, I've done him a bit of a favour.

SOCRATES: Have you just arrived, or have you been here some time?

CRITO: Quite some time.

SOCRATES: Then why on earth didn't you wake me up? What were you doing just b sitting there beside me in silence?

CRITO: I wouldn't have dreamt of it, Socrates. For my part, I wouldn't choose to be in this state of sleeplessness and misery; and for some time now it has astonished me to see how soundly you sleep. I deliberately didn't wake you because I wanted you to enjoy your rest. It has often struck me in the past, throughout my life in fact, how lucky you are in your temperament—and it strikes me much more forcibly in your present misfortune. You bear it so easily and calmly.

SOCRATES: Yes, Crito, I do. It wouldn't make much sense for a man my age to get upset at the prospect of dying.

CRITO: Other people your age, Socrates, find themselves in similar predicaments; c *their* age doesn't stop them getting upset at their misfortune.

SOCRATES: That's true. Anyway, why *have* you come so early?

CRITO: To bring news, Socrates, bad news. Not bad for you, as far as I can see, but for me and all your friends it is bad and hard to bear; and I think I shall find it as hard to bear as anybody.

SOCRATES: What sort of news? Has the boat from Delos arrived—the one my exe- d cution has been waiting for?

CRITO: It hasn't actually arrived, but I think it will today, judging by the reports of some people who've just come from Sunium. It was there when they left. It's clear from what they said that it will arrive today, and so tomorrow, Socrates, you will be forced to end your life.

SOCRATES: Well, Crito, if that is how the gods want it, I hope it will all turn out for the best. All the same, I don't think it will come today.

CRITO: What is that based on?

SOCRATES: I'll tell you. My death, I assume, is to take place on the day after the ship arrives.

CRITO: Yes. At least, that's what the prison authorities say.

SOCRATES: Then I think it will come tomorrow, not today. That's based on a dream I had last night, just before I woke up. So perhaps it was lucky you didn't wake me.

CRITO: What was the dream?

SOCRATES: I saw a woman, fair and beautiful, in a white cloak. She came up to b me, and called my name. "Socrates," she said, "On the third day shall you come to fertile Phthia."

CRITO: A strange dream, Socrates.

SOCRATES: Clear enough, though, I think, Crito.

CRITO: Only too clear, I'm afraid. Now listen, Socrates, it's not too late, even now, to do as I say and escape. For me, if you are put to death, it is a double disaster. Quite apart from losing a friend such as I shall never find again, there will also be

c   many who will think, those who don't know the two of us well, that I had the chance to save you if I'd been prepared to spend some money, and that I wasn't interested in doing so.

Can you think of a worse reputation than being thought to value money more highly than friends? Most people will never believe that it was you yourself who refused to leave here, and that we strongly encouraged you to do so.

SOCRATES: Really, Crito, why should we care so much about what "most people" believe? The best people, who are the ones we should worry about more, will realise that things were done in the way they actually were done.

d   CRITO: Yet you can see that we have no choice, Socrates, but to care about what most people think as well. The present situation is a clear example of how the many can injure us in ways which are not trivial, but just about as great as can be, if they are given the wrong impression about someone.

SOCRATES: If only the many *could* do us the greatest injuries, Crito. That would mean they were capable of doing us the greatest good as well, which would be excellent. As it is, they're incapable of doing either. They have no power to make a man either wise or foolish; nor do they care what effect they have.

e   CRITO: I dare say you are right. But tell me something, Socrates. Are you worried about me and the rest of your friends? Do you think, if you leave here, that we shall get into trouble with the people who make a living out of bringing private prosecutions, be-

45   cause we smuggled you out of here? Do you think we shall be forced to forfeit all our property, or pay a very large fine, and possibly undergo some further penalty in addition? If something like that is what you are afraid of, don't give it another thought. We are in duty bound to run this risk to save you—that goes without saying—and even greater risks, if need be. Listen to me. Don't say "no."

SOCRATES: It *is* something I worry about, Crito. That, and many other things besides.

CRITO: Well then, do not be afraid on that score. There are people prepared, for not a very large sum of money, to save you and get you out of here. And apart from them, can't you see how easily bought they are, the men who make their living out of

b   prosecutions? It wouldn't need a lot of money to take care of them. You have my resources at your disposal; that should be plenty, I imagine. And if you're worried about me, and feel you shouldn't spend my money, look at the people we've got here who are not Athenians, who are ready to spend theirs. One of them, Simmias the Theban, has actually brought enough money for just this purpose; Cebes too is fully prepared, and so are many others.

So as I say, you should not let these fears stop you saving yourself; and do not let it be an objection, as you claimed in court, that you would not know what to do with yourself if you went into exile. There are lots of places you can go where they'll be

c   glad to see you; if you want to go to Thessaly, for example, my family has friends there who will be delighted to see you, and who will give you sanctuary. Nobody in Thessaly will give you any trouble.

Apart from that, Socrates, it is actually wrong, in my opinion, to sacrifice yourself, as you are proposing to do, when you could escape. You seem to be voluntarily choosing for yourself the kind of fate your enemies would have chosen for you—and *did* choose for you when they were trying to destroy you. Worse still, I think, is the betrayal of your own sons, when there is nothing to stop you bringing them up and educating them—and yet you are going to go away and leave them, and for all you care they can turn out how they will. They will have, in all probability, the kind of life orphans generally have when they lose their parents. d

No. Either you shouldn't have children, or you should play your part, and go through with the labour of raising and educating them. You seem to me to be taking the easy way out. What you should do is choose what a decent and courageous man would choose—you who claim to have been concerned with human goodness all your life. Personally, I am ashamed both for you and for those of us who are your friends. I e think this whole business of yours will be thought to be the result of some lack of resolution on our part—first of all the fact that the case came to court when it needn't have done, then the actual conduct of the case in court, and now this, as the final absurdity 46 of the whole affair, that we shall be thought to have missed the opportunity—through our own cowardice and lack of resolution, since we didn't save you, nor did you save yourself, though it was possible, and within your power, with even a modest amount of help from us. Don't let all this be a humiliation, Socrates, both for you and for us, in addition to being an evil.

Think it over—or rather, the time for thinking it over is past, you should by now have thought it over—there is only one course of action. The whole thing must be done this coming night. If we wait any longer, it will be impossible; it will not be an option any longer. I cannot urge you too strongly, Socrates. Listen to me. Do as I say.

SOCRATES: My dear Crito, your enthusiasm is most commendable, so long as there is some justification for it. Otherwise, the greater your enthusiasm, the more out of place it is. We'd better look into whether this is the right thing to do or not. It has b been my practice, not just now but always, to trust, of all the guides at my disposal, only the principle which on reflection seems most appropriate. I cannot now throw overboard principles which I have put forward in the past, simply because of what has happened to me. They still seem to me very much the same as they always did; I still give pride of place to, and value, the same principles as before. Unless we can find some better principle than these to put forward on this occasion, you can be quite sure I am not going to agree with you, however many bugbears the power of the many produces to scare us with—as if we were children—letting loose on us its imprisonments, c its death sentences, and its fines.

What then is the best way of looking into this question? Why don't we start by going back to the argument you put forward based on what people will think? Were we right or wrong, all those times, when we said we should listen to some opinions, but not to others? Or were we right before I was sentenced to death, only for it now to become clear that it was a waste of breath, spoken simply for the sake of having something to say, and that it was really juvenile fantasy? Personally, Crito, I should very d much like to carry out a joint enquiry with you, to see whether the principle will seem rather different to me, now that I am in this situation, or whether it will seem the same—and whether we are going to forget about it, or follow it.

The principle so often put forward, I think, by those among us who thought they knew what they were talking about, was the one I referred to just now—that of the opinions held by men, we should regard some as important, and others not. Seriously, e Crito, don't you think this is a sound principle? You are, barring accidents, not in the position of having to die tomorrow, so you shouldn't be influenced by the present situation. Examine the question. Don't you think it a sound principle that we should not value all human opinions equally, but should value some highly, and others not? And the same with the people who hold the opinions. We should not value all of them, but should value some, and not others. What do you think? Isn't this a sound principle?

CRITO: Yes, it is.

SOCRATES: We should value the good opinions, but not the bad ones?

CRITO: Yes.

SOCRATES: Aren't good opinions the opinions of the wise, whereas bad opinions are those of the foolish?

CRITO: Obviously.

b SOCRATES: Well then, what was the kind of analogy we used to employ? If a man is taking physical exercise, and this is what he is interested in, does he listen to the praise and criticism and opinion of just anyone, or only of one person—the person who is in fact a medical expert or a physical training instructor?

CRITO: Only of one person.

SOCRATES: So he should worry about the criticisms, and welcome the praises, of this one person, but not those of the many?

CRITO: Clearly he should.

SOCRATES: In what he does, then—in the exercise he takes, in what he eats and drinks—he should be guided by the one man, the man in charge, the expert, rather than by everyone else.

CRITO: That is so.

c SOCRATES: All right. If he defies the one man, and doesn't value his opinion and his recommendations, but does value those of the many, those who are not experts, won't he do himself some harm?

CRITO: Of course he will.

SOCRATES: What is this harm? What is its extent? What part of the man who defies the expert does it attack?

CRITO: His body, obviously. That is what it damages.

SOCRATES: Quite right. Well then, is it the same also in other situations, Crito, to save us going through all the examples—and especially with right and wrong, foul and fair, good and bad, the things we are now discussing? Should we follow the opinion of the many, and fear that, or the opinion of the one man, if we can find an expert on the subject? Should we respect and fear this one man more than all the rest put together? And if we don't follow his advice, we shall injure and do violence to that part which we have often agreed improves with justice and is damaged by injustice. Or is this all wrong?

CRITO: No, I think it is right, Socrates.

SOCRATES: Very well. Take that part of us which improves with health, and is damaged by disease. If we ruin it by following advice other than that of the experts, is life worth living once that part is injured? This is the body, of course, isn't it?

CRITO: Yes.

SOCRATES: Is life worth living, then, if our body is in poor condition and injured?

CRITO: Certainly not.

SOCRATES: How about the part of us which is attacked by injustice, and helped by justice? Is life worth living when that is injured? Or do we regard it as less important than the body, this part of us—whichever of our faculties it is—the part to which justice and injustice belong?

CRITO: No, we certainly don't.

SOCRATES: More important, then?

CRITO: Much more important.

SOCRATES: In that case, my dear friend, we should not pay the slightest attention, as you suggested we should, to what most people will say about us. We should listen only to the expert on justice and injustice, to the one man, and to the truth itself. So you were wrong, for a start, in one of your recommendations—when you proposed that we should be concerned about the opinion of the many on the subject of justice, right, good, and their opposites. "Ah!" you might say, "but the many are liable to put us to death."

CRITO: That too is obviously true. You might well say that, Socrates. You are b
quite right.

SOCRATES: All the same, my learned friend, I think the principle we have elaborated still has the same force as it did. And what about this second principle? Tell me, does our belief—that the important thing is not being alive, but living a good life—still hold good, or not?

CRITO: It does still hold good.

SOCRATES: And that when we're talking about a life, good, right, and just are one and the same thing—does that still hold good, or not?

CRITO: It does.

SOCRATES: Well then, in the light of the points we have agreed, we must look into c
the question whether it is right, or not right, for me to attempt to leave here without the permission of the Athenians. If it appears to be right, let us make the attempt; otherwise let us forget about it. As for the considerations you raise—questions of expense, public opinion, the upbringing of children—I suspect that these, Crito, are really the concerns of those who readily put people to death, and would as readily bring them back to life again, if they could—for absolutely no reason. I am, of course, talking about the many.

For us, though, the thing is to follow where the argument leads us, and I rather think the only question we need ask is the one we asked just now: shall we act rightly if we give our money, and our thanks, to those who will arrange my escape from here? d
Shall we ourselves be acting rightly in arranging the escape, and allowing it to be arranged? Or shall we in fact be acting wrongly if we do all these things? If this is clearly the wrong way for us to behave, then I'm pretty sure that compared with the danger of acting wrongly, we should not take into account the certainty either of being put to death if we stay put and accept things quietly, or of suffering anything else at all.

CRITO: I am sure you are right, Socrates. You decide what we should do.

SOCRATES: Let us look into it together, my friend. And if you want to raise an ob- e
jection at any point while I'm talking, then raise it, and I will listen to you. Otherwise, my fine friend, stop repeating the same thing over and over again—that I should leave here in defiance of the wishes of the Athenians. I attach great importance to acting with your agreement, rather than against your wishes.

Now, think about the starting-point of our enquiry. Do you regard it as satisfac- 49
tory? And when you answer the question, mind you say what you really think.

CRITO: I will try.

SOCRATES: Do we agree that we should never deliberately do wrong, or should we sometimes do wrong, and sometimes not? Is wrong-doing absolutely contrary to what is good and fine, as has often been agreed among us in the past? Or have all those things we once agreed on become, in these last few days, so much water under the bridge? Did we, grown men and at the age we were, Crito, discuss things so enthusias- b
tically with one another, without realising we were no better than children? Or is what we said then more true now than ever? Whether "most people" agree or not, and

whether we have to undergo hardships more severe even than these—or possibly less severe—isn't wrong-doing in fact, for the person who does it, wholly evil and bad? Is this what we say, or not?

CRITO: It is.

SOCRATES: A man should never do wrong, then.

CRITO: No, he should not.

SOCRATES: So even if he is wronged, he should not do wrong in return, as most people think, since he ought not *ever* to do wrong.

c   CRITO: Apparently not.

SOCRATES: What about harming people, Crito? Should a man do that, or not?

CRITO: I suppose not, Socrates.

SOCRATES: How about harming people in retaliation, if he is injured by them first—which is what most people say he should do? Is that right or wrong?

CRITO: Completely wrong.

SOCRATES: And that, I imagine, is because injuring people is the same thing as doing them wrong.

CRITO: That is right.

SOCRATES: So he should not do wrong to anyone or injure them, in retaliation, no matter how he has been treated by them. And if you say "yes" to that, Crito, make sure

d   you are not saying "yes" against what you really think. I realise not many people accept this view—or ever will accept it. As a result, there is no common ground between those who do accept it and those who do not; each side necessarily regards the opinions of the other side with contempt. So you too must think very hard about it. Are you

e   on our side? Do you agree with us in accepting this view, and shall we base our argument on the premise that it is never legitimate to do wrong to people, nor do them wrong in retaliation, nor, if one is injured, defend oneself by harming them in return? Or do you disagree? Do you reject the original premise? Personally, I have held this view a long time, and I still hold it now. If you have been holding some other view, tell me; instruct me. But if you stand by what we said earlier, then listen to what follows from it.

CRITO: I do stand by it, and I do agree with you. Tell me what follows.

SOCRATES: Very well, I will tell you. Or rather, I'll ask you. If a man makes an agreement—a fair agreement—with someone, should he fulfil his side of the agreement, or should he try to get out of it?

CRITO: He should fulfil it.

50   SOCRATES: Then see what follows from that. If we leave here without persuading the city to change its mind, are we doing harm to anyone or anything—those we have least cause to injure—or not? Are we standing by our agreement—our fair agreement—or not?

CRITO: I can't answer your question, Socrates. I don't understand it.

SOCRATES: Look at it like this. Imagine that, just as we were about to run away, or whatever we are supposed to call it, from here, the laws of Athens and the state of Athens appeared before us, and said: "Tell me, Socrates, what are you trying to do?

b   Aren't you simply trying, by this action you are embarking on, to destroy both us, the laws, and the entire city, as far as lies within your power? Do you think it possible for a city to continue to exist, and not sink without trace, if the verdicts of its courts have no force, if they are rendered invalid, and nullified, by private citizens?"

What shall we say, Crito, to these questions and others like them? There's a lot that could be said, especially by the public advocate, in defence of this law we are trying to do away with—the law which lays down that verdicts arrived at in the courts

should be binding. Shall we say to the laws, "The city wronged us. It did not reach its   c
verdict fairly?" Shall we say that, or what?

CRITO: Yes, we most emphatically should say that, Socrates.

SOCRATES: Suppose then the laws say, "Was *that* what was agreed between us
and you, Socrates? Or was it to abide by the verdicts the city arrives at in its courts?"
And if we expressed surprise at their question, they might add: "Do not be surprised by
our question, Socrates. Answer it. You have had enough practice at question-and-   d
answer. Come on, then. What principle do you appeal to, against us and the city, to
allow you to try and destroy us? Did we not bring you into existence, for a start? Was it
not through us that your father married your mother, and fathered you? Tell us, then,
those of us who are the laws governing marriage, have you some criticism of us? Is
there something wrong with us?"

"I have no criticism," I should have to reply.   e

"All right, then. How about your upbringing and education after you were born?
How about the laws to do with those? Did we not give your father the right instructions—those of us whose job it is to attend to this—when we told him to educate you
by means of the arts and physical training?"

"No, they were the right instructions," I would say.

"Very well. Since you were born, and brought up, and educated, under our protection, you were our offspring and our slave—both you yourself and your parents.
Can you deny that, for a start? And if that is so, do you think that justice gives equivalent rights to you and to us? If we decide to do something to you, do you think you
have the right to do it to us in return?

"There was no equality of rights as between you and your father or your master,
if you had one, entitling you to do to him in retaliation what he did to you—to answer   51
him back if he spoke abusively to you, or beat him in retaliation if he beat you, or anything else like that. Will it then be legitimate for you to retaliate against your country
and its laws? And is the result that if we decide to destroy you, because we think it
right to do so, you in your turn, to the best of your ability, will set about destroying us,
the laws, and your country, in retaliation? Will you claim that in acting like this you
are doing what is right, you who are truly so concerned about human excellence? Are
you so clever that you fail to realise that your country is an object of greater value, an   b
object of greater respect and reverence, and altogether more important, both among
gods and among men, if they have any sense, than your mother and your father and all
the rest of your ancestors put together? That you should revere your country, submit to
it, mollify it when it is angry with you—more than you would your father—and either
persuade it to change its mind, or do what it tells you? That you should quietly accept
whatever treatment it ordains you should receive—beating, perhaps, or imprison-   c
ment—or if it takes you to war, to be wounded or killed, that is what you should do,
and that is what is right? That you should not give way, or retreat, or abandon your position, that in war, in the lawcourts, or anywhere else, you should do what your city
and your country tells you, or else convince it where justice naturally lies? And that the
use of force, against a mother or a father, is against god's law—still more so the use of
force against your country?"

What are we going to say in answer to this, Crito? Shall we say the laws are
right, or not?

CRITO: Well, *I* think they are right.

SOCRATES: "Consider, then, Socrates," the laws might perhaps say, "Are we right
in saying that you are not justified in embarking on the actions against us which you
are now embarking on? We fathered you, brought you up, educated you, gave you and   d

every other citizen a share in every good thing it was in our power to give. And even then, if there is any Athenian who reaches the age of majority, takes a look at his city's constitution, and at us, the laws, and finds we are not to his satisfaction, then by granting him permission we make a public declaration to anyone who wishes that he may take what is his, and go wherever he pleases. If a man chooses to go to one of your colonies, because we and the city are not to his liking, or to leave, emigrate to some other place, and go wherever he wants, with no loss of property, not one of us laws stands in his way, or forbids him.

"To those of you who stay, aware of our way of reaching verdicts in the courts, and of making our other political arrangements, we say that you have now entered into a formal agreement with us, to do what we tell you, and we say that the man who dis-
e   obeys us is doing wrong in three ways: he is disobeying us who fathered him; he is disobeying those who brought him up; and having made an agreement to obey us, he neither obeys, nor tries to make us change our minds, if we are doing something which is not right. When we make him a fair offer, not harshly demanding that he do whatever
52   we order, but allowing him a straight choice, either to make us change our minds, or to do as we say, he does neither. These are the charges, Socrates, to which we claim that you too will render yourself liable, if you do what you are proposing to do—you in particular, more than any of the Athenians."

If I asked them why me in particular, they might perhaps have a justifiable complaint against me in that I, as much as any of the Athenians, really have entered into
b   this agreement with them. They could say, "Socrates, we have convincing evidence to suggest that we and the city *were* to your liking. You could not possibly have spent more of your time living here in Athens than any other Athenian if the place had not been particularly to your liking; you would not have refused ever to leave the city to see famous places—except Corinth, once—or go anywhere else, unless it was to go somewhere on military service; you never went abroad, as other people do, nor were
c   you seized with a desire to know any other city, or any other laws. No, you were satisfied with us, and with our city. In fact, so strongly did you choose us, and agree to live your life as a citizen under us, that you even produced children in the city. You would not have done that if it had not been to your liking.

"Even at your trial, it was open to you to propose a penalty of exile, if you chose, and do then, with the city's permission, what you are now proposing to do without it. On that occasion you put a brave face on it; you said you didn't mind if you had to die; you preferred, so you said, death to exile. Do not those words now make you feel ashamed? Have you no feeling for us, the laws, as you set about destroying us, and do
d   what the meanest slave might do, trying to run away in breach of the contract and agreement by which you agreed to live your life as a citizen? Answer us this question, for a start: are we right in saying that you have agreed—not just verbally, but by your behaviour—to live your life as a citizen under us? Or are we wrong?"

What are we going to say to this, Crito? Can we do anything but agree?

CRITO: We have no choice, Socrates.

SOCRATES: "Aren't you simply breaking," they might say, "contracts and agree-
e   ments which you have with us? You did not enter into them under compulsion or false pretences. You were not forced to make up your mind on the spur of the moment, but over a period of seventy years, during which you were at liberty to leave, if we were
53   not to your liking, or if you thought the agreement was unfair. You did not choose Sparta or Crete instead, places which you have always described as well-governed; nor did you choose any other city, inside or outside Greece. Even people who are lame, or blind, or crippled in other ways, spend more time away from Athens than you did. *That*

is an indication, quite clearly, of how you, more than any of the Athenians, found the city, and us the laws, to your liking. After all, who could find a city to his liking, and not like its laws? And do you now not stand by what you agreed? You will if you take our advice, Socrates. That way you will avoid making yourself ridiculous by leaving the city.

"Think about it. If you break this agreement, and put yourself in the wrong in   b
this way, what good will you do yourself or your friends? That your friends will proba-
bly have to go into exile as well, be cut off from their city, and forfeit their property, is reasonably clear. And you? Well for a start, if you go to one of the cities nearby, say Thebes or Megara, both of which have good laws, you will come to them, Socrates, as an enemy of their constitution; those who care for their city will look at you with suspicion, believing you to be a subverter of the laws. You will also reinforce the opinion of   c
the jury about you. They will decide they did reach the right verdict. After all, there is a strong presumption that a man who subverts the laws will be a corrupting influence on people who are young and foolish.

"Will you then keep away from cities with good laws, and the most civilised part of mankind? If you do, will it be worth your while remaining alive? Or will you spend your time with them? And will you have the nerve, in your conversations with them—
what sort of conversations, Socrates? The ones you had here, about human excellence   d
and justice being the most valuable things for mankind, together with custom and the laws? Don't you think the whole idea of Socrates will be clearly seen to be a disgrace? You certainly should.

"Or will you leave this part of the world and go to Thessaly, to Crito's family friends? Up there you will find all sorts of anarchy and self-indulgence. I am sure they would be entertained by the amusing story of your running away from prison in some costume or other—wearing a leather jerkin, perhaps, or one of the other disguises   e
favoured by people running away—and altering your appearance. That an old man, in all probability with a small span of life remaining to him, could bring himself to cling to life in this limpet-like way, by transgressing the most important of the laws—will there be no-one who will say this? Perhaps not, if you can manage not to annoy anyone. Otherwise, Socrates, you will have to listen to a lot of unflattering comments about yourself. Are you going to spend your life ingratiating yourself with everyone, being a slave to them? Oh, yes, you will have a whale of a time up there in Thessaly, as if you had emigrated out to dinner in Thessaly. But what, please tell us, will become of   54
all those conversations about justice and other forms of human excellence?

"Or do you want to remain alive for your children's sake, so that you can bring them up and educate them? How do you feel about taking them to Thessaly, and bring-
ing them up and educating them there, turning them into foreigners, so you can give them that privilege as well? If not, if they are brought up here, will they be any better brought up and educated because you are alive and separated from them? Your friends will be looking after them. Will they look after them if you go to Thessaly to live, and not look after them if you go to the next world? If those who claim to be your friends   b
are any use at all, of course they will not.

"No, Socrates, obey us who brought you up. Do not regard your children, or life, or anything at all, as more important than justice; you do not want, when you come to the other world, to have to defend yourself on these charges to the rulers there. Neither in this world does it seem to be better, or more just or more godfearing, for you or any of your friends, if you behave like this; nor, when you come to the next world, will it be better for you there. As it is, you go there, if you do go, as one wronged—not by us,   c
the laws, but by men. If on the other hand you depart, after so shamefully returning

wrong for wrong, and injury for injury, breaking your own agreement and contract with us, and injuring those whom you had least cause to injure—yourself, your friends, your country, and us—then we shall be angry with you while you are alive, and in the next world our brothers, the laws in Hades, will not receive you kindly, since they will know that you tried, to the best of your ability, to destroy us. So do not let Crito persuade you to follow his advice rather than ours."

d

That, I assure you, Crito, my very dear friend, is what I think I hear them saying, just as those gripped by religious fervour think they hear the pipes; the sound of their words rings in my head, and stops me hearing anything else. Be in no doubt. As far as I can see at the moment, if you disagree with them, you will speak in vain. All the same, though, if you think it will do any good, then speak.

e

CRITO: Socrates, I have nothing to say.

SOCRATES: Then forget about it, Crito. Let us act in the way god points out to us.

PHAEDO (in part)

[Socrates is speaking] . . . My dear Cebes, if all things in which there is any life were to die, and when they were dead were to remain in that form and not come to life again, would not the necessary result be that everything at last would be dead, and nothing alive? For if living things were generated from other sources than death, and were to die, the result is inevitable that all things would be consumed by death. Is it not so?

72^d

It is indeed, I think, Socrates, said Cebes; I think that what you say is perfectly true.

Yes, Cebes, he said, I think it is certainly so. We are not misled into this conclusion. The dead do come to life again, and the living are generated from them, and the souls of the dead exist; and with the souls of the good it is well, and with the souls of the evil it is evil.

e

And besides, Socrates, rejoined Cebes, if the doctrine which you are fond of stating, that our learning is only a process of recollection, be true, then I suppose we must have learned at some former time what we recollect now. And that would be impossible unless our souls had existed somewhere before they came into this human form. So that is another reason for believing the soul immortal.

73

But, Cebes, interrupted Simmias, what are the proofs of that? Recall them to me; I am not very clear about them at present.

One argument, answered Cebes, and the strongest of all, is that if you question men about anything in the right way, they will answer you correctly of themselves. But they would not have been able to do that unless they had had within themselves knowledge and right reason. Again, show them such things as geometrical diagrams, and the proof of the doctrine is complete.*

b

*[For an example of this see Meno 82a–86b (pp. 68ff in this volume).]

Plato, *Phaedo,* translated by F.J. Church (New York: Macmillan/Library of the Liberal Arts, 1951).

And if that does not convince you, Simmias, said Socrates, look at the matter in another way and see if you agree then. You have doubts, I know, how what is called knowledge can be recollection.

Nay, replied Simmias, I do not doubt. But I want to recollect the argument about recollection. What Cebes undertook to explain has nearly brought your theory back to me and convinced me. But I am nonetheless ready to hear you undertake to explain it.

In this way, he returned. We are agreed, I suppose, that if a man remembers any- c thing, he must have known it at some previous time.

Certainly, he said.

And are we agreed that when knowledge comes in the following way, it is recollection? When a man has seen or heard anything, or has perceived it by some other sense, and then knows not that thing only, but has also in his mind an impression of some other thing, of which the knowledge is quite different, are we not right in saying d that he remembers the thing of which he has an impression in his mind?

What do you mean?

I mean this. The knowledge of a man is different from the knowledge of a lyre, is it not?

Certainly.

And you know that when lovers see a lyre, or a garment, or anything that their favorites are wont to use, they have this feeling. They know the lyre, and in their mind they receive the image of the youth whose the lyre was. That is recollection. For instance, someone seeing Simmias often is reminded of Cebes; and there are endless examples of the same thing.

Indeed there are, said Simmias.

Is not that a kind of recollection, he said; and more especially when a man has e this feeling with reference to things which the lapse of time and inattention have made him forget?

Yes, certainly, he replied.

Well, he went on, is it possible to recollect a man on seeing the picture of a horse, or the picture of a lyre? Or to recall Simmias on seeing a picture of Cebes?

Certainly.

And it is possible to recollect Simmias himself on seeing a picture of Simmias?

No doubt, he said.   74

Then in all these cases there is recollection caused by similar objects, and also by dissimilar objects?

There is.

But when a man has a recollection caused by similar objects, will he not have a further feeling and consider whether the likeness to that which he recollects is defective in any way or not?

He will, he said.

Now see if this is true, he went on. Do we not believe in the existence of equality—not the equality of pieces of wood or of stones, but something beyond that—equality in the abstract? Shall we say that there is such a thing, or not?

Yes indeed, said Simmias, most emphatically we will.   b

And do we know what this abstract equality is?

Certainly, he replied.

Where did we get the knowledge of it? Was it not from seeing the equal pieces of wood, and stones, and the like, which we were speaking of just now? Did we not form from them the idea of abstract equality, which is different from them? Or do you think that it is not different? Consider the question in this way. Do not equal pieces of wood and stones appear to us sometimes equal and sometimes unequal, though in fact they remain the same all the time?

Certainly they do.

c But did absolute equals ever seem to you to be unequal, or abstract equality to be inequality?

No, never, Socrates.

Then equal things, he said, are not the same as abstract equality?

No, certainly not, Socrates.

Yet it was from these equal things, he said, which are different from abstract equality, that you have conceived and got your knowledge of abstract equality?

That is quite true, he replied.

And that whether it is like them or unlike them?

Certainly.

d But that makes no difference, he said. As long as the sight of one thing brings another thing to your mind, there must be recollection, whether or no the two things are like.

That is so.

Well then, said he, do the equal pieces of wood, and other similar equal things, of which we have been speaking, affect us at all this way? Do they seem to us to be equal, in the way that abstract equality is equal? Do they come short of being like abstract equality, or not?

Indeed, they come very short of it, he replied.

Are we agreed about this? A man sees something and thinks to himself, "This

e thing that I see aims at being like some other thing, but it comes short and cannot be like that other thing; it is inferior"; must not the man who thinks that have known at some previous time that other thing, which he says that it resembles, and to which it is inferior?

He must.

Well, have we ourselves had the same sort of feeling with reference to equal things, and to abstract equality?

Yes, certainly.

75 Then we must have had knowledge of equality before we first saw equal things, and perceived that they all strive to be like equality, and all come short of it.

That is so.

And we are agreed also that we have not, nor could we have, obtained the idea of equality except from sight or touch or some other sense; the same is true of all the senses.

Yes, Socrates, for the purposes of the argument that is so.

b At any rate, it is by the senses that we must perceive that all sensible objects strive to resemble absolute equality, and are inferior to it. Is not that so?

Yes.

Then before we began to see, and to hear, and to use the other senses, we must have received the knowledge of the nature of abstract and real equality; otherwise we could not have compared equal sensible objects with abstract equality, and seen that the former in all cases strive to be like the latter, though they are always inferior to it?

That is the necessary consequence of what we have been saying, Socrates.

Did we not see, and hear, and possess the other senses as soon as we were born?

Yes, certainly.

c And we must have received the knowledge of abstract equality before we had these senses?

Yes.

Then, it seems, we must have received that knowledge before we were born?

It does.

Now if we received this knowledge before our birth, and were born with it, we knew, both before and at the moment of our birth, not only the equal, and the greater, and the less, but also everything of the same kind, did we not? Our present reasoning does not refer only to equality. It refers just as much to absolute good, and absolute   d
beauty, and absolute justice, and absolute holiness; in short, I repeat, to everything which we mark with the name of the real, in the questions and answers of our dialectic. So we must have received our knowledge of all realities before we were born.

That is so.

And we must always be born with this knowledge, and must always retain it throughout life, if we have not each time forgotten it, after having received it. For to know means to receive and retain knowledge, and not to have lost it. Do not we mean by forgetting, the loss of knowledge, Simmias?

Yes, certainly, Socrates, he said.   e

But, I suppose, if it be the case that we lost at birth the knowledge which we received before we were born, and then afterward, by using our senses on the objects of sense, recovered the knowledge which we had previously possessed, then what we call learning is the recovering of knowledge which is already ours. And are we not right in calling that recollection?

Certainly.

For we have found it possible to perceive a thing by sight, or hearing, or any   76
other sense, and thence to form a notion of some other thing, like or unlike, which had been forgotten, but with which this thing was associated. And therefore, I say, one of two things must be true. Either we are all born with this knowledge and retain it all our life; or, after birth, those whom we say are learning are only recollecting, and our knowledge is recollection.

Yes indeed, that is undoubtedly true, Socrates.

Then which do you choose, Simmias? Are we born with knowledge or do we recollect the things of which we have received knowledge before our birth?   b

I cannot say at present, Socrates.

Well, have you an opinion about this question? Can a man who knows give an account of what he knows, or not? What do you think about that?

Yes, of course he can, Socrates.

And do you think that everyone can give an account of the ideas of which we have been speaking?

I wish I did, indeed, said Simmias, but I am very much afraid that by this time to-morrow there will no longer be any man living able to do so as it should be done.

Then, Simmias, he said, you do not think that all men know these things?   c

Certainly not.

Then they recollect what they once learned?

Necessarily.

And when did our souls gain this knowledge? It cannot have been after we were born men.

No, certainly not.

Then it was before?

Yes.

Then, Simmias, our souls existed formerly, apart from our bodies, and possessed intelligence before they came into man's shape.

Unless we receive this knowledge at the moment of birth, Socrates. That time still remains.

d   Well, my friend, and at what other time do we lose it? We agreed just now that we are not born with it; do we lose it at the same moment that we gain it, or can you suggest any other time?

I cannot, Socrates. I did not see that I was talking nonsense.

Then, Simmias, he said, is not this the truth? If, as we are forever repeating,
e   beauty, and good, and the other ideas really exist, and if we refer all the objects of sensible perception to these ideas which were formerly ours, and which we find to be ours still, and compare sensible objects with them, then, just as they exist, our souls must have existed before ever we were born. But if they do not exist, then our reasoning will have been thrown away. Is it so? If these ideas exist, does it not at once follow that our souls must have existed before we were born, and if they do not exist, then neither did our souls?

Admirably put, Socrates, said Simmias. I think that the necessity is the same for
77   the one as for the other. The reasoning has reached a place of safety in the common proof of the existence of our souls before we were born and of the existence of the ideas of which you spoke. Nothing is so evident to me as that beauty, and good, and the other ideas which you spoke of just now have a very real existence indeed. Your proof is quite sufficient for me.

But what of Cebes? said Socrates. I must convince Cebes too.

I think that he is satisfied, said Simmias, though he is the most skeptical of men in argument. But I think that he is perfectly convinced that our souls existed before we were born.

But I do not think myself, Socrates, he continued, that you have proved that the
b   soul will continue to exist when we are dead. The common fear which Cebes spoke of, that she [the soul] may be scattered to the winds at death, and that death may be the end of her existence, still stands in the way. Assuming that the soul is generated and comes together from some other elements, and exists before she ever enters the human body, why should she not come to an end and be destroyed, after she has entered into the body, when she is released from it?

c   You are right, Simmias, said Cebes. I think that only half the required proof has been given. It has been shown that our souls existed before we were born; but it must also be shown that our souls will continue to exist after we are dead, no less than that they existed before we were born, if the proof is to be complete.

That has been shown already, Simmias and Cebes, said Socrates, if you will
d   combine this reasoning with our previous conclusion, that all life is generated from death. For if the soul exists in a previous state and if, when she comes into life and is born, she can only be born from death, and from a state of death, must she not exist after death too, since she has to be born again? So the point which you speak of has been already proved.

Still I think that you and Simmias would be glad to discuss this question further. Like children, you are afraid that the wind will really blow the soul away and disperse
e   her when she leaves the body, especially if a man happens to die in a storm and not in a calm.

Cebes laughed and said, Try and convince us as if we were afraid, Socrates; or rather, do not think that we are afraid ourselves. Perhaps there is a child within us who has these fears. Let us try and persuade him not to be afraid of death, as if it were a bugbear.

You must charm him every day, until you have charmed him away, said Socrates.

And where shall we find a good charmer, Socrates, he asked, now that you are 78 leaving us?

Hellas is a large country, Cebes, he replied, and good men may doubtless be found in it; and the nations of the Barbarians are many. You must search them all through for such a charmer, sparing neither money nor labor; for there is nothing on which you could spend money more profitably. And you must search for him among yourselves too, for you will hardly find a better charmer than yourselves.

That shall be done, said Cebes. But let us return to the point where we left off, if you will. b

Yes, I will: why not?

Very good, he replied.

Well, said Socrates, must we not ask ourselves this question? What kind of thing is liable to suffer dispersion, and for what kind of thing have we to fear dispersion? And then we must see whether the soul belongs to that kind or not, and be confident or afraid about our own souls accordingly.

That is true, he answered.

Now is it not the compound and composite which is naturally liable to be dis- c solved in the same way in which it was compounded? And is not what is uncompounded alone not liable to dissolution, if anything is not?

I think that that is so, said Cebes.

And what always remains in the same state and unchanging is most likely to be uncompounded, and what is always changing and never the same is most likely to be compounded, I suppose?

Yes, I think so.

Now let us return to what we were speaking of before in the discussion, he said. Does the being, which in our dialectic we define as meaning absolute existence, remain d always in exactly the same state, or does it change? Do absolute equality, absolute beauty, and every other absolute existence, admit of any change at all? Or does absolute existence in each case, being essentially uniform, remain the same and unchanging, and never in any case admit of any sort or kind of change whatsoever?

It must remain the same and unchanging, Socrates, said Cebes.

And what of the many beautiful things, such as men, and horses, and garments, and the like, and of all which bears the names of the ideas, whether equal, or beautiful, or anything else? Do they remain the same or is it exactly the opposite with them? In e short, do they never remain the same at all, either in themselves or in their relations?

These things, said Cebes, never remain the same.

You can touch them, and see them, and perceive them with the other senses, 79 while you can grasp the unchanging only by the reasoning of the intellect. These latter are invisible and not seen. Is it not so?

That is perfectly true, he said.

Let us assume then, he said, if you will, that there are two kinds of existence, the one visible, the other invisible.

Yes, he said.

And the invisible is unchanging, while the visible is always changing.

Yes, he said again.

Are not we men made up of body and soul? b

There is nothing else, he replied.

And which of these kinds of existence should we say that the body is most like, and most akin to?

The visible, he replied; that is quite obvious.

And the soul? Is that visible or invisible?

It is invisible to man, Socrates, he said.

But we mean by visible and invisible, visible and invisible to man; do we not?

Yes; that is what we mean.

Then what do we say of the soul? Is it visible or not visible?

It is not visible.

Then is it invisible?

Yes.

Then the soul is more like the invisible than the body; and the body is like the visible.

c   That is necessarily so, Socrates.

Have we not also said that, when the soul employs the body in any inquiry, and makes use of sight, or hearing, or any other sense—for inquiry with the body means inquiry with the senses—she is dragged away by it to the things which never remain the same, and wanders about blindly, and becomes confused and dizzy, like a drunken man, from dealing with things that are ever changing?

Certainly.

d   But when she investigates any question by herself, she goes away to the pure, and eternal, and immortal, and unchangeable, to which she is akin, and so she comes to be ever with it, as soon as she is by herself, and can be so; and then she rests from her wanderings and dwells with it unchangingly, for she is dealing with what is unchanging. And is not this state of the soul called wisdom?

Indeed, Socrates, you speak well and truly, he replied.

e   Which kind of existence do you think from our former and our present arguments that the soul is more like and more akin to?

I think, Socrates, he replied, that after this inquiry the very dullest man would agree that the soul is infinitely more like the unchangeable than the changeable.

And the body?

That is like the changeable.

Consider the matter in yet another way. When the soul and the body are united,
80   nature ordains the one to be a slave and to be ruled, and the other to be master and to rule. Tell me once again, which do you think is like the divine, and which is like the mortal? Do you not think that the divine naturally rules and has authority, and that the mortal naturally is ruled and is a slave?

I do.

Then which is the soul like?

That is quite plain, Socrates. The soul is like the divine, and the body is like the mortal.

Now tell me, Cebes, is the result of all that we have said that the soul is most like
b   the divine, and the immortal, and the intelligible, and the uniform, and the indissoluble, and the unchangeable; while the body is most like the human, and the mortal, and the unintelligible, and the multiform, and the dissoluble, and the changeable? Have we any other argument to show that this is not so, my dear Cebes?

We have not.

Then if this is so, is it not the nature of the body to be dissolved quickly, and of the soul to be wholly or very nearly indissoluble?

c   Certainly.

You observe, he said, that after a man is dead, the visible part of him, his body, which lies in the visible world and which we call the corpse, which is subject to dissolution and decomposition, is not dissolved and decomposed at once? It remains as it was for a considerable time, and even for a long time, if a man dies with his body in good condition and in the vigor of life. And when the body falls in and is embalmed, like the mummies of Egypt, it remains nearly entire for an immense time. And should it decay, yet some parts of it, such as the bones and muscles, may almost be said to be immortal. Is it not so?

Yes.

And shall we believe that the soul, which is invisible, and which goes hence to a place that is like herself, glorious, and pure, and invisible, to Hades, which is rightly called the unseen world, to dwell with the good and wise God, whither, if it be the will of God, my soul too must shortly go—shall we believe that the soul, whose nature is so glorious, and pure, and invisible, is blown away by the winds and perishes as soon as she leaves the body, as the world says? Nay, dear Cebes and Simmias, it is not so. I will tell you what happens to a soul which is pure at her departure, and which in her life has had no intercourse that she could avoid with the body, and so draws after her, when she dies, no taint of the body, but has shunned it, and gathered herself into herself, for such has been her constant study—and that only means that she has loved wisdom rightly, and has truly practiced how to die. Is not this the practice of death?

Yes, certainly.

Does not the soul, then, which is in that state, go away to the invisible that is like herself, and to the divine, and the immortal, and the wise, where she is released from error, and folly, and fear, and fierce passions, and all the other evils that fall to the lot of men, and is happy, and for the rest of time lives in very truth with the gods, as they say that the initiated do? Shall we affirm this, Cebes?

Yes, certainly, said Cebes.

But if she be defiled and impure when she leaves the body, from being ever with it, and serving it and loving it, and from being besotted by it and by its desires and pleasures, so that she thinks nothing true but what is bodily and can be touched, and seen, and eaten, and drunk, and used for men's lusts; if she has learned to hate, and tremble at, and fly from what is dark and invisible to the eye, and intelligible and apprehended by philosophy—do you think that a soul which is in that state will be pure and without alloy at her departure?

No, indeed, he replied.

She is penetrated, I suppose, by the corporeal, which the unceasing intercourse and company and care of the body has made a part of her nature.

Yes.

And, my dear friend, the corporeal must be burdensome, and heavy, and earthy, and visible; and it is by this that such a soul is weighed down and dragged back to the visible world, because she is afraid of the invisible world of Hades, and haunts, it is said, the graves and tombs, where shadowy forms of souls have been seen, which are the phantoms of souls which were impure at their release and still cling to the visible; which is the reason why they are seen.

That is likely enough, Socrates.

That is likely, certainly, Cebes; and these are not the souls of the good, but of the evil, which are compelled to wander in such places as a punishment for the wicked lives that they have lived; and their wanderings continue until, from the desire for the corporeal that clings to them, they are again imprisoned in a body.

And, he continued, they are imprisoned, probably, in the bodies of animals with habits similar to the habits which were theirs in their lifetime.

What do you mean by that, Socrates?

82 I mean that men who have practiced unbridled gluttony, and wantonness, and drunkenness probably enter the bodies of asses and suchlike animals. Do you not think so?

Certainly that is very likely.

And those who have chosen injustice, and tyranny, and robbery enter the bodies of wolves, and hawks, and kites. Where else should we say that such souls go?

No doubt, said Cebes, they go into such animals.

In short, it is quite plain, he said, whither each soul goes; each enters an animal with habits like its own.

Certainly, he replied, that is so.

And of these, he said, the happiest, who go to the best place, are those who have b practiced the popular and social virtues which are called temperance and justice, and which come from habit and practice, without philosophy or reason.

And why are they the happiest?

Because it is probable that they return into a mild and social nature like their own, such as that of bees, or wasps, or ants; or, it may be, into the bodies of men, and that from them are made worthy citizens.

Very likely.

c But none but the philosopher or the lover of knowledge, who is wholly pure when he goes hence, is permitted to go to the race of the gods; and therefore, my friends, Simmias and Cebes, the true philosopher is temperate and refrains from all the pleasures of the body, and does not give himself up to them. It is not squandering his substance and poverty that he fears, as the multitude and the lovers of wealth do; nor again does he dread the dishonor and disgrace of wickedness, like the lovers of power and honor. It is not for these reasons that he is temperate.

No, it would be unseemly in him if he were, Socrates, said Cebes.

d Indeed it would, he replied, and therefore all those who have any care for their souls, and who do not spend their lives in forming and molding their bodies, bid farewell to such persons, and do not walk in their ways, thinking that they know not whither they are going. They themselves turn and follow whithersoever philosophy leads them, for they believe that they ought not to resist philosophy, or its deliverance and purification.

How, Socrates?

I will tell you, he replied. The lovers of knowledge know that when philosophy e receives the soul, she is fast bound in the body, and fastened to it; she is unable to contemplate what is, by herself, or except through the bars of her prison house, the body; and she is wallowing in utter ignorance. And philosophy sees that the dreadful thing 83 about the imprisonment is that it is caused by lust, and that the captive herself is an accomplice in her own captivity. The lovers of knowledge, I repeat, know that philosophy takes the soul when she is in this condition, and gently encourages her, and strives to release her from her captivity, showing her that the perceptions of the eye, and the ear, and the other senses are full of deceit, and persuading her to stand aloof from the b senses and to use them only when she must, and exhorting her to rally and gather herself together, and to trust only to herself and to the real existence which she of her own self apprehends, and to believe that nothing which is subject to change, and which she perceives by other faculties, has any truth, for such things are visible and sensible, while what she herself sees is apprehended by reason and invisible. The soul of the true philosopher thinks that it would be wrong to resist this deliverance from captivity, and therefore she holds aloof, so far as she can, from pleasure, and desire, and pain, and $\quad$ c fear; for she reckons that when a man has vehement pleasure, or fear, or pain, or desire, he suffers from them not merely the evils which might be expected, such as sickness or some loss arising from the indulgence of his desires; he suffers what is the greatest and last of evils, and does not take it into account.

What do you mean, Socrates? asked Cebes.

I mean that when the soul of any man feels vehement pleasure or pain, she is forced at the same time to think that the object, whatever it be, of these sensations is the most distinct and truest, when it is not.

$$* \quad * \quad *$$

... A man should be of good cheer about his soul if in his life he has renounced the $\quad$ d pleasures and adornments of the body, because they were nothing to him, and because he thought that they would do him not good but harm; and if he has instead earnestly pursued the pleasures of learning, and adorned his soul with the adornment of temper- $\quad$ e ance, and justice, and courage, and freedom, and truth, which belongs to her and is her own, and so awaits his journey to the other world, in readiness to set forth whenever fate calls him. You, Simmias and Cebes, and the rest will set forth at some future day, $\quad$ 115 each at his own time. But me now, as a tragic poet would say, fate calls at once; and it is time for me to betake myself to the bath. I think that I had better bathe before I drink the poison, and not give the women the trouble of washing my dead body.

When he had finished speaking Crito said, Be it so, Socrates. But have you any $\quad$ b commands for your friends or for me about your children, or about other things? How shall we serve you best?

Simply by doing what I always tell you, Crito. Take care of your own selves, and you will serve me and mine and yourselves in all that you do, even though you make no promises now. But if you are careless of your own selves, and will not follow the path of life which we have pointed out in our discussions both today and at other times, all your promises now, however profuse and earnest they are, will be of no avail. $\quad$ c

We will do our best, said Crito. But how shall we bury you?

As you please, he answered; only you must catch me first and not let me escape you. And then he looked at us with a smile and said, My friends, I cannot convince Crito that I am the Socrates who has been conversing with you and arranging his argu- ments in order. He thinks that I am the body which he will presently see a corpse, and $\quad$ d he asks how he is to bury me. All the arguments which I have used to prove that I shall not remain with you after I have drunk the poison, but that I shall go away to the happi- ness of the blessed, with which I tried to comfort you and myself, have been thrown away on him. Do you therefore be my sureties to him, as he was my surety at the trial, but in a different way. He was surety for me then that I would remain; but you must be my sureties to him that I shall go away when I am dead, and not remain with you; then he will feel my death less; and when he sees my body being burned or buried, he will $\quad$ e not be grieved because he thinks that I am suffering dreadful things; and at my funeral he will not say that it is Socrates whom he is laying out, or bearing to the grave, or burying. For, dear Crito, he continued, you must know that to use words wrongly is not only a fault in itself, it also creates evil in the soul. You must be of good cheer, and say that you are burying my body; and you may bury it as you please and as you think $\quad$ 116 right.

The Death of Socrates, 1787, by Jacques-Louis David (1748–1825). (*Oil on canvas, 51 ×
77-1/4 inches. The Metropolitan Museum of Art, Wolfe Fund, 1931. Catharine Lorillard
Wolfe Collection. [31.45]*)

       With these words he rose and went into another room to bathe. Crito went with
him and told us to wait. So we waited, talking of the argument and discussing it, and
then again dwelling on the greatness of the calamity which had fallen upon us: it
b   seemed as if we were going to lose a father and to be orphans for the rest of our lives.
When he had bathed, and his children had been brought to him—he had two sons quite
little, and one grown up—and the women of his family were come, he spoke with them
in Crito's presence, and gave them his last instructions; then he sent the women and
children away and returned to us. By that time it was near the hour of sunset, for he
had been a long while within. When he came back to us from the bath he sat down, but
c   not much was said after that. Presently the servant of the Eleven came and stood before
him and said, "I know that I shall not find you unreasonable like other men, Socrates.
They are angry with me and curse me when I bid them drink the poison because the
authorities make me do it. But I have found you all along the noblest and gentlest and
best man that has ever come here; and now I am sure that you will not be angry with
d   me, but with those who you know are to blame. And so farewell, and try to bear what
must be as lightly as you can; you know why I have come." With that he turned away
weeping, and went out.

       Socrates looked up at him and replied, Farewell, I will do as you say. Then he
turned to us and said, How courteous the man is! And the whole time that I have
been here, he has constantly come in to see me, and sometimes he has talked to me,
and has been the best of men; and now, how generously he weeps for me! Come,
Crito, let us obey him; let the poison be brought if it is ready, and if it is not ready,
let it be prepared.

Crito replied: But, Socrates, I think that the sun is still upon the hills; it has not   e
set. Besides, I know that other men take the poison quite late, and eat and drink
heartily, and even enjoy the company of their chosen friends, after the announcement
has been made. So do not hurry; there is still time.

Socrates replied: And those whom you speak of, Crito, naturally do so, for they
think that they will be gainers by so doing. And I naturally shall not do so, for I think
that I should gain nothing by drinking the poison a little later, but my own contempt   117
for so greedily saving a life which is already spent. So do not refuse to do as I say.

Then Crito made a sign to his slave who was standing by; and the slave went out,
and after some delay returned with the man who was to give the poison, carrying it
prepared in a cup. When Socrates saw him, he asked, You understand these things, my
good man, what have I to do?

You have only to drink this, he replied, and to walk about until your legs feel
heavy, and then lie down; and it will act of itself.   b

With that he handed the cup to Socrates, who took it quite cheerfully,
Echecrates, without trembling, and without any change of color or of feature, and
looked up at the man with that fixed glance of his, and asked, What say you to making
a libation from this draught? May I, or not?

We only prepare so much as we think sufficient, Socrates, he answered.   c

I understand, said Socrates. But I suppose that I may, and must, pray to the gods
that my journey hence may be prosperous. That is my prayer; may it be so. With these
words he put the cup to his lips and drank the poison quite calmly and cheerfully.

Till then most of us had been able to control our grief fairly well; but when we
saw him drinking and then the poison finished, we could do so no longer: my tears
came fast in spite of myself, and I covered my face and wept for myself; it was not for
him, but at my own misfortune in losing such a friend. Even before that Crito had been   d
unable to restrain his tears, and had gone away; and Apollodorus, who had never once
ceased weeping the whole time, burst into a loud wail and made us one and all break
down by his sobbing, except Socrates himself.

What are you doing, my friends? he exclaimed. I sent away the women chiefly in   e
order that they might not behave in this way; for I have heard that a man should die in
silence. So calm yourselves and bear up.

When we heard that, we were ashamed, and we ceased from weeping. But he
walked about, until he said that his legs were getting heavy, and then he lay down on
his back, as he was told. And the man who gave the poison began to examine his feet
and legs from time to time. Then he pressed his foot hard and asked if there was any
feeling in it, and Socrates said, No; and then his legs, and so higher and higher, and   118
showed us that he was cold and stiff. And Socrates felt himself and said that when it
came to his heart, he should be gone. He was already growing cold about the groin,
when he uncovered his face, which had been covered, and spoke for the last time.
Crito, he said, I owe a cock to Asclepius; do not forget to pay it.*

It shall be done, replied Crito. Is there anything else that you wish? He made no
answer to this question; but after a short interval there was a movement, and the man
uncovered him, and his eyes were fixed. Then Crito closed his mouth and his eyes.

Such was the end, Echecrates, of our friend, a man, I think, who was the wisest
and justest, and the best man I have ever known.

---

*[Asclepius was the Greek god of healing. When one recovered from an illness it was customary to
offer a cock as a sacrifice, so Socrates' last words imply that death is a kind of healing. See, for instance 66b
ff., 67c.]

MENO

PERSONS OF THE DIALOGUE

    Meno
    A Slave of Meno
    Socrates
    Anytus

70   MENO: Can you tell me Socrates—is virtue something that can be taught? Or does it come by practice? Or is it neither teaching nor practice that gives it to a man but natural aptitude or something else?

    SOCRATES: Well Meno, in the old days the Thessalians had a great reputation

b among the Greeks for their wealth and their horsemanship. Now it seems they are philosophers as well—especially the men of Larissa, where your friend Aristippus comes from. It is Gorgias who has done it. He went to that city and captured the hearts of the foremost of the Aleuadae for his wisdom (among them your own admirer Aristippus), not to speak of other leading Thessalians. In particular he got you into the

c habit of answering any question you might be asked, with the confidence and dignity appropriate to those who know the answers, just as he himself invites questions of every kind from anyone in the Greek world who wishes to ask, and never fails to an-

71 swer them. But here at Athens, my dear Meno, it is just the reverse. There is a dearth of wisdom, and it looks as if it had migrated from our part of the country to yours. At any rate, if you put your question to any of our people, they will all alike laugh and say: "You must think I am singularly fortunate, to know whether virtue can be taught or how it is acquired. The fact is that far from knowing whether it can be taught, I have no idea what virtue itself is."

b   That is my own case. I share the poverty of my fellow-countrymen in this respect, and confess to my shame that I have no knowledge about virtue at all. And how can I know a property of something when I don't even know what it is? Do you suppose that somebody entirely ignorant who Meno is could say whether he is handsome and rich and well-born or the reverse? Is that possible, do you think?

    MENO: No. But is this true about yourself, Socrates, that you don't even know

c what virtue is? Is this the report that we are to take home about you?

    SOCRATES: Not only that; you may say also that, to the best of my belief, I have never yet met anyone who did know.

    MENO: What! Didn't you meet Gorgias when he was here?

    SOCRATES: Yes.

    MENO: And you still didn't think he knew?

    SOCRATES: I'm a forgetful sort of person, and I can't say just now what I thought at the time. Probably he did know, and I expect you know what he used to say about it.

d So remind me what it was, or tell me yourself if you will. No doubt you agree with him.

    MENO: Yes I do.

From *Protagoras and Meno,* translated with an introduction by W.K.C. Guthrie (Harmondsworth, Middlesex, England: Penguin Classics, 1956). Reprinted by permission of Penguin Books Ltd.

SOCRATES: Then let's leave him out of it, since after all he isn't here. What do you yourself say virtue is? I do ask you in all earnestness not to refuse me, but to speak out. I shall be only too happy to be proved wrong if you and Gorgias turn out to know this, although I said I had never met anyone who did.

MENO: But there is no difficulty about it. First of all, if it is manly virtue you are   e
after, it is easy to see that the virtue of a man consists in managing the city's affairs capably, and so that he will help his friends and injure his foes while taking care to come to no harm himself. Or if you want a woman's virtue, that is easily described. She must be a good housewife, careful with her stores and obedient to her husband. Then there is another virtue for a child, male or female, and another for an old man, free or slave as   72
you like; and a great many more kinds of virtue, so that no one need be at a loss to say what it is. For every act and every time of life, with reference to each separate function, there is a virtue for each one of us, and similarly, I should say, a vice.

SOCRATES: I seem to be in luck. I wanted one virtue and I find that you have a whole swarm of virtues to offer. But seriously, to carry on this metaphor of the swarm, suppose I asked you what a bee is, what is its essential nature, and you replied that bees were of many different kinds; what would you say if I went on to ask: "And is it in being bees that they are many and various and different from one another? Or would   b
you agree that it is not in this respect that they differ, but in something else, some other quality like size or beauty?"

MENO: I should say that in so far as they are bees, they don't differ from one another at all.

SOCRATES: Suppose I then continued: "Well, this is just what I want you to tell me. What is that character in respect of which they don't differ at all, but are all the   c
same?" I presume you would have something to say?

MENO: I should.

SOCRATES: Then do the same with the virtues. Even if they are many and various, yet at least they all have some common character which makes them virtues. That is what ought to be kept in view by anyone who answers the question: "What is virtue?"
Do you follow me?   d

MENO: I think I do, but I don't yet really grasp the question as I should wish.

SOCRATES: Well, does this apply in your mind only to virtue, that there is a different one for a man and a woman and the rest? Is it the same with health and size and strength, or has health the same character everywhere, if it is health, whether it be in a   e
man or any other creature?

MENO: I agree that health is the same in a man or in a woman.

SOCRATES: And what about size and strength? If a woman is strong, will it be the same thing, the same strength, that makes her strong? My meaning is that in its character as strength, it is no different, whether it be in a man or in a woman. Or do you think it is?

MENO: No.

SOCRATES: And will virtue differ, in its character as virtue, whether it be in a   73
child or an old man, a woman or a man?

MENO: I somehow feel that this is not on the same level as the other cases.

SOCRATES: Well then, didn't you say that a man's virtue lay in directing the city well, and a woman's in directing her household well?

MENO: Yes.

SOCRATES: And is it possible to direct anything well—city or household or anything else—if not temperately and justly?

MENO: Certainly not.

SOCRATES: And that means with temperance and justice?

MENO: Of course.

SOCRATES: Then both man and woman need the same qualities, justice and temperance, if they are going to be good.

MENO: It looks like it.

SOCRATES: And what about your child and old man? Could they be good if they were incontinent and unjust?

c   MENO: Of course not.

SOCRATES: They must be temperate and just?

MENO: Yes.

SOCRATES: So everyone is good in the same way, since they become good by possessing the same qualities.

MENO: So it seems.

SOCRATES: And if they did not share the same virtue, they would not be good in the same way.

MENO: No.

SOCRATES: Seeing then that they all have the same virtue, try to remember and tell me what Gorgias, and you who share his opinion, say it is.

d   MENO: It must be simply the capacity to govern men, if you are looking for one quality to cover all the instances.

SOCRATES: Indeed I am. But does this virtue apply to a child or a slave? Should a slave be capable of governing his master, and if he does, is he still a slave?

MENO: I hardly think so.

SOCRATES: It certainly doesn't sound likely. And here is another point. You speak of "capacity to govern." Shall we not add "justly but not otherwise"?

MENO: I think we should, for justice is virtue.

e   SOCRATES: Virtue, do you say, or *a* virtue?

MENO: What do you mean?

SOCRATES: Something quite general. Take roundness, for instance. I should say that it is a shape, not simply that it is shape, my reason being that there are other shapes as well.

MENO: I see your point, and I agree that there are other virtues besides justice.

74   SOCRATES: Tell me what they are. Just as I could name other shapes if you told me to, in the same way mention some other virtues.

MENO: In my opinion then courage is a virtue and temperance and wisdom and dignity and many other things.

SOCRATES: This puts us back where we were. In a different way we have discovered a number of virtues when we were looking for one only. This single virtue, which permeates each of them, we cannot find.

b   MENO: No, I cannot yet grasp it as you want, a single virtue covering them all, as I do in other instances.

SOCRATES: I'm not surprised, but I shall do my best to get us a bit further if I can. You understand, I expect, that the question applies to everything. If someone took the example I mentioned just now, and asked you: "What is shape?" and you replied that roundness is shape, and he then asked you as I did, "Do you mean it is shape or *a* shape?" you would reply of course that it is *a* shape.

MENO: Certainly.

c   SOCRATES: Your reason being that there are other shapes as well.

MENO: Yes.

SOCRATES: And if he went on to ask you what they were, you would tell him.

MENO: Yes.

SOCRATES: And the same with colour—if he asked you what it is, and on your re-plying "White," took you up with: "Is white colour or *a* colour?" you would say that it is *a* colour, because there are other colours as well.

MENO: I should.

SOCRATES: And if he asked you to, you would mention other colours which are   d
just as much colours as white is.

MENO: Yes.

SOCRATES: Suppose then he pursued the question as I did, and objected: "We al-ways arrive at a plurality, but that is not the kind of answer I want. Seeing that you call these many particulars by one and the same name, and say that every one of them is a shape, even though they are the contrary of each other, tell me what this is which em-braces round as well as straight, and what you mean by shape when you say that   e
straightness is a shape as much as roundness. You do say that?"

MENO: Yes.

SOCRATES: "And in saying it, do you mean that roundness is no more round than straight, and straightness no more straight than round?"

MENO: Of course not.

SOCRATES: "Yet you do say that roundness is no more a shape than straightness, and the other way about."

MENO: Quite true.

SOCRATES: "Then what is this thing which is called 'shape'? Try to tell me." If   75
when asked this question either about shape or colour you said: "But I don't under-stand what you want, or what you mean," your questioner would perhaps be surprised and say: "Don't you see that I am looking for what is the same in all of them?" Would you even so be unable to reply, if the question was: "What is it that is common to roundness and straightness and the other things which you call shapes?"

Do your best to answer, as practice for the question about virtue.

MENO: No, you do it, Socrates.   b

SOCRATES: Do you want me to give in to you?

MENO: Yes.

SOCRATES: And will you in your turn give me an answer about virtue?

MENO: I will.

SOCRATES: In that case I must do my best. It's in a good cause.

MENO: Certainly.

SOCRATES: Well now, let's try to tell you what shape is. See if you accept this definition. Let us define it as the only thing which always accompanies colour. Does that satisfy you, or do you want it in some other way? I should be content if your defin-   c
ition of virtue were on similar lines.

MENO: But that's a naïve sort of definition, Socrates.

SOCRATES: How?

MENO: Shape, if I understand what you say, is what always accompanies colour. Well and good—but if somebody says that he doesn't know what colour is, but is no better off with it than he is with shape, what sort of answer have you given him, do you think?

SOCRATES: A true one; and if my questioner were one of the clever, disputatious and quarrelsome kind, I should say to him: "You have heard my answer. If it is wrong,   d
it is for you to take up the argument and refute it." However, when friendly people, like you and me, want to converse with each other, one's reply must be milder and more conducive to discussion. By that I mean that it must not only be true, but must   e
employ terms with which the questioner admits he is familiar. So I will try to answer you like that. Tell me therefore, whether you recognize the term "end"; I mean limit or   51

boundary—all these words I use in the same sense. Prodicus might perhaps quarrel with us, but I assume you speak of something being bounded or coming to an end. That is all I mean, nothing subtle.

MENO: I admit the notion, and believe I understand your meaning.

SOCRATES: And again, you recognize "surface" and "solid," as they are used in geometry?

MENO: Yes.

SOCRATES: Then with these you should by this time understand my definition of shape. To cover all its instances, I say that shape is that in which a solid terminates, or more briefly, it is the limit of a solid.

MENO: And how do you define colour?

SOCRATES: What a shameless fellow you are, Meno. You keep bothering an old man to answer, but refuse to exercise your memory and tell me what was Gorgias's definition of virtue.

MENO: I will, Socrates, as soon as you tell me this.

SOCRATES: Anyone talking to you could tell blindfolded that you are a handsome man and still have your admirers.

MENO: Why so?

SOCRATES: Because you are forever laying down the law as spoilt boys do, who act the tyrant as long as their youth lasts. No doubt you have discovered that I can never resist good looks. Well, I will give in and let you have your answer.

MENO: Do by all means.

SOCRATES: Would you like an answer *à la* Gorgias, such as you would most readily follow?

MENO: Of course I should.

SOCRATES: You and he believe in Empedocles's theory of effluences, do you not?

MENO: Whole-heartedly.

SOCRATES: And passages to which and through which the effluences make their way?

MENO: Yes.

SOCRATES: Some of the effluences fit into some of the passages, whereas others are too coarse or too fine.

MENO: That is right.

SOCRATES: Now you recognize the term "sight"?

MENO: Yes.

SOCRATES: From these notions, then, "grasp what I would tell," as Pindar says. Colour is an effluence from shapes commensurate with sight and perceptible by it.

MENO: That seems to me an excellent answer.

SOCRATES: No doubt it is the sort you are used to. And you probably see that it provides a way to define sound and smell and many similar things.

MENO: So it does.

SOCRATES: Yes, it's a high-sounding answer, so you like it better than the one on shape.

MENO: I do.

SOCRATES: Nevertheless, son of Alexidemus, I am convinced that the other is better; and I believe you would agree with me if you had not, as you told me yesterday, to leave before the mysteries, but could stay and be initiated.*

---

*Evidently the Athenians are about to celebrate the famous rites of the Eleusinian Mysteries, but Meno has to return to Thessaly before they fall due. Plato frequently plays upon the analogy between religious initiation, which bestows a revelation of divine secrets, and the insight that comes from initiation into the truths of philosophy.

MENO: I would stay, Socrates, if you gave me more answers like this.

SOCRATES: You may be sure I shan't be lacking in keenness to do so, both for your sake and mine; but I'm afraid I may not be able to do it often. However, now it is your turn to do as you promised, and try to tell me the general nature of virtue. Stop making many out of one, as the humorists say when somebody breaks a plate. Just leave virtue whole and sound and tell me what it is, as in the examples I have given you.

MENO: It seems to me then, Socrates, that virtue is, in the words of the poet, "to rejoice in the fine and have power," and I define it as desiring fine things and being able to acquire them.

SOCRATES: When you speak of a man desiring fine things, do you mean it is good things he desires?

MENO: Certainly.

SOCRATES: Then do you think some men desire evil and others good? Doesn't everyone, in your opinion, desire good things?

MENO: No.

SOCRATES: And would you say that the others suppose evils to be good, or do they still desire them although they recognize them as evil?

MENO: Both, I should say.

SOCRATES: What? Do you really think that anyone who recognizes evils for what they are, nevertheless desires them?

MENO: Yes.

SOCRATES: Desires in what way? To possess them?

MENO: Of course.

SOCRATES: In the belief that evil things bring advantage to their possessor, or harm?

MENO: Some in the first belief, but some also in the second.

SOCRATES: And do you believe that those who suppose evil things bring advantage understand that they are evil?

MENO: No, that I can't really believe.

SOCRATES: Isn't it clear then that this class, who don't recognize evils for what they are, don't desire evil but what they think is good, though in fact it is evil; those who through ignorance mistake bad things for good obviously desire the good.

MENO: For them I suppose that is true.

SOCRATES: Now as for those whom you speak of as desiring evils in the belief that they do harm to their possessor, these presumably know that they will be injured by them?

MENO: They must.

SOCRATES: And don't they believe that whoever is injured is, in so far as he is injured, unhappy?

MENO: That too they must believe.

SOCRATES: And unfortunate?

MENO: Yes.

SOCRATES: Well, does anybody want to be unhappy and unfortunate?

MENO: I suppose not.

SOCRATES: Then if not, nobody desires what is evil; for what else is unhappiness but desiring evil things and getting them?

MENO: It looks as if you are right, Socrates, and nobody desires what is evil.

SOCRATES: Now you have just said that virtue consists in a wish for good things plus the power to acquire them. In this definition the wish is common to everyone, and in that respect no one is better than his neighbour.

MENO: So it appears.

SOCRATES: So if one man is better than another, it must evidently be in respect of the power, and virtue, according to your account, is the power of acquiring good things.

MENO: Yes, my opinion is exactly as you now express it.

SOCRATES: Let us see whether you have hit the truth this time. You may well be right. The power of acquiring good things, you say, is virtue?

MENO: Yes.

SOCRATES: And by good do you mean such things as health and wealth?

MENO: I include the gaining both of gold and silver and of high and honourable office in the State.

SOCRATES: Are these the only classes of goods that you recognize?

MENO: Yes, I mean everything of that sort.

SOCRATES: Right. In the definition of Meno, hereditary guest-friend of the Great King, the acquisition of gold and silver is virtue. Do you add "just and righteous" to the word "acquisition," or doesn't it make any difference to you? Do you call it virtue all the same even if they are unjustly acquired?

MENO: Certainly not.

SOCRATES: Vice then?

MENO: Most certainly.

SOCRATES: So it seems that justice or temperance or piety, or some other part of virtue, must attach to the acquisition. Otherwise, although it is a means to good things, it will not be virtue.

MENO: No, how could you have virtue without these?

SOCRATES: In fact lack of gold and silver, if it results from failure to acquire it—either for oneself or another—in circumstances which would have made its acquisition unjust, is itself virtue.

MENO: It would seem so.

SOCRATES: Then to have such goods is no more virtue than to lack them. Rather we may say that whatever is accompanied by justice is virtue, whatever is without qualities of that sort is vice.

MENO: I agree that your conclusion seems inescapable.

SOCRATES: But a few minutes ago we called each of these—justice, temperance, and the rest—a part of virtue?

MENO: Yes, we did.

SOCRATES: So it seems you are making a fool of me.

MENO: How so, Socrates?

SOCRATES: I have just asked you not to break virtue up into fragments, and given you models of the type of answer I wanted, but taking no notice of this you tell me that virtue consists in the acquisition of good things with justice; and justice, you agree, is a part of virtue.

MENO: True.

SOCRATES: So it follows from your own statements that to act with a part of virtue is virtue, if you call justice and all the rest parts of virtue. The point I want to make is that whereas I asked you to give me an account of virtue as a whole, far from telling me what it is itself you say that every action is virtue which exhibits a part of virtue, as if you had already told me what the whole is, so that I should recognize it even if you chop it up into bits. It seems to me that we must put the same old question to you, my dear Meno—the question: "What is virtue?"—if every act becomes virtue when combined with a part of virtue. That is, after all, what it means to say that every act performed with justice is virtue. Don't you agree that the same question

54

needs to be put? Does anyone know what a part of virtue is, without knowing the whole?

MENO: I suppose not.

SOCRATES: No, and if you remember, when I replied to you about shape just now,   d I believe we rejected the type of answer that employs terms which are still in question and not yet agreed upon.

MENO: We did, and rightly.

SOCRATES: Then please do the same. While the nature of virtue as a whole is still under question, don't suppose that you can explain it to anyone in terms of its parts, or by any similar type of explanation. Understand rather that the same question remains   e to be answered; you say this and that about virtue, but what *is* it? Does this seem nonsense to you?

MENO: No, to me it seems right enough.

SOCRATES: Then go back to the beginning and answer my question. What do you and your friend say that virtue is?

MENO: Socrates, even before I met you they told me that in plain truth you are a perplexed man yourself and reduce others to perplexity. At this moment I feel you are   80 exercising magic and witchcraft upon me and positively laying me under your spell until I am just a mass of helplessness. If I may be flippant, I think that not only in outward appearance but in other respects as well you are exactly like the flat stingray that one meets in the sea. Whenever anyone comes into contact with it, it numbs him, and that is the sort of thing that you seem to be doing to me now. My mind and my lips are literally numb, and I have nothing to reply to you. Yet I have spoken about virtue hun-   b dreds of times, held forth often on the subject in front of large audiences, and very well too, or so I thought. Now I can't even say what it is. In my opinion you are well advised not to leave Athens and live abroad. If you behaved like this as a foreigner in another country, you would most likely be arrested as a wizard.

SOCRATES: You're a real rascal, Meno. You nearly took me in.

MENO: Just what do you mean?

SOCRATES: I see why you used a simile about me.   c

MENO: Why, do you think?

SOCRATES: To be compared to something in return. All good-looking people, I know perfectly well, enjoy a game of comparisons. They get the best of it, for naturally handsome folk provoke handsome similes. But I'm not going to oblige you. As for myself, if the stingray paralyses others only through being paralysed itself, then the comparison is just, but not otherwise. It isn't that, knowing the answers myself, I perplex other people. The truth is rather that I infect them also with the perplexity I feel myself. So with virtue now. I don't know what it is. You may have known before you came   d into contact with me, but now you look as if you don't. Nevertheless I am ready to carry out, together with you, a joint investigation and inquiry into what it is.

MENO: But how will you look for something when you don't in the least know what it is? How on earth are you going to set up something you don't know as the object of your search? To put it another way, even if you come right up against it, how will you know that what you have found is the thing you didn't know?

SOCRATES: I know what you mean. Do you realize that what you are bringing up   e is the trick argument that a man cannot try to discover either what he knows or what he does not know? He would not seek what he knows, for since he knows it there is no need of the inquiry, nor what he does not know, for in that case he does not even know what he is to look for.

MENO: Well, do you think it a good argument?   81

SOCRATES: No.

MENO: Can you explain how it fails?

SOCRATES: I can. I have heard from men and women who understand the truths of religion—

[Here he presumably pauses to emphasize the solemn change of tone that the dialogue undergoes at this point.]

MENO: What did they say?

SOCRATES: Something true, I thought, and fine.

MENO: What was it, and who were they?

SOCRATES: Those who tell it are priests and priestesses of the sort who make it
b   their business to be able to account for the functions which they perform. Pindar speaks of it too, and many another of the poets who are divinely inspired. What they say is this—see whether you think they are speaking the truth. They say that the soul of man is immortal: At one time it comes to an end—that which is called death—and at another is born again, but is never finally exterminated. On these grounds a man must live all his days as righteously as possible. For those from whom

> Persephone receives requital for ancient doom,
> In the ninth year she restores again
> Their souls to the sun above.
> From whom rise noble kings
c   And the swift in strength and greatest in wisdom;
> And for the rest of time
> They are called heroes and sanctified by men.*

Thus the soul, since it is immortal and has been born many times, and has seen all things both here and in the other world, has learned everything that is. So we need not be surprised if it can recall the knowledge of virtue or anything else which, as we
d   see, it once possessed. All nature is akin, and the soul has learned everything, so that when a man has recalled a single piece of knowledge—*learned* it, in ordinary language—there is no reason why he should not find out all the rest, if he keeps a stout heart and does not grow weary of the search; for seeking and learning are in fact nothing but recollection.

We ought not then to be led astray by the contentious argument you quoted. It
e   would make us lazy, and is music in the ears of weaklings. The other doctrine produces energetic seekers after knowledge; and being convinced of its truth, I am ready, with your help, to inquire into the nature of virtue.

MENO: I see, Socrates. But what do you mean when you say that we don't learn anything, but that what we call learning is recollection? Can you teach me that it is so?

SOCRATES: I have just said that you're a rascal, and now you ask me if I can teach
82 you, when I say there is no such thing as teaching, only recollection. Evidently you want to catch me contradicting myself straight away.

MENO: No, honestly, Socrates, I wasn't thinking of that. It was just habit. If you can in any way make clear to me that what you say is true, please do.

SOCRATES: It isn't an easy thing, but still I should like to do what I can since you
b   ask me. I see you have a large number of retainers here. Call one of them, anyone you like, and I will use him to demonstrate it to you.

*The quotation is from Pindar.

56

MENO: Certainly. *(to a slave-boy)* Come here.

SOCRATES: He is a Greek and speaks our language?

MENO: Indeed yes—born and bred in the house.

SOCRATES: Listen carefully then, and see whether it seems to you that he is learning from me or simply being reminded.

MENO: I will.

SOCRATES: Now boy, you know that a square is a figure like this?

[Socrates begins to draw figures in the sand at his feet. He points to the square ABCD.]

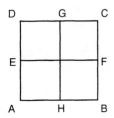

BOY: Yes.

SOCRATES: It has all these four sides equal?   c

BOY: Yes.

SOCRATES: And these lines which go through the middle of it are also equal? (The lines EF *and* GH.)

BOY: Yes.

SOCRATES: Such a figure could be either larger or smaller, could it not?

BOY: Yes.

SOCRATES: Now if this side is two feet long, and this side the same, how many feet will the whole be? Put it this way. If it were two feet in this direction and only one in that, must not the area be two feet taken once?

BOY: Yes.

SOCRATES: But since it is two feet this way also, does it not become twice two feet?   d

BOY: Yes.

SOCRATES: And how many feet is twice two? Work it out and tell me.

BOY: Four.

SOCRATES: Now could one draw another figure double the size of this, but similar, that is, with all its sides equal like this one?

BOY: Yes.

SOCRATES: It is on this line then, according to you, that we shall make the eight-foot square, by taking four of the same length?

BOY: Yes.

SOCRATES: How many feet will its area be?

BOY: Eight.

SOCRATES: Now then, try to tell me how long each of its sides will be. The present figure has a side of two feet. What will be the side of the double-sized one?   e

BOY: It will be double, Socrates, obviously.

SOCRATES: You see, Meno, that I am not teaching him anything, only asking. Now he thinks he knows the length of the side of the eight-foot square.

MENO: Yes.

SOCRATES: But does he?

MENO: Certainly not.

SOCRATES: He thinks it is twice the length of the other.

MENO: Yes.

SOCRATES: Now watch how he recollects things in order—the proper way to recollect.

You say that the side of double length produces the double-sized figure? Like this I mean, not long this way and short that. It must be equal on all sides like the first figure, only twice its size, that is eight feet. Think a moment whether you still expect to get it from doubling the side.

BOY: Yes, I do.

SOCRATES: Well now, shall we have a line double the length of this (AB) if we add another the same length at this end (BJ)?

BOY: Yes.

SOCRATES: It is on this line then, according to you, that we shall make the eight-foot square, by taking four of the same length?

BOY: Yes.

SOCRATES: Let us draw in four equal lines *(that is, counting* AJ, *and adding* JK, KL, *and* LA *made complete by drawing in its second half* LD*)*, using the first as a base. Does this not give us what you call the eight-foot figure?

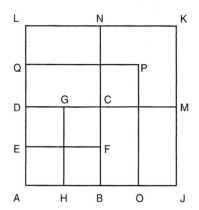

BOY: Certainly.

SOCRATES: But does it contain these four squares, each equal to the original four-foot one?

[Socrates has drawn in the lines CM, CN to complete the squares that he wishes to point out.]

BOY: Yes.

SOCRATES: How big is it then? Won't it be four times as big?

BOY: Of course.

SOCRATES: And is four times the same as twice?

BOY: Of course not.

SOCRATES: So doubling the side has given us not a double but a fourfold figure?

BOY: True.

SOCRATES: And four times four are sixteen, are they not?

BOY: Yes.

SOCRATES: Then how big is the side of the eight-foot figure? This one has given us four times the original area, hasn't it?

BOY: Yes.

SOCRATES: And a side half the length gave us a square of four feet?

BOY: Yes.

SOCRATES: Good. And isn't a square of eight feet double this one and half that?

BOY: Yes.

SOCRATES: Will it not have a side greater than this one but less than that?

BOY: I think it will.   d

SOCRATES: Right. Always answer what you think. Now tell me: was not this side two feet long, and this one four?

BOY: Yes.

SOCRATES: Then the side of the eight-foot figure must be longer than two feet but shorter than four?

BOY: It must.

SOCRATES: Try to say how long you think it is.   e

BOY: Three feet.

SOCRATES: If so, shall we add half of this bit (BO, *half of* BJ) and make it three feet? Here are two, and this is one, and on this side similarly we have two plus one; and here is the figure you want.

[Socrates completes the square AOPQ.*]*

BOY: Yes.

SOCRATES: If it is three feet this way and three that, will the whole area be three times three feet?

BOY: It looks like it.

SOCRATES: And that is how many?

BOY: Nine.

SOCRATES: Whereas the square double our first square had to be how many?

BOY: Eight.

SOCRATES: But we haven't yet got the square of eight feet even from a three-foot side?

BOY: No.

SOCRATES: Then what length will give it? Try to tell us exactly. If you don't want   84 to count it up, just show us on the diagram.

BOY: It's no use, Socrates, I just don't know.

SOCRATES: Observe, Meno, the stage he has reached on the path of recollection. At the beginning he did not know the side of the square of eight feet. Nor indeed does he know it now, but then he thought he knew it and answered boldly, as was appropriate—he felt no perplexity. Now however he does feel perplexed. Not only does he not know the answer; he doesn't even think he knows.

MENO: Quite true.   b

SOCRATES: Isn't he in a better position now in relation to what he didn't know?

MENO: I admit that too.

SOCRATES: So in perplexing him and numbing him like the sting-ray, have we done him any harm?

MENO: I think not.

SOCRATES: In fact we have helped him to some extent towards finding out the right answer, for now not only is he ignorant of it but he will be quite glad to look for it. Up to now, he thought he could speak well and fluently, on many occasions and before large audiences, on the subject of a square double the size of a given square, main-

c   taining that it must have a side of double the length.

MENO: No doubt.

SOCRATES: Do you suppose then that he would have attempted to look for, or learn, what he thought he knew (though he did not), before he was thrown into perplexity, became aware of his ignorance, and felt a desire to know?

MENO: No.

SOCRATES: Then the numbing process was good for him?

MENO: I agree.

SOCRATES: Now notice what, starting from this state of perplexity, he will discover by seeking the truth in company with me, though I simply ask him questions without teaching him. Be ready to catch me if I give him any instruction or explanation

d   instead of simply interrogating him on his own opinions.

[Socrates here rubs out the previous figures and starts again.]

Tell me, boy, is not this our square of four feet? *(ABCD.)* You understand?

BOY: Yes.

SOCRATES: Now we can add another equal to it like this? *(BCEF.)*

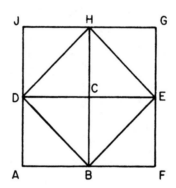

BOY: Yes.

SOCRATES: And a third here, equal to each of the others? *(CEGH.)*

BOY: Yes.

SOCRATES: And then we can fill in this one in the corner? *(DCHJ.)*

BOY: Yes.

SOCRATES: Then here we have four equal squares?

BOY: Yes.

e   SOCRATES: And how many times the size of the first square is the whole?

BOY: Four times.

SOCRATES: And we want one double the size. You remember?

BOY: Yes.

85   SOCRATES: Now does this line going from corner to corner cut each of these squares in half?

BOY: Yes.

SOCRATES: And these are four equal lines enclosing this area? *(BEHD.)*

BOY: They are.

SOCRATES: Now think. How big is this area?

BOY: I don't understand.

SOCRATES: Here are four squares. Has not each line cut off the inner half of each of them?

BOY: Yes.

SOCRATES: And how many such halves are there in this figure? *(BEHD.)*

BOY: Four.

SOCRATES: And how many in this one? *(ABCD.)*

BOY: Two.

SOCRATES: And what is the relation of four to two?   b

BOY: Double.

SOCRATES: How big is this figure then?

BOY: Eight feet.

SOCRATES: On what base?

BOY: This one.

SOCRATES: The line which goes from corner to corner of the square of four feet?

BOY: Yes.

SOCRATES: The technical name for it is "diagonal"; so if we use that name, it is your personal opinion that the square on the diagonal of the original square is double its area.

BOY: That is so, Socrates.

SOCRATES: What do you think, Meno? Has he answered with any opinions that   c
were not his own?

MENO: No, they were all his.

SOCRATES: Yet he did not know, as we agreed a few minutes ago.

MENO: True.

SOCRATES: But these opinions were somewhere in him, were they not?

MENO: Yes.

SOCRATES: So a man who does not know has in himself true opinions on a subject without having knowledge.

MENO: It would appear so.

SOCRATES: At present these opinions, being newly aroused, have a dream-like quality. But if the same questions are put to him on many occasions and in different ways, you can see that in the end he will have a knowledge on the subject as accurate   d
as anybody's.

MENO: Probably.

SOCRATES: This knowledge will not come from teaching but from questioning. He will recover it for himself.

MENO: Yes.

SOCRATES: And the spontaneous recovery of knowledge that is in him is recollection, isn't it?

MENO: Yes.

SOCRATES: Either then he has at some time acquired the knowledge which he now has, or he has always possessed it. If he always possessed it, he must always have known; if on the other hand he acquired it at some previous time, it cannot have been in this life, unless somebody has taught him geometry. He will behave in the same way   e
with all geometrical knowledge, and every other subject. Has anyone taught him all these? You ought to know, especially as he has been brought up in your household.

MENO: Yes, I know that no one ever taught him.

SOCRATES: And has he these opinions, or hasn't he?

MENO: It seems we can't deny it.

86 SOCRATES: Then if he did not acquire them in this life, isn't it immediately clear that he possessed and had learned them during some other period?

MENO: It seems so.

SOCRATES: When he was not in human shape?

MENO: Yes.

SOCRATES: If then there are going to exist in him, both while he is and while he is not a man, true opinions which can be aroused by questioning and turned into knowledge, may we say that his soul has been forever in a state of knowledge? Clearly he always either is or is not a man.

MENO: Clearly.

b SOCRATES: And if the truth about reality is always in our soul, the soul must be immortal, and one must take courage and try to discover—that is, to recollect—what one doesn't happen to know, or (more correctly) remember, at the moment.

MENO: Somehow or other I believe you are right.

SOCRATES: I think I am. I shouldn't like to take my oath on the whole story, but one thing I am ready to fight for as long as I can, in word and act: that is, that we shall be better, braver, and more active men if we believe it right to look for what we don't know than if we believe there is no point in looking because what we don't know we can never discover.

c know than if we believe there is no point in looking because what we don't know we can never discover.

MENO: There too I am sure you are right.

SOCRATES: Then, since we are agreed that it is right to inquire into something that one does not know, are you ready to face with me the question: what is virtue?

MENO: Quite ready. All the same, I would rather consider the question as I put it at the beginning, and hear your views on it; that is, are we to pursue virtue as some-

d thing that can be taught, or do men have it as a gift of nature or how?

SOCRATES: If I were your master as well as my own, Meno, we should not have inquired whether or not virtue can be taught until we had first asked the main question—what it is; but not only do you make no attempt to govern your own actions—you prize your freedom, I suppose—but you attempt to govern mine. And you succeed too, so I shall let you have your way. There's nothing else for it, and it seems we must

e inquire into a single property of something about whose essential nature we are still in the dark. Just grant me one small relaxation of your sway, and allow me, in considering whether or not it can be taught, to make use of a hypothesis—the sort of thing, I mean, that geometers often use in their inquiries. When they are asked, for example,

87 about a given area, whether it is possible for this area to be inscribed as a triangle in a given circle, they will probably reply: "I don't know yet whether it fulfils the conditions, but I think I have a hypothesis which will help us in the matter. It is this. If the area is such that, when one has applied it [e.g., as a rectangle] to the given line [i.e., the diameter] of the circle, it is deficient by another rectangle similar to the one which is applied, then, I should say, one result follows; if not, the result is different. If you ask

b me, then, about the inscription of the figure in the circle—whether it is possible or not—I am ready to answer you in this hypothetical way."*

---

*[It is very difficult to understand the geometrical illustration Socrates is giving here.] Sir Thomas Heath in his *History of Greek Mathematics* (1921), Vol. i, p. 298, says that C. Blass, writing in 1861, already knew of thirty different interpretations, and that many more had appeared since then. Fortunately it is not necessary to understand the example in order to grasp the hypothetical method Socrates is expounding.

Let us do the same about virtue. Since we don't know what it is or what it resembles, let us use a hypothesis in investigating whether it is teachable or not. We shall say: "What attribute of the soul must virtue be, if it is to be teachable or otherwise?" Well, in the first place, if it is anything else but knowledge, is there a possibility of anyone teaching it—or, in the language we used just now, reminding someone of it? We needn't worry about which name we are to give to the process, but simply ask: will c it be teachable? Isn't it plain to everyone that a man is not taught anything except knowledge?

MENO: That would be my view.

SOCRATES: If on the other hand virtue is some sort of knowledge, clearly it could be taught.

MENO: Certainly.

SOCRATES: So that question is easily settled; I mean, on what condition virtue would be teachable.

MENO: Yes.

SOCRATES: The next point then, I suppose, is to find out whether virtue is knowl- d edge or something different.

MENO: That is the next question, I agree.

SOCRATES: Well then, do we assert that virtue is something good? Is that assumption a firm one for us?

MENO: Undoubtedly.

SOCRATES: That being so, if there exists any good thing different from, and not associated with, knowledge, virtue will not necessarily be any form of knowledge. If on the other hand knowledge embraces everything that is good, we shall be right to suspect that virtue is knowledge.

MENO: Agreed.

SOCRATES: First then, is it virtue which makes us good? e

MENO: Yes.

SOCRATES: And if good, then advantageous. All good things are advantageous, are they not?

MENO: Yes.

SOCRATES: So virtue itself must be something advantageous?

MENO: That follows also.

SOCRATES: Now suppose we consider what are the sort of things that profit us. Take them in a list. Health, we may say, and strength and good looks, and wealth—these and their like we call advantageous, you agree?

MENO: Yes.

SOCRATES: Yet we also speak of these things as sometimes doing harm. Would 88 you object to that statement?

MENO: No, it is so.

SOCRATES: Now look here: what is the controlling factor which determines whether each of these is advantageous or harmful? Isn't it right use which makes them advantageous, and lack of it, harmful?

MENO: Certainly.

SOCRATES: We must also take spiritual qualities into consideration. You recognize such things as temperance, justice, courage, quickness of mind, memory, nobility of character and others?

MENO: Yes, of course I do.

SOCRATES: Then take any such qualities which in your view are not knowledge b but something different. Don't you think they may be harmful as well as advantageous? Courage for instance, if it is something thoughtless, is just a sort of confidence. Isn't it true that to be confident without reason does a man harm, whereas a reasoned confidence profits him?

MENO: Yes.

SOCRATES: Temperance and quickness of mind are no different. Learning and discipline are profitable in conjunction with wisdom, but without it harmful.

c MENO: That is emphatically true.

SOCRATES: In short, everything that the human spirit undertakes or suffers will lead to happiness when it is guided by wisdom, but to the opposite, when guided by folly.

MENO: A reasonable conclusion.

SOCRATES: If then virtue is an attribute of the spirit, and one which cannot fail to be beneficial, it must be wisdom; for all spiritual qualities in and by themselves are neither advantageous nor harmful, but become advantageous or harmful by the presence with them of wisdom or folly. If we accept this argument, then virtue, to be something advantageous, must be a sort of wisdom.

MENO: I agree.

SOCRATES: To go back to the other class of things, wealth and the like, of which we said just now that they are sometimes good and sometimes harmful, isn't it the same with them? Just as wisdom when it governs our other psychological impulses turns them to advantage, and folly turns them to harm, so the mind by its right use and control of these material assets makes them profitable, and by wrong use renders them harmful.

MENO: Certainly.

SOCRATES: And the right user is the mind of the wise man, the wrong user the mind of the foolish.

MENO: That is so.

SOCRATES: So we may say in general that the goodness of non-spiritual assets depends on our spiritual character, and the goodness of that on wisdom. This argument shows that the advantageous element must be wisdom; and virtue, we agree, is advantageous, so that amounts to saying that virtue, either in whole or in part, is wisdom.

89

MENO: The argument seems to me fair enough.

SOCRATES: If so, good men cannot be good by nature.

MENO: I suppose not.

b SOCRATES: There is another point. If they were, there would probably be experts among us who could recognize the naturally good at an early stage. They would point them out to us, and we should take them and shut them away safely in the Acropolis, sealing them up more carefully than bullion to protect them from corruption and ensure that when they came to maturity they would be of use to the State.

MENO: It would be likely enough.

c SOCRATES: Since then goodness does not come by nature, is it got by learning?

MENO: I don't see how we can escape the conclusion. Indeed it is obvious on our assumption that, if virtue is knowledge, it is teachable.

SOCRATES: I suppose so. But I wonder if we were right to bind ourselves to that.

MENO: Well, it seemed all right just now.

SOCRATES: Yes, but to be sound it has got to seem all right not only "just now" but at this moment and in the future.

d MENO: Of course. But what has occurred to you to make you turn against it and suspect that virtue may not be knowledge?

SOCRATES: I'll tell you. I don't withdraw from the position that if it is knowledge, it must be teachable; but as for its being knowledge, see whether you think my doubts on this point are well founded. If anything—not virtue only—is a possible subject of instruction, must there not be teachers and students of it?

MENO: Surely.

SOCRATES: And what of the converse, that if there are neither teachers nor students of a subject, we may safely infer that it cannot be taught? e

MENO: That is true. But don't you think there are teachers of virtue?

SOCRATES: All I can say is that I have often looked to see if there are any, and in spite of all my efforts I cannot find them, though I have had plenty of fellow-searchers, the kind of men especially whom I believe to have most experience in such matters. But look, Meno, here's a piece of luck. Anytus has just sat down beside us. We couldn't do better than make him a partner in our inquiry. In the first place, he is the 90 son of Anthemion, a man of property and good sense, who didn't get his money out of the blue or as a gift—like Ismenias of Thebes who has just come into the fortune of a Croesus—but earned it by his own brains and hard work. Besides this, he shows himself a decent, modest citizen with no arrogance or bombast or offensiveness about him. Also he brought up his son well and had him properly educated, as the Athenian people appreciate: look how they elect him into the highest offices in the State. This is b certainly the right sort of man with whom to inquire whether there are any teachers of virtue, and if so who they are.

Please help us, Anytus—Meno, who is a friend of your family, and myself—to find out who may be the teachers of this subject. Look at it like this. If we wanted Meno to become a good doctor, shouldn't we send him to the doctors to be taught? c

ANYTUS: Of course.

SOCRATES: And if we wanted him to become a shoemaker, to the shoemakers?

ANYTUS: Yes.

SOCRATES: And so on with other trades?

ANYTUS: Yes.

SOCRATES: Now another relevant question. When we say that to make Meno a doctor we should be right in sending him to the doctors, have we in mind that the sen- d sible thing is to send him to those who profess the subject rather than to those who don't, men who charge a fee as professionals, having announced that they are prepared to teach whoever likes to come and learn?

ANYTUS: Yes.

SOCRATES: The same is surely true of flute-playing and other accomplishments. If you want to make someone a performer on the flute it would be very foolish to refuse e to send him to those who undertake to teach the art and are paid for it, but to go and bother other people instead and have him try to learn from them—people who don't set up to be teachers or take any pupils in the subject which we want our young man to learn. Doesn't that sound very unreasonable?

ANYTUS: Sheer stupidity I should say.

SOCRATES: I agree. And now we can both consult together about our visitor 91 Meno. He has been telling me all this while that he longs to acquire the kind of wisdom and virtue which fits men to manage an estate or govern a city, to look after their parents, and to entertain and send off guests in proper style, both their own countrymen and foreigners. With this in mind, to whom would it be right to send him? What we have just said seems to show that the right people are those who profess to be teachers b of virtue and offer their services freely to any Greek who wishes to learn, charging a fixed fee for their instruction.

ANYTUS: Whom do you mean by that, Socrates?

SOCRATES: Surely you know yourself that they are the men called Sophists.

c   ANYTUS: Good heavens, what a thing to say! I hope no relative of mine or any of my friends, Athenian or foreign, would be so mad as to go and let himself be ruined by those people. That's what they are, the manifest ruin and corruption of anyone who comes into contact with them.

SOCRATES: What, Anytus? Can they be so different from other claimants to useful knowledge that they not only don't do good, like the rest, to the material that one puts in their charge, but on the contrary spoil it—and have the effrontery to take money for doing so? I for one find it difficult to believe you. I know that one of them alone, Pro-

d   tagoras, earned more money from being a Sophist than an outstandingly fine craftsman like Phidias and ten other sculptors put together. A man who mends old shoes or restores coats couldn't get away with it for a month if he gave them back in worse condition than he received them; he would soon find himself starving. Surely it is incredible

e   that Protagoras took in the whole of Greece, corrupting his pupils and sending them away worse than when they came to him, for more than forty years. I believe he was nearly seventy when he died, and had been practising for forty years, and all that time—indeed to this very day—his reputation has been consistently high; and there are

92   plenty of others besides Protagoras, some before his time and others still alive. Are we to suppose from your remark that they consciously deceive and ruin young men, or are they unaware of it themselves? Can these remarkably clever men—as some regard them—be mad enough for that?

ANYTUS: Far from it, Socrates. It isn't they who are mad, but rather the young men who hand over their money; and those responsible for them, who let them get into the Sophists' hands, are even worse. Worst of all are the cities who allow them in, or

b   don't expel them, whether it be a foreigner or one of themselves who tries that sort of game.

SOCRATES: Has one of the Sophists done you a personal injury, or why are you so hard on them?

ANYTUS: Heavens, no! I've never in my life had anything to do with a single one of them, nor would I hear of any of my family doing so.

SOCRATES: So you've had no experience of them at all?

ANYTUS: And don't want any either.

c   SOCRATES: You surprise me. How can you know what is good or bad in something when you have no experience of it?

ANYTUS: Quite easily. At any rate I know *their* kind, whether I've had experience or not.

SOCRATES: It must be second sight, I suppose; for how else you know about them, judging from what you tell me yourself, I can't imagine. However, we are not asking

d   whose instruction it is that would ruin Meno's character. Let us say that those are the Sophists if you like, and tell us instead about the ones we want. You can do a good turn to a friend of your father's house if you will let him know to whom in our great city he should apply for proficiency in the kind of virtue I have just described.

ANYTUS: Why not tell him yourself?

SOCRATES: Well, I did mention the men who in my opinion teach these things, but apparently I was talking nonsense. So you say, and you may well be right. Now it is

e   your turn to direct him; mention the name of any Athenian you like.

ANYTUS: But why mention a particular individual? Any decent Athenian gentleman whom he happens to meet, if he follows his advice, will make him a better man than the Sophists would.

93   SOCRATES: And did these gentlemen get their fine qualities spontaneously—self-taught, as it were, and yet [they are] able to teach this untaught virtue to others?

ANYTUS: I suppose they in their turn learned it from forebears who were gentlemen like themselves. Would you deny that there have been many good men in our city?

SOCRATES: On the contrary, there are plenty of good statesmen here in Athens, and have been as good in the past. The question is, have they also been good teachers of their own virtue? That is the point we are discussing now—not whether or not there are good men in Athens or whether there have been in past times, but whether virtue   b
can be taught. It amounts to the question whether the good men of this and former times have known how to hand on to someone else the goodness that was in themselves, or whether on the contrary it is not something that can be handed over, or that one man can receive from another. That is what Meno and I have long been puzzling over. Look at it from your own point of view. You would say that Themistocles was a   c
good man?

ANYTUS: Yes, none better.

SOCRATES: And that he, if anyone, must have been a good teacher of his own virtue?

ANYTUS: I suppose so, if he wanted to be.

SOCRATES: But don't you think he must have wanted others to become worthy men—above all, surely, his own son? Do you suppose he grudged him this and pur-   d
posely didn't pass on his own virtue to him? You must have heard that he had his son Cleophantus so well trained in horsemanship that he could stand upright on horseback and throw a javelin from that position; and many other wonderful accomplishments the young man had, for his father had him taught and made expert in every skill that a good instructor could impart. You must have heard this from older people?

ANYTUS: Yes.

SOCRATES: No one, then, could say that there was anything wrong with the boy's natural powers?

ANYTUS: Perhaps not.   e

SOCRATES: But have you ever heard anyone, young or old, say that Cleophantus the son of Themistocles was a good and wise man in the way that his father was?

ANYTUS: Certainly not.

SOCRATES: Must we conclude then that Themistocles' aim was to educate his son in other accomplishments, but not to make him any better than his neighbours in his own type of wisdom—that is, supposing that virtue could be taught?

ANYTUS: I hardly think we can.

SOCRATES: So much then for Themistocles as a teacher of virtue, whom you yourself agree to have been one of the best men of former times. Take another example, Aristides, son of Lysimachus. You accept him as a good man?   94

ANYTUS: Surely.

SOCRATES: He too gave his son Lysimachus the best education in Athens, in all subjects where a teacher could help; but did he make him a better man than his neighbour? You know him, I think, and can say what he is like. Or again there is Per-   b
icles, that great and wise man. He brought up two sons, Paralus and Xanthippus, and had them taught riding, music, athletics, and all the other skilled pursuits till they were as good as any in Athens. Did he then not want to make them good men? Yes, he wanted that, no doubt, but I am afraid it is something that cannot be done by teaching. And in case you should think that only very few, and those the most insignificant, lacked this power, consider that Thucydides also had two sons, Melesias and Stephanus, to whom he gave an excellent education. Among other things they   c
were the best wrestlers in Athens, for he gave one to Xanthias to train and the other

to Eudoxus—the two who, I understand, were considered the finest wrestlers of their time. You remember?

ANYTUS: I have heard of them.

d   SOCRATES: Surely then he would never have had his children taught these expensive pursuits and yet refused to teach them to be good men—which would have cost nothing at all—if virtue could have been taught? You are not going to tell me that Thucydides was a man of no account, or that he had not plenty of friends both at Athens and among the allies? He came of an influential family and was a great power both here and in the rest of Greece. If virtue could have been taught, he would have found the man to make his sons good, either among our own citizens or abroad, sup-

e   posing his political duties left him no time to do it himself. No, my dear Anytus, it looks as if it cannot be taught.

ANYTUS: You seem to me, Socrates, to be too ready to run people down. My advice to you, if you will listen to it, is to be careful. I dare say that in all cities it is easier

95   to do a man harm than good, and it is certainly so here, as I expect you know yourself.

SOCRATES: Anytus seems angry, Meno, and I am not surprised. He thinks I am slandering our statesmen, and moreover he believes himself to be one of them. He doesn't know what slander really is: if he ever finds out he will forgive me.

However, tell me this yourself: are there not similar fine characters in your country?

MENO: Yes, certainly.

b   SOCRATES: Do they come forward of their own accord to teach the young? Do they agree that they are teachers and that virtue can be taught?

MENO: No indeed, they don't agree on it at all. Sometimes you will hear them say that it can be taught, sometimes that it cannot.

SOCRATES: Ought we then to class as teachers of it men who are not even agreed that it can be taught?

MENO: Hardly, I think.

SOCRATES: And what about the Sophists, the only people who profess to teach it? Do you think they do?

c   MENO: The thing I particularly admire about Gorgias, Socrates, is that you will never hear him make this claim; indeed he laughs at the others when he hears them do so. In his view his job is to make clever speakers.

SOCRATES: So you too don't think the Sophists are teachers?

MENO: I really can't say. Like most people I waver—sometimes I think they are and sometimes I think they are not.

SOCRATES: Has it ever occurred to you that you and our statesmen are not alone in

d   this? The poet Theognis likewise says in one place that virtue is teachable and in another that it is not.

MENO: Really? Where?

SOCRATES: In the elegiacs in which he writes:

Eat, drink, and sit with men of power and weight,
Nor scorn to gain the favour of the great.
For fine men's teaching to fine ways will win thee:
Low company destroys what wit is in thee.

e   There he speaks as if virtue can be taught, doesn't he?

MENO: Clearly.

SOCRATES: But elsewhere he changes his ground a little:

Were mind by art created and instilled
Immense rewards had soon the pockets filled

of the people who could do this. Moreover

No good man's son would ever worthless be,
Taught by wise counsel. But no teacher's skill
Can turn to good what is created ill.   96

Do you see how he contradicts himself?

MENO: Plainly.

SOCRATES: Can you name any other subject, in which the professed teachers are
not only not recognized as teachers of others, but are thought to have no understanding
of it themselves, and to be no good at the very subject they profess to teach; whereas
those who are acknowledged to be the best at it are in two minds whether it can be   b
taught or not? When people are so confused about a subject, can you say that they are
in a true sense teachers?

MENO: Certainly not.

SOCRATES: Well, if neither the Sophists nor those who display fine qualities themselves are teachers of virtue, I am sure no one else can be, and if there are no teachers,
there can be no students either.   c

MENO: I quite agree.

SOCRATES: And we have also agreed that a subject of which there were neither
teachers nor students was not one which could be taught.

MENO: That is so.

SOCRATES: Now there turn out to be neither teachers nor students of virtue, so it
would appear that virtue cannot be taught.

MENO: So it seems, if we have made no mistake; and it makes me wonder,   d
Socrates, whether there are in fact no good men at all, or how they are produced when
they do appear.

SOCRATES: I have a suspicion, Meno, that you and I are not much good. Our masters Gorgias and Prodicus have not trained us properly. We must certainly take ourselves in hand, and try to find someone who will improve us by hook or by crook. I say
this with our recent discussion in mind, for absurdly enough we failed to perceive that   e
it is not only under the guidance of knowledge that human action is well and rightly
conducted. I believe that may be what prevents us from seeing how it is that men are
made good.

MENO: What do you mean?

SOCRATES: This: We were correct, were we not, in agreeing that good men must
be profitable or useful? It cannot be otherwise, can it?

MENO: No.

SOCRATES: And again that they will be of some use if they conduct our affairs
aright—that also was correct?   97

MENO: Yes.

SOCRATES: But in insisting that knowledge was a *sine qua non* [indispensible con-
dition] for right leadership, we look like being mistaken.

MENO: How so?

SOCRATES: Let me explain. If someone knows the way to Larissa, or anywhere
else you like, then when he goes there and takes others with him he will be a good and
capable guide, you would agree?

MENO: Of course.

b   SOCRATES: But if a man judges correctly which is the road, though he has never been there and doesn't know it, will he not also guide others aright?

MENO: Yes, he will.

SOCRATES: And as long as he has a correct opinion on the points about which the other has knowledge, he will be just as good a guide, believing the truth but not knowing it.

MENO: Just as good.

SOCRATES: Therefore true opinion is as good a guide as knowledge for the purpose of acting rightly. That is what we left out just now in our discussion of the nature of virtue, when we said that knowledge is the only guide to right action. There was also, it seems, true opinion.

c   MENO: It seems so.

SOCRATES: So right opinion is something no less useful than knowledge.

MENO: Except that the man with knowledge will always be successful, and the man with right opinion only sometimes.

SOCRATES: What? Will he not always be successful so long as he has the right opinion?

MENO: That must be so, I suppose. In that case, I wonder why knowledge should

d   be so much more prized than right opinion, and indeed how there is any difference between them.

SOCRATES: Shall I tell you the reason for your surprise, or do you know it?

MENO: No, tell me.

SOCRATES: It is because you have not observed the statues of Daedalus. Perhaps you don't have them in your country.

MENO: What makes you say that?

SOCRATES: They too, if no one ties them down, run away and escape. If tied, they

e   stay where they are put.

MENO: What of it?

SOCRATES: If you have one of his works untethered, it is not worth much: it gives you the slip like a runaway slave. But a tethered specimen is very valuable, for they are magnificent creations. And that, I may say, has a bearing on the matter of true opinions. True opinions are a fine thing and do all sorts of good so long as they stay in their

98   place; but they will not stay long. They run away from a man's mind, so they are not worth much until you tether them by working out the reason. That process, my dear Meno, is recollection, as we agreed earlier. Once they are tied down, they become knowledge, and are stable. That is why knowledge is something more valuable than right opinion. What distinguishes one from the other is the tether.

MENO: It does seem something like that, certainly.

b   SOCRATES: Well of course, I have only been using an analogy myself, not knowledge. But it is not, I am sure, a mere guess to say that right opinion and knowledge are different. There are few things that I should claim to know, but that at least is among them, whatever else is.

MENO: You are quite right.

SOCRATES: And is this right too, that true opinion when it governs any course of action produces as good a result as knowledge?

MENO: Yes, that too is right, I think.

c   SOCRATES: So that for practical purposes right opinion is no less useful than knowledge, and the man who has it is no less useful than the one who knows.

MENO: That is so.

SOCRATES: Now we have agreed that the good man is useful.

MENO: Yes.

SOCRATES: To recapitulate then: assuming that there are men good and useful to the community, it is not only knowledge that makes them so, but also right opinion, and neither of these comes by nature but both are acquired—or do you think either of them *is* natural? d

MENO: No.

SOCRATES: So if both are acquired, good men themselves are not good by nature.

MENO: No.

SOCRATES: That being so, the next thing we inquired was whether their goodness was a matter of teaching, and we decided that it would be, if virtue were knowledge, and conversely, that if it could be taught, it would be knowledge.

MENO: Yes.

SOCRATES: Next, that if there were teachers of it, it could be taught, but not if there were none. e

MENO: That was so.

SOCRATES: But we have agreed that there are no teachers of it, and so that it cannot be taught and is not knowledge.

MENO: We did.

SOCRATES: At the same time we agreed that it is something good, and that to be useful and good consists in giving right guidance.

MENO: Yes.

SOCRATES: And that these two, true opinion and knowledge, are the only things which direct us aright and the possession of which makes a man a true guide. We may except chance, because what turns out right by chance is not due to human direction, and say that where human control leads to right ends, these two principles are directive, true opinion and knowledge. 99

MENO: Yes, I agree.

SOCRATES: Now since virtue cannot be taught, we can no longer believe it to be knowledge, so that one of our two good and useful principles is excluded, and knowledge is not the guide in public life. b

MENO: No.

SOCRATES: It is not then by the possession of any wisdom that such men as Themistocles, and the others whom Anytus mentioned just now, became leaders in their cities. This fact, that they do not owe their eminence to knowledge, will explain why they are unable to make others like themselves.

MENO: No doubt it is as you say.

SOCRATES: That leaves us with the other alternative, that it is well-aimed conjecture which statesmen employ in upholding their countries' welfare. Their position in relation to knowledge is no different from that of prophets and tellers of oracles, who under divine inspiration utter many truths, but have no knowledge of what they are saying. c

MENO: It must be something like that.

SOCRATES: And ought we not to reckon those men divine who with no conscious thought are repeatedly and outstandingly successful in what they do or say?

MENO: Certainly.

SOCRATES: We are right therefore to give this title to the oracular priests and the prophets that I mentioned, and to poets of every description. Statesmen too, when by their speeches they get great things done yet know nothing of what they are saying, are to be considered as acting no less under divine influence, inspired and possessed by the divinity. d

MENO: Certainly.

SOCRATES: Women, you know, Meno, do call good men "divine," and the Spartans too, when they are singing a good man's praises, say "He is divine."

MENO: And it looks as if they are right—though our friend Anytus may be annoyed with you for saying so.

e

SOCRATES: I can't help that. We will talk to him some other time. If all we have said in this discussion, and the questions we have asked, have been right, virtue will be acquired neither by nature nor by teaching. Whoever has it gets it by divine dispensation without taking thought, unless he be the kind of statesman who can create another like himself. Should there be such a man, he would be among the living practically what Homer said Tiresias was among the dead, when he described him as the only one in the underworld who kept his wits—"the others are mere flitting shades." Where virtue is concerned such a man would be just like that, a solid reality among shadows.

100

MENO: That is finely put, Socrates.

SOCRATES: On our present reasoning then, whoever has virtue gets it by divine dispensation. But we shall not understand the truth of the matter until, before asking how men get virtue, we try to discover what virtue is in and by itself. Now it is time for me to go; and my request to you is that you will allay the anger of your friend Anytus by convincing him that what you now believe is true. If you succeed, the Athenians may have cause to thank you.

REPUBLIC (in part)

BOOK II

*   *   *

[Socrates is speaking]: Glaucon and the others begged me to step into the breach and carry through our inquiry into the real nature of justice and injustice, and the truth about their respective advantages. So I told them what I thought. This is a very obscure question, I said, and we shall need keen sight to see our way. Now, as we are not remarkably clever, I will make a suggestion as to how we should proceed. Imagine a rather short-sighted person told to read an inscription in small letters from some way off. He would think it a godsend if someone pointed out that the same inscription was written up elsewhere on a bigger scale, so that he could first read the larger characters and then make out whether the smaller ones were the same.

368^d

e

No doubt, said Adeimantus; but what analogy do you see in that to our inquiry?

I will tell you. We think of justice as a quality that may exist in a whole community as well as in an individual, and the community is the bigger of the two. Possibly, then, we may find justice there in larger proportions, easier to make out. So I suggest

The Republic of Plato (Book II, 368c–376e; Book III, 412c–417b; Book IV, 427c–445e; Book V, complete: 448e–480a; Books VI–VII, 502c–521b), translated by Francis MacDonald Cornford (Oxford: Oxford University Press, 1945). Reprinted by permission of Oxford University Press.

that we should begin by inquiring what justice means in a state. Then we can go on to look for its counterpart on a smaller scale in the individual.

That seems a good plan, he agreed.

Well then, I continued, suppose we imagine a state coming into being before our eyes. We might then be able to watch the growth of justice or of injustice within it. When that is done, we may hope it will be easier to find what we are looking for.

Much easier. b

Shall we try, then, to carry out this scheme? I fancy it will be no light undertaking; so you had better think twice.

No need for that, said Adeimantus. Don't waste any more time.

My notion is, said I, that a state comes into existence because no individual is self-sufficing; we all have many needs. But perhaps you can suggest some different origin for the foundation of a community?

No, I agree with you.

So, having all these needs, we call in one another's help to satisfy our various re- c quirements; and when we have collected a number of helpers and associates to live together in one place, we call that settlement a state.

Yes.

So if one man gives another what he has to give in exchange for what he can get, it is because each finds that to do so is for his own advantage.

Certainly.

Very well, said I. Now let us build up our imaginary state from the beginning. Apparently, it will owe its existence to our needs, the first and greatest need being the d provision of food to keep us alive. Next we shall want a house; and thirdly, such things as clothing.

True.

How will our state be able to supply all these demands? We shall need at least one man to be a farmer, another a builder, and a third a weaver. Will that do, or shall we add a shoemaker and one or two more to provide for our personal wants?

By all means.

The minimum state, then, will consist of four or five men.

Apparently. e

Now here is a further point. Is each one of them to bring the product of his work into a common stock? Should our one farmer, for example, provide food enough for four people and spend the whole of his working time in producing corn, so as to share with the rest; or should he take no notice of them and spend only a quarter of his time on growing just enough corn for himself, and divide the other three-quarters between building his house, weaving his clothes, and making his shoes, so as to save the trouble of sharing with others and attend himself to all his own concerns?

The first plan might be the easier, replied Adeimantus.

That may very well be so, said I; for, as you spoke, it occurred to me, for one thing, that no two people are born exactly alike. There are innate differences which fit b them for different occupations.

I agree.

And will a man do better working at many trades, or keeping to one only?

Keeping to one.

And there is another point: obviously work may be ruined, if you let the right time go by. The workman must wait upon the work; it will not wait upon his leisure and allow itself to be done in a spare moment. So the conclusion is that more things will be produced and the work be more easily and better done, when every man is set c   free from all other occupations to do, at the right time, the one thing for which he is naturally fitted.

That is certainly true.

We shall need more than four citizens, then, to supply all those necessaries we mentioned. You see, Adeimantus, if the farmer is to have a good plough and spade and other tools, he will not make them himself. No more will the builder and weaver and

d   shoemaker make all the many implements they need. So quite a number of carpenters and smiths and other craftsmen must be enlisted. Our miniature state is beginning to grow.

It is.

Still, it will not be very large, even when we have added cowherds and shepherds

e   to provide the farmers with oxen for the plough, and the builders as well as the farmers with draught-animals, and the weavers and shoemakers with wool and leather.

No; but it will not be so very small either.

And yet, again, it will be next to impossible to plant our city in a territory where it will need no imports. So there will have to be still another set of people, to fetch what it needs from other countries.

There will.

371   Moreover, if these agents take with them nothing that those other countries require in exchange, they will return as empty handed as they went. So, besides everything wanted for consumption at home, we must produce enough goods of the right kind for the foreigners whom we depend on to supply us. That will mean increasing the number of farmers and craftsmen.

Yes.

b   And then, there are these agents who are to import and export all kinds of goods—merchants, as we call them. We must have them; and if they are to do business overseas, we shall need quite a number of ship-owners and others who know about that branch of trading.

We shall.

Again, in the city itself how are the various sets of producers to exchange their products? That was our object, you will remember, in forming a community and so laying the foundation of our state.

Obviously, they must buy and sell.

c   That will mean having a market-place, and a currency to serve as a token for purposes of exchange.

Certainly.

Now suppose a farmer, or an artisan, brings some of his produce to market at a time when no one is there who wants to exchange with him. Is he to sit there idle, when he might be at work?

No, he replied; there are people who have seen an opening here for their services. In well-ordered communities they are generally men not strong enough to be of

d   use in any other occupation. They have to stay where they are in the market-place and take goods for money from those who want to sell, and money for goods from those who want to buy.

That, then, is the reason why our city must include a class of shopkeepers—so we call these people who sit still in the marketplace to buy and sell, in contrast with merchants who travel to other countries.

Quite so.

e   There are also the services of yet another class, who have the physical strength for heavy work, though on intellectual grounds they are hardly worth including in our society—hired labourers, as we call them, because they sell the use of their strength for wages. They will go to make up our population.

Yes.

Well, Adeimantus, has our state now grown to its full size?

Perhaps.

Then, where in it shall we find justice or injustice? If they have come in with one of the elements we have been considering, can you say with which one?

I have no idea, Socrates; unless it be somewhere in their dealings with one an- 372
other.

You may be right, I answered. Anyhow, it is a question which we shall have to face.

Let us begin, then, with a picture of our citizens' manner of life, with the provision we have made for them. They will be producing corn and wine, and making clothes and shoes. When they have built their houses, they will mostly work without their coats or shoes in summer, and in winter be well shod and clothed. For their food, b
they will prepare flour and barley-meal for kneading and baking, and set out a grand spread of loaves and cakes on rushes or fresh leaves. Then they will lie on beds of myrtle-boughs and bryony [a type of gourd vine] and make merry with their children, drinking their wine after the feast with garlands on their heads and singing the praises of the gods. So they will live pleasantly together; and a prudent fear of poverty or war c
will keep them from begetting children beyond their means.

Here Glaucon interrupted me: You seem to expect your citizens to feast on dry bread.

True, I said; I forgot that they will have something to give it a relish, salt, no doubt, and olives, and cheese, and country stews of roots and vegetables. And for dessert we will give them figs and peas and beans; and they shall roast myrtle-berries and acorns at the fire, while they sip their wine. Leading such a healthy life in peace, they will naturally come to a good old age, and leave their children to live after them in the same manner. d

That is just the sort of provender you would supply, Socrates, if you were founding a community of pigs.

Well, how are they to live, then, Glaucon?

With the ordinary comforts. Let them lie on couches and dine off tables on such dishes and sweets as we have nowadays. e

Ah, I see, said I; we are to study the growth, not just of a state, but of a luxurious one. Well, there may be no harm in that; the consideration of luxury may help us to discover how justice and injustice take root in society. The community I have described seems to me the ideal one, in sound health as it were: but if you want to see one suffering from inflammation, there is nothing to hinder us. So some people, it seems, will not be satisfied to live in this simple way; they must have couches and tables and 373
furniture of all sorts; and delicacies too, perfumes, unguents, courtesans, sweetmeats, all in plentiful variety. And besides, we must not limit ourselves now to those bare necessaries of house and clothes and shoes; we shall have to set going the arts of embroidery and painting, and collect rich materials, like gold and ivory.

Yes. b

Then we must once more enlarge our community. The healthy one will not be big enough now; it must be swollen up with a whole multitude of callings not ministering to any bare necessity: hunters and fishermen, for instance; artists in sculpture, painting, and music; poets with their attendant train of professional reciters, actors, c dancers, producers; and makers of all sorts of household gear, including everything for women's adornment. And we shall want more servants: children's nurses and attendants, lady's maids, barbers, cooks and confectioners. And then swineherds—there was no need for them in our original state, but we shall want them now; and a great quantity of sheep and cattle too, if people are going to live on meat.

Of course.

d And with this manner of life physicians will be in much greater request.

No doubt.

The country, too, which was large enough to support the original inhabitants, will now be too small. If we are to have enough pasture and plough land, we shall have to cut off a slice of our neighbours' territory; and if they too are not content with necessaries, but give themselves up to getting unlimited wealth, they will want a slice of ours.

e That is inevitable, Socrates.

So the next thing will be, Glaucon, that we shall be at war.

No doubt.

We need not say yet whether war does good or harm, but only that we have discovered its origin in desires which are the most fruitful source of evils both to individuals and to states.

Quite true.

374 This will mean a considerable addition to our community—a whole army, to go out to battle with any invader, in defence of all this property and of the citizens we have been describing.

Why so? Can't they defend themselves?

Not if the principle was right, which we all accepted in framing our society. You remember we agreed that no one man can practise many trades or arts satisfactorily.

True.

b Well, is not the conduct of war an art, quite as important as shoemaking?

Yes.

But we would not allow our shoemaker to try to be also a farmer or weaver or builder, because we wanted our shoes well made. We gave each man one trade, for c which he was naturally fitted; he would do good work, if he confined himself to that all his life, never letting the right moment slip by. Now in no form of work is efficiency so important as in war; and fighting is not so easy a business that a man can follow an- d other trade, such as farming or shoemaking, and also be an efficient soldier. Why, even a game like draughts or dice must be studied from childhood; no one can become a fine player in his spare moments. Just taking up a shield or other weapon will not make a man capable of fighting that very day in any sort of warfare, any more than taking up a tool or implement of some kind will make a man a craftsman or an athlete, if he does not understand its use and has never been properly trained to handle it.

No; if that were so, tools would indeed be worth having.

These guardians of our state, then, inasmuch as their work is the most important e of all, will need the most complete freedom from other occupations and the greatest amount of skill and practice.

I quite agree.

And also a native aptitude for their calling.

Certainly.

So it is our business to define, if we can, the natural gifts that fit men to be guardians of a commonwealth, and to select them accordingly. It will certainly be a formidable task; but we must grapple with it to the best of our power. Yes.

Don't you think then, said I, that, for the purpose of keeping guard, a young man should have much the same temperament and qualities as a well-bred watch-dog? I mean, for instance, that both must have quick senses to detect an enemy, swiftness in pursuing him, and strength, if they have to fight when they have caught him.

Yes, they will need all those qualities.

And also courage, if they are to fight well.

Of course.

And courage, in dog or horse or any other creature, implies a spirited disposition. You must have noticed that a high spirit is unconquerable. Every soul possessed of it is b fearless and indomitable in the face of any danger.

Yes, I have noticed that.

So now we know what physical qualities our Guardian must have, and also that he must be of a spirited temper.

Yes.

Then, Glaucon, how are men of that natural disposition to be kept from behaving pugnaciously to one another and to the rest of their countrymen?

It is not at all easy to see.

And yet they must be gentle to their own people and dangerous only to enemies; c otherwise they will destroy themselves without waiting till others destroy them.

True.

What are we to do, then? If gentleness and a high temper are contraries, where d shall we find a character to combine them? Both are necessary to make a good Guardian, but it seems they are incompatible. So we shall never have a good Guardian.

It looks like it.

Here I was perplexed, but on thinking over what we had been saying, I remarked that we deserved to be puzzled, because we had not followed up the comparison we had just drawn.

What do you mean? he asked.

We never noticed that, after all, there are natures in which these contraries are combined. They are to be found in animals, and not least in the kind we compared to e our Guardian. Well-bred dogs, as you know, are by instinct perfectly gentle to people whom they know and are accustomed to, and fierce to strangers. So the combination of qualities we require for our Guardian is, after all, possible and not against nature.

Evidently.

Do you further agree that, besides this spirited temper, he must have a philosophical element in his nature?

I don't see what you mean.

This is another trait you will see in the dog. It is really remarkable how the crea- 376 ture gets angry at the mere sight of a stranger and welcomes anyone he knows, though he may never have been treated unkindly by the one or kindly by the other. Did that never strike you as curious?

I had not thought of it before; but that certainly is how a dog behaves.

Well, but that shows a fine instinct, which is philosophic in the true sense. b

How so?

Because the only mark by which he distinguishes a friendly and an unfriendly face is that he knows the one and does not know the other; and if a creature makes that the test of what it finds congenial or otherwise, how can you deny that it has a passion for knowledge and understanding?

Of course, I cannot.

And that passion is the same thing as philosophy—the love of wisdom.

Yes.

Shall we boldly say, then, that the same is true of human beings? If a man is to
c be gentle towards his own people whom he knows, he must have an instinctive love of
wisdom and understanding.

Agreed.

So the nature required to make a really noble Guardian of our commonwealth
will be swift and strong, spirited, and philosophic.

Quite so.

Given those natural qualities, then, how are these Guardians to be brought up
and educated? First, will the answer to that question help the purpose of our whole in-
d quiry, which is to make out how justice and injustice grow up in a state? We want to be
thorough, but not to draw out this discussion to a needless length.

Glaucon's brother answered: I certainly think it will help.

If so, I said, we must not think of dropping it, though it may be rather a long
business.

I agree.

Come on then. We will take our time and educate our imaginary citizens.
e Yes, let us do so.

* * *

Book III

* * *

Good, said I; and what is the next point to be settled? Is it not the question, which of
these Guardians are to be rulers and which are to obey?
412^c No doubt.

Well, it is obvious that the elder must have authority over the young, and that the
rulers must be the best.

Yes.

And as among farmers the best are those with a natural turn for farming, so, if we
want the best among our Guardians, we must take those naturally fitted to watch over a
commonwealth. They must have the right sort of intelligence and ability; and also they
must look upon the commonwealth as their special concern—the sort of concern that is
d felt for something so closely bound up with oneself that its interests and fortunes, for
good or ill, are held to be identical with one's own.

Exactly.

So the kind of men we must choose from among the Guardians will be those
who, when we look at the whole course of their lives, are found to be full of zeal to do
whatever they believe is for the good of the commonwealth and never willing to act
e against its interest.

Yes, they will be the men we want.

We must watch them, I think, at every age and see whether they are capable of
preserving this conviction that they must do what is best for the community, never forgetting it or allowing themselves to be either forced or bewitched into throwing it over.

How does this throwing over come about?

I will explain. When a belief passes out of the mind, a man may be willing to part with it, if it is false and he has learnt better, or unwilling, if it is true.   413

I see how he might be willing to let it go; but you must explain how he can be unwilling.

Where is your difficulty? Don't you agree that men are unwilling to be deprived of good, though ready enough to part with evil? Or that to be deceived about the truth is evil, to possess it good? Or don't you think that possessing truth means thinking of things as they really are?

You are right. I do agree that men are unwilling to be robbed of a true belief.

When that happens to them, then, it must be by theft, or violence, or bewitch-   b
ment.

Again I do not understand.

Perhaps my metaphors are too high-flown. I call it theft when one is persuaded out of one's belief or forgets it. Argument in the one case, and time in the other, steal it away without one's knowing what is happening. You understand now?

Yes.

And by violence I mean being driven to change one's mind by pain or suffering.

That too I understand, and you are right.

And bewitchment, as I think you would agree, occurs when a man is beguiled   c
out of his opinion by the allurements of pleasure or scared out of it under the spell of panic.

Yes, all delusions are like a sort of bewitchment.

As I said just now, then, we must find out who are the best guardians of this in-ward conviction that they must always do what they believe to be best for the com-monwealth. We shall have to watch them from earliest childhood and set them tasks in which they would be most likely to forget or to be beguiled out of this duty. We shall then choose only those whose memory holds firm and who are proof against delusion.   d

Yes.

We must also subject them to ordeals of toil and pain and watch for the same qualities there. And we must observe them when exposed to the test of yet a third kind of bewitchment. As people lead colts up to alarming noises to see whether they are timid, so these young men must be brought into terrifying situations and then into scenes of pleasure, which will put them to severer proof than gold tried in the furnace.   e
If we find one bearing himself well in all these trials and resisting every enchantment, a true guardian of himself, preserving always that perfect rhythm and harmony of being which he has acquired from his training in music and poetry, such a one will be of the greatest service to the commonwealth as well as to himself. Whenever we find one who has come unscathed through every test in childhood, youth, and manhood, we   414
shall set him as a Ruler to watch over the commonwealth; he will be honoured in life, and after death receive the highest tribute of funeral rites and other memorials. All who do not reach this standard we must reject. And that, I think, my dear Glaucon, may be taken as an outline of the way in which we shall select Guardians to be set in authority as Rulers.

I am very much of your mind.

These, then, may properly be called Guardians in the fullest sense, who will en-   b
sure that neither foes without shall have the power, nor friends within the wish, to do harm. Those young men whom up to now we have been speaking of as Guardians, will be better described as Auxiliaries, who will enforce the decisions of the Rulers.

I agree.

Now, said I, can we devise something in the way of those convenient fictions we
c   spoke of earlier, a single bold flight of invention,* which we may induce the community in general, and if possible the Rulers themselves, to accept?

What kind of fiction?

Nothing new; something like an Eastern tale of what, according to the poets, has happened before now in more than one part of the world. The poets have been believed; but the thing has not happened in our day, and it would be hard to persuade anyone that it could ever happen again.

You seem rather shy of telling this story of yours.

With good reason, as you will see when I have told it.

Out with it; don't be afraid.

d   Well, here it is; though I hardly know how to find the courage or the words to express it. I shall try to convince, first the Rulers and the soldiers, and then the whole community, that all that nurture and education which we gave them was only something they seemed to experience as it were in a dream. In reality they were the whole time down inside the earth, being moulded and fostered while their arms and all their equipment were being fashioned also; and at last, when they were complete, the earth sent them up from her womb into the light of day. So now they must think of the land
e   they dwell in as a mother and nurse, whom they must take thought for and defend against any attack, and of their fellow citizens as brothers born of the same soil.

You might well be bashful about coming out with your fiction.

415   No doubt; but still you must hear the rest of the story. It is true, we shall tell our people in this fable, that all of you in this land are brothers; but the god who fashioned you mixed gold in the composition of those among you who are fit to rule, so that they are of the most precious quality; and he put silver in the Auxiliaries, and iron and brass in the farmers and craftsmen. Now, since you are all of one stock, although your chil-
b   dren will generally be like their parents, sometimes a golden parent may have a silver child or a silver parent a golden one, and so on with all the other combinations. So the first and chief injunction laid by heaven upon the Rulers is that, among all the things of which they must show themselves good guardians, there is none that needs to be so carefully watched as the mixture of metals in the souls of the children. If a child of
c   their own is born with an alloy of iron or brass, they must, without the smallest pity, assign him the station proper to his nature and thrust him out among the craftsmen or the farmers. If, on the contrary, these classes produce a child with gold or silver in his composition, they will promote him, according to his value, to be a Guardian or an Auxiliary. They will appeal to a prophecy that ruin will come upon the state when it passes into the keeping of a man of iron or brass. Such is the story; can you think of any device to make them believe it?

d   Not in the first generation; but their sons and descendants might believe it, and finally the rest of mankind.

Well, said I, even so it might have a good effect in making them care more for the commonwealth and for one another; for I think I see what you mean.

---

*[What Cornford translates as "bold flight of invention" is usually rendered "noble lie." Cornford claims this common translation is unfair to "Plato's harmless allegory." Other scholars are not so generous. For a discussion of the issues, see the bibliography for books on the *Republic*.]

So, I continued, we will leave the success of our story to the care of popular tradition; and now let us arm these sons of Earth and lead them, under the command of their Rulers, to the site of our city. There let them look round for the best place to fix their camp, from which they will be able to control any rebellion against the laws from within and to beat off enemies who may come from without like wolves to attack the fold. When they have pitched their camp and offered sacrifice to the proper divinities, they must arrange their sleeping quarters; and these must be sufficient to shelter them from winter cold and summer heat.

Naturally. You mean they are going to live there?

Yes, said I; but live like soldiers, not like men of business.

What is the difference?

I will try to explain. It would be very strange if a shepherd were to disgrace himself by keeping, for the protection of his flock, dogs who were so ill-bred and badly trained that hunger or unruliness or some bad habit or other would set them worrying the sheep and behaving no better than wolves. We must take every precaution against our Auxiliaries treating the citizens in any such way and, because they are stronger, turning into savage tyrants instead of friendly allies; and they will have been furnished with the best of safeguards, if they have really been educated in the right way.

But surely there is nothing wrong with their education.

We must not be too positive about that, my dear Glaucon; but we can be sure of what we said not long ago, that if they are to have the best chance of being gentle and humane to one another and to their charges, they must have the right education, whatever that may be.

We were certainly right there.

Then besides that education, it is only common sense to say that the dwellings and other belongings provided for them must be such as will neither make them less perfect Guardians nor encourage them to maltreat their fellow citizens.

True.

With that end in view, let us consider how they should live and be housed. First, none of them must possess any private property beyond the barest necessaries. Next, no one is to have any dwelling or store-house that is not open for all to enter at will. Their food, in the quantities required by men of temperance and courage who are in training for war, they will receive from the other citizens as the wages of their guardianship, fixed so that there shall be just enough for the year with nothing over; and they will have meals in common and all live together like soldiers in a camp. Gold and silver, we shall tell them, they will not need, having the divine counterparts of those metals always in their souls as a god-given possession, whose purity it is not lawful to sully by the acquisition of that mortal dross, current among mankind, which has been the occasion of so many unholy deeds. They alone of all the citizens are forbidden to touch and handle silver or gold, or to come under the same roof with them, or wear them as ornaments, or drink from vessels made of them. This manner of life will be their salvation and make them the saviours of the commonwealth. If ever they should come to possess land of their own and houses and money, they will give up their guardianship for the management of their farms and households and become tyrants at enmity with their fellow citizens instead of allies. And so they will pass all their lives in hating and being hated, plotting and being plotted against, in much greater fear of their enemies at home than of any foreign foe, and fast heading for the destruction that will soon overwhelm their country with themselves. For all these rea-

416

b

c

d

e

417

b

sons let us say that this is how our Guardians are to be housed and otherwise provided for, and let us make laws accordingly.

By all means, said Glaucon.

Book IV

* * *

So now at last, son of Ariston, said I, your commonwealth is established. The 427^d next thing is to bring to bear upon it all the light you can get from any quarter, with the help of your brother and Polemarchus and all the rest, in the hope that we may see where justice is to be found in it and where injustice, how they differ, and which of the two will bring happiness to its possessor, no matter whether gods and men see that he has it or not.

e   Nonsense, said Glaucon; you promised to conduct the search yourself, because it would be a sin not to uphold justice by every means in your power.

That is true; I must do as you say, but you must all help.

We will.

I suspect, then, we may find what we are looking for in this way. I take it that our state, having been founded and built up on the right lines, is good in the complete sense of the word.

It must be.

Obviously, then, it is wise, brave, temperate, and just.

Obviously.

Then if we find some of these qualities in it, the remainder will be the one we 428 have not found. It is as if we were looking somewhere for one of any four things: if we detected that one immediately, we should be satisfied; whereas if we recognized the other three first, that would be enough to indicate the thing we wanted; it could only be the remaining one. So here we have four qualities. Had we not better follow that method in looking for the one we want?

Surely.

To begin then: the first quality to come into view in our state seems to be its wis-
b dom; and there appears to be something odd about this quality.

What is there odd about it?

I think the state we have described really has wisdom; for it will be prudent in counsel, won't it?

Yes.

And prudence in counsel is clearly a form of knowledge; good counsel cannot be due to ignorance and stupidity.

Clearly.

c   But there are many and various kinds of knowledge in our commonwealth. There is the knowledge possessed by the carpenters or the smiths, and the knowledge how to raise crops. Are we to call the state wise and prudent on the strength of these forms of skill?

No; they would only make it good at furniture-making or working in copper or agriculture.

Well then, is there any form of knowledge, possessed by some among the citizens of our new-founded commonwealth, which will enable it to take thought, not for some particular interest, but for the best possible conduct of the state as a whole in its internal and external relations? d

Yes, there is.

What is it, and where does it reside?

It is precisely that art of guardianship which resides in those Rulers whom we just now called Guardians in the full sense.

And what would you call the state on the strength of that knowledge?

Prudent and truly wise. e

And do you think there will be more or fewer of these genuine Guardians in our state than there will be smiths?

Far fewer.

Fewer, in fact, than any of those other groups who are called after the kind of skill they possess?

Much fewer.

So, if a state is constituted on natural principles, the wisdom it possesses as a whole will be due to the knowledge residing in the smallest part, the one which takes the lead and governs the rest. Such knowledge is the only kind that deserves the name 429 of wisdom, and it appears to be ordained by nature that the class privileged to possess it should be the smallest of all.

Quite true.

Here then we have more or less made out one of our four qualities and its seat in the structure of the commonwealth.

To my satisfaction, at any rate.

Next there is courage. It is not hard to discern that quality or the part of the community in which it resides so as to entitle the whole to be called brave.

Why do you say so?

Because anyone who speaks of a state as either brave or cowardly can only be b thinking of that part of it which takes the field and fights in its defence; the reason being, I imagine, that the character of the state is not determined by the bravery or cowardice of the other parts.

No.

Courage, then, is another quality which a community owes to a certain part of itself. And its being brave will mean that, in this part, it possesses the power of preserving, in all circumstances, a conviction about the sort of things that it is right to be c afraid of—the conviction implanted by the education which the law-giver has established. Is not that what you mean by courage?

I do not quite understand. Will you say it again?

I am saying that courage means preserving something.

Yes, but what?

The conviction, inculcated by lawfully established education, about the sort of things which may rightly be feared. When I added "in all circumstances," I meant preserving it always and never abandoning it, whether under the influence of pain or of pleasure, of desire or of fear. If you like, I will give an illustration. d

Please do.

You know how dyers who want wool to take a purple dye, first select the white wool from among all the other colours, next treat it very carefully to make it take the dye in its full brilliance, and only then dip it in the vat. Dyed in that way, wool gets a

fast colour, which no washing, even with soap, will rob of its brilliance; whereas if
they choose wool of any colour but white, or if they neglect to prepare it, you know
what happens.

Yes, it looks washed-out and ridiculous.

That illustrates the result we were doing our best to achieve when we were
choosing our fighting men and training their minds and bodies. Our only purpose was
to contrive influences whereby they might take the colour of our institutions like a dye,
so that, in virtue of having both the right temperament and the right education, their
convictions about what ought to be feared and on all other subjects might be indelibly
fixed, never to be washed out by pleasure and pain, desire and fear, solvents more terribly effective than all the soap and fuller's earth in the world. Such a power of constantly preserving, in accordance with our institutions, the right conviction about the
things which ought, or ought not, to be feared, is what I call courage. That is my position, unless you have some objection to make.

None at all, he replied; if the belief were such as might be found in a slave or an
animal—correct, but not produced by education—you would hardly describe it as in
accordance with our institutions, and you would give it some other name than courage.

Quite true.

Then I accept your account of courage.

You will do well to accept it, at any rate as applying to the courage of the ordinary
citizen; if you like we will go into it more fully some other time. At present we are in
search of justice, rather than of courage; and for that purpose we have said enough.

I quite agree.

Two qualities, I went on, still remain to be made out in our state, temperance
and the object of our whole inquiry, justice. Can we discover justice without troubling
ourselves further about temperance?

I do not know, and I would rather not have justice come to light first, if that
means that we should not go on to consider temperance. So if you want to please me,
take temperance first.

Of course I have every wish to please you.

Do go on then.

I will. At first sight, temperance seems more like some sort of concord or harmony than the other qualities did.

How so?

Temperance surely means a kind of orderliness, a control of certain pleasures
and appetites. People use the expression, "master of oneself," whatever that means,
and various other phrases that point the same way.

Quite true.

Is not "master of oneself" an absurd expression? A man who was master of himself would presumably be also subject to himself, and the subject would be master; for
all these terms apply to the same person.

No doubt.

I think, however, the phrase means that within the man himself, in his soul, there
is a better part and a worse; and that he is his own master when the part which is better
by nature has the worse under its control. It is certainly a term of praise; whereas it is
considered a disgrace, when, through bad breeding or bad company, the better part is
overwhelmed by the worse, like a small force outnumbered by a multitude. A man in
that condition is called a slave to himself and intemperate.

Probably that is what is meant.

Then now look at our newly founded state and you will find one of these two conditions realized there. You will agree that it deserves to be called master of itself, if temperance and self-mastery exist where the better part rules the worse.

Yes, I can see that is true.

It is also true that the great mass of multifarious appetites and pleasures and pains will be found to occur chiefly in children and women and slaves, and, among free men so called, in the inferior multitude; whereas the simple and moderate desires which, with the aid of reason and right belief, are guided by reflection, you will find only in a few, and those with the best inborn dispositions and the best educated.

Yes, certainly.

Do you see that this state of things will exist in your commonwealth, where the desires of the inferior multitude will be controlled by the desires and wisdom of the superior few? Hence, if any society can be called master of itself and in control of pleasures and desires, it will be ours.

Quite so.

On all these grounds, then, we may describe it as temperate. Furthermore, in our state, if anywhere, the governors and the governed will share the same conviction on the question of who ought to rule. Don't you think so?

I am quite sure of it.

Then, if that is their state of mind, in which of the two classes of citizens will temperance reside—in the governors or in the governed?

In both, I suppose.

So we were not wrong in divining a resemblance between temperance and some kind of harmony. Temperance is not like courage and wisdom, which made the state wise and brave by residing each in one particular part. Temperance works in a different way; it extends throughout the whole gamut of the state, producing a consonance of all its elements from the weakest to the strongest as measured by any standard you like to take—wisdom, bodily strength, numbers, or wealth. So we are entirely justified in identifying with temperance this unanimity or harmonious agreement between the naturally superior and inferior elements on the question which of the two should govern, whether in the state or in the individual.

I fully agree.

Good, said I. We have discovered in our commonwealth three out of our four qualities, to the best of our present judgment. What is the remaining one, required to make up its full complement of goodness? For clearly this will be justice.

Clearly.

Now is the moment, then, Glaucon, for us to keep the closest watch, like huntsmen standing round a covert, to make sure that justice does not slip through and vanish undetected. It must certainly be somewhere hereabouts; so keep your eyes open for a view of the quarry, and if you see it first, give me the alert.

I wish I could, he answered; but you will do better to give me a lead and not count on me for more than eyes to see what you show me.

Pray for luck, then, and follow me.

I will, if you will lead on.

The thicket looks rather impenetrable, said I; too dark for it to be easy to start up the game. However, we must push on.

Of course we must.

Here I gave the view halloo. Glaucon, I exclaimed, I believe we are on the track and the quarry is not going to escape us altogether.

That is good news.

Really, I said, we have been extremely stupid. All this time the thing has been under our very noses from the start, and we never saw it. We have been as absurd as a person who hunts for something he has all the time got in his hand. Instead of looking at the thing, we have been staring into the distance. No doubt that is why it escaped us.

What do you mean?

I believe we have been talking about the thing all this while without ever understanding that we were giving some sort of account of it.

Do come to the point. I am all ears.

Listen, then, and judge whether I am right. You remember how, when we first began to establish our commonwealth and several times since, we have laid down, as a universal principle, that everyone ought to perform the one function in the community for which his nature best suited him. Well, I believe that that principle, or some form of it, is justice.

We certainly laid that down.

Yes, and surely we have often heard people say that justice means minding one's own business and not meddling with other men's concerns; and we have often said so ourselves.

We have.

Well, my friend, it may be that this minding of one's own business, when it takes a certain form, is actually the same thing as justice. Do you know what makes me think so?

No, tell me.

I think that this quality which makes it possible for the three we have already considered, wisdom, courage, and temperance, to take their place in the commonwealth, and so long as it remains present secures their continuance, must be the remaining one. And we said that, when three of the four were found, the one left over would be justice.

It must be so.

Well now, if we had to decide which of these qualities will contribute most to the excellence of our commonwealth, it would be hard to say whether it was the unanimity of rulers and subjects, or the soldier's fidelity to the established conviction about what is, or is not, to be feared, or the watchful intelligence of the Rulers; or whether its excellence were not above all due to the observance by everyone, child or woman, slave or freeman or artisan, ruler or ruled, of this principle that each one should do his own proper work without interfering with others.

It would be hard to decide, no doubt.

It seems, then, that this principle can at any rate claim to rival wisdom, temperance, and courage as conducive to the excellence of a state. And would you not say that the only possible competitor of these qualities must be justice?

Yes, undoubtedly.

Here is another thing which points to the same conclusion. The judging of law-suits is a duty that you will lay upon your Rulers, isn't it?

Of course.

And the chief aim of their decisions will be that neither party shall have what belongs to another or be deprived of what is his own.

Yes.

Because that is just?

Yes.

So here again justice admittedly means that a man should possess and concern himself with what properly belongs to him.

True.

Again, do you agree with me that no great harm would be done to the community by a general interchange of most forms of work, the carpenter and the cobbler exchanging their positions and their tools and taking on each other's jobs, or even the same man undertaking both?

Yes, there would not be much harm in that.

But I think you will also agree that another kind of interchange would be disastrous. Suppose, for instance, someone whom nature designed to be an artisan or trades- b man should be emboldened by some advantage, such as wealth or command of votes or bodily strength, to try to enter the order of fighting men; or some member of that order should aspire, beyond his merits, to a seat in the council-chamber of the Guardians. Such interference and exchange of social positions and tools, or the attempt to combine all these forms of work in the same person, would be fatal to the commonwealth.

Most certainly.

Where there are three orders, then, any plurality of functions or shifting from one order to another is not merely utterly harmful to the community, but one might fairly c call it the extreme of wrongdoing. And you will agree that to do the greatest of wrongs to one's own community is injustice.

Surely.

This, then, is injustice. And, conversely, let us repeat that when each order—tradesman, Auxiliary, Guardian—keeps to its own proper business in the commonwealth and does its own work, that is justice and what makes a just society.

I entirely agree. d

We must not be too positive yet, said I. If we find that this same quality when it exists in the individual can equally be identified with justice, then we can at once give our assent; there will be no more to be said; otherwise, we shall have to look further. For the moment, we had better finish the inquiry which we began with the idea that it would be easier to make out the nature of justice in the individual if we first tried to study it in something on a larger scale. That larger thing we took to be a state, and so e we set about constructing the best one we could, being sure of finding justice in a state that was good. The discovery we made there must now be applied to the individual. If it is confirmed, all will be well; but if we find that justice in the individual is something different, we must go back to the state and test our new result. Perhaps if we brought 435 the two cases into contact like flint and steel, we might strike out between them the spark of justice, and in its light confirm the conception in our own minds.

A good method. Let us follow it.

Now, I continued, if two things, one large, the other small, are called by the same name, they will be alike in that respect to which the common name applies. Accord- b ingly, in so far as the quality of justice is concerned, there will be no difference between a just man and a just society.

No.

Well, but we decided that a society was just when each of the three types of human character it contained performed its own function; and again, it was temperate and brave and wise by virtue of certain other affections and states of mind of those same types.

True.

Accordingly, my friend, if we are to be justified in attributing those same virtues to the individual, we shall expect to find that the individual soul contains the same c three elements and that they are affected in the same way as are the corresponding types in society.

That follows.

Here, then, we have stumbled upon another little problem: Does the soul contain these three elements or not?

Not such a very little one, I think. It may be a true saying, Socrates, that what is worthwhile is seldom easy.

Apparently; and let me tell you, Glaucon, it is my belief that we shall never reach the exact truth in this matter by following our present methods of discussion; the road leading to that goal is longer and more laborious. However, perhaps we can find an answer that will be up to the standard we have so far maintained in our speculations.

Is not that enough? I should be satisfied for the moment.

Well, it will more than satisfy me, I replied.

Don't be disheartened, then, but go on.

Surely, I began, we must admit that the same elements and characters that appear in the state must exist in every one of us; where else could they have come from? It would be absurd to imagine that among peoples with a reputation for a high-spirited character, like the Thracians and Scythians and northerners generally, the states have not derived that character from their individual members; or that it is otherwise with the love of knowledge, which would be ascribed chiefly to our own part of the world, or with the love of money, which one would specially connect with Phoenicia and Egypt.

Certainly.

So far, then, we have a fact which is easily recognized. But here the difficulty begins. Are we using the same part of ourselves in all these three experiences, or a different part in each? Do we gain knowledge with one part, feel anger with another, and with yet a third desire the pleasures of food, sex, and so on? Or is the whole soul at work in every impulse and in all these forms of behaviour? The difficulty is to answer that question satisfactorily.

I quite agree.

Let us approach the problem whether these elements are distinct or identical in this way. It is clear that the same thing cannot act in two opposite ways or be in two opposite states at the same time, with respect to the same part of itself, and in relation to the same object. So if we find such contradictory actions or states among the elements concerned, we shall know that more than one must have been involved.

Very well.

Consider this proposition of mine, then. Can the same thing, at the same time and with respect to the same part of itself, be at rest and in motion?

Certainly not.

We had better state this principle in still more precise terms, to guard against misunderstanding later on. Suppose a man is standing still, but moving his head and arms. We should not allow anyone to say that the same man was both at rest and in motion at the same time, but only that part of him was at rest, part in motion. Isn't that so?

Yes.

An ingenious objector might refine still further and argue that a peg-top, spinning with its peg fixed at the same spot, or indeed any body that revolves in the same place, is both at rest and in motion as a whole. But we should not agree, because the parts in respect of which such a body is moving and at rest are not the same. It contains an axis and a circumference; and in respect of the axis it is at rest inasmuch as the axis is not inclined in any direction, while in respect of the circumference it revolves; and if, while it is spinning, the axis does lean out of the perpendicular in all directions, then it is in no way at rest.

That is true.

No objection of that sort, then, will disconcert us or make us believe that the same thing can ever act or be acted upon in two opposite ways, or be two opposite things, at the same time, in respect of the same part of itself, and in relation to the same object. 437

I can answer for myself at any rate.

Well, anyhow, as we do not want to spend time in reviewing all such objections to make sure that they are unsound, let us proceed on this assumption, with the understanding that, if we ever come to think otherwise, all the consequences based upon it will fall to the ground.

Yes, that is a good plan.

Now, would you class such things as assent and dissent, striving after something b and refusing it, attraction and repulsion, as pairs of opposite actions or states of mind—no matter which?

Yes, they are opposites.

And would you not class all appetites such as hunger and thirst, and again willing and wishing, with the affirmative members of those pairs I have just mentioned? For instance, you would say that the soul of a man who desires something is striving c after it, or trying to draw to itself the thing it wishes to possess, or again, in so far as it is willing to have its want satisfied, it is giving its assent to its own longing, as if to an inward question.

Yes.

And, on the other hand, disinclination, unwillingness, and dislike, we should class on the negative side with acts of rejection or repulsion.

Of course. d

That being so, shall we say that appetites form one class, the most conspicuous being those we call thirst and hunger?

Yes.

Thirst being desire for drink, hunger for food?

Yes.

Now, is thirst, just in so far as it is thirst, a desire in the soul for anything more than simply drink? Is it, for instance, thirst for hot drink or for cold, for much drink or for little, or in a word for drink of any particular kind? Is it not rather e true that you will have a desire for cold drink only if you are feeling hot as well as thirsty, and for hot drink only if you are feeling cold; and if you want much drink or little, that will be because your thirst is a great thirst or a little one? But, just in itself, thirst or hunger is a desire for nothing more than its natural object, drink or food, pure and simple.

Yes, he agreed, each desire, just in itself, is simply for its own natural object. When the object is of such and such a particular kind, the desire will be correspondingly qualified.

We must be careful here, or we might be troubled by the objection that no one 438 desires mere food and drink, but always wholesome food and drink. We shall be told that what we desire is always something that is good; so if thirst is a desire, its object must be, like that of any other desire, something—drink or whatever it may be—that will be good for one.

Yes, there might seem to be something in that objection.

But surely, wherever you have two correlative terms, if one is qualified, the other
b must always be qualified too; whereas if one is unqualified, so is the other.

I don't understand.

Well, "greater" is a relative term; and the greater is greater than the less; if it is much greater, then the less is much less; if it is greater at some moment, past or future, then the less is less at that same moment. The same principle applies to all such correl-
c atives, like "more" and "fewer," "double" and "half"; and again to terms like "heavier" and "lighter," "quicker" and "slower," and to things like hot and cold.

Yes.

Or take the various branches of knowledge: is it not the same there? The object of knowledge pure and simple is the knowable—if that is the right word—without any qualification; whereas a particular kind of knowledge has an object of a particular kind.
d For example, as soon as men learnt how to build houses, their craft was distinguished from others under the name of architecture, because it had a unique character, which was itself due to the character of its object; and all other branches of craft and knowledge were distinguished in the same way.

True.

This, then, if you understand me now, is what I meant by saying that, where there are two correlatives, the one is qualified if, and only if, the other is so. I am not
e saying that the one must have the same quality as the other—that the science of health and disease is itself healthy and diseased, or the knowledge of good and evil is itself good and evil—but only that, as soon as you have a knowledge that is restricted to a particular kind of object, namely health and disease, the knowledge itself becomes a particular kind of knowledge. Hence we no longer call it merely knowledge, which would have for its object whatever can be known, but we add the qualification and call it medical science.

I understand now and I agree.

439 Now, to go back to thirst: is not that one of these relative terms? It is essentially thirst for something.

Yes, for drink.

And if the drink desired is of a certain kind, the thirst will be correspondingly qualified. But thirst which is just simply thirst is not for drink of any particular sort—much or little, good or bad—but for drink pure and simple.

Quite so.

We conclude, then, that the soul of a thirsty man, just in so far as he is thirsty,
b has no other wish than to drink. That is the object of its craving, and towards that it is impelled.

That is clear.

Now if there is ever something which at the same time pulls it the opposite way, that something must be an element in the soul other than the one which is thirsting and driving it like a beast to drink; in accordance with our principle that the same thing cannot behave in two opposite ways at the same time and towards the same object with the same part of itself. It is like an archer drawing the bow: it is not accurate to say that his hands are at the same time both pushing and pulling it. One hand does the pushing, the other the pulling.

c Exactly.

Now, is it sometimes true that people are thirsty and yet unwilling to drink?

Yes, often.

What, then, can one say of them, if not that their soul contains something which urges them to drink and something which holds them back, and that this latter is a distinct thing and overpowers the other?

I agree.

And is it not true that the intervention of this inhibiting principle in such cases always has its origin in reflection; whereas the impulses driving and dragging the soul are engendered by external influences and abnormal conditions?

Evidently.

We shall have good reason, then, to assert that they are two distinct principles. We may call that part of the soul whereby it reflects, rational; and the other, with which it feels hunger and thirst and is distracted by sexual passion and all the other desires, we will call irrational appetite, associated with pleasure in the replenishment of certain wants.

Yes, there is good ground for that view.

Let us take it, then, that we have now distinguished two elements in the soul. What of that passionate element which makes us feel angry and indignant? Is that a third, or identical in nature with one of those two?

It might perhaps be identified with appetite.

I am more inclined to put my faith in a story I once heard about Leontius, son of Aglaion. On his way up from the Piraeus outside the north wall, he noticed the bodies of some criminals lying on the ground, with the executioner standing by them. He wanted to go and look at them, but at the same time he was disgusted and tried to turn away. He struggled for some time and covered his eyes, but at last the desire was too much for him. Opening his eyes wide, he ran up to the bodies and cried, "There you are, curse you; feast yourselves on this lovely sight!"

Yes, I have heard that story too.

The point of it surely is that anger is sometimes in conflict with appetite, as if they were two distinct principles. Do we not often find a man whose desires would force him to go against his reason, reviling himself and indignant with this part of his nature which is trying to put constraint on him? It is like a struggle between two factions, in which indignation takes the side of reason. But I believe you have never observed, in yourself or anyone else, indignation make common cause with appetite in behaviour which reason decides to be wrong.

No, I am sure I have not.

Again, take a man who feels he is in the wrong. The more generous his nature, the less can he be indignant at any suffering, such as hunger and cold, inflicted by the man he has injured. He recognizes such treatment as just, and, as I say, his spirit refuses to be roused against it.

That is true.

But now contrast one who thinks it is he that is being wronged. His spirit boils with resentment and sides with the right as he conceives it. Persevering all the more for the hunger and cold and other pains he suffers, it triumphs and will not give in until its gallant struggle has ended in success or death; or until the restraining voice of reason, like a shepherd calling off his dog, makes it relent.

An apt comparison, he said; and in fact it fits the relation of our Auxiliaries to the Rulers: they were to be like watch-dogs obeying the shepherds of the commonwealth.

Yes, you understand very well what I have in mind. But do you see how we have changed our view? A moment ago we were supposing this spirited element to be something of the nature of appetite; but now it appears that, when the soul is divided into factions, it is far more ready to be up in arms on the side of reason.

Quite true.

Is it, then, distinct from the rational element or only a particular form of it, so that the soul will contain no more than two elements, reason and appetite? Or is the soul like the state, which had three orders to hold it together, traders, Auxiliaries, and counsellors? Does the spirited element make a third, the natural auxiliary of reason, when not corrupted by bad upbringing?

It must be a third.

Yes, I said, provided it can be shown to be distinct from reason, as we saw it was from appetite.

That is easily proved. You can see that much in children: they are full of passionate feelings from their very birth; but some, I should say, never become rational, and most of them only late in life.

A very sound observation, said I, the truth of which may also be seen in animals. And besides, there is the witness of Homer in that line I quoted before: "He smote his breast and spoke, chiding his heart." The poet is plainly thinking of the two elements as distinct, when he makes the one which has chosen the better course after reflection rebuke the other for its unreasoning passion.

I entirely agree.

And so, after a stormy passage, we have reached the land. We are fairly agreed that the same three elements exist alike in the state and in the individual soul.

That is so.

Does it not follow at once that state and individual will be wise or brave by virtue of the same element in each and in the same way? Both will possess in the same manner any quality that makes for excellence.

That must be true.

Then it applies to justice: we shall conclude that a man is just in the same way that a state was just. And we have surely not forgotten that justice in the state meant that each of the three orders in it was doing its own proper work. So we may henceforth bear in mind that each one of us likewise will be a just person, fulfilling his proper function, only if the several parts of our nature fulfil theirs.

Certainly.

And it will be the business of reason to rule with wisdom and forethought on behalf of the entire soul; while the spirited element ought to act as its subordinate and ally. The two will be brought into accord, as we said earlier, by that combination of mental and bodily training which will tune up one string of the instrument and relax the other, nourishing the reasoning part on the study of noble literature and allaying the other's wildness by harmony and rhythm. When both have been thus nurtured and trained to know their own true functions, they must be set in command over the appetites, which form the greater part of each man's soul and are by nature insatiably covetous. They must keep watch lest this part, by battening on the pleasures that are called bodily, should grow so great and powerful that it will no longer keep to its own work, but will try to enslave the others and usurp a dominion to which it has no right, thus turning the whole of life upside down. At the same time, those two together will be the best of guardians for the entire soul and for the body against all enemies from without: the one will take counsel, while the other will do battle, following its ruler's commands and by its own bravery giving effect to the ruler's designs.

Yes, that is all true.

And so we call an individual brave in virtue of this spirited part of his nature,   c
when, in spite of pain or pleasure, it holds fast to the injunctions of reason about what
he ought or ought not to be afraid of.

True.

And wise in virtue of that small part which rules and issues these injunctions,
possessing as it does the knowledge of what is good for each of the three elements and
for all of them in common.

Certainly.

And, again, temperate by reason of the unanimity and concord of all three, when   d
there is no internal conflict between the ruling element and its two subjects, but all are
agreed that reason should be ruler.

Yes, that is an exact account of temperance, whether in the state or in the individual.

Finally, a man will be just by observing the principle we have so often stated.

Necessarily.

Now is there any indistinctness in our vision of justice, that might make it seem
somehow different from what we found it to be in the state?   e

I don't think so.

Because, if we have any lingering doubt, we might make sure by comparing it
with some commonplace notions. Suppose, for instance, that a sum of money were entrusted to our state or to an individual of corresponding character and training, would   443
anyone imagine that such a person would be specially likely to embezzle it?

No.

And would he not be incapable of sacrilege and theft, or of treachery to friend or
country; never false to an oath or any other compact; the last to be guilty of adultery or
of neglecting parents or the due service of the gods?

Yes.

And the reason for all this is that each part of his nature is exercising its proper   b
function, of ruling or of being ruled.

Yes, exactly.

Are you satisfied, then, that justice is the power which produces states or individuals of whom that is true, or must we look further?

There is no need; I am quite satisfied.

And so our dream has come true—I mean the inkling we had that, by some
happy chance, we had lighted upon a rudimentary form of justice from the very mo-   c
ment when we set about founding our commonwealth. Our principle that the born
shoemaker or carpenter had better stick to his trade turns out to have been an adumbra-
tion of justice; and that is why it has helped us. But in reality justice, though evidently
analogous to this principle, is not a matter of external behaviour, but of the inward self
and of attending to all that is, in the fullest sense, a man's proper concern. The just man   d
does not allow the several elements in his soul to usurp one another's functions; he is
indeed one who sets his house in order, by self-mastery and discipline coming to be at
peace with himself, and bringing into tune those three parts, like the terms in the proportion of a musical scale, the highest and lowest notes and the mean between them,
with all the intermediate intervals. Only when he has linked these parts together in
well-tempered harmony and has made himself one man instead of many, will he be   e
ready to go about whatever he may have to do, whether it be making money and satisfying bodily wants, or business transactions, or the affairs of state. In all these fields
when he speaks of just and honourable conduct, he will mean the behaviour that helps

to produce and to preserve this habit of mind; and by wisdom he will mean the knowledge which presides over such conduct. Any action which tends to break down this habit will be for him unjust; and the notions governing it he will call ignorance and folly.

That is perfectly true, Socrates.

Good, said I. I believe we should not be thought altogether mistaken, if we claimed to have discovered the just man and the just state, and wherein their justice consists.

Indeed we should not.

Shall we make that claim, then?

Yes, we will.

So be it, said I. Next, I suppose, we have to consider injustice.

Evidently.

This must surely be a sort of civil strife among the three elements, whereby they usurp and encroach upon one another's functions and some one part of the soul rises up in rebellion against the whole, claiming a supremacy to which it has no right because its nature fits it only to be the servant of the ruling principle. Such turmoil and aberration we shall, I think, identify with injustice, intemperance, cowardice, ignorance, and in a word with all wickedness.

Exactly.

And now that we know the nature of justice and injustice, we can be equally clear about what is meant by acting justly and again by unjust action and wrongdoing.

How do you mean?

Plainly, they are exactly analogous to those wholesome and unwholesome activities which respectively produce a healthy or unhealthy condition in the body; in the same way just and unjust conduct produce a just or unjust character. Justice is produced in the soul, like health in the body, by establishing the elements concerned in their natural relations of control and subordination, whereas injustice is like disease and means that this natural order is inverted.

Quite so.

It appears, then, that virtue is as it were the health and comeliness and well-being of the soul, as wickedness is disease, deformity, and weakness.

True.

And also that virtue and wickedness are brought about by one's way of life, honourable or disgraceful.

That follows.

So now it only remains to consider which is the more profitable course: to do right and live honourably and be just, whether or not anyone knows what manner of man you are, or to do wrong and be unjust, provided that you can escape the chastisement which might make you a better man.

But really, Socrates, it seems to me ridiculous to ask that question now that the nature of justice and injustice has been brought to light. People think that all the luxury and wealth and power in the world cannot make life worth living when the bodily constitution is going to rack and ruin; and are we to believe that, when the very principle whereby we live is deranged and corrupted, life will be worth living so long as a man can do as he will, and wills to do anything rather than to free himself from vice and wrong doing and to win justice and virtue?

Yes, I replied, it is a ridiculous question.

Nevertheless, I continued, we are now within sight of the clearest possible proof of our conclusions, and we ought not to slacken our efforts.

No, anything rather than that.

If you will take your stand with me, then, on this point of vantage to which we have climbed, you shall see all the forms that evil takes, or at least all that it seems worthwhile to look at. c

Lead the way and tell me what you see.

What I see is that, whereas there is only one form of excellence, imperfection exists in innumerable shapes, of which there are four that specially deserve notice.

What do you mean?

It looks as if there were as many types of character as there are distinct varieties of political constitution.

How many?

Five of each. d

Will you define them?

Yes, I said. One form of constitution will be the form we have been describing, though it may be called by two names: monarchy, when there is one man who stands out above the rest of the Rulers; aristocracy, when there are more than one.

True.

That, then, I regard as a single form; for, so long as they observe our principles of upbringing and education, whether the Rulers be one or more, they will not subvert the important institutions in our commonwealth. e

Naturally not.

Book V

Such, then, is the type of state or constitution that I call good and right, and the corresponding type of man. By this standard, the other forms in which a state or an individual character may be organized are depraved and wrong. There are four of these vicious forms. 449

What are they?

Here I was going on to describe these forms in the order in which, as I thought, they develop one from another, when Polemarchus, who was sitting a little way from Adeimantus, reached out his hand and took hold of his garment by the shoulder. Leaning forward and drawing Adeimantus towards him, he whispered something in his ear, of which I only caught the words: What shall we do? Shall we leave it alone? b

Certainly not, said Adeimantus, raising his voice.

What is this, I asked, that you are not going to leave alone?

You, he replied.

Why, in particular? I inquired. c

Because we think you are shirking the discussion of a very important part of the subject and trying to cheat us out of an explanation. Everyone, you said, must of course see that the maxim "friends have all things in common" applies to women and children. You thought we should pass over such a casual remark!

But wasn't that right, Adeimantus? said I.

Yes, he said, but "right" in this case, as in others, needs to be defined. There may be many ways of having things in common, and you must tell us which you mean. We have been waiting a long time for you to say something about the conditions in which children are to be born and brought up and your whole plan of having wives and chil- d dren held in common. This seems to us a matter in which right or wrong management will make all the difference to society; and now, instead of going into it thoroughly, you are passing on to some other form of constitution. So we came to the resolution which you overheard, not to let you off discussing it as fully as all the other institutions.

I will vote for your resolution too, said Glaucon.

In fact, Socrates, Thrasymachus added, you may take it as carried unanimously.

You don't know what you are doing, I said, in holding me up like this. You want to start, all over again, on an enormous subject, just as I was rejoicing at the idea that we had done with this form of constitution. I was only too glad that my casual remark should be allowed to pass. And now, when you demand an explanation, you little know what a swarm of questions you are stirring up. I let it alone, because I foresaw no end of trouble.

Well, said Thrasymachus, what do you think we came here for—to play pitch-and-toss or to listen to a discussion?

A discussion, no doubt, I replied; but within limits.

No man of sense, said Glaucon, would think the whole of life too long to spend on questions of this importance. But never mind about us; don't be faint-hearted yourself. Tell us what you think about this question: how our Guardians are to have wives and children in common, and how they will bring up the young in the interval between their birth and education, which is thought to be the most difficult time of all. Do try to explain how all this is to be arranged.

I wish it were as easy as you seem to think, I replied. These arrangements are even more open to doubt than any we have so far discussed. It may be questioned whether the plan is feasible, and even if entirely feasible, whether it would be for the best. So I have some hesitation in touching on what may seem to be an idle dream.

You need not hesitate, he replied. This is not an unsympathetic audience; we are neither incredulous nor hostile.

Thank you, I said; I suppose that remark is meant to be encouraging.

Certainly it is.

Well, I said, it has just the opposite effect. You would do well to encourage me, if I had any faith in my own understanding of these matters. If one knows the truth, there is no risk to be feared in speaking about the things one has most at heart among intelligent friends; but if one is still in the position of a doubting inquirer, as I am now, talking becomes a slippery venture. Not that I am afraid of being laughed at—that would be childish—but I am afraid I may miss my footing just where a false step is most to be dreaded and drag my friends down with me in my fall. I devoutly hope, Glaucon, that no nemesis will overtake me for what I am going to say; for I really believe that to kill a man unintentionally is a lighter offence than to mislead him concerning the goodness and justice of social institutions. Better to run that risk among enemies than among friends; so your encouragement is out of place.

Glaucon laughed at this. No, Socrates, he said, if your theory has any untoward effect on us, our blood shall not be on your head; we absolve you of any intention to mislead us. So have no fear.

Well, said I, when a homicide is absolved of all intention, the law holds him clear of guilt; and the same principle may apply to my case.

Yes, so far as that goes, you may speak freely.

We must go back, then, to a subject which ought, perhaps, to have been treated earlier in its proper place; though, after all, it may be suitable that the women should have their turn on the stage when the men have quite finished their performance, especially since you are so insistent. In my judgement, then, the question under what conditions people born and educated as we have described should possess wives and children, and how they should treat them, can be rightly settled only by keeping to the course on which we started them at the outset. We undertook to put these men in the position of watch-dogs guarding a flock. Suppose we follow up the analogy and imagine them bred and reared in the same sort of way. We can then see if that plan will suit our purpose.   d

How will that be?

In this way. Which do we think right for watch-dogs: should the females guard the flock and hunt with the males and take a share in all they do, or should they be kept within doors as fit for no more than bearing and feeding their puppies, while all the hard work of looking after the flock is left to the males?

They are expected to take their full share, except that we treat them as not quite   e
so strong.

Can you employ any creature for the same work as another, if you do not give them both the same upbringing and education?

No.

Then, if we are to set women to the same tasks as men, we must teach them the   452
same things. They must have the same two branches of training for mind and body and also be taught the art of war, and they must receive the same treatment.

That seems to follow.

Possibly, if these proposals were carried out, they might be ridiculed as involving a good many breaches of custom.

They might indeed.

The most ridiculous—don't you think?—being the notion of women exercising naked along with the men in the wrestling-schools; some of them elderly women too,   b
like the old men who still have a passion for exercise when they are wrinkled and not very agreeable to look at.

Yes, that would be thought laughable, according to our present notions.

Now we have started on this subject, we must not be frightened of the many witticisms that might be aimed at such a revolution, not only in the matter of bodily exercise but in the training of women's minds, and not least when it comes to their bearing   c
arms and riding on horseback. Having begun upon these rules, we must not draw back from the harsher provisions. The wits may be asked to stop being witty and try to be serious; and we may remind them that it is not so long since the Greeks, like most foreign nations of the present day, thought it ridiculous and shameful for men to be seen naked. When gymnastic exercises were first introduced in Crete and later at Sparta, the   d
humorists had their chance to make fun of them; but when experience had shown that nakedness is better uncovered than muffled up, the laughter died down and a practice which the reason approved ceased to look ridiculous to the eye. This shows how idle it is to think anything ludicrous but what is base. One who tries to raise a laugh at any spectacle save that of baseness and folly will also, in his serious moments, set before   e
himself some other standard than goodness of what deserves to be held in honour.

Most assuredly.

The first thing to be settled, then, is whether these proposals are feasible; and it   453
must be open to anyone, whether a humorist or serious-minded, to raise the question whether, in the case of mankind, the feminine nature is capable of taking part with the other sex in all occupations, or in none at all, or in some only; and in particular under which of these heads this business of military service falls. Well begun is half done, and would not this be the best way to begin?

Yes.

Shall we take the other side in this debate and argue against ourselves? We do not want the adversary's position to be taken by storm for lack of defenders.

b   I have no objection.

Let us state his case for him. "Socrates and Glaucon," he will say, "there is no need for others to dispute your position; you yourselves, at the very outset of founding your commonwealth, agreed that everyone should do the one work for which nature fits him." Yes, of course; I suppose we did. "And isn't there a very great difference in nature between man and woman?" Yes, surely. "Does not that natural difference imply a corresponding difference in the work to be given to each?" Yes. "But if so, surely you must be mistaken now and contradicting yourselves when you say that men and women, having such widely divergent natures, should do the same things? What is your answer to that, my ingenious friend?"

It is not easy to find one at the moment. I can only appeal to you to state the case on our own side, whatever it may be.

d   This, Glaucon, is one of many alarming objections which I foresaw some time ago. That is why I shrank from touching upon these laws concerning the possession of wives and the rearing of children.

It looks like anything but an easy problem.

True, I said; but whether a man tumbles into a swimming-pool or into mid-ocean, he has to swim all the same. So must we, and try if we can reach the shore, hoping for some Arion's dolphin or other miraculous deliverance to bring us safe to land.

e   I suppose so.

Come then, let us see if we can find the way out. We did agree that different natures should have different occupations, and that the natures of man and woman are different; and yet we are now saying that these different natures are to have the same occupations. Is that the charge against us?

Exactly.

454   It is extraordinary, Glaucon, what an effect the practice of debating has upon people.

Why do you say that?

Because they often seem to fall unconsciously into mere disputes which they mistake for reasonable argument, through being unable to draw the distinctions proper to their subject; and so, instead of a philosophical exchange of ideas, they go off in chase of contradictions which are purely verbal.

I know that happens to many people; but does it apply to us at this moment?

b   Absolutely. At least I am afraid we are slipping unconsciously into a dispute about words. We have been strenuously insisting on the letter of our principle that different natures should not have the same occupations, as if we were scoring a point in a debate; but we have altogether neglected to consider what sort of sameness or difference we meant and in what respect these natures and occupations were to be defined as

c   different or the same. Consequently, we might very well be asking one another whether there is not an opposition in nature between bald and long-haired men, and, when that was admitted, forbid one set to be shoemakers, if the other were following that trade.

That would be absurd.

Yes, but only because we never meant any and every sort of sameness or difference in nature, but the sort that was relevant to the occupations in question. We meant, for instance, that a man and a woman have the same nature if both have a talent for medicine; whereas two men have different natures if one is a born physician, the other a born carpenter.

Yes, of course.

If, then, we find that either the male sex or the female is specially qualified for any particular form of occupation, then that occupation, we shall say, ought to be assigned to one sex or the other. But if the only difference appears to be that the male begets and the female brings forth, we shall conclude that no difference between man and woman has yet been produced that is relevant to our purpose. We shall continue to think it proper for our Guardians and their wives to share in the same pursuits.

And quite rightly.

The next thing will be to ask our opponent to name any profession or occupation in civic life for the purposes of which woman's nature is different from man's.

That is a fair question.

He might reply, as you did just now, that it is not easy to find a satisfactory answer on the spur of the moment, but that there would be no difficulty after a little reflection.

Perhaps.

Suppose, then, we invite him to follow us and see if we can convince him that there is no occupation concerned with the management of social affairs that is peculiar to women. We will confront him with a question: When you speak of a man having a natural talent for something, do you mean that he finds it easy to learn, and after a little instruction can find out much more for himself; whereas a man who is not so gifted learns with difficulty and no amount of instruction and practice will make him even remember what he has been taught? Is the talented man one whose bodily powers are readily at the service of his mind, instead of being a hindrance? Are not these the marks by which you distinguish the presence of a natural gift for any pursuit?

Yes, precisely.

Now do you know of any human occupation in which the male sex is not superior to the female in all these respects? Need I waste time over exceptions like weaving and watching over saucepans and batches of cakes, though women are supposed to be good at such things and get laughed at when a man does them better?

It is true, he replied, in almost everything one sex is easily beaten by the other. No doubt many women are better at many things than many men; but taking the sexes as a whole, it is as you say.

To conclude, then, there is no occupation concerned with the management of social affairs which belongs either to woman or to man, as such. Natural gifts are to be found here and there in both creatures alike; and every occupation is open to both, so far as their natures are concerned, though woman is for all purposes the weaker.

Certainly.

Is that a reason for making over all occupations to men only?

Of course not.

No, because one woman may have a natural gift for medicine or for music, another may not.

Surely.

Is it not also true that a woman may, or may not, be warlike or athletic?

I think so.

And again, one may love knowledge, another hate it; one may be high-spirited, another spiritless?

Steps in Cloth-Making. Black-figure lekythos (oil jug) attributed to the potter Amasis (sixth century B.C.). The women on the left are hand spinning thread; those in the center are weaving wool. Given that Greek women generally remained at home fulfilling such domestic occupations, Plato's suggestions in the *Republic* were quite revolutionary. Though he claims that women are "for all purposes the weaker [sex]," Plato's character, Socrates, concludes, "There is no occupation concerned with the management of social affairs which belongs to woman or to man, as such. Natural gifts are to be found here and there in both . . . alike; and every occupation is open to both. . . ." (*The Metropolitan Museum of Art, Fletcher Fund, 1931*)(31.11.10)Greek vases. Attic, Black-figure. VI ca. 560 BC. Attributed to the Amasis painter, Lekthyos. Women-working wool on a loom. H. 6 3/4 in. Said to have been found in Attica.

True again.

It follows that one woman will be fitted by nature to be a Guardian, another will not; because these were the qualities for which we selected our men Guardians. So for the purpose of keeping watch over the commonwealth, woman has the same nature as man, save in so far as she is weaker.

So it appears.

b It follows that women of this type must be selected to share the life and duties of Guardians with men of the same type, since they are competent and of a like nature, and the same natures must be allowed the same pursuits.

Yes.

We come round, then, to our former position, that there is nothing contrary to c nature in giving our Guardians' wives the same training for mind and body. The practice we proposed to establish was not impossible or visionary, since it was in accordance with nature. Rather, the contrary practice which now prevails turns out to be unnatural.

So it appears.

Well, we set out to inquire whether the plan we proposed was feasible and also the best. That it is feasible is now agreed; we must next settle whether it is the best.

Obviously.

Now, for the purpose of producing a woman fit to be a Guardian, we shall not have one education for men and another for women, precisely because the nature to be taken in hand is the same. d

True.

What is your opinion on the question of one man being better than another? Do you think there is no such difference?

Certainly I do not.

And in this commonwealth of ours which will prove the better men—the Guardians who have received the education we described, or the shoemakers who have been trained to make shoes?

It is absurd to ask such a question.

Very well. So these Guardians will be the best of all the citizens? e

By far.

And these women the best of all the women?

Yes.

Can anything be better for a commonwealth than to produce in it men and women of the best possible type?

No.

And that result will be brought about by such a system of mental and bodily 457 training as we have described?

Surely.

We may conclude that the institution we proposed was not only practicable, but also the best for the commonwealth.

Yes.

The wives of our Guardians, then, must strip for exercise, since they will be clothed with virtue, and they must take their share in war and in the other social duties of guardianship. They are to have no other occupation; and in these duties the lighter part must fall to the women, because of the weakness of their sex. The man who laughs b at naked women, exercising their bodies for the best of reasons, is like one that "gathers fruit unripe," for he does not know what it is that he is laughing at or what he is doing. There will never be a finer saying than the one which declares that whatever does good should be held in honour, and the only shame is in doing harm.

That is perfectly true.

So far, then, in regulating the position of women, we may claim to have come safely through with one hazardous proposal, that male and female Guardians shall c have all occupations in common. The consistency of the argument is an assurance that the plan is a good one and also feasible. We are like swimmers who have breasted the first wave without being swallowed up.

Not such a small wave either.

You will not call it large when you see the next.

Let me have a look at the next one, then.

Here it is: a law which follows from that principle and all that has gone before, d namely that, of these Guardians, no one man and one woman are to set up house together privately: wives are to be held in common by all; so too are the children, and no parent is to know his own child, nor any child his parent.

It will be much harder to convince people that that is either a feasible plan or a good one.

As to its being a good plan, I imagine no one would deny the immense advantage of wives and children being held in common, provided it can be done. I should expect dispute to arise chiefly over the question of whether it is possible.

e   There may well be a good deal of dispute over both points.

You mean, I must meet attacks on two fronts. I was hoping to escape one by running away: if you agreed it was a good plan, then I should only have had to inquire whether it was feasible.

No, we have seen through that manoeuvre. You will have to defend both positions.

Well, I must pay the penalty for my cowardice. But grant me one favour. Let me
458   indulge my fancy, like one who entertains himself with idle day-dreams on a solitary walk. Before he has any notion how his desires can be realized, he will set aside that question, to save himself the trouble of reckoning what may or may not be possible. He will assume that his wish has come true, and amuse himself with settling all the details of what he means to do then. So a lazy mind encourages itself to be lazier than ever;
b   and I am giving way to the same weakness myself. I want to put off till later that question, how the thing can be done. For the moment, with your leave, I shall assume it to be possible, and ask how the Rulers will work out the details in practice; and I shall argue that the plan, once carried into effect, would be the best thing in the world for our commonwealth and for its Guardians. That is what I shall now try to make out with your help, if you will allow me to postpone the other question.

Very good; I have no objection.

Well, if our Rulers are worthy of the name, and their Auxiliaries likewise, these
c   latter will be ready to do what they are told, and the Rulers, in giving their commands, will themselves obey our laws and will be faithful to their spirit in any details we leave to their discretion.

No doubt.

It is for you, then, as their lawgiver, who has already selected the men, to select for association with them women who are so far as possible of the same natural capac-
d   ity. Now since none of them will have any private home of his own, but they will share the same dwelling and eat at common tables, the two sexes will be together; and meeting without restriction for exercise and all through their upbringing, they will surely be drawn towards union with one another by a necessity of their nature—necessity is not too strong a word, I think?

Not too strong for the constraint of love, which for the mass of mankind is more persuasive and compelling than even the necessity of mathematical proof.

Exactly. But in the next place, Glaucon, anything like unregulated unions would
e   be a profanation in a state whose citizens lead the good life. The Rulers will not allow such a thing.

No, it would not be right.

Clearly, then, we must have marriages, as sacred as we can make them; and this sanctity will attach to those which yield the best results.

Certainly.
459   How are we to get the best results? You must tell me, Glaucon, because I see you keep sporting dogs and a great many game birds at your house; and there is something about their mating and breeding that you must have noticed.

What is that?

In the first place, though they may all be of good stock, are there not some that turn out to be better than the rest?

There are.

And do you breed from all indiscriminately? Are you not careful to breed from the best so far as you can?

Yes.

And from those in their prime, rather than the very young or the very old?   b
Yes.

Otherwise, the stock of your birds or dogs would deteriorate very much, wouldn't it?

It would.

And the same is true of horses or of any animal?

It would be very strange if it were not.

Dear me, said I; we shall need consummate skill in our Rulers, if it is also true of the human race.

Well, it is true. But why must they be so skilful?   c

Because they will have to administer a large dose of that medicine we spoke of earlier. An ordinary doctor is thought good enough for a patient who will submit to be dieted and can do without medicine; but he must be much more of a man if drugs are required.

True, but how does that apply?

It applies to our Rulers: it seems they will have to give their subjects a consider- able dose of imposition and deception for their good. We said, if you remember, that   d such expedients would be useful as a sort of medicine.

Yes, a very sound principle.

Well, it looks as if this sound principle will play no small part in this matter of marriage and child-bearing.

How so?

It follows from what we have just said that, if we are to keep our flock at the highest pitch of excellence, there should be as many unions of the best of both sexes, and as few of the inferior, as possible, and that only the offspring of the better unions   e should be kept. And again, no one but the Rulers must know how all this is being ef- fected; otherwise our herd of Guardians may become rebellious.

Quite true.

We must, then, institute certain festivals at which we shall bring together the brides and the bridegrooms. There will be sacrifices, and our poets will write songs be-   460 fitting the occasion. The number of marriages we shall leave to the Rulers' discretion. They will aim at keeping the number of the citizens as constant as possible, having re- gard to losses caused by war, epidemics, and so on; and they must do their best to see that our state does not become either great or small.

Very good.

I think they will have to invent some ingenious system of drawing lots, so that, at each pairing off, the inferior candidate may blame his luck rather than the Rulers.

Yes, certainly.

Moreover, young men who acquit themselves well in war and other duties,   b should be given, among other rewards and privileges, more liberal opportunities to sleep with a wife, for the further purpose that, with good excuse, as many as possible of the children may be begotten of such fathers.

Yes.

As soon as children are born, they will be taken in charge by officers appointed for the purpose, who may be men or women or both, since offices are to be shared by both sexes. The children of the better parents they will carry to the creche to be reared   c in the care of nurses living apart in a certain quarter of the city. Those of the inferior parents and any children of the rest that are born defective will be hidden away, in some appropriate manner that must be kept secret.

They must be, if the breed of our Guardians is to be kept pure.

These officers will also superintend the nursing of the children. They will bring the mothers to the creche when their breasts are full, while taking every precaution that no mother shall know her own child; and if the mothers have not enough milk, they will provide wet-nurses. They will limit the time during which the mothers will suckle their children, and hand over all the hard work and sitting up at night to nurses and attendants.

That will make child-bearing an easy business for the Guardians' wives.

So it should be. To go on with our scheme: we said that children should be born from parents in the prime of life. Do you agree that this lasts about twenty years for a woman, and thirty for a man? A woman should bear children for the commonwealth from her twentieth to her fortieth year; a man should begin to beget them when he has passed "the racer's prime in swiftness," and continue till he is fifty-five.

Those are certainly the years in which both the bodily and the mental powers of man and woman are at their best.

If a man either above or below this age meddles with the begetting of children for the commonwealth, we shall hold it an offence against divine and human law. He will be begetting for his country a child conceived in darkness and dire incontinence, whose birth, if it escape detection, will not have been sanctioned by the sacrifices and prayers offered at each marriage festival, when priests and priestesses join with the whole community in praying that the children to be born may be even better and more useful citizens than their parents.

You are right.

The same law will apply to any man within the prescribed limits who touches a woman also of marriageable age when the Ruler has not paired them. We shall say that he is foisting on the commonwealth a bastard, unsanctioned by law or by religion.

Perfectly right.

As soon, however, as the men and the women have passed the age prescribed for producing children, we shall leave them free to form a connexion with whom they will, except that a man shall not take his daughter or daughter's daughter or mother or mother's mother, nor a woman her son or father or her son's son or father's father; and all this only after we have exhorted them to see that no child, if any be conceived, shall be brought to light, or, if they cannot prevent its birth, to dispose of it on the understanding that no such child can be reared.

That too is reasonable. But how are they to distinguish fathers and daughters and those other relations you mentioned?

They will not, said I. But, reckoning from the day when he becomes a bridegroom, a man will call all children born in the tenth or the seventh month sons and daughters, and they will call him father. Their children again he will call grandchildren, and they will call his group grandfathers and grandmothers; and all who are born within the period during which their mothers and fathers were having children will be called brothers and sisters. This will provide for those restrictions on unions that we mentioned; but the law will allow brothers and sisters to live together, if the lot so falls out and the Delphic oracle also approves.

Very good.

This, then, Glaucon, is the manner in which the Guardians of your commonwealth are to hold their wives and children in common. Must we not next find arguments to establish that it is consistent with our other institutions and also by far the best plan?

Yes, surely.

We had better begin by asking what is the greatest good at which the lawgiver should aim in laying down the constitution of a state, and what is the worst evil. We can then consider whether our proposals are in keeping with that good and irreconcilable with the evil.

By all means.

Does not the worst evil for a state arise from anything that tends to rend it asunder and destroy its unity, while nothing does it more good than whatever tends to bind it together and make it one?

That is true.

And are not citizens bound together by sharing in the same pleasures and pains, all feeling glad or grieved on the same occasions of gain or loss; whereas the bond is broken when such feelings are no longer universal, but any event of public or personal concern fills some with joy and others with distress?

Certainly.

And this disunion comes about when the words "mine" and "not mine," "another's" and "not another's" are not applied to the same things throughout the community. The best ordered state will be the one in which the largest number of persons use these terms in the same sense, and which accordingly most nearly resembles a single person. When one of us hurts his finger, the whole extent of those bodily connexions which are gathered up in the soul and unified by its ruling element is made aware and it all shares as a whole in the pain of the suffering part; hence we say that the man has a pain in his finger. The same thing is true of the pain or pleasure felt when any other part of the person suffers or is relieved.

Yes; I agree that the best organized community comes nearest to that condition.

And so it will recognize as a part of itself the individual citizen to whom good or evil happens, and will share as a whole in his joy or sorrow.

It must, if the constitution is sound.

It is time now to go back to our own commonwealth and see whether these conclusions apply to it more than to any other type of state. In all alike there are rulers and common people, all of whom will call one another fellow citizens.

Yes.

But in other states the people have another name as well for their rulers, haven't they?

Yes; in most they call them masters; in democracies, simply the government.

And in ours?

The people will look upon their rulers as preservers and protectors.

And how will our rulers regard the people?

As those who maintain them and pay them wages.

And elsewhere?

As slaves.

And what do rulers elsewhere call one another?

Colleagues.

And ours?

Fellow Guardians.

And in other states may not a ruler regard one colleague as a friend in whom he has an interest, and another as a stranger with whom he has nothing in common?

Yes, that often happens.

But that could not be so with your Guardians? None of them could ever treat a fellow Guardian as a stranger.

105

Certainly not. He must regard everyone whom he meets as brother or sister, father or mother, son or daughter, grandchild or grandparent.

d Very good; but here is a further point. Will you not require them, not merely to use these family terms, but to behave as a real family? Must they not show towards all whom they call "father" the customary reverence, care, and obedience due to a parent, if they look for any favour from gods or men, since to act otherwise is contrary to divine and human law? Should not all the citizens constantly reiterate in the hearing of the children from their earliest years such traditional maxims of conduct towards those whom they are taught to call father and their other kindred?

e They should. It would be absurd that terms of kinship should be on their lips without any action to correspond.

In our community, then, above all others, when things go well or ill with any individual everyone will use that word "mine" in the same sense and say that all is going well or ill with him and his.

Quite true.

464 And, as we said, this way of speaking and thinking goes with fellow-feeling; so that our citizens, sharing as they do in a common interest which each will call his own, will have all their feelings of pleasure or pain in common.

Assuredly.

A result that will be due to our institutions, and in particular to our Guardians' holding their wives and children in common.

Very much so.

b But you will remember how, when we compared a well-ordered community to the body which shares in the pleasures and pains of any member, we saw in this unity the greatest good that a state can enjoy. So the conclusion is that our commonwealth owes to this sharing of wives and children by its protectors its enjoyment of the greatest of all goods.

Yes, that follows.

Moreover, this agrees with our principle that they were not to have houses

c or lands or any property of their own, but to receive sustenance from the other citizens, as wages for their guardianship, and to consume it in common. Only so will they keep to their true character; and our present proposals will do still more to make them genuine Guardians. They will not rend the community asunder by each apply-

d ing that word "mine" to different things and dragging off whatever he can get for himself into a private home, where he will have his separate family, forming a centre of exclusive joys and sorrows. Rather they will all, so far as may be, feel together and aim at the same ends, because they are convinced that all their interests are identical.

Quite so.

Again, if a man's person is his only private possession, lawsuits and prosecutions will all but vanish, and they will be free of those quarrels that arise from ownership of property and from having family ties. Nor would they be justified even in bringing ac-

e tions for assault and outrage; for we shall pronounce it right and honourable for a man to defend himself against an assailant of his own age, and in that way they will be compelled to keep themselves fit.

That would be a sound law.

465 And it would also have the advantage that, if a man's anger can be satisfied in this way, a fit of passion is less likely to grow into a serious quarrel.

True.

But an older man will be given authority over all younger persons and power to correct them; whereas the younger will, naturally, not dare to strike the elder or do him any violence, except by command of a Ruler. He will not show him any sort of disrespect. Two guardian spirits, fear and reverence, will be enough to restrain him—reverence forbidding him to lay hands on a parent, and fear of all those others who as sons b or brothers or fathers would come to the rescue.

Yes, that will be the result.

So our laws will secure that these men will live in complete peace with one another; and if they never quarrel among themselves, there is no fear of the rest of the community being divided either against them or against itself.

No.

There are other evils they will escape, so mean and petty that I hardly like to mention them: the poor man's flattery of the rich, and all the embarrassments and vex- c ations of rearing a family and earning just enough to maintain a household; now borrowing and now refusing to repay, and by any and every means scraping together money to be handed over to wife and servants to spend. These sordid troubles are familiar and not worth describing.

Only too familiar. d

Rid of all these cares, they will live a more enviable life than the Olympic victor, who is counted happy on the strength of far fewer blessings than our Guardians will enjoy. Their victory is the nobler, since by their success the whole commonwealth is preserved; and their reward of maintenance at the public cost is more complete, since their prize is to have every need of life supplied for themselves and for their children; their country honours them while they live, and when they die they receive a worthy burial. e

Yes, they will be nobly rewarded.

Do you remember, then, how someone who shall be nameless reproached us for not making our Guardians happy: they were to possess nothing, though all the wealth 466 of their fellow citizens was within their grasp? We replied, I believe, that we would consider that objection later, if it came in our way: for the moment we were bent on making our Guardians real guardians, and moulding our commonwealth with a view to the greatest happiness, not of one section of it, but of the whole.

Yes, I remember.

Well, it appears now that these protectors of our state will have a life better and more honourable than that of any Olympic victor; and we can hardly rank it on a level b with the life of a shoemaker or other artisan or of a farmer.

I should think not.

However, it is right to repeat what I said at the time: if ever a Guardian tries to make himself happy in such a way that he will be a guardian no longer; if, not content with the moderation and security of this way of living which we think the best, he becomes possessed with some silly and childish notion of happiness, impelling him to make his power a means to appropriate all the citizens' wealth, then he will learn the c wisdom of Hesiod's saying that the half is more than the whole.

My advice would certainly be that he should keep to his own way of living.

You do agree, then, that women are to take their full share with men in education, in the care of children, and in the guardianship of the other citizens; whether they stay at home or go out to war, they will be like watch-dogs which take their part either in guarding the fold or in hunting and share in every task so far as their strength allows. Such conduct will not be unwomanly, but all for the best and in accordance with the d natural partnership of the sexes.

Yes, I agree.

It remains to ask whether such a partnership can be established among human beings, as it can among animals, and if so, how.

I was just going to put that question.

e So far as fighting is concerned, it is easy to see how they will go out to war.

How?

Men and women will take the field together and moreover bring with them the children who are sturdy enough, to learn this trade, like any other, by watching what they will have to do themselves when they are grown up; and besides looking on, they will fetch and carry for their fathers and mothers and see to all their needs in time of

467 war. You must have noticed how, in the potter's trade for example, the children watch their fathers and wait on them long before they may touch the wheel. Ought our Guardians to be less careful to train theirs by letting them look on and become familiar with their duties?

No, that would be absurd.

b Moreover, any creature will fight better in the presence of its young.

That is so. But in case of defeat, which may always happen in war, there will be serious danger of their children's lives being lost with their own, so that the country could never recover.

True; but, in the first place, do you think we must make sure that they never run any risk?

No, far from it.

c Well, if they are ever to take their chance, should it not be on some occasion when, if all goes well, they will be the better for it?

No doubt.

And is it of no importance that men who are to be warriors should see something of war in childhood? Is that not worth some danger?

Yes; it is important.

Granted, then, that the children are to go to war as spectators, all will be well if

d we can contrive that they shall do so in safety. To begin with, their fathers will not be slow to judge, so far as human foresight can, which expeditions are hazardous and which are safe; and they will be careful not to take the children into danger. Also they will put them in charge of officers qualified by age and experience to lead and take care of them.

Yes, that would be the proper way.

All the same, the unexpected often happens; and to guard against such chances we must see that they have, from their earliest years, wings to fly away with if need be.

e What do you mean by wings?

Horses, which they must be taught to ride at the earliest possible age; then, when they are taken to see the fighting, their mounts must not be spirited chargers but the swiftest we can find and the easiest to manage. In that way they will get a good view of their future business, and in case of need they will be able to keep up with their older leaders and escape in safety.

That seems an excellent plan.

468 Now, as to the conduct of war and your soldiers' relations to one another and to the enemy: am I right in thinking that anyone guilty of an act of cowardice, such as deserting his post or throwing away his arms, should be reduced to the artisan or farmer class; while if any fall alive into the enemy's hands, we shall make them a present of him, and they may do what they like with their prey?

b Certainly.

And what shall be done to the hero who has distinguished himself by his valour? First, should he not be crowned on the field by the youths and children each in turn?

Surely.

And they might shake his hand?

Yes.

But you would stop there, no doubt. I am sure you would not approve of his ex- c changing kisses with them all?

I am all for that; indeed I would add to the law the provision that, so long as they are on the campaign, no one whom he wishes to kiss may refuse. That would make any soldier who chanced to be in love with a youth or a girl all the more eager to win the prize of valour.

Very well. We have already said that the brave man is to be selected for marriage more frequently than the rest, so that as many children as possible may have such a man for their father. But besides that, these valiant youths may well be rewarded in the d Homeric manner. When Ajax distinguished himself in the war, he was "honoured with slices of the chine's full length," a suitable compliment to a lusty young hero, and one that would at the same time strengthen his muscles.

An excellent idea.

Then here at any rate we will follow Homer. At sacrificial feasts and all such occasions, we shall reward the brave, in proportion to their merit, not only with songs and those privileges we mentioned but "with seats of honour, meat, and cups brimful"; and so e at once pay tribute to the bravery of these men and women and improve their physique.

Nothing could be better.

Good. And of those who are slain in the field, we shall say that all who fell with honour are of that Golden Race, who, when they die,

Dwell here on earth, pure spirits, beneficent.   469
Guardians to shield us mortal men from harm.

Shall we not believe those words of Hesiod?

We shall.

Then we shall ask the Oracle with what special rites these men of more than human mould should be buried, and we shall do as it prescribes. And for all time to b come we shall reverence their tombs and worship them as demigods. Others, too, who die in the natural course of old age or otherwise shall be honoured in the same way, if they are judged to have led an exceptionally noble life.

That is but fair.

And next, how will our soldiers deal with enemies?

In what respect?

First take slavery. Is it right that Greek states should sell Greeks into slavery? Ought they not rather to do all they can to stop this practice and substitute the custom c of sparing their own race, for fear of falling into bondage to foreign nations?

That would be better, beyond all comparison.

They must not, then, hold any Greek in slavery themselves, and they should advise the rest of Greece not to do so.

Certainly. Then they would be more likely to keep their hands off one another and turn their energies against foreigners.

Next, is it well to strip the dead, after a victory, of anything but their arms? It only gives cowards an excuse for not facing the living enemy, as if they were usefully d employed in poking about over a dead body. Many an army has been lost through this pillaging. There is something mean and greedy in plundering a corpse; and a sort of womanish pettiness in treating the body as an enemy, when the spirit, the real enemy, has flown, leaving behind only the instrument with which he fought. It is to behave no better than a dog who growls at the stone that has hit him and leaves alone the man who threw it.

True.

So we will have no stripping of the slain and we shall not prevent their comrades from burying them. Nor shall we dedicate in the temples trophies of their weapons, least of all those of Greeks, if we are concerned to show loyalty towards the rest of Hellas. We shall rather be afraid of desecrating a sanctuary by bringing to it such spoils of our own people, unless indeed the Oracle should pronounce otherwise.

That is very right.

And what of ravaging Greek lands and burning houses? How will your soldiers deal with their enemies in this matter?

I should like to hear your own opinion.

I think they should do neither, but only carry off the year's harvest. Shall I tell you why?

Please do.

It seems to me that war and civil strife differ in nature as they do in name, according to the two spheres in which disputes may arise: at home or abroad, among men of the same race or with foreigners. War means fighting with a foreign enemy; when the enemy is of the same kindred, we call it civil strife.

That is a reasonable distinction.

Is it not also reasonable to assert that Greeks are a single people, all of the same kindred and alien to the outer world of foreigners?

Yes.

Then we shall speak of war when Greeks fight with foreigners, whom we may call their natural enemies. But Greeks are by nature friends of Greeks, and when they fight, it means that Hellas is afflicted by dissension which ought to be called civil strife.

I agree with that view.

Observe, then, that in what is commonly known as civil strife, that is to say, when one of our Greek states is divided against itself, it is thought an abominable outrage for either party to ravage the lands or burn the houses of the other. No lover of his country would dare to mangle the land which gave him birth and nursed him. It is thought fair that the victors should carry off the others' crops, but do no more. They should remember that the war will not last forever; some day they must make friends again.

That is a much more civilized state of mind.

Well then, is not this commonwealth you are founding a Greek state, and its citizens good and civilized people?

Very much so.

And lovers of Greece, who will think of all Hellas as their home, where they share in one common religion with the rest?

Most certainly.

Accordingly, the Greeks being their own people, a quarrel with them will not be called a war. It will only be civil strife, which they will carry on as men who will some day be reconciled. So they will not behave like a foreign enemy seeking to enslave or destroy, but will try to bring their adversaries to reason by well-meant correction. As Greeks they will not devastate the soil of Greece or burn the homesteads; nor will they allow that all the inhabitants of any state, men, women, and children, are their enemies, but only the few who are responsible for the quarrel. The greater number are friends, whose land and houses, on all these accounts, they will not consent to lay waste and destroy. They will pursue the quarrel only until the guilty are compelled by the innocent sufferers to give satisfaction.

For my part, I agree that our citizens should treat their adversaries in that way, and deal with foreigners as Greeks now deal with one another.

We will make this a law, then, for our Guardians: they are not to ravage lands or burn houses.

Yes, we will; it is as satisfactory as all our other laws.

But really, Socrates, Glaucon continued, if you are allowed to go on like this, I am afraid you will forget all about the question you thrust aside some time ago: whether a society so constituted can ever come into existence, and if so, how. No doubt, if it did exist, all manner of good things would come about. I can even add some that you have passed over. Men who acknowledged one another as fathers, sons, or brothers and always used those names among themselves would never desert one another; so they would fight with unequaled bravery. And if their womenfolk went out with them to war, either in the ranks or drawn up in the rear to intimidate the enemy and act as a reserve in case of need, I am sure all this would make them invincible. At home, too, I can see many advantages you have not mentioned. But, since I admit that our commonwealth would have all these merits and any number more, if once it came into existence, you need not describe it in further detail. All we have now to do is to convince ourselves that it can be brought into being and how.

This is a very sudden onslaught, said I; you have no mercy on my shilly-shally-ing. Perhaps you do not realize that, after I have barely escaped the first two waves, the third, which you are now bringing down upon me, is the most formidable of all. When you have seen what it is like and heard my reply, you will be ready to excuse the very natural fears which made me shrink from putting forward such a paradox for discussion.

The more you talk like that, he said, the less we shall be willing to let you off from telling us how this constitution can come into existence; so you had better waste no more time.

Well, said I, let me begin by reminding you that what brought us to this point was our inquiry into the nature of justice and injustice.

True; but what of that?

Merely this: suppose we do find out what justice is, are we going to demand that a man who is just shall have a character which exactly corresponds in every respect to the ideal of justice? Or shall we be satisfied if he comes as near to the ideal as possible and has in him a larger measure of that quality than the rest of the world?

That will satisfy me.

If so, when we set out to discover the essential nature of justice and injustice and what a perfectly just and a perfectly unjust man would be like, supposing them to exist, our purpose was to use them as ideal patterns: we were to observe the degree of happiness or unhappiness that each exhibited, and to draw the necessary inference that our own destiny would be like that of the one we most resembled. We did not set out to show that these ideals could exist in fact.

That is true.

Then suppose a painter had drawn an ideally beautiful figure complete to the last touch, would you think any the worse of him, if he could not show that a person as beautiful as that could exist?

No, I should not.

e   Well, we have been constructing in discourse the pattern of an ideal state. Is our theory any the worse, if we cannot prove it possible that a state so organized should be actually founded?

Surely not.

That, then, is the truth of the matter. But if, for your satisfaction, I am to do my best to show under what conditions our ideal would have the best chance of being real-

473   ized, I must ask you once more to admit that the same principle applies here. Can theory ever be fully realized in practice? Is it not in the nature of things that action should come less close to truth than thought? People may not think so; but do you agree or not?

I do.

Then you must not insist upon my showing that this construction we have traced in thought could be reproduced in fact down to the last detail. You must admit that we shall have found a way to meet your demand for realization, if we can discover how a

b   state might be constituted in the closest accordance with our description. Will not that content you? It would be enough for me.

And for me too.

Then our next attempt, it seems, must be to point out what defect in the working of existing states prevents them from being so organized, and what is the least change that would effect a transformation into this type of government—a single change if possible, or perhaps two; at any rate let us make the changes as few and insignificant as may be.

c   By all means.

Well, there is one change which, as I believe we can show, would bring about this revolution—not a small change, certainly, nor an easy one, but possible.

What is it?

I have now to confront what we called the third and greatest wave. But I must state my paradox, even though the wave should break in laughter over my head and drown me in ignominy. Now mark what I am going to say.

Go on.

Unless either philosophers become kings in their countries or those who are now called kings and rulers come to be sufficiently inspired with a genuine desire for wis-

d   dom; unless, that is to say, political power and philosophy meet together, while the many natures who now go their several ways in the one or the other direction are

e   forcibly debarred from doing so, there can be no rest from troubles, my dear Glaucon, for states, nor yet, as I believe, for all mankind; nor can this commonwealth which we have imagined ever till then see the light of day and grow to its full stature. This it was that I have so long hung back from saying; I knew what a paradox it would be, because it is hard to see that there is no other way of happiness either for the state or for the individual.

Socrates, exclaimed Glaucon, after delivering yourself of such a pronouncement as that, you must expect a whole multitude of by no means contemptible assailants to fling off their coats, snatch up the handiest weapon, and make a rush at you, breathing

474   fire and slaughter. If you cannot find arguments to beat them off and make your escape, you will learn what it means to be the target of scorn and derision.

Well, it was you who got me into this trouble.

Yes, and a good thing too. However, I will not leave you in the lurch. You shall have my friendly encouragement for what it is worth; and perhaps you may find me

more complaisant than some would be in answering your questions. With such backing b
you must try to convince the unbelievers.

I will, now that I have such a powerful ally.

Now, I continued, if we are to elude those assailants you have described, we must, I think, define for them whom we mean by these lovers of wisdom who, we have dared to assert, ought to be our rulers. Once we have a clear view of their character, we shall be able to defend our position by pointing to some who are naturally fitted to c combine philosophic study with political leadership, while the rest of the world should accept their guidance and let philosophy alone.

Yes, this is the moment for a definition.

Here, then, is a line of thought which may lead to a satisfactory explanation. Need I remind you that a man will deserve to be called a lover of this or that, only if it is clear that he loves that thing as a whole, not merely in parts?

You must remind me, it seems; for I do not see what you mean. d

That answer would have come better from someone less susceptible to love than yourself, Glaucon. You ought not to have forgotten that any boy in the bloom of youth will arouse some sting of passion in a man of your amorous temperament and seem worthy of his attentions. Is not this your way with your favourites? You will praise a snub nose as piquant and a hooked one as giving a regal air, while you call a straight e nose perfectly proportioned; the swarthy, you say, have a manly look, the fair are children of the gods; and what do you think is that word "honey-pale," if not the euphemism of some lover who had no fault to find with sallowness on the cheek of youth? In a word, you will carry pretence and extravagance to any length sooner than 475 reject a single one that is in the flower of his prime.

If you insist on taking me as an example of how lovers behave, I will agree for the sake of argument.

Again, do you not see the same behaviour in people with a passion for wine? They are glad of any excuse to drink wine of any sort. And there are the men who covet honour, who, if they cannot lead an army, will command a company, and if they b cannot win the respect of important people, are glad to be looked up to by nobodies, because they must have someone to esteem them.

Quite true.

Do you agree, then, that when we speak of a man as having a passion for a certain kind of thing, we mean that he has an appetite for everything of that kind without discrimination?

Yes.

So the philosopher, with his passion for wisdom, will be one who desires all wisdom, not only some part of it. If a student is particular about his studies, especially while he is too young to know which are useful and which are not, we shall say he is c no lover of learning or of wisdom; just as, if he were dainty about his food, we should say he was not hungry or fond of eating, but had a poor appetite. Only the man who has a taste for every sort of knowledge and throws himself into acquiring it with an insatiable curiosity will deserve to be called a philosopher. Am I not right?

That description, Glaucon replied, would include a large and ill assorted com- d pany. It is curiosity, I suppose, and a delight in fresh experience that gives some people a passion for all that is to be seen and heard at theatrical and musical performances. But they are a queer set to reckon among philosophers, considering that they would never go near anything like a philosophical discussion, though they run round at all the Dionysiac festivals in town or country as if they were under contract to listen to every

company of performers without fail. Will curiosity entitle all these enthusiasts, not to
e   mention amateurs of the minor arts, to be called philosophers?

Certainly not; though they have a certain counterfeit resemblance.

And whom do you mean by the genuine philosophers?

Those whose passion it is to see the truth.

That must be so; but will you explain?

It would not be easy to explain to everyone; but you, I believe, will grant my
premise.

Which is—?

That since beauty and ugliness are opposite, they are two things; and conse-
476   quently each of them is one. The same holds of justice and injustice, good and bad, and
all the essential Forms: each in itself is one; but they manifest themselves in a great variety of combinations, with actions, with material things, and with one another, and so
each seems to be many.

That is true.

On the strength of this premise, then, I can distinguish your amateurs of the arts
b   and men of action from the philosophers we are concerned with, who are alone worthy
of the name.

What is your distinction?

Your lovers of sights and sounds delight in beautiful tones and colours and
shapes and in all the works of art into which these enter; but they have not the power of
thought to behold and to take delight in the nature of Beauty itself. That power to approach Beauty and behold it as it is in itself, is rare indeed.
c   Quite true.

Now if a man believes in the existence of beautiful things, but not of Beauty itself, and cannot follow a guide who would lead him to a knowledge of it, is he not living in a dream? Consider: does not dreaming, whether one is awake or asleep, consist
in mistaking a semblance for the reality it resembles?

I should certainly call that dreaming.

Contrast with him the man who holds that there is such a thing as Beauty
d   itself and can discern that essence as well as the things that partake of its character,
without ever confusing the one with the other—is he a dreamer or living in a waking
state?

He is very much awake.

So may we say that he knows, while the other has only a belief in appearances;
and might we call their states of mind knowledge and belief?

Certainly.

But this person who, we say, has only belief without knowledge may be ag-
e   grieved and challenge our statement. Is there any means of soothing his resentment and
converting him gently, without telling him plainly that he is not in his right mind?

We surely ought to try.

Come then, consider what we are to say to him. Or shall we ask him a question,
assuring him that, far from grudging him any knowledge he may have, we shall be
only too glad to find that there is something he knows? But, we shall say, tell us this:
When a man knows, must there not be something that he knows? Will you answer for
him, Glaucon?

My answer will be, that there must.

Something real or unreal?

477   Something real; how could a thing that is unreal ever be known?

Are we satisfied, then, on this point, from however many points of view we might examine it: that the perfectly real is perfectly knowable, and the utterly unreal is entirely unknowable?

Quite satisfied.

Good. Now if there is something so constituted that it both *is* and *is not,* will it not lie between the purely real and the utterly unreal?

It will.

Well then, as knowledge corresponds to the real, and absence of knowledge necessarily to the unreal, so, to correspond to this intermediate thing, we must look for   b
something between ignorance and knowledge, if such a thing there be.

Certainly.

Is there not a thing we call belief?

Surely.

A different power from knowledge, or the same?

Different.

Knowledge and belief, then, must have different objects, answering to their respective powers.

Yes.

And knowledge has for its natural object the real—to know the truth about reality. However, before going further, I think we need a definition. Shall we distinguish   c
under the general name of "faculties" those powers which enable us—or anything else—to do what we can do? Sight and hearing, for instance, are what I call faculties, if that will help you to see the class of things I have in mind.

Yes, I understand.

Then let me tell you what view I take of them. In a faculty I cannot find any of those qualities, such as colour or shape, which, in the case of many other things, enable me to distinguish one thing from another. I can only look to its field of objects and the state of mind it produces, and regard these as sufficient to identify it and to distinguish   d
it from faculties which have different fields and produce different states. Is that how you would go to work?

Yes.

Let us go back, then, to knowledge. Would you class that as a faculty?

Yes; and I should call it the most powerful of all.

And is belief also a faculty?   e

It can be nothing else, since it is what gives us the power of believing.

But a little while ago you agreed that knowledge and belief are not the same thing.

Yes; there could be no sense in identifying the infallible with the fallible.

Good. So we are quite clear that knowledge and belief are different things?   478

They are.

If so, each of them, having a different power, must have a different field of objects.

Necessarily.

The field of knowledge being the real; and its power, the power of knowing the real as it is.

Yes.

Whereas belief, we say, is the power of believing. Is its object the same as that which knowledge knows? Can the same things be possible objects both of knowledge and of belief?

b   Not if we hold to the principles we agreed upon. If it is of the nature of a different faculty to have a different field, and if both knowledge and belief are faculties and, as we assert, different ones, it follows that the same things cannot be possible objects of both.

So if the real is the object of knowledge, the object of belief must be something other than the real.

Yes.

c   Can it be thè unreal? Or is that an impossible object even for belief? Consider: if a man has a belief, there must be something before his mind; he cannot be believing nothing, can he?

No.

He is believing something, then; whereas the unreal could only be called nothing at all.

Certainly.

Now we said that ignorance must correspond to the unreal, knowledge to the real. So what he is believing cannot be real nor yet unreal.

True.

Belief, then, cannot be either ignorance or knowledge.

It appears not.

d   Then does it lie outside and beyond these two? Is it either more clear and certain than knowledge or less clear and certain than ignorance?

No, it is neither.

It rather seems to you to be something more obscure than knowledge, but not so dark as ignorance, and so to lie between the two extremes?

Quite so.

Well, we said earlier that if some object could be found such that it both *is* and at the same time *is not,* that object would lie between the perfectly real and the utterly unreal; and that the corresponding faculty would be neither knowledge nor ignorance, but a faculty to be found situated between the two.

Yes.

And now what we have found between the two is the faculty we call belief.

True.

e   It seems, then, that what remains to be discovered is that object which can be said both to be and not to be and cannot properly be called either purely real or purely unreal. If that can be found, we may justly call it the object of belief, and so give the intermediate faculty the intermediate object, while the two extreme objects will fall to the extreme faculties.

Yes.

479   On these assumptions, then, I shall call for an answer from our friend who denies the existence of Beauty itself or of anything that can be called an essential Form of Beauty remaining unchangeably in the same state forever, though he does recognize the existence of beautiful things as a plurality—that lover of things seen who will not listen to anyone who says that Beauty is one, Justice is one, and so on. I shall say to him, Be so good as to tell us: of all these many beautiful things is there one which will not appear ugly? Or of these many just or righteous actions, is there one that will not appear unjust or unrighteous?

b   No, replied Glaucon, they must inevitably appear to be in some way both beautiful and ugly; and so with all the other terms your question refers to.

And again the many things which are doubles are just as much halves as they are doubles. And the things we call large or heavy have just as much right to be called small or light.

Yes; any such thing will always have a claim to both opposite designations.

Then, whatever any one of these many things may be said to be, can you say that it absolutely *is* that, any more than that it *is not* that?

They remind me of those punning riddles people ask at dinner parties, or the child's puzzle about what the eunuch threw at the bat and what the bat was perched on. These things have the same ambiguous character, and one cannot form any stable conception of them either as being or as not being, or as both being and not being, or as neither.   c

Can you think of any better way of disposing of them than by placing them between reality and unreality? For I suppose they will not appear more obscure and so less real than unreality, or clearer and so more real than reality.   d

Quite true.

It seems, then, we have discovered that the many conventional notions of the mass of mankind about what is beautiful or honourable or just and so on are adrift in a sort of twilight between pure reality and pure unreality.

We have.

And we agreed earlier that, if any such object were discovered, it should be called the object of belief and not of knowledge. Fluctuating in that half-way region, it would be seized upon by the intermediate faculty.

Yes.

So when people have an eye for the multitude of beautiful things or of just actions or whatever it may be, but can neither behold Beauty or Justice itself nor follow a guide who would lead them to it, we shall say that all they have is beliefs, without any real knowledge of the objects of their belief.   e

That follows.

But what of those who contemplate the realities themselves as they are forever in the same unchanging state? Shall we not say that they have, not mere belief, but knowledge?

That too follows.

And, further, that their affection goes out to the objects of knowledge, whereas the others set their affections on the objects of belief; for it was they, you remember, who had a passion for the spectacle of beautiful colours and sounds, but would not hear of Beauty itself being a real thing.   480

I remember.

So we may fairly call them lovers of belief rather than of wisdom—not philosophical, in fact, but philodoxical. Will they be seriously annoyed by that description?

Not if they will listen to my advice. No one ought to take offence at the truth.

The name of philosopher, then, will be reserved for those whose affections are set, in every case, on the reality.

By all means.

BOOK VI

*   *   *

One difficulty, then, has been surmounted. It remains to ask how we can make sure of having men who will preserve our constitution. What must they learn, and at what age should they take up each branch of study?   502^{d}

Yes, that is the next point.

I gained nothing by my cunning in putting off those thorny questions of the possession of wives and children and the appointment of Rulers. I knew that the ideal plan would give offence and be hard to carry out; none the less I have had to discuss these matters. We have now disposed of the women and children, but we must start all over again upon the training of the Rulers. You remember how their love for their country was to be proved, by the tests of pain and pleasure, to be a faith that no toil or danger, no turn of fortune could make them abandon. All who failed were to be rejected; only the man who came out flawless, like gold tried in the fire, was to be made a Ruler with privileges and rewards in life and after death. So much was said, when our argument turned aside, as if hoping, with veiled face, to slip past the danger that now lies in our path.

Quite true, I remember.

Yes, I shrank from the bold words which have now been spoken; but now we have ventured to declare that our Guardians in the fullest sense must be philosophers. So much being granted, you must reflect how few are likely to be available. The natural gifts we required will rarely grow together into one whole; they tend to split apart.

How do you mean?

Qualities like ready understanding, a good memory, sagacity, quickness, together with a high-spirited, generous temper, are seldom combined with willingness to live a quiet life of sober constancy. Keen wits are apt to lose all steadiness and to veer about in every direction. On the other hand, the steady reliable characters, whose impassivity is proof against the perils of war, are equally proof against instruction. Confronted with intellectual work, they become comatose and do nothing but yawn.

That is true.

But we insist that no one must be given the highest education or hold office as Ruler, who has not both sets of qualities in due measure. This combination will be rare. So, besides testing it by hardship and danger and by the temptations of pleasure, we may now add that its strength must be tried in many forms of study, to see whether it has the courage and endurance to pursue the highest kind of knowledge, without flinching as others flinch under physical trials.

By all means; but what kinds of study do you call the highest?

You remember how we deduced the definitions of justice, temperance, courage, and wisdom by distinguishing three parts of the soul?

If I had forgotten that, I should not deserve to hear any more.

Do you also remember my warning you beforehand that in order to gain the clearest possible view of these qualities we should have to go round a longer way, although we could give a more superficial account in keeping with our earlier argument. You said that would do; and so we went on in a way which seemed to me not sufficiently exact; whether you were satisfied, it is for you to say.

We all thought you gave us a fair measure of truth.

No measure that falls in the least degree short of the whole truth can be quite fair in so important a matter. What is imperfect can never serve as a measure; though people sometimes think enough has been done and there is no need to look further.

Yes, indolence is common enough.

But the last quality to be desired in the Guardian of a commonwealth and its laws. So he will have to take the longer way and work as hard at learning as at training his body; otherwise he will never reach the goal of the highest knowledge, which most of all concerns him.

Why, are not justice and the other virtues we have discussed the highest? Is there something still higher to be known?

There is; and of those virtues themselves we have as yet only a rough outline, where nothing short of the finished picture should content us. If we strain every nerve to reach precision and clearness in things of little moment, how absurd not to demand the highest degree of exactness in the things that matter most.

Certainly. But what do you mean by the highest kind of knowledge and with what is it concerned? You cannot hope to escape that question.

I do not; you may ask me yourself. All the same, you have been told many a time; but now either you are not thinking or, as I rather suspect, you mean to put me to some trouble with your insistence. For you have often been told that the highest object of knowledge is the essential nature of the Good, from which everything that is good and right derives its value for us. You must have been expecting me to speak of this now, and to add that we have no sufficient knowledge of it. I need not tell you that, without that knowledge, to know everything else, however well, would be of no value to us, just as it is of no use to possess anything without getting the good of it. What advantage can there be in possessing everything except what is good, or in understanding everything else while of the good and desirable we know nothing?

None whatever.

Well then, you know too that most people identify the Good with pleasure, whereas the more enlightened think it is knowledge.

Yes, of course.

And further that these latter cannot tell us what knowledge they mean, but are reduced at last to saying, "knowledge of the Good."

That is absurd.

It is; first they reproach us with not knowing the Good, and then tell us that it is knowledge of the Good, as if we did after all understand the meaning of that word "Good" when they pronounce it.

Quite true.

What of those who define the Good as pleasure? Are they any less confused in their thoughts? They are obliged to admit that there are bad pleasures; from which it follows that the same things are both good and bad.

Quite so.

Evidently, then, this is a matter of much dispute. It is also evident that, although many are content to do what seems just or honourable without really being so, and to possess a mere semblance of these qualities, when it comes to good things, no one is satisfied with possessing what only seems good: here all reject the appearance and demand the reality.

Certainly.

A thing, then, that every soul pursues as the end of all her actions, dimly divining its existence, but perplexed and unable to grasp its nature with the same clearness and assurance as in dealing with other things, and so missing whatever value those other things might have—a thing of such supreme importance is not a matter about which those chosen Guardians of the whole fortunes of our commonwealth can be left in the dark.

Most certainly not.

At any rate, institutions or customs which are desirable and right will not, I imagine, find a very efficient guardian in one who does not know in what way they are good. I should rather guess that he will not be able to recognize fully that they are right and desirable.

No doubt.

So the order of our commonwealth will be perfectly regulated only when it is watched over by a Guardian who does possess this knowledge.

That follows. But, Socrates, what is your own account of the Good? Is it knowledge, or pleasure, or something else?

There you are! I exclaimed; I could see all along that you were not going to be content with what other people think.

Well, Socrates, it does not seem fair that you should be ready to repeat other people's opinions but not to state your own, when you have given so much thought to this subject.

c   And do you think it fair of anyone to speak as if he knew what he does not know?

No, not as if he knew, but he might give his opinion for what it is worth.

Why, have you never noticed that opinion without knowledge is always a shabby sort of thing? At the best it is blind. One who holds a true belief without intelligence is just like a blind man who happens to take the right road, isn't he?

No doubt.

d   Well, then, do you want me to produce one of these poor blind cripples, when others could discourse to you with illuminating eloquence?

No, really, Socrates, said Glaucon, you must not give up within sight of the goal. We should be quite content with an account of the Good like the one you gave us of justice and temperance and the other virtues.

So should I be, my dear Glaucon, much more than content! But I am afraid it is beyond my powers; with the best will in the world I should only disgrace myself and

e   be laughed at. No, for the moment let us leave the question of the real meaning of good; to arrive at what I at any rate believe it to be would call for an effort too ambitious for an inquiry like ours. However, I will tell you, though only if you wish it, what I picture to myself as the offspring of the Good and the thing most nearly resembling it.

Well, tell us about the offspring, and you shall remain in our debt for an account of the parent.

507   I only wish it were within my power to offer, and within yours to receive, a settlement of the whole account. But you must be content now with the interest only; and you must see to it that, in describing this offspring of the Good, I do not inadvertently cheat you with false coin.

We will keep a good eye on you. Go on.

First we must come to an understanding. Let me remind you of the distinction we

b   drew earlier and have often drawn on other occasions, between the multiplicity of things that we call good or beautiful or whatever it may be and, on the other hand, Goodness itself or Beauty itself and so on. Corresponding to each of these sets of many things, we postulate a single Form or real essence, as we call it.

Yes, that is so.

Further, the many things, we say, can be seen, but are not objects of rational thought; whereas the Forms are objects of thought, but invisible.

c   Yes, certainly.

And we see things with our eyesight, just as we hear sounds with our ears and, to speak generally, perceive any sensible thing with our sense-faculties.

Of course.

Have you noticed, then, that the artificer who designed the senses has been exceptionally lavish of his materials in making the eyes able to see and their objects visible?

That never occurred to me.

Well, look at it in this way. Hearing and sound do not stand in need of any third

d   thing, without which the ear will not hear nor sound be heard; and I think the same is true of most, not to say all, of the other senses. Can you think of one that does require anything of the sort?

No, I cannot.

But there is this need in the case of sight and its objects. You may have the power of vision in your eyes and try to use it, and colour may be there in the objects; but sight will see nothing and the colours will remain invisible in the absence of a third   e thing peculiarly constituted to serve this very purpose.

By which you mean—?

Naturally I mean what you call light; and if light is a thing of value, the sense of sight and the power of being visible are linked together by a very precious bond, such   508 as unites no other sense with its object.

No one could say that light is not a precious thing.

And of all the divinities in the skies is there one whose light, above all the rest, is responsible for making our eyes see perfectly and making objects perfectly visible?

There can be no two opinions: of course you mean the Sun.

And how is sight related to this deity? Neither sight nor the eye which contains it is the Sun, but of all the sense-organs it is the most sun-like; and further, the power it   b possesses is dispensed by the Sun, like a stream flooding the eye. And again, the Sun is not vision, but it is the cause of vision and also is seen by the vision it causes.

Yes.

It was the Sun, then, that I meant when I spoke of that offspring which the Good has created in the visible world, to stand there in the same relation to vision and visible things as that which the Good itself bears in the intelligible world to intelligence and to   c intelligible objects.

How is that? You must explain further.

You know what happens when the colours of things are no longer irradiated by the daylight, but only by the fainter luminaries of the night: when you look at them, the eyes are dim and seem almost blind, as if there were no unclouded vision in them. But   d when you look at things on which the Sun is shining, the same eyes see distinctly and it becomes evident that they do contain the power of vision.

Certainly.

Apply this comparison, then, to the soul. When its gaze is fixed upon an object irradiated by truth and reality, the soul gains understanding and knowledge and is manifestly in possession of intelligence. But when it looks towards that twilight world of things that come into existence and pass away, its sight is dim and it has only opinions and beliefs which shift to and fro, and now it seems like a thing that has no intelligence.

That is true.

This, then, which gives to the objects of knowledge their truth and to him who knows them his power of knowing, is the Form or essential nature of Goodness. It is   e the cause of knowledge and truth; and so, while you may think of it as an object of knowledge, you will do well to regard it as something beyond truth and knowledge and, precious as these both are, of still higher worth. And, just as in our analogy light and vision were to be thought of as like the Sun, but not identical with it, so here both   509 knowledge and truth are to be regarded as like the Good, but to identify either with the Good is wrong. The Good must hold a yet higher place of honour.

You are giving it a position of extraordinary splendour, if it is the source of knowledge and truth and itself surpasses them in worth. You surely cannot mean that it is pleasure.

Heaven forbid, I exclaimed. But I want to follow up our analogy still further.   b You will agree that the Sun not only makes the things we see visible, but also brings them into existence and gives them growth and nourishment; yet he is not the same thing as existence. And so with the objects of knowledge: these derive from the Good not only their power of being known, but their very being and reality; and Goodness is not the same thing as being, but even beyond being, surpassing it in dignity and power.

c   Glaucon exclaimed with some amusement at my exalting Goodness in such extravagant terms.

It is your fault, I replied; you forced me to say what I think.

Yes, and you must not stop there. At any rate, complete your comparison with the Sun, if there is any more to be said.

There is a great deal more, I answered.

Let us hear it, then; don't leave anything out.

I am afraid much must be left unspoken. However, I will not, if I can help it, leave out anything that can be said on this occasion.

Please do not.

d   Conceive, then, that there are these two powers I speak of, the Good reigning over the domain of all that is intelligible, the Sun over the visible world—or the heaven as I might call it; only you would think I was showing off my skill in etymology. At any rate you have these two orders of things clearly before your mind: the visible and the intelligible?

I have.

Now take a line divided into two unequal parts, one to represent the visible order, the other the intelligible; and divide each part again in the same proportion, e   symbolizing degrees of comparative clearness or obscurity. Then (A) one of the two 510   sections in the visible world will stand for images. By images I mean first shadows, and then reflections in water or in close-grained, polished surfaces, and everything of that kind, if you understand.

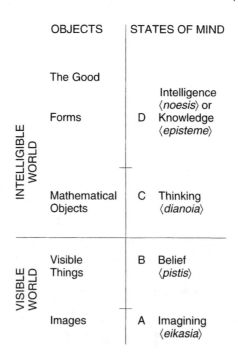

	OBJECTS	STATES OF MIND
	The Good	
INTELLIGIBLE WORLD	Forms	D Intelligence ⟨*noesis*⟩ or Knowledge ⟨*episteme*⟩
	Mathematical Objects	C Thinking ⟨*dianoia*⟩
VISIBLE WORLD	Visible Things	B Belief ⟨*pistis*⟩
	Images	A Imagining ⟨*eikasia*⟩

Yes, I understand.

Let the second section (B) stand for the actual things of which the first are likenesses, the living creatures about us and all the works of nature or of human hands.

So be it.

Will you also take the proportion in which the visible world has been divided as corresponding to degrees of reality and truth, so that the likeness shall stand to the original in the same ratio as the sphere of appearances and belief to the sphere of knowledge?

Certainly.   b

Now consider how we are to divide the part which stands for the intelligible world. There are two sections. In the first (C) the mind uses as images those actual things which themselves had images in the visible world; and it is compelled to pursue its inquiry by starting from assumptions and travelling, not up to a principle, but down to a conclusion. In the second (D) the mind moves in the other direction, from an assumption up towards a principle which is not hypothetical; and it makes no use of the images employed in the other section, but only of Forms, and conducts its inquiry solely by their means.

I don't quite understand what you mean.

Then we will try again; what I have just said will help you to understand. (C)   c
You know, of course, how students of subjects like geometry and arithmetic begin by postulating odd and even numbers, or the various figures and the three kinds of angle, and other such data in each subject. These data they take as known; and, having adopted them as assumptions, they do not feel called upon to give any account of them to themselves or to anyone else, but treat them as self-evident. Then, starting from these assumptions, they go on until they arrive, by a series of consistent steps, at all the   d
conclusions they set out to investigate.

Yes, I know that.

You also know how they make use of visible figures and discourse about them, though what they really have in mind is the originals of which these figures are images: they are not reasoning, for instance, about this particular square and diagonal which they have drawn, but about *the* Square and *the* Diagonal; and so in all cases. The diagrams they draw and the models they make are actual things, which may have their   e
shadows or images in water; but now they serve in their turn as images, while the student is seeking to behold those realities which only thought can apprehend.

True.   511

This, then, is the class of things that I spoke of as intelligible, but with two qualifications: first, that the mind, in studying them, is compelled to employ assumptions, and, because it cannot rise above these, does not travel upwards to a first principle; and second, that it uses as images those actual things which have images of their own in the section below them and which, in comparison with those shadows and reflections, are reputed to be more palpable and valued accordingly.

I understand: you mean the subject-matter of geometry and of the kindred arts.   b

(D) Then by the second section of the intelligible world you may understand me to mean all that unaided reasoning apprehends by the power of dialectic, when it treats its assumptions, not as first principles, but as *hypotheses* in the literal sense, things "laid down" like a flight of steps up which it may mount all the way to something that is not hypothetical, the first principle of all; and having grasped this, may turn back and, holding on to the consequences which depend upon it, descend at last to a conclusion, never making use of any sensible object, but only of Forms, moving through   c
Forms from one to another, and ending with Forms.

I understand, he said, though not perfectly; for the procedure you describe sounds like an enormous undertaking. But I see that you mean to distinguish the field of intelligible reality studied by dialectic as having a greater certainty and truth than the subject-matter of the "arts," as they are called, which treat their assumptions as first principles. The students of these arts are, it is true, compelled to exercise thought in

d contemplating objects which the senses cannot perceive; but because they start from assumptions without going back to a first principle, you do not regard them as gaining true understanding about those objects, although the objects themselves, when connected with a first principle, are intelligible. And I think you would call the state of mind of the students of geometry and other such arts, not intelligence, but thinking, as being something between intelligence and mere acceptance of appearances.

You have understood me quite well enough, I replied. And now you may take, as

e corresponding to the four sections, these four states of mind: *intelligence* for the highest, *thinking* for the second, *belief* for the third, and for the last *imagining*. These you may arrange as the terms in a proportion, assigning to each a degree of clearness and certainty corresponding to the measure in which their objects possess truth and reality.

I understand and agree with you. I will arrange them as you say.

BOOK VII

514 Next, said I, here is a parable to illustrate the degrees in which our nature may be enlightened or unenlightened. Imagine the condition of men living in a sort of cavernous chamber underground, with an entrance open to the light and a long passage all down the cave. Here they have been from childhood, chained by the leg and also by the neck, so that they cannot move and can see only what is in front of them, because the chains

b will not let them turn their heads. At some distance higher up is the light of a fire burning behind them; and between the prisoners and the fire is a track with a parapet built along it, like the screen at a puppet-show, which hides the performers while they show their puppets over the top.

I see, said he.

Now behind this parapet imagine persons carrying along various artificial ob-

c jects, including figures of men and animals in wood or stone or other materials, which
515 project above the parapet. Naturally, some of these persons will be talking, others silent.

It is a strange picture, he said, and a strange sort of prisoners.

Like ourselves, I replied; for in the first place prisoners so confined would have seen nothing of themselves or of one another, except the shadows thrown by the fire-light on the wall of the Cave facing them, would they?

b Not if all their lives they had been prevented from moving their heads.

And they would have seen as little of the objects carried past.

Of course.

Now, if they could talk to one another, would they not suppose that their words referred only to those passing shadows which they saw?

Necessarily.

And suppose their prison had an echo from the wall facing them? When one of the people crossing behind them spoke, they could only suppose that the sound came from the shadow passing before their eyes.

No doubt.

In every way, then, such prisoners would recognize as reality nothing but the shadows of those artificial objects. c

Inevitably.

Now consider what would happen if their release from the chains and the healing of their unwisdom should come about in this way. Suppose one of them were set free and forced suddenly to stand up, turn his head, and walk with eyes lifted to the light; all these movements would be painful, and he would be too dazzled to make out the objects whose shadows he had been used to seeing. What do you think he would say, if someone told him that what he had formerly seen was meaningless illusion, but now, being somewhat nearer to reality and turned towards more real objects, he was getting a truer d view? Suppose further that he were shown the various objects being carried by and were made to say, in reply to questions, what each of them was. Would he not be perplexed and believe the objects now shown him to be not so real as what he formerly saw?

Yes, not nearly so real.

And if he were forced to look at the firelight itself, would not his eyes ache, so e that he would try to escape and turn back to the things which he could see distinctly, convinced that they really were clearer than these other objects now being shown to him?

Yes.

And suppose someone were to drag him away forcibly up the steep and rugged ascent and not let him go until he had hauled him out into the sunlight, would he not suffer pain and vexation at such treatment, and, when he had come out into the light, find his eyes so full of its radiance that he could not see a single one of the things that 516 he was now told were real?

Certainly he would not see them all at once.

He would need, then, to grow accustomed before he could see things in that upper world. At first it would be easiest to make out shadows, and then the images of men and things reflected in water, and later on the things themselves. After that, it would be easier to watch the heavenly bodies and the sky itself by night, looking at the b light of the moon and stars rather than the Sun and the Sun's light in the day-time.

Yes, surely.

Last of all, he would be able to look at the Sun and contemplate its nature, not as it appears when reflected in water or any alien medium, but as it is in itself in its own domain.

No doubt.

And now he would begin to draw the conclusion that it is the Sun that produces the seasons and the course of the year and controls everything in the visible world, and moreover is in a way the cause of all that he and his companions used to see. c

Clearly he would come at last to that conclusion.

Then if he called to mind his fellow prisoners and what passed for wisdom in his former dwelling-place, he would surely think himself happy in the change and be sorry for them. They may have had a practice of honouring and commending one another, with prizes for the man who had the keenest eye for the passing shadows and the best memory for the order in which they followed or accompanied one another, so that he d could make a good guess as to which was going to come next. Would our released prisoner be likely to covet those prizes or to envy the men exalted to honour and power in the Cave? Would he not feel like Homer's Achilles, that he would far sooner "be on earth as a hired servant in the house of a landless man" or endure anything rather than go back to his old beliefs and live in the old way?

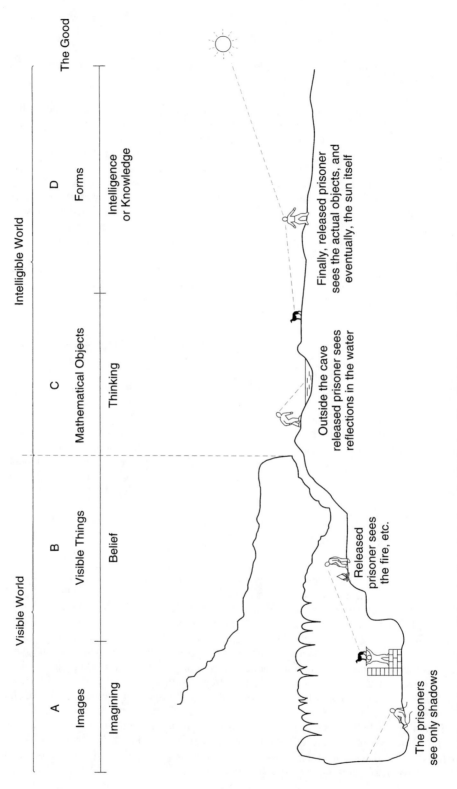

Visible World		Intelligible World	
A	B	C	D
Images	Visible Things	Mathematical Objects	Forms
Imagining	Belief	Thinking	Intelligence or Knowledge

The Good

Finally, released prisoner sees the actual objects, and eventually, the sun itself

Outside the cave released prisoner sees reflections in the water

Released prisoner sees the fire, etc.

The prisoners see only shadows

Adapted from N. Jordan, *Western Philosophy: From Antiquity to the Middle Ages* (New York: Macmillan, 1987), p. 95.

Yes, he would prefer any fate to such a life.   e

Now imagine what would happen if he went down again to take his former seat in the Cave. Coming suddenly out of the sunlight, his eyes would be filled with dark-   517
ness. He might be required once more to deliver his opinion on those shadows, in com-
petition with the prisoners who had never been released, while his eyesight was still
dim and unsteady; and it might take some time to become used to the darkness. They
would laugh at him and say that he had gone up only to come back with his sight ruined; it was worth no one's while even to attempt the ascent. If they could lay hands on
the man who was trying to set them free and lead them up, they would kill him.

Yes, they would.

Every feature in this parable, my dear Glaucon, is meant to fit our earlier analy-
sis. The prison dwelling corresponds to the region revealed to us through the sense of   b
sight, and the firelight within it to the power of the Sun. The ascent to see the things in
the upper world you may take as standing for the upward journey of the soul into the
region of the intelligible; then you will be in possession of what I surmise, since that is
what you wish to be told. Heaven knows whether it is true; but this, at any rate, is how
it appears to me. In the world of knowledge, the last thing to be perceived and only
with great difficulty is the essential Form of Goodness. Once it is perceived, the conclusion must follow that, for all things, this is the cause of whatever is right and good;   c
in the visible world it gives birth to light and to the lord of light, while it is itself sovereign in the intelligible world and the parent of intelligence and truth. Without having
had a vision of this Form no one can act with wisdom, either in his own life or in matters of state.

So far as I can understand, I share your belief.

Then you may also agree that it is no wonder if those who have reached this
height are reluctant to manage the affairs of men. Their souls long to spend all their   d
time in that upper world—naturally enough, if here once more our parable holds true.
Nor, again, is it at all strange that one who comes from the contemplation of divine
things to the miseries of human life should appear awkward and ridiculous when, with
eyes still dazed and not yet accustomed to the darkness, he is compelled, in a law-court
or elsewhere, to dispute about the shadows of justice or the images that cast those
shadows, and to wrangle over the notions of what is right in the minds of men who   e
have never beheld Justice itself.

It is not at all strange.

No; a sensible man will remember that the eyes may be confused in two   518
ways—by a change from light to darkness or from darkness to light; and he will recognize that the same thing happens to the soul. When he sees it troubled and unable to
discern anything clearly, instead of laughing thoughtlessly, he will ask whether, coming from a brighter existence, its unaccustomed vision is obscured by the darkness, in
which case he will think its condition enviable and its life a happy one; or whether,
emerging from the depths of ignorance, it is dazzled by excess of light. If so, he will   b
rather feel sorry for it; or, if he were inclined to laugh, that would be less ridiculous
than to laugh at the soul which has come down from the light.

That is a fair statement.

If this is true, then, we must conclude that education is not what it is said to be by
some, who profess to put knowledge into a soul which does not possess it, as if they   c
could put sight into blind eyes. On the contrary, our own account signifies that the soul
of every man does possess the power of learning the truth and the organ to see it with;
and that, just as one might have to turn the whole body round in order that the eye
should see light instead of darkness, so the entire soul must be turned away from this

changing world, until its eye can bear to contemplate reality and that supreme splen-
d   dour which we have called the Good. Hence there may well be an art whose aim would
be to effect this very thing, the conversion of the soul, in the readiest way; not to put
the power of sight into the soul's eye, which already has it, but to ensure that, instead
of looking in the wrong direction, it is turned the way it ought to be.

Yes, it may well be so.

It looks, then, as though wisdom were different from those ordinary virtues, as
they are called, which are not far removed from bodily qualities, in that they can be
produced by habituation and exercise in a soul which has not possessed them from the
e   first. Wisdom, it seems, is certainly the virtue of some diviner faculty, which never
loses its power, though its use for good or harm depends on the direction towards
519 which it is turned. You must have noticed in dishonest men with a reputation for
sagacity the shrewd glance of a narrow intelligence piercing the objects to which it is
directed. There is nothing wrong with their power of vision, but it has been forced into
the service of evil, so that the keener its sight, the more harm it works.

Quite true.

And yet if the growth of a nature like this had been pruned from earliest child-
b   hood, cleared of those clinging overgrowths which come of gluttony and all luxurious
pleasure and, like leaden weights charged with affinity to this mortal world, hang upon
the soul, bending its vision downwards; if, freed from these, the soul were turned
round towards true reality, then this same power in these very men would see the truth
as keenly as the objects it is turned to now.

Yes, very likely.

Is it not also likely, or indeed certain after what has been said, that a state can
never be properly governed either by the uneducated who know nothing of truth or by
c   men who are allowed to spend all their days in the pursuit of culture? The ignorant
have no single mark before their eyes at which they must aim in all the conduct of their
own lives and of affairs of state; and the others will not engage in action if they can
help it, dreaming that, while still alive, they have been translated to the Islands of the
Blest.

Quite true.

It is for us, then, as founders of a commonwealth, to bring compulsion to bear on
the noblest natures. They must be made to climb the ascent to the vision of Goodness,
d   which we called the highest object of knowledge; and, when they have looked upon it
long enough, they must not be allowed, as they now are, to remain on the heights, refusing to come down again to the prisoners or to take any part in their labours and rewards, however much or little these may be worth.

Shall we not be doing them an injustice, if we force on them a worse life than
they might have?

e   You have forgotten again, my friend, that the law is not concerned to make any
one class specially happy, but to ensure the welfare of the commonwealth as a whole.
520 By persuasion or constraint it will unite the citizens in harmony, making them share
whatever benefits each class can contribute to the common good; and its purpose in
forming men of that spirit was not that each should be left to go his own way, but that
they should be instrumental in binding the community into one.

True, I had forgotten.

You will see, then, Glaucon, that there will be no real injustice in compelling our
philosophers to watch over and care for the other citizens. We can fairly tell them that
b   their compeers in other states may quite reasonably refuse to collaborate: there they
have sprung up, like a self-sown plant, in despite of their country's institutions; no one

has fostered their growth, and they cannot be expected to show gratitude for a care they have never received. "But," we shall say, "it is not so with you. We have brought you into existence for your country's sake as well as for your own, to be like leaders and king-bees in a hive; you have been better and more thoroughly educated than those others and hence you are more capable of playing your part both as men of thought and as men of action. You must go down, then, each in his turn, to live with the rest and let c your eyes grow accustomed to the darkness. You will then see a thousand times better than those who live there always; you will recognize every image for what it is and know what it represents, because you have seen justice, beauty, and goodness in their reality; and so you and we shall find life in our commonwealth no mere dream, as it is in most existing states, where men live fighting one another about shadows and quar- d relling for power, as if that were a great prize; whereas in truth government can be at its best and free from dissension only where the destined rulers are least desirous of holding office."

Quite true.

Then will our pupils refuse to listen and to take their turns at sharing in the work of the community, though they may live together for most of their time in a purer air?

No; it is a fair demand, and they are fair-minded men. No doubt, unlike any ruler e of the present day, they will think of holding power as an unavoidable necessity.

Yes, my friend; for the truth is that you can have a well-governed society only if you can discover for your future rulers a better way of life than being in office; then 521 only will power be in the hands of men who are rich, not in gold, but in the wealth that brings happiness, a good and wise life. All goes wrong when, starved for lack of anything good in their own lives, men turn to public affairs hoping to snatch from thence the happiness they hunger for. They set about fighting for power, and this internecine conflict ruins them and their country. The life of true philosophy is the only one that looks down upon offices of state; and access to power must be confined to men who are not in love with it; otherwise rivals will start fighting. So whom else can you com- pel to undertake the guardianship of the commonwealth, if not those who, besides un- b derstanding best the principles of government, enjoy a nobler life than the politician's and look for rewards of a different kind?

There is indeed no other choice.

ARISTOTLE
384–322 B.C.

Aristotle was born in Stagira, on the border of Macedonia. His mother, Phaestis, was from a family of doctors, and his father, Nicomachus, was the court physician to the king of Macedonia. At seventeen, Aristotle was sent to Athens. There he studied in Plato's Academy for two decades, but, as he later wrote, he loved the truth more than he loved Plato, and so he had no mind to remain a mere disciple. In 347 B.C., after Plato's death, he left Athens and spent the next four years conducting zoological investigations on the islands of Assos and Lesbos.

About 343 B.C., he was called to Macedonia by King Philip to tutor the king's son—the future Alexander the Great. Upon Alexander's ascension to the throne seven years later, Aristotle returned to Athens to set up the Lyceum, a rival to the Academy. Aristotle did much of his teaching walking up and down the colonnades with advanced students. As a result, his school and philosophy came to be called by the Greek word for walking around: *peripatetikos*, from which we get our word "peripatetic." Tradition has it that as Alexander the Great moved east, conquering Persia and moving into India, he would send back biological specimens for Aristotle's school. Although most scholars doubt this popular story, it is nevertheless clear that under Alexander's patronage, the Lyceum flourished.

However, the connection to Alexander proved a liability in the end. On Alexander's death in 323 B.C., Athenians went on a rampage against any and all associated with him. Indicted on charges of impiety, Aristotle fled Athens, "lest," as he put it, "the Athenians sin twice against philosophy" (referring, of course, to the unjust trial and death of Socrates). Aristotle died a year later. A popular but again highly questionable story says he drowned investigating marine life.

There is no doubt that after Plato, Aristotle is the most influential philosopher of all time. In the early Middle Ages, his thought was preserved and commented upon by the great Arab philosophers. He dominated later medieval philosophy to such an extent that St. Thomas Aquinas referred to him simply as *philosophus*, the "philosopher." Logic, as taught until about the time of World War II, was essentially Aristotle's logic. His *Poetics* is still a classic of literary criticism, and his dicta on tragedy are widely accepted even today. Criticism of Aristotle's metaphysical and epistemological views has spread ever since Bacon and Descartes inaugurated modern philosophy; but for all that, the problems Aristotle saw, the distinctions he introduced, and the terms he defined are still central in many, if not most, philosophical discussions. His influence and prestige, like Plato's, are international and beyond all schools.

* * *

Aristotle found Plato's theory of Forms unacceptable. Like Plato, he wanted to discover universals, but he did not believe they existed apart from particulars. The form of a chair, for instance, can be thought of apart from the matter out of which the chair is made, but the form does not subsist as a separate invisible entity. The universal of "chairness" exists only in particular chairs—there is no other-worldly "Form of Chairness." Accordingly, Aristotle began his philosophy not with reflection on or dialogue about eternal Forms but with observations of particular objects.

In observing the world, Aristotle saw four "causes" responsible for making an object what it is: the material, formal, efficient, and final. In the case of a chair, for example, the chair's material cause is its wood and cloth, its formal cause is the structure or form given in its plan or blueprint, its efficient cause is the worker who made it, and its final cause is sitting. The material cause, then, is that *out of which* a thing is made, the formal cause is that *into which* a thing is made, the efficient cause is that *by which* a thing is made, and the final cause is that *for which* a thing is made. It is the last of these, the final cause, that Aristotle held to be most important, for it determined the other three. The "goal" or "end" (*telos* in Greek), the final cause, of any given substance is the key to its understanding. This means that all nature is to be understood in terms of final causes or purposes. This is known as a "teleological" explanation of reality.

As Aristotle applied these insights to human beings, he asked what the *telos* of a person could be. By observing what is unique to persons and what they, in fact, do seek, Aristotle came to the conclusion that the highest good or end for humans is *eudaimonia*. While this word is generally translated as "happiness," one must be careful to acknowledge that Aristotle's understanding of "happiness" is rather different from ours. *Eudaimonia* happiness is not a feeling of euphoria—in fact, it is not a feeling at all. It is rather "activity in accordance with virtue." Much of the material from the *Nicomachean Ethics* presented here is devoted both to clarifying the word and to discovering how this kind of "happiness" is to be achieved.

* * *

Aristotle's extant works lack the literary grace of Plato's. Like Plato, Aristotle is said to have written popular dialogues—the "exoteric" writings intended for those who were not students at the Lyceum—but they have not survived. What we have instead are the difficult "esoteric" works: lecture notes for classes at school. According to some scholars, these are not even Aristotle's notes, but the notes of students collected by editors. In any case, the writings as we have them contain much overlapping, repetition, and apparent contradiction.

The first five chapters of the *Categories*, with which we begin, help clear up a number of questions about Aristotle's conception of substance. Written as a treatise on language, the *Categories* makes clear why Aristotle rejected Plato's approach to knowledge of the Forms.

The *Physics* deals with some of the main questions of physical science. In Book II, reprinted here (complete), Aristotle makes a distinction between physics and mathematics and discusses the four causes. This work is translated by R.P. Hardie and R.K. Gaye.

The *Metaphysics* probably consists of several independent treatises. Book I (*Alpha*) of this collection develops Aristotle's four causes and reviews the history of philosophy to his time. Book XII (*Lambda*) employs many of the concepts previously introduced, such as substance, actuality, and potency, and then moves to Aristotle's theology of the Unmoved Mover. The work concludes with Aristotle's rejection of Platonic Forms as separate, mathematical entities. Apparently Aristotle was responding to Plato's successors, who emphasized the mathematical nature of the Forms. W.D. Ross is the translator.

The first part of the selection presented from Aristotle's *On the Soul (De Anima)* gives a definition of the soul and distinguishes its faculties. The second part discusses the passive and the active mind. As this selection makes clear, Aristotle rejected Plato's view of a soul separate from the body. The selection is given in the translation by J.A. Smith.

Our final selection, the *Nicomachean Ethics*, is still considered one of the greatest works in ethics. Named for Aristotle's son, Nicomachus, it discusses the nature of the good and of moral and intellectual virtues, as well as investigating specific virtues. The lengthy selection presented here (about one-half of the complete work) reflects this vast range of topics and includes discussions of the subject matter and nature of ethics; of the good for an individual; of moral virtue; of the mean; of the conditions of responsibility for an action; of pride, vanity, humility, and the great-souled man (Aristotle's ideal); of the superiority of loving over being loved; and finally, of human happiness. The translation is Martin Ostwald's.

The marginal page numbers, with their "a" and "b," are those of all scholarly editions—Greek, English, German, French, and others.

* * *

Timothy A. Robinson, *Aristotle in Outline* (Indianapolis, IN: Hackett, 1995) provides an excellent short introduction for the beginning student. W.K.C. Guthrie, *A History of Greek Philosophy, VI: Aristotle: An Encounter* (Cambridge: Cambridge University Press, 1981) and the classic W.D. Ross, *Aristotle* (1923; reprinted in New York: Meridian Books, 1959) are more advanced studies. John Herman Randall, Jr., *Aristotle* (New York: Columbia University Press, 1960); Marjorie Grene, *A Portrait of Aristotle* (Chicago: University of Chicago Press, 1963); J.L. Ackrill, *Aristotle the Philosopher* (Oxford: Oxford University Press, 1981); Jonathan Barnes, *Aristotle* (Oxford: Oxford University Press, 1982); Jonathan Lear, *Aristotle: The Desire to Understand* (Cambridge: Cambridge

University Press, 1988); Terence Irwin, *Aristotle's First Principles* (Oxford: Oxford University Press, 1988); and Jonathan Barnes, ed., *The Cambridge Companion to Aristotle* (Cambridge: Cambridge University Press, 1995) also provide helpful overviews of Aristotle's life and thought. For general collections of essays, see R. Bambrough, ed., *New Essays on Plato and Aristotle* (London: Routledge & Kegan Paul, 1965); J.M.E. Moravcsik, ed., *Aristotle: A Collection of Critical Essays* (New York: Anchor Doubleday, 1967); J. Barnes, M. Schofield, and R. Sorabji, eds., *Articles on Aristotle*, four volumes. (London: Duckworth, 1979); Terence Irwin, ed., *Aristotle's Ethics, Aristotle: Substance, Form, and Matter* and *Aristotle: Metaphysics, Epistemology, Natural Philosophy* (all three, Hamden, CT: Garland Publishing, 1995); and Cynthia A. Freeland, ed., *Feminist Interpretations of Aristotle* (College Park, PA: Pennsylvania State University Press, 1998). For help with specific works (besides the *Nicomachean Ethics*), see Lindsay Judson, ed., *Aristotle's Physics: A Collection of Essays* (Oxford: Oxford University Press, 1991); Helen S. Lang, *Aristotle's Physics and Its Medieval Varieties* (Albany: SUNY Press, 1992); Martha C. Nussbaum and Amelie O. Rorty, eds., *Essays on Aristotle's De Anima* (Oxford: Oxford University Press, 1992); Michael Durrant, ed., *Aristotle's De Anima in Focus* (Oxford: Routledge, 1993); Michael Davis, *The Politics of Philosophy: A Commentary on Aristotle's Politics,* (Lanham, MD: Rowan & Littlefield, 1996); and Helen S. Lang, *The Order of Nature in Aristotle's Physics* (Cambridge: Cambridge University Press, 1998). The *Nichomachean Ethics* has been such an influential book that many commentaries and essays have been written about it. Among these are H.H. Joachim, *Aristotle: The Nicomachean Ethics*, edited by D.A. Rees (Oxford: Clarendon Press, 1951); W.F.R. Hardie, *Aristotle's Ethical Theory*, 2nd edition (Oxford: Oxford University Press, 1980); Amelie O. Rorty, ed., *Essays on Aristotle's Ethics* (Berkeley: University of California Press, 1980); J.O. Urmson, *Aristotle's Ethics* (Oxford: Basil Blackwell, 1988); Sarah Brodie, *Ethics with Aristotle* (Oxford: Oxford University Press, 1991); and Francis Sparshott, *Taking Life Seriously: A Study of the Argument of the Nichomachean Ethics* (Toronto: University of Toronto Press, 1994). Alasdair C. MacIntyre's pair of books, *After Virtue: A Study in Moral Theory* (Notre Dame, IN: University of Notre Dame Press, 1981) and *Whose Justice? Which Rationality?* (Notre Dame, IN: University of Notre Dame Press, 1988) are interesting examples of recent attempts to apply Aristotle's ethics to contemporary moral problems.

CATEGORIES (in part)

1. When things have only a name in common and the definition of being which corresponds to the name is different, they are called *homonymous*. Thus, for example, both a man and a picture are animals. These have only a name in common and the definition   1ᵃ

Aristotle, *Categories*, Chapters 1–5 from *Aristotle's Categories and De Interpretatione*, translated by J.L. Ackrill (Oxford: Oxford University Press, 1963). Reprinted by permission of Oxford University Press.

of being which corresponds to the name is different; for if one is to say what being an
animal is for each of them, one will give two distinct definitions.

When things have the name in common and the definition of being which corresponds to the name is the same, they are called *synonymous*. Thus, for example, both a man and an ox are animals. Each of these is called by a common name, "animal," and the definition of being is also the same; for if one is to give the definition of each—what being an animal is for each of them—one will give the same definition.

When things get their name from something, with a difference of ending, they are called *paronymous*. Thus, for example, the grammarian gets his name from grammar, the brave get theirs from bravery.

2. Of things that are said, some involve combination while others are said without combination. Examples of those involving combination are "man runs," "man wins"; and of those without combination "man," "ox," "runs," "wins."

Of things there are: (*a*) some are *said of* a subject but are not in any subject. For example, man is said of a subject, the individual man, but is not in any subject. (*b*) Some are in a subject but are not said of any subject. (By "in a subject" I mean what is in something, not as a part, and cannot exist separately from what it is in.) For example, the individual knowledge-of-grammar is in a subject, the soul, but is not said of any subject; and the individual white is in a subject, the body (for all colour is in a body), but is not said of any subject. (*c*) Some are both said of a subject and in a subject. For example, knowledge is in a subject, the soul, and is also said of a subject, knowledge-of-grammar. (*d*) Some are neither in a subject nor said of a subject, for example, the individual man or individual horse—for nothing of this sort is either in a subject or said of a subject. Things that are individual and numerically one are, without exception, not said of any subject, but there is nothing to prevent some of them from being in a subject—the individual knowledge-of-grammar is one of the things in a subject.

3. Whenever one thing is predicated of another as of a subject, all things said of what is predicated will be said of the subject also. For example, man is predicated of the individual man, and animal of man; so animal will be predicated of the individual man also—for the individual man is both a man and an animal.

The differentiae of genera which are different and not subordinate one to the other are themselves different in kind. For example, animal and knowledge: footed, winged, aquatic, two-footed, are differentiae of animal, but none of these is a differentia of knowledge; one sort of knowledge does not differ from another by being two-footed. However, there is nothing to prevent genera subordinate one to the other from having the same differentiae. For the higher are predicated of the genera below them, so that all differentiae of the predicated genus will be differentiae of the subject also.

4. Of things said without any combination, each signifies either substance or quantity or qualification or a relative or where or when or being-in-a-position or having or doing or being-affected. To give a rough idea, examples of substance are man, horse; of quantity: four-foot, five-foot; of qualification: white, grammatical; of a relative: double, half, larger; of where: in the Lyceum, in the market-place; of when: yesterday, last-year; of being-in-a-position: is-lying, is-sitting; of having: has-shoes-on, has-armour-on; of doing: cutting, burning; of being-affected: being-cut, being-burned.

None of the above is said just by itself in any affirmation, but by the combination of these with one another an affirmation is produced. For every affirmation, it seems, is either true or false; but of things said without any combination none is either true or false (e.g., "man," "white," "runs," "wins").   10

5. A *substance*—that which is called a substance most strictly, primarily, and most of all—is that which is neither said of a subject nor in a subject, e.g., the individual man   15 or the individual horse. The species in which the things primarily called substances are, are called *secondary substances,* as also are the genera of these species. For example, the individual man belongs in a species, man, and animal is a genus of the species; so these—both man and animal—are called secondary substances.

It is clear from what has been said that if something is said of a subject both its name and its definition are necessarily predicated of the subject. For example, man is   20 said of a subject, the individual man, and the name is of course predicated (since you will be predicating man of the individual man), and also the definition of man will be predicated of the individual man (since the individual man is also a man). Thus both   25 the name and the definition will be predicated of the subject. But as for things which are in a subject, in most cases neither the name nor the definition is predicated of the subject. In some cases there is nothing to prevent the name from being predicated of   30 the subject, but it is impossible for the definition to be predicated. For example, white, which is in a subject (the body), is predicated of the subject; for a body is called white. But the definition of white will never be predicated of the body.

All the other things are either said of the primary substances as subjects or in   35 them as subjects. This is clear from an examination of cases. For example, animal is predicated of man and therefore also of the individual man; for were it predicated of none of the individual men it would not be predicated of man at all. Again, colour is in body and therefore also in an individual body; for were it not in some individual body   2^b it would not be in body at all. Thus all the other things are either said of the primary substances as subjects or in them as subjects. So if the primary substances did not exist   5 it would be impossible for any of the other things to exist.

Of the secondary substances the species is more a substance than the genus, since it is nearer to the primary substance. For if one is to say of the primary substance what it is, it will be more informative and apt to give the species than the genus. For   10 example, it would be more informative to say of the individual man that he is a man than that he is an animal (since the one is more distinctive of the individual man while the other is more general); and more informative to say of the individual tree that it is a tree than that it is a plant. Further, it is because the primary substances are subjects for   15 all the other things and all the other things are predicated of them or are in them, that they are called substances most of all. But as the primary substances stand to the other things, so the species stands to the genus: the species is a subject for the genus (for the   20 genera are predicated of the species but the species are not predicated reciprocally of the genera). Hence for this reason too the species is more a substance than the genus.

But of the species themselves—those which are not genera—one is no more a substance than another: it is no more apt to say of the individual man that he is a man than to say of the individual horse that it is a horse. And similarly of the primary sub-   25 stances one is no more a substance than another: the individual man is no more a substance than the individual ox.

It is reasonable that, after the primary substances, their species and genera should be the only other things called (secondary) substances. For only they, of things predi-   30 cated, reveal the primary substance. For if one is to say of the individual man what he is, it will be in place to give the species or the genus (though more informative to give man than animal); but to give any of the other things would be out of place—for exam-

35   ple, to say "white" or "runs" or anything like that. So it is reasonable that these should be the only other things called substances. Further, it is because the primary substances are subjects for everything else that they are called substances most strictly. But as the

3ª   primary substances stand to everything else, so the species and genera of the primary substances stand to all the rest: all the rest are predicated of these. For if you will call the individual man grammatical it follows that you will call both a man and an animal

5   grammatical; and similarly in other cases.

    It is a characteristic common to every substance not to be in a subject. For a pri-

10   mary substance is neither said of a subject nor in a subject. And as for secondary substances, it is obvious at once that they are not in a subject. For man is said of the individual man as subject but is not in a subject: man is not *in* the individual man.

15   Similarly, animal also is said of the individual man as subject but animal is not in the individual man. Further, while there is nothing to prevent the name of what is in a subject from being sometimes predicated of the subject, it is impossible for the definition to be predicated. But the definition of the secondary substances, as well as the name, is

20   predicated of the subject: you will predicate the definition of man of the individual man, and also that of animal. No substance, therefore, is in a subject.

    This is not, however, peculiar to substance; the differentia also is not in a subject.

25   For footed and two-footed are said of man as subject but are not in a subject; neither two-footed nor footed is in man. Moreover, the definition of the differentia is predicated of that of which the differentia is said. For example, if footed is said of man the definition of footed will also be predicated of man; for man is footed.

30   We need not be disturbed by any fear that we may be forced to say that the parts of a substance, being in a subject (the whole substance), are not substances. For when we spoke of things *in a subject* we did not mean things belonging in something as *parts*.

    It is a characteristic of substances and differentiae that all things called from them are so called synonymously. For all the predicates from them are predicated ei-

35   ther of the individuals or of the species. (For from a primary substance there is no predicate, since it is said of no subject; and as for secondary substances, the species is

3ᵇ   predicated of the individual, the genus both of the species and of the individual. Similarly, differentiae too are predicated both of the species and of the individuals.) And the primary substances admit the definition of the species and of the genera, and the

5   species admits that of the genus; for everything said of what is predicated will be said of the subject also. Similarly, both the species and the individuals admit the definition of the differentiae. But synonymous things were precisely those with both the name in common and the same definition. Hence all the things called from substances and differentiae are so called synonymously.

10   Every substance seems to signify a certain "this." As regards the primary substances, it is indisputably true that each of them signifies a certain "this"; for the thing revealed is individual and numerically one. But as regards the secondary substances,

15   though it appears from the form of the name—when one speaks of man or animal— that a secondary substance likewise signifies a certain "this," this is not really true; rather, it signifies a certain qualification, for the subject is not, as the primary substance is, one, but man and animal are said of many things. However, it does not signify sim-

20   ply a certain qualification, as white does. White signifies nothing but a qualification, whereas the species and the genus mark off the qualification of substance—they signify substance of a certain qualification. (One draws a wider boundary with the genus than with the species, for in speaking of animal one takes in more than in speaking of man.)

Another characteristic of substances is that there is nothing contrary to them. For what would be contrary to a primary substance? For example, there is nothing contrary 25 to an individual man, nor yet is there anything contrary to man or to animal. This, however, is not peculiar to substance but holds of many other things also, for example, of quantity. For there is nothing contrary to four-foot or to ten or to anything of this kind—unless someone were to say that many is contrary to few or large to small; but 30 still there is nothing contrary to any *definite* quantity.

Substance, it seems, does not admit of a more and a less. I do not mean that one substance is not more a substance than another (we have said that it is), but that any 35 given substance is not called more, or less, than that which it is. For example, if this substance is a man, it will not be more a man or less a man either than itself or than another man. For one man is not more a man than another, as one pale thing is more pale 4ᵃ than another and one beautiful thing more beautiful than another. Again, a thing is called more, or less, such-and-such than itself; for example, the body that is pale is called more pale now than before, and the one that is hot is called more, or less, hot. Substance, however, is not spoken of thus. For a man is not called more a man now 5 than before, nor is anything else that is a substance. Thus substance does not admit of a more and a less.

It seems most distinctive of substance that what is numerically one and the same 10 is able to receive contraries. In no other case could one bring forward anything, numerically one, which is able to receive contraries. For example, a colour which is numerically one and the same will not be black and white, nor will numerically one and the same action be bad and good; and similarly with everything else that is not substance. 15 A substance, however, numerically one and the same, is able to receive contraries. For example, an individual man—one and the same—becomes pale at one time and dark at another, and hot and cold, and bad and good. 20

Nothing like this is to be seen in any other case, unless someone might object and say that statements and beliefs are like this. For the same statement seems to be both true and false. Suppose, for example, that the statement that somebody is sitting is true; after he has got up this same statement will be false. Similarly with beliefs. Sup- 25 pose you believe truly that somebody is sitting; after he has got up you will believe falsely if you hold the same belief about him. However, even if we were to grant this, there is still a difference in the way contraries are received. For in the case of sub- 30 stances it is by themselves changing that they are able to receive contraries. For what has become cold instead of hot, or dark instead of pale, or good instead of bad, has changed (has altered); similarly in other cases too it is by itself undergoing change that each thing is able to receive contraries. Statements and beliefs, on the other hand, 35 themselves remain completely unchangeable in every way; it is because the actual thing changes that the contrary comes to belong to them. For the statement that some- 4ᵇ body is sitting remains the same; it is because of a change in the actual thing that it comes to be true at one time and false at another. Similarly with beliefs. Hence at least the way in which it is able to receive contraries— through a change in itself—would be distinctive of substance, even if we were to grant that beliefs and statements are able to receive contraries. However, this is not true. For it is not because they themselves re- 5 ceive anything that statements and beliefs are said to be able to receive contraries, but because of what has happened to something else. For it is because the *actual thing* ex- 10 ists or does not exist that the statement is said to be true or false, not because it is able itself to receive contraries. No statement, in fact, or belief is changed at all by anything. So, since nothing happens in them, they are not able to receive contraries. A sub-

Diskobolos, by Myron. A Roman copy after a bronze original of ca. 450 B.C. Myron's athlete epitomizes the ideal Olympian goals of godlike perfection and rational beauty. *(Museo del Terme, Rome)*

15   stance, on the other hand, is said to be able to receive contraries because it itself receives contraries. For it receives sickness and health, and paleness and darkness; and because it itself receives the various things of this kind it is said to be able to receive contraries. It is, therefore, distinctive of substance that what is numerically one and the same is able to receive contraries. This brings to an end our discussion of substance.

PHYSICS (in part)

BOOK II

1. Of things that exist, some exist by nature, some from other causes. By nature the an- $\quad$ 192^b
imals and their parts exist, and the plants and the simple bodies (earth, fire, air,
water)—for we say that these and the like exist by nature.

All the things mentioned plainly differ from things which are not constituted by
nature. For each of them has within itself a principle of motion and of stationariness (in
respect of place, or of growth and decrease, or by way of alteration). On the other $\quad$ 15
hand, a bed and a coat and anything else of that sort, *qua* receiving these designations—i.e., in so far as they are products of art—have no innate impulse to change. But
in so far as they happen to be composed of stone or of earth or of a mixture of the two, $\quad$ 20
they do have such an impulse, and just to that extent—which seems to indicate that nature is a principle or cause of being moved and of being at rest in that to which it belongs primarily, in virtue of itself and not accidentally.

I say "not accidentally," because (for instance) a man who is a doctor might himself be a cause of health to himself. Nevertheless it is not in so far as he is a patient that $\quad$ 25
he possesses the art of medicine: it merely has happened that the same man is doctor
and patient—and that is why these attributes are not always found together. So it is
with all other artificial products. None of them has in itself the principle of its own production. But while in some cases (for instance houses and the other products of manual $\quad$ 30
labour) that principle is in something else external to the thing, in others—those which
may cause a change in themselves accidentally—it lies in the things themselves (but
not in virtue of what they are).

Nature then is what has been stated. Things have a nature which have a principle of
this kind. Each of them is a substance; for it is a subject, and nature is always in a subject.

The term "according to nature" is applied to all these things and also to the at- $\quad$ 35
tributes which belong to them in virtue of what they are, for instance the property of
fire to be carried upwards—which is not a nature nor has a nature but is by nature or $\quad$ 193^a
according to nature.

What nature is, then, and the meaning of the terms "by nature" and "according to
nature," has been stated. *That* nature exists, it would be absurd to try to prove; for it is
obvious that there are many things of this kind, and to prove what is obvious by what is
not is the mark of a man who is unable to distinguish what is self-evident from what $\quad$ 5
is not. (This state of mind is clearly possible. A man blind from birth might reason
about colours.) Presumably therefore such persons must be talking about words without any thought to correspond.

Some identify the nature or substance of a natural object with that immediate $\quad$ 10
constituent of it which taken by itself is without arrangement, e.g., the wood is the nature of the bed, and the bronze the nature of the statue.

As an indication of this Antiphon points out that if you planted a bed and the rot-
ting wood acquired the power of sending up a shoot, it would not be a bed that would

15   come up, but *wood* which shows that the arrangement in accordance with the rules of the art is merely an accidental attribute, whereas the substance is the other, which, further, persists continuously through the process.

20   But if the material of each of these objects has itself the same relation to something else, say bronze (or gold) to water, bones (or wood) to earth and so on, *that* (they say) would be their nature and substance. Consequently some assert earth, others fire or air or water or some or all of these, to be the nature of the things that are. For whatever any one of them supposed to have this character—whether one thing or more than
25   one thing—this or these he declared to be the whole of substance, all else being its affections, states, or dispositions. Every such thing they held to be eternal (for it could not pass into anything else), but other things to come into being and cease to be times without number.

This then is one account of nature, namely that it is the primary underlying matter of things which have in themselves a principle of motion or change.

30   Another account is that nature is the shape or form which is specified in the definition of the thing.

For the word "nature" is applied to what is according to nature and the natural in the same way as "art" is applied to what is artistic or a work of art. We should not say in the latter case that there is anything artistic about a thing, if it is a bed only poten-
35   tially, not yet having the form of a bed; nor should we call it a work of art. The same is true of natural compounds. What is potentially flesh or bone has not yet its own nature,
193^b and does not exist by nature, until it receives the form specified in the definition, which we name in defining what flesh or bone is. Thus on the second account of nature, it
5   would be the shape or form (not separable except in statement) of things which have in themselves a principle of motion. (The combination of the two, e.g. man, is not nature but by nature.)

The form indeed is nature rather than the matter; for a thing is more properly said to be what it is when it exists in actuality than when it exists potentially. Again man is born from man but not bed from bed. That is why people say that the shape is not the
10   nature of a bed, but the wood is—if the bed sprouted, not a bed but wood would come up. But even if the shape *is* art, then on the same principle the shape of man is his nature. For man is born from man.

Again, nature in the sense of a coming-to-be proceeds towards nature. For it is not like doctoring, which leads not to the art of doctoring but to health. Doctoring must
15   start from the art, not lead to it. But it is not in this way that nature is related to nature. What grows *qua* growing grows from something into something. Into what then does it grow? Not into that from which it arose but into that to which it tends. The shape then is nature.

Shape and nature are used in two ways. For the privation too is in a way form.
20   But whether in unqualified coming to be there is privation, i.e., a contrary, we must consider later.

2. We have distinguished, then, the different ways in which the term "nature" is used.

The next point to consider is how the mathematician differs from the student of nature; for natural bodies contain surfaces and volumes, lines and points, and these are
25   the subject-matter of mathematics.

Further, is astronomy different from natural science or a department of it? It seems absurd that the student of nature should be supposed to know the nature of sun or moon, but not to know any of their essential attributes, particularly as the writers on nature obvi-
30   ously do discuss their shape and whether the earth and the world are spherical or not.

Now the mathematician, though he too treats of these things, nevertheless does not treat of them as the limits of a natural body; nor does he consider the attributes indicated as the attributes of such bodies. That is why he separates them, for in thought they are separable from motion, and it makes no difference, nor does any falsity result, if they are separated. The holders of the theory of Forms do the same, though they are not aware of it; for they separate the objects of natural science, which are less separable than those of mathematics. This becomes plain if one tries to state in each of the two cases the definitions of the things and of their attributes. Odd and even, straight and curved, and likewise number, line, and figure, do not involve motion; not so flesh and bone and man—*these* are defined like snub nose, not like curved.

Similar evidence is supplied by the more natural of the branches of mathematics, such as optics, harmonics, and astronomy. These are in a way the converse of geometry. While geometry investigates natural lines but not *qua* natural, optics investigates mathematical lines, but *qua* natural, not *qua* mathematical.

Since two sorts of thing are called nature, the form and the matter, we must investigate its objects as we would the essence of snubness, that is neither independently of matter nor in terms of matter only. Here too indeed one might raise a difficulty. Since there are two natures, with which is the student of nature concerned? Or should he investigate the combination of the two? But if the combination of the two, then also each severally. Does it belong then to the same or to different sciences to know each severally?

If we look at the ancients, natural science would seem to be concerned with the *matter*. (It was only very slightly that Empedocles and Democritus touched on form and essence.)

But if on the other hand art imitates nature, and it is the part of the same discipline to know the form and the matter up to a point (e.g., the doctor has a knowledge of health and also of bile and phlegm, in which health is realized and the builder both of the form of the house and of the matter, namely that it is bricks and beams, and so forth): if this is so, it would be the part of natural science also to know nature in both its senses.

Again, that for the sake of which, or the end, belongs to the same department of knowledge as the means. But the nature is the end or that for the sake of which. For if a thing undergoes a continuous change toward some end, that last stage is actually that for the sake of which. (That is why the poet was carried away into making an absurd statement when he said "he has the end for the sake of which he was born." For not every stage that is last claims to be an end, but only that which is best.)

For the arts make their material (some simply make it, others make it serviceable), and we use everything as if it was there for our sake. (We also are in a sense an end. "That for the sake of which" may be taken in two ways, as we said in our work *On Philosophy*.) The arts, therefore, which govern the matter and have knowledge are two, namely the art which uses the product and the art which directs the production of it. That is why the using art also is in a sense directive; but it differs in that it knows the form, whereas the art which is directive as being concerned with production knows the matter. For the helmsman knows and prescribes what sort of form a helm should have, the other from what wood it should be made and by means of what operations. In the products of art, however, we make the material with a view to the function, whereas in the products of nature the matter is there all along.

Again, matter is a relative thing—for different forms there is different matter.

How far then must the student of nature know the form or essence? Up to a point, perhaps, as the doctor must know sinew or the smith bronze (i.e., until he understands the purpose of each); and the student of nature is concerned only with things

whose forms are separable indeed, but do not exist apart from matter. Man is begotten
by man and by the sun as well. The mode of existence and essence of the separable it is
the business of first philosophy to define.

3. Now that we have established these distinctions, we must proceed to consider causes, their character and number. Knowledge is the object of our inquiry, and men do not think they know a thing till they have grasped the "why" of it (which is to grasp its primary cause). So clearly we too must do this as regards both coming to be and passing away and every kind of natural change, in order that, knowing their principles, we may try to refer to these principles each of our problems.

In one way, then, that out of which a thing comes to be and which persists, is called a cause, e.g., the bronze of the statue, the silver of the bowl, and the genera of which the bronze and the silver are species.

In another way, the form or the archetype, i.e., the definition of the essence, and its genera, are called causes (e.g., of the octave the relation of 2:1, and generally number), and the parts in the definition.

Again, the primary source of the change or rest; e.g., the man who deliberated is a cause, the father is cause of the child, and generally what makes of what is made and what changes of what is changed.

Again, in the sense of end or that for the sake of which a thing is done, e.g., health is the cause of walking about. ("Why is he walking about?" We say: "To be healthy," and, having said that, we think we have assigned the cause.) The same is true also of all the intermediate steps which are brought about through the action of something else as means towards the end, e.g., reduction of flesh, purging, drugs, or surgical instruments are means towards health. All these things are for the sake of the end, though they differ from one another in that some are activities, others instruments.

This then perhaps exhausts the number of ways in which the term "cause" is used.

As things are called causes in many ways, it follows that there are several causes of the same thing (not merely accidentally), e.g., both the art of the sculptor and the bronze are causes of the statue. These are causes of the statue *qua* statue, not in virtue of anything else that it may be—only not in the same way, the one being the material cause, the other the cause whence the motion comes. Some things cause each other reciprocally, e.g., hard work causes fitness and *vice versa*, but again not in the same way, but the one as end, the other as the principle of motion. Further the same thing is the cause of contrary results. For that which by its presence brings about one result is sometimes blamed for bringing about the contrary by its absence. Thus we ascribe the wreck of a ship to the absence of the pilot whose presence was the cause of its safety.

All the causes now mentioned fall into four familiar divisions. The letters are the causes of syllables, the material of artificial products, fire and the like of bodies, the parts of the whole, and the premises of the conclusion, in the sense of "that from which." Of these pairs the one set are causes in the sense of what underlies, e.g., the parts, the other set in the sense of essence—the whole and the combination and the form. But the seed and the doctor and the deliberator, and generally the maker, are all sources whence the change or stationariness originates, which the others are causes in the sense of the end or the good of the rest; for that for the sake of which tends to be what is best and the end of the things that lead up to it. (Whether we call it good or apparently good makes no difference.)

Such then is the number and nature of the kinds of cause.

Now the modes of causation are many, though when brought under heads they too can be reduced in number. For things are called causes in many ways and even

within the same kind one may be prior to another: e.g., the doctor and the expert are 30
causes of health, the relation 2:1 and number of the octave, and always what is inclu-
sive to what is particular. Another mode of causation is the accidental and its genera,
e.g., in one way Polyclitus, in another a sculptor is the cause of a statue, because being
Polyclitus and a sculptor are accidentally conjoined. Also the classes in which the acci- 35
dental attribute is included; thus a man could be said to be the cause of a statue or, generally, a living creature. An accidental attribute too may be more or less remote, e.g., 195[b]
suppose that a pale man or a musical man were said to be the cause of the statue.

All causes, both proper and accidental, may be spoken of either as potential or as
actual; e.g., the cause of a house being built is either a house-builder or a house-builder 5
building.

Similar distinctions can be made in the things of which the causes are causes,
e.g., of this statue or of a statue or of an image generally, of this bronze or of bronze or
of material generally. So too with the accidental attributes. Again we may use a com- 10
plex expression for either and say, e.g., neither "Polyclitus" nor a "sculptor" but "Polyclitus, the sculptor."

All these various uses, however, come to six in number, under each of which
again the usage is twofold. It is either what is particular or a genus, or an accidental attribute or a genus of that, and these either as a complex or each by itself; and all either 15
as actual or as potential. The difference is this much, that causes which are actually at
work and particular exist and cease to exist simultaneously with their effect, e.g., this
healing person with this being-healed person and that housebuilding man with that
being-built house; but this is not always true of potential causes—the house and the 20
housebuilder do not pass away simultaneously.

In investigating the cause of each thing it is always necessary to seek what is
most precise (as also in other things): thus a man builds because he is a builder, and a
builder builds in virtue of his art of building. This last cause then is prior; and so gener- 25
ally.

Further, generic effects should be assigned to generic causes, particular effects to
particular causes, e.g., statue to sculptor, this statue to this sculptor; and powers are relative to possible effects, actually operating causes to things which are actually being
effected.

This must suffice for our account of the number of causes and the modes of cau- 30
sation.

4. But chance and spontaneity are also reckoned among causes: many things are said
both to be and to come to be as a result of chance and spontaneity. We must inquire
therefore in what manner chance and spontaneity are present among the causes enu- 35
merated, and whether they are the same or different, and generally what chance and
spontaneity are.

Some people even question whether there are such things or not. They say that
nothing happens by chance, but that everything which we ascribe to chance or spon- 196[a]
taneity has some definite cause, e.g., coming by chance into the market and finding
there a man whom one wanted but did not expect to meet is due to one's wish to go
and buy in the market. Similarly, in other so-called cases of chance it is always possi- 5
ble, they maintain, to find something which is the cause; but not chance, for if chance
were real, it would seem strange indeed, and the question might be raised, why on
earth none of the wise men of old in speaking of the causes of generation and decay 10
took account of chance; whence it would seem that they too did not believe that anything is by chance. But there is a further circumstance that is surprising. Many things

both come to be and are by chance and spontaneity, and although all know that each of them can be ascribed to some cause (as the old argument said which denied chance), nevertheless they all speak of some of these things as happening by chance and others not. For this reason they ought to have at least referred to the matter in some way or other.

Certainly the early physicists found no place for chance among the causes which they recognized—love, strife, mind, fire, or the like. This is strange, whether they supposed that there is no such thing as chance or whether they thought there is but omitted to mention it—and that too when they sometimes used it, as Empedocles does when he says that the air is not always separated into the highest region, but as it may chance. At any rate he says in his cosmogony that "it happened to run that way at that time, but it often ran otherwise." He tells us also that most of the parts of animals came to be by chance.

There are some who actually ascribe this heavenly sphere and all the worlds to spontaneity. They say that the vortex arose spontaneously, i.e., the motion that separated and arranged the universe in its present order. This statement might well cause surprise. For they are asserting that chance is not responsible for the existence or generation of animals and plants, nature or mind or something of the kind being the cause of them (for it is not any chance thing that comes from a given seed but an olive from one kind and a man from another); and yet at the same time they assert that the heavenly sphere and the divinest of visible things arose spontaneously, having no such cause as is assigned to animals and plants. Yet if this is so, it is a fact which deserves to be dwelt upon, and something might well have been said about it. For besides the other absurdities of the statement, it is the more absurd that people should make it when they see nothing coming to be spontaneously in the heavens, but much happening by chance among the things which as they say are not due to chance; whereas we should have expected exactly the opposite.

Others there are who believe that chance is a cause, but that it is inscrutable to human intelligence, as being a divine thing and full of mystery.

Thus we must inquire what chance and spontaneity are, whether they are the same or different, and how they fit into our division of causes.

5. First then we observe that some things always come to pass in the same way, and others for the most part. It is clearly of neither of these that chance, or the result of chance, is said to be the cause—neither of that which is by necessity and always, nor of that which is for the most part. But as there is a third class of events besides these two—events which all say are by chance—it is plain that there is such a thing as chance and spontaneity; for we know that things of this kind are due to chance and that things due to chance are of this kind.

Of things that come to be, some come to be for the sake of something, others not. Again, some of the former class are in accordance with intention, others not, but both are in the class of things which are for the sake of something. Hence it is clear that even among the things which are outside what is necessary and what is for the most part, there are some in connexion with which the phrase "for the sake of something" is applicable. (Things that are for the sake of something include whatever may be done as a result of thought or of nature.) Things of this kind, then, when they come to pass accidentally are said to be by chance. For just as a thing is something either in virtue of itself or accidentally, so may it be a cause. For instance, the housebuilding faculty is in virtue of itself a cause of a house, whereas the pale or the musical is an accidental cause. That which is per se cause is determinate, but the accidental cause is indeterminable; for the possible attributes of an individual are innumerable. As we said, then, when a thing of this kind comes to pass among events which are for the sake of some- 30 thing, it is said to be spontaneous or by chance. (The distinction between the two must be made later—for the present it is sufficient if it is plain that both are in the sphere of things done for the sake of something.)

Example: A man is engaged in collecting subscriptions for a feast. He would have gone to such and such a place for the purpose of getting the money, if he had known. He actually went there for another purpose, and it was only accidentally that he 35 got his money by going there; and this was not due to the fact that he went there as a rule or necessarily, nor is the end effected (getting the money) a cause present in him- 197ᵃ self—it belongs to the class of things that are objects of choice and the result of thought. It is when these conditions are satisfied that the man is said to have gone by chance. If he had chosen and gone for the sake of this—if he always or normally went there when he was collecting payments—he would not be said to have gone by chance. 5

It is clear then that chance is an accidental cause in the sphere of those actions for the sake of something which involves choice. Thought, then, and chance are in the same sphere, for choice implies thought.

It is necessary, no doubt, that the causes of what comes to pass by chance be in- definite; and that is why chance is supposed to belong to the class of the indefinite and to be inscrutable to man, and why it might be thought that, in a way, nothing occurs by 10 chance. For all these statements are correct, as might be expected. Things *do*, in a way, occur by chance, for they occur accidentally and chance is an accidental cause. But it is not the cause without qualification of anything; for instance, a housebuilder is the 15 cause of a house; accidentally, a fluteplayer may be so.

And the causes of the man's coming and getting the money (when he did not come for the sake of that) are innumerable. He may have wished to see somebody or been following somebody or avoiding somebody, or may have gone to see a spectacle. Thus to say that chance is unaccountable is correct. For an account is of what holds al- ways or for the most part, whereas chance belongs to a third type of event. Hence, 20 since causes of this kind are indefinite, chance too is indefinite. (Yet in some cases one might raise the question whether *any* chance fact might be the cause of the chance oc- currence, e.g., of health the fresh air or the sun's heat may be the cause, but having had one's hair cut *cannot*; for some accidental causes are more relevant to the effect than others.)

Chance is called good when the result is good, evil when it is evil. The terms 25 "good fortune" and "ill fortune" are used when either result is of considerable magni- tude. Thus one who comes within an ace of some great evil or great good is said to be fortunate or unfortunate. The mind affirms the presence of the attribute, ignoring the hair's breadth of difference. Further, it is with reason that good fortune is regarded as 30 unstable; for chance is unstable, as none of the things which result from it can hold al- ways or for the most part.

Both are then, as I have said, accidental causes—both chance and spontaneity— in the sphere of things which are capable of coming to pass not simply, nor for the most part and with reference to such of these as might come to pass for the sake of 35 something.

6. They differ in that spontaneity is the wider. Every result of chance is from what is spontaneous, but not everything that is from what is spontaneous is from chance.

Chance and what results from chance are appropriate to agents that are capable 197ᵇ of good fortune and of action generally. Therefore necessarily chance is in the sphere

145

of actions. This is indicated by the fact that good fortune is thought to be the same, or
nearly the same, as happiness, and happiness to be a kind of action, since it is well-
doing. Hence what is not capable of action cannot do anything by chance. Thus an
inanimate thing or a beast or a child cannot do anything by chance, because it is incapable of choice; nor can good fortune or ill fortune be ascribed to them, except
metaphorically, as Protarchus, for example, said that the stones of which altars are
made are fortunate because they are held in honour, while their fellows are trodden
under foot. Even these things, however, can in a way be affected by chance, when one
who is dealing with them does something to them by chance, but not otherwise.

The spontaneous on the other hand is found both in the beasts and in many inanimate objects. We say, for example, that the horse came spontaneously, because,
though his coming saved him, he did not come for the sake of safety. Again, the tripod
fell spontaneously, because, though it stood on its feet so as to serve for a seat, it did
not fall so as to serve for a seat.

Hence it is clear that events which belong to the general class of things that may
come to pass for the sake of something, when they come to pass not for the sake of
what actually results, and have an external cause, may be described by the phrase
"from spontaneity." These spontaneous events are said to be from chance if they have
the further characteristics of being the objects of choice and happening to agents capable of choice. This is indicated by the phrase "in vain," which is used when one thing
which is for the sake of another, does not result in it. For instance, taking a walk is for
the sake of evacuation of the bowels; if this does not follow after walking, we say that
we have walked in vain and that the walking was vain. This implies that what is naturally for the sake of an end is in vain, when it does not effect the end for the sake of
which it was the natural means—for it would be absurd for a man to say that he had
bathed in vain because the sun was not eclipsed, since the one was not done for the
sake of the other. Thus the spontaneous is even according to its derivation the case in
which the thing itself happens in vain. The stone that struck the man did not fall for the
sake of striking him; therefore it fell spontaneously, because it might have fallen by the
action of an agent and for the sake of striking. The difference between spontaneity and
what results by chance is greatest in things that come to be by nature; for when anything comes to be contrary to nature, we do not say that it came to be by chance, but by
spontaneity. Yet strictly this too is different from the spontaneous proper; for the cause
of the latter is external, that of the former internal.

198ᵃ We have now explained what chance is and what spontaneity is, and in what they
differ from each other. Both belong to the mode of causation "source of change," for
either some natural or some intelligent agent is always the cause; but in this sort of
causation the number of possible causes is infinite.

Spontaneity and chance are causes of effects which, though they might result
from intelligence or nature, have in fact been caused by something accidentally. Now
since nothing which is accidental is prior to what is *per se*, it is clear that no accidental
cause can be prior to a cause *per se*. Spontaneity and chance, therefore, are posterior to
intelligence and nature. Hence, however true it may be that the heavens are due to
spontaneity, it will still be true that intelligence and nature will be prior causes of this
universe and of many things in it besides.

7. It is clear then that there are causes, and that the number of them is what we have
stated. The number is the same as that of the things comprehended under the question
"why." The "why" is referred ultimately either, in things which do not involve motion,
e.g., in mathematics, to the "what" (to the definition of straight line or commensurable

or the like); or to what initiated a motion, e.g., "why did they go to war?—because there had been a raid"; or we are inquiring "for the sake of what?"—"that they may rule"; or in the case of things that come into being, we are looking for the matter. The causes, therefore, are these and so many in number. 20

Now, the causes being four, it is the business of the student of nature to know about them all, and if he refers his problems back to all of them, he will assign the "why" in the way proper to his science—the matter, the form, the mover, that for the sake of which. The last three often coincide; for the what and that for the sake of which are one, while the primary source of motion is the same in species as these. For man generates man—and so too, in general, with all things which cause movement by being themselves moved; and such as are not of this kind are no longer inside the province of natural science, for they cause motion not by possessing motion or a source of motion in themselves, but being themselves incapable of motion. Hence there are three branches of study, one of things which are incapable of motion, the second of things in motion, but indestructible, the third of destructible things. 30

The question "why," then, is answered by reference to the matter, to the form, and to the primary moving cause. For in respect of coming to be it is mostly in this last way that causes are investigated—"what comes to be after what? what was the primary agent or patient?" and so at each step of the series. 35

Now the principles which cause motion in a natural way are two, of which one is not natural, as it has no principle of motion in itself. Of this kind is whatever causes 198ᵇ movement, not being itself moved, such as that which is completely unchangeable, the primary reality, and the essence of a thing, i.e., the form; for this is the end or that for the sake of which. Hence since nature is for the sake of something, we must know this cause also. We must explain the "why" in all the senses of the term, namely, that from 5 this that will necessarily result ("from this" either without qualification or for the most part); that this must be so if that is to be so (as the conclusion presupposes the premises); that this was the essence of the thing; and because it is better thus (not without qualification, but with reference to the substance in each case).

8. We must explain then first why nature belongs to the class of causes which act for 10 the sake of something; and then about the necessary and its place in nature, for all writers ascribe things to this cause, arguing that since the hot and the cold and the like are of such and such a kind, therefore certain things *necessarily* are and come to be—and if they mention any other cause (one friendship and strife, another mind), it is only to 15 touch on it, and then good-bye to it.

A difficulty presents itself: why should not nature work, not for the sake of something, nor because it is better so, but just as the sky rains, not in order to make the corn grow, but of necessity? (What is drawn up must cool, and what has been cooled must become water and descend, the result of this being that the corn grows.) Similarly 20 if a man's crop is spoiled on the threshing-floor, the rain did not fall for the sake of this—in order that the crop might be spoiled—but that result just followed. Why then should it not be the same with the parts in nature, e.g., that our teeth should come up of necessity—the front teeth sharp, fitted for tearing, the molars broad and useful for 25 grinding down the food—since they did not arise for this end, but it was merely a coincident result; and so with all other parts in which we suppose that there is purpose? Wherever then all the parts came about just what they would have been if they had come to be for an end, such things survived, being organized spontaneously in a fitting 30 way; whereas those which grew otherwise perished and continue to perish, as Empedocles says his "man-faced ox-progeny" did.

Such are the arguments (and others of the kind) which may cause difficulty on this point. Yet it is impossible that this should be the true view. For teeth and all other

35 natural things either invariably or for the most part come about in a given way; but of not one of the results of chance or spontaneity is this true. We do not ascribe to chance or mere coincidence the frequency of rain in winter, but frequent rain in summer we

199ᵃ do; nor heat in summer but only if we have it in winter. If then, it is agreed that things are either the result of coincidence or for the sake of something, and these cannot be

5 the result of coincidence or spontaneity, it follows that they must be for the sake of something; and that such things are all due to nature even the champions of the theory which is before us would agree. Therefore action for an end is present in things which come to be and are by nature.

Further, where there is an end, all the preceding steps are for the sake of that.

10 Now surely as in action, so in nature; and as in nature, so it is in each action, if nothing interferes. Now action is for the sake of an end; therefore the nature of things also is so. Thus if a house, e.g. had been a thing made by nature, it would have been made in the same way as it is now by art; and if things made by nature were made not only by na-

15 ture but also by art, they would come to be in the same way as by nature. The one, then, is for the sake of the other; and generally art in some cases completes what nature cannot bring to a finish, and in others imitates nature. If, therefore, artificial products are for the sake of an end, so clearly also are natural products. The relation of the later to the earlier items is the same in both.

20 This is most obvious in the animals other than man: they make things neither by art nor after inquiry or deliberation. That is why people wonder whether it is by intelligence or by some other faculty that these creatures work,—spiders, ants, and the like. By gradual advance in this direction we come to see clearly that in plants too that is

25 produced which is conducive to the end—leaves, e.g. grow to provide shade for the fruit. If then it is both by nature and for an end that the swallow makes its nest and the spider its web, and plants grow leaves for the sake of the fruit and send their roots

30 down (not up) for the sake of nourishment, it is plain that this kind of cause is operative in things which come to be and are by nature. And since nature is twofold, the matter and the form, of which the latter is the end, and since all the rest is for the sake of the end, the form must be the cause in the sense of that for the sake of which.

Now mistakes occur even in the operations of art: the literate man makes a mis-

199ᵇ take in writing and the doctor pours out the wrong dose. Hence clearly mistakes are possible in the operations of nature also. If then in art there are cases in which what is rightly produced serves a purpose, and if where mistakes occur there was a purpose in what was attempted, only it was not attained, so must it be also in natural products, and

5 monstrosities will be failures in the purposive effort. Thus in the original combinations the "ox-progeny," if they failed to reach a determinate end must have arisen through the corruption of some principle, as happens now when the seed is defective.

Further, seed must have come into being first, and not straightway the animals: what was "undifferentiated first" was seed.

10 Again, in plants too we find that for the sake of which, though the degree of organization is less. Were there then in plants also olive-headed vine-progeny, like the "man-headed ox-progeny," or not? An absurd suggestion; yet there must have been, if there were such things among animals.

Moreover, among the seeds anything must come to be at random. But the person

15 who asserts this entirely does away with nature and what exists by nature. For those things are natural which, by a continuous movement originated from an internal principle, arrive at some end: the same end is not reached from every principle; nor any

chance end, but always the tendency in each is towards the same end, if there is no impediment.

The end and the means towards it may come about by chance. We say, for instance, that a stranger has come by chance, paid the ransom, and gone away, when he does so as if he had come for that purpose, though it was not for that that he came. This is accidental, for chance is an accidental cause, as I remarked before. But when an event takes place always or for the most part, it is not accidental or by chance. In natural products the sequence is invariable, if there is no impediment.

It is absurd to suppose that purpose is not present because we do not observe the agent deliberating. Art does not deliberate. If the ship-building art were in the wood, it would produce the same results by nature. If, therefore, purpose is present in art, it is present also in nature. The best illustration is a doctor doctoring himself: nature is like that.

It is plain then that nature is a cause, a cause that operates for a purpose.

9. As regards what is of necessity, we must ask whether the necessity is hypothetical, or simple as well. The current view places what is of necessity in the process of production, just as if one were to suppose that the wall of a house necessarily comes to be because what is heavy is naturally carried downwards and what is light to the top, so that the stones and foundations take the lowest place, with earth above because it is lighter, and wood at the top of all as being the lightest. Whereas, though the wall does not come to be *without* these, it is not *due* to these, except as its material cause: it comes to be for the sake of sheltering and guarding certain things. Similarly in all other things which involve that for the sake of which: the product cannot come to be without things which have a necessary nature, but it is not due to these (except as its material); it comes to be for an end. For instance, why is a saw such as it is? To effect so-and-so and for the sake of so-and-so. This end, however, cannot be realized unless the saw is made of iron. It is, therefore, necessary for it to be of iron, if we are to have a saw and perform the operation of sawing. What is necessary then, is necessary on a hypothesis, not as an end. Necessity is in the matter, while that for the sake of which is in the definition.

Necessity in mathematics is in a way similar to necessity in things which come to be through the operation of nature. Since a straight line is what it is, it is necessary that the angles of a triangle should equal two right angles. But not conversely; though if the angles are *not* equal to two right angles, then the straight line is not what it is either. But in things which come to be for an end, the reverse is true. If the end is to exist or does exist, that also which precedes it will exist or does exist; otherwise just as there, if the conclusion is not true, the principle will not be true, so here the end or that for the sake of which will not exist. For this too is itself a principle, but of the reasoning, not of the action. (In mathematics the principle is the principle of the reasoning only, as there is no action.) If then there is to be a house, such-and-such things must be made or be there already or exist, or generally the matter relative to the end, bricks and stones if it is a house. But the end is not due to these except as the matter, nor will it come to exist because of them. Yet if they do not exist at all, neither will the house, or the saw—the former in the absence of stones, the latter in the absence of iron—just as in the other case the principles will not be true, if the angles of the triangle are not equal to two right angles.

The necessary in nature, then, is plainly what we call by the name of matter, and the changes in it. Both causes must be stated by the student of nature, but especially the end; for that is the cause of the matter, not *vice versa*; and the end is that for the sake of which, and the principle starts from the definition or essence: as in artificial products, since a house is of such-and-such a kind, certain things must necessarily come to be or be there already, or since health is this, these things must *necessarily* come to be or be there already, so too if man is this, then these; if these, then those. Perhaps the necessary is present also in the definition. For if one defines the operation of sawing as being a certain kind of dividing, then this cannot come about unless the saw has teeth of a certain kind; and these cannot be unless it is of iron. For in the definition too there are some parts that stand as matter.

METAPHYSICS (in part)

Book XII

* * *

1071^b 6. Since there were three kinds of substance, two of them natural and one unmovable, regarding the latter we must assert that it is necessary that there should be an eternal
5   unmovable substance. For substances are the first of existing things, and if they are all destructible, all things are destructible. But it is impossible that movement should either come into being or cease to be; for it must always have existed. Nor can time come into being or cease to be; for there could not be a before and an after if time did not exist. Movement also is continuous, then, in the sense in which time is; for time is

either the same thing as movement or an attribute of movement. And there is no con- 10
tinuous movement except movement in place, and of this only that which is circular is
continuous.

But if there is something which is capable of moving things or acting on them,
but is not actually doing so, there will not be movement; for that which has a capacity
need not exercise it. Nothing, then, is gained even if we suppose eternal substances, as
the believers in the Forms do, unless there is to be in them some principle which can 15
cause movement; and even this is not enough, nor is another substance besides the
Forms enough; for if it does not *act*, there will be no movement. Further, even if it acts,
this will not be enough, if its substance is potentiality; for there will not be *eternal*
movement; for that which is potentially may possibly not be. There must, then, be such
a principle, whose very substance is actuality. Further, then, these substances must be 20
without matter; for they must be eternal, at least if anything else is eternal. Therefore
they must be actuality.

Yet there is a difficulty; for it is thought that everything that acts is able to act,
but that not everything that is able to act acts, so that the potentiality is prior. But if
this is so, nothing at all will exist; for it is possible for things to be capable of existing 25
but not yet to exist. Yet if we follow the mythologists who generate the world from
night, or the natural philosophers who say that all things were together, the same impossible result ensues. For how will there be movement, if there is no actual cause?
Matter will surely not move itself—the carpenter's art must act on it; nor will the 30
menstrual fluids nor the earth set themselves in motion, but the seeds and the semen
must act on them.

This is why some suppose eternal actuality—e.g. Leucippus and Plato; for they
say there is always movement. But why and what this movement is they do not say,
nor, if the world moves in this way or that, do they tell us the cause of its doing so.
Now nothing is moved at random, but there must always be something present, e.g. as 35
a matter of fact a thing moves in one way by nature, and in another by force or through
the influence of thought or something else. Further, what sort of movement is primary?
This makes a vast difference. But again Plato, at least, cannot even say what it is that
he sometimes supposes to be the source of movement—that which moves itself; for the 1072ᵃ
soul is later, and simultaneous with the heavens, according to his account. To suppose
potentiality prior to actuality, then, is in a sense right, and in a sense not; and we have
specified these senses.

That actuality is prior is testified by Anaxagoras (for his thought is actuality) and 5
by Empedocles in his doctrine of love and strife, and by those who say that there is always movement, e.g. Leucippus.

Therefore chaos or night did not exist for any infinite time, but the same things
have always existed (either passing through a cycle of changes or in some other way),
since actuality is prior to potentiality. If, then, there is a constant cycle, something
must always remain, acting in the same way. And if there is to be generation and de- 10
struction, there must be something else which is always acting in different ways. This
must, then, act in one way in virtue of itself, and in another in virtue of something
else—either of a third agent, therefore, or of the first. But it must be in virtue of the
first. For otherwise this again causes the motion both of the third agent and of the second. Therefore it is better to say the first. For it was the cause of eternal movement; 15
and something else is the cause of variety, and evidently both together are the cause of
eternal variety. This, accordingly, is the character which the motions actually exhibit.
What need then is there to seek for other principles?

7. Since this is a possible account of the matter, and if it were not true, the world would
20　have proceeded out of night and "all things together" and out of non-being, these difficulties may be taken as solved. There is, then, something which is always moved with
an unceasing motion, which is motion in a circle; and this is plain not in theory only
but in fact. Therefore the first heavens must be eternal. There is therefore also something which moves them. And since that which is moved and moves is intermediate,
25　there is a mover which moves without being moved, being eternal, substance, and actuality. And the object of desire and the object of thought move in this way; they move
without being moved. The primary objects of desire and of thought are the same. For
the apparent good is the object of appetite, and the real good is the primary object of
wish. But desire is consequent on opinion rather than opinion on desire; for the think-
30　ing is the starting-point. And thought is moved by the object of thought, and one side
of the list of opposites is in itself the object of thought; and in this, substance is first,
and in substance, that which is simple and exists actually. (The one and the simple are
not the same; for "one" means a measure, but "simple" means that the thing itself has a
35　certain nature.) But the good, also, and that which is in itself desirable are on this same
side of the list; and the first in any class is always best, or analogous to the best.

1072^b　　　That that for the sake of which is found among the unmovables is shown by
making a distinction; for that for the sake of which is both that *for* which and that *to-*
wards which, and of these the one is unmovable and the other is not. Thus it produces
motion by being loved, and it moves the other moving things. Now if something is
5　moved it is capable of being otherwise than as it is. Therefore if the actuality of the
heavens is primary motion, then in so far as they are in motion, in *this* respect they are
capable of being otherwise,—in place, even if not in substance. But since there is
something which moves while itself unmoved, existing actually, this can in no way be
otherwise than as it is. For motion in space is the first of the kinds of change, and mo-
10　tion in a circle the first kind of spatial motion; and this the first mover *produces*. The
first mover, then, of necessity exists; and in so far as it is necessary, it is good, and in
this sense a first principle. For the necessary has all these senses—that which is necessary perforce because it is contrary to impulse, that without which the good is impossible, and that which cannot be otherwise but is *absolutely* necessary.

　　　On such a principle, then, depend the heavens and the world of nature. And its
15　life is such as the best which we enjoy, and enjoy for but a short time. For it is ever in
this state (which we cannot be), since its actuality is also pleasure. (And therefore waking, perception, and thinking are most pleasant, and hopes and memories are so because of their reference to these.) And thought in itself deals with that which is best in
itself, and that which is thought in the fullest sense with that which is best in the fullest
20　sense. And thought thinks itself because it shares the nature of the object of thought;
for it becomes an object of thought in coming into contact with and thinking its objects, so that thought and object of thought are the same. For that which is *capable* of
receiving the object of thought, i.e. the substance, is thought. And it is active when it
possesses this object. Therefore the latter rather than the former is the divine element
which thought seems to contain, and the act of contemplation is what is most pleasant
25　and best. If, then, God is always in that good state in which we sometimes are, this
compels our wonder; and if in a better this compels it yet more. And God *is* in a better
state. And life also belongs to God; for the actuality of thought is life, and God is that
actuality; and God's essential actuality is life most good and eternal. We say therefore
that God is a living being, eternal, most good, so that life and duration continuous and
30　eternal belong to God; for this *is* God.

Those who suppose, as the Pythagoreans and Speusippus do, that supreme beauty and goodness are not present in the beginning, because the beginnings both of plants and of animals are *causes*, but beauty and completeness are in the *effects* of these, are wrong in their opinion. For the seed comes from other individuals which are prior and complete, and the first thing is not seed but the complete being, e.g. we must say that before the seed there is a man,—not the man produced from the seed, but another from whom the seed comes.

It is clear then from what has been said that there is a substance which is eternal and unmovable and separate from sensible things. It has been shown also that this substance cannot have any magnitude, but is without parts and indivisible. For it produces movement through infinite time, but nothing finite has infinite power. And, while every magnitude is either infinite or finite, it cannot, for the above reason, have finite magnitude, and it cannot have infinite magnitude because there is no infinite magnitude at all. But it is also clear that it is impassive and unalterable; for all the other changes are posterior to change of place. It is clear, then, why the first mover has these attributes.

8. We must not ignore the question whether we have to suppose one such substance or more than one, and if the latter, how many; we must also mention, regarding the opinions expressed by others, that they have said nothing that can even be clearly stated about the number of the substances. For the theory of Ideas has no special discussion of the subject; for those who believe in Ideas say the Ideas are numbers, and they speak of numbers now as unlimited, now as limited by the number ten; but as for the reason why there should be just so many numbers, nothing is said with any demonstrative exactness.

We however must discuss the subject, starting from the presuppositions and distinctions we have mentioned. The first principle or primary being is not movable either in itself or accidentally, but produces the primary eternal and single movement. And since that which is moved must be moved by something, and the first mover must be in itself unmovable, and eternal movement must be produced by something eternal and a single movement by a single thing, and since we see that besides the simple spatial movement of the universe, which we say the first and unmovable substance produces, there are other spatial movements—those of the planets—which are eternal (for the body which moves in a circle is eternal and unresting; we have proved these points in the *Physics*), each of these movements also must be caused by a substance unmovable in itself and eternal. For the nature of the stars is eternal, being a kind of substance, and the mover is eternal and prior to the moved, and that which is prior to a substance must be a substance. Evidently, then, there must be substances which are of the same number as the movements of the stars, and in their nature eternal, and in themselves unmovable, and without magnitude, for the reason before mentioned.

That the movers are substances, then, and that one of these is first and another second according to the same order as the movements of the stars, is evident. But in the number of movements we reach a problem which must be treated from the standpoint of that one of the mathematical sciences which is most akin to philosophy—viz. of astronomy; for this science speculates about substance which is perceptible but eternal, but the other mathematical sciences, i.e. arithmetic and geometry, treat of no substance. That the movements are more numerous than the bodies that are moved, is evident to those who have given even moderate attention to the matter; for each of the planets has more than one movement. But as to the actual number of these movements, we now—to give some notion of the subject—quote what some of the mathematicians

1073ᵃ

5

10

15

20

25

30

35

1073ᵇ

5

10

154

say, that our thought may have some definite number to grasp; but, for the rest, we
must partly investigate for ourselves, partly learn from other investigators, and if those
who study this subject form an opinion contrary to what we have now stated, we must
esteem both parties indeed, but follow the more accurate.

Eudoxus supposed that the motion of the sun or of the moon involves, in either
case, three spheres, of which the first is the sphere of the fixed stars, and the second
moves in the circle which runs along the middle of the zodiac, and the third in the circle which is inclined across the breadth of the zodiac; but the circle in which the moon
moves is inclined at a greater angle than that in which the sun moves. And the motion
of the planets involves, in each case, four spheres, and of these also the first and second
are the same as the first two mentioned above (for the sphere of the fixed stars is that
which moves all the other spheres, and that which is placed beneath this and has its
movement in the circle which bisects the zodiac is common to all), but the *poles* of the
third sphere of each planet are in the circle which bisects the zodiac, and the motion of
the fourth sphere is in the circle which is inclined at an angle to the equator of the third
sphere; and the poles of the third spheres are different for the other planets, but those
of Venus and Mercury are the same.

Callippus made the position of the spheres the same as Eudoxus did, but while
he assigned the same number as Eudoxus did to Jupiter and to Saturn, he thought two
more spheres should be added to the sun and two to the moon, if we were to explain
the phenomena, and one more to each of the other planets.

But it is necessary, if all the spheres combined are to explain the phenomena,
that for each of the planets there should be other spheres (one fewer than those hitherto
assigned) which counteract those already mentioned and bring back to the same position the first sphere of the star which in each case is situated below the star in question;
for only thus can all the forces at work produce the motion of the planets. Since, then,
the spheres by which the planets themselves are moved are eight and twenty-five, and
of these only those by which the lowest-situated planet is moved need not be counter-
acted, the spheres which counteract those of the first two planets will be six in number,
and the spheres which counteract those of the next four planets will be sixteen, and the
number of all the spheres—those which move the planets and those which counteract
these—will be fifty-five. And if one were not to add to the moon and to the sun the
movements we mentioned, all the spheres will be forty-nine in number.

Let this then be taken as the number of the spheres, so that the unmovable substances and principles may reasonably be taken as just so many; the assertion of *necessity* must be left to more powerful thinkers.

If there can be no spatial movement which does not conduce to the moving of a
star, and if further every being and every substance which is immune from change and
in virtue of itself has attained to the best must be considered an end, there can be no
other being apart from these we have named, but this must be the number of the substances. For if there are others, they will cause change as being an end of movement;
but there *cannot* be other movements besides those mentioned. And it is reasonable to
infer this from a consideration of the bodies that are moved; for if everything that
moves is for the sake of that which is moved, and every movement belongs to something that is moved, no movement can be for the sake of itself or of another movement,
but all movements must be for the sake of the stars. For if a movement is to be for the
sake of a movement, this latter also will have to be for the sake of something else; so
that since there cannot be an infinite regress, the end of every movement will be one of
the divine bodies which move through the heaven.

Evidently there is but one heaven. For if there are many heavens as there are many men, the moving principles, of which each heaven will have one, will be one in form but in number many. But all things that are many in number have matter. (For one and the same formula applies to *many* things, e.g. the formula of man; but Socrates is *one*.) But the primary essence has not matter; for it is fulfillment. So the unmovable first mover is one both in formula and in number; therefore also that which is moved always and continuously is one alone; therefore there is one heaven alone.

Our forefathers in the most remote ages have handed down to us their posterity a tradition, in the form of a myth, that these substances are gods and that the divine encloses the whole of nature. The rest of the tradition has been added later in mythical form with a view to the persuasion of the multitude and to its legal and utilitarian expediency; they say these gods are in the form of men or like some of the other animals, and they say other things consequent on and similar to these which we have mentioned. But if we were to separate the first point from these additions and take it alone—that they thought the first substances to be gods—we must regard this as an inspired utterance, and reflect that, while probably each art and science has often been developed as far as possible and has again perished, these opinions have been preserved like relics until the present. Only thus far, then, is the opinion of our ancestors and our earliest predecessors clear to us.

9. The nature of the divine thought involves certain problems; for while thought is held to be the most divine of phenomena, the question what it must be in order to have that character involves difficulties. For if it thinks nothing, what is there here of dignity? It is just like one who sleeps. And if it thinks, but this depends on something else, then (as that which is its substance is not the act of thinking, but a capacity) it cannot be the best substance; for it is through thinking that its value belongs to it. Further, whether its substance is the faculty of thought or the act of thinking, what does it think? Either itself or something else; and if something else, either the same always or something different. Does it matter, then, or not, whether it thinks the good or any chance thing? Are there not some things about which it is incredible that it should think? Evidently, then, it thinks that which is most divine and precious, and it does not change; for change would be change for the worse, and this would be already a movement. First, then, if it is not the act of thinking but a capacity, it would be reasonable to suppose that the continuity of its thinking is wearisome to it. Secondly, there would evidently be something else more precious than thought, viz. that which is thought. For both thinking and the act of thought will belong even to one who has the worst of thoughts. Therefore if this ought to be avoided (and it ought, for there are even some things which it is better not to see than to see), the act of thinking cannot be the best of things. Therefore it must be itself that thought thinks (since it is the most excellent of things), and its thinking is a thinking on thinking.

But evidently knowledge and perception and opinion and understanding have always something else as their object, and themselves only by the way. Further, if thinking and being thought are different, in respect of which does goodness belong to thought? For being an act of thinking and being an object of thought are not the same. We answer that in some cases the knowledge is the object. In the productive sciences (if we abstract from the matter) the substance in the sense of essence, and in the theoretical sciences the formula or the act of thinking, is the object. As, then, thought and the object of thought are not different in the case of things that have not matter, they will be the same, i.e. the thinking will be one with the object of its thought.

5   A further question is left—whether the object of the thought is composite; for if
it were, thought would change in passing from part to part of the whole. We answer
that everything which has not matter is indivisible. As human thought, or rather the
thought of composite objects, is in a certain period of time (for it does not possess the
good at this moment or at that, but its best, being something different from it, is at-
10   tained only in a whole period of time), so throughout eternity is the thought which has
itself for its object.

ON THE SOUL (in part)

BOOK II

412ª   1. Let the foregoing suffice as our account of the views concerning the soul which have
been handed on by our predecessors; let us now make as it were a completely fresh
5   start, endeavouring to answer the question, What is soul? i.e. to formulate the most
general possible account of it.
       We say that substance is one kind of what is, and that in several senses: in the
sense of matter or that which in itself is not a this, and in the sense of form or essence,
which is that precisely in virtue of which a thing is called a this, and thirdly in the
10   sense of that which is compounded of both. Now matter is potentiality, form actuality;
and actuality is of two kinds, one as e.g. knowledge, the other as e.g. reflecting.
       Among substances are by general consent reckoned bodies and especially natural
bodies; for they are the principles of all other bodies. Of natural bodies some have life
15   in them, others not; by life we mean self-nutrition and growth and decay. It follows
that every natural body which has life in it is a substance in the sense of a composite.
       Now given that there are bodies of such and such a kind, viz. having life, the soul
cannot be a body; for the body is the subject or matter, not what is attributed to it.
20   Hence the soul must be a substance in the sense of the form of a natural body having
life potentially within it. But substance is actuality, and thus soul is the actuality of a
body as above characterized. Now there are two kinds of actuality corresponding to
knowledge and to reflecting. It is obvious that the soul is an actuality like knowledge;
for both sleeping and waking presuppose the existence of soul, and of these waking
25   corresponds to reflecting, sleeping to knowledge possessed but not employed, and
knowledge of something is temporally prior.
       That is why the soul is an actuality of the first kind of a natural body having life
412ᵇ   potentially in it. The body so described is a body which is organized. The parts of plants
in spite of their extreme simplicity are organs; e.g. the leaf serves to shelter the pericarp,
the pericarp to shelter the fruit, while the roots of plants are analogous to the mouth of
animals, both serving for the absorption of food. If, then, we have to give a general for-
5   mula applicable to all kinds of soul, we must describe it as an actuality of the first kind

Aristotle, *On the Soul*, Book II, 1–3; Book III, 4–5, translated by J.A. Smith from *Complete Works of Aristotle*, edited by Jonathan Barnes. Copyright © 1984 by PUP. Reprinted by permission of Princeton University
Press.

of a natural organized body. That is why we can dismiss as unnecessary the question whether the soul and the body are one: it is as though we were to ask whether the wax and its shape are one, or generally the matter of a thing and that of which it is the matter. Unity has many senses (as many as "is" has), but the proper one is that of actuality.

We have now given a general answer to the question, What is soul? It is substance in the sense which corresponds to the account of a thing. That means that it is what it is to be for a body of the character just assigned. Suppose that a tool, e.g. an axe, were a natural body, then being an axe would have been its essence, and so its soul; if this disappeared from it, it would have ceased to be an axe, except in name. As it is, it is an axe; for it is not of a body of that sort that what it is to be, i.e. its account, is a soul, but of a natural body of a particular kind, viz. one having in itself the power of setting itself in movement and arresting itself. Next, apply this doctrine in the case of the parts of the living body. Suppose that the eye were an animal—sight would have been its soul, for sight is the substance of the eye which corresponds to the account, the eye being merely the matter of seeing; when seeing is removed the eye is no longer an eye, except in name—no more than the eye of a statue or of a painted figure. We must now extend our consideration from the parts to the whole living body; for what the part is to the part, that the whole faculty of sense is to the whole sensitive body as such.

We must not understand by that which is potentially capable of living what has lost the soul it had, but only what still retains it; but seeds and fruits are bodies which are potentially of that sort. Consequently, while waking is actuality in a sense corresponding to the cutting and the seeing, the soul is actuality in the sense corresponding to sight and the power in the tool; the body corresponds to what is in potentiality; as the pupil *plus* the power of sight constitutes the eye, so the soul *plus* the body constitutes the animal.

From this it is clear that the soul is inseparable from its body, or at any rate that certain parts of it are (if it has parts)—for the actuality of some of them is the actuality of the parts themselves. Yet some may be separable because they are not the actualities of any body at all. Further, we have no light on the problem whether the soul may not be the actuality of its body in the sense in which the sailor is the actuality of the ship.

This must suffice as our sketch or outline of the nature of soul.

2. Since what is clear and more familiar in account emerges from what in itself is confused but more observable by us, we must reconsider our results from this point of view. For it is not enough for a definitional account to express as most now do the mere fact; it must include and exhibit the cause also. At present definitions are given in a form analogous to the conclusion of an argument; e.g. What is squaring? The construction of an equilateral rectangle equal to a given oblong rectangle. Such a definition is in form equivalent to a conclusion. One that tells us that squaring is the discovery of a mean proportional discloses the cause of what is defined.

We resume our inquiry from a fresh starting-point by calling attention to the fact that what has soul in it differs from what has not in that the former displays life. Now this word has more than one sense, and provided any one alone of these is found in a thing we say that thing is living—viz. thinking or perception or local movement and rest, or movement in the sense of nutrition, decay and growth. Hence we think of plants also as living, for they are observed to possess in themselves an originative power through which they increase or decrease in all spatial directions; they do not grow up but not down—they grow alike in both, indeed in all, directions; and that holds for everything which is constantly nourished and continues to live, so long as it can absorb nutriment.

This power of self-nutrition can be separated from the other powers mentioned, but not they from it—in mortal beings at least. The fact is obvious in plants; for it is the only psychic power they possess.

This is the originative power the possession of which leads us to speak of things as *living* at all, but it is the possession of sensation that leads us for the first time to speak of living things as *animals*; for even those beings which possess no power of local movement but do possess the power of sensation we call animals and not merely living things.

The primary form of sense is touch, which belongs to all animals. Just as the
5 power of self-nutrition can be separated from touch and sensation generally, so touch can be separated from all other forms of sense. (By the power of self-nutrition we mean that part of the soul which is common to plants and animals: all animals whatso-ever are observed to have the sense of touch.) What the explanation of these two facts
10 is, we must discuss later. At present we must confine ourselves to saying that soul is the source of these phenomena and is characterized by them, viz. by the powers of self-nutrition, sensation, thinking, and movement.

Is each of these a soul or a part of a soul? And if a part, a part merely distinguish-
15 able by definition or a part distinct in local situation as well? In the case of certain of these powers, the answers to these questions are easy, in the case of others we are puz-zled what to say. Just as in the case of plants which when divided are observed to con-tinue to live though separated from one another (thus showing that in *their* case the soul of each individual plant was actually one, potentially many), so we notice a simi-
20 lar result in other varieties of soul, i.e. in insects which have been cut in two; each of the segments possesses both sensation and local movement; and if sensation, necessar-ily also imagination and appetition; for, where there is sensation, there is also pleasure and pain, and, where these, necessarily also desire.
25 We have no evidence as yet about thought or the power of reflexion; it seems to be a different kind of soul, differing as what is eternal from what is perishable; it alone is capable of being separated. All the other parts of soul, it is evident from what we have said, are, in spite of certain statements to the contrary, incapable of separate exis-tence though, of course, distinguishable by definition. If opining is distinct from per-
30 ceiving, to be capable of opining and to be capable of perceiving must be distinct, and so with all the other forms of living above enumerated. Further, some animals possess all these parts of soul, some certain of them only, others one only (this is what enables
us to classify animals); the cause must be considered later. A similar arrangement is found also within the field of the senses; some classes of animals have all the senses, some only certain of them, others only one, the most indispensable, touch.

Since the expression "that whereby we live and perceive" has two meanings, just
5 like the expression "that whereby we know"—that may mean either knowledge or the soul, for we can speak of knowing *by* either, and similarly that whereby we are in health may be either health or the body or some part of the body; and since of these knowledge or health is a form, essence, or account, or if we so express it an activity of
10 a recipient matter—knowledge of what is capable of knowing, health of what is capa-ble of being made healthy (for the activity of that which is capable of originating change seems to take place in what is changed or altered); further, since it is the soul by which primarily we live, perceive, and think:—it follows that the soul must be an account and essence, not matter or a subject. For, as we said, the word substance has
15 three meanings—form, matter, and the complex of both—and of these matter is poten-tiality, form actuality. Since then the complex here is the living thing, the body cannot be the actuality of the soul; it is the soul which is the actuality of a certain kind of

body. Hence the rightness of the view that the soul cannot *be* without a body, while it 20
cannot be a body; it is not a body but something relative to a body. That is why it is *in*
a body, and a body of a definite kind. It was a mistake, therefore, to do as former
thinkers did, merely to fit it into a body without adding a definite specification of the
kind or character of that body, although evidently one chance thing will not receive an- 25
other. It comes about as reason requires: the actuality of any given thing can only be
realized in what is already potentially that thing, i.e. in a matter of its own appropriate
to it. From all this it is plain that soul is an actuality or account of something that possesses a potentiality of being such.

3. Of the psychic powers above enumerated some kinds of living things, as we have
said, possess all, some less than all, others one only. Those we have mentioned are the 30
nutritive, the appetitive, the sensory, the locomotive, and the power of thinking. Plants
have none but the first, the nutritive, while another order of living things has this *plus*
the sensory. If any order of living things has the sensory, it must also have the appeti- 414^b
tive; for appetite is the genus of which desire, passion, and wish are the species; now
all animals have one sense at least, viz. touch, and whatever has a sense has the capacity for pleasure and pain and therefore has pleasant and painful objects present to it,
and wherever these are present, there is desire, for desire is appetition of what is pleas- 5
ant. Further, all animals have the sense for food (for touch is the sense for food); the
food of all living things consists of what is dry, moist, hot, cold, and these are the qualities apprehended by touch; all other sensible qualities are apprehended by touch only
indirectly. Sounds, colours, and odours contribute nothing to nutriment; flavours fall 10
within the field of tangible qualities. Hunger and thirst are forms of desire, hunger a
desire for what is dry and hot, thirst a desire for what is cold and moist; flavour is a sort
of seasoning added to both. We must later clear up these points, but at present it may
be enough to say that all animals that possess the sense of touch have also appetition. 15
The case of imagination is obscure; we must examine it later. Certain kinds of animals
possess in addition the power of locomotion, and still others, i.e. man and possibly another order like man or superior to him, the power of thinking and thought. It is now
evident that a single definition can be given of soul only in the same sense as one can 20
be given of figure. For, as in that case there is no figure apart from triangle and those
that follow in order, so here there is no soul apart from the forms of soul just enumerated. It is true that a common definition can be given for figure which will fit all figures
without expressing the peculiar nature of any figure. So here in the case of soul and its
specific forms. Hence it is absurd in this and similar cases to look for a common defini- 25
tion which will not express the peculiar nature of anything that is and will not apply to
the approrate indivisible species, while at the same time omitting to look for an account which will. The cases of figure and soul are exactly parallel; for the particulars
subsumed under the common name in both cases—figures and living beings—consti- 30
tute a series, each successive term of which potentially contains its predecessor, e.g.
the square the triangle, the sensory power the self-nutritive. Hence we must ask in the
case of each order of living things, What is its soul, i.e. What is the soul of plant, man,
beast? Why the terms are related in this serial way must form the subject of examina- 415^a
tion. For the power of perception is never found apart from the power of self-nutrition,
while—in plants—the latter is found isolated from the former. Again, no sense is
found apart from that of touch, while touch *is* found by itself; many animals have nei- 5
ther sight, hearing, nor smell. Again, among living things that possess sense some have
the power of locomotion, some not. Lastly, certain living beings—a small minority—
possess calculation and thought, for (among mortal beings) those which possess calcu-

10   lation have all the other powers above mentioned, while the converse does not hold—indeed some live by imagination alone, while others have not even imagination. Reflective thought presents a different problem.

It is evident that the way to give the most adequate definition of soul is to seek in the case of *each* of its forms for the most appropriate definition.

* * *

Book III

* * *

429ᵃ   4. Turning now to the part of the soul with which the soul knows and (whether this is separable from the others in definition only, or spatially as well) we have to inquire what differentiates this part, and how thinking can take place.

If thinking is like perceiving, it must be either a process in which the soul is acted upon by what is capable of being thought, or a process different from but analo-
15   gous to that. The thinking part of the soul must therefore be, while impassible, capable of receiving the form of an object; that is, must be potentially identical in character with its object without being the object. Thought must be related to what is thinkable, as sense is to what is sensible.

Therefore, since everything is a possible object of thought, mind in order, as Anaxagoras says, to dominate, that is, to know, must be pure from all admixture; for
20   the co-presence of what is alien to its nature is a hindrance and a block: it follows that it can have no nature of its own, other than that of having a certain capacity. Thus that in the soul which is called thought (by thought I mean that whereby the soul thinks and judges) is, before it thinks, not actually any real thing. For this reason it cannot reason-
25   ably be regarded as blended with the body: if so, it would acquire some quality, e.g. warmth or cold, or even have an organ like the sensitive faculty: as it is, it has none. It was a good idea to call the soul "the place of forms," though this description holds only of the thinking soul, and even this is the forms only potentially, not actually.

Observation of the sense-organs and their employment reveals a distinction be-
30   tween the impassibility of the sensitive faculty and that of the faculty of thought. After strong stimulation of a sense we are less able to exercise it than before, as e.g. in the
429ᵇ   case of a loud sound we cannot hear easily immediately after, or in the case of a bright colour or a powerful odour we cannot see or smell, but in the case of thought thinking about an object that is highly thinkable renders it more and not less able afterwards to think of objects that are less thinkable: the reason is that while the faculty of sensation
5   is dependent upon the body, thought is separable from it.

When thought has become each thing in the way in which a man who actually knows is said to do so (this happens when he is now able to exercise the power on his own initiative), its condition is still one of potentiality, but in a different sense from the potentiality which preceded the acquisition of knowledge by learning or discovery; and thought is then able to think of itself.
10   Since we can distinguish between a magnitude and what it is to be a magnitude, and between water and what it is to be water, and so in many other cases (though not in all; for in certain cases the thing and its form are identical), flesh and what it is to be flesh are discriminated either by different faculties, or by the same faculty in two different states; for flesh necessarily involves matter and is like what is snub-nosed, a *this* in a *this*. Now it is by means of the sensitive faculty that we discriminate the hot and

the cold, i.e. the factors which combined in a certain ratio constitute flesh: the essential $\quad$ 15
character of flesh is apprehended by something different either wholly separate from
the sensitive faculty or related to it as a bent line to the same line when it has been
straightened out.

Again in the case of abstract objects what is straight is analogous to what is
snub-nosed; for it necessarily implies a continuum: its constitutive essence is different,
if we may distinguish between straightness and what is straight: let us take it to be two-
ness. It must be apprehended, therefore, by a different power or by the same power in a $\quad$ 20
different state. To sum up, in so far as the realities it knows are capable of being separated from their matter, so it is also with the powers of thought.

The problem might be suggested: if thinking is a passive affection, then if
thought is simple and impassible and has nothing in common with anything else, as
Anaxagoras says, how can it come to think at all? For interaction between two factors $\quad$ 25
is held to require a precedent community of nature between the factors. Again it might
be asked, is thought a possible object of thought to itself? For if thought is thinkable
per se and what is thinkable is in kind one and the same, then either thought will belong to everything, or it will contain some element common to it with all other realities
which makes them all thinkable.

Have not we already disposed of the difficulty about interaction involving a $\quad$ 30
common element, when we said that thought is in a sense potentially whatever is thinkable, though actually it is nothing until it has thought? What it thinks must be in it just
as characters may be said to be on a writing-table on which as yet nothing actually $\quad$ 430ª
stands written: this is exactly what happens with thought.

Thought is itself thinkable in exactly the same way as its objects are. For in the
case of objects which involve no matter, what thinks and what is thought are identical;
for speculative knowledge and its object are identical. (Why thought is not always $\quad$ 5
thinking we must consider later.) In the case of those which contain matter each of the
objects of thought is only potentially present. It follows that while they will not have
thought in them (for thought is a potentiality of them only in so far as they are capable
of being disengaged from matter) thought may yet be thinkable.

5. Since in every class of things, as in nature as a whole, we find two factors involved, $\quad$ 10
a matter which is potentially all the particulars included in the class, a cause which is
productive in the sense that it makes them all (the latter standing to the former, as e.g.
an art to its material), these distinct elements must likewise be found within the soul.

And in fact thought, as we have described it, is what it is by virtue of becoming
all things, while there is another which is what it is by virtue of making all things: this $\quad$ 15
is a sort of positive state like light; for in a sense light makes potential colours into actual colours.

Thought in this sense of it is separable, impassible, unmixed, since it is in its essential nature activity (for always the active is superior to the passive factor, the originating force to the matter).

Actual knowledge is identical with its object: in the individual, potential knowl- $\quad$ 20
edge is in time prior to actual knowledge, but absolutely it is not prior even in time. It
does not sometimes think and sometimes not think. When separated it is alone just
what it is, and this above is immortal and eternal (we do not remember because, while
this is impossible, passive thought is perishable); and without this nothing thinks.

CHRISTIANITY AND MEDIEVAL PHILOSOPHY

With only a few exceptions, European medieval thought was deeply imbued with Christian faith. As a result, it is not possible to understand medieval philosophy without at least a rudimentary understanding of Christian beliefs as presented in the Bible. Whether or not today's reader accepts the veracity of the claims put forth in these writings, most medievals did believe them, and that belief formed the foundation of their thought.

Beginning as a Jewish sect, Christianity continued to hold a number of beliefs in common with Judaism, including the following bedrock convictions: that the Hebrew Bible (called the "Old Testament" by Christians) is the revealed Word of God; that God is superior to and distinct from the created world; that the world was created by God at a specific point in time and that the world will come to an end; that God is personal and desires a special relationship with the human race; that humans have sinned against God's Law and need God's forgiveness; that God requires righteousness as a means of a right relationship with God and others; and that God would send the Anointed One ("Messiah" in Hebrew, "Christ" in Greek) to set the people of God free.

But while Christians accepted the foundational beliefs of their Jewish ancestors, they differed on one key point: the identity of the Messiah. Whereas the Jews anticipated a spiritual-political figure to save them from the oppression of their enemies, Christians believed the Christ saved his people mainly from the spiritual oppressors of sin and death. Whereas the Jews believed the Messiah would scrupulously follow the Law, favoring and associating only with those who did likewise, the Christ of the Christians seemed to enjoy a remarkable freedom in relation to several of Israel's most venerable institutions—for example,

Sabbath observances, the Temple, and ritual purity—while associating with the "lowlifes" of society. In short, whereas the Jewish people were (and still are) awaiting the Messiah, Christians believed (and still believe) Jesus of Nazareth was the Messiah.

Christians held that after his death by crucifixion, Jesus rose from the dead (the Resurrection) and taught his followers for forty days before ascending into heaven. As part of that teaching, Jesus promised that he would return again (the Second Coming ⟨*parousia*⟩) and that in the meantime his followers should spread the Christian faith to all the world.

The basic Christian belief was (and still is) that Jesus is the Son of God who became a human (the Incarnation) to atone for human sin (Redemption). The severed relationship between the Holy God and sinful humanity could be restored only through the sacrifice of one who was consummate righteousness. As the Word (⟨*Logos*⟩) of God made flesh, Jesus was that righteousness, made that sacrifice, and offered that restoration. Through faith, Christians accept this work done on their behalf (Justification) and receive the power of God's spirit to overcome sin and to serve others (Sanctification).

As Christians spread this message throughout the Roman Empire, they encountered resistance and persecution from both Jewish and Roman authorities. Many Jewish leaders objected to the Christian identification of Jesus with God; Roman authorities objected to the Christians' unwillingness to participate in emperor worship. Jews, too, had refused to participate in state religion and had often been persecuted. But Christians posed a unique threat to the Romans because, unlike the Jews, Christians proclaimed a supranational, supraracial, universal Lord—one very much in competition with Caesar. And Christians indefatigably sought converts to their universal Savior. Accordingly, they were persecuted on and off for three centuries.

Despite persecution, Christianity grew steadily in the centuries after Christ. There have been many explanations for that growth. The eighteenth-century historian Edward Gibbon* listed five causes: (1) Christianity's inheritance of the zeal of the Jews; (2) its connection to the philosophical doctrine of the immortality of the soul; (3) its claim of miracles; (4) the virtue of the early Christians; and (5) the organization of the church. Recent historians have pointed to the moral exclusivity of Christians, who demanded deep commitment; the definite and absolute character of Christian belief in an age of uncertainty; and the social dimensions of Christianity, which made it attractive to women, the poor, and the oppressed.**

As Christianity grew, doctrinal disputes inevitably arose. What was true Christianity? The answers tended to reflect deep convictions about two essential issues: the nature of the person and work of Jesus Christ and the relationship between faith and reason. What was the relationship between Jesus and God? Did Jesus have two distinct natures: one divine and one human? Or were they merged into a single unique nature? Moreover, if there is only one God, how could God also be three (Father, Son, and Holy Spirit)? And how could reason resolve issues of faith?

The Decline and Fall of the Roman Empire, Chapter XV.

**Of course, Christians have always claimed that none of these reasons is entirely adequate and that the most acceptable explanation for the rise of Christianity is a supernatural one.

The first issue, the nature of Christ, was resolved at the Council of Nicea, convened and presided over by the first Christian emperor, Constantine, in A.D. 325. The Council determined that the Son was exactly the same substance, "consubstantial" ⟨*homoousios*⟩, and not just "of like substance" ⟨*homoiousios*⟩, with God the Father. (The single Greek letter "iota," meant a great deal more than "one iota of difference" to the early church.) By the middle of the first millenium, the "Nicene Creed" was confessed by virtually all Christendom as the orthodox answer to the nature-of-Christ question. The Nicene Creed is still authoritative in Orthodox, Catholic, and Protestant churches.

Even though the Christological question was answered at Nicea, the question of the right relation between faith and reason continued to be argued throughout the medieval period. The early Christians had a simple faith in Jesus as Messiah (if they were Jewish Christians) and as Lord (if they were Gentile Christians), and they believed Jesus had lived, taught, died, and risen for them and all others. But almost immediately, that simple faith encountered sophisticated Hellenistic thought throughout the Roman Empire. How much should Christian faith concede to the competence of philosophic reason? What was the relation between sacred writings (i.e., the Bible) and secular writings (e.g., philosophy)? In Acts 17, the Apostle Paul, the early Christian convert, used reason and quoted pagan poets to help him preach the gospel to Epicurean and Stoic philosophers in Athens. Yet later, in Colossians 2:8, he warned, "See to it that no one takes you captive through philosophy and empty deceit. . . ." Some early Church Fathers, such as Justin Martyr, used philosophy to help interpret Christian faith. Other Church Fathers, such as Tertullian, argued that reason could be inimical to faith: "What has Jerusalem to do with Athens?" he asked.

Some in the early church even claimed to have special esoteric knowledge not available to the rabble either in the sacred Scriptures or secular reason. They were known as "Gnostics," from the Greek word for knowledge ⟨*gnosis*⟩. These Gnostics emphasized the Platonic belief in the soul as good and the body as evil, and they sought to free the soul from the body by extreme ascetic practices. Some of the Gnostics taught that Jesus was not *really* a physical person (since the body is evil) and that the Old Testament God, Yahweh, who had created bodies and matter, was really the devil. Manicheaism, which rivaled Christianity in the third and fourth centuries, and for a time claimed Augustine as one of its believers, was based on Gnostic thought.

For the most part, the early medieval philosophers sought to resolve these theological issues within the broad framework of Platonic thought. Augustine (as either the last classical thinker or the first medieval one), Boethius, and Anselm all used Neoplatonic concepts. In the early Middle Ages, most of Aristotle's writings were not available in the West. But in the East, Islamic philosophers, such as Ibn-Sina and Ibn Rushd (or Averroës), and Jewish thinkers, such as Moses Maimonides, read and commented on a wide range of Aristotelian works. These works, along with the Muslim and Jewish commentaries on them, were reintroduced to Western Europe in the late–Middle Ages and became the basis for the monumental work of Thomas Aquinas.

While Thomas lived during a period of relative calm and well-being, the centuries following his death were filled with tumult and upheaval. As a part of the often vicious conflict between church and state, Philip IV of France captured Pope Boniface VIII in 1303 and soon thereafter moved the papal court to Avignon, France—the so-called Babylonian Captivity of the Church. Beginning in

1347, the bubonic plague, or Black Death, struck Western Europe. Responses to the plague ranged from fanatical anti-intellectual apocalypticism to self-indulgent hedonism. Some even blamed the plague on intellectuals such as Thomas Aquinas, saying they provoked divine wrath by explaining God's ways rationally; others simply counselled, "Let us eat, drink, and be merry, for tomorrow we die." Many turned to superstition or to scapegoating Jews. At the same time, England and France were involved in the Hundred Years' War (1337–1453), which brought enormous casualties. Because of the plague and the war, in the years from 1300 to 1450, the population of Western Europe was reduced by half—perhaps by as much as two-thirds. In 1378, the Great Schism divided the Catholic Church as the Italians reinstituted the papacy in Rome, while a second pope reigned in Avignon. For over thirty years, rival popes condemned and excommunicated one another. In 1409, an attempt to end the schism with a compromise pope led only to a third pope and thus a third claimant to St. Peter's universal chair. Finally, in 1417, the church united around one pope ruling in Rome. But by now the power and prestige of the papacy had been severely diminished, and a hundred years later, in the Protestant Reformation, the Western church split decisively.

The philosophy of this later medieval period is commonly viewed in the light of these social upheavals, and, indeed, there does seem to be some connection. Thomas had harmonized philosophy and theology in a systematic way reflective of the relative peacefulness of the thirteenth century. Just as social stability—particularly in the relationship between church and state—deteriorated in the centuries following Thomas, so also the philosophies that developed during this period tended to separate reason and faith. William of Ockham, for example, held that philosophy and theology were separate realms with separate rules. The Renaissance thinker Pico della Mirandola developed a philosophy essentially excluding faith while using reason to draw from sources both within and outside Christendom. In Pico's philosophy, reason and faith were no longer systematically conjoined: Reason stood supremely alone. Clearly the coherent, rational Christian synthesis of Thomas had unraveled.

But as Frederick Copleston has pointed out, there are other ways of understanding this transition. Instead of seeing late-medieval–early-Renaissance philosophy as destructive to a grand synthesis or as reactive to societal chaos, "one can see . . . philosophy being reborn and growing up under the shadow and care of theology, reaching a more or less adult stage and then tending to go its own way and assert its independence" (*A History of Medieval Philosophy*, p. 314). While acknowledging the disintegration of the peculiarly Thomistic approach to synthesis, this view sees the late-medieval period as a natural development of Western European thought.

* * *

For discussions of the interaction between Christianity and its surrounding culture, see A.H. Armstrong and R.A. Markus, *Christian Faith and Greek Philosophy* (New York: Sheed and Ward, 1960); E.R. Dodds, *Pagan and Christian in an Age of Anxiety* (Cambridge: Cambridge University Press, 1965); Jaroslav Pelikan, *The Christian Tradition: A History of the Development of Doctrine*, five volumes (Chicago: University of Chicago Press, 1971–1989); and R.A. Markus, *Christianity in the Roman World* (London: Thames & Hudson, 1974). For a discussion of Christian beliefs in their historical context, see J.N.D. Kelly, *Early Christian Doctrines*, 5th edition (London: Black, 1978). For basic introductions to traditional Christian beliefs, see John R.W. Stott, *Basic Christianity* (Downers Grove, IL: Inter-Varsity Press, 1971), and Hans Küng, *On Being a Christian*, translated by Edward Quinn (Garden City, NY: Doubleday, 1976).

Étienne Gilson's work, *History of Christian Philosophy in the Middle Ages* (New York: Random House, 1955), is the classic study of this time period, while Maurice De Wulf, *History of Mediaeval Philosophy* (New York: Dover, 1952); Armand A. Maurer, *Medieval Philosophy* (New York: Random House, 1962); Michael Haren, *Medieval Thought: The Western Intellectual Tradition from Antiquity to the Thirteenth Century* (New York: St. Martin's Press, 1985); B.B. Price, *Medieval Thought* (Oxford: Blackwell, 1992); and John Marenbon, ed., *Medieval Philosophy* (London: Routledge & Kegan Paul, 1997) are also useful. Frederick Copleston's work on medieval philosophy includes several volumes of his multi-volume set, *A History of Philosophy* (1950; reprinted Garden City, NY: Image Doubleday, 1962–1963), as well as the later single volume, *A History of Medieval Philosophy* (New York: Harper & Row, 1972). Hans-Werner Goetz, *Life in the Middle Ages*, translated by Albert Wimmer (Notre Dame, IN: Notre Dame University Press, 1994) provides historical context.

For books specifically on the early medieval period, see A.H. Armstrong, ed., *The Cambridge History of Later Greek and Early Medieval Philosophy* (Cambridge: Cambridge University Press, 1967); and John Marenbon, *Early Medieval Philosophy (480–1150): An Introduction* (London: Routledge & Kegan Paul, 1983). For books on the later medieval period, see Ray C. Petry, ed., *Late Medieval Mysticism* (Philadelphia: Westminster Press, 1957); Gordon Leff, *The Dissolution of the Medieval Outlook: An Essay on Intellectual and Spiritual Change in the Fourteenth Century* (New York: New York University Press, 1976); Norman Kretzmann et al., eds., *The Cambridge History of Later Medieval Philosophy: From the Rediscovery of Aristotle to the Disintegration of Scholasticism 1100–1600* (Cambridge: Cambridge University Press, 1982); and John Marenbon, *Later Medieval Philosophy (1150–1350): An Introduction* (London: Routledge & Kegan Paul, 1987).

AUGUSTINE

A.D. 354–430

------◄○►------

Aurelius Augustinus, Saint Augustine, was born of a Christian mother and a pagan father in Thagaste, a small town in what is now Algeria, North Africa. In many ways, his family's mixed religious background represented the crumbling Roman Empire. Even though the influence of Christianity had grown since Emperor Constantine's edict of religious toleration in A.D. 313, there were still many rivals to his mother's faith.

As a boy, Augustine showed intellectual promise, and at seventeen he was sent to Carthage to study rhetoric. While there, Augustine found philosophy, rejected Christianity, took a mistress (who bore him a son), and began to investigate some of the religions of the time. He turned first to the followers of the prophet Mani—the Manichaeans. Mani was a third-century prophet who called himself "the apostle of God." He developed the ancient Persian teaching of Zoroaster (or Zarathustra), which said that there are two great forces in the world, one good and one evil, and that neither can overcome the other. Living a life of sensual indulgence, Augustine took comfort from the idea that God could no more overcome evil in the universe than Augustine could in his own life.

In 375, Augustine returned to Thagaste to begin teaching rhetoric. When his mother, Monica (later sainted for her perseverance in prayer for her son), discovered that he had become a Manichaean, she expelled him from her house. Finding Thagaste boring, and his mother difficult, Augustine returned to Carthage. Over the next seven years, he grew disenchanted with Manichaeism. In 384, he left Carthage for teaching positions in Rome and finally Milan. In Milan, Augustine encountered the writings of Plotinus and was converted to Neoplatonism. At the same time, he came into contact with a group of Christians led by the Bishop of Milan, Ambrose. Under the influence of this group, Augustine was forced to reconsider his earlier rejection of Christianity, yet he was still unwilling to give up his life of self-gratification. In 386, while sitting in a friend's garden, he heard what he thought was a child's voice saying, "Pick it up and read, pick it up and read." Augustine later recounted what happened:

> I returned to the place where Alypius was sitting, for on leaving it I had put down there the book of the apostle's letters. I snatched it up, opened it and read in silence the passsage on which my eyes first lighted: "Not in dissipation and drunkenness, nor in debauchery and lewdness, nor in arguing and jealousy; but put on the Lord Jesus Christ, and make no provision for the flesh or the gratification of your desires." [Rom. 13:13–14] I had no wish to read further, nor was there need. No sooner had I reached the end of the verse than the light of certainty flooded my heart and all dark shades of doubt fled away.*

The following year, Augustine was baptized and returned to Africa to found a monastic community. Within two years he left the cloister, answering the church's call to priesthood. He served as a priest, and later as bishop, in the African town of Hippo for the rest of his life.

*   *   *

While at Hippo, Augustine wrote voluminously on a variety of theological and philosophical topics. Many of his works sought to define exactly what was and wàs not "Christian." His doctrinal works, such as *The Trinity*, established Christian essentials; whereas his polemical works, directed against "heresies" (positions unacceptable to the church), outlined what was not admissible. Augustine fought two major heresies: the Pelagian and the Donatist. The Pelagians held that sin had affected only Adam, that the will is free from sin, and that God's grace is given on the basis of human merit. The Donatists maintained that the sacraments were effective only when administered by a priest in a state of grace. Augustine argued passionately that both heresies put too much emphasis on human ability and not enough on God's grace.

Augustine's most famous work, the *Confessions*, invented the genre of introspective autobiography. The *Confessions* are full of both psychological and spiritual insight and so can be read as either devotional tract or philosophical essay. Books I through IX are Augustine's life story from the perspective of Christian conversion (detailed in our selection from Book VIII). As Augustine reflects on his life, he sees both his sinfulness and his intellectual aimlessness apart from God's grace. He also gives early glimpses of his mature epistemological position that God must illumine the mind in order for an individual to gain wisdom. Following his conversion, Augustine continued to seek understanding—though now firmly founded on faith. Books X to XII illustrate this "faith seeking understanding," as Augustine examines the questions of memory, time, and creation. Our selection from Book XI explores the nature of time and God's relation to it. Augustine argues that God must be "outside" time in an eternal present. This view of God as timelessly eternal was developed by Boethius and is still influential

---

*Saint Augustine, *Confessions*, Book VIII. See reading on p. 293.

today (see the suggested readings that follow). I am pleased to offer this selection in the outstanding new translation by Maria Boulding.

Of Augustine's many other works, *The City of God* is by far the most influential. During the fourth century, Christianity had become the state religion of the Roman Empire; in 410, Rome fell to the Visigoths, and the eternal city was sacked for the first time. Naturally, many considered the sack of Rome a punishment for the betrayal of the old Roman religion. Augustine wrote *The City of God* to answer this charge and in so doing he developed yet another first: the first Western philosophy of history. Rather than a cycle of repeated events, Augustine described history as being linear—from creation to consummation and final judgment. As history moves from beginning to end, we can observe two cities: the City of God, consisting of those who love God; and the City of Man, those who love self rather than God.

The second selection, from Book XII, explains the origin of evil and of the City of Man. Augustine begins by insisting, against the Manichaeans, that there is no being capable of opposing God: God is all-powerful. But, despite the presence of evil, God is also all-good and everything God created is good. Evil arises when a moral agent (angel or human) wills to love a lesser good (self) rather than the highest good (God). There is no evil "thing" to choose—there is only evil choosing. This leads to the question of what caused the will to choose evilly—a question Augustine says cannot be answered.

Augustine's impact has been enormous. Medieval Catholic philosophers, such as Anselm and Thomas Aquinas, as well as Protestant reformers, such as Martin Luther and John Calvin, wanted to be Augustine's heirs. Many contemporary Christian thinkers still appeal to Augustine's ideas, such as his defense of grace and his explanation of evil. But Augustine's influence has not been limited to theologians and philosophers of religion. Ludwig Wittgenstein began his *Philosophical Investigations* by examining Augustine's theory of language, and Bertrand Russell claimed Augustine's theory of time superior even to that of Kant. Echoes of Augustine's understanding of history as the unfolding of divine purpose can be heard in the writings of Hegel, whereas Augustine's idea that some kind of faith must precede fruitful understanding has been adapted by thinkers in such fields as the sociology of knowledge and philosophy of science.

*　　*　　*

The best general account of Augustine's philosophy remains Étienne Gilson, *The Christian Philosophy of Saint Augustine,* translated by L.E.M. Lynch (New York: Random House, 1960); Peter Brown, *Augustine of Hippo: A Biography* (Berkeley: University of California Press, 1967), provides an excellent biography. For a brief introduction to Augustine's life and thought, see Henry Chadwick, *Augustine* (Oxford: Oxford University Press, 1986). For more extensive discussions of Augustine's thought, see Robert E. Meagher, *An Introduction to Augustine* (New York: New York University Press, 1978), and Christopher Kirwan, *Augustine* (London: Routledge, 1989). J.N. Figgis, *The Political Aspects of St. Augustine's City of God* (London: Longmans, Green, 1921); Ronald H. Nash, *The Light of the Mind: St. Augustine's Theory of Knowledge* (Lexington: University Press of Kentucky, 1969); R.A. Markus, *Saeculum: History and Society in the Theology of St. Augustine* (Cambridge: Cambridge University Press, 1970); and Brian Stock, *Augustine the Reader* (Cambridge, MA; Harvard University

Press, 1996) deal with the specialized topics indicated by their respective titles. John M. Rist, *Augustine: Ancient Thought Baptized* (Cambridge: Cambridge University Press, 1994) explores the connections between Augustine and Platonic thought. For collections of essays, see M.C. D'Arcy et al., *Saint Augustine* (New York: Meridian, 1957), and R.A. Markus, ed., *Augustine: A Collection of Critical Essays* (Garden City, NY: Anchor, Doubleday, 1972).

CONFESSIONS (in part)

Book VIII—Conversion

5, 10. . . . It was no iron chain imposed by anyone else that fettered me, but the iron of my own will. The enemy had my power of willing in his clutches, and from it had forged a chain to bind me. The truth is that disordered lust springs from a perverted will; when lust is pandered to, a habit is formed; when habit is not checked, it hardens into compulsion. These were like interlinking rings forming what I have described as a chain, and my harsh servitude used it to keep me under duress.

A new will had begun to emerge in me, the will to worship you disinterestedly and enjoy you, O God, our only sure felicity; but it was not yet capable of surmounting that earlier will strengthened by inveterate custom. And so the two wills fought it out—the old and the new, the one carnal, the other spiritual—and·in their struggle tore my soul apart.

*   *   *

8, 19. Within the house of my spirit the violent conflict raged on, the quarrel with my soul that I had so powerfully provoked in our secret dwelling, my heart, and at the height of it I rushed to Alypius with my mental anguish plain upon my face. "What is happening to us?" I exclaimed. "What does this mean? What did you make of it? The untaught are rising up and taking heaven by Storm, while we with all our dreary teachings are still groveling in this world of flesh and blood! Are we ashamed to follow, just because they have taken the lead, yet not ashamed of lacking the courage even to follow?" Some such words as these I spoke, and then my frenzy tore me away from him, while he regarded me in silent bewilderment. Unusual, certainly, was my speech, but my brow, cheeks and eyes, my flushed countenance and the cadences of my voice expressed my mind more fully than the words I uttered.

Adjacent to our lodgings was a small garden. We were free to make use of it as well as of the house, for our host, who owned the house, did not live there. The tumult in my breast had swept me away to this place, where no one would interfere with the blazing dispute I had engaged in with myself until it should be resolved. What the out-

Saint Augustine, *Confessions*, Book VIII (5, 8–12) and XI (14–28), translated by Maria Boulding (New York: New City Press, 1997). ©1997 by the Augustinian Heritage Institute.

come would be you knew, not I. All I knew was that I was going mad, but for the sake of my sanity, and dying that I might live, aware of the evil that I was but unaware of the good I was soon to become. So I went out into the garden and Alypius followed at my heels; my privacy was not infringed by his presence, and, in any case, how could he abandon me in that state? We sat down as far as possible from the house. I was groaning in spirit and shaken by violent anger because I could form no resolve to enter into a covenant with you, though in my bones I knew that this was what I ought to do, and everything in me lauded such a course to the skies. It was a journey not to be undertaken by ship or carriage or on foot, nor need it take me even that short distance I had walked from the house to the place where we were sitting; for to travel—and more, to reach journey's end—was nothing else but to want to go there, but to want it valiantly and with all my heart, not to whirl and toss this way and that a will half crippled by the struggle, as part of it rose up to walk while part sank down.

20. While this vacillation was at its most intense many of my bodily gestures were of the kind that people sometimes want to perform but cannot, either because the requisite limbs are missing, or because they are bound and restricted, or paralyzed through illness, or in some other way impeded. If I tore out my hair, battered my forehead, entwined my fingers and clasped them round my knee, I did so because I wanted to. I might have wanted to but found myself unable, if my limbs had not been mobile enough to obey. So then, there were plenty of actions that I performed where willing was not the same thing as being able; yet I was not doing the one thing that was incomparably more desirable to me, the thing that I would be able to do as soon as I willed, because as soon as I willed—why, then, I would be willing it! For in this sole instance the faculty to act and the will to act precisely coincide, and the willing is already the doing. Yet this was not happening. My body was more ready to obey the slightest whim of my soul in the matter of moving my limbs, than the soul was to obey its own command in carrying out this major volition, which was to be accomplished within the will alone.

9, 21. How did this bizarre situation arise, how develop? May your mercy shed light on my inquiry, so that perhaps an answer may be found in the mysterious punishments meted out to humankind, those utterly baffling pains that afflict the children of Adam. How then did this bizarre situation arise, how develop? The mind commands the body and is instantly obeyed; the mind commands itself, and meets with resistance. When the mind orders the hand to move, so smooth is the compliance that command can scarcely be distinguished from execution; yet the mind is mind, while the hand is body. When the mind issues its command that the mind itself should will something (and the mind so commanded is no other than itself), it fails to do so. How did this bizarre situation arise, how develop? As I say, the mind commands itself to will something: it would not be giving the order if it did not want this thing; yet it does not do what it commands.

Evidently, then, it does not want this thing with the whole of itself, and therefore the command does not proceed from an undivided mind. Inasmuch as it issues the command, it does will it, but inasmuch as the command is not carried out, it does not will it. What the will is ordering is that a certain volition should exist, and this volition is not some alien thing, but its very self. Hence it cannot be giving the order with its whole self. It cannot be identical with that thing which it is commanding to come into existence, for if it were whole and entire it would not command itself to be, since it would be already.

This partial willing and partial non-willing is thus not so bizarre, but a sickness of the mind, which cannot rise with its whole self on the wings of truth because it is heavily burdened by habit. There are two wills, then, and neither is the whole: what one has the other lacks.

10, 22. Some there are who on perceiving two wills engaged in deliberation assert that in us there are two natures, one good, the other evil, each with a mind of its own. Let them perish from your presence, O God, as perish all who talk wildly and lead our minds astray. They are evil themselves as long as they hold these opinions, yet these same people will be good if they embrace true opinions and assent to true teaching, and so merit the apostle's commendation, You were darkness once, but now you are light in the Lord. The trouble is that they want to be light not in the Lord but in themselves, with their notion that the soul is by nature divine, and so they have become denser darkness still, because by their appalling arrogance they have moved further away from you, the true Light, who enlighten everyone who comes into the world. I warn these people, Take stock of what you are saying, and let it shame you; but once draw near to him and be illumined, and your faces will not blush with shame.

When I was making up my mind to serve the Lord my God at last, as I had long since purposed, I was the one who wanted to follow that course, and I was the one who wanted not to. I was the only one involved. I neither wanted it wholeheartedly nor turned from it wholeheartedly. I was at odds with myself, and fragmenting myself. This disintegration was occurring without my consent, but what it indicated was not the presence in me of a mind belonging to some alien nature but the punishment undergone by my own. In this sense, and this sense only, it was not I who brought it about, but the sin that dwelt within me as penalty for that other sin committed with greater freedom;* for I was a son of Adam.

23. Moreover, if we were to take the number of conflicting urges to signify the number of natures present in us, we should have to assume that there are not two, but many. If someone is trying to make up his mind whether to go to a Manichean conventicle or to the theater, the Manichees declare, "There you are, there's the evidence for two natures: the good one is dragging him our way, the bad one is pulling him back in the other direction. How else explain this dithering between contradictory wills?" But I regard both as bad, the one that leads him to them and the one that lures him back to the theater. They, on the contrary, think that an inclination toward them can only be good.

But consider this: suppose one of our people is deliberating, and as two desires clash he is undecided whether to go to the theater or to our church, will not our opponents too be undecided what attitude to take? Either they will have to admit that it is good will that leads a person to our church, just as good as that which leads to theirs the people who are initiated into their sacred rites and trapped there—and this they are unwilling to admit; or they will conclude that two evil natures and two bad minds are pitted against each other within one person, in which case their habitual assertion of one good and one evil nature will be erroneous; or, finally, they will be brought round to the truth and no longer deny that when a person is deliberating there is but one soul, thrown into turmoil by divergent impulses.

24. When, therefore, they observe two conflicting impulses within one person, let them stop saying that two hostile minds are at war, one good, the other evil, and that these derive from two hostile substances and two hostile principles. For you are

*[That is, by Adam. Augustine uses the comparative to suggest a relative freedom enjoyed by Adam, superior to our own but short of perfect freedom. He was to spell out the distinction later in *Correction and Grace* XII, 33 between *posse non peccare* (the ability not to sin, Adam's privilege), and *non posse peccare* (the perfection of freedom in heaven)].

true, O God, and so you chide and rebuke them and prove them wrong. The choice may lie between two impulses that are both evil, as when a person is debating whether to murder someone with poison or a dagger; whether to annex this part of another man's property or that, assuming he cannot get both; whether to buy himself pleasure by extravagant spending or hoard his money out of avarice; whether to go to the circus or the theater if both performances are on the same day—and I would even add a third possibility: whether to go and steal from someone else's house while he has the chance, and a fourth as well: whether to commit adultery while he is about it. All these impulses may occur together, at exactly the same time, and all be equally tempting, but they cannot all be acted upon at once. The mind is then rent apart by the plethora of desirable objects as four inclinations, or even more, do battle among themselves; yet the Manichees do not claim that there are as many disparate substances in us as this.

The same holds true for good impulses. I would put these questions to them: Is it good to find delight in a reading from the apostle? To enjoy the serenity of a psalm? To discuss the gospel? To each point they will reply, "Yes, that is good." Where does that leave us? If all these things tug at our will with equal force, and all together at the same time, will not these divergent inclinations put a great strain on the human heart, as we deliberate which to select? All are good, but they compete among themselves until one is chosen, to which the will, hitherto distracted between many options, may move as a united whole. So too when the joys of eternity call us from above, and pleasure in temporal prosperity holds us fast below, our one soul is in no state to embrace either with its entire will. Claimed by truth for the one, to the other clamped by custom, the soul is torn apart in its distress.

11, 25. Such was the sickness in which I agonized, blaming myself more sharply than ever, turning and twisting in my chain as I strove to tear free from it completely, for slender indeed was the bond that still held me. But hold me it did. In my secret heart you stood by me, Lord, redoubling the lashes of fear and shame in the severity of your mercy, lest I give up the struggle and that slender, fragile bond that remained be not broken after all, but thicken again and constrict me more tightly. "Let it be now," I was saying to myself. "Now is the moment, let it be now," and merely by saying this I was moving toward the decision. I would almost achieve it, but then fall just short; yet I did not slip right down to my starting-point, but stood aside to get my breath back. Then I would make a fresh attempt, and now I was almost there, almost there . . . I was touching the goal, grasping it . . . and then I was not there, not touching, not grasping it. I shrank from dying to death and living to life, for ingrained evil was more powerful in me than new-grafted good. The nearer it came, that moment when I would be changed, the more it pierced me with terror. Dismayed, but not quite dislodged, I was left hanging.

26. The frivolity of frivolous aims, the futility of futile pursuits, these things that had been my cronies of long standing, still held me back, plucking softly at my garment of flesh and murmuring in my ear, "Do you mean to get rid of us? Shall we never be your companions again after that moment . . . never . . . never again? From that time onward so-and-so will be forbidden to you, all your life long." And what was it that they were reminding me of by those words, "so-and-so," O my God, what were they bringing to my mind? May your mercy banish such memories far from me! What foul deeds were they not hinting at, what disgraceful exploits! But now their voices were less than half as loud, for they no longer confronted me directly to argue their case, but muttered behind my back and slyly tweaked me as I walked away, trying to make me look back. Yet they did slow me down, for I could not bring myself to

tear free and shake them off and leap across to that place whither I was summoned, while aggressive habit still taunted me: "Do you imagine you will be able to live without these things?"

27. The taunts had begun to sound much less persuasive, however; for a revelation was coming to me from that country toward which I was facing, but into which I trembled to cross. There I beheld the chaste, dignified figure of Continence. Calm and cheerful was her manner, though modest, pure and honorable her charm as she coaxed me to come and hesitate no longer, stretching kindly hands to welcome and embrace me, hands filled with a wealth of heartening examples. A multitude of boys and girls were there, a great concourse of youth and persons of every age, venerable widows and women grown old in their virginity, and in all of them I saw this that this same Continence was by no means sterile, but the fruitful mother of children conceived in joy from you, her Bridegroom. She was smiling at me, but with a challenging smile, as though to say, "Can you not do what these men have done, these women? Could any of them achieve it by their own strength, without the Lord their God? He it was, the Lord their God, who granted me to them. Why try to stand by yourself, only to lose your footing? Cast yourself on him and do not be afraid: he will not step back and let you fall. Cast yourself upon him trustfully; he will support and heal you." And I was bitterly ashamed, because I could still hear the murmurs of those frivolities, and I was still in suspense, still hanging back. Again she appealed to me, as though urging, "Close your ears against those unclean parts of you which belong to the earth and let them be put to death. They tell you titillating tales, but have nothing to do with the law of the Lord your God."

All this argument in my heart raged only between myself and myself. Alypius stood fast at my side, silently awaiting the outcome of my unprecedented agitation.

12, 28. But as this deep meditation dredged all my wretchedness up from the secret profundity of my being and heaped it all together before the eyes of my heart, a huge storm blew up within me and brought on a heavy rain of tears. In order to pour them out unchecked with the sobs that accompanied them I arose and left Alypius, for solitude seemed to me more suitable for the business of weeping. I withdrew far enough to ensure that his presence—even his—would not be burdensome to me. This was my need, and he understood it, for I think I had risen to my feet and blurted out something, my voice already choked with tears. He accordingly remained, in stunned amazement, at the place where we had been sitting. I flung myself down somehow under a fig-tree and gave free rein to the tears that burst from my eyes like rivers, as an acceptable sacrifice to you. Many things I had to say to you, and the gist of them, though not the precise words, was: "O Lord, how long? How long? Will you be angry for ever? Do not remember our age-old sins." For by these I was conscious of being held prisoner. I uttered cries of misery: "Why must I go on saying, 'Tomorrow . . . tomorrow'? Why not now? Why not put an end to my depravity this very hour?"

29. I went on talking like this and weeping in the intense bitterness of my broken heart. Suddenly I heard a voice from a house nearby—perhaps a voice of some boy or girl, I do not know—singing over and over again, "Pick it up and read, pick it up and read." My expression immediately altered and I began to think hard whether children ordinarily repeated a ditty like this in any sort of game, but I could not recall ever having heard it anywhere else. I stemmed the flood of tears and rose to my feet, believing that this could be nothing other than a divine command to open the Book and read the first passage I chanced upon; for I had heard the story of how Antony had been in-

structed by a gospel text. He happened to arrive while the gospel was being read, and took the words to be addressed to himself when he heard, "Go and sell all you possess and give the money to the poor: you will have treasure in heaven. Then come, follow me" [Matt. 19:21]. So he was promptly converted to you by this plainly divine message. Stung into action, I returned to the place where Alypius was sitting, for on leaving it I had put down there the book of the apostle's letters. I snatched it up, opened it and read in silence the passage on which my eyes first lighted: "Not in dissipation and drunkenness, nor in debauchery and lewdness, nor in arguing and jealousy; but put on the Lord Jesus Christ, and make no provision for the flesh or the gratification of your desires" [Rom. 13:13–14]. I had no wish to read further, nor was there need. No sooner had I reached the end of the verse than the light of certainty flooded my heart and all dark shades of doubt fled away.

30. I closed the book, marking the place with a finger between the leaves or by some other means, and told Alypius what had happened. My face was peaceful now. He in return told me what had been happening to him without my knowledge. He asked to see what I had read: I showed him, but he looked further than my reading had taken me. I did not know what followed, but the next verse was, "Make room for the person who is weak in faith." He referred this text to himself and interpreted it to me. Confirmed by this admonition he associated himself with my decision and good purpose without any upheaval or delay, for it was entirely in harmony with his own moral character, which for a long time now had been far, far better than mine.

We went indoors and told my mother, who was overjoyed. When we related to her how it had happened she was filled with triumphant delight and blessed you, who have power to do more than we ask or understand, for she saw that you had granted her much more in my regard than she had been wont to beg of you in her wretched, tearful groaning. Many years earlier you had shown her a vision of me standing on the rule of faith; and now indeed I stood there, no longer seeking a wife or entertaining any worldly hope, for you had converted me to yourself. In so doing you had also converted her grief into a joy far more abundant than she had desired, and much more tender and chaste than she could ever have looked to find in grandchildren from my flesh.

Book XI—Time and Eternity

14, 17. There was therefore never any time when you had not made anything, because you made time itself. And no phases of time are coeternal with you, for you abide, and if they likewise were to abide, they would not be time. For what is time? Who could find any quick or easy answer to that? Who could even grasp it in his thought clearly enough to put the matter into words? Yet is there anything to which we refer in conversation with more familiarity, any matter of more common experience, than time? And we know perfectly well what we mean when we speak of it, and understand just as well when we hear someone else refer to it. What, then, is time? If no one asks me, I know; if I want to explain it to someone who asks me, I do not know. I can state with confidence, however, that this much I do know: if nothing passed away there would be no past time; if there was nothing still on its way there would be no future time; and if nothing existed, there would be no present time.

God in Act of Creation, from a thirteenth-century French Bible. In the *Confessions,* Augustine argues that God created the world *ex nihilo* (out of nothing) and that God is outside of time. *(Corbis-Bettmann)*

Now, what about those two times, past and future: in what sense do they have real being, if the past no longer exists and the future does not exist yet? As for present time, if that were always present and never slipped away into the past, it would not be time at all; it would be eternity. If, therefore, the present's only claim to be called "time" is that it is slipping away into the past, how can we assert that this thing *is,* when its only title to being is that it will soon cease to be? In other words, we cannot really say that time exists, except because it tends to non-being.*

15, 18. Nonetheless we speak of a long time or a short time, and we do so only of time past or time in the future. For example, we call a hundred years ago a long time in the past, and likewise a hundred years hence a long time in the future; but we call—say—ten days ago a short time past, and ten days hence a short time in the future. But on what grounds can something that does not exist be called long or short? The past no longer exists and the future does not exist yet. We ought not, therefore, to say, "That is a long time," but, when speaking of the past, we should say, "That was long," and of the future, "That will be long."

O my Lord, my light, will your truth not deride us humans for speaking so? This long time in the past: was it long when it was already past, or earlier than that, when it was still present? If the latter, yes, then it might have been long, because there was something to be long; but if it was already past it no longer existed, and therefore could not have been long, since it was not in existence at all. We ought not, therefore, to say, "That era in the past was a long one," for we shall not find anything that was long, for since that point at which it became past time it has no longer had any being. Rather, we ought to say, "That era of time was long while present," because while it was present it was long. It had not yet passed away and so passed out of existence, and so there was something there which could be long. But when it passed away it ceased to be long at that very point when it ceased to be at all.

19. Now, human mind, let us consider whether present time can be long, as you seem to think it can, since you have been granted the power to be aware of duration and to measure it. Answer my questions, then. Is the present century a long period of time? Before you say yes, reflect whether a hundred years can be present. If the first of them is running its course, that year is present, but ninety-nine others are future and therefore as yet have no being. If the second year is running its course, one year is already past, another is present, and the remainder are still to come. In the same fashion we may represent any one of the intervening years of the century as present, and always the years that preceded it will be past, and those that follow it future. Evidently, then, a hundred years cannot be present.

Well then, consider whether the one current year at least can be present. If we are in the first month of it, the other months are in the future; if we are in the second, the first month is already past and the rest do not yet exist. Even the current year, then, is not present in its totality, and if it is not present in its totality, the year is not present; for a year consists of twelve months, and while any one of them is current that one is present, but the others are either past or future.

But we must go further, and notice that the current month is not in fact present, because only one day of it is: if we are on the first day, the rest are future; if on the last,

---

*[This is the heart of the matter for Augustine. He pursues the argument relentlessly throughout the rest of this Book XI, revealing time as something elusive that slips the more swiftly through our fingers the more we try to analyze it or justify our habit of measuring it. The inexorable rush of time toward non-being reveals the fragility of time-bound, time-conditioned creatures, whose only refuge from their native nothingness is the eternity of God.]

the others are past; if on any day in the middle, we shall be midway between past and future days.

20. Look where this leaves us. We saw earlier that present time was the only one of the three that might properly be called long, and now this present time has been pared down to the span of a bare day. But let us take the discussion further, because not even a single day is present all at once. It is made up of night hours and day hours, twenty-four in all. From the standpoint of the first hour all the rest are still future; the last hour looks to all those already past; and any one we pick in between has some before it, others to follow. Even a single hour runs its course through fleeing minutes: whatever portion of it has flown is now past, and what remains is future. If we can conceive of a moment in time which cannot be further divided into even the tiniest of minute particles, that alone can be rightly termed the present; yet even this flies by from the future into the past with such haste that it seems to last no time at all. Even if it has some duration, that too is divisible into past and future; hence the present is reduced to vanishing-point.

What kind of time, then, can be referred to as "a long time"? Future time, perhaps? Then we must not say, "That is a long time," because there is as yet nothing to be long; we will have to say, "That will be long." But when will it be so? If at the point of speaking that period is still in the future, it will not be long, because nothing yet exists to be long; if, however, at the moment when we speak it has begun to exist by emerging from the non-existent future, and so has become present, so that there is something in existence to be long, then this present time proclaims itself incapable of being long for the reasons already discussed.

16, 21. All the same, Lord, we are conscious of intervals of time, and we compare them with each other and pronounce some longer, others shorter. We also calculate by how much this period of time is longer or shorter than that other, and we report that the one is twice or three times as long as the other, or that it is the same length. But when we measure periods of time by our awareness of them, what we measure is passing time. Could anyone measure past periods that no longer exist, or future periods that do not yet exist? Only someone who is bold enough to claim that what has no being can be measured. So then, while time is passing it can be felt and measured, but once past it cannot, because it no longer exists.

17, 22. I am asking questions, Father, not making assertions: rule me, O my God, and shepherd me. For who would make so bold as to tell me that there are not really three tenses or times—past, present and future—as we learned as children and as we in our turn have taught our children, but that there is only present, since the other two do not exist? Or is the truth perhaps that they do exist, but that when a future thing becomes present it emerges from some hiding-place, and then retreats into another hiding-place when it moves from the present into the past? Where, otherwise, did soothsayers see future events, if they do not yet exist? What has no being cannot be seen. Nor would people who tell stories about the past be telling true tales if they had no vision of those past events in their minds; and if the events in question were non-existent they could not be seen. The future and the past must exist, then?

18, 23. Allow me, Lord, to press the question further: O my hope, do not let me lose the thread. If future and past things do exist, I want to know where they are. If this is not yet within my compass, I do know at any rate that, wherever they are, they are not there as future or past, but as present. For if in that place too future things are future, they are not there yet; and if there too past things are past, they are there no longer. Clearly, then, wherever they are and whatever they are, they can only be present. Nonetheless, when a true account is given of past events, what is brought forth from the memory is not the events themselves, which have passed away, but words formed from images of those events which as they happened and went on their way left some kind of traces in the mind through the medium of the senses. This is the case with my childhood, which no longer exists: it belongs to past time which exists no longer, but when I recall it and tell the story I contemplate the image of it which is still in my memory.

Whether something similar occurs in the prediction of future events, in that the seer has a presentiment of images which exist already, I confess, O my God, that I do not know. But this I undoubtedly do know, that we often plan our future actions beforehand, and that the plans in our mind are present to us, though the action we are planning has as yet no being, because it is future. When we set about it, and begin to do what we were planning, then the action will have real being, because then it will be not future but present.

24. However the mysterious presentiment of future events may be explained, only what exists can be seen. But what already exists is not future but present. Therefore when it is claimed that future events are seen, it is not that these things are seen in themselves, because they have as yet no existence, being still future. It may be, however, that their causes, or signs of them, are seen, because these already exist; hence they are not future but present to the people who discern them, and from them future events may take shape in the mind and can be foretold. These ideas in the mind also exist already, and can be inwardly contemplated by people who predict the future.

Let me take an example from a wealth of such occurrences. I watch the dawn, and I give advance notice that the sun is about to rise. What I am looking at is present; what I foretell is future. Not that the sun is future, of course—no, that exists already, but its rising is future; it has not yet happened, yet unless I could imagine the sunrise in my mind, as I do now while I speak of it, I would be unable to forecast it. The dawn, which I am watching in the sky, is not the sunrise, but only precedes it; and similarly the picture I have in my mind is not the sunrise either. But these two realities are present and open to observation, so that the future event can be announced before its time.

We must conclude, then, that future events have no being as yet, and if they have no being yet they do not exist, and if they do not exist it is absolutely impossible for anyone to see them. But they can be predicted on the basis of other things which are already present and hence can be seen.

19, 25. You are the king of your creation; tell me, then: how do you instruct people's minds about the future? You did so teach the prophets. What method can you adopt for teaching what is future, when to you nothing is future at all? Would it be better to say that you teach what is present but has a bearing on the future? Yes, because what does not exist obviously cannot be taught. This method of yours is far above the reach of my mind; it is too much for me and of myself I cannot see it, but I will see it with your help, when you grant me this gift, O gracious light of my secret eyes.

20, 26. What is now clear and unmistakable is that neither things past nor things future have any existence, and that it is inaccurate to say, "There are three tenses or times: past, present and future," though it might properly be said, "There are three tenses or times: the present of past things, the present of present things, and the present of future things." These are three realities in the mind, but nowhere else as far as I can see, for the present of past things is memory, the present of present things is attention, and the present of future things is expectation. If we are allowed to put it that way, I do see three tenses or times, and admit that they are three. Very well, then, let the phrase pass: "There are three tenses or times: past, present and future," as common usage improperly has it: let people go on saying this. I do not mind, nor will I put up any opposition or offer correction, provided we understand what we are saying, and do not assert that either the future or the past exists now. There are few things, in fact, which we state accurately; far more we express loosely, but what we mean is understood.

21, 27. I said just now* that we measure periods of time as they pass, so as to declare this interval twice as long as that, or this equal to that, and report anything else about segments of time that our measurements have revealed. It follows, then, that we measure these intervals of time as they are passing by, as I remarked, and if anyone asks me, "How do you know that?" I must be allowed to reply, "I know it because we do in fact measure them; but what does not exist we cannot measure, and past and future do not exist." But how can we measure present time, when it has no extension?** We can only hope to measure it as it passes by, because once it has passed by there will be no measuring; it will not exist to be measured.

But when it is measured, where does it come from, by what path does it pass, and whither go? Where from, if not from the future? By what path, if not the present? Whither, if not into the past? It comes, then, from what is not yet real, travels through what occupies no space, and is bound for what is no longer real. But what are we trying to measure, if not time that does have some extension? We speak of "half as long," "double the time," "three times as long," "equal in length," and make similar statements about time only in reference to extended time, or duration. Where then is this duration which will give us a chance to measure passing time? In the future, whence it has come to pass us by? But we do not measure what does not yet exist. In the present, perhaps, through which it passes on its way? But where there is no extension we cannot measure. In the past, then, to which it has gone? But we cannot measure what no longer exists.

22, 28. My mind is on fire to solve this most intricate enigma. O Lord, my God, my good Father, through Christ I beg you not to shut against me the door to these truths, so familiar yet so mysterious. Do not slam the door in the face of my desire, nor forbid me entrance to that place where I may watch these things grow luminous as your mercy sheds its light upon them, Lord. To whom should I put my questions about them? And to whom should I confess my stupidity with greater profit than to you, who do not weary of my intense, burning interest in your scriptures? Give me what I love; for I love indeed, and this love you have given me. Give this to me, Father, for you truly know how to give good gifts to your children; give me this gift, for I have only just begun to understand, and the labor is too much for me until you open the door. Through Christ I implore you, in the name of that holy of holies, let no noisy person stand in my way. I too have believed, and so I too speak. This is my hope, for this I live: to contemplate the delight of the Lord. See how old you have made my days; they are slipping away and I know not how.

We speak of one time and another time, of this period of time or that; we ask, "How long did that man speak?" or "How long did he take to do it?" We say, "What a long time it is since I saw so-and-so," and "This syllable has twice the length of that short one." We say these things and listen to them, we are understood and we understand. They are perfectly plain and fully familiar, yet at the same time deeply mysterious, and we still need to discover their meaning.

23, 29. I was once told by a certain learned man that the movements of the sun, moon and stars themselves constitute time. I did not agree with him. Why, in that case,

*[That is, in XI, 16, 21.]
**[That is, the ideal present is a point, which has position but no magnitude.]

182

should not the movements of all corporeal things constitute time? Suppose the luminaries of heaven were to halt, but a potter's wheel went on turning, would there not still be time by which we could measure those rotations, and say either that all of them took the same time, or (if the speed of the wheel varied) that some were of longer duration, others shorter? And when we said this, would we too not be speaking within time; and in the words we used, would there not be some long syllables and some short; and why could that be said of them, unless because some of them had taken a longer time to pronounce than others?

Through this small thing, O God, grant our human minds insight into the principles common to small things and great. The stars and the other luminaries in the sky are there to mark our times and days and years. Yes, granted; but as I would not assert that the revolution of that little wooden wheel itself constituted a day, so my learned informant on the other hand had no business to say that its gyrations did not occupy a space of time.

30. I want to know the essence and nature of time, whereby we measure the movement of bodies and say, for instance, that one movement lasts twice as long as another. Now I have a question to ask. Taking the word "day" to apply not only to the period of sunlight on earth—day as opposed to night, that is—but to the sun's whole course from the east and back to the east again, in the sense that we say, "So many days elapsed," meaning to include the nights, and not reckoning the nights as extra time over and above the days; taking it, then, that the movement of the sun in its circular course from the east back to the east completes a day, this is my question: is it the movement itself that constitutes a day? Or the time it takes? Or both? If the movement constitutes a day, then it would still be one day if the sun were to achieve its circuit in an interval of time equivalent to a single hour. If it is the time it takes, there would not be a day if the space between one sunrise and the next were as short as an hour; the sun would have to go round twenty-four times to make up a day. If both were required complete circuit of the sun and the customary duration of this—we could not call it a day if the sun traveled through its whole circuit in the space of an hour, nor could we if the sun stopped and as much time elapsed as it usually takes to run its whole course from morning to morning.

My question now is not, therefore, what is it that we call a day, but what is time itself, the time whereby we would be able to measure the sun's revolution and say that it had been completed in only half the usual time, if the circuit had occupied only that space of time represented by twelve hours? We could compare the two periods in terms of time and say that one was twice the length of the other, and this would still be possible even if the sun sometimes took the single period, and sometimes the double, to circle from the east and back to the east again. Let no one tell me, then, that time is simply the motion of the heavenly bodies. After all, at the prayer of a certain man the sun halted so that he could press home the battle to victory. The sun stood still, but time flowed on its way, and that fight had all the time it needed to be carried through to the finish.

I see, therefore, that time is a kind of strain or tension. But do I really see it? Or only seem to see? You will show me, O Light, O Truth.

24, 31. Are you commanding me to agree with someone who says that time is the motion of a body? You do not so command me. No corporeal object moves except within time: this is what I hear; this is what you tell me. But that a corporeal object's movement is itself time I do not hear; this you do not say. When a body moves, I measure in terms of time how long it is in motion, from the moment when it begins until its motion ceases. If I did not notice when it began, and it continues to move without my seeing when it stops, I cannot measure the time, except perhaps the interval between the moment when I began to watch and that when I ceased to observe it. If my observation is prolonged, I can only say that the process went on for a long time; I cannot say exactly how long, because when we add a definite indication of a length of time we do so by reference to some agreed standard. "This is as long as that," we say; or "This is twice as long as that other," or something similar. If, on the other hand, we have been able to note the position of some corporeal object when it moves (or when parts of it move, if, for example, it is being turned on a lathe), and we have observed its starting-point and its point of arrival, then we are able to state how much time has elapsed while the movement of the object was effected from the one place to the other, or how long it has taken to revolve on its axis.

Therefore if the motion of an object is one thing, and the standard by which we measure its duration another, is it not obvious which of the two has the stronger claim to be called time? Moreover, if the motion is irregular, so that the object is sometimes moving and sometimes stationary, we measure not only its motion but also its static periods in terms of time, and say, "Its stationary periods were equivalent in length to its phases of motion," or "It was stationary for two or three times as long as it was in motion," or whatever else our calculation has ascertained or estimated roughly—more or less, as we customarily say. Clearly, then, time is not the movement of any corporeal object.

25, 32. I confess to you, Lord, that even today I am still ignorant of what time is; but I praise you, Lord, for the fact that I know I am making this avowal within time, and for my realization that within time I am talking about time at such length, and that I know this "length" itself is long only because time has been passing all the while. But how can I know that, when I do not know what time is? Or perhaps I simply do not know how to articulate what I know? Woe is me, for I do not even know what I do not know!

Behold me here before you, O my God; see that I do not lie. As I speak, this is the true state of my heart. You, you alone, will light my lamp, O Lord; O my God, you will illumine my darkness.

26, 33. Am I not making a truthful confession to you when I praise you for my ability to measure time? But this must mean, O my God, that though I can measure it, I do not know what I am measuring! I measure the movement of a body in terms of time, but surely I am by that same calculation measuring time itself? Would it be possible for me to measure a body's motion, to calculate how long it lasts and how long the object takes to travel from here to there, without also measuring the time within which the motion occurs? With what, then, do I measure time itself? Do we measure a longer time by the standard of a shorter, as we use the cubit to measure the span of a crossbeam? That indeed seems to be how we measure the quantity of a long syllable by that of a short syllable, and decide that the former is twice as long. Similarly we measure the length of poems by the length of their lines, and the length of the lines by the length of the feet, and the length of each foot by the length of its syllables, and the length of a long syllable by that of a short syllable. We do not reckon by the number of pages— that would be to impose a spatial, not a temporal standard—but by the pronunciation as voices recite them and die away. We declare, "That is a lengthy poem, for it consists of so many lines; the lines are long, since each is composed of so many feet; the feet are long, since each extends over so many syllables; and a syllable is long, when it is twice the quantity of a short one."

But the mensuration of time by these methods yields no result that is absolute, since it may happen that the sound of a shorter line, spoken with a drawl, actually lasts longer than that of a longer one hurried over. The same holds for the whole poem, a foot, and a syllable.

I have therefore come to the conclusion that time is nothing other than tension: but tension of what, I do not know, and I would be very surprised if it is not tension of consciousness itself. What am I measuring, I beg you to tell me, my God, when I say in imprecise terms, "This is longer than that," or even, precisely, "This is twice that"? That I am measuring time, I know; but I am not measuring future time, because it does not yet exist, not present time, which is a point without extension, nor past time, which exists no more. What, then, am I measuring? Time as it passes by, but not once it has passed? That was what I said earlier.

27, 34. Stick to it, now, my mind, and pay close attention. God is our ally; and he made us, not we ourselves. Mark where truth brightens to the dawn!

Suppose now that a physical voice begins to sound . . . and goes on sounding . . . and is still sounding . . . and now stops. Now there is silence, and that voice is past and is a voice no longer. Before it sounded forth it was a future thing, so it could not be measured because it did not yet exist; neither can it be now, because it exists no more. Perhaps, then, it could be measured while it was sounding forth, because something did then exist that could be measured? But at that time it was not standing still; it was but a fleeting thing that was speeding on its way. Was it therefore any more measurable while sounding than before or after? Only as something transient was it extended over a period of time whereby it might be measured—only as transient, because the present moment has no duration. If it is argued that the sound could, nevertheless, be measured while it lasted, consider this: another voice begins to sound and is still sounding in a continuous, steady tone. Let us measure it, then, while it is sounding, for once it has fallen silent it will be a thing of the past, and nothing measurable will then exist. By all means let us measure it now, and state how long it lasts.

Ah, but it is still sounding, and there is no way of timing it except from its beginning, when the sound originated, to its end, when it ceases. Obviously we measure any interval of time from some inception to some ending. Hence the sound of a voice which has not yet finished cannot be measured in such a way that anyone can say how long or how short it is, nor can it be declared to be of the same length as something else, or half the length, or twice the length, or anything of the kind. But once finished, it will not exist. So by what criteria will it then be subject to measurement?

All the same we do measure periods of time, not periods which as yet have no being, nor those which have ceased to be, nor those which have no duration, nor those which have no terminus. We measure neither future nor past nor present nor passing time. Yet time we do measure.

35. Take the line, *Deus, creator omnium.** This line consists of eight syllables, short and long alternating. The four short ones—the first, third, fifth and seventh—are thus half the length of the four long ones—the second, fourth, sixth and eighth. Each of these latter lasts twice as long as each of the former; I have only to pronounce the line to report that this is the case, insofar as clear sense-perception can verify it. Relying on this unmistakable evidence of my ear I measure each long syllable by the criterion of a short one, and perceive that it is twice the quantity. But the syllables make themselves heard in succession; and if the first is short and the second long, how am I to hold on to the short one, how am I to apply it to the long one as a measuring-rod in order to discover that the long one has twice the quantity, when the long one does not begin to

*[Ambrose's evening hymn: "God, Creator of all."]

185

sound until the short one has ceased? Am I to measure the long one while it is present? Impossible, because I cannot measure something unfinished. But its completion is its passing away, so what now exists for me to measure? Where is the short syllable I was going to use as a standard? What has become of the long one I want to measure? Both have made their sound, and flown away, and passed by, and exist no more; yet I do my calculation and confidently assert that insofar as the testimony of my trained ear can be trusted, the short is half the long, the long twice the short; and obviously I am speaking about a space of time. I can only do this because the syllables have passed away and are completed. Evidently, then, what I am measuring is not the syllables themselves, which no longer exist, but something in my memory, something fixed and permanent there.

36. In you, my mind, I measure time. Do not interrupt me by clamoring that time has objective existence, nor hinder yourself with the hurly-burly of your impressions. In you, I say, do I measure time. What I measure is the impression which passing phenomena leave in you, which abides after they have passed by: that is what I measure as a present reality, not the things that passed by so that the impression could be formed. The impression itself is what I measure when I measure intervals of time. Hence either time is this impression, or what I measure is not time.

What about when we measure silences, and say that this silent pause lasted as long as that sound? Do we not strain our thought to retain the feeling of a sound's duration, as though it were still audible, so as to be able to estimate the intervals of silence in relation to the whole space of time in question? Without any articulate word or even opening our mouths we go over in our minds poems, their lines, a speech, and we assess their developmental patterns and the time they occupied in relation to one another; and our estimate is no different from what it would have been if we had been reciting them aloud.

Suppose a person wishes to utter a fairly long sound, and has determined beforehand in his own mind how long it is to be. He must have first thought through that period of time in silence and committed the impression of it to memory; then he begins to utter the sound, which continues until it reaches the predetermined end. Or rather, it does not "continue," because the sound is evidently both something already heard and something still to be heard, for the part of it already completed is sound that has been, but the part that remains is sound still to be. Thus it is carried through as our present awareness drags what is future into the past. As the future dwindles the past grows, until the future is used up altogether and the whole thing is past.

28, 37. But how can a future which does not yet exist dwindle or be used up, and how can a past which no longer exists grow? Only because there are three realities in the mind which conducts this operation. The mind expects, and attends, and remembers, so that what it expects passes by way of what it attends to into what it remembers. No one, surely, would deny that the future is as yet non-existent? Yet an expectation of future events does exist in the mind. And would anyone deny that the past has ceased to be? Yet the memory of past events still lives on in the mind. And who would deny that the present has no duration, since it passes in an instant? Yet our attention does endure, and through our attention what is still to be makes its way into the state where it is no more. It is not, therefore, future time which is long, for it does not exist; a long future is simply an expectation of the future which represents it as long. Nor is the past a long period of time, because it does not exist at all; a long past is simply a memory of the past which represents it as long.

38. Suppose I have to recite a poem I know by heart. Before I begin, my expectation is directed to the whole poem, but once I have begun, whatever I have plucked

away from the domain of expectation and tossed behind me to the past becomes the business of my memory, and the vital energy of what I am doing is in tension between the two of them: it strains toward my memory because of the part I have already recited, and to my expectation on account of the part I still have to speak. But my attention is present all the while, for the future is being channeled through it to become the past. As the poem goes on and on, expectation is curtailed and memory prolonged, until expectation is entirely used up, when the whole completed action has passed into memory.

What is true of the poem as a whole is true equally of its individual stanzas and syllables. The same is true of the whole long performance, in which this poem may be a single item. The same thing happens in the entirety of a person's life, of which all his actions are parts; and the same in the entire sweep of human history, the parts of which are individual human lives.

BOETHIUS
ca. A.D. 480–ca. A.D. 524

Anicius Manlius Severinus Boethius was the son of a Roman high-government official. Possibly educated in Athens or Alexandria, Boethius had a special interest in the writings of Plato and Aristotle. His intention was to translate all their works into Latin and provide full commentary. He hoped to show the essential unity between Plato and Aristotle, but he finished only Aristotle's logical works. In 510, Boethius became consul and first minister to King Theodoric, the Ostrogothic ruler of Italy. Boethius served the next twelve years in government, wrote commentaries on Porphyry and Cicero, and began his work on Plato and Aristotle. Boethius's sons were named consuls in 522, and Boethius was made the important "master of the offices." But within a year, tragedy struck. Boethius was accused of treason, imprisoned, and executed sometime around 524. The specific charges are not known, but religious differences were probably involved. Theodoric followed the teachings of Arius (ca. A.D. 256–336) that Jesus Christ was neither coeternal with God the Father nor of the same substance. Boethius, as a Catholic, accepted the conclusions of the Council of Nicea (A.D. 325), which condemned Arian theology.

While in prison, Boethius wrote his most famous work, *The Consolation of Philosophy*. Written as a dialogue between Boethius and Lady Philosophy, it begins with Boethius protesting innocence and complaining of God's injustice and fortune's caprice. Using arguments rooted in both Stoic and Platonic thought, Philosophy replies that fortune is indeed fickle, but that the highest Good is found not in circumstances but in God. The selection given here, translated by Richard Green, is from the final book of the *Consolation* and examines how God's foreknowledge is compatible with free will. Boethius asks how one could be free to perform an action if God knew *beforehand* what one would do. Using a conception of time similar to Augustine's in Book XI of the *Confessions,* Lady Philosophy explains that God is completely outside time. This means that God "sees all things in his eternal present as you see some things in your temporal present. . . . This divine foreknowledge does not change the nature and properties of things; it simply sees things present before it as they will later turn out to be in what we regard as the future." For example, just as I know what my son is doing now even though his action is free, so God can know what I will do tomorrow though I act freely—because for God tomorrow *is* now.

It may seem odd that a devout Catholic presented his final thoughts in Neoplatonic and Stoic terms, without any specifically Christian references. Yet Boethius's *magnum opus* was a source of great comfort to Christians in the Middle Ages for, as Étienne Gilson points out, "even when he is speaking only as a philosopher Boethius, thinks as a Christian."

*   *   *

For background work on Boethius, see Howard Rollin Patch, *The Tradition of Boethius: A Study of His Importance in Medieval Culture* (New York: Oxford University Press, 1935) and Helen Marjorie Barrett, *Boethius: Some Aspects of His Times and Work* (Cambridge: Cambridge University Press, 1940). Henry Chadwick, *Boethius: The Consolations of Music, Logic, Theology, and Philosophy* (Oxford: Clarendon Press, 1981) and Edmund Reiss, *Boethius* (Boston: Twayne, 1982) study Boethius's writings, whereas Ralph M. McInerny, *Boethius and Aquinas* (Washington, DC: Catholic University of America Press, 1990) shows his influence on Thomas Aquinas. For collections of essays, see Michael Masi, ed., *Boethius and the Liberal Arts: A Collection of Essays* (Las Vegas, NV: Peter Lang, 1981), and Margaret Gibson, ed., *Boethius, His Life, Thought, and Influence* (Oxford: Blackwell, 1981).

In recent years, there has been renewed interest in the problems posed by Boethius's conception of God's timelessness and foreknowledge. Paul Helm, *Eternal God: A Study of God Without Time* (Oxford: Clarendon Press, 1988), for example, argues in favor of Boethius's position, whereas Richard Swinburne, *The Coherence of Theism* (Oxford: Clarendon Press, 1977) and Stephen T. Davis, *Logic and the Nature of God* (Grand Rapids, MI: Eerdmans, 1983) oppose it. Much of the most interesting work in this area is found only in journals such as the *Journal of Philosophy* and *Faith and Philosophy.*

Theodoric exiles Boethius from Rome to Padua, 1521, woodcut. Boethius was consul and first minister to King Theodoric, the Ostrogothic ruler of Italy. But in 522 Boethius was accused of treason, imprisoned, and executed sometime around 524. The specific charges are not known, but probably involved religious differences between the Catholic Boethius and the Arian Theodoric. *(Library of Congress/Instructional Resources Corp.)*

THE CONSOLATION OF PHILOSOPHY
(in part)

BOOK V

CHAPTER 6: PHILOSOPHY SOLVES THE PROBLEM OF PROVIDENCE AND FREE WILL BY DISTINGUISHING BETWEEN SIMPLE AND CONDITIONAL NECESSITY

"Since, as we have shown, whatever is known is known according to the nature of the knower, and not according to its own nature, let us now consider as far as is lawful the nature of the Divine Being, so that we may discover what its knowledge is. The common judgment of all rational creatures holds that God is eternal. Therefore let us consider what eternity is, for this will reveal both the divine nature and the divine knowledge.

"Eternity is the whole, perfect, and simultaneous possession of endless life. The meaning of this can be made clearer by comparison with temporal things. For whatever

Boethius, *The Consolation of Philosophy,* Book V, Chapters (prose) 2, 3, 6, translated by Richard Green (New York: Macmillan/Library of the Liberal Arts, 1962).

lives in time lives in the present, proceeding from past to future, and nothing is so constituted in time that it can embrace the whole span of its life at once. It has not yet arrived at tomorrow, and it has already lost yesterday; even the life of this day is lived only in each moving, passing moment. Therefore, whatever is subject to the condition of time, even that which—as Aristotle conceived the world to be—has no beginning and will have no end in a life coextensive with the infinity of time, is such that it cannot rightly be thought eternal. For it does not comprehend and include the whole of infinite life all at once, since it does not embrace the future which is yet to come. Therefore, only that which comprehends and possesses the whole plenitude of endless life together, from which no future thing nor any past thing is absent, can justly be called eternal. Moreover, it is necessary that such a being be in full possession of itself, always present to itself, and hold the infinity of moving time present before itself.

"Therefore, they are wrong who, having heard that Plato held that this world did not have a beginning in time and would never come to an end, suppose that the created world is coeternal with its Creator. For it is one thing to live an endless life, which is what Plato ascribed to the world, and another for the whole of unending life to be embraced all at once as present, which is clearly proper to the divine mind. Nor should God be thought of as older than His creation in extent of time, but rather as prior to it by virtue of the simplicity of His nature. For the infinite motion of temporal things imitates the immediate present of His changeless life and, since it cannot reproduce or equal life, it sinks from immobility to motion and declines from the simplicity of the present into the infinite duration of future and past. And, since it cannot possess the whole fullness of its life at once, it seems to imitate to some extent that which it cannot completely express, and it does this by somehow never ceasing to be. It binds itself to a kind of present in this short and transitory period which, because it has a certain likeness to that abiding, unchanging present, gives everything it touches a semblance of existence. But, since this imitation cannot remain still, it hastens along the infinite road of time, and so it extends by movement the life whose completeness it could not achieve by standing still. Therefore, if we wish to call things by their proper names, we should follow Plato in saying that God indeed is eternal, but the world is perpetual.

"Since, then, every judgment comprehends the subjects presented to it according to its own nature, and since God lives in the eternal present, His knowledge transcends all movement of time and abides in the simplicity of its immediate present. It encompasses the infinite sweep of past and future, and regards all things in its simple comprehension as if they were now taking place. Thus, if you will think about the foreknowledge by which God distinguishes all things, you will rightly consider it to be not a foreknowledge of future events, but knowledge of a never changing present. For this reason, divine knowledge is called providence, rather than prevision, because it resides above all inferior things and looks out on all things from their summit.

"Why then do you imagine that things are necessary which are illuminated by this divine light, since even men do not impose necessity on the things they see? Does your vision impose any necessity upon things which you see present before you?"

"Not at all," I answered.

"Then," Philosophy went on, "if we may aptly compare God's present vision with man's, He sees all things in his eternal present as you see some things in your temporal present. Therefore, this divine foreknowledge does not change the nature and properties of things; it simply sees things present before it as they will later turn out to be in what we regard as the future. His judgment is not confused; with a single intuition of his mind He knows all things that are to come, whether necessarily or not. Just as, when you happen to see simultaneously a man walking on the street and the sun shining in the sky, even though you see both at once, you can distinguish between them and realize that one action is voluntary, the other necessary; so the divine mind, looking down on all things, does not disturb the nature of the things which are present before it but are future with respect to time. Therefore, when God knows that something will happen in the future, and at the same time knows that it will not happen through necessity, this is not opinion but knowledge based on truth.

"If you should reply that whatever God foresees as happening cannot help but happen, and that whatever must happen is bound by necessity—if you pin me down to this word 'necessity'—I grant that you state a solid truth, but one which only a profound theologian can grasp. I would answer that the same future event is necessary with respect to God's knowledge of it, but free and undetermined if considered in its own nature. For there are two kinds of necessity: one is simple, as the necessity by which all men are mortals; the other is conditional, as is the case when, if you know that someone is walking, he must necessarily be walking. For whatever is known, must be as it is known to be; but this condition does not involve that other, simple necessity. It is not caused by the peculiar nature of the person in question, but by an added condition. No necessity forces the man who is voluntarily walking to move forward; but as long as he is walking, he is necessarily moving forward. In the same way, if Providence sees anything as present, that thing must necessarily be, even though it may have no necessity by its nature. But God sees as present those future things which result from free will. Therefore, from the standpoint of divine knowledge these things are necessary because of the condition of their being known by God; but, considered only in themselves, they lose nothing of the absolute freedom of their own natures.

"There is no doubt, then, that all things will happen which God knows will happen; but some of them happen as a result of free will. And, although they happen, they do not, by their existence, lose their proper natures by which, before they happened, they were able not to happen. But, you may ask, what does it mean to say that these events are not necessary, since by reason of the condition of divine knowledge they happen just as if they were necessary? The meaning is the same as in the example I used a while ago of the sun rising and the man walking. At the time they are happening, they must necessarily be happening; but the sun's rising is governed by necessity even before it happens, while the man's walking is not. Similarly, all the things God sees as present will undoubtedly come to pass; but some will happen by the necessity of their natures, others by the power of those who make them happen. Therefore, we quite properly said that these things are necessary if viewed from the standpoint of divine knowledge, but if they are considered in themselves, they are free of the bonds of necessity. In somewhat the same way, whatever is known by the senses is singular in itself, but universal as far as the reason is concerned.

"But, you may say, if I can change my mind about doing something, I can frustrate Providence, since by chance I may change something which Providence foresaw. My answer is this: you can indeed alter what you propose to do, but, because the present truth of Providence sees that you can, and whether or not you will, you cannot frustrate the divine knowledge any more than you can escape the eye of someone who is present and watching you, even though you may, by your free will, vary your actions. You may still wonder, however, whether God's knowledge is changed by your decisions, so that when you wish now one thing, now another, the divine knowledge undergoes corresponding changes. This is not the case. For divine Providence anticipates every future action and converts it to its own present knowledge. It does not change, as you imagine, foreknowing this or that in succession, but in a single instant, without being changed itself, anticipates and grasps your changes.

God has this present comprehension and immediate vision of all things not from the outcome of future events, but from the simplicity of his own nature. In this way, the problem you raised a moment ago is settled. You observed that it would be unworthy of God if our future acts were said to be the cause of divine knowledge. Now you see that this power of divine knowledge, comprehending all things as present before it, itself constitutes the measure of all things and is in no way dependent on things that happen later.

"Since this is true, the freedom of the human will remains inviolate, and laws are just since they provide rewards and punishments to human wills which are not controlled by necessity. God looks down from above, knowing all things, and the eternal present of his vision concurs with the future character of our actions, distributing rewards to the good and punishments to the evil. Our hopes and prayers are not directed to God in vain, for if they are just they cannot fail. Therefore, stand firm against vice and cultivate virtue. Lift up your soul to worthy hopes, and offer humble prayers to heaven. If you will face it, the necessity of virtuous action imposed upon you is very great, since all your actions are done in the sight of a Judge who sees all things."

ANSELM (AND GAUNILO)
1033–1109

Saint Anselm was born to a noble family in Aosta, in what is now Italy. Following a youth of travel and learning, Anselm joined the Benedictine monastery in the town of Bec, Normandy (in modern France). He remained in this monastery for the next thirty-three years, the last fifteen as abbot. During this time, he wrote a number of books on theological and philosophical topics. In 1093, Anselm was coerced into leaving the monastery to become Archbishop of Canterbury. Most of his sixteen years in Canterbury were spent skirmishing with the king of England for control of the church (a pattern that continued for five centuries until Henry VIII severed the English church from Rome entirely in 1534). Anselm died in 1109 and was canonized in 1494.

Anselm's thought can be summed up in the Augustinian phrase, "faith seeking understanding." Anselm was a deeply devoted Christian who began his thinking with the assumption that the doctrines of Christianity are true. And this faith drove him to seek understanding, to find rational explanations for the Christian teachings he already believed. His writings reflected this yearning to understand rationally particular problems in faith; he wrote a number of short treatises on such subjects as the Incarnation and the Trinity. He believed that he could demonstrate the truth of these revealed doctrines.

Anselm's most famous work is his attempt to prove the existence of God in Chapters II to IV of the *Proslogion* (or *Discourse*) known now as the "ontological argument" (from Immanuel Kant's description). The ontological argument attempts to show that if one can conceive of "something-than-which-nothing-greater-can-be-thought," one must also acknowledge that this being exists in reality as well as in the understanding. That is, if God is thought of, then God must exist. Recent scholars have pointed out that there are actually two arguments here: one, in Chapter II, that proves that God exists in reality; and another, in Chapters III to IV, that proves that God's existence is necessary.

Anselm's argument was immediately attacked by a fellow monk named Gaunilo. Anselm's exchange with Gaunilo has been preserved and the key sections are reprinted here, along with the *Proslogion,* Chapters II to IV, in the M.J. Charlesworth translation.

Despite the fact that this argument has fascinated thinkers for over nine hundred years, a student's first response to this passage is often one of confusion or simple denial: "He can't do that!" The student is not alone in being confused; the history of the argument is full of misrepresentations and misinterpretations. To be sure, careful thinkers such as Hume and Kant have attacked this argument. But it is notoriously difficult to say exactly what is wrong with Anselm's logic, and many purported refutations have actually been refutations of arguments quite different from Anselm's.

In recent years, there has been renewed interest in the argument, with Charles Hartshorne, Norman Malcom, and Alvin Plantinga claiming that it is successful. There has also been a tradition, beginning with the medieval thinker Bonaventure and continuing through Karl Barth in this century, that claims the *Proslogion*, Chapters II to IV, is not a philosophical argument at all. These theologians are convinced that Anselm is not "proving" anything, that he is simply showing the implications of God's self-revelation.

While the debate continues to rage, one fact is clear: Anselm raised some of the most basic questions in the history of philosophy. Questions about modes of existence, possible beings, necessity and contingency, as well as a range of issues in logic, all emerge in discussions of this provocative passage.

* * *

For a study of the complete *Proslogion,* see M.J. Charlesworth, *St. Anselm's Proslogion* (Oxford: Clarendon Press, 1965). For the rest of Anselm's major works see, Anselm, *Basic Writings,* translated by S.N. Deane (1902; reprinted LaSalle, IL: Open Court, 1962). For a study of Anselm's life and times, see R.W. Southern's books *Saint Anselm and His Biographer* (Cambridge: Cambridge University Press, 1963) and *Saint Anselm: A Portrait in a Landscape* (Cambridge: Cambridge University Press, 1990). Jasper Hopkins, *A Companion to the Study of St. Anselm* (Minneapolis: University of Minnesota Press, 1972), provides a comprehensive discussion of Anselm and his work.

For further reading on the ontological argument, the best source is John Hick and Arthur C. McGill, eds., *The Many-Faced Argument* (New York: Macmillan, 1967). Charles Hartshorne, *Anselm's Discovery: A Re-Examination of the Ontological Argument for God's Existence* (LaSalle, IL: Open Court, 1965); Alvin Plantinga, *The Nature of Necessity* (Oxford: Clarendon Press, 1974)—and his "simplified" version of this difficult work, Alvin Plantinga, *God, Freedom, and Evil* (Grand Rapids, MI: Eerdmans, 1977); and Richard Campbell, *From Belief to Understanding* (Canberra: Australian National University Press, 1976), all defend the argument. For theological interpretations, see Karl Barth, *Anselm: Fides Quaren Intellectum,* translated by Ian W. Robinson (London: SCM Press, 1960) (Key chapters from this work are included in Hick and McGill's *The Many-Faced Argument.*)

PROSLOGION (in part)

CHAPTER 2: THAT GOD TRULY EXISTS

Well then, Lord, You who give understanding to faith, grant me that I may understand, as much as You see fit, that You exist as we believe You to exist, and that You are what we believe You to be. Now we believe that You are something than which nothing greater can be thought. Or can it be that a thing of such a nature does not exist, since "the Fool has said in his heart, there is no God" (Ps. xiii. 1, lii. 1)? But surely, when this same Fool hears what I am speaking about, namely, "something-than-which-nothing-greater-can-be-thought," he understands what he hears, and what he understands is in his mind, even if he does not understand that it actually exists. For it is one thing for an object to exist in the mind, and another thing to understand that an object actually exists. Thus, when a painter plans beforehand what he is going to execute, he has [the picture] in his mind, but he does not yet think that it actually exists because he has not yet executed it. However, when he has actually painted it, then he both has it in his mind and understands that it exists because he has now made it. Even the Fool, then, is forced to agree that something-than-which-nothing-greater-can-be-thought exists in the mind, since he understands this when he hears it, and whatever is understood is in the mind. And surely that-than-which-a-greater-cannot-be-thought cannot exist in the mind alone. For if it exists solely in the mind even, it can be thought to exist in reality also, which is greater. If then that-than-which-a-greater-cannot-be-thought exists in the mind alone, this same that-than-which-a-greater-*cannot*-be-thought is that-than-which-a-greater-*can*-be-thought. But this is obviously impossible. Therefore there is absolutely no doubt that something-than-which-a-greater-cannot-be-thought exists both in the mind and in reality.

CHAPTER 3: THAT GOD CANNOT BE THOUGHT NOT TO EXIST

And certainly this being so truly exists that it cannot be even thought not to exist. For something can be thought to exist that cannot be thought not to exist, and this is greater than that which can be thought not to exist. Hence, if that-than-which-a-greater-cannot-be-thought can be thought not to exist, then that-than-which-a-greater-cannot-be-thought is not the same as that-than-which-a-greater-cannot-be-thought, which is absurd. Something-than-which-a-greater-cannot-be-thought exists so truly then, that it cannot be even thought not to exist. And You, Lord our God, are this being. You exist so truly, Lord my God, that You cannot even be thought not to exist. And this is as it should be, for if some intelligence could think of something better than You, the creature would be above its creator and would judge its creator—and that is completely absurd. In fact, everything else there is, except You alone, can be thought of as not existing. You alone, then, of all things most truly exist and therefore of all things possess existence to the highest degree; for anything else does not exist as truly, and so possesses existence to a lesser degree. Why then did "the Fool say in his heart, there is no

From M.J. Charlesworth, *St. Anselm's Proslogion* (Oxford: Oxford University Press, 1965). Reprinted by permission of Oxford University Press.

God" (Ps. xiii. 1, lii. 1) when it is so evident to any rational mind that You of all things exist to the highest degree? Why indeed, unless because he was stupid and a fool?

CHAPTER 4: HOW "THE FOOL SAID IN HIS HEART" WHAT CANNOT BE THOUGHT

How indeed has he "said in his heart" what he could not think; or how could he not think what he "said in his heart," since to "say in one's heart" and to "think" are the same? But if he really (indeed, since he really) both thought because he "said in his heart" and did not "say in his heart" because he could not think, there is not only one sense in which something is "said in one's heart" or thought. For in one sense a thing is thought when the word signifying it is thought; in another sense when the very object which the thing is is understood. In the first sense, then, God can be thought not to exist, but not at all in the second sense.* No one, indeed, understanding what God is can think that God does not exist, even though he may say these words in his heart either without any [objective] signification or with some peculiar signification. For God is that-than-which-nothing-greater-can-be-thought. Whoever really understands this understands clearly that this same being so exists that not even in thought can it not exist. Thus whoever understands that God exists in such a way cannot think of Him as not existing.

I give thanks, good Lord, I give thanks to You, since what I believed before through Your free gift I now so understand through Your illumination, that if I did not want to *believe* that You existed, I should nevertheless be unable not to *understand* it.

GAUNILO AND ANSELM: DEBATE**

GAUNILO

[5.] That, however, [this nature] necessarily exists in reality is demonstrated to me from the fact that, unless it existed, whatever exists in reality would be greater than it and consequently it would not be that which is greater than everything that undoubtedly had already been proved to exist in the mind. To this I reply as follows: if something that cannot even be thought in the true and real sense must be said to exist in the mind, then I do not deny that this also exists in my mind in the same way. But since from this one cannot in any way conclude that it exists also in reality, I certainly do not yet concede that it actually exists, until this is proved to me by an indubitable argu-

---

*[Later manuscripts insert the following: "For no one who understands what fire and water are can think that the reality of fire is the reality of water. At the level of words, however, this confusion is possible."

**[I have followed the procedure of John Hick, *Classical and Contemporary Readings in the Philosophy of Religion* (Englewood Cliffs, NJ: Prentice Hall, 1964) and put the main points of Gaunilo's critique together with Anselm's replies. The numbers before each section refer to the paragraph numbers of Gaunilo's *A Reply to the Foregoing by a Certain Writer on Behalf of the Fool* (in Arabic numbers) and Anselm's *Reply to the Foregoing by the Author of the Book in Question* (in Roman numerals).]

a.   b.

The Romanesque Cathedral
a. Exterior view of the Abbey Church of the Madeleine, Vezelay, France, built in the twelfth century. This church typifies the Romanesque style that flourished from about 1000 to 1200. The rounded arches above the portals are reminiscent of the arches of Roman construction. The thickness of the stone walls, together with the relatively simple facade, gives the structure the impression of solidity and solemnity. *(French Government Tourist Office)*
b. The nave. The rounded interior arches distribute the weight of the roof outward as well as downward, necessitating thick stone walls. As a result, only a few small windows are possible in a Romanesque church—adding to the fortress-like feel of the architecture. *(Caisse Nationale des Monuments Historique)*

ment. For he who claims that it actually exists because otherwise it would not be that which is greater than everything does not consider carefully enough whom he is addressing. For I certainly do not yet admit this greater [than everything] to be any truly existing thing; indeed I doubt or even deny it. And I do not concede that it exists in a different way from that—if one ought to speak of "existence" here—when the mind tries to imagine a completely unknown thing on the basis of the spoken words alone. How then can it be proved to me on that basis that that which is greater than everything truly exists in reality (because it is evident that it is greater than all others) if I keep on denying and also doubting that this is evident and do not admit that this greater [than everything] is either in my mind or thought, not even in the sense in which many doubtfully real and unreal things are? It must first of all be proved to me then that this same greater than everything truly exists in reality somewhere, and then only will the fact that it is greater than everything make it clear that it also subsists in itself.

ANSELM

[II.] I said further that if a thing exists even in the mind alone, it can be thought to exist also in reality, which is greater. If, then, it (namely, "that-than-which-a-greater-cannot-be-thought") exists in the mind alone, it is something than which a greater can be thought. What, I ask you, could be more logical? For if it exists even in the mind alone, cannot it be thought to exist also in reality? And if it can [be so thought], is it not the case that he who thinks this thinks of something greater than it, if it exists in the mind alone? What, then, could follow more logically than that, if "that-than-which-a-greater-*cannot*-be-thought" exists in the mind alone, it is the same as that-than-which-a-greater-*can*-be-thought? But surely "that-than-which-a-greater-*can*-be-thought" is not for any mind [the same as] "that-than-which-a-greater-*cannot*-be-thought." Does it not follow, then, that "that-than-which-a-greater-*cannot*-be-thought," if it exists in anyone's mind, does not exist in the mind alone? For if it exists in the mind alone, it is that-than-which-a-greater-*can*-be-thought, which is absurd.

*   *   *

[IX.] It is evident, moreover, that in the same way one can think of and understand that which cannot not exist. And one who thinks of this thinks of something greater than one who thinks of what can not exist. When, therefore, one thinks of that-than-which-a-greater-cannot-be-thought, if one thinks of what can not exist, one does not think of that-than-which-a-greater-cannot-be-thought. Now the same thing cannot at the same time be thought of and not thought of. For this reason he who thinks of that-than-which-a-greater-cannot-be-thought does not think of something that can not exist but something that cannot not exist. Therefore what he thinks of exists necessarily, since whatever can not exist is not what he thinks of.

GAUNILO

[6.] They say that there is in the ocean somewhere an island which, because of the difficulty (or rather the impossibility) of finding that which does not exist, some have called the "Lost Island." And the story goes that it is blessed with all manner of priceless riches and delights in abundance, much more even than the Happy Isles, and, having no owner or inhabitant, it is superior everywhere in abundance of riches to all those other lands that men inhabit. Now, if anyone tells me that it is like this, I shall easily understand what is said, since nothing is difficult about it. But if he should then go on to say, as though it were a logical consequence of this: You cannot any more doubt that this island that is more excellent than all other lands truly exists somewhere in reality than you can doubt that it is in your mind; and since it is more excellent to exist not only in the mind alone but also in reality, therefore it must needs be that it exists. For if it did not exist, any other land existing in reality would be more excellent than it, and so this island, already conceived by you to be more excellent than others, will not be more excellent. If, I say, someone wishes thus to persuade me that this island really exists beyond all doubt, I should either think that he was joking, or I should find it hard to decide which of us I ought to judge the bigger fool—I, if I agreed with him, or he, if he thought that he had proved the existence of this island with any certainty, unless he had first convinced me that its very excellence exists in my mind precisely as a thing existing truly and indubitably and not just as something unreal or doubtfully real.

ANSELM

[III.] You claim, however, that this is as though someone asserted that it cannot be doubted that a certain island in the ocean (which is more fertile than all other lands and which, because of the difficulty or even the impossibility of discovering what does not exist, is called the "Lost Island") truly exists in reality since anyone easily understands it when it is described in words. Now, I truly promise that if anyone should discover for me something existing either in reality or in the mind alone—except "that-than-which-a-greater-cannot-be-thought"—to which the logic of my argument would apply, then I shall find that Lost Island and give it, never more to be lost, to that person.

GAUNILO

[7.] If then someone should assert [to the Fool in *Proslogion* III] that this greater [than everything] is such that it cannot be thought not to exist (again without any other proof than that otherwise it would not be greater than everything), then he could make this same reply and say: When have I said that there truly existed some being that is "greater than everything," such that from this it could be proved to me that this same being really existed to such a degree that it could not be thought not to exist? That is why it must first be conclusively proved by argument that there is some higher nature, namely that which is greater and better than all the things that are, so that from this we can also infer everything else which necessarily cannot be wanting to what is greater and better than everything.

ANSELM

[III.] It has already been clearly seen, however, that "that-than-which-a-greater-cannot-be-thought" cannot be thought not to exist, because it exists as a matter of such certain truth. Otherwise it would not exist at all. In short, if anyone says that he thinks that this being does not exist, I reply that, when he thinks of this, either he thinks of something than which a greater cannot be thought, or he does not think of it. If he does not think of it, then he does not think that what he does not think of does not exist. If, however, he does think of it, then indeed he thinks of something which cannot be even thought not to exist. For if it could be thought not to exist, it could be thought to have a beginning and an end—but this cannot be. Thus, he who thinks of it thinks of something that cannot be thought not to exist; indeed, he who thinks of this does not think of it as not existing, otherwise he would think what cannot be thought. Therefore "that-than-which-a-greater-cannot-be-thought" cannot be thought not to exist.

[7.] When, however, it is said that this supreme being cannot be *thought* not to exist, it would perhaps be better to say that it cannot be *understood* not to exist nor even to be able not to exist. For, strictly speaking, unreal things cannot be *understood,* though certainly they can be *thought* of in the same way as the Fool *thought* that God does not exist. I know with complete certainty that I exist, but I also know at the same time nevertheless that I can not-exist. And I *understand* without any doubt that that which exists to the highest degree, namely God, both exists and cannot not exist. I do not know, however, whether I can think of myself as not existing while I know with absolute certainty that I do exist; but if I can, why cannot [I do the same] with regard to anything else I know with the same certainty? If however I cannot, this will not be the distinguishing characteristic of God [namely, to be such that He cannot be thought not to exist].

[IV.] You say, moreover, that when it is said that this supreme reality cannot be *thought* not to exist, it would perhaps be better to say that it cannot be *understood* not to exist or even to be able not to exist. However, it must rather be said that it cannot be *thought.* For if I had said that the thing in question could not be *understood* not to exist, perhaps you yourself (who claim that we cannot understand—if this word is to be taken strictly—things that are unreal) would object that nothing that exists can be understood not to exist. For it is false [to say that] what exists does not exist, so that it is not the distinguishing characteristic of God not to be able to be understood not to exist. But, if any of those things which exist with absolute certainty can be understood not to exist, in the same way other things that certainly exist can be understood not to exist. But, if the matter is carefully considered, this objection cannot be made apropos [the term] "thought." For even if none of those things that exist can be *understood* not to exist, all however can be *thought* as not existing, save that which exists to a supreme degree. For in fact all those things (and they alone) that have a beginning or end or are made up of parts and, as I have already said, all those things that do not exist as a whole in a particular place or at a particular time can be thought as not existing. Only that being in which there is neither beginning nor end nor conjunction of parts, and that thought does not discern save as a whole in every place and at every time, cannot be thought as not existing.

Know then that you can think of yourself as not existing while yet you are absolutely sure that you exist. I am astonished that you have said that you do not know this. For we think of many things that we know to exist, as not existing; and [we think of] many things that we know not to exist, as existing—not judging that it is really as we think but imagining it to be so. We *can,* in fact, think of something as not existing while knowing that it does exist, since we can [think of] the one and know the other at the same time. And we *cannot* think of something as not existing if yet we know that it does exist, since we cannot think of it as existing and not existing at the same time. He, therefore, who distinguishes these two senses of this assertion will understand that [in one sense] nothing can be thought as not existing while yet it is known to exist, and that [in another sense] whatever exists, save that-than-which-a-greater-cannot-be-thought, can be thought of as not existing even when we know that it does exist. Thus it is that, on the one hand, it is the distinguishing characteristic of God that He cannot be thought of as not existing [in the one sense], and that, on the other hand, many things, the while they do exist, cannot be thought of as not existing [in the other sense]. In what sense, however, one can say that God can be thought of as not existing I think I have adequately explained in my tract.

THOMAS AQUINAS
1225–1274

Saint Thomas Aquinas was indisputably the greatest of the medieval philosophers. He was born in his family's castle of Roccasecca near the town of Aquino, about halfway between Rome and Naples. The seventh son of the Count of Aquino, Landolfo, and his wife Teodora, at the age of five Thomas was sent to the Benedictine monastery of Monte Casino, where his uncle was the abbot. His parents hoped he would get a good education at the monastery and perhaps one day become abbot of Monte Casino. However, political struggles between the pope and the emperor made the monastery unsafe, and at age fourteen Thomas moved to the Imperial University in Naples.

At this university, Thomas came under the influence of the Dominicans, a mendicant, or begging, order of friars. Even though the Dominicans were admired by many for their religious commitment, Thomas's family was appalled when in 1244 he announced his plans to join the order. They considered the Dominicans religious fanatics, virtually a cult, with none of the sophistication, prestige, or power of the long-established Benedictines. At his parents' instigation, Thomas's brothers kidnapped him and held him captive in the family castle. For a year they tried reasoning, shouting, intimidating—even tempting him with a prostitute—but Thomas would not be swayed. He eventually managed to escape and became a Dominican friar.

Thomas went to Paris, where he studied with Albertus Magnus (Albert the Great), an advocate of the newly rediscovered Aristotelian writings, and he even followed his teacher to Cologne to continue his study of Aristotle. As a student, Thomas was so stolid and methodical that many of his peers thought he was dull or downright stupid. Given his deliberate manner and his portly build, his classmates dubbed him "the Dumb Ox." But Albertus saw his potential and turned this cruel epithet into a prophecy, saying, "You call him a Dumb Ox; I tell you the Dumb Ox will bellow so loud his bellowing will fill the world." In 1252, Thomas returned to Paris for graduate studies, eventually receiving the magistrate (doctorate) in theology in 1256.

On concluding his studies, it seemed natural that Thomas would join the faculty of the University of Paris. However, scholars from the mendicant orders were held in suspicion by the regular faculty of the university. Along with the great Franciscan friar Bonaventure, Thomas was not allowed to teach in Paris until the pope himself intervened.

The rest of Thomas's life was spent teaching in France and Italy and writing extensively on philosophical and theological subjects. His complete works in Latin comprise twenty-five volumes. Thomas was also called upon to intervene in several disputes. In addition to defending his Dominican order, he was forced to articulate a middle position between those who rejected Aristotelian philosophy as anti-Christian and those who accepted Aristotle (or, rather, a version of Averroës' interpretation of Aristotle) too uncritically. Throughout his writings, Thomas negotiated a middle path of critical admiration for Aristotle.

Like other Christian thinkers, Thomas was concerned with the relation between reason and faith. Using basically Aristotelian categories, Thomas taught that natural reason could establish some of the truths of religion (such as the existence, unity, and goodness of God), but other truths were accessible only through faith. Contrary to some of the Latin Averroists, Thomas taught that there

The Benedictine Monastery of Monte Casino. At the age of five, St. Thomas Aquinas was sent here to study. His parents hoped that he might someday become abbot of the monastery, but he chose to join the Dominican order instead. *(AP/Wide World Photos)*

was no conflict between the teachings of philosophy and those of theology. To use a later analogy, Thomas believed that "the book of nature" (i.e., the created world) and the "Book of Scripture" were in perfect harmony.

In December 1273, Thomas suddenly stopped writing, apparently the result of a mystical experience. He reported to a friend that "all I have written seems like straw to me." A few months later, he was called to a church council in Lyon, France. On the way there his health forced him to stop at Fossanova (south of Rome) where he died on March 7, 1274, at the age of forty-nine.

Three years after his death, several of Thomas's teachings were condemned by the Bishop of Paris. However, the condemnation did not stand long, and in 1323, Saint Thomas Aquinas was canonized. In 1879, Pope Leo XII commended the study of Aquinas's philosophy in an encyclical, *Aeterni Patris*. This papal proclamation did not launch a revival of Thomism, as is often said, but it did lend an enormous prestige to the study of Thomas and his work. The encyclical praises the saint in the highest terms: "As far as man is concerned, reason can now hardly rise higher than she rose, borne up in the flight of Thomas; and Faith can hardly gain more help from reason than those which Thomas gave her." Despite the encouragement of Leo XII and others, not all Catholic philosophers are by any means Thomists; many twentieth-century Catholic thinkers have shown more interest in existentialism and phenomenology. Today Thomas is studied and admired as much by Protestants and non-Christians as he is by Catholics.

*   *   *

Thomas's most famous work, the *Summa Theologica*, is one of the most comprehensive and systematic works of theology ever written. It has often been likened in its complexity and grandeur to a Gothic cathedral. This monumental classic is divided into four sections that, collectively, include 512 "Questions." Each Question raises a topic or area of investigation and is, in turn, made up of several "Articles" that explore specific concerns. These Articles range from abstract philosophical issues, such as "Whether one can intend two things at the same time," to such minutiae of theology as "Whether one angel can speak to another in such a way that others will not know what he is saying." Each Article is examined in the same manner, beginning with a question, offering an answer that Thomas considers inadequate, then supporting this answer with several "objections." At this point, a quotation or argument that contradicts the position taken thus far is introduced with the words "On the contrary (*sed contra*) . . ." The dramatic tension between two opposing positions is then resolved by the author's concise and straightforward *Respondeo,* or "I answer that . . . ," which introduces his own view. In presenting his answer, Thomas tries to avoid directly denying the preceding objections, seeing them instead as limited truths that his *Respondeo* supersedes. Finally, Thomas moves on to answer, one by one, each of the initial objections. (The reader should keep in mind that the *first* things Thomas says about a subject are the *opposite* of the position he will subsequently defend.)

The selections from the *Summa Theologica* given here include readings from Thomas's "Treatise on God" (including his famous "Five Ways" or five arguments for God's existence); "Treatise on Man" (including a discussion of the nature of the soul); "Treatise on Human Acts" (including his definition of happiness); "Treatise on Law" (describing the kinds of law); and "Treatise on War" (describing his arguments for a just war). The translation is that of the Fathers of the English Dominican Province.

*   *   *

The classic introductions to Thomas Aquinas are F.C. Copleston, *Aquinas* (Baltimore, MD: Penguin Books, 1955), and Étienne Gilson, *The Christian Philosophy of St. Thomas Aquinas* (New York: Random House, 1956). More recent helpful studies include Josef Pieper, *Guide to Thomas Aquinas* (New York: Pantheon, 1962); Ralph McInerny, *St. Thomas Aquinas* (Boston: Twayne, 1977); Anthony Kenny, *Aquinas* (New York: Hill and Wang, 1980); and Brian Davies, *The Thought of Thomas Aquinas* (Oxford: Oxford University Press, 1992). James A. Weisheipl, *Friar Thomas D'Aquino: His Life, Thought, and Works* (Garden City, NY: Doubleday, 1974) offers a biography. G.K. Chesterton's impressionistic study entitled *St. Thomas Aquinas: The "Dumb Ox"* (1933; reprinted New York: Doubleday Image, 1956) is also a good place to become acquainted with Thomas. For collections of general essays, see Anthony Kenny, ed., *Aquinas: A Collection of Critical Essays* (Garden City, NY: Anchor Doubleday, 1969), and Norman Kretzmann and Eleonore Stump, eds., *The Cambridge Companion to Aquinas* (Cambridge: Cambridge University Press, 1993).

There are many studies on aspects of Thomas's thought. For example, a sampling of works on the "Five Ways" includes A.G.N. Flew, *God and Philosophy* (London: Hutchinson, 1966); Anthony Kenny, *The Five Ways: St. Thomas Aquinas' Proofs of God's Existence* (London: Routledge & Kegan Paul, 1969); Richard Swinburne, *The Existence of God* (Oxford: Clarendon Press, 1979); and J.L. Mackie, *The Miracle of Theism: Arguments for and against the Existence of God* (Oxford: Clarendon Press, 1982).

SUMMA THEOLOGICA (in part)

TREATISE ON GOD

QUESTION 2: THE EXISTENCE OF GOD
(IN THREE ARTICLES)

Because the chief aim of sacred doctrine is to teach the knowledge of God, not only as He is in Himself, but also as He is the beginning of things and their last end, and especially of rational creatures, as is clear from what has been already said, therefore, in our endeavor to expound this science, we shall treat: (1) Of God; (2) Of the rational creature's advance towards God; (3) Of Christ, Who as man, is our way to God.

In treating of God there will be a threefold division:—

For we shall consider (1) Whatever concerns the Divine Essence; (2) Whatever concerns the distinctions of Persons; (3) Whatever concerns the procession of creatures from Him.

Concerning the Divine Essence, we must consider:—

(1) Whether God exists? (2) The manner of His existence, or, rather, what is *not* the manner of His existence; (3) Whatever concerns His operations—namely, His knowledge, will, power.

Concerning the first, there are three points of inquiry:—

(1) Whether the proposition "God exists" is self-evident? (2) Whether it is demonstrable? (3) Whether God exists?

First Article

WHETHER THE EXISTENCE OF GOD IS SELF-EVIDENT?

We Proceed Thus to the First Article:—

Objection 1. It seems that the existence of God is self-evident. Now those things are said to be self-evident to us the knowledge of which is naturally implanted in us, as we can see in regard to first principles. But as Damascene says (*De Fid. Orth.* i. 1, 3), *the knowledge of God is naturally implanted in all.* Therefore the existence of God is self-evident.

Obj. 2. Further, those things are said to be self-evident which are known as soon as the terms are known, which the Philosopher (1 *Poster.* iii) says is true of the first principles of demonstration. Thus, when the nature of a whole and of a part is known, it is at once recognized that every whole is greater than its part. But as soon as the

From St. Thomas Aquinas, *Summa Theologica,* Treatise on God (Part I, Q.2); Treatise on Man (Part I, Q. 75, a. 2; Q. 76, a. 1); Treatise on Human Acts (Part I–II, Q. 2, a. 8; Q. 3, a. 4, 8; Q. 5, a. 5); Treatise on Law (Part I–II, Q. 94, a. 2, 4, 5; Q. 95, a. 1, 2; Q. 96, a. 2); Treatise on War (Part II–II, q. 40, a. 1), translated by the Fathers of the English Dominican Province (New York: Benziger Brothers, 1947). Reprinted by permission.

signification of the word "God" is understood, it is at once seen that God exists. For by this word is signified that thing than which nothing greater can be conceived. But that which exists actually and mentally is greater than that which exists only mentally. Therefore, since as soon as the word "God" is understood it exists mentally, it also follows that it exists actually. Therefore the proposition "God exists" is self-evident.

Obj. 3. Further, the existence of truth is self-evident. For whoever denies the existence of truth grants that truth does not exist: and if truth does not exist, then the proposition "Truth does not exist" is true: and if there is anything true, there must be truth. But God is truth itself: *I am the way, the truth, and the life* (John xiv. 6). Therefore "God exists" is self-evident.

On the contrary, No one can mentally admit the opposite of what is self-evident; as the Philosopher (*Metaph.* iv., lect. vi) states concerning the first principles of demonstration. But the opposite of the proposition "God is" can be mentally admitted: *The fool said in his heart, There is no God* (Ps. lii. 1). Therefore, that God exists is not self-evident.

I answer that, A thing can be self-evident in either of two ways; on the one hand, self-evident in itself, though not to us; on the other, self-evident in itself, and to us. A proposition is self-evident because the predicate is included in the essence of the subject, as "Man is an animal," for animal is contained in the essence of man. If, therefore the essence of the predicate and subject be known to all, the proposition will be self-evident to all; as is clear with regard to the first principles of demonstration, the terms of which are common things that no one is ignorant of, such as being and non-being, whole and part, and such like. If, however, there are some to whom the essence of the predicate and subject is unknown, the proposition will be self-evident in itself, but not to those who do not know the meaning of the predicate and subject of the proposition. Therefore, it happens, as Boethius says (*Hebdom., the title of which is: "Whether all that is, is good"*), "that there are some mental concepts self-evident only to the learned, as that incorporeal substances are not in space." Therefore I say that this proposition, "God exists," of itself is self-evident, for the predicate is the same as the subject; because God is His own existence as will be hereafter shown (Q. 3, A. 4). Now because we do not know the essence of God, the proposition is not self-evident to us; but needs to be demonstrated by things that are more known to us, though less known in their nature—namely, by effects.

Reply Obj. 1. To know that God exists in a general and confused way is implanted in us by nature, inasmuch as God is man's beatitude. For man naturally desires happiness, and what is naturally desired by man must be naturally known to him. This, however, is not to know absolutely that God exists; just as to know that someone is approaching is not the same as to know that Peter is approaching, even though it is Peter who is approaching; for many there are who imagine that man's perfect good which is happiness, consists in riches, and others in pleasures, and others in something else.

Reply Obj. 2. Perhaps not everyone who hears this word "God" understands it to signify something than which nothing greater can be thought, seeing that some have believed God to be a body. Yet, granted that everyone understands that by this word "God" is signified something than which nothing greater can be thought, nevertheless, it does not therefore follow that he understands that what the word signifies exists actually, but only that it exists mentally. Nor can it be argued that it actually exists, unless it be admitted that there actually exists something than which nothing greater can be thought; and this precisely is not admitted by those who hold that God does not exist.

Reply Obj. 3. The existence of truth in general is self-evident but the existence of a Primal Truth is not self-evident to us.

Second Article

WHETHER IT CAN BE DEMONSTRATED THAT GOD EXISTS?

We Proceed Thus to the Second Article:—

Objection 1. It seems that the existence of God cannot be demonstrated. For it is an article of faith that God exists. But what is of faith cannot be demonstrated, because a demonstration produces scientific knowledge; whereas faith is of the unseen (Heb. xi. 1). Therefore it cannot be demonstrated that God exists.

Obj. 2. Further, the essence is the middle term of demonstration. But we cannot know in what God's essence consists, but solely in what it does not consist; as Damascene says (*De Fid. Orth.* i. 4). Therefore we cannot demonstrate that God exists.

Obj. 3. Further, if the existence of God were demonstrated, this could only be from His effects. But His effects are not proportionate to Him, since He is infinite and His effects are finite; and between the finite and infinite there is no proportion. Therefore, since a cause cannot be demonstrated by an effect not proportionate to it, it seems that the existence of God cannot be demonstrated.

On the contrary, The Apostle says: *The invisible things of Him are clearly seen, being understood by the things that are made* (Rom. i. 20). But this would not be unless the existence of God could be demonstrated through the things that are made; for the first thing we must know of anything is, whether it exists.

I answer that, Demonstration can be made in two ways: One is through the cause, and is called *a priori*, and this is to argue from what is prior absolutely. The other is through the effect, and is called a demonstration *a posteriori;* this is to argue from what is prior relatively only to us. When an effect is better known to us than its cause, from the effect we proceed to the knowledge of the cause. And from every effect the existence of its proper cause can be demonstrated, so long as its effects are better known to us; because since every effect depends upon its cause, if the effect exists, the cause must pre-exist. Hence the existence of God, in so far as it is not self-evident to us, can be demonstrated from those of His effects which are known to us.

Reply Obj. 1. The existence of God and other like truths about God, which can be known by natural reason, are not articles of faith, but are preambles to the articles; for faith presupposes natural knowledge, even as grace presupposes nature, and perfection supposes something that can be perfected. Nevertheless, there is nothing to prevent a man, who cannot grasp a proof, accepting, as a matter of faith, something which in itself is capable of being scientifically known and demonstrated.

Reply Obj. 2. When the existence of a cause is demonstrated from an effect, this effect takes the place of the definition of the cause in proof of the cause's existence. This is especially the case in regard to God, because, in order to prove the existence of anything, it is necessary to accept as a middle term the meaning of the word, and not its essence, for the question of its essence follows on the question of its existence. Now the names given to God are derived from His effects; consequently, in demonstrating the existence of God from His effects, we may take for the middle term the meaning of the word "God."

Reply Obj. 3. From effects not proportionate to the cause no perfect knowledge of that cause can be obtained. Yet from every effect the existence of the cause can be clearly demonstrated, and so we can demonstrate the existence of God from His effects; though from them we cannot perfectly know God as He is in His essence.

Third Article

WHETHER GOD EXISTS?

We Proceed Thus to the Third Article:—

Objection 1. It seems that God does not exist; because if one of two contraries be infinite, the other would be altogether destroyed. But the word "God" means that He is infinite goodness. If, therefore, God existed, there would be no evil discoverable; but there is evil in the world. Therefore God does not exist.

Obj. 2. Further, it is superfluous to suppose that what can be accounted for by a few principles has been produced by many. But it seems that everything we see in the world can be accounted for by other principles, supposing God did not exist. For all natural things can be reduced to one principle, which is nature; and all voluntary things can be reduced to one principle, which is human reason, or will. Therefore there is no need to suppose God's existence.

On the contrary, It is said in the person of God: *I am Who am* (Exod. iii. 14).

I answer that, The existence of God can be proved in five ways.

The first and more manifest way is the argument from motion. It is certain, and evident to our senses, that in the world some things are in motion. Now whatever is in motion is put in motion by another, for nothing can be in motion except it is in potentiality to that towards which it is in motion; whereas a thing moves inasmuch as it is in act. For motion is nothing else than the reduction of something from potentiality to actuality. But nothing can be reduced from potentiality to actuality, except by something in a state of actuality. Thus that which is actually hot, as fire, makes wood, which is potentially hot, to be actually hot, and thereby moves and changes it. Now it is not possible that the same thing should be at once in actuality and potentiality in the same respect, but only in different respects. For what is actually hot cannot simultaneously be potentially hot; but it is simultaneously potentially cold. It is therefore impossible that in the same respect and in the same way a thing should be both mover and moved, *i.e.,* that it should move itself. Therefore, whatever is in motion must be put in motion by another. If that by which it is put in motion be itself put in motion, then this also must needs be put in motion by another, and that by another again. But this cannot go on to infinity, because then there would be no first mover, and, consequently, no other mover; seeing that subsequent movers move only inasmuch as they are put in motion by the first mover; as the staff moves only because it is put in motion by the hand. Therefore it is necessary to arrive at a first mover, put in motion by no other; and this everyone understands to be God.

The second way is from the nature of the efficient cause. In the world of sense we find there is an order of efficient causes. There is no case known (neither is it, indeed, possible) in which a thing is found to be the efficient cause of itself; for so it would be prior to itself, which is impossible. Now in efficient causes it is not possible to go on to infinity, because in all efficient causes following in order, the first is the cause of the intermediate cause, and the intermediate is the cause of the ultimate cause, whether the intermediate cause be several, or one only. Now to take away the cause is to take away the effect. Therefore if there be no first cause among efficient causes, there will be no ultimate, nor any intermediate cause. But if in efficient causes it is possible to go on to infinity, there will be no first efficient cause, neither will there be an ultimate effect, nor any intermediate efficient causes; all of which is plainly false.

Therefore it is necessary to admit a first efficient cause, to which everyone gives the name of God.

The third way is taken from possibility and necessity, and runs thus. We find in nature things that are possible to be and not to be, since they are found to be generated, and to corrupt, and consequently, they are possible to be and not to be. But it is impossible for these always to exist, for that which is possible not to be at some time is not. Therefore, if everything is possible not to be, then at one time there could have been nothing in existence. Now if this were true, even now there would be nothing in existence, because that which does not exist only begins to exist by something already existing. Therefore, if at one time nothing was in existence, it would have been impossible for anything to have begun to exist; and thus even now nothing would be in existence—which is absurd. Therefore, not all beings are merely possible, but there must exist something the existence of which is necessary. But every necessary thing either has its necessity caused by another, or not. Now it is impossible to go on to infinity in necessary things which have their necessity caused by another, as has been already proved in regard to efficient causes. Therefore we cannot but postulate the existence of some being having of itself its own necessity, and not receiving it from another, but rather causing in others their necessity. This all men speak of as God.

The fourth way is taken from the gradation to be found in things. Among beings there are some more and some less good, true, noble, and the like. But "more" and "less" are predicated of different things, according as they resemble in their different ways something which is the maximum, as a thing is said to be hotter according as it more nearly resembles that which is hottest; so that there is something which is truest, something best, something noblest, and, consequently, something which is uttermost being; for those things that are greatest in truth are greatest in being, as it is written in *Metaph.* ii. Now the maximum in any genus is the cause of all in that genus; as fire, which is the maximum of heat, is the cause of all hot things. Therefore there must also be something which is to all beings the cause of their being, goodness, and every other perfection; and this we call God.

The fifth way is taken from the governance of the world. We see that things which lack intelligence, such as natural bodies, act for an end, and this is evident from their acting always, or nearly always, in the same way, so as to obtain the best result. Hence it is plain that not fortuitously, but designedly, do they achieve their end. Now whatever lacks intelligence cannot move towards an end, unless it be directed by some being endowed with knowledge and intelligence; as the arrow is shot to its mark by the archer. Therefore some intelligent being exists by whom all natural things are directed to their end; and this being we call God.

Reply Obj. 1. As Augustine says (*Enchir.* xi): *Since God is the highest good, He would not allow any evil to exist in His works, unless His omnipotence and goodness were such as to bring good even out of evil.* This is part of the infinite goodness of God, that He should allow evil to exist, and out of it produce good.

Reply Obj. 2. Since nature works for a determinate end under the direction of a higher agent, whatever is done by nature must needs be traced back to God, as to its first cause. So also whatever is done voluntarily must also be traced back to some higher cause other than human reason or will, since these can change and fail; for all things that are changeable and capable of defect must be traced back to an immovable and self-necessary first principle, as was shown in the body of the *Article.*

* * *

QUESTION 75: OF MAN WHO IS COMPOSED OF A SPIRITUAL AND A CORPOREAL SUBSTANCE: AND IN THE FIRST PLACE CONCERNING WHAT BELONGS TO THE ESSENCE OF THE SOUL

* * *

Second Article

WHETHER THE HUMAN SOUL IS SOMETHING SUBSISTENT?

We Proceed Thus to the Second Article:—

Objection 1. It would seem that the human soul is not something subsistent. For that which subsists is said to be *this particular thing*. Now *this particular thing* is said not of the soul, but of that which is composed of soul and body. Therefore the soul is not something subsistent.

Obj. 2. Further, everything subsistent operates. But the soul does not operate; for, as the Philosopher says (*De Anima* i. 4), *to say that the soul feels or understands is like saying that the soul weaves or builds.* Therefore the soul is not subsistent.

Obj. 3. Further, if the soul were subsistent, it would have some operation apart from the body. But it has no operation apart from the body, not even that of understanding: for the act of understanding does not take place without a phantasm, which cannot exist apart from the body. Therefore the human soul is not something subsistent.

On the contrary, Augustine says (*de Trin.* x. 7): *Whoever understands that the nature of the soul is that of a substance and not that of a body, will see that those who maintain the corporeal nature of the soul, are led astray through associating with the soul those things without which they are unable to think of any nature—i.e., imaginary pictures of the corporal things.* Therefore the nature of the human intellect is not only incorporeal, but it is also a substance, that is, something subsistent.

I answer that, It must necessarily be allowed that the principle of intellectual operation which we call the soul, is a principle both incorporeal and subsistent. For it is clear that by means of the intellect man can have knowledge of all corporeal things. Now whatever knows certain things cannot have any of them in its own nature; because that which is in it naturally would impede the knowledge of anything else. Thus we observe that a sick man's tongue being vitiated by a feverish and bitter humor, is insensible to anything sweet and everything seems bitter to it. Therefore if the intellectual principle contained the nature of a body it would be unable to know all bodies. Now every body has its own determinate nature. Therefore it is impossible for the intellectual principle to be a body. It is likewise impossible for it to understand by means of a bodily organ; since the determinate nature of that organ would impede knowledge of all bodies; as when a certain determinate color is not only in the pupil of the eye, but also in a glass vase, the liquid in the vase seems to be of that same color.

Therefore the intellectual principle which we call the mind or the intellect has the operation *per se* apart from the body. Now only that which subsists can have an operation *per se*. For nothing can operate but what is actual: wherefore a thing operates according as it is; for which reason we do not say that heat imparts heat, but that what is hot gives heat. We must conclude, therefore, that the human soul, which is called the intellect or the mind, is something incorporeal and subsistent.

Reply Obj. 1. This particular thing can be taken in two senses. Firstly, for anything subsistent; secondly, for that which subsists, and is complete in a specific nature. The former sense excludes the inherence of an accident or of a material form; the latter excludes also the imperfection of the part, so that a hand can be called *this particular thing* in the first sense, but not in the second. Therefore as the human soul is a part of human nature, it can indeed be called *this particular thing,* in the first sense, as being something subsistent; but not in the second, for in this sense, what is composed of body and soul is said to be *this particular thing.*

Reply Obj. 2. Aristotle wrote those words as expressing not his own opinion, but the opinion of those who said that to understand is to be moved, as is clear from the context. Or we may reply that to operate *per se* belongs to what exists *per se*. But for a thing to exist *per se,* it suffices sometimes that it be not inherent, as an accident or a material form; even though it be part of something. Nevertheless, that is rightly said to subsist *per se,* which is neither inherent in the above sense nor part of anything else. In this sense, the eye or the hand cannot be said to subsist *per se;* nor can it for that reason be said to operate *per se.* Hence the operation of the parts is through each part attributed to the whole. For we say that the man sees with the eye, and feels with the hand and, and not in the same sense as when we say that what is hot gives heat by its heat; for heat, strictly speaking, does not give heat. We may therefore say that the soul understands, as the eye sees; but it is more correct to say that man understands through the soul.

Reply Obj. 3. The body is necessary for intellect, not as its origin of action, but on the part of the object; for the phantasm is to the intellect what color is to the sight. Neither does such a dependence on the body prove the intellect to be non-subsistent; otherwise it would follow that an animal is not subsistent, since it requires external objects of the senses in order to perform its act of perception.

* * *

*   *   *

First Article

<small>WHETHER THE INTELLECTUAL PRINCIPLE IS UNITED TO THE BODY AS ITS FORM?</small>

We Proceed Thus to the First Article:—

Objection 1. It seems that the intellectual principle is not united to the body as its form. For the Philosopher says (*De Anima* iii. 4) that "the intellect is separate," and that it is not the act of any body. Therefore it is not united to the body as its form.

Obj. 2. Further, every form is determined according to the nature of the matter of which it is the form; otherwise no proportion would be required between matter and form. Therefore if the intellect were united to the body as its form since every body has a determinate nature it would follow that the intellect has a determinate nature; and thus, it would not be capable of knowing all things, as is clear from what has been said (Q. 75, A. 2), which is contrary to the notion of intellect. Therefore the intellect is not united to the body as its form.

Obj. 3. Further, whatever receptive power is an act of a body receives a form materially and individually; for what is received must be received according to the mode of the receiver. But the form of the thing understood is not received into the intellect materially and individually, but rather immaterially and universally; otherwise the intellect would not be capable of the knowledge of immaterial and universal objects, but only of individuals, like the senses. Therefore the intellect is not united to the body as its form.

Obj. 4. Further, power and action have the same subject; for the same subject is what can, and does, act. But the intellectual action is not the action of a body, as appears from above (Q. 75, A. 2). Therefore neither is the intellectual power a power of the body. But virtue or power cannot be more abstract or more simple than the essence from which the virtue or power is derived. Therefore neither is the substance of the intellect the form of a body.

Obj. 5. Further, whatever has *per se* being is not united to the body as its form, because a form is that by which a thing is, so that the very being of a form does not belong to the form by itself. But the intellectual principle has *per se* being and is subsistent, as was said above (Q. 75, A. 2). Therefore it is not united to the body as its form.

Obj. 6. Further, whatever exists in a thing by reason of its nature exists in it always. But to be united to matter belongs to the form by reason of its nature. For form is the act of matter not by any accidental quality, but by its own essence; otherwise matter and form would not make a thing substantially one, but only accidentally one. Therefore a form cannot be without its own proper matter. But the intellectual principle, since it is incorruptible, as was shown above (Q. 75, A. 6), remains separate from the body after the dissolution of the body. Therefore the intellectual principle is not united to the body as its form.

On the contrary, According to the Philosopher (*Metaph.* vii. 2), difference is derived from the form. But the difference which constitutes man is *rational* which is applied to man on account of his intellectual principle. Therefore the intellectual principle is the form of man.

I answer that, We must assert that the intellect which is the principle of intellectual operation is the form of the human body. For that whereby primarily anything acts is a form of the thing to which the act is to be attributed; for instance, that whereby a body is primarily healed is health and that whereby the soul knows primarily is knowledge; hence health is a form of the body, and knowledge is a form of the soul. The reason is because nothing acts except so far as it is in act; hence a thing acts by that whereby it is in act. Now it is clear that the first thing by which the body lives is the soul. And as life appears through various operations in different degrees of living things, that whereby we primarily perform each of all these vital actions is the soul. For the soul is the primary principle of our nourishment, sensation, and local movement; and likewise of our understanding. Therefore this principle by which we primarily understand, whether it be called the intellect or the intellectual soul, is the form of the body. This is the demonstration used by Aristotle (*De Anima* ii. 2).

But if anyone say that the intellectual soul is not the form of the body he must first explain how it is that this action of understanding is the action of this particular man; for each one is conscious that it is himself who understands. Now an action may be attributed to anyone in three ways, as is clear from the Philosopher. "For a thing is said to move or act either by virtue of its whole self, for instance, as a physician heals; or by virtue of a part, as a man sees by his eye; or through an accidental quality, as when we say that something that is white build, because it is accidental to the builder to be white" (*Phys.* v. 1) So when we say that Socrates or Plato understands, it is clear that this is not attributed to him accidentally, since it is ascribed to him as man, which is predicated of him essentially. We must therefore say either that Socrates understands by virtue of his whole self, as Plato maintained, holding that man is an intellectual soul, or that the intellect is a part of Socrates. The first cannot stand, as was shown above (Q. 75, A. 4), for this reason, that it is one and the same man who is conscious both that he understands, and that he senses. But one cannot sense without a body; therefore the body must be some part of man. It remains therefore that the intellect by which Socrates understands is a part of Socrates, so that in some way it is united to the body of Socrates.

The Commentator [Averroës] held that this union is through the intelligible species, as having a double subject: in the possible intellect, and in the phantasms which are in the corporeal organs (*De Anima* iii, Comm. 5). Thus through the intelligible species the possible intellect is linked to the body of this or that particular man. But this link or union does not sufficiently explain the fact that the act of the intellect is the act of Socrates. This can be clearly seen from comparison with the sensitive power, from which Aristotle proceeds to consider things relating to the intellect. For the relation of phantasms to the intellect is like the relation of colours to the sense of sight, as he says in the book on the *Soul* (iii. 7). Therefore, as the species of colours are in the sight, so are the species of phantasms in the possible-intellect. Now it is clear that because the colours, the likenesses of which are in the sight, are on a wall, the action of seeing is not attributed to the wall, for

a.

b.

c.

d.

The Gothic Cathedral

a. The Cathedral of Notre Dame de Chartres, Chartres, France, begun in the 1140s. The word "Gothic" was originally a perjorative term coined by Renaissance thinkers who considered this style to be a barbaric break from classical tradition. The two towers shown here, for example, are not symmetrical. Even though the overall design of the cathedral may not be symmetrical, each of its elements was designed to reflect the harmony and beauty of God's creation. (*Lauros-Giraudon/Art Resource*)

b. Interior, Chartres Cathedral. By using pointed arches, it was possible to make soaring open spaces in the nave (main sanctuary) of the Gothic cathedral. The weight was shifted downward instead of outward. (*Bildarchiv Foto Marburg/Art Resource*) we do not say that the wall sees, but rather that it is seen. Therefore, from the fact that the species of phantasms are in the possible intellect it does not follow that Socrates, in whom are the phantasms, understands, but that he or his phantasms are understood.

Some, however, tried to maintain that the intellect is united to the body as its mover, and hence that the intellect and body form one thing so that the act of the intellect could be attributed to the whole. This is groundless however, for many reasons. First, because the intellect does not move the body except through desire, the movement of which presupposes the operation of the intellect. The reason therefore why Socrates understands is not because he is moved by his intellect, but rather, contrariwise, he is moved by his intellect because he understands. Secondly, because, since Socrates is an individual in a nature of one essence composed of matter and form, if the intellect be not the form, it follows that it must be outside the essence, and then the intellect is to the whole Socrates as a mover to the thing moved. The act of intellect however remains in the agent, and does not pass into something else, as does the action of heating. Therefore the act of understanding cannot be attributed to Socrates for the reason that he is moved by his intellect. Thirdly, because the action of a mover is never attributed to the thing moved, except as to an instrument; as the action of a carpenter to a saw. Therefore if understanding is attributed to Socrates, as the action of what moves him, it follows that it is attributed to him as to an instrument. This is contrary to the teaching of the Philosopher, who holds that understanding is not possible through a corporeal instrument (*De Anima* iii. 4). Fourthly, because, although the action of a part be attributed to the whole, as the action of the eye is attributed to a man, yet it is never attributed to another part, except perhaps accidentally; for we do not say that the hand sees because the eye sees. Therefore if the intellect and Socrates are united in the above manner, the action of the intellect cannot be attributed to Socrates. If, however, Socrates be a whole composed of a union of the intellect with whatever else belongs to Socrates, while nevertheless the intellect is united to those other things only as a mover, it follows that Socrates is not one absolutely, and consequently neither a being absolutely, for a thing is a being according as it is one.

There remains, therefore, no other explanation than that given by Aristotle (*De Anima* ii. 2)—namely, that this particular man understands because the intellectual principle is his form. Thus from the very operation of the intellect it is made clear that the intellectual principle is united to the body as its form.

The same can be clearly shown from the nature of the human species. For the nature of each thing is shown by its operation. Now the proper operation of man as man is to understand, because he thereby surpasses all other animals. From this, too,

---

c. Flying Buttresses at Reims Cathedral, ca. 1230–1235, by Villard De Honnecourt. To leave the interior unencumbered, the remaining outward stresses were often buttressed from outside the building. In some cathedrals exterior buttresses could not be built directly along the outside walls because of side aisles. Instead they were built outside the side aisles and connected to the pillars of the nave by stone ribs. These supporting ribs appear to "fly" over the side aisles. (*Villard de Honnecourt/Giraudon, Art Resource*)

d. The Rose Window, Notre Dame Cathedral, Paris, thirteenth century. By using pointed arches and flying buttresses, the walls of a cathedral did not have to bear the weight of the roof. Instead they could be used as screens for stained glass ornamentation such as this. (*Giraudon/Art Resource*)

Aristotle concludes (*Ethic.* x. 7) that the ultimate happiness of man must consist in this operation as properly belonging to him. Man must therefore derive his species from that which is the principle of this operation. But the species of anything is derived from its form. It follows therefore that the intellectual principle is the proper form of man.

But we must observe that the nobler a form is, the more it rises above corporeal matter, the less it is merged in matter, and the more it excels matter by its power and its operation; hence we find that the form of a mixed body has another operation not caused by its elemental qualities. And the higher we advance in the nobility of forms, the more we find that the power of the form excels the elementary matter; as the vegetative soul excels the form of the metal, and the sensitive soul excels the vegetative soul. Now the human soul is the highest and noblest of forms. Therefore it excels corporeal matter in its power by the fact that it has an operation and a power in which corporeal matter has no share whatever. This power is called the intellect.

It is well to remark that if anyone holds that the soul is composed of matter and form, it would follow that in no way could the soul be the form of the body. For since the form is an act, and matter is only a being in potency, that which is composed of matter and form cannot be the form of another by virtue of itself as a whole. But if it is a form by virtue of some part of itself, then that part which is the form we call the soul, and that of which it is the form we call the first thing animated, as was said above (Q. 75, A. 5).

Reply Obj. 1. As the Philosopher Says (*Phys.* ii. 2), the ultimate natural form to which the consideration of the natural philosopher is directed, namely, the human soul, is indeed separate; yet it exists in matter. He proves this from the fact that "man and the sun generate man from matter." It is separate indeed according to its intellectual power, because the intellectual power does not belong to a corporeal organ, as the power of seeing is the act of the eye; for understanding is an act which cannot be performed by a corporeal organ, like the act of seeing. But it exists in matter so far as the soul itself, to which this power belongs, is the form of the body, and the term of human generation. And so the Philosopher says (*De Anima* ii. 2) that "the intellect is separate" because it is not the power of a corporeal organ.

From this it is clear how to answer the *Second and Third objections.* For, in order that man may be able to understand all things by means of his intellect, and that his intellect may understand all things immaterial and universal, it is sufficient that the intellectual power be not the act of the body.

Reply Obj. 4. The human soul, by reason of its perfection, is not a form merged in matter, or entirely embraced by matter. Therefore there is nothing to prevent one of its powers not being the act of the body, although the soul is essentially the form of the body.

Reply Obj. 5. The soul communicates that being in which it subsists to the corporeal matter, out of which, combined with the intellectual soul, there results unity of being so that the being of the whole composite is also the being of the soul. This is not the case with other nonsubsistent forms. For this reason the human soul retains its own being after the dissolution of the body, though this is not so with other forms.

Reply Obj. 6. To be united to the body pertains to the soul by reason of itself, as it pertains to a light body by reason of itself to be raised up. And as a light body remains light when removed from its proper place, retaining meanwhile an aptitude and an inclination for its proper place, so the human soul retains its proper being when separated from the body, having an aptitude and a natural inclination to be united to the body.

* * *

FIRST PART OF THE SECOND PART (I–II)

TREATISE ON HUMAN ACTS

* * *

QUESTION 2: OF THOSE THINGS IN WHICH MAN'S HAPPINESS CONSISTS

* * *

Eighth Article

WHETHER ANY CREATED GOOD CONSTITUTES MAN'S HAPPINESS?

We Proceed Thus to the Eighth Article:—

Objection 1. It would seem that some created good constitutes man's happiness. For Dionysius says (*Div. Nom.* vii) that Divine wisdom *unites the ends of first things to the beginnings of second things,* from which we may gather that the summit of a lower nature touches the base of the higher nature. But man's highest good is happiness. Since then the angel is above man in the order of nature, as stated in the First Part (Q. 111, A. 1), it seems that man's happiness consists in man somehow reaching the angel.

Obj. 2. Further, the last end of each thing is that which, in relation to it, is perfect: hence the part is for the whole, as for its end. But the universe of creatures which is called the macrocosm, is compared to man who is called the microcosm (*Phys.* viii. 2), as perfect to imperfect. Therefore man's happiness consists in the whole universe of creatures.

Obj. 3. Further, man is made happy by that which lulls his natural desire. But man's natural desire does not reach out to a good surpassing his capacity. Since then man's capacity does not include that good which surpasses the limits of all creation, it seems that man can be made happy by some created good. Consequently some created good constitutes man's happiness.

On the contrary, Augustine says (*De Civ. Dei* xix. 26): *As the soul is the life of the body, so God is man's life of happiness: of Whom it is written: "Happy is that people whose God is the Lord"* (Ps. cxliii. 15).

I answer that, It is impossible for any created good to constitute man's happiness. For happiness is the perfect good, which lulls the appetite altogether; else it would not be the last end, if something yet remained to be desired. Now the object of the will, *i.e.*, of man's appetite, is the universal good; just as the object of the intellect is the universal true. Hence it is evident that naught can lull man's will, save the universal good. This is to be found, not in any creature, but in God alone; because every creature has goodness by participation. Wherefore God alone can satisfy the will of man, according to the words of Ps. cii. 5: *Who satisfieth thy desire with good things.* Therefore God alone constitutes man's happiness.

Reply Obj. 1. The summit of man does indeed touch the base of the angelic nature, by a kind of likeness; but man does not rest there as in his last end, but reaches out to the universal fount itself of good, which is the common object of happiness of all the blessed, as being the infinite and perfect good.

Reply Obj. 2. If a whole be not the last end, but ordained to a further end, then the last end of a part thereof is not the whole itself, but something else. Now the universe of creatures, to which man is compared as part to whole, is not the last end, but is ordained to God, as to its last end. Therefore the last end of man is not the good of the universe, but God himself.

Reply Obj. 3. Created good is not less than that good of which man is capable, as of something intrinsic and inherent to him: but it is less than the good of which he is capable, as of an object, and which is infinite. And the participated good which is in an angel, and in the whole universe, is a finite and restricted good.

* * *

QUESTION 3: WHAT IS HAPPINESS?

* * *

Fourth Article

WHETHER, IF HAPPINESS IS IN THE INTELLECTIVE PART, IT IS AN OPERATION OF THE INTELLECT OR OF THE WILL?

We Proceed Thus to the Fourth Article:—

Objection 1. It would seem that happiness consists in an act of the will. For Augustine says (*De Civ. Dei* xix. 10, 11), that man's happiness consists in peace; wherefore it is written (Ps. cxlvii. 3): *Who hath placed peace in thy end.* But peace pertains to the will. Therefore man's happiness is in the will.

Obj. 2. Further, happiness is the supreme good. But good is the object of the will. Therefore happiness consists in an operation of the will.

Obj. 3. Further, the last end corresponds to the first mover: thus the last end of the whole army is victory, which is the end of the general, who moves all the men. But the first mover in regard to operations is the will: because it moves the other powers, as we shall state further on (Q. 9, AA. 1, 3). Therefore happiness regards the will.

Obj. 4. Further, if happiness be an operation, it must needs be man's most excellent operation. But the love of God, which is an act of the will, is a more excellent operation than knowledge, which is an operation of the intellect, as the Apostle declares (1 Cor. xiii). Therefore it seems that happiness consists in an act of the will.

Obj. 5. Further, Augustine says (*De Trin.* xiii. 5) that *happy is he who has whatever he desires, and desires nothing amiss.* And a little further on (6) he adds: *He is almost happy who desires well, whatever he desires: for good things make a man happy, and such a man already possesses some good—i.e., a good will.* Therefore happiness consists in an act of the will.

On the contrary, Our Lord said (Jo. xvii. 3): *This is eternal life: that they may know Thee, the only true God.* Now eternal life is the last end, as stated above (A. 2 *ad* 1). Therefore man's happiness consists in the knowledge of God, which is an act of the intellect.

I answer that, As stated above (Q. 2, A. 6) two things are needed for happiness: one, which is the essence of happiness: the other, that is, as it were, its proper accident, *i.e.,* the delight connected with it. I say, then, that as to the very essence of happiness, it is impossible for it to consist in an act of the will. For it is evident from what has been said (AA. 1, 2; Q. 2, A. 7) that happiness is the attainment of the last end. But the attainment of the end does not consist in the very act of the will. For the will is directed to the end, both absent, when it desires it; and present, when it is delighted by resting therein. Now it is evident that the desire itself of the end is not the attainment of the end, but is a movement towards the end: while delight comes to the will from the end being present; and not conversely, is a thing made present, by the fact that the will delights in it. Therefore, that the end be present to him who desires it, must be due to something else than an act of the will.

This is evidently the case in regard to sensible ends. For if the acquisition of money were through an act of the will, the covetous man would have it from the very moment that he wished for it. But at that moment it is far from him; and he attains it, by grasping it in his hand, or in some like manner; and then he delights in the money got. And so it is with an intelligible end. For at first we desire to attain an intelligible end; we attain it, through its being made present to us by an act of the intellect; and then the delighted will rests in the end when attained.

So, therefore, the essence of happiness consists in an act of the intellect: but the delight that results from happiness pertains to the will. In this sense Augustine says (*Conf.* x. 23) that happiness is *joy in truth,* because, to wit, joy itself is the consummation of happiness.

Reply Obj. 1. Peace pertains to man's last end, not as though it were the very essence of happiness; but because it is antecedent and consequent thereto: antecedent, in so far as all those things are removed which disturb and hinder man in attaining the last end: consequent, inasmuch as, when man has attained his last end, he remains at peace, his desire being at rest.

Reply Obj. 2. The will's first object is not its act: just as neither is the first object of the sight, vision, but a visible thing. Wherefore, from the very fact that happiness belongs to the will, as the will's first object, it follows that it does not belong to it as its act.

Reply Obj. 3. The intellect apprehends the end before the will does: yet motion towards the end begins in the will. And therefore to the will belongs that which last of all follows the attainment of the end, viz., delight or enjoyment.

Reply Obj. 4. Love ranks above knowledge in moving, but knowledge precedes love in attaining: *for naught is loved save what is known,* as Augustine says (*De Trin.* x. 1). Consequently we first attain an intelligible end by an act of the intellect; just as we first attain a sensible end by an act of sense.

Reply Obj. 5. He who has whatever he desires, is happy, because he has what he desires: and this indeed is by something other than the act of his will. But to desire nothing amiss is needed for happiness, as a necessary disposition thereto. And a good will is reckoned among the good things which make a man happy, forasmuch as it is an inclination of the will: just as a movement is reduced to the genus of its terminus, for instance, *alteration* to the genus *quality.*

Eighth Article

WHETHER MAN'S HAPPINESS CONSISTS IN THE VISION OF THE DIVINE ESSENCE?

We Proceed Thus to the Eighth Article:—

Objection 1. It would seem that man's happiness does not consist in the vision of the Divine Essence. For Dionysius says (*Myst. Theol.* i) that by that which is highest in his intellect, man is united to God as to something altogether unknown. But that which is seen in its essence is not altogether unknown. Therefore the final perfection of the intellect, namely, happiness, does not consist in God being seen in His Essence.

Obj. 2. Further, the higher perfection belongs to the higher nature. But to see His own Essence is the perfection proper to the Divine intellect. Therefore the final perfection of the human intellect does not reach to this, but consists in something less.

On the contrary, It is written (1 Jo. iii. 2): *When He shall appear, we shall be like to Him; and we shall see Him as He is.*

I answer that, Final and perfect happiness can consist in nothing else than the vision of the Divine Essence. To make this clear, two points must be observed. First, that man is not perfectly happy, so long as something remains for him to desire and seek: secondly, that the perfection of any power is determined by the nature of its object. Now the object of the intellect is *what a thing is, i.e.,* the essence of a thing, according to *De Anima* iii. 6. Wherefore the intellect attains perfection, in so far as it knows the essence of a thing. If therefore an intellect know the essence of some effect, whereby it is not possible to know the essence of the cause, *i.e.* to know of the cause *what it is;* that intellect cannot be said to reach that cause simply, although it may be able to gather from the effect the knowledge that the cause is. Consequently, when man knows an effect, and knows that it has a cause, there naturally remains in man the desire to know about that cause, *what it is.* And this desire is one of wonder, and causes inquiry, as is stated in the beginning of the *Metaphysics* (i. 2). For instance, if a man, knowing the eclipse of the sun, consider that it must be due to some cause, and know not what that cause is, he wonders about it, and from wondering proceeds to inquire. Nor does this inquiry cease until he arrive at a knowledge of the essence of the cause.

If therefore the human intellect, knowing the essence of some created effect, knows no more of God than *that He is;* the perfection of that intellect does not yet reach simply the First Cause, but there remains in it the natural desire to seek the cause. Wherefore it is not yet perfectly happy. Consequently, for perfect happiness the intellect needs to reach the very Essence of the First Cause. And thus it will have its perfection through union with God as with that object, in which alone man's happiness consists, as stated above (AA. 1, 7; Q. 2, A. 8).

Reply Obj. 1. Dionysius speaks of the knowledge of wayfarers journeying towards happiness.

Reply Obj. 2. As stated above (Q. 1, A. 8), the end has a twofold acceptation. First, as to the thing itself which is desired: and in this way, the same thing is the end of the higher and of the lower nature, and indeed of all things, as stated above *(ibid.).* Secondly, as to the attainment of this thing; and thus the end of the higher nature is different from that of the lower, according to their respective habitudes to that thing. So then the happiness of God, Who, in understanding his Essence, comprehends It, is higher than that of a man or angel who sees It indeed, but comprehends It not.

* * *

QUESTION 5: OF THE ATTAINMENT OF HAPPINESS

* * *

Fifth Article

Whether Man Can Attain Happiness by His Natural Powers?

We Proceed Thus to the Fifth Article:—

Objection 1. It would seem that man can attain Happiness by his natural powers. For nature does not fail in necessary things. But nothing is so necessary to man as that by which he attains the last end. Therefore this is not lacking to human nature. Therefore man can attain Happiness by his natural powers.

Obj. 2. Further, since man is more noble than irrational creatures, it seems that he must be better equipped than they. But irrational creatures can attain their end by their natural powers. Much more therefore can man attain Happiness by his natural powers.

Obj. 3. Further, Happiness is a *perfect operation,* according to the Philosopher (*Ethic.* vii. 13). Now the beginning of a thing belongs to the same principle as the perfecting thereof. Since, therefore, the imperfect operation, which is as the beginning in human operations, is subject to man's natural power, whereby he is master of his own actions; it seems that he can attain to perfect operation, *i.e.,* Happiness, by his natural powers.

On the contrary, Man is naturally the principle of his action, by his intellect and will. But final Happiness prepared for the saints, surpasses the intellect and will of man; for the Apostle says (1 Cor. ii. 9): *Eye hath not seen, nor ear heard, neither hath it entered into the heart of man, what things God hath prepared for them that love Him.* Therefore man cannot attain Happiness by his natural powers.

I answer that, Imperfect happiness that can be had in this life, can be acquired by man by his natural powers, in the same way as virtue, in whose operation it consists: on this point we shall speak further on (Q. 63). But man's perfect Happiness, as stated above (Q. 3, A. 8), consists in the vision of the Divine Essence. Now the vision of God's Essence surpasses the nature not only of man, but also of every creature, as was shown in the First Part (Q. 12, A. 4). For the natural knowledge of every creature is in keeping with the mode of his substance: thus it is said of the intelligence (*De Causis;* Prop. viii.) that *it knows things that are above it, and things that are below it, according to the mode of its substance.* But every knowledge that is according to the mode of created substance, falls short of the vision of the Divine Essence, which infinitely surpasses all created substance. Consequently neither man, nor any creature, can attain final Happiness by his natural powers.

Reply Obj. 1. Just as nature does not fail man in necessaries, although it has not provided him with weapons and clothing, as it provided other animals, because it gave him reason and hands, with which he is able to get these things for himself; so neither did it fail man in things necessary, although it gave him not the wherewithal to attain Happiness: since this it could not do. But it did give him freewill, with which he can turn to God, that He may make him happy. *For what we do by means of our friends, is done, in a sense, by ourselves (Ethic.* iii. 3).

Reply Obj. 2. The nature that can attain perfect good, although it needs help from without in order to attain it, is of more noble condition than a nature which cannot attain perfect good, but attains some imperfect good, although it need no help from without in order to attain it, as the Philosopher says (*De Cælo* ii. 12). Thus he is better disposed to health who can attain perfect health, albeit by means of medicine, than he who can attain but imperfect health, without the help of medicine. And therefore the rational creature, which can attain the perfect good of happiness, but needs the Divine assistance for the purpose, is more perfect than the irrational creature, which is not capable of attaining this good, but attains some imperfect good by its natural powers.

Reply Obj. 3. When imperfect and perfect are of the same species, they can be caused by the same power. But this does not follow of necessity, if they be of different species: for not everything, that can cause the disposition of matter, can produce the final perfection. Now the imperfect operation, which is subject to man's natural power, is not of the same species as that perfect operation which is man's happiness: since operation takes its species from its object. Consequently the argument does not prove.

* * *

QUESTION 94: OF THE NATURAL LAW

*   *   *

Second Article

WHETHER THE NATURAL LAW CONTAINS SEVERAL PRECEPTS, OR ONE ONLY?

We Proceed Thus to the Second Article:—

Objection 1. It would seem that the natural law contains, not several precepts, but one only. For law is a kind of precept, as stated above (Q. 92, A. 2). If therefore there were many precepts of the natural law, it would follow that there are also many natural laws.

Obj. 2. Further, the natural law is consequent to human nature. But human nature, as a whole, is one; though, as to its parts, it is manifold. Therefore, either there is but one precept of the law of nature, on account of the unity of nature as a whole; or there are many, by reason of the number of parts of human nature. The result would be that even things relating to the inclination of the concupiscible faculty belong to the natural law.

Obj. 3. Further, law is something pertaining to reason, as stated above (Q. 90, A. 1). Now reason is but one in man. Therefore there is only one precept of the natural law.

On the contrary, The precepts of the natural law in man stand in relation to practical matters, as the first principles to matters of demonstration. But there are several first indemonstrable principles. Therefore there are also several precepts of the natural law.

I answer that, As stated above (Q. 91, A. 3), the precepts of the natural law are to the practical reason, what the first principles of demonstrations are to the speculative reason; because both are self-evident principles. Now a thing is said to be self-evident in two ways: first, in itself; secondly, in relation to us. Any proposition is said to be self-evident in itself, its predicate is contained in the notion of the subject: although, to one who knows not the definition of the subject, it happens that such a proposition is not self-evident. For instance, this proposition, *Man is a rational being,* is, in its very nature, self-evident, since who says *man,* says *a rational being:* and yet to one who knows not what a man is, this proposition is not self-evident. Hence it is that, as Boethius says *(De Hebdom.),* certain axioms or propositions are universally self-evident to all; and such are those propositions whose terms are known to all, as, *Every whole is greater than its part,* and, *Things equal to one and the same are equal to one another.* But some propositions are self-evident only to the wise, who understand the meaning of the terms of such propositions: thus to one who understands that an angel is not a body, it is self-evident that an angel is not circumscriptively in a place: but this is not evident to the unlearned, for they cannot grasp it.

Now a certain order is to be found in those things that are apprehended universally. For that which, before aught else, falls under apprehension, is *being,* the notion of which is included in all things whatsoever a man apprehends. Wherefore the first indemonstrable principle is that *the same thing cannot be affirmed and denied at the same time,* which is based on the notion of being and not-being: and on this principle all others are based, as is stated in *Metaph.* iv, text. 9. Now as being is the first thing that falls under the apprehension simply, so *good* is the first thing that falls under the apprehension of the practical reason, which is directed to action: since every agent acts for an end under the aspect of good. Consequently the first principle in the practical reason is one founded on the notion of good, viz., that *good is that which all things seek after.* Hence this is the first precept of law, that *good is to be done and pursued, and evil is to be avoided.* All other precepts of the natural law are based upon this: so that whatever the practical reason naturally apprehends as man's good (or evil) belongs to the precepts of the natural law as something to be done or avoided.

Since, however, good has the nature of an end, and evil, the nature of a contrary, hence it is that all those things to which man has a natural inclination, are naturally apprehended by reason as being good, and consequently as objects of pursuit, and their contraries as evil, and objects of avoidance. Wherefore according to the order of natural inclinations, is the order of the precepts of the natural law. Because in man there is first of all an inclination to good in accordance with the nature which he has in common with all substances: inasmuch as every substance seeks the preservation of its own being, according to its nature: and by reason of this inclination, whatever is a means of preserving human life, and of warding off its obstacles, belongs to the natural law. Secondly, there is in man an inclination to things that pertain to him more specially, according to that nature which he has in common with other animals: and in virtue of this inclination, those things are said to belong to the natural law, *which nature has taught to all animals,* such as sexual intercourse, education of offspring and so forth. Thirdly, there is in man an inclination to good, according to the nature of his reason, which nature is proper to him: thus man has a natural inclination to know the truth about God, and to live in society: and in this respect, whatever pertains to this inclination belongs to the natural law; for instance, to shun ignorance, to avoid offending those among whom one has to live, and other such things regarding the above inclination.

Reply Obj. 1. All these precepts of the law of nature have the character of one natural law, inasmuch as they flow from one first precept.

Reply Obj. 2. All the inclinations of any parts whatsoever of human nature, *e.g.,* of the concupiscible and irascible parts, in so far as they are ruled by reason, belong to the natural law, and are reduced to one first precept, as stated above: so that the precepts of the natural law are many in themselves, but are based on one common foundation.

Reply Obj. 3. Although reason is one in itself, yet it directs all things regarding man; so that whatever can be ruled by reason, is contained under the law of reason.

*   *   *

Fourth Article

WHETHER THE NATURAL LAW IS THE SAME IN ALL MEN?

We Proceed Thus to the Fourth Article:—

Objection 1. It would seem that the natural law is not the same in all. For it is stated in the Decretals (*Dist.* i) that *the natural law is that which is contained in the*

Law and the Gospel. But this is not common to all men; because, as it is written (Rom. x. 16), *all do not obey the gospel.* Therefore the natural law is not the same in all men.

Obj. 2. Further, *Things which are accordingly to the law are said to be just,* as stated in *Ethic.* v. But it is stated in the same book that nothing is so universally just as not to be subject to change in regard to some men. Therefore even the natural law is not the same in all men.

Obj. 3. Further, as stated above (AA. 2, 3), to the natural law belongs everything to which a man is inclined according to his nature. Now different men are naturally inclined to different things; some to the desire of pleasures, others to the desire of honors, and other men to other things. Therefore there is not one natural law for all.

On the contrary, Isidore says (*Etym.* v. 4): *The natural law is common to all nations.*

I answer that, As stated above (AA. 2, 3), to the natural law belongs those things to which a man is inclined naturally: and among these it is proper to man to be inclined to act according to reason. Now the process of reason is from the common to the proper, as stated in *Phys.* i. The speculative reason, however, is differently situated in this matter, from the practical reason. For, since the speculative reason is busied chiefly with necessary things, which cannot be otherwise than they are, its proper conclusions, like the universal principles, contain the truth without fail. The practical reason, on the other hand, is busied with contingent matters, about which human actions are concerned: and consequently, although there is necessity in the general principles, the more we descend to matters of detail, the more frequently we encounter defects. Accordingly then in speculative matters truth is the same in all men, both as to principles and as to conclusions: although the truth is not known to all as regards the conclusions, but only as regards the principles which are called *common notions.* But in matters of action, truth or practical rectitude is not the same for all, as to matters of detail, but only as to the general principles: and where there is the same rectitude in matters of detail, it is not equally known to all.

It is therefore evident that, as regards the general principles whether of speculative or of practical reason, truth or rectitude is the same for all, and is equally known by all. As to the proper conclusions of the speculative reason, the truth is the same for all, but is not equally known to all: thus it is true for all that the three angles of a triangle are together equal to two right angles, although it is not known to all. But as to the proper conclusions of the practical reason, neither is the truth or rectitude the same for all, nor, where it is the same, is it equally known by all. Thus it is right and true for all to act according to reason: and from this principle it follows as a proper conclusion, that goods entrusted to another should be restored to their owner. Now this is true for the majority of cases: but it may happen in a particular case that it would be injurious, and therefore unreasonable, to restore goods held in trust; for instance if they are claimed for the purpose of fighting against one's country. And this principle will be found to fail the more, according as we descend further into detail, e.g., if one were to say that goods held in trust should be restored with such and such a guarantee, or in such and such a way; because the greater the number of conditions added, the greater the number of ways in which the principle may fail, so that it be not right to restore or not to restore.

Consequently we must say that the natural law, as to general principles, is the same for all, both as to rectitude and as to knowledge. But as to certain matters of detail, which are conclusions, as it were, of those general principles, it is the same for all in the majority of cases, both as to rectitude and as to knowledge; and yet in some few cases it may fail, both as to rectitude, by reason of certain obstacles (just as natures subject to generation and corruption fail in some few cases on account of some obstacle), and as to knowledge, since in some the reason is perverted by passion, or evil habit, or an evil disposition of nature; thus formerly, theft, although it is expressly contrary to the natural law, was not considered wrong among the Germans, as Julius Caesar relates (*De Bello Gall.* vi).

Reply Obj. 1. The meaning of the sentence quoted is not that whatever is contained in the Law and the Gospel belongs to the natural law, since they contain many things that are above nature; but that whatever belongs to the natural law is fully contained in them. Wherefore Gratian, after saying that *the natural law is what is contained in the Law and the Gospel,* adds at once, by way of example, *by which everyone is commanded to do to others as he would be done by.*

Reply Obj. 2. The saying of the Philosopher is to be understood of things that are naturally just, not as general principles, but as conclusions drawn from them, having rectitude in the majority of cases, but failing in a few.

Reply Obj. 3. As, in man, reason rules and commands the other powers, so all the natural inclinations belonging to the other powers must needs be directed according to reason. Wherefore it is universally right for all men, that all their inclinations should be directed according to reason.

Fifth Article

WHETHER THE NATURAL LAW CAN BE CHANGED?

We Proceed Thus to the Fifth Article:—

Objection 1. It would seem that the natural law can be changed. Because on Ecclus. xvii. 9, *He gave them instructions, and the law of life,* the gloss says: *He wished the law of the letter to be written, in order to correct the law of nature.* But that which is corrected is changed. Therefore the natural law can be changed.

Obj. 2. Further, the slaying of the innocent, adultery, and theft are against the natural law. But we find these things changed by God: as when God commanded Abraham to slay his innocent son (Gen. xxii. 2); and when he ordered the Jews to borrow and purloin the vessels of the Egyptians (Exod. xii. 35); and when He commanded Osee to take to himself *a wife of fornications* (Osee i. 2). Therefore the natural law can be changed.

Obj. 3. Further, Isidore says (*Etym.* v. 4) that *the possession of all things in common, and universal freedom, are matters of natural law.* But these things are seen to be changed by human laws. Therefore it seems that the natural law is subject to change.

On the contrary, It is said in the Decretals (*Dist.* v): *The natural law dates from the creation of the rational creature. It does not vary according to time, but remains unchangeable.*

I answer that, A change in the natural law may be understood in two ways. First, by way of addition. In this sense nothing hinders the natural law from being changed: since many things for the benefit of human life have been added over and above the natural law, both by the Divine law and by human laws.

Secondly, a change in the natural law may be understood by way of subtraction, so that what previously was according to the natural law, ceases to be so. In this sense, the natural law is altogether unchangeable in its first principles: but in its secondary principles, which, as we have said (A. 4), are certain detailed proximate conclusions drawn from the first principles, the natural law is not changed so that what it prescribes be not right in most cases. But it may be changed in some particular cases of rare occurrence, through some special causes hindering the observance of such precepts, as stated above (A. 4).

Reply Obj. 1. The written law is said to be given for the correction of the natural law, either because it supplies what was wanting to the natural law; or because the natural law was perverted in the hearts of some men, as to certain matters, so that they esteemed those things good which are naturally evil; which perversion stood in need of correction.

Reply Obj. 2. All men alike, both guilty and innocent, die the death of nature: which death of nature is inflicted by the power of God on account of original sin, according to 1 Kings ii. 6: *The Lord killeth and maketh alive.* Consequently, by the command of God, death can be inflicted on any man, guilty or innocent, without any injustice whatever.—In like manner adultery is intercourse with another's wife; who is allotted to him by the law emanating from God. Consequently intercourse with any woman, by the command of God, is neither adultery nor fornication.—The same applies to theft, which is the taking of another's property. For whatever is taken by the command of God, to Whom all things belong, is not taken against the will of its owner, whereas it is in this that theft consists.—Nor is it only in human things, that whatever is commanded by God is right; but also in natural things, whatever is done by God, is, in some way, natural, as stated in the First Part (Q. 105, A. 6 *ad* 1).

Reply Obj. 3. A thing is said to belong to the natural law in two ways. First, because nature inclines thereto: *e.g.,* that one should not do harm to another. Secondly, because nature did not bring in the contrary: thus we might say that for man to be naked is of the natural law, because nature did not give him clothes, but art invented them. In this sense, *the possession of all things in common and universal freedom* are said to be of the natural law, because, to wit, the distinction of possessions and slavery were not brought in by nature, but devised by human reason for the benefit of human life. Accordingly the law of nature was not changed in this respect, except by addition.

* * *

QUESTION 95: OF HUMAN LAW

* * *

First Article

WHETHER IT WAS USEFUL FOR LAWS TO BE FRAMED BY MEN?

We Proceed Thus to the First Article:—

Objection 1. It would seem that it was not useful for laws to be framed by men. Because the purpose of every law is that man be made good thereby, as stated above (Q. 92, A. 1). But men are more to be induced to be good willingly by means of admonitions, than against their will, by means of laws. Therefore there was no need to frame laws.

Obj. 2. Further, as the Philosopher says (*Ethic.* v. 4), *men have recourse to a judge as to animate justice.* But animate justice is better than inanimate justice, which is contained in laws. Therefore it would have been better for the execution of justice to be entrusted to the decision of judges, than to frame laws in addition.

Obj. 3. Further, every law is framed for the direction of human actions, as is evident from what has been stated above (Q. 90, AA. 1, 2). But since human actions are about singulars, which are infinite in number, matters pertaining to the direction of human actions cannot be taken into sufficient consideration except by a wise man, who looks into each one of them. Therefore it would have been better for human acts to be directed by the judgment of wise men, than by the framing of laws. Therefore there was no need of human laws.

On the contrary, Isidore says (*Etym.* v. 20): *Laws were made that in fear thereof human audacity might be held in check, that innocence might be safeguarded in the midst of wickedness, and that the dread of punishment might prevent the wicked from doing harm.* But these things are most necessary to mankind. Therefore it was necessary that human laws should be made.

I answer that, As stated above (Q. 63, A. 1; Q. 94, A. 3), man has a natural aptitude for virtue; but the perfection of virtue must be acquired by man by means of some kind of training. Thus we observe that man is helped by industry in his necessities, for instance, in food and clothing. Certain beginnings of these he has from nature, viz., his reason and his hands; but he has not the full complement, as other animals have, to whom nature has given sufficiency of clothing and food. Now it is difficult to see how man could suffice for himself in the matter of this training: since the perfection of virtue consists chiefly in withdrawing man from undue pleasures, to which above all man is inclined, and especially the young, who are more capable of being trained. Consequently a man needs to receive this training from another, whereby to arrive at the perfection of virtue. And as to those young people who are inclined to acts of virtue, by their good natural disposition, or by custom, or rather by the gift of God, paternal training suffices, which is by admonitions. But since some are found to be depraved, and prone to vice, and not easily amenable to words, it was necessary for such to be restrained from evil by force and fear, in order that, at least, they might desist from evildoing, and leave others in peace, and that they themselves, by being habituated in this way, might be brought to do willingly what hitherto they did from fear, and thus become virtuous. Now this kind of training, which compels through fear of punishment, is the discipline of laws. Therefore, in order that man might have peace and virtue, it was necessary for laws to be framed: for, as the Philosopher says (Polit. i. 2), *as man is the most noble of animals if he be perfect in virtue, so is he the lowest of all, if he be severed from law and righteousness;* because man can use his reason to devise means of satisfying his lusts and evil passions, which other animals are unable to do.

Reply Obj. 1. Men who are well disposed are led willingly to virtue by being admonished better than by coercion: but men who are evilly disposed are not led to virtue unless they are compelled.

Reply Obj. 2. As the Philosopher says (*Rhet.* i. 1), *it is better that all things be regulated by law, than left to be decided by judges: and this for three reasons. First, because it is easier to find a few wise men competent to frame right laws, than to find the many who would be necessary to judge aright of each single case.—Secondly, because those who make laws consider long beforehand* what laws to make; whereas judgment on each single case has to be pronounced as soon as it arises: and it is easier for man to see what is right, by taking many instances into consideration, than by considering one solitary fact.—Thirdly, because lawgivers judge in the abstract and of future events; whereas those who sit in judgment judge of things present, towards which they are affected by love, hatred, or some kind of cupidity; wherefore their judgment is perverted.

Since then the animated justice of the judge is not found in every man, and since it can be deflected, therefore it was necessary, whenever possible, for the law to determine how to judge, and for very few matters to be left to the decision of men.

Reply Obj. 3. Certain individual facts which cannot be covered by the law *have necessarily to be committed to judges,* as the Philosopher says in the same passage: for instance, *concerning something that has happened or not happened,* and the like.

Second Article

WHETHER EVERY HUMAN LAW IS DERIVED FROM THE NATURAL LAW?

We Proceed Thus to the Second Article:—

Objection 1. It would seem that not every human law is derived from the natural law. For the Philosopher says (*Ethic.* v. 7) that *the legal just is that which originally was a matter of indifference.* But those things which arise from the natural law are not matters of indifference. Therefore the enactments of human laws are not all derived from the natural law.

Obj. 2. Further, positive law is contrasted with natural law, as stated by Isidore (*Etym.* v. 4) and the Philosopher *(Ethic.* v, *loc. cit.).* But those things which flow as conclusion from the general principles of the natural law belong to the natural law, as stated above (Q. 94, A. 4). Therefore that which is established by human law does not belong to the natural law.

Obj. 3. Further, the law of nature is the same for all; since the Philosopher says (*Ethic.* v. 7) that *the natural just is that which is equally valid everywhere.* If therefore human laws were derived from the natural law, it would follow that they too are the same for all: which is clearly false.

Obj. 4. Further, it is possible to give a reason for things which are derived from the natural law. But *it is not possible to give the reason for all the legal enactments of the lawgivers,* as the jurist says. Therefore not all human laws are derived from the natural law.

On the contrary, Tully says (*Rhetor.* ii): *Things which emanated from nature and were approved by custom, were sanctioned by fear and reverence for the laws.*

I answer that, As Augustine says (*De Lib. Arb.* i. 5), *that which is not just seems to be no law at all: wherefore the force of a law depends on the extent of its justice.* Now in human affairs a thing is said to be just, from being right, according to the rule of reason. But the first rule of reason is the law of nature, as is clear from what has been stated above (Q. 91, A. 2 *ad* 2). Consequently every human law has just so much of the nature of law, as it is derived from the law of nature. But if in any point it deflects from the law of nature, it is no longer a law but a perversion of law.

But it must be noted that something may be derived from the natural law in two ways: first, as a conclusion from premises, secondly, by way of determination of certain generalities. The first way is like to that by which, in sciences, demonstrated conclusions are drawn from the principles: while the second mode is likened to that whereby, in the arts, general forms are particularized as to details: thus the craftsman needs to determine the general form of a house to some particular shape. Some things are therefore derived from the general principles of the natural law, by way of conclusions; *e.g.,* that *one must not kill* may be derived as a conclusion from the principle that one should do harm to no man: while some are derived therefrom by way of determination; *e.g.,* the law of nature has it that the evil-doer should be punished; but that he be punished in this or that way, is a determination of the law of nature.

Accordingly both modes of derivation are found in the human law. But those things which are derived in the first way, are contained in human law not as emanating therefrom exclusively, but have some force from the natural law also. But those things which are derived in the second way, have no other force than that of human law.

Reply Obj. 1. The Philosopher is speaking of those enactments which are by way of determination or specification of the precepts of the natural law.

Reply Obj. 2. This argument avails for those things that are derived from the natural law, by way of conclusions.

Reply Obj. 3. The general principles of the natural law cannot be applied to all men in the same way on account of the great variety of human affairs: and hence arises the diversity of positive laws among various people.

Reply Obj. 4. These words of the Jurist are to be understood as referring to decisions of rulers in determining particular points of the natural law: on which determinations the judgment of expert and prudent men is based as on its principles; in so far, to wit, as they see at once what is the best thing to decide.

Hence the Philosopher says (*Ethic.* vi. 11) that in such matters, *we ought to pay as much attention to the undemonstrated sayings and opinions of persons who surpass us in experience, age and prudence, as to their demonstrations.*

*   *   *

QUESTION 96: OF THE POWER OF HUMAN LAW

*   *   *

Second Article

WHETHER IT BELONGS TO THE HUMAN LAW TO REPRESS ALL VICES?

We Proceed Thus to the Second Article:—

Objection 1. It would seem that it belongs to human law to repress all vices. For Isidore says (*Etym.* v. 20) that *laws were made in order that, in fear thereof, man's audacity might be held in check.* But it would not be held in check sufficiently, unless all evils were repressed by law. Therefore human law should repress all evils.

Obj. 2. Further, the intention of the lawgiver is to make the citizens virtuous. But a man cannot be virtuous unless he forbear from all kinds of vice. Therefore it belongs to human law to repress all vices.

Obj. 3. Further, human law is derived from the natural law, as stated above (Q. 95, A. 2). But all vices are contrary to the law of nature. Therefore human law should repress all vices.

On the contrary, We read in *De Lib. Arb.* i. 5: *It seems to me that the law which is written for the governing of the people rightly permits these things, and that Divine providence punishes them.* But Divine providence punishes nothing but vices. Therefore human law rightly allows some vices, by not repressing them.

I answer that, As stated above (Q. 90, AA. I, 2), law is framed as a rule or measure of human acts. Now a measure should be homogeneous with that which it measures, as stated in *Metaph.* x, text. 3, 4, since different things are measured by different measures. Wherefore laws imposed on men should also be in keeping with their condition, for, as Isidore says (*Etym.* v. 21), law should be *possible both according to nature, and according to the customs of the country.* Now possibility or faculty of action is due to an interior habit or disposition: since the same thing is not possible to one who has not a virtuous habit, as is possible to one who has. Thus the same is not possible to a child as to a full-grown man: for which reason the law for children is not the same as for adults, since many things are permitted to children, which in an adult are punished by law or at any rate are open to blame. In like manner many things are permissible to men not perfect in virtue, which would be intolerable in a virtuous man.

Now human law is framed for a number of human beings, the majority of whom are not perfect in virtue. Wherefore human laws do not forbid all vices, from which the virtuous abstain, but only the more grievous vices, from which it is possible for the majority to abstain; and chiefly those that are to the hurt of others, without the prohibition of which human society could not be maintained: thus human law prohibits murder, theft and such like.

Reply Obj. 1. Audacity seems to refer to the assailing of others. Consequently it belongs to those sins chiefly whereby one's neighbor is injured: and these sins are forbidden by human law, as stated.

Reply Obj. 2. The purpose of human law is to lead men to virtue, not suddenly, but gradually. Wherefore it does not lay upon the multitude of imperfect men the burdens of those who are already virtuous, viz., that they should abstain from all evil. Otherwise these imperfect ones, being unable to bear such precepts, would break out into yet greater evils: thus it is written (Prov. xxx. 33): *He that violently bloweth his nose, bringeth out blood;* and (Matth. ix. 17) that if *new wine,* i.e., precepts of a perfect life, *is put into old bottles,* i.e., into imperfect men, *the bottles break, and the wine runneth out,* i.e., the precepts are despised, and those men, from contempt, break out into evils worse still.

Reply Obj. 3. The natural law is a participation in us of the eternal law: while human law falls short of the eternal law. Now Augustine says (*De Lib. Arb.* i. 5): *The law which is framed for the government of states, allows and leaves unpunished many things that are punished by Divine providence. Nor, if this law does not attempt to do everything, is this a reason why it should be blamed for what it does.* Wherefore, too, human law does not prohibit everything that is forbidden by the natural law.

*   *   *

SECOND PART OF THE SECOND PART (II–II)

* * *

QUESTION 40: OF WAR

* * *

First Article

WHETHER IT IS ALWAYS SINFUL TO WAGE WAR?

We Proceed Thus to the First Article:—

Objection 1. It would seem that it is always sinful to wage war. Because punishment is not inflicted except for sin. Now those who wage war are threatened by Our Lord with punishment, according to Matth. xxvi. 52: *All that take the sword shall perish with the sword.* Therefore all wars are unlawful.

Obj. 2. Further, whatever is contrary to a Divine precept is a sin. But war is contrary to a Divine precept, for it is written (Matth. v. 39): *But I say to you not to resist evil;* and (Rom. xii. 19): *Not revenging yourselves, my dearly beloved, but give place unto wrath.* Therefore war is always sinful.

Obj. 3. Further, nothing, except sin, is contrary to an act of virtue. But war is contrary to peace. Therefore war is always a sin.

Obj. 4. Further, the exercise of a lawful thing is itself lawful, as is evident in scientific exercises. But warlike exercises which take place in tournaments are forbidden by the Church, since those who are slain in these trials are deprived of ecclesiastical burial. Therefore it seems that war is a sin in itself.

On the contrary, Augustine says in a sermon on the son of the centurion [*Ep. ad Marcel.,* cxxxviii.]: *If the Christian Religion forbade war altogether, those who sought salutary advice in the Gospel would rather have been counselled to cast aside their arms, and to give up soldiering altogether. On the contrary, they were told: "Do violence to no man; . . . and be content with your pay." [Luke iii. 14] If he commanded them to be content with their pay, he did not forbid soldiering.*

I answer that, In order for a war to be just, three things are necessary. First, the authority of the sovereign by whose command the war is to be waged. For it is not the business of a private individual to declare war, because he can seek for redress of his rights from the tribunal of his superior. Moreover it is not the business of a private individual to summon together the people, which has to be done in wartime. And as the care of the common weal is committed to those who are in authority, it is their business to watch over the common weal of the city, kingdom or province subject to them. And just as it is lawful for them to have recourse to the sword in defending that common weal against internal disturbances, when they punish evil-doers, according to the words of the Apostle (Rom. xiii. 4): *He beareth not the sword in vain: for he is God's minister, an avenger to execute wrath upon him that doth evil;* so too, it is their busi-

Three Orders of Society, from *L'image du monde,* Franco-Flemish, late-thirteenth century. This detail from an illustrated manuscript page shows the hierarchy of medieval society with monk, knight, and peasant. (*British Museum*)

ness to have recourse to the sword of war in defending the common weal against external enemies. Hence it is said to those who are in authority (Ps. lxxxi. 4): *Rescue the poor: and deliver the needy out of the hand of the sinner;* and for this reason Augustine says (*Contra Faust.* xxii. 75): *The natural order conducive to peace among mortals demands that the power to declare and counsel war should be in the hands of those who hold the supreme authority.*

Secondly, a just cause is required, namely that those who are attacked, should be attacked because they deserve it on account of some fault. Wherefore Augustine says (*QQ. in Hept.,* qu. x, *super Jos.*): *A just war is wont to be described as one that avenges wrongs, when a nation or state has to be punished, for refusing to make amends for the wrongs inflicted by its subjects, or to restore what it has seized unjustly.*

Thirdly, it is necessary that the belligerents should have a rightful intention, so that they intend the advancement of good, or the avoidance of evil. Hence Augustine says *De Verb. Dom: True religion looks upon as peaceful those wars that are waged not for motives of aggrandizement or cruelty, but with the object of securing peace, of punishing evil-doers, and of uplifting the good.* For it may happen that the war is declared by the legitimate authority, and for a just cause, and yet be rendered unlawful through a wicked intention. Hence Augustine says (*Contra Faust.* xxii. 74): *The passion for inflicting harm, the cruel thirst for vengeance, an unpacific and relentless spirit, the fever of revolt, the lust of power, and such like things, all these are rightly condemned in war.*

Reply Obj. 1. As Augustine says (*Contra Faust.* xxii. 70): *To take the sword is to arm oneself in order to take the life of anyone, without the command or permission of superior or lawful authority.* On the other hand, to have recourse to the sword (as a private person) by the authority of the sovereign or judge, or (as a public person) through zeal for justice, and by the authority, so to speak, of God, is not to *take the sword,* but to use it as commissioned by another, wherefore it does not deserve punishment. And yet even those who make sinful use of the sword are not always slain with the sword, yet they always perish with their own sword, because, unless they repent, they are punished eternally for their sinful use of the sword.

Reply Obj. 2. Such like precepts, as Augustine observes (*De Serm. Dom. in Monte* i. 19), should always be borne in readiness of mind, so that we be ready to obey them, and, if necessary, to refrain from resistance or self-defense. Nevertheless it is necessary sometimes for a man to act otherwise for the common good, or for the good of those with whom he is fighting. Hence Augustine says (*Ep. ad Marcellin.* cxxxviii): *Those whom we have to punish with a kindly severity, it is necessary to handle in many ways against their will. For when we are stripping a man of the lawlessness of sin, it is good for him to be vanquished, since nothing is more hopeless than the happiness of sinners, whence arises a guilty impunity, and an evil will, like an internal enemy.*

Reply Obj. 3. Those who wage war justly aim at peace, and so they are not opposed to peace, except to the evil peace, which Our Lord *came not to send upon earth* (Matth. x. 34). Hence Augustine says (*Ep. ad Bonif.* clxxxix): *We do not seek peace in order to be at war, but we go to war that we may have peace. Be peaceful, therefore, in warring, so that you may vanquish those whom you war against, and bring them to the prosperity of peace.*

Reply Obj. 4. Manly exercises in warlike feats of arms are not all forbidden, but those which are inordinate and perilous, and end in slaying or plundering. In olden times warlike exercises presented no such danger, and hence they were called *exercises of arms* or bloodless wars, as Jerome states in an epistle.

MODERN PHILOSOPHY

———◀◯▶———

To a large extent, modern philosophy begins with a rejection of tradition. Whereas medieval philosophers such as Thomas Aquinas had taken great pains to incorporate and reconcile ancient writings, early modern philosophers such as René Descartes encouraged their readers to make a clean sweep of the past. Previous thinkers had been deluded by errors in thinking or had relied too heavily on authority. In the modern age, the wisdom of the past was to be discarded as error-prone. As Descartes observed in his *Meditations*,

> Some years ago I was struck by the large number of falsehoods that I had accepted as true in my childhood, and by the highly doubtful nature of the whole edifice that I had subsequently based on them. I realized that it was necessary, once in the course of my life, to demolish everything completely and start again right from the foundations if I wanted to establish anything at all in the sciences that was stable and likely to last.

This quest to establish a stable intellectual foundation on which to build something "likely to last" characterized seventeenth- and eighteenth-century European philosophy. "British Empiricists," such as Thomas Hobbes, John Locke, and David Hume found such a foundation in sensory experience and developed their thought on that basis. On the other hand, the "Continent Rationalists," philosophers such as Descartes, Baruch Spinoza, and Gottfried Leibniz, thought the senses inadequate for such a task. They considered reason superior to experience and sought to establish their philosophies on the basis of more certain principles. The greatest of the modern philosophers, Immanuel Kant, sought to combine these two approaches and in so doing developed a uniquely influential system of philosophy.

Contemporary thinkers in the West are still trying to come to grips with these modern philosophers. For better or for worse, their ideas have influenced virtually all areas of Euro-American civilization. The subtlety and clarity with which these thinkers wrote continues to demand careful study even in this "postmodern" age.

*   *   *

There are a number of fine introductions to modern philosophy. Among the classics in this area are Étienne Gilson, *Modern Philosophy: Descartes to Kant* (New York: Random House, 1963); the appropriate works from Frederick Copleston, *A History of Philosophy, Volume IV: Descartes to Leibniz; Volume V: Hobbes to Hume;* and *Volume VI: Wolff to Kant* (1950; reprinted New York: Image Doubleday, 1959–1960); and W.T. Jones's books, *Hobbes to Hume*, 2nd edition and *Kant and the Nineteenth Century*, 2nd edition, revised (both New York: Harcourt, Brace & World, 1969 and 1975). More recent general surveys include Roger Scruton, *A Short History of Modern Philosophy: From Descartes to Wittgenstein* (London: Routledge, 1984), and Wallace I. Matson, *A New History of Philosophy, Volume II: Modern* (San Diego, CA: Harcourt Brace Jovanovich, 1987). The following volumes from the *Routledge History of Philosophy* series include essays on this period: G.H.R. Parkinson, ed., *Volume 4: The Renaissance and Seventeenth Century Rationalism*; Stuart Brown, ed., *Volume 5: British Empiricism and the Enlightenment*; and Robert Solomon and Kathleen Higgins, eds., *Volume 6: The Age of German Idealism* (all London: Routledge, 1993). A sampling of the many specialized books on specific topics from this era includes Louis E. Loeb, *From Descartes to Hume: Continental Metaphysics and the Development of Modern Philosophy* (Ithaca, NY: Cornell University Press, 1981); Robert C. Solomon, *Continental Philosophy Since 1750: The Rise and Fall of the Self* (Oxford: Oxford University Press, 1988); and Iain Hampshire-Monk, *A History of Modern Political Thought* (Oxford: Blackwell, 1992).

René Descartes
1596–1650

René Descartes was born into the family of a minor noble in the town of La Haye in Touraine, France. At ten, René began a nine-year course of studies at the Royal Jesuit College of La Flèche. There he studied the humanities, theology, and philosophy (which included morals, logic, mathematics, metaphysics, and science). Though he did well in school, he was disillusioned by the uncertainty of his studies and their contradictory conclusions. Like modern students, he felt overwhelmed by the many opinions he encountered. He later wrote in his *Discourse on Method* that upon completing of his course of study, "I found myself embarrassed with so many doubts and errors that it seemed to me that the effort to instruct myself had no effect other than the increasing discovery of my own ignorance."

However, one discipline contained the certainty he was seeking: mathematics. The truths of mathematics were assured regardless of one's metaphysical or epistemological assumptions: $2 + 2 = 4$ whether one is a Platonist or an Aristotelian; $3 \times 3 = 9$ whether one is a Roman Catholic or a Protestant. Given mathematical certainty, Descartes found it odd that on such a firm basis "no loftier edifice had been reared."

Left a modest inheritance by his father, Descartes spent the rest of his life seeking the certainty not found in college. After receiving a law degree at Poitiers in 1616, he served as a gentleman volunteer in the army of Maurice of Nassau. While soldiering, he began to develop the idea of connecting mathematical certainty with philosophy. In 1619, he had a series of dreams convincing him that the "spirit of truth" was leading him and that he had divine approval for his studies. For the next ten years, while traveling and serving in the army, he developed his ideas. In 1628, he had a debate with Chandoux, a scientist who claimed that science could only be founded on probability. Descartes argued eloquently that knowledge must be based on certainty and that he had a system that provided that basis. Encouraged by others to develop his system, he retired to Holland, where he found a greater degree of intellectual freedom and spent the next twenty years writing and publishing his ideas. His major philosophical works include *Rules for the Direction of the Mind* (written 1628, but not published until 1701), *Discourse on Method* (published in 1637 as a preface to the essays *Geometry, Dioptric,* and *Meteors*), and *Meditations on First Philosophy* (1641). Descartes also published seven sets of *Objections to the Meditations* of such thinkers as Hobbes, Arnauld, and Gassendi, accompanied by his *Reply to Objections.* In addition to his work in philosophy, Descartes made major contributions to the fields of optics, anatomy, physiology, and mathematics (especially analytic geometry in which "Cartesian coordinates" are still used).

Descartes chose to write his works in French as well as Latin in order to reach beyond the academics to a wider audience. His writings did, indeed, reach learned people throughout Europe and that fact, unfortunately, led indirectly to his death. In 1649, Queen Christina of Sweden invited Descartes to join a circle of leading thinkers to instruct her in philosophy. Although he initially resisted the invitation, he finally felt compelled to accept. Upon arriving in Sweden, Descartes discovered that Queen Christina had time to see him only at five each morning. Descartes had been used to lying in bed until late in the morning, reflecting and philosophizing. Within a year the rigorous new schedule, together with Sweden's harsh weather, led to his death.

* * *

Descartes began his philosophy by sweeping away what he considered the "errors of the past." Using the methods of mathematics, specifically geometry, he began by establishing twenty-one *Rules for the Direction of the Mind.* He would begin by finding knowledge that he could "clearly and evidently intuit, or deduce with certainty." Then he would build from this knowledge deductively, one step at a time. This procedure would parallel the geometrical method of moving with deductive certainty from postulates to axioms. His *Meditations on First Philosophy,* reprinted here (complete) in the Laurence J. Lafleur translation, chronicles this process.

The key was to find the knowledge that he could "clearly and evidently intuit" that could serve as his starting point. Although uncertainty and doubt were the enemies, Descartes hit upon the idea of using doubt as a tool or a weapon. Instead of fighting doubt, he would use it to find certainty. He would use doubt as an acid to pour over every "truth" to see if there was anything that would not be dissolved, any "truth" that could not be doubted. Some of his doubts may seem extreme (such as that the earth may not exist or that I may be dreaming all this), but in order to find 100-percent certainty he had to find a starting point with zero-percent doubt.

After subjecting all his knowledge to the acid of doubt, he concluded that there was one thing he could not doubt: that he was doubting. The one fact the acid of doubt could not dissolve was doubt itself. This meant there had to be an "I" who was doing the doubting. Even if he were deceived about everything else, he had to exist in order to be deceived. This led Descartes to his famous statement, *Cogito ergo sum,* meaning "I think, therefore I am" (although these exact words do not appear in the *Meditations*). Here was the "clearly and evidently intuited" knowledge, the starting point, that Descartes had been seeking.

Having established that there is an "I," a self, a starting point, Descartes began to explore the nature of this "I":

> But what then am I? A thing that thinks. What is that? A thing that doubts, understands, affirms, denies, is willing, is unwilling, and also imagines and has sensory perceptions.

Among the ideas of this "thinking thing" called the "I" is the idea of a perfect God. Descartes went on to argue that nothing less than God could have caused the idea of God. He therefore concluded with a second certainty: God exists.

From here Descartes moved to his third certainty: We have a strong tendency to believe in the existence of a reality beyond our consciousness. If there is no such external world, then we are terribly deceived. But a perfect God would not allow us to be unavoidably deceived, since deceit implies imperfection. Accordingly, we can conclude that we are not misled about those natural beliefs, such as the existence of an external world, so long as they can withstand the scrutiny of reason and are not willfully disregarded.

Descartes had now established a basis for accepting the "obvious" truths he had thrown out earlier by his method of doubt. He had at the same time identified the criterion needed to distinguish the foundational truths upon which his knowl-

The Anatomy Lesson, 1632, by Rembrandt (1606–1669). Members of the Surgeons and Physicians Guild personify the Age of Observation with their intense scientific inquiry into human anatomy. Descartes was also interested in anatomy, making such important discoveries as that muscles work in opposition to each other. (*Mauritshuis, The Hague*)

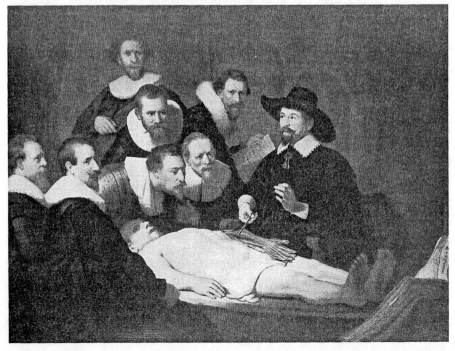

edge rested, namely, the criterion that a truth must be "clearly and distinctly perceived." An example of his rationalistic dependence upon such intuitions is his claim that the essential nature of a material object can only be known intuitively, not through sense perceptions.

One final point needs to be noted. The "I" that Descartes found at the end of his methodological doubting was "entirely distinct from the body." This "I" was an immaterial mind, a "spiritual" thing. The body is an "extended, nonthinking thing." As such, it is part of the material world, subject to the same laws of motion as a billiard ball. The "I," or the mind, on the other hand, is not bound by physical laws. This Cartesian distinction leads to a problem about the relationship between body and mind with which we still struggle today.

* * *

For a concise treatment of Descartes' thought in its historical context, see Alexandre Koyré, "Introduction," in E. Anscombe and P.T. Geach, eds., *René Descartes' Philosophical Writings* (Edinburgh: Nelson, 1954). Among the best of several excellent general studies of Descartes are Anthony Kenny, *Descartes: A Study of His Philosophy* (New York: Random House, 1968); Margaret Dauler Wilson, *Descartes* (Oxford: Routledge, 1983); John Cottingham, *Descartes* (Oxford: Basil Blackwell, 1986); and Stephen Gauktoger, *Descartes: An Intellectual Biography* (Oxford: Oxford University Press, 1995). For discussions of Descartes' *Meditations*, see L.J. Beck, *The Metaphysics of Descartes: A Study of the Meditations* (Oxford: Clarendon Press, 1965); E.M. Curley, *Descartes Against the Skeptics* (Cambridge, MA: Harvard University Press, 1978); Stanley Tweyman, ed., *Rene Descartes' Meditations on First Philosophy in Focus* (Oxford: Routledge, 1993); Georges Dicker, *Descartes* (Oxford: Oxford University Press, 1993). Roger Ariew and Marjorie Grene, eds., *Descartes and his Contemporaries: Meditations, Objections, and Replies* (Chicago: University of Chicago Press, 1995 and Vere Chappel, ed., *Descartes's Meditations: Critical Essays* (Lanham, MD: Rowan & Littlefield, 1997) includes the responses of Descartes' contemporaries to the *Meditations*. S. Woolhouse, *Descartes, Spinoza, Leibniz: The Concept of Substance in Seventeenth-Century Metaphysics* (London: Routledge, 1993) provides a comparative study, whereas John Cottingham, *A Descartes Dictionary* (Oxford: Basil Blackwell, 1993) provides a helpful reference work. For collections of essays on Descartes, see Willis Doney, ed., *Descartes: A Collection of Critical Essays* (Garden City, NY: Doubleday, 1967); Michael Hooker, ed., *Descartes: Critical and Interpretive Essays* (Baltimore, MD: Johns Hopkins University Press, 1978); Amelie O. Rorty, ed., *Essays on Descartes' Meditations* (Berkeley: University of California Press, 1986); Georges J.D. Moyal, ed., *René Descartes: Critical Assessments* (London: Routledge, 1991); Vere Chappell, ed., *Essays on Early Modern Philosophers: René Descartes* (Hamden, CT: Garland, 1992); John Cottingham, ed., *The Cambridge Companion to Descartes* (Cambridge: Cambridge University Press, 1992); the multi-volume George J.D. Moyal, *Rene Descartes: Critical Assessments* (Oxford: Routledge, 1992); and Stephen Voss, *Essays on the Philosophy and Science of René Descartes* (Oxford: Oxford University Press, 1993). Gilbert Ryle, *The Concept of Mind* (London: Hutchinson's University Library, 1949) is the classic critique of Descartes' views on body and mind.

MEDITATIONS ON THE FIRST PHILOSOPHY

[Dedicatory letter to the Sorbonne]

To those most learned and most illustrious men, the Dean and Doctors of the Sacred Faculty of Theology of Paris

Gentlemen:
My reason for offering you this work is so logical, and after you have learned its plan you will also, I am sure, have so logical a reason to take it under your protection, that I believe nothing will recommend it to you more than a brief statement of what I herein propose to do.

I have always thought that the two questions, of God and of the soul, were the principal questions among those that should be demonstrated by rational philosophy rather than theology. For although it may suffice us faithful ones to believe by faith that there is a God and that the human soul does not perish with the body, (2) certainly it does not seem possible ever to persuade those without faith to accept any religion, nor even perhaps any moral virtue, unless they can first be shown these two things by means of natural reason. And since in this life one frequently finds greater rewards offered for vice than for virtue, few persons would prefer the just to the useful if they were not restrained either by the fear of God or by the expectation of another life. It is absolutely true, both that we must believe that there is a God because it is so taught in the Holy Scriptures, and, on the other hand, that we must believe the Holy Scriptures because they come from God. The reason for this is that faith is a gift of God, and the very God that gives us the faith to believe other things can also give us the faith to believe that he exists. Nevertheless, we could hardly offer this argument to those without faith, for they might suppose that we were committing the fallacy that logicians call circular reasoning.

And truly I have noticed that you, gentlemen, along with all other theologians, assure us not only that the existence of God can be proved by natural reason, but also that we can infer from the Holy Scriptures that our knowledge of God is much clearer and easier than our knowledge of various created things, so clear in fact, so absolutely easy to attain, that those who do not possess it are blameworthy. This is evidenced in the words of the Book of the Wisdom of Solomon, Chapter XIII, where it is said: "Howbeit they are not to be excused; for if their understanding was so great that they could discern the world and the creatures, why did they not rather find out the Lord thereof?" And in the Epistle to the Romans, Chapter 1, where it is said that they are "without excuse," and again in the same place in these words: "That which may be known of God is manifest in them." It seems that we are being told that all that can be known of God can be demonstrated by reasons that we do not need to seek elsewhere than in ourselves, and that our minds alone are capable of furnishing us. That is why I

René Descartes, *Meditations on First Philosophy,* translated by Laurence J. Lafleur (New York: Macmillan/Library of the Liberal Arts, 1951).

have believed that it would not be inappropriate if I showed here how that can be done, and by what means we can know God more easily and more certainly than we know the things of the world.

And as for the soul, many have believed that it is not easy to understand its nature, (3) and some have even dared to say that human reasoning would convince us that it perishes with the body, and that faith alone can teach us the contrary. Nevertheless, as the Lateran Council, held under Leo X, Session 8, condemns these persons, and expressly orders Christian philosophers to refute their arguments and to employ all their intellectual abilities to make the truth known, I have decided to make the attempt in this work.

Moreover, the principal reason why many outside the Church do not wish to believe that there is a God and that the human soul is distinct from the body is that they claim that no one has so far been able to demonstrate these two things. I do not share their opinion; on the contrary, I hold that almost all of the arguments brought to bear on these two questions by so many illustrious men are valid demonstrations when they are properly understood, and that it is practically impossible to invent new ones. So I believe that there is nothing more useful to be done in philosophy than critically and carefully to seek out, once and for all, the best and most reliable of such arguments, and to give them so clear and exact a presentation that it would thenceforward be evident to everyone that they are valid demonstrations. And finally, several persons have urged me to do this, since they knew that I have been practicing a certain method of solving all sorts of difficulties in the sciences—a method which really is not new, for nothing is older than the truth, but which they knew I was using rather successfully in other matters. I have therefore considered it my duty to see what I could achieve in this field. (4)

I have put in this treatise everything that I was able to discover about this subject. That is not to say that I have collected here all the various arguments which might be adduced as proofs in our subject, for I have never thought that that would be necessary unless no certain proof existed. I have only treated here of the most basic and principal ones in such a way that I can reasonably venture to maintain that they are very evident and very certain demonstrations. And I shall say further that they are such that I do not think there is any way in which the human mind can ever find better ones; for the importance of the subject, and the glory of God, to which all this relates, constrain me to speak somewhat more freely of myself here than I usually do. Nevertheless, whatever certainty and obviousness I find in my own arguments, I cannot convince myself that everyone will be able to understand them. There is a similar situation in geometry, where there are several proofs, left to us by Archimedes, Apollonius, Pappus, and several others, that are accepted by everyone as very certain and evident because they contain nothing but what, considered separately, is very easy to understand, and because there is no place where the consequences do not have an exact connection with and dependence upon their antecedents. Nevertheless, because these proofs are rather long and demand undivided attention, they are comprehended and understood by only a very few persons. In the same way, although I consider that the arguments I use here equal or even surpass in certainty and obviousness the demonstrations of geometry, I nevertheless appreciate that they cannot be sufficiently well understood by many persons, partly because they also are somewhat lengthy and involved, but principally because they require a mind entirely free of all prejudice and one that can readily free itself from its attachment to the senses. And to tell the truth, there are not so many people in the world who are fitted for metaphysical speculations as there are those who are fitted for geometry. (5) There is this further difference, that in geometry everyone is persuaded that nothing should be written for which there is no certain proof. Therefore, those who are not well versed in the field are much more apt to make the mistake of accepting false demonstrations in order to make others believe that they understand them than they are to make the mistake of rejecting good ones. It is different in philosophy, where it is believed that there is nothing about which it is not possible to argue on either side. Thus few people engage in the search for truth, and many, who wish to acquire a reputation as clever thinkers, bend all their efforts to arrogant opposition to the most obvious truths.

That is why, gentlemen, since my arguments belong to philosophy, however strong they may be, I do not suppose that they will have any great effect unless you take them under your protection. But the esteem which everyone has for your Faculty is so great, and the name of the Sorbonne carries such authority, that not only is it more deferred to in matter of faith than any other group except the sacred councils, but even in human philosophy everyone agrees that it is impossible to find anywhere else so much reliability and knowledge, as well as prudence and integrity in the pronouncement of a judgment. Therefore, I do not doubt that if you will deign to give enough attention to this work so as to correct it—for, knowing not only my human fallibility but also my ignorance, I would not dare to affirm that it was free of error—and then to add to it whatever it lacks, to complete whatever is imperfect, and yourselves either to take the trouble to give a more adequate explanation of those points that need it or at least to advise me of them so that I may work on them; and finally, after the reasons by which I prove that there is a God and that the human soul differs from the body have been brought to such a degree of clarity and obviousness, which I am sure is possible, (6) that they should be considered very exact demonstrations, if you then will deign to give them the authority of your approbation and publicly testify to their truth and certitude—I do not doubt, I say, that when this has been done, all the errors and false opinions which have ever been entertained on these two questions will soon be effaced from the minds of men. For the expression of the truth will cause all learned and wise men to subscribe to your judgment, and your authority will cause the atheists, who are ordinarily more arrogant than learned and judicious, to set aside their spirit of contradiction, or perhaps themselves defend the arguments which they see being accepted as demonstrations by all intelligent people, for fear of appearing not to understand them. And finally, everyone else will easily accept the testimony of so many witnesses, and there will no longer be anyone who dares to doubt the existence of God and the real and true distinction between the human soul and the body.

It is for you, who now see the disorders which doubt of these things produces, in your great wisdom to judge the fruit which would grow out of such belief, once it were well established; but it would not be fitting for me further to commend the cause of God and religion to those who have always been the firmest supporters of them and of the Catholic Church. (7)

PREFACE

I have already touched upon these two questions of God and of the human soul in the *Discourse on the Method of Rightly Conducting the Reason and Seeking Truth in the Sciences*, which I published in French in the year 1637. Then I was not concerned to give a complete discussion of the subjects, but only to treat of them in passing, in order to learn from the judgments of the readers in what way I should treat them afterward. For these questions have always seemed to me so important that I judged it appropriate to deal with them more than once. And the road I take to explain them is so little traveled and so far from the ordinary route that I did not think it would be useful to explain it in French in a discourse that might be read by anyone, for fear that those of feeble intellect would think it permissible for them to make the same attempt.

In the *Discourse on Method*, I requested everyone who found in my writings something worthy of criticism to do me the favor of informing me thereof. There were no noteworthy objections concerning these subjects except two, to which I shall here make a short reply before undertaking a more detailed presentation of them later.

The first objection is that it does not follow from the fact that the human mind, reflecting upon its own nature, (8) knows itself solely as a thinking being, that its nature or essence is only to think. The trouble is that this word "only" excludes all those other qualities that might perhaps also pertain to the nature of the mind.

To this objection I reply that it was not my intention at this point to exclude those qualities from the realm of objective reality, with which I was not then concerned, but only from the realm of my thought. My intention was to say that I knew nothing to pertain to my essence except that I was a being which thinks, that is, a being having in itself the faculty of thinking. Nevertheless, I shall show further on how it follows from the fact that I know nothing else which belongs to my essence that nothing else really does belong to it.

The second objection is that it does not follow from the fact that I have in my mind the idea of a thing more perfect than I am that this idea is more perfect than myself, much less that what is represented by this idea exists.

But I reply that in this word "idea" there is here an equivocation. For it can be taken materially, as an operation of my intellect, and in this sense it cannot be said to be more perfect than myself; or it can be taken objectively for the body which is represented by this operation, which, even though it is not supposed to exist outside of my understanding, can nevertheless be more perfect than myself in respect to its essence. In the rest of this treatise I shall show more fully how it follows from the mere fact that I have in my mind an idea of something more perfect than myself that this thing really exists.

In addition, I have seen two other rather long works on this subject which did not so much oppose my reasons as my conclusions, and this by arguments drawn from the commonplaces of the atheists. (9) But since arguments of this type cannot make any impression in the minds of those who fully understand my reasoning, and since the judgment of many persons is so weak and irrational that they much more often let themselves be convinced by the first opinions they hear on a subject, however false and unreasonable they may be, than by a refutation of their opinions which is valid and true but which is heard later, I do not wish to reply to the arguments here, for fear of being obliged first to report them.

I shall only say, in general, that the arguments which atheists use to combat the existence of God always depend either upon the assumption that God has human characteristics, or else upon the assumption that our own minds have so much ability and wisdom that we presume to delimit and comprehend what God can and should do. Thus all that atheists allege will give us no difficulty if only we remind ourselves that we should consider our minds to be finite and limited, and God to be an infinite and incomprehensible Being.

Now, having paid sufficient attention to the opinions of men, I undertake directly to treat of God and of the human mind, and at the same time to lay the foundations of first philosophy. I do this without expecting any praise for it from the vulgar, and without hoping that my book will be read by many. On the contrary, I would not recommend it to any except to those who would want to meditate seriously along with me, and who are capable of freeing the mind from attachment to the senses and clearing it entirely of all sorts of prejudices; and I know only too well that there are very few people of this sort. But as for those who do not care much about the order and connection of my arguments, and who amuse themselves by making clever remarks on the several parts, as (10) some will do—those persons, I say, will not profit much from reading this work. And although they may find opportunities for caviling in many places, they will hardly be able to make any objections which are important or which are worthy of reply.

And since I do not promise others to satisfy them wholly at the first attempt, and since I do not so far presume as to believe that I can foresee all that may entail difficulties for some people, I shall first present in these *Meditations* the same thoughts by which I think I have reached a certain and evident knowledge of the truth, in order to see whether I will be able to persuade others by means of the same reasons that have persuaded me. After that I shall reply to the objections which have been offered to me by people of insight and learning to whom I sent my *Meditations* to be examined before committing them to the press. These have been so numerous and so varied that I feel secure in believing that it would be difficult for anyone else to find an objection of consequence that has not already been treated.

That is why I beg my readers to suspend their judgment upon the *Meditations* until they have taken the trouble of reading all these objections and the replies that I have made to them. (11)

SYNOPSIS OF THE SIX FOLLOWING MEDITATIONS

In the First Meditation, I offer the reasons why we can doubt all things in general, and particularly material objects, at least as long as we do not have other foundations for the sciences than those we have hitherto possessed. And although it is not immediately apparent that so general a doubt can be useful, it is in fact very much so, since it delivers us from all sorts of prejudices and makes available to us an easy method of accustoming our minds to become independent of the senses. Finally, it is useful in making it subsequently impossible to doubt those things which we discover to be true after we have taken doubt into consideration.

In the Second, the mind, which in its intrinsic freedom supposes that everything which is open to the least doubt is nonexistent, recognizes that it is nevertheless absolutely impossible that it does not itself exist. This is also of the highest utility, since by this means the mind can easily distinguish between those qualities which belong to it—that is to say, to its intellectual nature—and those which belong to the body.

But because it might happen that some persons will expect me to offer at this point reasons to prove the immortality of the soul, I think it my duty to warn them now (13) that, since I have tried to write nothing in this treatise for which I did not have very exact demonstrations, I have found myself obliged to follow an order similar to that used by geometricians, which is to present first all those things on which the proposition one is seeking to prove depends, before reaching any conclusions about the proposition itself.

But the first and principal thing required in order to recognize the immortality of the soul is to form the clearest possible conception of it, and one which is entirely distinct from all the conceptions one can have of the body, which has been done in this Second Meditation. It is necessary, in addition, to know that all things which we conceive clearly and distinctly are true in the manner in which we conceive them, and this cannot be proved before the Fourth Meditation. Furthermore, we must have a distinct conception of corporeal nature, which we acquire partly in the Second, and partly in the Fifth and Sixth Meditations. And finally, we must conclude from all this that things which we clearly and distinctly perceive to be diverse substances, as we conceive the mind and the body, are in fact substances which are really distinct from each other; which is what we conclude in the Sixth Meditation. This is confirmed again, in the same Meditation, by the fact that we cannot conceive any body except as divisible, while the mind or soul of man can only be conceived as indivisible. For in reality we cannot conceive of half of any soul, as we can of the smallest possible body, so that we recognize that their natures are not only different but even in some sense contrary. I have not treated this subject further in this treatise, partly because we have already discovered enough to show with sufficient clarity that the corruption of the body does not entail the death of the soul, and so to give men the hope of a second life after death; and partly because the premises from which the immortality of the soul may be concluded depend upon the explanation of the whole of physics. First, (14) we must know that all substances in general—that is to say, all those things which cannot exist without being created by God—are by nature incorruptible and can never cease to be, unless God himself, by denying them his usual support, reduces them to nothingness. And secondly, we must notice that body, taken in general, is a substance, and that it therefore will never perish. But the human body, however much it may differ from other bodies, is only a composite, produced by a certain configuration of members and by other similar accidents, whereas the human soul is not thus dependent upon any accidents, but is a pure substance. For even if all its accidents change—as, for example, if it conceives of certain things, wills others, and receives sense impressions of still others—nevertheless it still remains the same soul. But the human body becomes a different entity from the mere fact that the shape of some of its parts has been changed. From this it follows that the human body may very easily perish, but that the mind or soul of man, between which I find no distinction, is immortal by its very nature.

In the Third Meditation, I have explained at sufficient length, it seems to me, the principal argument I use to prove the existence of God. Nevertheless, I did not want to use at that point any comparisons drawn from physical things, in order that the minds of the readers should be as far as possible withdrawn from the use of and commerce with the senses. There may, therefore, be many obscurities remaining, which I hope will be completely elucidated in my replies to the objections which have since been made to me. One of these obscurities is this: how can the idea of a supremely perfect Being, which we find in ourselves, contain so much objective reality, that is to say, how can it participate by representation in so many degrees of being and of perfection, that it must have come from a supremely perfect cause? This I have explained in these replies by means of a comparison with a very ingenious and artificial machine, the idea of which occurs in the mind of some worker. For as the real cleverness of this idea must have some cause, I conclude it to be either the knowledge of this worker or that of some other from whom he has received this idea. In the same way (15) it is impossible that the idea of God, which is in us, does not have God himself as its cause.

In the Fourth, it is proved that all things which we conceive or perceive very clearly and very distinctly are wholly true. At the same time I explain the nature of error or falsity, which nature we ought to discover, as much to confirm the preceding truths as to understand better those that follow. Nevertheless, it should be noticed that I do not in any way treat here of sin—that is, of error committed in the pursuit of good and evil—but only of that which occurs in the judgment and discernment of the true and the false; and that I do not intend to speak of beliefs which belong to faith or to the conduct of life, but only of those which pertain to speculative truth and which can be known by the aid of the light of nature alone.

In the Fifth Meditation, besides the explanation of corporeal nature in general, the existence of God is again demonstrated by a new argument. There may also be some difficulties in this argument, but the solution will be found in the replies to the objections which have been made to me. In addition, I show how it is true that even the certainty of geometrical demonstrations themselves depends on the knowledge of God.

Finally, in the Sixth, I distinguish the action of the understanding from that of the imagination, and the marks of this distinction are described. Here I show that the mind or soul of man is really distinct from the body, and that nevertheless it is so tightly bound and united with it that it forms with it what is almost a single entity. All the errors which arise from the senses are here exposed, together with the methods of avoiding them. And finally, I here bring out all the arguments from which we may conclude the existence of material things; not because I judge them very useful, in that they prove what (16) they do prove—namely, that there is a world, that men have bodies, and other similar things which have never been doubted by any man of good sense—but because, in considering these arguments more closely, we come to recognize that they are not as firm and as evident as those which lead us to the knowledge of God and of our soul, so that the latter are the most certain and most evident truths which can become known to the human mind. That is all that I had planned to prove in these *Meditations*, which leads me to omit here many other questions with which I have dealt incidentally in this treatise. (17)

FIRST MEDITATION
CONCERNING THINGS THAT CAN BE DOUBTED

There is no novelty to me in the reflection that, from my earliest years, I have accepted many false opinions as true, and that what I have concluded from such badly assured premises could not but be highly doubtful and uncertain. From the time that I first recognized this fact, I have realized that if I wished to have any firm and constant knowledge in the sciences, I would have to undertake, once and for all, to set aside all the opinions which I had previously accepted among my beliefs and start again from the very beginning. But this enterprise appeared to me to be of very great magnitude, and so I waited until I had attained an age so mature that I could not hope for a later time when I would be more fitted to execute the project. Now, however, I have delayed so long that henceforward I should be afraid that I was committing a fault if, in continuing to deliberate, I expended time which should be devoted to action.

The present is opportune for my design; I have freed my mind of all kinds of cares; (18) I feel myself, fortunately, disturbed by no passions; and I have found a serene retreat in peaceful solitude. I will therefore make a serious and unimpeded effort to destroy generally all my former opinions. In order to do this, however, it will not be necessary to

251

show that they are all false, a task which I might never be able to complete; because, since reason already convinces me that I should abstain from the belief in things which are not entirely certain and indubitable no less carefully than from the belief in those which appear to me to be manifestly false, it will be enough to make me reject them all if I can find in each some ground for doubt. And for that it will not be necessary for me to examine each one in particular, which would be an infinite labor; but since the destruction of the foundation necessarily involves the collapse of all the rest of the edifice, I shall first attack the principles upon which all my former opinions were founded.

Everything which I have thus far accepted as entirely true and assured has been acquired from the senses or by means of the senses. But I have learned by experience that these senses sometimes mislead me, and it is prudent never to trust wholly those things which have once deceived us.

But it is possible that, even though the senses occasionally deceive us about things which are barely perceptible and very far away, there are many other things which we cannot reasonably doubt, even though we know them through the senses—as, for example, that I am here, seated by the fire, wearing a winter dressing gown, holding this paper in my hands, and other things of this nature. And how could I deny that these hands and this body are mine, unless I am to compare myself with certain lunatics (19) whose brain is so troubled and befogged by the black vapors of the bile that they continually affirm that they are kings while they are paupers, that they are clothed in gold and purple while they are naked; or imagine that their head is made of clay, or that they are gourds, or that their body is glass? But this is ridiculous; such men are fools, and I would be no less insane than they if I followed their example.

Nevertheless, I must remember that I am a man, and that consequently I am accustomed to sleep and in my dreams to imagine the same things that lunatics imagine when awake, or sometimes things which are even less plausible. How many times has it occurred that the quiet of the night made me dream of my usual habits: that I was here, clothed tin a dressing gown, and sitting by the fire, although I was in fact lying undressed in bed! It seems apparent to me now, that I am not looking at this paper with my eyes closed, that this head that I shake is not drugged with sleep, that it is with design and deliberate intent that I stretch out this hand and perceive it. What happens in sleep seems not at all as clear and as distinct as all this. But I am speaking as though I never recall having been misled, while asleep, by similar illusions. When I consider these matters carefully, I realize so clearly that there are no conclusive indications by which waking life can be distinguished from sleep that I am quite astonished, and my bewilderment is such that it is almost able to convince me that I am sleeping.

So let us suppose now that we are asleep and that all these details, such as opening the eyes, shaking the head, extending the hands, and similar things, are merely illusions; and let us think that perhaps our hands and our whole body are not such as we see them. Nevertheless, we must at least admit that these things which appear to us in sleep are like painted scenes and portraits which can only be formed in imitation of something real and true, and so, at the very least, these types of things—namely, eyes, head, hands, and the whole body—are not imaginary entities, but real and existent. For in truth painters, even when (20) they use the greatest ingenuity in attempting to portray sirens and satyrs in bizarre and extraordinary ways, nevertheless cannot give them wholly new shapes and natures, but only invent some particular mixture composed of parts of various animals; or even if perhaps their imagination is sufficiently extravagant that they invent something so new that nothing like it has ever been seen, and so their work represents something purely imaginary and absolutely false, certainly at the very least the colors of which they are composed must be real.

And for the same reason, even if these types of things—namely, a body, eyes, head, hands, and other similar things—could be imaginary, nevertheless, we are bound to confess that there are some other still more simple and universal concepts which are true and existent], from the mixture of which, neither more nor less than in the case of the mixture of real colors, all these images of things are formed in our minds, whether they are true and real or imaginary and fantastic.

Of this class of entities is corporeal nature in general and its extension, including the shape of extended things, their quantity, or size and number, and also the place where they are, the time that measures their duration, and so forth. That is why we will perhaps not be reasoning badly if we conclude that physics, astronomy, medicine, and all the other sciences which follow from the consideration of composite entities are very dubious and uncertain; whereas arithmetic, geometry, and the other sciences of this nature, which treat only of very simple and general things without concerning themselves as to whether they occur in nature or not, contain some element of certainty and sureness. For whether I am awake or whether I am asleep, two and three together will always make the number five, and the square will never have more than four sides; and it does not seem possible that truths so clear and so apparent can ever be suspected of any falsity for uncertainty. (21)

Nevertheless, I have long held the belief that there is a God who can do anything, by whom I have been created and made what I am. But how can I be sure but that he has brought it to pass that there is no earth, no sky, no extended bodies, no shape, no size, no place, and that nevertheless I have the impressions of all these things and cannot imagine that things might be other than as I now see them? And furthermore, just as I sometimes judge that others are mistaken about those things which they think they know best, how can I be sure but that God has brought it about that I am always mistaken when I add two and three or count the sides of a square, or when I judge of something else even easier, if I can imagine anything easier than that? But perhaps God did not wish me to be deceived in that fashion, since he is said to be supremely good. But if it was repugnant to his goodness to have made me so that I was always mistaken, it would seem also to be inconsistent for him to permit me to be sometimes mistaken, and nevertheless I cannot doubt that he does permit it.

At this point there will perhaps be some persons who would prefer to deny the existence of so powerful a God, rather than to believe that everything else is uncertain. Let us not oppose them for the moment, and let us concede according to their point of view that everything which I have stated here about God is fictitious. Then in whatever way they suppose that I have reached the state of being that I now have, whether they attribute it to some destiny or fate or refer it to chance, or whether they wish to explain it as the result of a continual interplay of events or in any other manner; nevertheless, since to err and be mistaken is a kind of imperfection, to whatever degree less powerful they consider the author to whom they at-tribute my origin, in that degree it will be more probable that I am so imperfect that I am always mistaken. To this reasoning, certainly, I have nothing to reply; and I am at last constrained to admit that there is nothing in what I formerly believed to be true which I cannot somehow doubt, and this not for lack of thought and attention, but for weighty and well-considered reasons. Thus I find that, in the future, I should withhold and suspend my judgment about these matters, and guard myself no less carefully from believing them than I should from be-lieving what is manifestly false (22) if I wish to find any certain and assured knowl-edge in the sciences.

It is not enough to have made these observations; it is also necessary that I should take care to bear them in mind. For these customary and long-standing beliefs will frequently recur in my thoughts, my long and familiar acquaintance with them giving them the right to occupy my mind against my will and almost to make themselves masters of my beliefs. I will never free myself of the habit of deferring to them and having faith in them as long as I consider that they are what they really are—that is, somewhat doubtful, as I have just shown, even if highly probable—so that there is much more reason to believe than to deny them. That is why I think that I would not do badly if I deliberately took the opposite position and deceived myself in pretending for some time that all these opinions are entirely false and imaginary, until at last I will have so balanced my former and my new prejudices that they cannot incline my mind more to one side than the other, and my judgment will not be mastered and turned by bad habits from the correct perception of things and the straight road leading to the knowledge of the truth. For I feel sure that I cannot overdo this distrust, since it is not now a question of acting, but only of meditating and learning.

I will therefore suppose that, not a true God, who is very good and who is the supreme source of truth, but a certain evil spirit, not less clever and deceitful than powerful, has bent all his efforts to deceiving me. I will suppose that the sky, the air, the earth, colors, shapes, sounds, and all other objective things that we see are nothing but illusions and dreams that he has used to trick my credulity. I will consider (23) myself as having no hands, no eyes, no flesh, no blood, nor any senses, yet falsely believing that I have all these things. I will remain resolutely attached to this hypothesis; and if I cannot attain the knowledge of any truth by this method, at any rate it is in my power to suspend my judgment. That is why I shall take great care not to accept any falsity among my beliefs and shall prepare my mind so well for all the ruses of this great deceiver that, however powerful and artful he may be, he will never be able to mislead me in anything.

But this undertaking is arduous, and a certain laziness leads me insensibly into the normal paths of ordinary life. I am like a slave who, enjoying an imaginary liberty during sleep, begins to suspect that his liberty is only a dream; he fears to wake up and conspires with his pleasant illusions to retain them longer. So insensibly to myself I fall into my former opinions; and I am slow to wake up from this slumber for fear that the labors of waking life which will have to follow the tranquillity of this sleep, instead of leading me into the daylight of the knowledge of the truth, will be insufficient to dispel the darkness of all the difficulties which have just been raised.

SECOND MEDITATION
OF THE NATURE OF THE HUMAND MIND, AND THAT IT IS
MORE EASILY KNOWN THAN THE BODY

Yesterday's Meditation has filled my mind with so many doubts that it is no longer in my power to forget them. Nor do I yet see how I will be able to resolve them; I feel as though (24) I were suddenly thrown into deep water, being so disconcerted that I can neither plant my feet on the bottom nor swim on the surface. I shall nevertheless make every effort to conform precisely to the plan commenced yesterday and put aside every belief in which I could imagine the least doubt, just as though I knew that it was absolutely false. And I shall continue in this manner until I have found something certain, or at least, if I can do nothing else, until I have learned with certainty that there is nothing certain in this world. Archimedes, to move the earth from its orbit and place it in a new position, demanded nothing more than a fixed and immovable fulcrum; in a similar manner I shall have the right to entertain high hopes if I am fortunate enough to find a single truth which is certain and indubitable.

I suppose, accordingly, that everything that I see is false; I convince myself that nothing has ever existed of all that my deceitful memory recalls to me. I think that I have no senses; and I believe that body, shape, extension, motion, and location are merely inventions of my mind. What then could still be thought true? Perhaps nothing else, unless it is that there is nothing certain in the world.

But how do I know that there is not some entity, of a different nature from what I have just judged uncertain, of which there cannot be the least doubt? Is there not some God or some other power who gives me these thoughts? But I need not think this to be true, for possibly I am able to produce them myself. Then, at the very least, am I not an entity myself? But I have already denied that I had any senses or any body. However, at this point I hesitate, for what (25) follows from that? Am I so dependent upon the body and the senses that I could not exist without them? I have just convinced myself that nothing whatsoever existed in the world that there was no sky, no earth, no minds, and no bodies; have I not thereby convinced myself that I did not exist? Not at all; without doubt I existed if I was convinced or even if I thought anything. Even though there may be a deceiver of some sort, very powerful and very tricky, who bends all his efforts to keep me perpetually deceived, there can be no slightest doubt that I exist, since he deceives me; and let him deceive me as much as he will, he can never make me be nothing as long as I think that I am something. Thus, after having thought well on this matter, and after examining all things with care, I must finally conclude and maintain that this proposition: *I am, I exist*, is necessarily true every time that I pronounce it or conceive it in my mind.

But I do not yet know sufficiently clearly what I am, I who am sure that I exist. So I must henceforth take very great care that I do not incautiously mistake some other thing for myself, and so make an error even in that knowledge which I maintain to be more certain and more evident than all other knowledge that I previously had. That is why I shall now consider once more what I thought myself to be before I began these last deliberations. Of my former opinions I shall reject all that are rendered even slightly doubtful by the arguments that I have just now offered, so that there will remain just that part alone which is entirely certain and indubitable.

What then have I previously believed myself to be? Clearly, I believed that I was a man. But what is a man? Shall I say a rational animal? Certainly not, for I would have to determine what an "animal" is and what is meant by "rational"; and so, from a single question, I would find myself gradually enmeshed in an infinity of others more difficult and more inconvenient, and I would not care to waste the little time and leisure remaining to me in disentangling such difficulties. I shall rather pause here to consider the ideas which previously arose naturally and of themselves (26) in my mind whenever I considered what I was. I thought of myself first as having a face, hands, arms, and all this mechanism composed of bone and flesh and members, just as it appears in a corpse, and which I designated by the name of "body." In addition, I thought of the fact that I consumed nourishment, that I walked, that I perceived and thought, and I ascribed all these actions to the soul. But either I did not stop to consider what this soul was or else, if I did, I imagined that it was something very rarefied and subtle, such as a wind, a flame, or a very much expanded air which penetrated into and was infused throughout my grosser components. As for what body was, I did not realize that there could be any doubt about it, for I thought that I recognized its nature very distinctly. If I had wished to explain it according to the notions that I then entertained, I would have described it somewhat in this way: By "body" I understand all that can be bounded by some figure; that can be located in some place and occupy space in such a way that every other body is excluded from it; that can be perceived by touch or sight or hearing or taste or smell; that can be moved in various ways, not by itself but by some other object by which it is touched and from which it receives an impulse. For to possess the power to move itself, and also to feel or to think, I did not believe at all that these are attributes of corporeal nature; on the contrary, rather, I was astonished to see a few bodies possessing such abilities.

But I, what am I, on the basis of the present hypothesis that there is a certain spirit who is extremely powerful and, if I may dare to say so, malicious and tricky, and who uses all his abilities and efforts in order to deceive me? Can I be sure that I possess the smallest fraction of all those characteristics which I have just now said belonged to the nature of body? (27) I pause to consider this attentively. I pass and repass in review in my mind each one of all these things—it is not necessary to pause to take the time to list them—and I do not find any one of them which I can pronounce to be part of me. Let us move on to the attributes of the soul and see if any of these are in me. Is it characteristic of me to consume nourishment and to walk? But if it is true that I do not have a body, these also are nothing but figments of the imagination. To perceive? But once more, I cannot perceive without the body, except in the sense that I have thought I perceived various things during sleep, which I recognized upon waking not to have been really perceived. To think? Here I find the answer. Thought is an attribute that belongs to me; it alone is inseparable from my nature.

I am, I exist—that is certain; but for how long do I exist? For as long as I think; for it might perhaps happen, if I totally ceased thinking, that I would at the same time completely cease to be. I am now admitting nothing except what is necessarily true. I am therefore, to speak precisely, only a thinking being, that is to say, a mind, an understanding, or a reasoning, being, which are terms whose meaning was previously unknown to me.

I am something real and really existing, but what thing am I? I have already given the answer: a thing which thinks. And what more? I will stimulate my imagination to see if I am not something else beyond this. I am not this assemblage of members which is called a human body; I am not a rarefied and penetrating air spread throughout all these members; I am not a wind, a flame, a breath, a vapor, or anything at all that I can imagine and picture to myself—since I have supposed that all that was nothing, and since, without abandoning this supposition, I find that I do not cease to be certain that I am something.

But perhaps it is true that those same things which I suppose not to exist because I do not know them are really no different from the self which I do know. As to that I cannot decide; I am not discussing that question at the moment, since I can pass judgment only upon those things which are known to me: I know that I exist and I am seeking to discover what I am, that "I" that I know to be. Now it is very certain that this notion and knowledge of my being, thus precisely understood, does not depend on things whose existence (28) is not yet known to me; and consequently and even more certainly, it does not depend on any of those things that I can picture in my imagination. And even these terms, "picture" and "imagine," warn me of my error. For I would be imagining falsely indeed were I to picture myself as something; since to imagine is nothing else than to contemplate the shape or image of a bodily entity, and I already know both that I certainly exist and that it is altogether possible that all these images, and everything in general which is involved in the nature of body, are only dreams and illusions. From this I see clearly that there was no more sense in saying that I would stimulate my imagination to learn more distinctly what I am than if I should say: I am now awake, and I see something real and true; but because I do not yet perceive it sufficiently clearly, I will go to sleep on purpose, in order that my dreams will show it to me with more truth and evidence. And thus I know manifestly that nothing of all that I can understand by means of the imagination is pertinent to the knowledge which I have of myself, and that I must remember this and prevent my mind from thinking in this fashion, in order that it may clearly perceive its own nature.

But what then am I? A thinking being. What is a thinking being? It is a being which doubts, which understands, which conceives, which affirms, which denies, which wills, which rejects, which imagines also, and which perceives. It is certainly not a trivial matter if all these things belong to my nature. But why should they not belong to it? Am I not that same person who now doubts almost everything, who nevertheless understands and conceives certain things, who is sure of and affirms the truth of this one thing alone, who denies all the others, who wills and desires to know more about them, who rejects error, who imagines many things, sometimes even against my will, and who also perceives many things, as through the medium of the senses or the organs of the body? Is there anything in all that which is not just as true as it is certain that I am and that I exist, even though I were always asleep (29) and though the one who created me directed all his efforts to deluding me? And is there any one of these attributes which can be distinguished from my thinking or which can be said to be separable from my nature? For it is so obvious that it is I who doubt, understand, and desire, that nothing could be added to make it more evident. And I am also certainly the same one who imagines; for once more, even though it could happen that the things I imagine are not true, nevertheless this power of imagining cannot fail to be real, and it is part of my thinking. Finally I am the same being which perceives—that is, which observes certain objects as though by means of the sense organs, because I do really see light, hear noises, feel heat. Will it be said that these appearances are false and that I am sleeping? Let it be so; yet at the very least it is certain that it seems to me that I see light, hear noises, and feel heat. This much cannot be false, and it is this, properly considered, which in my nature is called perceiving, and that, again speaking precisely, is nothing else but thinking.

As a result of these considerations, I begin to recognize what I am somewhat better and with a little more clarity and distinctness than heretofore. But nevertheless it still seems to me, and I cannot keep myself from believing that corporeal things, images of which are formed by thought and which the senses themselves examine, are much more distinctly known than that indescribable part of myself which cannot be pictured by the imagination. Yet it would truly be very strange to say that I know and comprehend more distinctly things whose existence seems doubtful to me, that are unknown to me and do not belong to me, than those of whose truth I am persuaded, which are known to me, and which belong to my real nature—to say, in a word, that I know them better than myself. But I see well what is the trouble: my mind is a vagabond who likes to wander and is not yet able to stay within the strict bounds of truth. Therefore, let us give it the rein once more and allow it every kind of liberty, (30) permitting it to consider the objects which appear to be external, so that when a little later we come to restrain it gently and at the right time and force it to the consideration of its own nature and of the things that it finds in itself, it will more readily permit itself to be ruled and guided.

Let us now consider the commonest things, which are commonly believed to be the most distinctly known and the easiest of all to know, namely, the bodies which we touch and see. I do not intend to speak of bodies in general, for general notions are usually somewhat more confused; let us rather consider one body in particular. Let us take, for example, this bit of wax which has just been taken from the hive. It has not yet completely lost the sweetness of the honey it contained; it still retains something of the odor of the flowers from which it was collected; its color, shape, and size are apparent; it is hard and cold; it can easily be touched; and, if you knock on it, it will give out some sound. Thus everything which can make a body distinctly known are found in this example.

But now while I am talking I bring it close to the fire. What remains of the taste evaporates; the odor vanishes; its color changes; its shape is lost; its size increases; it becomes liquid; it grows hot; one can hardly touch it; and although it is knocked upon, it will give out no sound. Does the same wax remain after this change? We must admit that it does; no one denies it, no one judges otherwise. What is it then in this bit of wax that we recognize with so much distinctness? Certainly it cannot be anything that I observed by means of the senses, since everything in the field of taste, smell, sight, touch, and hearing are changed, and since the same wax nevertheless remains.

The truth of the matter perhaps, as I now suspect, is that this wax was neither that sweetness of honey, nor that pleasant odor of flowers, nor that whiteness, nor that shape, nor that sound, but only a body which a little while ago appeared to my senses under these forms and which now makes itself felt under others. But what is it, to speak precisely, that I imagine when I conceive it in this fashion? Let us consider it attentively (31) and, rejecting everything that does not belong to the wax, see what remains. Certainly nothing is left but something extended, flexible, and movable. But what is meant by flexible and movable? Does it consist in my picturing that this wax, being round, is capable of becoming square and of passing from the square into a triangular shape? Certainly not; it is not that, since I conceive it capable of undergoing an infinity of similar changes, and I could not compass this infinity in my imagination. Consequently this conception that I have of the wax is not achieved by the faculty of imagination.

Now what is this extension? Is it not also unknown? For it becomes greater in the melting wax, still greater when it is completely melted, and much greater again when the heat increases still more. And I would not conceive clearly and truthfully what wax was if I did not think that even this bit of wax is capable of receiving more variations in extension than I have ever imagined. We must therefore agree that I cannot even conceive what this bit of wax is by means of the imagination, and that there is nothing but my understanding alone which does conceive it. I say this bit of wax in particular, for as to wax in general, it is still more evident. But what is this bit of wax which cannot be comprehended except by the understanding, or by the mind? Certainly it is the same as the one that I see, that I touch, that I imagine; and finally it is the same as I always believed it to be from the beginning. But what is here important to notice is that perception, or the action by which we perceive, is not a vision, a touch, nor an imagination, and has never been that, even though it formerly appeared so; but is solely an inspection by the mind, which can be imperfect and confused as it was formerly, or clear and distinct as it is at present, as I attend more or less to the things which are in it and of which it is composed.

Now I am truly astonished when I consider how weak my mind is and how apt I am to fall into error. For even though I consider all this in my mind without speaking, (32) still words impede me, and I am nearly deceived by the terms of ordinary language. For we say that we see the same wax if it is present, and not that we judge that it is the same from the fact that it has the same color or shape. Thus I might be tempted to conclude that one knows the wax by means of eyesight, and not uniquely by the perception of the mind. So I may by chance look out of a window and notice some men passing in the street, at the sight of whom I do not fail to say that I see men, just as I say that I see wax; and nevertheless what do I see from this window except hats and cloaks which might cover ghosts, or automata which move only by springs? But I judge that they are men, and thus I comprehend, solely by the faculty of judgment which resides in my mind, that which I believed I saw with my eyes.

A person who attempts to improve his understanding beyond the ordinary ought to be ashamed to go out of his way to criticize the forms of speech used by ordinary men. I prefer to pass over this matter and to consider whether I understood what wax was more evidently and more perfectly when I first noticed it and when I thought I knew it by means of the external senses, or at the very least by common sense, as it is called, or the imaginative faculty; or whether I conceive it better at present, after having more carefully examined what it is and how it can be known. Certainly it would be ridiculous to doubt the superiority of the latter method of knowing. For what was there in that first perception which was distinct and evident? What was there which might not occur similarly to the senses of the lowest of the animals? But when I distinguished the real wax from its superficial appearances, and when, just as though I had removed its garments, I consider it all naked, it is certain that although there might still be some

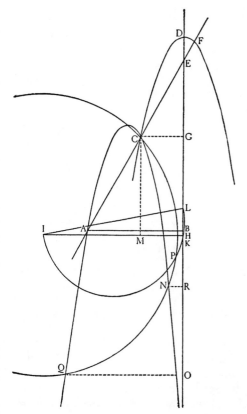

Geometry formula from Descartes' *Geometry* (1637). The X–Y axes in analytic geometry, which Descartes invented, are still called "Cartesian coordinates." (*Library of Congress*)

error in my judgment, I could not conceive it in this fashion without a human mind. (33)

And now what shall I say of the mind, that is to say, of myself? For so far I do not admit in myself anything other than the mind. Can it be that I, who seem to perceive this bit of wax so clearly and distinctly, do not know my own self, not only with much more truth and certainty, but also much more distinctly and evidently? For if I judge that the wax exists because I see it, certainly it follows much more evidently that I exist myself because I see it. For it might happen that what I see is not really wax; it might also happen that I do not even possess eyes to see anything; but it could not happen that, when I see, or what amounts to the same thing, when I think I see, I who think am not something. For a similar reason, if I judge that the wax exists because I touch it, the same conclusion follows once more, namely, that I am. And if I hold to this judgment because my imagination, or whatever other entity it might be, persuades me of it, I will still reach the same conclusion. And what I have said here about the wax can be applied to all other things which are external to me.

Furthermore, if the idea or knowledge of the wax seems clearer and more distinct to me after I have investigated it, not only by sight or touch, but also in many other ways, with how much more evidence, distinctness and clarity must it be admitted that I now know myself; since all the reasons which help me to know and conceive the nature of the wax, or of any other body whatsoever, serve much better to show the nature of my mind! And we also find so many other things in the mind itself which can contribute to the clarification of its nature, that those which depend on the body, such as the ones I have just mentioned, hardly deserve to be taken into account.

And at last here I am, having insensibly returned to where (34) I wished to be; for since it is at present manifest to me that even bodies are not properly known by the senses nor by the faculty of imagination, but by the understanding alone; and since they are not known in so far as they are seen or touched, but only in so far as they are understood by thinking, I see clearly that there is nothing easier for me to understand than my mind. But since it is almost impossible to rid oneself so soon of an opinion of long standing, it would be wise to stop a while at this point, in order that, by the length of my meditation, I may impress this new knowledge more deeply upon my memory.

THIRD MEDITATION
OF GOD: THAT HE EXISTS

Now I shall close my eyes, I shall stop my ears, I shall disregard my senses, I shall even efface from my mind all the images of corporeal things; or at least, since that can hardly be done, I shall consider them vain and false. By thus dealing only with myself and considering what is included in me, I shall try to make myself, little by little, better known and more familiar to myself.

I am a thing which thinks, that is to say, which doubts, which affirms, which denies, which knows a few things, which is ignorant of many, which loves, which hates, which wills, which rejects, which imagines also, and which senses. For as I have previously remarked, although the things which I sense and which I imagine are perhaps nothing at all apart from me and in themselves, I am nevertheless sure that those modes of thought which I call sensations and imaginations, (35) only just as far as they are modes of thought, reside and are found with certainty in myself.

And in this short statement I think I have reported all that I truly know, or at least all that I have so far noticed that I know. Now, in order to try to extend my knowledge further, I shall be circumspect and consider with care if I cannot still discover in myself some other bits of knowledge which I have not yet observed. I am sure that I am a thinking being; but do I not then know what is required to make me sure of something? Certainly, in this first conclusion, there is nothing else which assures me of its truth but the clear and distinct perception of what I affirm. But this would really not be sufficient to assure me that what I affirm is true if it could ever happen that something which I conceived just as clearly and distinctly should prove false. And therefore it seems to me that I can already establish as a general principle that everything which we conceive very clearly and very distinctly is wholly true.

I have, however, previously accepted and admitted several things as very certain and very obvious which I have nevertheless subsequently recognized to be doubtful and uncertain. What, then, were those things? They were the earth, the sky, the stars, and all the other things I perceived through the medium of my senses. But what did I conceive clearly and distinctly in them? Nothing, certainly, unless that the ideas or thoughts of those things were present to my mind. And even now I do not deny the occurrence of these ideas in me. But there was still another thing of which I was sure and which, because of my habit of believing it, I thought I perceived very clearly, although in truth I did not perceive it at all—namely, that there were things outside of myself from which these ideas came and to which they were completely similar. That was the point in which, perhaps, I was mistaken; or at any rate, even if my judgment was in accord with the truth, it was no knowledge of mine which produced the truth of my judgment.

But when I considered something very simple and very easy concerning arithmetic and geometry, (36) as, for example, that two and three joined together produce the number five, and other similar things, did I not conceive them at least sufficiently clearly to guarantee that they were true? Certainly, if I have since judged that these things might be doubted, it was for no other reason than that it occurred to me that some God might perhaps have given me such a nature that I would be mistaken even about those things that seemed most obvious to me. Every time that this idea of the supreme power of a God, as previously conceived, occurs to me, I am constrained to admit that it is easy for him, if he wishes it, to bring it about that I am wrong even in those matters which I believe I perceive with the mind's eye with the greatest possible obviousness. And on the other hand, every time I turn to the things I think I conceive very clearly, I am so convinced by them that I am spontaneously led to proclaim: "Let him deceive me who can; he will never be able to bring it about that I am nothing while I think I am something, or, it being true that I now am, that it will some day be true that I have never been, or that two and three joined together make more or less than five, or similar things in which I recognize a manifest contradiction and which I see clearly could not be otherwise than as I conceive them."

And certainly, since I have no reason to believe that there is a God who is a deceiver, and since I have not yet even considered those reasons that prove that there is a God, the argument for doubting which depends only on this opinion is very tenuous and, so to speak, metaphysical. But in order to remove it altogether I must examine whether there is a God as soon as an opportunity occurs, and if I find that there is one I must also investigate whether he can be a deceiver; for as long as this is unknown, I do not see that I can ever be certain of anything. And now, in order that I shall have an opportunity to examine this question without interrupting the order of thought which I have proposed for myself, which is to pass by degrees from the notions which I discover to be most basic in my mind to those that I can discover afterwards, order seems to demand that I should first classify all (37) my thoughts into certain types and consider in which of these types there is, properly, truth or error.

Among my thoughts some are like images of objects, and it is to these alone that the name of "idea" properly applies, as when I picture to myself a man, or a chimera, or the sky, or an angel, or God himself. Then there are others with different forms, as when I wish, or fear, or affirm, or deny. In these cases I do conceive something as the object of the action of my mind, but I also add something else by this action to the idea which I have of the entity; and of this type of thought, some are called volitions or emotions, and others judgments.

Now as far as ideas are concerned, if we consider them only in themselves and do not relate them to something else, they cannot, properly speaking, be false; for whether I imagine a sage or a satyr, it is no less true that I imagine the one than the other. Similarly, we must not fear to encounter falsity in the emotions or volitions; for even though I may desire bad things, or even things which never existed, nevertheless it is no less true on that account that I desire them. So there is nothing left but judgments alone, in which I must take very great care not to make a mistake. But the principal and most common error which can be encountered here consists in judging that the ideas which are in myself are similar to, or conformable to, things outside of myself; for certainly, if I considered the ideas only as certain modes or aspects of my thought, without intending them to refer to some other exterior object, they could hardly offer me a chance of making a mistake.

Among these ideas, some seem to be born with me, others to be alien to me and to come from without, (38) and the rest to be made and invented by myself. For I have the ability to conceive what is generally called a thing, or a truth, or a thought; and it seems to me that I do not conceive this from anything but my own nature. But if I now hear some noise, if I see the sun, if I feel heat, I have hitherto judged that these feelings proceeded from some things which exist outside of myself; and finally, it seems to me that sirens, hippogriffs, and all other similar chimeras are fictions and inventions of my mind. Perhaps I might persuade myself that all these ideas are of the type of those I call alien and which come from without, or perhaps they are all innate, or perhaps they might all be invented; for I have not yet clearly discovered their true origin. And what I must principally do at this point is to consider, concerning those which seem to me to come from objects outside of me, what evidence obliges me to believe that they resemble those objects.

The first of these reasons is that it seems to me that nature teaches me so, and the second that I have direct experience that these ideas are not dependent upon my will nor upon myself. For often they come to me despite my wishes; just as now, whether I wish it or not, I feel heat, and for that reason I conclude that this sensation, or rather this idea, of heat is produced in me by something different from myself, namely, by the heat of the fire near which I am sitting. And I see nothing which appears more reasonable to me than to judge that this alien entity sends to me and imposes upon me its likeness rather than anything else.

Now I must see whether these reasons are sufficiently strong and convincing. When I say that it seems to me that nature teaches me so, I understand by this word "nature" only a certain inclination which leads me to believe it, and not the light of nature which makes me know that it is true. But these two expressions are very different from each other; for I could not doubt in any way what the light of nature made me see to be true, just as it made me see, a little while ago, that from the fact that I doubted I could conclude that I existed. And there is no way in which this could be doubted, because I have no other faculty or power to distinguish the true from the false which could teach me that what this light of nature shows me as true is not so, and in which I could trust as much as in the light of nature itself. (39) But as for inclinations, which also seem to me to be natural, I have often noticed, when it was a question of choosing between virtues and vices, that they led me to the bad no less than to the good; and for this reason I have not been inclined to follow them even in what concerns the true and the false.

As for the other reason, which is that these ideas must come from elsewhere, since they do not depend upon my will, I do not find this convincing either. For just as the inclinations which we are now considering occur in me, despite the fact that they are not always in accord with my will, so perhaps there is in me some faculty or power adequate to produce these ideas without the aid of any external objects, even though it is not yet known to me; just as it has so far always seemed to me that when I sleep, these ideas are formed in me without the aid of the objects which they represent. And finally, even if I should agree that the ideas are caused by these objects, it does not necessarily follow that they should be similar to them. On the contrary, I have often observed in many instances that there was a great difference between the object and its idea. Thus, for example, I find in myself two completely different ideas of the sun: the one has its origin in the senses, and must be placed in the class of those that, as I said before, came from without, according to which it seems to me extremely small; the other is derived from astronomical considerations that is, from certain innate ideas—or at least is formed by myself in whatever way it may be, according to which it seems to me many times greater than the whole earth. Certainly, these two ideas of the sun cannot both be similar to the same sun existing outside of me, and reason makes me believe that the one which comes directly from its appearance is that which least resembles it.

All this makes me recognize sufficiently well that up to now it has not been by (40) a valid and considered judgment, but only by a blind and rash impulse, that I have believed that there were things outside of myself and different from my own being which, through the organs of my senses or by whatever other method it might be, sent into me their ideas or images and impressed upon me their resemblances.

But there is still another path by which to seek if, among the things of which I possess ideas, there are some which exist outside of myself. If these ideas are considered only in so far as they are particular modes of thought, I do not recognize any difference or inequality among them, and all of them appear to arise from myself in the same fashion. But considering them as images, of which some represent one thing and some another, it is evident that they differ greatly among themselves. For those that represent substances are undoubtedly something more, and contain in themselves, so to speak, more objective reality, or rather, participate by representation in a higher degree of being or perfection, than those that represent only modes or accidents. Furthermore, that by which I conceive a supreme God, eternal, infinite, rimmutable, omniscient, omnipotent, and the universal creator of all things that exist outside of himself—that idea, I say, certainly contains in itself more objective reality than do those by which finite substances are represented.

Now it is obvious, according to the light of nature, that there must be at least as much reality in the total efficient cause as in its effect, for whence can the effect derive its reality, if not from its cause? And how could this cause communicate reality to the effect, unless it possessed it in itself?

And from this it follows, not only that something cannot be derived from nothing, but also that the more perfect—that is to say, that which contains in itself more reality (41)—cannot be a consequence of and dependent upon the less perfect. This truth is not only clear and evident in regard to the effects which have what philosophers call actual or formal reality, but also in regard to the ideas where one considers only what they call objective reality. For example, the stone which has not yet existed cannot now begin to be, unless it is produced by a being that possesses in itself formally or eminently all that enters into the composition of stone—that is, which contains in itself the same things as, or others more excellent than, those which are in stone. Heat cannot be produced in a being that previously lacked it, unless by something which is of an order, a degree, or a type at least as perfect as heat, and so forth. But still, in addition, the idea of heat or of stone cannot be in me, unless it was put there by something which contains in itself at least as much reality as I conceive there is in heat or stone; for even though that cause does not transfer to my idea anything of its actual or formal reality, we must not therefore suppose that such a cause is any less real, nor that the nature of an idea, since it is a work of the mind, is such that it does not require any other formal reality than what it receives and borrows from thought or mind, of which it is only a mode—that is, a way or manner of thinking. In order that an idea should contain one particular objective reality rather than another, it should no doubt obtain it from some cause in which there is at least as much formal reality as the idea contains objective reality. For if we suppose that there is some element in an idea which is not present in its cause, this element must then arise from nothing. However imperfect may be this mode of being, by which a thing exists objectively or is represented by a concept of it in the understanding, certainly we can nevertheless say that this mode and manner of being is not nothing, and consequently the idea cannot derive its origin from nothingness.

Nor must I imagine that, since the reality that I consider to be in my ideas is only objective, the same reality need not (42) be present formally or actually in the causes of these ideas, but that it is sufficient that it should be objectively present in them. For just as this manner of existing objectively belongs to ideas as part of their own nature, so also the manner or fashion of existing formally belongs to the causes of these ideas, or at the very least to their first and principal causes, as part of their own nature. And even though it might happen that one idea gives birth to another idea, that could not continue indefinitely; but we must finally reach a first idea, the cause of which is like an archetype or source, in which is contained formally and in actuality all the reality or perfection that is found only objectively or by representation in the ideas. Thus the light of nature makes me clearly recognize that ideas in me are like paintings or pictures, which can, truly, easily fall short of the perfection of the original from which they have been drawn, but which can never contain anything greater or more perfect. And the longer and the more carefully I consider all these arguments, the more clearly and distinctly I know that they are true.

What, then, shall I conclude from all this evidence? Clearly, that if the objective reality or perfection of some one of my ideas is such that I recognize clearly that this same reality or perfection does not exist in me, either formally or eminently, and consequently that I cannot myself be its cause, it necessarily follows that I am not alone in the world, but that there is also some other entity that exists and is the cause of this idea. On the other hand, if I find no such idea in myself, I will have no argument which can convince me and make me certain of the existence of any entity other than myself; for I have diligently searched for all such arguments and have been thus far unable to find any other.

Among all these ideas which exist in me, besides that which represents myself to myself, concerning which there can be no difficulty here, (43) there is another which represents a God, others corporeal and inanimate things, others angels, others animals, and still others which represent men similar to myself. But as far as the ideas which represent other men, or animals, or angels are concerned, I can easily imagine that they could be formed by the mixture and combination of my other ideas, of myself, of corporeal objects, and of God, even though outside of me there were no other men in the world, nor any animals, nor any angels. And as far as the ideas of corporeal objects are concerned, I recognize nothing in them so great or so excellent that it seems impossible that they could arise from myself. For if I consider them more closely and examine them in the same way that I examined the idea of wax yesterday, I find that there are only a few elements in them which I conceive clearly and distinctly—namely, size, or extension in length, width and depth; shape, which results from the termination and limitation of this extension; location, which the variously shaped objects have with respect to one another; and movement, or the changing of this location. To this one may add substance, duration, and number. As for other elements, such as light, colors, sounds, odors, tastes, heat, cold, and the other qualities involved in the sense of touch, they occur in my thought with so much obscurity and confusion that I do not even know whether they are true or false and only apparent, that is, whether my ideas of these qualities are really ideas of actual bodies or of non-bodies, which are only chimerical and cannot exist. For even though I have previously stated that true and formal falsity can characterize judgments only, there can exist nevertheless a certain material falsity in ideas, as when they represent that which is nothing as though it were something. For example, my ideas of cold and heat are so little clear (44) and distinct that I cannot determine from them whether cold is only the absence of heat or heat the absence of cold, or whether both of them are real qualities, or whether neither is such. Besides, since ideas are like pictures, there can be no ideas which do not seem to us to represent objects; and if it is true to say that cold is nothing but an absence of heat, the idea of cold which represents it as something real and positive could, riot inappropriately, be called false, and so for other similar ideas.

And assuredly, it is not necessary for me to attribute to such ideas any other source than myself. For if they are false—that is, if they represent entities which do not exist—the light of nature lets me know that they proceed from nothingness; that is, that they occur in me only because something is lacking in my nature and that the latter is not altogether perfect. And if these ideas are true, nevertheless, since they show me so little reality that I cannot even clearly distinguish the object represented from the nonexistent, I do not see why they could not be produced by myself and why I could not be their author.

As for my clear and distinct ideas of corporeal things, there are some of them which, it seems to me, might have been derived from my ideas of myself, such as my ideas of substance, duration, number, and other similar things. For I think that stone is a substance, or a thing which is capable of existing by itself, and that I myself am also a substance, even though I understand perfectly that I am a being that thinks and that is not extended, and that stone, on the contrary, is an extended being which does not think. Nevertheless, even though there is a notable difference between these two conceptions, they seem to agree in this fact that both of them represent substances. In the same way, when I think I exist now and remember in addition having existed formerly, or when I conceive various thoughts of which I recognize the number, I acquire (45) the ideas of duration and number which I afterward am able to apply to any other things I wish. As for the other qualities of which the ideas of material entities are composed—namely, extension, shape, location, and movement—it is true that they are not formally in my nature, since I am only a thinking being; but since these are only particular modes of substance, or, as it were, the garments in which corporeal substance appears to us, and since I am myself a substance, it seems that they might be contained in my nature eminently.

Thus there remains only the idea of God, in which we must consider if there is something which could not have come from myself. By the word "God" I mean an infinite substance, eternal, immutable, independent, omniscient, omnipotent, and that by which I myself and all other existent things, if it is true that there are other existent things, have been created and produced. But these attributes are such—they are so great and so eminent—that the more attentively I consider them, the less I can persuade myself that I could have derived them from my own nature. And consequently we must necessarily conclude from all that I have previously said that God exists. For even though the idea of substance exists in me from the very fact that I am a substance, I would nevertheless have no idea of an infinite substance, I who am a finite being, unless the idea had been placed in me by some substance which was in fact infinite.

And I must not imagine that I do not conceive infinity as a real idea, but only through the negation of what is finite in the manner that I comprehend rest and darkness as the negation of movement and light. On the contrary, I see manifestly that there is more reality in infinite substance than in finite substance, and my notion of the infinite is somehow prior to that of the finite, that is, the notion of God is prior to that of myself. For how would it be possible for me to know that I doubt and that I (46) desire—that is, that I lack something and am not all perfect—if I did not have in myself any idea of a being more perfect than my own, by comparison with which I might recognize the defects of my own nature?

And we cannot say that this idea of God might be materially false, and that in consequence I might derive it from nothingness, or, in other words, that it might be in me as a deficiency, as I have just now said about the ideas of heat and cold, and other similar things. For, on the contrary, this idea is very clear and very distinct and contains more objective reality than does any other, so that there is no other which is more true from its very nature, nor which is less open to the suspicion of error and falsity.

This idea, I say, of a supremely perfect and infinite being, is entirely true; for even though one might imagine that such a being does not exist, nevertheless one cannot imagine that the idea of it does not represent anything real, as I have just said of the idea of cold. It is also very clear and very distinct, since everything real and true which my mind conceives clearly and distinctly, and which contains some perfection, is contained and wholly included in this idea. And this will be no less true even though I do not comprehend the infinite and though there is in God an infinity of things which I cannot comprehend, or even perhaps suggest in thought, for it is the nature of infinity that I, who am finite and limited, cannot comprehend it. It is enough that I understand this and that I judge that all qualities which I conceive clearly and in which I know that there is some perfection, and possibly also an infinity of other qualities of which I am ignorant, are in God formally or eminently. Then the idea which I have of God is seen to be the truest, the clearest, and the most distinct of all the ideas which I have in my mind.

But possibly I am something more than I suppose myself to be. Perhaps all the perfections which I attribute to the nature of a God are somehow potentially in me, although they are not yet actualized and do not yet appear (47) and make themselves known by their actions. Experience shows, in fact, that my knowledge increases and improves little by little, and I see nothing to prevent its increasing thus, more and more, to infinity; nor even why, my knowledge having thus been augmented and perfected, I could not thereby acquire all the other perfections of divinity; nor finally, why my potentiality of acquiring these perfections, if it is true that I possess it, should not be sufficient to produce the ideas of them and introduce them into my mind.

Nevertheless, considering the matter more closely, I see that this could not be the case. For, first, even if it were true that my knowledge was always achieving new degrees of perfection and that there were in my nature many potentialities which had not yet been actualized, nevertheless none of these qualities belong to or approach in any way my idea of divinity, in which nothing is merely potential and everything is actual and real. Is it not even a most certain and infallible proof of the imperfection of my knowledge that it can grow little by little and increase by degrees? Furthermore, even if my knowledge increased more and more, I am still unable to conceive how it could ever become actually infinite, since it would never arrive at such a high point of perfection that it would no longer be capable of acquiring some still greater increase. But I conceive God to be actually infinite in such a high degree that nothing could be added to the supreme perfection that he already possesses. And finally, I understand very well that the objective existence of an idea can never be produced by a being that is merely potential and that, properly speaking, is nothing, but only by a formal or actual being.

And certainly there is nothing in all that I have just said which is not easily known by the light of nature to all those who will consider it carefully. But when I relax my attention somewhat, my mind is obscured, as though blinded by the images of sensible objects, and does not easily recall the reason why my idea of a being more perfect than my own must necessarily have been imparted to me by a being that is actually more perfect. (48)

That is why I wish to pass on now to consider whether I myself, who have this idea of God, could exist if there had been no God. And I ask, from what source would I have derived my existence? Possibly from myself, or from my parents, or from some other causes less perfect than God; for we could think of or imagine nothing more perfect, nor even equal to him. But if I were independent of anything else and were the author of my own being, I would doubt nothing, I would experience no desires, and finally I would lack no perfection. For I would have endowed myself with all those perfections of which I had any notion, and thus I would be God himself.

And I must not imagine that what I lack might be more difficult to acquire than what I already possess; for, on the contrary, it is very certain that it was far more difficult for this ego—that is, this being or substance that thinks—to emerge from nothingness than it would be for me to acquire the insight into and knowledge of various matters about which I am ignorant, since this knowledge would only be an accident of this substance. And certainly if I had given myself all the qualities that I have just mentioned and more, that is, if I were myself the author of my birth and of my being, I would at least not have denied to myself those things which could be obtained with greater facility as are an infinity of items of information, of which my nature happens to be deprived. I would not even have denied myself any of the qualities which I see are included in the idea of God, because there is no one of them which seems to me to be more difficult to create or acquire. And if there were one of them which was more difficult, certainly it would have appeared so to me, because, on the assumption that all my other qualities were self-given, I would see in this one quality a limitation of my power since I would not be able to acquire it.

Even if I could suppose that possibly I have always been as I am now, still I could not evade the force of this argument since it would not follow that no author of my existence need then be sought and I would still have to recognize that it is necessary that God is the author of my existence. For the whole duration of my life can be divided into (49) an infinite number of parts, no one of which is in any way dependent upon the others; and so it does not follow from the fact that I have existed a short while before that I should exist now, unless at this very moment some cause produces and creates me, as it were, anew or, more properly, conserves me.

Actually it is quite clear and evident to all who will consider attentively the nature of time that a substance, to be conserved at every moment that it endures, needs the same power and the same action which would be necessary to produce it and create it anew if it did not yet exist. Thus the light of nature makes us see clearly that conservation and creation differ only in regard to our manner of thinking and not in reality.

It is therefore only necessary here for me to question myself and consider my own nature to see whether I possess some power and ability by means of which I can bring it about that I, who exist now, shall still exist a moment later. For since I am nothing but a being which thinks, or at least since we are so far concerned only with that part of me, if such a power resided in me, certainly I should at least be conscious of it and recognize it. But I am aware of no such thing, and from that fact I recognize evidently that I am dependent upon some other being different from myself.

But possibly that being upon whom I am dependent is not God, and I am produced either by my parents or by some other causes less perfect than he. Not at all, that cannot be the case. For, as I have already said, it is very evident that there must be at least as much reality in the cause as in the effect; and since I am a being who thinks and who has some idea of God, whatever turns out to be the cause of my existence must be admitted to be also a being who thinks and which has in itself the idea of all the perfections which I attribute to the divine nature of God. Thus we can in turn inquire whether this cause derives its origin and existence from itself or from something else. For if it is self-caused, it follows, for the reasons that I have previously given, that this cause must be God himself, (50) since, to have the capacity to be or exist by itself, it must also, without doubt, have the power to possess in actuality all the perfections which it can imagine, that is, all those that I conceive to be in God. But if it derives its existence from something else, we ask once more, for the same reason, whether this second cause is caused by itself or by another, until step by step we finally arrive at an ultimate cause which will turn out to be God. And it is very obvious that in this case there cannot be an infinite regress, since it is not so much a question of the cause which produced me in the past as of that which conserves me in the present.

Nor can we pretend that possibly several partial causes have concurred to produce me, and that from one of them I received the idea of one of the perfections which I attribute to God, and from another the idea of some other, so that each of these perfections would actually be found somewhere in the universe, but would nowhere be joined together and assembled in one entity which would be God. For, on the contrary, the unity, simplicity, or inseparability of all the qualities which are in God is one of the principal perfections which I conceive to be in him. And certainly the idea of this unity of all God's perfections could not have been placed in me by any cause from which I had not also received the ideas of all the other perfections. For nothing could have brought it about that I understood these qualities as joined together and inseparable, without having brought it about at the same time that I know what qualities they were and that I knew something about each one of them.

Finally, concerning my parents, from whom it seems that I derive my birth, even if all that I could ever have believed of them should be true, that would still not imply that it is they who conserve me, nor even that they made and produced me in so far as I am a thinking being, there being no relation between the bodily activity by which I have been accustomed to believe I was engendered and the production of a thinking substance. The most that they can have contributed to my birth is that they have produced certain arrangements in the matter within which I have so far believed that the real I, that is, my mind, (51) is enclosed. Thus the existence of my parents is no objection to the argument, and we must necessarily conclude from the mere fact that I exist and that I have an idea of a supremely perfect Being, or God, that the existence of God is very clearly demonstrated.

The only task left is to consider how I received this idea from God; for I did not get it through the senses, nor has it ever appeared to me unexpectedly, as the ideas of sensible objects are wont to do, when these objects are presented or seem to be presented to my external sense organs. Nor is it only a product for fiction of my mind, for it is not in my power to diminish it or to add anything to it. No possibility remains, consequently, except that this idea is born and produced with me from the moment that I was created, just as was the idea of myself.

And truly it must not be thought strange that God, in creating me, put this idea in my nature in much the same way as an artisan imprints his mark on his work. Nor is it necessary that this mark be something different from the work itself. From the very fact that God has created me, it is very credible that he has made me, in some sense, in his own image and similitude, and that I conceive this similitude, in which the idea of God is contained, by the same faculty by which I conceive myself. In other words, when I reflect upon myself, I not only know that I am ran imperfect being, incomplete and dependent upon some other being, and a being which strives and aspires incessantly to become something better and greater than I now am, but also and at the same time I know that the being upon which I depend possesses in itself all these great qualities to which I aspire and the ideas of which I find in myself, and possesses these qualities, not indefinitely and merely potentially, but really, actually, and infinitely, and so that it is God. And the whole force of the argument I have here used to prove the existence of God consists in the fact that I recognize that it would not be possible (52) for my nature to be what it is, possessing the idea of a God, unless God really existed—the same God, I say, the idea of whom I possess, the God who possesses all these high perfections of which my mind can have some slight idea, without however being able fully to comprehend them; who is subject to no defect and who has no part of all those qualities which involve imperfection. And from this it is quite evident that he cannot be a deceiver, since the light of nature teaches us that deception must always be the result of some deficiency.

But before I examine this more carefully and pass on to the consideration of other truths which may follow from this one, it seems proper to pause for a while to contemplate this all-perfect God, to weigh at leisure his marvelous attributes, to consider, admire, and adore the incomparable beauty of this immense magnificence, as far at least as the power of my mind, which is somewhat overwhelmed by it, permits.

For just as faith teaches that the supreme felicity of the next life consists only in this contemplation of divine majesty, so let us try from now on whether a similar contemplation, although incomparably less perfect, will not make us enjoy the greatest happiness that we are capable of experiencing in this life.

FOURTH MEDITATION
OF THE TRUE AND THE FALSE

In these last few days I have become so accustomed to ignoring my senses, and I have so carefully noticed that we know very little (53) with certainty about corporeal things and that we know much more about the human mind, and still more again about God himself, that it is easy for me now to turn my consideration from sensible or picturable things to those which, being wholly dissociated from matter, are purely intelligible. And certainly my idea of the human mind, in so far as it is a thinking being, not extended in length, breadth, and depth, and participating in none of the qualities of body, is incomparably more distinct than my idea of anything corporeal. And when I consider that I doubt, that is to say, that I am an incomplete and dependent being, the idea of a complete and independent being, that is, of God, occurs to my mind with very great distinctness and clearness. And from the very fact that such an idea occurs in me, or that I who possess this idea exist, I so evidently conclude that God exists and that my own existence depends entirely upon him every moment of my life that I am confident that the human mind can know nothing with greater evidence and certainty. And I already seem to have discovered a path that will lead us from this contemplation of the true God, in whom all the treasures of science and wisdom are contained, to the knowledge of all other beings in the universe.

For first, I recognize that it is impossible for God ever to deceive me, since in all fraud and deception there is some kind of imperfection. And although it seems that to be able to deceive is a mark of acumen, subtlety, or power, nevertheless to wish to deceive testifies without question to weakness or malice, which could not be found in God.

Then, I know by my own experience that I have some ability to judge, or to distinguish the true from the false, an ability which I have no doubt received from God just as I have received all the other qualities which are part of me and which I possess. (54) Furthermore, since it is impossible that God wishes to deceive me, it is also certain that he has not given me an ability of such a sort that I could ever go wrong when I use it properly.

And no doubt on this subject would remain, except that we could apparently then draw the conclusion that I can never commit an error. For if everything in me is derived from God, and if he has not given me any ability to make errors, it seems that I should never be mistaken. It is true that when I consider myself only as a creature of God, and when I orient myself completely upon him, I discover in myself no cause of error or falsity. But when, a little later, I think of myself, experience convinces me that I am nevertheless subject to innumerable errors. And when I try to discover the reason for this, I notice that there is present in my thought not only a real and positive idea of God, or rather of a supremely perfect being, but also, so to speak, a certain negative idea of nothingness, or of what is infinitely removed from every kind of perfection. And I see that I am, as it were, a mean between God and nothingness, that is, so placed between the supreme Being and not-being that, in so far as a supreme Being has produced me, there is truly nothing in me which could lead me into error; but if I consider myself as somehow participating in nothingness or not-being, that is, in so far as I am not myself the supreme being and am lacking many things, I find myself exposed to an infinity of defects, so that I should not be astonished if I go wrong.

Thus I clearly recognize that error as such is not something real which depends upon God, but only a deficiency. Thus, in order to err, I do not need a faculty I which God has given to me expressly for the purpose; mistakes on my part occur because the power that God has given me to discriminate between the true and the false is not infinite.

Nevertheless I am not yet altogether satisfied, for error is not (55) a pure negation—that is, it is not a simple deficiency or lack of some perfection which is not my duel, but rather a privation or lack of some knowledge which it seems to me that I should possess. And in considering the nature of God, it does not seem possible that he should have endowed me with any faculty which is not perfect of its kind, or which lacks some perfection which is its due. For if it is true that the more expert the artisan, the more perfect and finished the artifacts produced by his hands, what could we imagine to have been produced by this supreme creator of the universe that is not perfect and entirely complete in all its parts? Certainly there is no doubt but that God could have created me such that I would never be mistaken; it is also certain that he always wills that which is best. Is it therefore a better thing to be able to make a mistake than not to be able to do so?

Considering this question with attention, it occurs to me, to begin with, that I should not be astonished at not being able to understand why God does what he does; and that I must not for this reason doubt his existence, since I may perchance observe in my experience many other beings that exist, even though I cannot understand why or how they were made. For, knowing by now that my nature is extremely weak and limited and that God's, on the contrary, is immense, incomprehensible, and infinite, I no longer have any difficulty in recognizing that there are an infinity of things within his power the causes of which lie beyond the powers of my mind. And this consideration alone is sufficient to persuade me that all causes of the type we are accustomed to call final are useless in physical or natural affairs, for it does not seem possible for me, without presumption, to seek and undertake to discover the impenetrable purposes of God.

Furthermore, it occurs to me that we should not consider a single creation separately when we investigate whether the works of God are perfect, but generally all created objects together. For the same thing which might perhaps, with some sort of justification, appear to be very imperfect if it were alone in the world (56) is seen to be very perfect when considered as constituting a part of this whole universe. And although, since I undertook to doubt everything, I have so far only learned with certainty of my existence and of God's, nevertheless, since I have recognized the infinite power of God, I could not deny that he has produced many other things, or at least that he could produce them, in such a way that I exist and am placed in the world as forming a part of the universality of all beings.

Consequently, when I come to examine myself more closely and to consider what are my errors, which alone testify that there is imperfection in me, I find that they depend upon two joint causes, namely, the faculty of knowing which I possess and the faculty of choice, or rather of free will—that is to say, of my understanding together with my will. For by the understanding alone I neither assert nor deny anything, but I only conceive the ideas of things which I may assert or deny. Nor in considering the understanding thus precisely can we say that any error is ever found in it, provided that we take the word "error" in its proper sense. And even if there might be in the world an infinity of things of which my understanding has no idea, we cannot therefore say that it is deprived of these ideas as of something which is owed to its nature, but only that it does not possess them, because in reality there is no argument which can prove that God ought to have given me a greater and more ample faculty of knowing than what lie has given me; and however adroit and able a worker I consider him to be, I must not therefore think that he ought to have put in each of his works all the perfections which lie is able to bestow upon some. Thus I cannot complain because God has not given me a sufficiently ample and perfect free will or volition, since, as a matter of fact, I experience it to be so ample and extended that there are no limits which restrict it.

And it appears to me to be very remarkable that, of all the other qualities which I possess, there is none (57) so perfect or so great that I do not clearly recognize that it could be even greater or more perfect. Thus for example, if I consider my faculty of conceiving, I immediately recognize that it is of very small extent and greatly limited; and at the same time there occurs to me the idea of another faculty, much more ample, indeed immensely greater and even infinite, and from the very fact that I can imagine this I recognize without difficulty that it belongs to the nature of God. In the same way, if I examine memory, imagination, or any other faculty of mine, I find no one of them which is not quite small and limited and which is not, in God, immense and infinite. There is only volition alone, or the liberty of the free will, which I experience to be so great in myself that I cannot conceive the idea of any other more ample and extended, so that this is what principally indicates to me that I am made in the image and likeness of God. For even though the will may be incomparably greater in God than in myself, either because of the knowledge and the power which are joined with it and which make it surer and more efficacious, or because of its object, since it extends to infinitely more things, nevertheless it does not appear any greater when I consider it formally and precisely by itself. For it consists only in the fact that we can make a choice; we can do a given thing or not do it—that is to say, we can affirm or deny, pursue or avoid. Or more properly, our free will consists only in the fact that in affirming or denying, pursuing or avoiding the things suggested by the understanding, we behave in such a way that we do not feel that any external force has constrained us in our decision.

For in order to be free, it is not necessary for me to be indifferent about the choice of one or the other of the two contraries, but rather, the more I lean to one, either because I see clearly that it contains the preponderance (58) of both goodness and truth or because God so guides my private thoughts, the more freely do I choose and embrace it. And certainly, divine grace and natural understanding, far from diminishing my liberty, rather augment and strengthen it. Moreover, that indifference which I feel when I am not more moved toward one side than the other by the weight of some reason is the lowest degree of liberty, and is rather a defect in the understanding than a perfection of the will. For if I always understood clearly what is true and what is good, I would never need to deliberate about what judgment and what choice I ought to make, and so I would be entirely free without ever being indifferent.

From all this I recognize, on the one hand, that the cause of my errors is not the power of willing considered by itself, which I have received from God, for it is very ample and perfect in its own kind. Nor, on the other hand, is it the power of understanding or conceiving; for since I conceive nothing except by means of this power which God has given me in order to conceive, no doubt everything I conceive I conceive properly, and it is not possible for me to be deceived in that respect.

Whence, then, do my errors arise? Only from the fact that the will is much more ample and far-reaching than the understanding, so that I do not restrain it within the same limits but extend it even to those things which I do not understand. Being by its nature indifferent about such matters, it very easily is turned aside from the true and the good and chooses the false and the evil. And thus it happens that I make mistakes and that I sin.

For example, when I recently examined the question whether anything in the world existed, and I recognized from the very fact that I examined this question that it was very evident that I myself existed, I could not refrain from concluding that what I conceived so clearly was true. Not that I found myself forced to this conclusion by any (59) external cause, but only because the great clarity which was in my understanding produced a great inclination of my will, and I was led to this conviction all the more spontaneously and freely as I experienced in myself less indifference. Now, on the contrary, I know not only that I exist, in so far as I am something that thinks, but there is also present in my mind a certain idea of corporeal nature. In consequence, I wonder whether this nature that thinks, which is in me, or rather which is myself, is different from this corporeal nature, or if both are one and the same. I am supposing, here, that I do not yet know any argument to convince me of one possibility rather than the other, so it follows that I am entirely indifferent as to denying or affirming it, or even as to abstaining from making any judgment.

And this indifference extends not only to those things with which the understanding has no acquaintance, but also to all those generally that it does not comprehend with sufficiently perfect clarity at the moment when the will is deliberating the issue. For however probable may be the conjectures which incline me to a particular judgment, the mere recognition that they are only conjectures and not certain and indubitable reasons is enough to give me grounds for making the contrary judgment. I have had sufficient experience of this in these past few days when I assumed as false all that I had previously held to be very true, merely because I noticed that it was somehow possible to doubt it.

Now, if I abstain from making a judgment upon a topic when I do not conceive it sufficiently clearly and distinctly, it is evident that I do well and am not making a mistake; but if I decide to deny or affirm it, then I am not making a proper use of my free will. And (60) if in this situation I affirm what is not true, it is evident that I am making a mistake; and even when I judge according to the truth, it is only by chance, and I am not for that reason free of blame for misusing my freedom. For the light of nature dictates that the understanding should always know before the will makes a decision.

It is in this improper use of the free will that we find the privation which constitutes the essence of error. Privation, I say, is found in the operation in so far as it proceeds from me, but not in the faculty which I have received from God, nor even in the operation in so far as it depends upon him. For certainly I have no reason to complain because God has not given me a more ample intelligence or a more perfect insight than what he has bestowed upon me, since it is actually the nature of a finite understanding not to comprehend many things, and it is the nature of a created understanding to be finite. On the contrary, far from conceiving such unjust sentiments as to imagine that he has deprived me or unjustly kept from me the other perfections with which he has not endowed me, I have every reason to give him thanks because, never having any obligation to me, he has nevertheless given me those few perfections that I have.

Nor have I any reason to complain because he has given me a volition more ample than my understanding. For as the volition consists of just one body, its subject being apparently indivisible, it seems that its nature is such that nothing could be taken from it without destroying it. And, certainly, the more ample it is, the more reason I have to give thanks for the generosity of the One who has given it to me.

Nor, finally, have I any reason to complain that God concurs with me to perform the acts of this volition, that is, the judgments in which I am mistaken. For those acts are entirely true and absolutely good in so far as they depend upon God, and there is somehow more perfection in my nature because I can perform them than there would be if I could not. As for privation; in which alone is found the formal cause (61) of error and sin, it has no need of any concurrence on the part of God, since it is not a thing of a being and since, if it is referred to God as to its cause, it should not be called privation but only negation according to the significance attached to these words in the schools. For actually it is not an imperfection in God that he has given me the liberty of judging or not judging, or giving or withholding my assent, on certain matters of which he has given me no clear and distinct knowledge. It is, without doubt, an imperfection in myself not to make proper use of this liberty, and rashly to pass judgment on matters which I do not rightly understand and conceive only obscurely and confusedly.

I perceive, nevertheless, that it would have been easy for God to contrive that I would never make mistakes, even though I remained free and with limited knowledge.

He might, for example, have given my understanding a clear and distinct comprehension of all the things about which I should ever deliberate, or he might simply have engraved so deeply in my memory the resolution never to pass judgment on anything without conceiving it clearly and distinctly that I could never forget this rule. And I readily recognize in so far as I possess the comprehension of any whole, that when I consider myself alone, as if I were the only person in the world, I would have been much more perfect than I am if God had so created me that I never made a mistake; nevertheless I cannot therefore deny that the universe may be somehow more perfect because some of its parts are not free from defect while others are, than it would be if all its parts were alike.

And I have no right to complain because God, having put me in the world, has not wished to place me in the ranks of the noblest and most perfect beings. I indeed have reason to rejoice because, even if I do not have the power of avoiding error by the first method which I have just described, which depends upon a clear and evident knowledge of all the things about which I can deliberate, the other method, at least, is within my power. This is, (62) firmly to adhere to the resolution never to pass judgment upon things whose truth is not clearly known to me. For even though I experience in myself the weakness of not being able to keep my mind continuously faithful to a fixed resolution, I can nevertheless, by attentive and frequently repeated meditation, so strongly impress it upon my memory that I will never fail to recollect it whenever there is need, and thus I can acquire the habit of not erring. And since this comprises the greatest and principal perfection of man, I consider that I have benefited not a little by today's meditation, in having discovered the cause of error and falsity.

And certainly, there can be no other cause than the one I have just explained, for whenever I restrict my volition within the bounds of my knowledge, whenever my volition makes no judgment except upon matters clearly and distinctly reported to it by the understanding, it cannot happen that I err. For every clear and distinct conception is without doubt something real and positive, and thus cannot derive its origin from nothingness, but must have God for its author—God, I say, who, being supremely perfect, cannot be the cause of any error—and consequently we must conclude that such a conception or such a judgment is true.

For the rest, I have not only learned today what I must avoid in order not to err, but also what I ought to do to arrive at the knowledge of the truth. For I shall certainly achieve this goal if I hold my attention sufficiently fixed upon all those things which I conceive perfectly and if I distinguish these from the others which I conceive only confusedly and obscurely. And from now on I shall take particular care to act accordingly. (63)

Fifth Meditation
Of the Essence of Material Things and, Once More,
of God: That he Exists

There are many other questions for me to inquire into concerning the attributes of God and concerning my own nature, or the nature of my mind. I may, perhaps, pursue this investigation some other time; for the present, having noticed what must be done or avoided in order to arrive at the knowledge of the truth, my principal task is to attempt to escape from and relieve myself of All the doubts into which I have fallen in these last few days, and to see if we cannot know anything certain about material objects. But before examining whether such objects exist outside of myself, I must consider the concepts of these objects, in so far as they occur in my thought, and see which of them are distinct and which of them are confused.

In the first place, I picture distinctly that quantity which philosophers commonly call the "continuum," or extension in length, width, and depth which exists in this quantity, or rather in the body to which we attribute it. Furthermore, I can distinguish in it various different parts and attribute to each of these parts all sorts of sizes, shapes, positions, and movements; and, finally, I can assign to each of these movements all degrees of duration.

And I not only know these things distinctly when I consider them thus in general, but also, however little I am applying my attention to it, I come to recognize an infinity of details concerning numbers, shapes, movements, and other similar things, the truth of which makes itself so apparent (64) and accords so well with my nature that when I discover them for the first time it does not seem to me as though I were learning anything new, but rather as though I were remembering what I had previously known—that is, that I am perceiving things which were already in my mind, even though I had not yet focussed my attention upon them.

And what I believe to be more important here is that I find in myself an infinity of ideas of certain things which cannot be assumed to be pure nothingness, even though they may perhaps have no existence outside of my thought. These things are not figments of my imagination, even though it is within my power to think of them or not to think of them; on the contrary, they have their own true and immutable natures. Thus, for example, when I imagine a triangle, even though there may perhaps be no such figure anywhere in the world outside of my thought, nor ever have been, nevertheless the figure cannot help having a certain determinate nature, or form, or essence, which is immutable and eternal, which I have not invented and which does not in any way depend upon my mind. This is evidenced by the fact that we can demonstrate various properties of this triangle, namely, that its three angles are equal to two right angles, that the greatest angle subtends the longest side, and other similar properties. Whether I wish it or not, I now recognize very clearly and evidently that these are properties of the triangle, even though I had never previously thought of them in any way when I first imagined one. And therefore it cannot be said that I have imagined or invented them.

Nor can I raise the objection here that possibly this idea of the triangle came to my mind from external things through the medium of my senses, since I have sometimes seen triangularly shaped objects; for I can picture in my mind an infinity of other shapes such that I cannot have the least suspicion that they have ever been present to my senses, and I am still (65) no less able to demonstrate various properties about their nature than I am about that of the triangle. These properties, certainly, must be wholly true, since I conceive them clearly. And thus they are something, and not pure negation, since it is quite evident that everything which is true is something, as truth is the same as being. I have already amply demonstrated that everything that I recognize clearly and distinctly is true; and even if I had not demonstrated this, the nature of my mind is such that I can not help believing things to be true while I am conceiving them clearly and distinctly. And I recollect that even when I was still strongly attached to the objects of sense, I numbered among the most constant truths that which I conceived clearly and distinctly about the shapes, numbers, and other properties which belong to the fields of arithmetic and geometry or, in general, to pure and abstract mathematics.

Now, if from the very fact that I can derive from my thoughts the idea of something, it follows that all that I clearly and distinctly recognize as characteristic of this thing does in reality characterize it, can I not derive from this an argument which will demonstratively prove the existence of God? It is certain that I find in my mind the idea of God, of a supremely perfect Being, no less than that of any shape or number whatsoever; and I recognize that an actual and eternal existence belongs to his nature no less clearly and distinctly than I recognize that all I can demonstrate about some figure or number actually belongs to the nature of that figure or number. Thus, even if everything that I concluded in the preceding Meditations were by chance not true, the existence of God should pass in my mind as at least as certain (66) as I have hitherto considered all the truths of mathematics, which deal only with numbers and figures.

And this is true even though I must admit that it does not at first appear entirely obvious, but seems to have some appearance of sophistry. For since in all other matters I have become accustomed to make a distinction between existence and essence, I am easily convinced that the existence of God can be separated from his essence, and that thus I can conceive of God as not actually existing. Nevertheless, when I consider this with more attention, I find it manifest that we can no more separate the existence of God from his essence than we can separate from the essence of a rectilinear triangle the fact that the size of its three angles equals two right angles, or from the idea of a mountain the idea of a valley. Thus it is no less self-contradictory to conceive of a God, a supremely perfect Being, who lacks existence—that is, who lacks some perfection—than it is to conceive of a mountain for which there is no valley.

But even though in fact I cannot conceive of a God without existence, any more than of a mountain without a valley, nevertheless, just as from the mere fact that I conceive a mountain with a valley, it does not follow that any mountain exists in the world, so likewise, though I conceive of God as existing, it does not seem to follow for this reason that God exists. For my thought does not impose any necessity upon things; and just as I can at my pleasure imagine a winged horse, even though no horse has wings, so I could perhaps attribute existence to God, even though no God existed.

This is far from the truth; it is here that there is sophistry hidden under the guise of a valid objection. For from the fact that I cannot conceive a mountain without a valley it does not follow that there is a mountain or a valley anywhere in the world, but only that the mountain (67) and the valley, whether they exist or not, are inseparable from each other. From the fact alone that I cannot conceive God except as existing, it follows that existence is inseparable from him, and consequently that he does, in truth, exist. Not that my thought can bring about this result or that it imposes any necessity upon things; on the contrary, the necessity which is in the thing itself—that is, the necessity of the existence of God—determines me to have this thought. For it is not in my power to conceive of a God without existence—that is to say, of a supremely perfect Being without a supreme perfection—as it is in my power to imagine a horse either with or without wings.

And it must not be said here that it is only necessary that I admit that God exists after I have supposed that he possesses all sorts of perfections, since existence is one of them, but that my first supposition was not really necessary. Thus it is not necessary to think that all four-sided figures can be inscribed in a circle; but if we suppose that I do have this idea, I am forced to admit that a rhombus can be inscribed in one, since it is a four-sided figure, and by this I will be forced to admit what is clearly false. We must not, I say, argue thus; for even though it is not necessary that I should ever have any thought about God, nevertheless, whenever I do choose to think of a first and supreme being and to derive, so to speak, the idea of God from the treasure house of my mind, it is necessary that I attribute to him all kinds of perfections, even though it does not occur to me to mention them all and to pay attention to each one of them severally. And this necessity is enough to bring it about that afterward, as soon as I come to recognize that existence is a perfection, I conclude very properly that this first and supreme Being truly exists; just as it is not necessary that I should ever imagine any triangle, but every time that I wish to consider a rectilinear figure containing three angles only, it is absolutely necessary that I attribute to it everything that leads (68) to the conclusion that these three angles are not greater than two right angles, even if perhaps I do not then consider this matter in particular. But when I wish to determine what figures can be inscribed in a circle, it is in no way necessary that I think that all four-sided figures are of this number; on the contrary, I cannot even pretend that this is the case as long as I do not wish to accept anything but what I can conceive clearly and distinctly. Consequently, there is a vast difference between false suppositions, such as this one, and the true ideas which are inborn in me, of which the first and chief one is that of God. For actually I have several reasons for recognizing that this idea is not something imaginary or fictitious, depending only on my thought, but that it is the image of a true and immutable nature. The first reason is that I cannot conceive anything but God alone, to whose essence existence belongs with necessity. Another reason is that it is not possible for me to conceive in the same way two or more gods such as he. Again, assuming that there is now a God who exists, I see clearly that he must have existed before from all eternity and that he should be eternally in the future. And a final reason is that I conceive various other qualities in God, of which I can neither diminish nor change a particle.

For the rest, whatever proof or argument I use, I must always come back to this conclusion: that it is only the things that I conceive clearly and distinctly which have the power to convince me completely. And although among the things which I conceive in this way there are, in truth, some which are obviously known to everyone, while others of them only become known to those who consider them more closely and examine them more carefully, nevertheless, after they have once been discovered, none of them can be esteemed less certain than the rest. Thus, for example, in every right-angled triangle, even though it is not so readily apparent (69) that the square of the hypotenuse is equal to the squares of the other two sides as it is that this hypotenuse is opposite the greatest angle, nevertheless, after this fact has once been recognized, we are as much convinced of the truth of the one proposition as of the other. And as for the question of God, certainly, if my mind were not prejudiced and if my thought were not distracted by the constant presence on all sides of images of sensible objects, there would be nothing that I would recognize sooner or more easily than God. For is there anything clearer and more obvious in itself than to think that there is a God, that is to say, a supreme and perfect Being, in whom uniquely necessary for eternal existence is included in essence, and who consequently exists?

And although, in order thoroughly to understand this truth, I have bad to make a great mental effort, nevertheless I find myself at present not only as certain of this as of everything which seems to me most certain, but even beyond that I notice that the certainty of all other things depends upon this so absolutely that, without this knowledge, it is impossible ever to be able to know anything perfectly.

For even though my nature is such that as soon as I understand anything very clearly and very distinctly I cannot help but believe it to be true, nevertheless, because I am also of such a nature that I cannot always confine my attention to one thing and frequently remember having judged a thing to be true when I have ceased considering the reasons which forced me to that conclusion, it can happen at such a time that other reasons occur to me which would easily make me change my mind if I did not know that there was a God. And so I would never have true and certain knowledge concerning anything at all, but only vague and fluctuating opinions.

Thus, for example, when I consider the nature of the rectilinear triangle, I recognize most evidently, I, who am somewhat skilled in geometry, that its three angles are equal to two right angles; nor can I disbelieve this while I am paying attention to (70) its demonstration. But as soon as I turn my attention away from the demonstration, even while I remember having clearly understood it, it can easily happen that I doubt its truth, if I do not know that there is a God. For I can persuade myself that I was so made by nature that I could easily make mistakes, even in those matters which I believe I understand with the greatest evidence and certainty, especially because I remember having often judged many things true and certain, which, later, other reasons constrained me to consider absolutely false.

But after having recognized that there is a God, and having recognized at the same time that all things arc dependent upon him and that he is not a deceiver, I can infer as a consequence that everything which I conceive clearly and distinctly is necessarily true. Therefore, even if I am no longer thinking of the reasons why I have judged something to be true, provided only I remember having understood it clearly and distinctly, there can never be a reason on the other side which can make me consider the matter doubtful. Thus I have a true and certain body of knowledge on this matter. And this same body of knowledge extends also to all the other things which I remember having formerly demonstrated such as the truths of geometry and other similar matters. For what reason can anyone give to make me doubt them? Would it be that my nature is such that I am very likely to be frequently deceived? But I know already that I cannot go wrong in judgments for which I clearly know the reasons. Would it be that I have formerly considered many things true and certain which I later recognized to be false? But I had not clearly or distinctly known any of those things; and not yet knowing this rule by which I am certain of truth, I had been led to believe them by reasons that I have since recognized to be less strong than I had then imagined them. What further objections could be raised? Would it be that possibly I am asleep, as I had myself argued earlier, or that all the thoughts that I now have are no more true than the dreams we imagine when asleep? But even so, nothing would be altered. For (71) even if I were asleep, all that appears evident to my mind is absolutely true.

And thus I recognize very clearly that the certainty and truth of all knowledge depends solely on the knowledge of the true God, so that before I knew him I could not know any other thing perfectly. And now that I know him, I have the means of acquiring clear and certain and perfect knowledge about an infinity of things, not only about God himself and about other intellectual matters, but also about that which pertains to corporeal nature, in so far as it can be the object of pure mathematics—that is, of the demonstrations of geometricians who are not concerned with its existence.

SIXTH MEDITATION
OF THE EXISTENCE OF CORPOREAL THINGS
AND OF THE REAL DISTINCTION BETWEEN
THE MIND AND BODY OF MAN

Nothing more is now left for me to do except to examine whether corporeal things exist; and I already know for certain that they can exist at least in so far as they are considered as the objects of pure mathematics, or of the demonstrations of geometry, since I conceive them in this way very clearly and very distinctly. For there is no doubt but that God has the power of producing everything that I am able to conceive with distinctness; and I have never supposed that it was impossible for him to do anything, except only when I found a contradiction in being able to conceive it well. Furthermore, my faculty of imagination, which I find by experience that I use when I apply myself to the consideration of material objects, is capable of persuading me of their existence. For when I consider attentively what the imagination is, (72) I find that it is nothing else than a particular application of the faculty of knowledge to a body which is intimately present to it and which therefore exists.

And to make this very obvious, I take note of the difference between imagination and pure intellection or conception. For example, when I imagine a triangle, not only do I conceive that it is a figure composed of three lines, but along with that I envision these three lines as present, by the force and the internal effort of my mind; and it is just this that I call "imagination." But if I wish to think of a chiliogon, I recognize quite well, indeed, that it is a figure composed of a thousand sides, as easily as I conceive that a triangle is a figure composed of only three sides, but I cannot imagine the thousand sides of a chiliogon as I can the three of a triangle, nor, so to speak, look at them as though they were present to the eyes of my mind. And although, following my habit of always using my imagination when I think of corporeal things, it may happen that in conceiving a chiliogon I confusedly picture some figure to myself, nevertheless it is quite evident that this figure is not a chiliogon, since it is in no way different from what I would picture to myself if I thought of a myriogon or of some other figure of many sides, and that it in no way serves to bring out the properties which constitute the difference between the chiliogon and the other polygons. But if it is a question of considering a pentagon, it is quite true that I can conceive its shape, just as well as that of a chiliogon, without the aid of the imagination; but I can also imagine it by applying my mind attentively to each of its five sides, and at the same time collectively to the area or space that they enclose.

Thus I recognize clearly that I have need of a special (73) mental effort in order to imagine, which I do not require in order to conceive or understand, and this special mental effort clearly shows the difference that exists between imagination and pure intellection or conception. In addition, I notice that this ability to imagine which I possess, in so far as it differs from the power of conceiving, is in no way necessary to my nature or essence, that is to say, to the essence of my mind. For even if I did not possess it, there is no doubt that I would still remain the same person I now am, from which it seems to follow that it depends upon something other than my mind. And I readily conceive that if some body exists with which my mind is so joined and united] that it can consider it whenever it wishes, it could be that by this means it imagines corporeal things. Thus this method of thinking only differs from pure intellection in that the mind, in conceiving, turns somehow toward itself and considers some one of the ideas which it possesses in itself, whereas in imagining it turns toward the body and considers in the latter something conformable to the idea which it has either thought of by itself or perceived through the senses. I easily conceive, I say, that the imagination can work in this fashion, if it is true that there are bodies; and because I cannot find any other way in which this can be explained equally well, I therefore conjecture that bodies probably exist. But this is only a probability; and although I carefully consider all aspects of the question, I nevertheless do not see that from this distinct idea of corporeal nature which I find in my imagination, I can derive any argument which necessarily proves the existence of any body. (74)

But I have become accustomed to imagine many other things besides that corporeal nature which is the object of pure mathematics or geometry, although less distinctly, such as colors, sounds, tastes, pain, and other similar qualities. And inasmuch as I perceive those qualities much better by the senses, through the medium of which, with the help of the memory, they seem to have reached my imagination, I believe that in order to examine them more readily it is appropriate to consider at the same time the nature of the sensation and to see whether, from those ideas which are perceived by the method of thinking which I call "sensation," I will not be able to derive some certain proof of the existence of corporeal things.

First, I shall recall in my memory what are the things which I formerly held to be true because I had received them through the senses, and what were the bases on which my belief was founded. Afterward I shall examine the reasons which since then have obliged me to consider them doubtful, and finally, I shall consider what I ought now to believe about them.

First, then, I felt that I had a head, hands, feet, and all the other members which compose this body which I thought of as a part, or possibly even as the whole, of myself. Furthermore, I felt that this body was one of a world of bodies, from which it was capable of receiving various advantages and disadvantages; and I identified these advantages by a certain feeling of pleasure or enjoyment, and the disadvantages by a feeling of pain. Besides this pleasure and pain, I also experienced hunger, thirst, and other similar appetites, as well as certain bodily tendencies toward gaiety, sadness, anger, and other similar emotions. And externally, in addition to the extension, shapes, and (75) movements of bodies, I observed in them hardness, warmth, and all the other qualities perceived by touch. Furthermore, I noticed in them light, colors, odors, tastes, and sounds, the variety of which enabled me to distinguish the sky, the earth, the sea, and, in general, all other bodies, one from another.

And certainly, considering the ideas of all these qualities which were presented to my mind and which alone I directly sensed, in the true significance of that term, it was not without reason that I believed I had sensory knowledge of things entirely different from my thought—of bodies, namely, from which these ideas came. For I was aware that these ideas occurred without the necessity of my consent, so that I could not perceive any object, however much I wished, unless it was present to one of my sense organs; nor was it in my power not to perceive it when it was present. And because the ideas I received through the senses were much more vivid, more detailed, and even in their own way more distinct than any of those which I could picture to myself with conscious purpose while meditating, or even than those which I found impressed upon my memory, it seemed that they could not be derived from my own mind, and therefore they must have been produced in me by some other things. Of these things I have no knowledge whatsoever, except that derived from the ideas themselves, so nothing else could occur to my mind except that those things were similar to the ideas they caused. And since I remembered that I had used my senses earlier than my reason, and since I recognized that the ideas I formed by myself were not as detailed as those I received through the senses and were most commonly composed. of the latter as parts, I easily became persuaded that I had no idea in my mind which I had not previously acquired through my senses.

It was also not without reason that I believed that this body, which by a certain particular privilege I called mine, (76) belonged to me more properly and strictly than any other. For in fact I could never be separated from it, as I could be from other bodies; I felt in it and for it all my appetites and all my emotions; and finally I experienced the sensations of pain and the thrill of pleasure in its parts, and not in those of other bodies which are separated from it.

But when I inquired why any particular sensation of pain should be followed by unhappiness in the mind and the thrill of pleasure should give rise to happiness, or even why a particular feeling of the stomach, which I call hunger, makes us want to eat, and the dryness of the throat makes us want to drink, and so on, I could give no reason except that nature teaches me so. For there is certainly no affinity and no relationship, or at least none that I can understand, between the feeling in the stomach and the desire to eat, no more than between the perception of the, object which causes pain and the feeling of displeasure produced by it. And in the same way, it seemed to me that I had learned from nature all the other beliefs which I held about the objects of my senses, since I noticed that the judgments I habitually made about these objects took form in my mind before I had the opportunity to weigh and consider any reasons which could oblige me to make them.

Later on, various experiences gradually destroyed all my faith in my senses. For I often observed that towers which, viewed from far away, had appeared round to me, seemed at close range to be square, and that colossal statues placed on the highest summits of these towers appeared small when viewed from below. And similarly in a multitude of other experiences, I encountered errors in judgments based on the external senses. And not only on the external senses, but even on the internal ones, (77) for is there anything more intimate or more internal than pain? Yet I have learned from certain persons whose arms or legs had been amputated that it still seemed to them sometimes that they felt pain in the parts which they no longer possessed. This gives me reason to think that I could not be entirely sure either that there was something wrong with one of my limbs, even though I felt a pain in it.

And to these reasons for doubting I have recently added two other very general ones. The first is that I have never thought I perceived anything when awake that I might not sometimes also think I perceived when I am asleep; and since I do not believe that the things I seem to perceive when asleep proceed from objects outside of myself, I did not see any better reason why I ought to believe this about what I seem to perceive when awake. The other reason was that, not yet knowing, or rather pretending not to know the author of my being, I saw nothing to make it impossible that I was so constructed by nature that I should be mistaken even in the things which seemed to me most true.

And as for the reasons which had previously persuaded me that sensible objects truly existed, I did not find it very difficult to answer them. For as nature seemed to lead me to many conclusions from which reason dissuaded me, I did not believe that I ought to have much faith in the teachings of this nature. And although my sense perceptions do not depend upon my volition, I did not think that I should therefore conclude that they proceeded from things different from myself, since there might perhaps be some faculty in myself even though it has been thus far unknown to me, which could bwe their cause and produce them.

But now that I am beginning to know myself better and to discover more clearly the author of my origin, I do not think in truth that I ought rashly to admit everything which the senses seem to teach us, (78) but on the other hand I do not think that I should doubt them all in general.

First, since I know that all the things I conceive clearly and distinctly can be produced by God exactly as I conceive them, it is sufficient that I can clearly and distinctly conceive one thing apart from another to be certain that the one is distinct or different from the other. For they can be made to exist separately, at least by the omnipotence of God, and we are obliged to consider them different no matter what power produces this separation. From the very fact that I know with certainty that I exist, and that I find that absolutely nothing else belongs necessarily to my nature or essence except that I am a thinking being, I readily conclude that my essence consists solely in being a body which thinks or a substance whose whole essence or nature is only to think. And although perhaps, or rather certainly, as I will soon show, I have a body with which I am very closely united, nevertheless, since on the one hand I have a clear and distinct idea of myself in so far as I am only a thinking and not an extended being, and since on the other hand I have a distinct idea of body in so far as it is only an extended being which does not think, it is certain that this "I"—that is to say, my soul, by virtue of which I am what I am—is entirely and truly distinct from my body and that it can be or exist without it.

Furthermore, I find in myself various faculties of thinking which each have their own particular characteristics and are distinct from myself. For example, I find in myself the faculties of imagination and of perception, without which I might no doubt conceive of myself, clearly and distinctly, as a whole being; but I could not I, conversely, conceive of those faculties without me, that is to say, without an intelligent substance to which they are attached or in which they inhere. For in our notion of them or, to use the scholastic vocabulary, in their formal concept, they embrace some type of intellection. From all this I reach the conception that these faculties are distinct from me as shapes, movements, and other modes or accidents of objects are distinct from the very objects that sustain them.

I also recognize in myself some other faculties, such as the power of changing location, of assuming various postures, and other similar ones; which cannot be conceived without some substance in which they inhere, any more than the preceding ones, (79) and which therefore cannot exist without such a substance. But it is quite evident that these faculties, if it is true that they exist, must inhere in some corporeal or extended substance, and not in an intelligent substance, since their clear and distinct concept does actually involve some sort of extension, but no sort of intelligence whatsoever. Furthermore, I cannot doubt that there is in me a certain passive faculty of perceiving, that is, of receiving and recognizing the ideas of sensible objects; but it would be valueless to me, and I could in no way use it if there were not also in me, or in something else, another active faculty capable of forming and producing these ideas. But this active faculty cannot be in me, in so far as I am a thinking being, since it does not at all presuppose my intelligence and also since those ideas often occur to me without my contributing to them in any way, and even frequently against my will. Thus it must necessarily exist in some substance different from myself, in which all the reality that exists objectively in the ideas produced by this faculty is formally or eminently contained, as I have said before. This substance is either a body—that is, a corporeal nature—in which is formally and actually contained all that which is contained objectively and by representation in these ideas; or else it is God himself, or some other creation more noble than the body, in which all this is eminently contained.

But since God is not a deceiver, it is very manifest that he does not send me these ideas directly by his own agency, nor by the mediation of some creation in which their objective reality does not exist formally but only eminently. For since he has not given me any faculty for recognizing what that creation might be, but on the contrary a very great (80) inclination to believe that these ideas come from corporeal objects, I do not see how we could clear God of the charge of deceit if these ideas did in fact come from some other source or were produced by other causes than corporeal objects. Therefore we must conclude that corporeal objects exist. Nevertheless, they are not perhaps entirely what our senses perceive them to be, for there are many ways in which this sense perception is very obscure and confused; but we must at least admit that everything which I conceive clearly and distinctly as occuring in them—that is to say, everything,

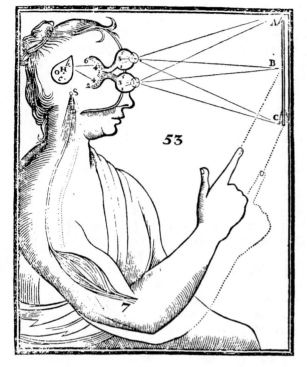

A diagram from Descartes'
Tractatus de Homine (1677)
showing how the pineal gland
(shown here at the back of the head)
connects sensory images from the
eyes to the muscles of the arm.
(*Library of Congress*)

generally speaking, which is discussed in pure mathematics or geometry—does in truth occur in them.

As for the rest, there are other beliefs, which are very doubtful and uncertain, which are either merely particular—as, for example, that the sun is of such a size and such a shape—or else are conceived less clearly and less distinctly—such as light, sound, pain, and other similar things. Nevertheless, from the mere fact that God is not a deceiver, and that in consequence he has not permitted any falsity in my opinions without having given me some faculty capable of correcting it, I think I can conclude with assurance that I have some hope of learning the truth even about these matters and the means of knowing them with certainty.

First, there is no doubt but that all that nature teaches me contains some truth. For by nature, considered in general, I now understand nothing else but God himself, or else the order and! system that God has established for created things; and by my nature in particular I understand nothing else but the arrangement or assemblage of all that God has given me.

Now there is nothing that this nature teaches me more expressly or more obviously than that I have a body which is in poor condition when I feel pain, which needs food or drink when I have the feelings of hunger or thirst, and so on. And therefore I ought to have no doubt that in this there is some truth. (81)

Nature also teaches me by these feelings of pain, hunger, thirst, and so on that I am not only residing in my body, as a pilot in his ship, but furthermore, that I am intimately connected with it, and that the mixture is so blended, as it were, that something like a single whole is produced. For if that were not the case, when my body is wounded I would not therefore feel pain, I, who am only a thinking being; but I would perceive that wound by the understanding alone, as a pilot perceives by sight if something in his vessel is broken. And when my body needs food or drink, I would simply know the fact itself, instead of receiving notice of it by having confused feelings of hunger and thirst. For actually all these feelings of hunger, thirst, pain, and so on are nothing else but certain confused modes of thinking, which have their origin in and depend upon the union and apparent fusion of the mind with the body.

Furthermore, nature teaches me that many other bodies exist in the vicinity of my own, of which I must seek some and avoid others. And certainly, from the fact that I perceive different kinds of colors, odors, tastes, sounds, heat, hardness, and so on, I very readily conclude that in the objects from which these various sense perceptions proceed there are some corresponding variations, although perhaps these variations are not really similar to the perceptions. And from the fact that some of these various sense. perceptions are agreeable to me and others are disagreeable, there is absolutely no doubt that my body, or rather my whole self, in so far as I am composed of body and mind, can in various ways be benefited or harmed by the other objects which surround it. (82)

But there are many other opinions that nature has apparently taught me which, however, I have not truly learned from her, but which were introduced into my mind by my habit of judging things inattentively. Thus it can easily happen that these opinions contain some falsity—as, for example, my opinion that all spaces in which there is nothing which affects and makes an impression on my senses are empty; that in an object which is hot there is some quality similar to my idea of heat; that in a white, or black, or green object there is the same whiteness, or blackness, for greenness that I perceive; that in a bitter or sweet object there is the same taste or the same flavor, and so on for the other senses; and that stars, towers, and all other distant objects are the same shape and size that they appear from afar to our eyes, and so forth.

In order that there should be nothing in this matter that I do not conceive sufficiently distinctly, I should define more precisely what I properly mean when I say that nature teaches me something. For I am here using the word "nature" in a more restricted sense than when I use it to mean a combination or assemblage of everything God has given me, seeing that this assemblage or combination includes many things which pertain to the mind alone, to which I do not intend to refer here when speaking of nature—as for example my knowledge of this truth: that what has once been done can never after not have been done, and all of an infinity of other similar truths known to me by the light of nature without any aid of the body. Such an assemblage also includes many other things which belong to body alone and are not here included under the name of "nature," such as its quality of being heavy and many other similar ones; for I am not concerned with these either, but only with those things which God has presented to me as a being composed of mind and body. This nature effectively teaches me to avoid things which produce in me the feeling of pain and to seek those which make me have some feeling of pleasure and so on. But I do not see that beyond this it teaches me that I should ever conclude anything from these various sense perceptions concerning things outside of ourselves, unless the mind has carefully and maturely examined them. For it seems to me that it is the business of the mind alone, and not of the being composed of mind and body, to decide the truth of such matters. (83)

Thus, although a star makes no more impression on my eye than the flame of a candle, and there is no real or positive inclination or natural faculty in me that leads me to believe that it is larger than this flame, nevertheless I have so judged it from infancy for no adequate reason. And although in approaching the flame I feel heat, and even though in approaching it a little too closely I feel pain, there is still no reason that can convince me that there is some quality in the flame similar to this heat, any more than to this pain. I only have reason to believe there is some quality in it, whatever it may be, which arouses in me these feelings of heat or pain.

Similarly, although there are parts of space in which I find nothing that excites and affects my senses, I ought not therefore to conclude that they contain no objects. Thus I see that both here and in many other similar cases I am accustomed to misunderstand and misconstrue the order of nature, because although these sensations or sense perceptions were given to me only to indicate to my mind which objects are useful or harmful to the composite body of which it is a part, and are for that purpose sufficiently clear and distinct, I nevertheless use them as though they were very certain rules by which I could obtain direct information about the essence and the nature of external objects, about which they can of course give me no information except very obscurely and confusedly.

In the previous discussion I have already explained sufficiently how it happens, despite the supreme goodness of God, that error occurs in my judgments. One further difficulty, though, presents itself here. This concerns objects which I am taught by nature to seek or avoid and also the internal sensations which she has given me. For it seems to me that I have noticed error here and thus that I am sometimes directly deceived by my nature—as, for example, when the pleasant taste of some food in which poison has been mixed can induce me to take the poison, and so misleads me. (84) It is nevertheless true that in this case nature can be excused, for it only leads me to desire the food in which a pleasant taste is found, and not to desire the poison which is unknown to it. Thus I cannot conclude anything from this except that my nature is not entirely and universally cognizant of all things. And at this there is no reason to be surprised, since man, being of a finite nature, is also restricted to a knowledge of a limited perfection.

But we also make mistakes sufficiently frequently even about matters of which we are directly informed by nature, as happens to sick people when they desire to drink or eat things which can later harm them. It might be argued here that the reason that they err is that their nature is corrupted. But this does not remove the difficulty, for a sick man is in truth no less the creation of God than is a man in full health, and therefore it is just as inconsistent with the goodness of God for him as for the other to have a misleading and faulty nature. A clock, composed of wheels and counterweights, is no less exactly obeying all the laws of nature when it is badly made and does not mark the time correctly than when it completely fulfills the intention of its maker; so also, the human body may be considered as a machine, so built and composed of bones, nerves, muscles, veins, blood, and skin that even if there were no mind in it, it would not cease to move in all the ways that it does at present when it is not moved under the direction of the will, nor consequently with the aid of the mind, but only by the condition of its organs I readily recognize that it is quite natural, for example, for this body to suffer dryness in the throat as a result of a dropsical condition, and thus to produce a feeling of thirst in the mind and a consequent disposition on the part of the mind to stimulate the nerves and other parts in the manner requisite for drinking, and so to increase the body's illness and injure itself. It is just as natural, I say, as it is for it to be beneficially influenced to drink by a similar dryness of the throat, when it is not ill at all. (85)

And although in considering the purpose for which a clock has been intended by its designer, I can say that it is false to its nature when it does not correctly indicate the time, and although in considering the mechanism of the human body in the same way as having been formed by God to provide all the customary activities, I have reason to think that it is not functioning according to its nature when its throat is dry and drinking injures its chances of self-preservation, I nevertheless recognize that this last usage of the word "nature" is very different from the other. For the latter is nothing else but an arbitrary appellation which depends entirely on my own idea in comparing a sick man and a poorly made clock, and contrasting them with my idea of a healthy man and a wellmade clock; this appellation refers to nothing which is actually found in the objects of which we are talking. On the contrary, by the other usage of the word "nature," I mean something which is actually found in objects and which therefore is not without some truth.

But certainly, although as far as a dropsical body is concerned, it is only an arbitrary appellation to say that its nature is corrupted when, without needing to drink, it still has a dry and and throat; nevertheless, when we consider the composite body as a whole—that is to say, the mind or soul United with the body—it is not a pure appellation, but truly an actual error on the part of nature that it is thirsty when it is very harmful to it to drink. Therefore we must examine how it is that the goodness of God does not prevent man's nature, so considered, from being faulty and deceptive.

To begin this examination, I first take notice here that there is a great difference between the mind and the body, in that the body, from its nature, is always divisible and the mind is completely (86) indivisible. For in reality, when I consider the mind—that is, when I consider myself in so far as I am only a thinking being—I cannot distinguish any parts, but I recognize and conceive very clearly that I am a thing which is absolutely unitary and entire. And although the whole mind seems to be united with the whole body, nevertheless when a foot or an arm or some other part of the body is amputated, I recognize quite well that nothing has been lost to my mind on that account. Nor can the faculties of willing, perceiving, understanding, and so forth be any more properly called parts of the mind, for it is one and the same mind which as a complete unit wills, perceives, and understands, and so forth. But just the contrary is the case with corporeal or extended objects, for I cannot imagine any, however small they might be, which my mind does not very easily divide into several parts, and I consequently recognize these objects to be divisible. This alone would suffice to show me that the mind or soul. of man is altogether different from the body, if I did not already know it sufficiently well for other reasons.

I also take notice that the mind does not receive impressions from all parts of the body directly, but only from the brain, or perhaps even from one of its smallest parts—the one, namely, where the senses in common have their seat. This makes the mind feel the same thing whenever it is in the same condition, even though the other parts of the body can be differently arranged, as is proved by an infinity of experiments which it is not necessary to describe here.

I furthermore notice that the nature of the body is such that no one of its parts can be moved by another part some little distance away without its being possible for it to be moved in the same way by any one of the intermediate parts, even when the more distant part does not act. For example, in the cord ABCD which is thoroughly stretched, if (87) we pull and move the last part D, the first part A will not be moved in any different manner from that in which it could also be moved if we pulled one of the middle parts B or C, while the last part D remained motionless. And in the same way, when I feel pain in my foot, physics teaches me that this sensation is communicated by means of nerves distributed through the foot. When these nerves are pulled in the foot, being stretched like cords from there to the brain, they likewise pull at the same time the internal part of the brain from which they come and where they terminate, and there produce a certain movement which nature has arranged to make my mind feel pain as though that pain were in my foot. But because these nerves must pass through the leg, the thigh, the loins, the back, and the neck, in order to extend from the foot to the brain, it can happen that even when the nerve endings in the foot are not stimulated, but only some of the lintermediate parts located in the loins or the neck, precisely the same movements are nevertheless produced in the brain that could be produced there by a wound received in the foot, as a result of which it necessarily follows that the mind feels the same pain in the foot as though the foot had been wounded. And we must make the same judgment about all our other sense perceptions.

Finally, I notice that since each one of the movements that occurs in the part of the brain from which the mind receives impressions directly can only produce in the mind a single sensation, we cannot desire or imagine any better arrangement than that this movement should cause the mind to feel that sensation, of all the sensations the movement is capable of causing, which is most effectively and frequently useful for the preservation of the human body when it is in full health. But experience shows us that all the sensations which nature has given us are such as I have just stated, and therefore there is nothing in their nature which does not show the power and the goodness of the God who has produced them.

Thus, for example, (88) when the nerves of the foot are stimulated violently and more than is usual, their movement, passing through the marrow of the backbone up to the interior of the brain, produces there an impression upon the mind which makes the mind feel something—namely, pain as though in the foot—by which the mind is warned and stimulated to do whatever it can to remove the cause, taking it to be very dangerous and harmful to the foot.

It is true that God could establish the nature of man in such a way that this same brain event would make the mind feel something quite different; for example, it might cause the movement to be felt as though it were in the brain, or in the foot, or else in some other intermediate location between the foot and the brain, or finally it might produce any other feeling that can exist; but none of those would have contributed so well to the preservation of the body as that which it does produce.

In the same way, when we need to drink, there results a certain dryness in the throat which affects its nerves and, by means of them, the interior of the brain. This brain event makes the mind feel the sensation of thirst, because under those conditions there is nothing more useful to us than to know that we need to drink for the conservation of our health. And similar reasoning applies to other sensations.

From this it is entirely manifest that, despite the supreme goodness of God, the nature of man, in so far as he is composed of mind and body, cannot escape being sometimes faulty and deceptive. For if there is some cause which produces, not in the foot, but in some other part of the nerve which is stretched from the foot to the brain, or even in the brain itself, the same effect which ordinarily occurs when the foot is injured, we will feel pain as though it were in the foot, and we will naturally be deceived by the sensation. The reason for this is that the same brain event can cause only a single sensation in the mind; and this sensation being much more frequently produced by a cause which wounds the foot than by another acting in a different location, it is much more reasonable (89) that it should always convey to the mind a pain in the foot rather than one in any other part of the body. And if it happens that sometimes the dryness of the throat does not come in the usual manner from the fact that drinking is necessary for the health of the body, but from some quite contrary cause, as in the case of those afflicted with dropsy, nevertheless it is much better that we should be deceived in that instance than if, on the contrary, we were always deceived when the body was in health; and similarly for the other sensations.

And certainly this consideration is very useful to me, not only so that I can recognize all the errors to which my nature is subject, but also so that I may avoid them or correct them more easily. For knowing that each of my senses conveys truth to me more often than falsehood concerning whatever is useful or harmful to the body, and being almost always able to use several of them to examine the same object, and being in addition able to use my memory to bind and join together present information with what is past, and being able to use my understanding, which has already discovered all the causes of my errors, I should no longer fear to encounter falsity in the objects which are most commonly represented to me by my senses.

And I should reject all the doubts of these last few days as exaggerated and ridiculous, particularly that very general uncertainty about sleep, which I could not distinguish from waking life. For now I find in them a very notable difference, in that our memory can never bind and join our dreams together one with another and all with the course of our lives, as it habitually joins together what happens to us when we are awake. And so, in effect, if someone suddenly appeared to me when I was awake and afterward disappeared in the same way, as do images that I see in my sleep, so that I could not determine where he came from or where he went, it would not be without reason that I would consider it a ghost (90) or a phantom produced in my brain and similar to those produced there when I sleep, rather than truly a man.

But when I perceive objects in such a way that I distinctly recognize both the place from which they come and the place where they are, as well as the time when they appear to me; and when, without any hiatus, I can relate my perception of them with all the rest of my life, I am entirely certain that I perceive them wakefully and not in sleep. And I should not in any way doubt the truth of these things if, having made use of all my senses, my memory, and my understanding, to examine them, nothing is reported to me by any of them which is inconsistent with what is reported by the others. For, from the fact that God is not a deceiver, it necesarily follows that in this matter I am not deceived.

But because the exigencies of action frequently oblige us to make decisions and do not always allow us the leisure to examine these things with sufficient care, we must admit that human life is very often subject to error in particular matters; and we must in the end recognize the infirmity and weakness of our nature.

GEORGE BERKELEY
1685–1753

George Berkeley was born near Kilkenny, Ireland, and, although an Anglican of English descent, he emphatically considered himself Irish. He studied at Kilkenny College and in 1700 went on to Trinity College, Dublin. There he read Descartes, Newton, and Locke. In 1707, he became a Fellow of the College and was ordained in the Anglican church. The next six years were the most philosophically productive in his life. In 1709, he published his *New Theory of Vision,* and in the following year his most important philosophic work, *A Treatise Concerning the Principles of Human Knowledge.* In 1711, he wrote *Discourse on Passive Obedience.* Two years later, he published a more popular exposition of the doctrine of his *Principles* in the form of *Three Dialogues Between Hylas and Philonous.*

For the next eleven years, Berkeley traveled widely, visiting with many of the great thinkers of his day. He became Dean of Derry in 1724, though most of his energy at this time seems to have been given to the founding of a college in the Bermudas. With promises of financial support, he sailed for Rhode Island in 1728 to establish farms for supplying his future college with food. Berkeley spent two and a half years in Rhode Island with his new wife and friends, waiting for the twenty-thousand pounds the government had promised. When the funds never arrived, he finally gave up and returned to London.

In 1733, he published *Alciphron,* or *The Minute Philosopher,* against the freethinkers (agnostics), and in the following year *The Analyst,* a criticism of Newton. That same year, he was made Bishop of Cloyne. For the next eighteen years, he energetically served his remote, poor diocese. Among the works he wrote during this period are *The Querist* (1737), which used questions to propose public works and education as remedies to the crushing poverty he observed, and *Siris* (1744), an unusual work dealing with the medicinal value of tar water. In 1751, he lost his eldest son, and the next year he moved to Oxford, where another son was beginning his studies. On January 14, 1753, Berkeley died suddenly; he was buried at Christ Church, Oxford.

* * *

Like Locke before him, Berkeley accepted the empiricist doctrine that all we can know are ideas and that ideas come from perception or reflection. But Berkeley saw a problem in Locke's assertion of an external world of material "substances" giving rise to perceptions. If all we can know are ideas, how can we know there is a world "out there" giving rise to our ideas? Locke had said that the primary qualities of an "external object" (such as extension and solidity) are "utterly inseparable" from the objects themselves, whereas this is not the case with secondary qualities (such as color, taste, etc.). But again, asked Berkeley, how can Locke know this? He cannot get "outside himself" to see which of his perceptions are actually a part of objects "out there." Berkeley concluded that Locke's philosophy will lead to skepticism, whereby we must admit that we cannot really know anything about the world "out there."

To avoid this skepticism, Berkeley made the radical claim that there is no "out there," or, more precisely, there is no *matter*. Berkeley's position, which is called "idealism," can be summed up in his famous phrase "*esse* is *percipi*": to be is to be perceived. What we call "bodies," or physical objects, are simply stable collections of perceptions to which we give names such as "apples," "trees," and so on. These collections of perceptions have no existence apart from a perceiving mind. The answer to the famous conundrum "If a tree falls in the forest and no one hears it, does it make a sound?" is that if no one is perceiving it, it not only does not make a sound, the tree does not even exist!

Does this mean that trees go out of existence when no one is left in the forest to perceive them and that they come back into existence when someone enters the forest to perceive them again? It would seem that Berkeley must accept this odd conclusion were it not for one important point: God never leaves the forest, and God is *always* perceiving the trees. By always holding all collections of perceptions in the divine mind, God ensures their continued existence and the perceived regularity in what we call "nature." This point has been classically formulated in the following limericks:

> There was a young man who said, "God,
> Must think it exceedingly odd
> If he finds that this tree
> Continues to be
> When there's no one about in the Quad."

> REPLY:
> "Dear Sir: Your astonishment's odd:
> I am always about in the Quad.
> And that's why the tree
> Continues to be,
> Since observed by, Yours faithfully, God."

Berkeley saw his philosophy as a commonsense attack on the metaphysical excesses of medieval Scholastics, Continental Rationalists, and even fellow empiricists such as Hobbes and Locke. Although Berkeley understood his philosophy to be common sense, his readers drew different conclusions. One prominent physician of his day claimed Berkeley was insane. The great Dr. Samuel Johnson dismissed Berkeley's ideas with his famous "I refute Berkeley *thus*" and then he kicked a rock. Of course, this did not refute Berkeley at all. It only proved Johnson had not understood Berkeley's point. Berkeley did not claim the non-existence of stones or that kicking a stone will not produce sensation. He claimed the rock did not exist apart from the perception of its solidity or the perception of pain when struck, and so on. An oft-repeated epitaph summarizes the general reaction to Berkeley: "His arguments produce no conviction, though they cannot be refuted."

* * *

In Berkeley's *Three Dialogues between Hylas and Philonous*, reprinted here complete, Hylas argues for materialism, whereas Philonous presents Berkeley's own position. The dialogue form allows Berkeley to expound his own philosophy while meeting various anticiated objections.

For general introductions to Berkeley, see G.J. Warnock, *Berkeley* (Harmondsworth, Middlesex: Penguin Books, 1953); Harry M. Bracken, *Berkeley* (New York: St. Martin's Press, 1974); J.O. Urmson, *Berkeley* (Oxford: Oxford University Press, 1982)—part of the Past Masters series, now reprinted in the combined volume John Dunn et al., eds., *The British Empiricists* (Oxford: Oxford University Press, 1992); and David Berman, *George Berkeley: Idealism and the Man* (Oxford: Oxford University Press, 1994). For interesting but difficult discussions of Berkeley's arguments, see George Pitcher, *Berkeley* (London: Routledge, 1977) or Kenneth Winkler, *Berkeley: An Interpretation* (Oxford: Oxford University Press, 1989). For collections of essays, see Gale W. Engle and Gabriele Taylor, eds., *Berkeley's Principles of Human Knowledge* (Belmont, CA: Wadsworth, 1968); Colin M. Turbayne, ed., *Berkeley: Critical and Interpretive Essays* (Minneapolis: University of Minnesota Press, 1982); John Foster and Howard Robinson, eds., *Essays on Berkeley: A Tercentennial Celebration* (Oxford: Oxford University Press, 1985); and D.M. Armstrong and C.B. Martin, *Berkeley: A Collection of Critical Essays* (Hamden, CT: Garland, 1992)—a reprint of the second half of *Locke and Berkeley: A Collection of Critical Essays* (Garden City, NY: Doubleday, 1968).

THREE DIALOGUES BETWEEN HYLAS AND PHILONOUS, IN OPPOSITION TO SCEPTICS AND ATHEISTS

THE FIRST DIALOGUE

PHILONOUS: Good morrow, Hylas: I did not expect to find you abroad so early.

HYLAS: It is indeed something unusual; but my thoughts were so taken up with a subject I was discoursing of last night, that finding I could not sleep, I resolved to rise and take a turn in the garden.

PHILONOUS: It happened well, to let you see what innocent and agreeable pleasures you lose every morning. Can there be a pleasanter time of the day, or a more delightful season of the year? That purple sky, those wild but sweet notes of birds, the fragrant bloom upon the trees and flowers, the gentle influence of the rising sun, these

Fruits and Dishes on the Table, by Jan Davids de Heem (1606–1683). The underlying theme of *Vanitas* in Dutch still life presents a dual message in the arrangement of fine and rare objects. On the one hand, the objects represent the joy of possessions and the good life, yet the half-eaten pie and the peeled fruit cause reflection on the brevity of human existence and the fleeting nature of material objects. Berkeley takes this a step further by denying material substance and claiming that such objects do not exist apart from a perceiving mind. (*Lauros-Giraudon/Art Resource*)

and a thousand nameless beauties of nature inspire the soul with secret transports; its faculties too being at this time fresh and lively, are fit for those meditations, which the solitude of a garden and tranquillity of the morning naturally dispose us to. But I am afraid I interrupt your thoughts: for you seemed very intent on something.

HYLAS: It is true, I was, and shall be obliged to you if you will permit me to go on in the same vein; not that I would by any means deprive myself of your company, for my thoughts always flow more easily in conversation with a friend, than when I am alone: but my request is, that you would suffer me to impart my reflexions to you.

PHILONOUS: With all my heart, it is what I should have requested myself if you had not prevented me.

HYLAS: I was considering the odd fate of those men who have in all ages, through an affectation of being distinguished from the vulgar, or some unaccountable turn of thought, pretended either to believe nothing at all, or to believe the most extravagant things in the world. This however might be borne, if their paradoxes and scepticism did not draw after them some consequences of general disadvantage to mankind. But the mischief lies here; that when men of less leisure see them who are supposed to have spent their whole time in the pursuits of knowledge professing an entire igno-rance of all things, or advancing such notions as are repugnant to plain and commonly received principles, they will be tempted to entertain suspicions concerning the most important truths, which they had hitherto held sacred and unquestionable.

PHILONOUS: I entirely agree with you, as to the ill tendency of the affected doubts of some philosophers, and fantastical conceits of others. I am even so far gone of late in this way of thinking, that I have quitted several of the sublime notions I had got in their schools for vulgar opinions. And I give it you on my word; since this revolt from metaphysical notions to the plain dictates of nature and common sense, I find my un-derstanding strangely enlightened, so that I can now easily comprehend a great many things which before were all mystery and riddle.

HYLAS: I am glad to find there was nothing in the accounts I heard of you.

PHILONOUS: Pray, what were those?

HYLAS: You were represented, in last night's conversation, as one who main-tained the most extravagant opinion that ever entered into the mind of man, to wit, that there is no such thing as *material substance* in the world.

PHILONOUS: That there is no such thing as what philosophers call *material sub-stance,* I am seriously persuaded: but, if I were made to see anything absurd or scepti-cal in this, I should then have the same reason to renounce this that I imagine I have now to reject the contrary opinion.

HYLAS: What! Can anything be more fantastical, more repugnant to common sense, or a more manifest piece of scepticism, than to believe there is no such thing as *matter?*

PHILONOUS: Softly, good Hylas. What if it should prove that you, who hold there is, are, by virtue of that opinion, a greater *sceptic,* and maintain more paradoxes and re-pugnances to common sense, than I who believe no such thing?

HYLAS: You may as soon persuade me, the part is greater than the whole, as that, in order to avoid absurdity and scepticism, I should ever be obliged to give up my opinion in this point

PHILONOUS: Well then, are you content to admit that opinion for true, which upon examination shall appear most agreeable to common sense, and remote from scepticism?

HYLAS: With all my heart. Since you are for raising disputes about the plainest things in nature, I am content for once to hear what you have to say.

PHILONOUS: Pray, Hylas, what do you mean by a *sceptic?*

HYLAS: I mean what all men mean—one that doubts of everything.

PHILONOUS: He then who entertains no doubts concerning some particular point, with regard to that point cannot be thought a *sceptic*.

HYLAS: I agree with you.

PHILONOUS: Whether does doubting consist in embracing the affirmative or negative side of a question?

HYLAS: In neither; for whoever understands English cannot but know that doubting signifies a suspense between both.

PHILONOUS: He then that denies any point, can no more be said to doubt of it, than he who affirms it with the same degree of assurance.

HYLAS: True.

PHILONOUS: And, consequently, for such his denial is no more to be esteemed a *sceptic* than the other.

HYLAS: I acknowledge it.

PHILONOUS: How comes it to pass then, Hylas, that you pronounce me a *sceptic,* because I deny what you affirm, to wit the existence of matter? Since, for aught you can tell I am as peremptory in my denial, as you in your affirmation.

HYLAS: Hold, Philonous, I have been a little out in my definition; but every false step a man makes in discourse is not to be insisted on. I said indeed that a sceptic was one who doubted of everything; but I should have added, or who denies the reality and truth of things.

PHILONOUS: What things? Do you mean the principles and theorems of sciences? But these you know are universal intellectual notions, and consequently independent of matter. The denial therefore of this does not imply the denying them.

HYLAS: I grant it. But are there no other things? What think you of distrusting the senses, of denying the real existence of sensible things, or pretending to know nothing of them. Is not this sufficient to denominate a man a *sceptic?*

PHILONOUS: Shall we therefore examine which of us it is that denies the reality of sensible things, or professes the greatest ignorance of them; since, if I take you rightly, he is to be esteemed the greatest *sceptic?*

HYLAS: That is what I desire.

PHILONOUS: What mean you by Sensible Things?

HYLAS: Those things which are perceived by the senses. Can you imagine that I mean anything else?

PHILONOUS: Pardon me, Hylas, if I am desirous clearly to apprehend your notions, since this may much shorten our inquiry. Suffer me then to ask you this farther question. Are those things only perceived by the senses which are perceived immediately? Or, may those things properly be said to be *sensible* which are perceived mediately, or not without the intervention of others?

HYLAS: I do not sufficiently understand you.

PHILONOUS: In reading a book, what I immediately perceive are the letters; but mediately, or by means of these, are suggested to my mind the notions of God, virtue, truth, &c. Now, that the letters are truly sensible things, or perceived by sense, there is no doubt: but I would know whether you take the things suggested by them to be so too.

HYLAS: No, certainly: it were absurd to think *God* or *virtue* sensible things; though they may be signified and suggested to the mind by sensible marks, with which they have an arbitrary connexion.

PHILONOUS: It seems then, that by *sensible things* you mean those only which can be perceived immediately by sense?

HYLAS: Right.

PHILONOUS: Does it not follow from this, that though I see one part of the sky red, and another blue, and that my reason does thence evidently conclude there must be some cause of that diversity of colours, yet that cause cannot be said to be a sensible thing, or perceived by the sense of seeing?

HYLAS: It does.

PHILONOUS: In like manner, though I hear variety of sounds, yet I cannot be said to hear the causes of those sounds?

HYLAS: You cannot.

PHILONOUS: And when by my touch I perceive a thing to be hot and heavy, I cannot say, with any truth or propriety, that I feel the cause of its heat or weight?

HYLAS: To prevent any more questions of this kind, I tell you once for all, that by *sensible things* I mean those only which are perceived by sense; and that in truth the senses perceive nothing which they do not perceive immediately: for they make no inferences. The deducing therefore of causes or occasions from effects and appearances, which alone are perceived by sense, entirely relates to reason.

PHILONOUS: This point then is agreed between us—That *sensible things are those only which are immediately perceived by sense.* You will farther inform me, whether we immediately perceive by sight anything beside light, and colours, and figures; or by hearing, anything but sounds; by the palate, anything beside tastes; by the smell, beside odours; or by the touch, more than tangible qualities.

HYLAS: We do not.

PHILONOUS: It seems, therefore, that if you take away all sensible qualities, there remains nothing sensible?

HYLAS: I grant it.

PHILONOUS: Sensible things therefore are nothing else but so many sensible qualities, or combinations of sensible qualities?

HYLAS: Nothing else.

PHILONOUS: Heat then is a sensible thing?

HYLAS: Certainly.

PHILONOUS: Does the reality of sensible things consist in being perceived? Or, is it something distinct from their being perceived, and that bears no relation to the mind?

HYLAS: To *exist* is one thing, and to be *perceived* is another.

PHILONOUS: I speak with regard to sensible things only. And of these I ask, whether by their real existence you mean a subsistence exterior to the mind, and distinct from their being perceived?

HYLAS: I mean a real absolute being, distinct from, and without any relation to, their being perceived.

PHILONOUS: Heat therefore, if it be allowed a real being, must exist without the mind?

HYLAS: It must.

PHILONOUS: Tell me, Hylas, is this real existence equally compatible to all degrees of heat, which we perceive; or is there any reason why we should attribute it to some, and deny it to others? And if there be, pray let me know that reason.

HYLAS: Whatever degree of heat we perceive by sense, we may be sure the same exists in the object that occasions it.

PHILONOUS: What! The greatest as well as the least?

HYLAS: I tell you, the reason is plainly the same in respect of both. They are both perceived by sense; nay, the greater degree of heat is more sensibly perceived, and consequently, if there is any difference, we are more certain of its real existence than we can be of the reality of a lesser degree.

PHILONOUS: But is not the most vehement and intense degree of heat a very great pain?

HYLAS: No one can deny it.

PHILONOUS: And is any unperceiving thing capable of pain or pleasure?

HYLAS: No, certainly.

PHILONOUS: Is your material substance a senseless being, or a being endowed with sense and perception?

HYLAS: It is senseless without doubt.

PHILONOUS: It cannot therefore be the subject of pain?

HYLAS: By no means.

PHILONOUS: Nor consequently of the greatest heat perceived by sense, since you acknowledge this to be no small pain?

HYLAS: I grant it.

PHILONOUS: What shall we say then of your external object; is it a material substance, or no?

HYLAS: It is a material substance with the sensible qualities inhering in it.

PHILONOUS: How then can a great heat exist in it, since you own it cannot in a material substance? I desire you would clear this point.

HYLAS: Hold, Philonous, I fear I was out in yielding intense heat to be a pain. It should seem rather, that pain is something distinct from heat, and the consequence or effect of it.

PHILONOUS: Upon putting your hand near the fire, do you perceive one simple uniform sensation, or two distinct sensations?

HYLAS: But one simple sensation.

PHILONOUS: Is not the heat immediately perceived?

HYLAS: It is.

PHILONOUS: And the pain?

HYLAS: True.

PHILONOUS: Seeing therefore they are both immediately perceived at the same time, and the fire affects you only with one simple or uncompounded idea, it follows that this same simple idea is both the intense heat immediately perceived, and the pain; and, consequently, that the intense heat immediately perceived is nothing distinct from a particular sort of pain.

HYLAS: It seems so.

PHILONOUS: Again, try in your thoughts, Hylas, if you can conceive a vehement sensation to be without pain or pleasure.

HYLAS: I cannot.

PHILONOUS: Or can you frame to yourself an idea of sensible pain or pleasure in general, abstracted from every particular idea of heat, cold, tastes, smells? &c.

HYLAS: I do not find that I can.

PHILONOUS: Does it not therefore follow, that sensible pain is nothing distinct from those sensations or ideas, in an intense degree?

HYLAS: It is undeniable; and, to speak the truth, I begin to suspect a very great heat cannot exist but in a mind perceiving it.

PHILONOUS: What! Are you then in that *sceptical* state of suspense, between affirming and denying?

HYLAS: I think I may be positive in the point. A very violent and painful heat cannot exist without the mind.

PHILONOUS: It hath not therefore, according to you, any real being?

HYLAS: I own it.

PHILONOUS: Is it therefore certain, that there is no body in nature really hot?

HYLAS: I have not denied there is any real heat in bodies. I only say, there is no such thing as an intense real heat.

PHILONOUS: But, did you not say before that all degrees of heat were equally real; or, if there was any difference, that the greater were more undoubtedly real than the lesser?

HYLAS: True: but it was because I did not then consider the ground there is for distinguishing between them, which I now plainly see. And it is this: because intense heat is nothing else but a particular kind of painful sensation; and pain cannot exist but in a perceiving being; it follows that no intense heat can really exist in an unperceiving corporeal substance. But this is no reason why we should deny heat in an inferior degree to exist in such a substance.

PHILONOUS: But how shall we be able to discern those degrees of heat which exist only in the mind from those which exist without it?

HYLAS: That is no difficult matter. You know the least pain cannot exist unperceived; whatever, therefore, degree of heat is a pain exists only in the mind. But, as for all other degrees of heat, nothing obliges us to think the same of them.

PHILONOUS: I think you granted before that no unperceiving being was capable of pleasure, any more than of pain.

HYLAS: I did.

PHILONOUS: And is not warmth, or a more gentle degree of heat than what causes uneasiness, a pleasure?

HYLAS: What then?

PHILONOUS: Consequently, it cannot exist without the mind in an unperceiving substance, or body.

HYLAS: So it seems.

PHILONOUS: Since, therefore, as well those degrees of heat that are not painful, as those that are, can exist only in a thinking substance; may we not conclude that external bodies are absolutely incapable of any degree of heat whatsoever?

HYLAS: On second thoughts, I do not think it so evident that warmth is a pleasure as that a great degree of heat is a pain.

PHILONOUS: I do not pretend that warmth is as great a pleasure as heat is a pain. But, if you grant it to be even a small pleasure, it serves to make good my conclusion.

HYLAS: I could rather call it an *indolence*. It seems to be nothing more than a privation of both pain and pleasure. And that such a quality or state as this may agree to an unthinking substance, I hope you will not deny.

PHILONOUS: If you are resolved to maintain that warmth, or a gentle degree of heat, is no pleasure, I know not how to convince you otherwise than by appealing to your own sense. But what think you of cold?

HYLAS: The same that I do of heat. An intense degree of cold is a pain; for to feel a very great cold, is to perceive a great uneasiness: it cannot therefore exist without the mind; but a lesser degree of cold may, as well as a lesser degree of heat.

PHILONOUS: Those bodies, therefore, upon whose application to our own, we perceive a moderate degree of heat, must be concluded to have a moderate degree of heat or warmth in them—and those, upon whose application we feel a like degree of cold, must be thought to have cold in them.

HYLAS: They must.

PHILONOUS: Can any doctrine be true that necessarily leads a man into an absurdity?

HYLAS: Without doubt it cannot.

PHILONOUS: Is it not an absurdity to think that the same thing should be at the same time both cold and warm?

HYLAS: It is.

PHILONOUS: Suppose now one of your hands hot, and the other cold, and that they are both at once put into the same vessel of water, in an intermediate state; will not the water seem cold to one hand, and warm to the other?

HYLAS: It will.

PHILONOUS: Ought we not therefore, by your principles, to conclude it is really both cold and warm at the same time, that is, according to your own concession, to believe an absurdity?

HYLAS: I confess it seems so.

PHILONOUS: Consequently, the principles themselves are false, since you have granted that no true principle leads to an absurdity.

HYLAS: But, after all, can anything be more absurd than to say, *there is no heat in the fire?*

PHILONOUS: To make the point still clearer; tell me whether, in two cases exactly alike, we ought not to make the same judgment?

HYLAS: We ought.

PHILONOUS: When a pin pricks your finger, does it not rend and divide the fibres of your flesh?

HYLAS: It does.

PHILONOUS: And when a coal burns your finger, does it any more?

HYLAS: It does not.

PHILONOUS: Since, therefore, you neither judge the sensation itself occasioned by the pin, nor anything like it to be in the pin; you should not, conformably to what you have now granted, judge the sensation occasioned by the fire, or anything like it, to be in the fire.

HYLAS: Well, since it must be so, I am content to yield this point, and acknowledge that heat and cold are only sensations existing in our minds. But there still remain qualities enough to secure the reality of external things.

PHILONOUS: But what will you say, Hylas, if it shall appear that the case is the same with regard to all other sensible qualities, and that they can no more be supposed to exist without the mind, than heat and cold?

HYLAS: Then indeed you will have done something to the purpose; but that is what I despair of seeing proved.

PHILONOUS: Let us examine them in order. What think you of tastes—do they exist without the mind, or no?

HYLAS: Can any man in his senses doubt whether sugar is sweet, or wormwood bitter?

PHILONOUS: Inform me, Hylas. Is a sweet taste a particular kind of pleasure or pleasant sensation, or is it not?

HYLAS: It is.

PHILONOUS: And is not bitterness some kind of uneasiness or pain?

HYLAS: I grant it.

PHILONOUS: If therefore sugar and wormwood are unthinking corporeal substances existing without the mind, how can sweetness and bitterness, that is, pleasure and pain, agree to them?

HYLAS: Hold, Philonous, I now see what it was deluded me all this time. You asked whether heat and cold, sweetness and bitterness, were not particular sorts of pleasure and pain; to which I answered simply, that they were. Whereas I should have thus distinguished:—those qualities, as perceived by us, are pleasures or pains; but not as existing in the external objects. We must not therefore conclude absolutely, that there is no heat in the fire, or sweetness in the sugar, but only that heat or sweetness, as perceived by us, are not in the fire or sugar. What say you to this?

PHILONOUS: I say it is nothing to the purpose. Our discourse proceeded altogether concerning sensible things, which you defined to be, the things we *immediately perceive by our senses.* Whatever other qualities, therefore, you speak of as distinct from these, I know nothing of them, neither do they at all belong to the point in dispute. You may, indeed, pretend to have discovered certain qualities which you do not perceive, and assert those insensible qualities exist in fire and sugar. But what use can be made of this to your present purpose, I am at a loss to conceive. Tell me then once more, do you acknowledge that heat and cold, sweetness and bitterness (meaning those qualities which are perceived by the senses), do not exist without the mind?

HYLAS: I see it is to no purpose to hold out, so I give up the cause as to those mentioned qualities. Though I profess it sounds oddly, to say that sugar is not sweet.

PHILONOUS: But, for your farther satisfaction, take this along with you: that which at other times seems sweet, shall, to a distempered palate, appear bitter. And, nothing can be plainer than that divers persons perceive different tastes in the same food; since that which one man delights in, another abhors. And how could this be, if the taste was something really inherent in the food?

HYLAS: I acknowledge I know not how.

PHILONOUS: In the next place, *odours* are to be considered. And, with regard to these, I would fain know whether what hath been said of tastes does not exactly agree to them? Are they not so many pleasing or displeasing sensations?

HYLAS: They are.

PHILONOUS: Can you then conceive it possible that they should exist in an unperceiving thing?

HYLAS: I cannot.

PHILONOUS: Or, can you imagine that filth and ordure affect those brute animals that feed on them out of choice, with the same smells which we perceive in them?

HYLAS: By no means.

PHILONOUS: May we not therefore conclude of smells, as of the other forementioned qualities, that they cannot exist in any but a perceiving substance or mind?

HYLAS: I think so.

PHILONOUS: Then as to *sounds,* what must we think of them: are they accidents really inherent in external bodies, or not?

HYLAS: That they inhere not in the sonorous bodies is plain from hence: because a bell struck in the exhausted receiver of an air- pump sends forth no sound. The air, therefore, must be thought the subject of sound.

PHILONOUS: What reason is there for that, Hylas?

HYLAS: Because, when any motion is raised in the air, we perceive a sound greater or lesser, according to the air's motion; but without some motion in the air, we never hear any sound at all.

PHILONOUS: And granting that we never hear a sound but when some motion is produced in the air, yet I do not see how you can infer from thence, that the sound itself is in the air.

HYLAS: It is this very motion in the external air that produces in the mind the sensation of *sound.* For, striking on the drum of the ear, it causes a vibration, which by the auditory nerves being communicated to the brain, the soul is thereupon affected with the sensation called *sound.*

PHILONOUS: What! Is sound then a sensation?

HYLAS: I tell you, as perceived by us, it is a particular sensation in the mind.

PHILONOUS: And can any sensation exist without the mind?

HYLAS: No, certainly.

PHILONOUS: How then can sound, being a sensation, exist in the air, if by the *air* you mean a senseless substance existing without the mind?

HYLAS: You must distinguish, Philonous, between sound as it is perceived by us, and as it is in itself; or (which is the same thing) between the sound we immediately perceive, and that which exists without us. The former, indeed, is a particular kind of sensation, but the latter is merely a vibrative or undulatory motion in the air.

PHILONOUS: I thought I had already obviated that distinction, by the answer I gave when you were applying it in a like case before. But, to say no more of that, are you sure then that sound is really nothing but motion?

HYLAS: I am.

PHILONOUS: Whatever therefore agrees to real sound, may with truth be attributed to motion?

HYLAS: It may.

PHILONOUS: It is then good sense to speak of *motion* as of a thing that is *loud, sweet, acute,* or *grave.*

HYLAS: I see you are resolved not to understand me. Is it not evident those accidents or modes belong only to sensible sound, or *sound* in the common acceptation of the word, but not to *sound* in the real and philosophic sense; which, as I just now told you, is nothing but a certain motion of the air?

PHILONOUS: It seems then there are two sorts of sound—the one vulgar, or that which is heard, the other philosophical and real?

HYLAS: Even so.

PHILONOUS: And the latter consists in motion?

HYLAS: I told you so before.

PHILONOUS: Tell me, Hylas, to which of the senses, think you, the idea of motion belongs? To the hearing?

HYLAS: No, certainly; but to the sight and touch.

PHILONOUS: It should follow then, that, according to you, real sounds may possibly be *seen* or *felt,* but never *heard.*

HYLAS: Look you, Philonous, you may, if you please, make a jest of my opinion, but that will not alter the truth of things. I own, indeed, the inferences you draw me into sound something oddly, but common language, you know, is framed by, and for the use of the vulgar: we must not therefore wonder if expressions adapted to exact philosophic notions seem uncouth and out of the way.

PHILONOUS: Is it come to that? I assure you, I imagine myself to have gained no small point, since you make so light of departing from common phrases and opinions; it being a main part of our inquiry, to examine whose notions are widest of the common road, and most repugnant to the general sense of the world. But, can you think it no more than a philosophical paradox, to say that *real sounds are never heard,* and that the idea of them is obtained by some other sense? And is there nothing in this contrary to nature and the truth of things?

HYLAS: To deal ingenuously, I do not like it. And, after the concessions already made, I had as well grant that sounds too have no real being without the mind.

PHILONOUS: And I hope you will make no difficulty to acknowledge the same of colours.

HYLAS: Pardon me: the case of colours is very different. Can anything be plainer than that we see them on the objects?

PHILONOUS: The objects you speak of are I suppose, corporeal substances existing without the mind?

HYLAS: They are.

PHILONOUS: And have true and real colours inhering in them?

HYLAS: Each visible object hath that colour which we see in it.

PHILONOUS: How! Is there anything visible but what we perceive by sight?

HYLAS: There is not.

PHILONOUS: And, do we perceive anything by sense which we do not perceive immediately?

HYLAS: How often must I be obliged to repeat the same thing? I tell you, we do not.

PHILONOUS: Have patience, good Hylas; and tell me once more, whether there is anything immediately perceived by the senses, except sensible qualities. I know you asserted there was not; but I would now be informed, whether you still persist in the same opinion.

HYLAS: I do.

PHILONOUS: Pray, is your corporeal substance either a sensible quality, or made up of sensible qualities?

HYLAS: What a question that is! Who ever thought it was?

PHILONOUS: My reason for asking was, because in saying, *each visible object hath that colour which we see in it,* you make visible objects to be corporeal substances; which implies either that corporeal substances are sensible qualities, or else that there is something besides sensible qualities perceived by sight: but, as this point was formerly agreed between us, and is still maintained by you, it is a clear consequence, that your corporeal substance is nothing distinct from sensible qualities.

HYLAS: You may draw as many absurd consequences as you please, and endeavour to perplex the plainest things; but you shall never persuade me out of my senses. I clearly understand my own meaning.

PHILONOUS: I wish you would make me understand it too. But, since you are unwilling to have your notion of corporeal substance examined, I shall urge that point no farther. Only be pleased to let me know, whether the same colours which we see exist in external bodies, or some other.

HYLAS: The very same.

PHILONOUS: What! Are then the beautiful red and purple we see on yonder clouds really in them? Or do you imagine, they have in themselves any other form than that of a dark mist or vapour?

HYLAS: I must own, Philonous, those colours are not really in the clouds as they seem to be at this distance. They are only apparent colours.

PHILONOUS: *Apparent* call you them? How shall we distinguish these apparent colours from real?

HYLAS: Very easily. Those are to be thought apparent which, appearing only at a distance, vanish upon a nearer approach.

PHILONOUS: And those, I suppose, are to be thought real which are discovered by the most near and exact survey.

HYLAS: Right.

PHILONOUS: Is the nearest and exactest survey made by the help of a microscope, or by the naked eye?

HYLAS: By a microscope, doubtless.

PHILONOUS: But a microscope often discovers colours in an object different from those perceived by the unassisted sight. And, in case we had microscopes magnifying to any assigned degree, it is certain that no object whatsoever, viewed through them, would appear in the same colour which it exhibits to the naked eye.

HYLAS: And what will you conclude from all this? You cannot argue that there are really and naturally no colours on objects: because by artificial managements they may be altered, or made to vanish.

PHILONOUS: I think it may evidently be concluded from your own concessions, that all the colours we see with our naked eyes are only apparent as those on the clouds, since they vanish upon a more close and accurate inspection which is afforded us by a microscope. Then, as to what you say by way of prevention: I ask you whether the real and natural state of an object is better discovered by a very sharp and piercing sight, or by one which is less sharp?

HYLAS: By the former without doubt.

PHILONOUS: Is it not plain from *Dioptrics* that microscopes make the sight more penetrating, and represent objects as they would appear to the eye in case it were naturally endowed with a most exquisite sharpness?

HYLAS: It is.

PHILONOUS: Consequently the microscopical representation is to be thought that which best sets forth the real nature of the thing, or what it is in itself. The colours, therefore, by it perceived are more genuine and real than those perceived otherwise.

HYLAS: I confess there is something in what you say.

PHILONOUS: Besides, it is not only possible but manifest, that there actually are animals whose eyes are by nature framed to perceive those things which by reason of their minuteness escape our sight. What think you of those inconceivably small animals perceived by glasses? Must we suppose they are all stark blind? Or, in case they see, can it be imagined their sight hath not the same use in preserving their bodies from injuries, which appears in that of all other animals? And if it hath, is it not evident they must see particles less than their own bodies; which will present them with a far different view in each object from that which strikes our senses? Even our own eyes do not always represent objects to us after the same manner. In the jaundice every one knows that all things seem yellow. Is it not therefore highly probable those animals in whose eyes we discern a very different texture from that of ours, and whose bodies abound with different humors, do not see the same colours in every object that we do? From all which, should it not seem to follow that all colours are equally apparent, and that none of those which we perceive are really inherent in any outward object?

HYLAS: It should.

PHILONOUS: The point will be past all doubt, if you consider that, in case colours were real properties or affections inherent in external bodies, they could admit of no alteration without some change wrought in the very bodies themselves: but, is it not evident from what hath been said that, upon the use of microscopes, upon a change happening in the humors of the eye, or a variation of distance, without any manner of real alteration in the thing itself, the colours of any object are either changed, or totally disappear? Nay, all other circumstances remaining the same, change but the situation of some objects, and they shall present different colours to the eye. The same thing happens upon viewing an object in various degrees of light. And what is more known than that the same bodies appear differently colored by candle-light from what they do in the open day? Add to these the experiment of a prism which, separating the heterogeneous rays of light, alters the colour of any object, and will cause the whitest to appear of a deep blue or red to the naked eye. And now tell me whether you are still of opinion that every body hath its true real colour inhering in it; and, if you think it hath, I would fain know farther from you, what certain distance and position of the object, what peculiar texture and formation of the eye, what degree or kind of light is necessary for ascertaining that true colour, and distinguishing it from apparent ones.

HYLAS: I own myself entirely satisfied, that they are all equally apparent, and that there is no such thing as colour really inhering in external bodies, but that it is altogether in the light. And what confirms me in this opinion is, that in proportion to the light colours are still more or less vivid; and if there be no light, then are there no colours perceived. Besides, allowing there are colours on external objects, yet, how is it possible for us to perceive them? For no external body affects the mind, unless it acts first on our organs of sense. But the only action of bodies is motion; and motion cannot be communicated otherwise than by impulse. A distant object therefore cannot act on the eye, nor consequently make itself or its properties perceivable to the soul. Whence it plainly follows that it is immediately some contiguous substance, which, operating on the eye, occasions a perception of colours: and such is light.

PHILONOUS: How! Is light then a substance?

HYLAS: I tell you, Philonous, external light is nothing but a thin fluid substance, whose minute particles being agitated with a brisk motion, and in various manners reflected from the different surfaces of outward objects to the eyes, communicate different motions to the optic nerves; which, being propagated to the brain, cause therein various impressions; and these are attended with the sensations of red, blue, yellow, &c.

PHILONOUS: It seems then the light does no more than shake the optic nerves.

HYLAS: Nothing else.

PHILONOUS: And consequent to each particular motion of the nerves, the mind is affected with a sensation, which is some particular colour.

HYLAS: Right.

PHILONOUS: And these sensations have no existence without the mind.

HYLAS: They have not.

PHILONOUS: How then do you affirm that colours are in the light; since by light you understand a corporeal substance external to the mind?

HYLAS: Light and colours, as immediately perceived by us, I grant cannot exist without the mind. But in themselves they are only the motions and configurations of certain insensible particles of matter.

PHILONOUS: Colours then, in the vulgar sense, or taken for the immediate objects of sight, cannot agree to any but a perceiving substance.

HYLAS: That is what I say.

PHILONOUS: Well then, since you give up the point as to those sensible qualities which are alone thought colours by all mankind beside, you may hold what you please with regard to those invisible ones of the philosophers. It is not my business to dispute about them; only I would advise you to bethink yourself, whether, considering the inquiry we are upon, it be prudent for you to affirm—*the red and blue which we see are not real colours, but certain unknown motions and figures which no man ever did or can see are truly so.* Are not these shocking notions, and are not they subject to as many ridiculous inferences, as those you were obliged to renounce before in the case of sounds?

HYLAS: I frankly own, Philonous, that it is in vain to stand out any longer. Colours, sounds, tastes, in a word all those termed *secondary qualities,* have certainly no existence without the mind. But by this acknowledgment I must not be supposed to derogate anything from the reality of matter, or external objects; seeing it is no more than several philosophers maintain, who nevertheless are the farthest imaginable from denying matter. For the clearer understanding of this, you must know sensible qualities are by philosophers divided into *primary* and *secondary*. The former are extension, figure, solidity, gravity, motion, and rest; and these they hold exist really in bodies. The latter are those above enumerated; or, briefly, all sensible qualities beside the primary; which they assert are only so many sensations or ideas existing nowhere but in the mind. But all this, I doubt not, you are apprised of. For my part, I have been a long time sensible there was such an opinion current among philosophers, but was never thoroughly convinced of its truth until now.

PHILONOUS: You are still then of opinion that extension and figures are inherent in external unthinking substances?

HYLAS: I am.

PHILONOUS: But what if the same arguments which are brought against secondary qualities will hold good against these also?

HYLAS: Why then I shall be obliged to think, they too exist only in the mind.

PHILONOUS: Is it your opinion the very figure and extension which you perceive by sense exist in the outward object or material substance?

HYLAS: It is.

PHILONOUS: Have all other animals as good grounds to think the same of the figure and extension which they see and feel?

HYLAS: Without doubt, if they have any thought at all.

PHILONOUS: Answer me, Hylas. Think you the senses were bestowed upon all animals for their preservation and well-being in life? Or were they given to men alone for this end?

HYLAS: I make no question but they have the same use in all other animals.

PHILONOUS: If so, is it not necessary they should be enabled by them to perceive their own limbs, and those bodies which are capable of harming them?

HYLAS: Certainly.

PHILONOUS: A mite therefore must be supposed to see his own foot, and things equal or even less than it, as bodies of some considerable dimension, though at the same time they appear to you scarce discernible, or at best as so many visible points?

HYLAS: I cannot deny it.

PHILONOUS: And to creatures less than the mite they will seem yet larger?

HYLAS: They will.

PHILONOUS: Insomuch that what you can hardly discern will to another extremely minute animal appear as some huge mountain?

HYLAS: All this I grant.

PHILONOUS: Can one and the same thing be at the same time in itself of different dimensions?

HYLAS: That were absurd to imagine.

PHILONOUS: But, from what you have laid down it follows that both the extension by you perceived, and that perceived by the mite itself, as likewise all those perceived by lesser animals, are each of them the true extension of the mite's foot; that is to say, by your own principles you are led into an absurdity.

HYLAS: There seems to be some difficulty in the point.

PHILONOUS: Again, have you not acknowledged that no real inherent property of any object can be changed without some change in the thing itself?

HYLAS: I have.

PHILONOUS: But, as we approach to or recede from an object, the visible extension varies, being at one distance ten or a hundred times greater than another. Does it not therefore follow from hence likewise that it is not really inherent in the object?

HYLAS: I own I am at a loss what to think.

PHILONOUS: Your judgment will soon be determined, if you will venture to think as freely concerning this quality as you have done concerning the rest. Was it not admitted as a good argument, that neither heat nor cold was in the water, because it seemed warm to one hand and cold to the other?

HYLAS: It was.

PHILONOUS: Is it not the very same reasoning to conclude, there is no extension or figure in an object, because to one eye it shall seem little, smooth, and round, when at the same time it appears to the other, great, uneven, and regular?

HYLAS: The very same. But does this latter fact ever happen?

PHILONOUS: You may at any time make the experiment, by looking with one eye bare, and with the other through a microscope.

HYLAS: I know not how to maintain it; and yet I am loath to give up *extension,* I see so many odd consequences following upon such a concession.

PHILONOUS: Odd, say you? After the concessions already made, I hope you will stick at nothing for its oddness. But, on the other hand, should it not seem very odd, if the general reasoning which includes all other sensible qualities did not also include extension? If it be allowed that no idea, nor anything like an idea, can exist in an unperceiving substance, then surely it follows that no figure, or mode of extension, which we can either perceive, or imagine, or have any idea of, can be really inherent in matter; not to mention the peculiar difficulty there must be in conceiving a material substance, prior to and distinct from extension to be the *substratum* of extension. Be the sensible quality what it will—figure, or sound, or colour, it seems alike impossible it should subsist in that which does not perceive it.

HYLAS: I give up the point for the present, reserving still a right to retract my opinion, in case I shall hereafter discover any false step in my progress to it.

PHILONOUS: That is a right you cannot be denied. Figures and extension being dispatched, we proceed next to *motion.* Can a real motion in any external body be at the same time very swift and very slow?

HYLAS: It cannot.

PHILONOUS: Is not the motion of a body swift in a reciprocal proportion to the time it takes up in describing any given space? Thus a body that describes a mile in an hour moves three times faster than it would in case it described only a mile in three hours.

HYLAS: I agree with you.

PHILONOUS: And is not time measured by the succession of ideas in our minds?

HYLAS: It is.

PHILONOUS: And is it not possible ideas should succeed one another twice as fast in your mind as they do in mine, or in that of some spirit of another kind?

HYLAS: I own it.

PHILONOUS: Consequently the same body may to another seem to perform its motion over any space in half the time that it does to you. And the same reasoning will hold as to any other proportion: that is to say, according to your principles (since the motions perceived are both really in the object) it is possible one and the same body shall be really moved the same way at once, both very swift and very slow. How is this consistent either with common sense, or with what you just now granted?

HYLAS: I have nothing to say to it.

PHILONOUS: Then as for *solidity;* either you do not mean any sensible quality by that word, and so it is beside our inquiry: or if you do, it must be either hardness or resistance. But both the one and the other are plainly relative to our senses: it being evident that what seems hard to one animal may appear soft to another, who hath greater force and firmness of limbs. Nor is it less plain that the resistance I feel is not in the body.

HYLAS: I own the very sensation of resistance, which is all you immediately perceive, is not in the *body;* but the cause of that sensation is.

PHILONOUS: But the causes of our sensations are not things immediately perceived, and therefore are not sensible. This point I thought had been already determined.

HYLAS: I own it was; but you will pardon me if I seem a little embarrassed: I know not how to quit my old notions.

PHILONOUS: To help you out, do but consider that if extension be once acknowledged to have no existence without the mind, the same must necessarily be granted of motion, solidity, and gravity; since they all evidently suppose extension. It is therefore superfluous to inquire particularly concerning each of them. In denying extension, you have denied them all to have any real existence.

HYLAS: I wonder, Philonous, if what you say be true, why those philosophers who deny the secondary qualities any real existence should yet attribute it to the primary. If there is no difference between them, how can this be accounted for?

PHILONOUS: It is not my business to account for every opinion of the philosophers. But, among other reasons which may be assigned for this, it seems probable that pleasure and pain being rather annexed to the former than the latter may be one. Heat and cold, tastes and smells, have something more vividly pleasing or disagreeable than the ideas of extension, figure, and motion affect us with. And, it being too visibly absurd to hold that pain or pleasure can be in an unperceiving substance, men are more easily weaned from believing the external existence of the secondary than the primary qualities. You will be satisfied there is something in this, if you recollect the difference you made between an intense and more moderate degree of heat; allowing the one a real existence, while you denied it to the other. But, after all, there is no rational ground for that distinction; for, surely an indifferent sensation is as truly a *sensation* as one more pleasing or painful; and consequently should not any more than they be supposed to exist in an unthinking subject.

HYLAS: It is just come into my head, Philonous, that I have somewhere heard of a distinction between absolute and sensible extension. Now, though it be acknowledged that *great* and *small,* consisting merely in the relation which other extended beings have to the parts of our own bodies, do not really inhere in the substances themselves; yet nothing obliges us to hold the same with regard to *absolute extension,* which is something abstracted from *great* and *small,* from this or that particular magnitude or figure. So likewise as to motion; *swift* and *slow* are altogether relative to the succession of ideas in our own minds. But, it does not follow, because those modifications of motion exist not without the mind, that therefore absolute motion abstracted from them does not.

PHILONOUS: Pray what is it that distinguishes one motion, or one part of extension, from another? Is it not something sensible, as some degree of swiftness or slowness, some certain magnitude or figure peculiar to each?

HYLAS: I think so.

PHILONOUS: These qualities, therefore, stripped of all sensible properties, are without all specific and numerical differences, as the schools call them.

HYLAS: They are.

PHILONOUS: That is to say, they are extension in general, and motion in general.

HYLAS: Let it be so.

PHILONOUS: But it is a universally received maxim that *Everything which exists is particular.* How then can motion in general, or extension in general, exist in any corporeal substance?

HYLAS: I will take time to solve your difficulty.

PHILONOUS: But I think the point may be speedily decided. Without doubt you can tell whether you are able to frame this or that idea. Now I am content to put our dispute on this issue. If you can frame in your thoughts a distinct abstract idea of motion or extension, divested of all those sensible modes, as swift and slow, great and small, round and square, and the like, which are acknowledged to exist only in the mind, I will then yield the point you contend for. But if you cannot, it will be unreasonable on your side to insist any longer upon what you have no notion of.

HYLAS: To confess ingenuously, I cannot.

PHILONOUS: Can you even separate the ideas of extension and motion from the ideas of all those qualities which they who make the distinction term *secondary?*

HYLAS: What! Is it not an easy matter to consider extension and motion by themselves, abstracted from all other sensible qualities? Pray how do the mathematicians treat of them?

PHILONOUS: I acknowledge, Hylas, it is not difficult to form general propositions and reasonings about those qualities, without mentioning any other; and, in this sense, to consider or treat of them abstractedly. But, how does it follow that, because I can pronounce the word *motion* by itself, I can form the idea of it in my mind exclusive of body? Or, because theorems may be made of extension and figures, without any mention of *great* or *small,* or any other sensible mode or quality, that therefore it is possible such an abstract idea of extension, without any particular size or figure, or sensible quality, should be distinctly formed, and apprehended by the mind? Mathematicians treat of quantity, without regarding what other sensible qualities it is attended with, as being altogether indifferent to their demonstrations. But, when laying aside the words, they contemplate the bare ideas, I believe you will find, they are not the pure abstracted ideas of extension.

HYLAS: But what say you to *pure intellect?* May not abstracted ideas be framed by that faculty?

PHILONOUS: Since I cannot frame abstract ideas at all, it is plain I cannot frame them by the help of *pure intellect;* whatsoever faculty you understand by those words. Besides, not to inquire into the nature of pure intellect and its spiritual objects, as *virtue, reason, God,* or the like, thus much seems manifest—that sensible things are only to be perceived by sense, or represented by the imagination. Figures, therefore, and extension, being originally perceived by sense, do not belong to pure intellect: but, for your farther satisfaction, try if you can frame the idea of any figure, abstracted from all particularities of size, or even from other sensible qualities.

HYLAS: Let me think a little—I do not find that I can.

PHILONOUS: And can you think it possible that should really exist in nature which implies a repugnancy in its conception?

HYLAS: By no means.

PHILONOUS: Since therefore it is impossible even for the mind to disunite the ideas of extension and motion from all other sensible qualities, does it not follow, that where the one exist there necessarily the other exist likewise?

HYLAS: It should seem so.

PHILONOUS: Consequently, the very same arguments which you admitted as conclusive against the secondary qualities are, without any farther application of force, against the primary too. Besides, if you will trust your senses, is it not plain all sensible qualities coexist, or to them appear as being in the same place? Do they ever represent a motion, or figure, as being divested of all other visible and tangible qualities?

HYLAS: You need say no more on this head. I am free to own, if there be no secret error or oversight in our proceedings hitherto, that all sensible qualities are alike to be denied existence without the mind. But, my fear is that I have been too liberal in my former concessions, or overlooked some fallacy or other. In short, I did not take time to think.

PHILONOUS: For that matter, Hylas, you may take what time you please in reviewing the progress of our inquiry. You are at liberty to recover any slips you might have made, or offer whatever you have omitted which makes for your first opinion.

HYLAS: One great oversight I take to be this—that I did not sufficiently distinguish the *object* from the *sensation.* Now though this latter may not exist without the mind, yet it will not thence follow that the former cannot.

PHILONOUS: What object do you mean? The object of the senses?

HYLAS: The same.

PHILONOUS: It is then immediately perceived?

HYLAS: Right.

PHILONOUS: Make me to understand the difference between what is immediately perceived and a sensation.

HYLAS: The sensation I take to be an act of the mind perceiving; besides which, there is something perceived, and this I call the *object.* For example, there is red and yellow on that tulip. But then the act of perceiving those colours is in me only, and not in the tulip.

PHILONOUS: What tulip do you speak of? Is it that which you see?

HYLAS: The same.

PHILONOUS: And what do you see beside colour, figure, and extension?

HYLAS: Nothing.

PHILONOUS: What you would say then is that the red and yellow are coexistent with the extension; is it not?

HYLAS: That is not all; I would say they have a real existence without the mind, in some unthinking substance.

PHILONOUS: That the colours are really in the tulip which I see is manifest. Neither can it be denied that this tulip may exist independent of your mind or mine; but, that any immediate object of the senses—that is, any idea, or combination of ideas—should exist in an unthinking substance, or exterior to all minds, is in itself an evident contradiction. Nor can I imagine how this follows from what you said just now, to wit, that the red and yellow were on the tulip *you saw,* since you do not pretend to see that unthinking substance.

HYLAS: You have an artful way, Philonous, of diverting our inquiry from the subject.

PHILONOUS: I see you have no mind to be pressed that way. To return then to your distinction between *sensation* and *object;* if I take you right, you distinguish in every perception two things, the one an action of the mind, the other not.

HYLAS: True.

PHILONOUS: And this action cannot exist in, or belong to, any unthinking thing; but, whatever beside is implied in a perception may?

HYLAS: That is my meaning.

PHILONOUS: So that if there was a perception without any act of the mind, it were possible such a perception should exist in an unthinking substance?

HYLAS: I grant it. But it is impossible there should be such a perception.

PHILONOUS: When is the mind said to be active?

HYLAS: When it produces, puts an end to, or changes, anything.

PHILONOUS: Can the mind produce, discontinue, or change anything, but by an act of the will?

HYLAS: It cannot.

PHILONOUS: The mind therefore is to be accounted active in its perceptions so far forth as volition is included in them?

HYLAS: It is.

PHILONOUS: In plucking this flower I am *active;* because I do it by the motion of my hand, which was consequent upon my *volition;* so likewise in applying it to my nose. But is either of these smelling?

HYLAS: No.

PHILONOUS: I act too in drawing the air through my nose; because my breathing so rather than otherwise is the effect of my volition. But neither can this be called *smelling:* for, if it were, I should smell every time I breathed in that manner?

HYLAS: True.

PHILONOUS: Smelling then is somewhat consequent to all this?

HYLAS: It is.

PHILONOUS: But I do not find my will concerned any farther. Whatever more there is—as that I perceive such a particular smell, or any smell at all—this is independent of my will, and therein I am altogether passive. Do you find it otherwise with you, Hylas?

HYLAS: No, the very same.

PHILONOUS: Then, as to seeing, is it not in your power to open your eyes, or keep them shut; to turn them this or that way?

HYLAS: Without doubt.

PHILONOUS: But does it in like manner depend on your will that in looking on this flower you perceive *white* rather any other colour? Or, directing your open eyes towards yonder part of the heaven, can you avoid seeing the sun? Or is light or darkness the effect of your volition?

HYLAS: No, certainly.

PHILONOUS: You are then in these respects altogether passive?

HYLAS: I am.

PHILONOUS: Tell me now, whether *seeing* consists in perceiving light and colours, or in opening and turning the eyes?

HYLAS: Without doubt, in the former.

PHILONOUS: Since therefore you are in the very perception of light and colours altogether passive, what is become of that action you were speaking of as an ingredient in every sensation? And, does it not follow from your own concessions, that the perception of light and colours, including no action in it, may exist in an unperceiving substance? And is not this a plain contradiction?

HYLAS: I know not what to think of it.

PHILONOUS: Besides, since you distinguish the *active* and *passive* in every perception, you must do it in that of pain. But how is it possible that pain, be it as little active as you please, should exist in an unperceiving substance? In short, do but consider the point, and then confess ingenuously, whether light and colours, tastes, sounds, &c. are not all equally passions or sensations in the soul. You may indeed call them *external objects,* and give them in words what subsistence you please. But, examine your own thoughts, and then tell me whether it be not as I say?

HYLAS: I acknowledge, Philonous, that, upon a fair observation of what passes in my mind I can discover nothing else but that I am a thinking being, affected with variety of sensations; neither is it possible to conceive how a sensation should exist in an unperceiving substance.—But then, on the other hand, when I look on sensible things in a different view, considering them as so many modes and qualities, I find it necessary to suppose a *material* substratum, without which they cannot be conceived to exist.

PHILONOUS: *Material substratum* call you it? Pray, by which of your senses came you acquainted with that being?

HYLAS: It is not itself sensible; its modes and qualities only being perceived by the senses.

PHILONOUS: I presume then it was by reflexion and reason you obtained the idea of it?

HYLAS: I do not pretend to any proper positive idea of it. However, I conclude it exists, because qualities cannot be conceived to exist without a support.

PHILONOUS: It seems then you have only a relative notion of it, or that you conceive it not otherwise than by conceiving the relation it bears to sensible qualities?

HYLAS: Right.

PHILONOUS: Be pleased therefore to let me know wherein that relation consists.

HYLAS: Is it not sufficiently expressed in the term *substratum,* or *substance?*

PHILONOUS: If so, the word *substratum* should import that it is spread under the sensible qualities or accidents?

HYLAS: True.

PHILONOUS: And consequently under extension?

HYLAS: I own it.

PHILONOUS: It is therefore somewhat in its own nature entirely distinct from extension?

HYLAS: I tell you, extension is only a mode, and matter is something that supports modes. And is it not evident the thing supported is different from the thing supporting?

PHILONOUS: So that something distinct from, and exclusive of, extension is supposed to be the substratum of extension?

HYLAS: Just so.

PHILONOUS: Answer me, Hylas. Can a thing be spread without extension? or is not the idea of extension necessarily included in *spreading?*

HYLAS: It is.

PHILONOUS: Whatsoever therefore you suppose spread under anything must have in itself an extension distinct from the extension of that thing under which it is spread?

HYLAS: It must.

PHILONOUS: Consequently, every corporeal substance, being the *substratum* of extension, must have in itself another extension, by which it is qualified to be a *substratum:* and so on to infinity. And I ask whether this be not absurd in itself, and repugnant to what you granted just now, to wit, that the *substratum* was something distinct from and exclusive of extension?

HYLAS: Aye but, Philonous, you take me wrong. I do not mean that matter is *spread* in a gross literal sense under extension. The word *substratum* is used only to express in general the same thing with *substance.*

PHILONOUS: Well then, let us examine the relation implied in the term *substance.* Is it not that it stands under accidents?

HYLAS: The very same.

PHILONOUS: But, that one thing may stand under or support another, must it not be extended?

HYLAS: It must.

PHILONOUS: Is not therefore this supposition liable to the same absurdity with the former?

HYLAS: You still take things in a strict literal sense. That is not fair, Philonous.

PHILONOUS: I am not for imposing any sense on your words: you are at liberty to explain them as you please. Only, I beseech you, make me understand something by them. You tell me matter supports or stands under accidents. How! is it as your legs support your body?

HYLAS: No; that is the literal sense.

PHILONOUS: Pray let me know any sense, literal or not literal, that you understand it in.—How long must I wait for an answer, Hylas?

HYLAS: I declare I know not what to say. I once thought I understood well enough what was meant by matter's supporting accidents. But now, the more I think on it the less can I comprehend it: in short I find that I know nothing of it.

PHILONOUS: It seems then you have no idea at all, neither relative nor positive, of matter; you know neither what it is in itself, nor what relation it bears to accidents?

HYLAS: I acknowledge it.

PHILONOUS: And yet you asserted that you could not conceive how qualities or accidents should really exist, without conceiving at the same time a material support of them?

HYLAS: I did.

PHILONOUS: That is to say, when you conceive the real existence of qualities, you do withal conceive something which you cannot conceive?

HYLAS: It was wrong, I own. But still I fear there is some fallacy or other. Pray what think you of this? It is just come into my head that the ground of all our mistake lies in your treating of each quality by itself. Now, I grant that each quality cannot singly subsist without the mind. Colour cannot without extension, neither can figure without some other sensible quality. But, as the several qualities united or blended together form entire sensible things, nothing hinders why such things may not be supposed to exist without the mind.

PHILONOUS: Either, Hylas, you are jesting, or have a very bad memory. Though indeed we went through all the qualities by name one after another, yet my arguments or rather your concessions, nowhere tended to prove that the secondary qualities did not subsist each alone by itself; but, that they were not *at all* without the mind. Indeed, in treating of figure and motion we concluded they could not exist without the mind, because it was impossible even in thought to separate them from all secondary qualities, so as to conceive them existing by themselves. But then this was not the only argument made use of upon that occasion. But (to pass by all that hath been hitherto said, and reckon it for nothing, if you will have it so) I am content to put the whole upon this issue. If you can conceive it possible for any mixture or combination of qualities, or any sensible object whatever, to exist without the mind, then I will grant it actually to be so.

HYLAS: If it comes to that the point will soon be decided. What more easy than to conceive a tree or house existing by itself, independent of, and unperceived by, any mind whatsoever? I do at this present time conceive them existing after that manner.

PHILONOUS: How say you, Hylas, can you see a thing which is at the same time unseen?

HYLAS: No, that were a contradiction.

PHILONOUS: Is it not as great a contradiction to talk of *conceiving* a thing which is *unconceived?*

HYLAS: It is.

PHILONOUS: The tree or house therefore which you think of is conceived by you?

HYLAS: How should it be otherwise?

PHILONOUS: And what is conceived is surely in the mind?

HYLAS: Without question, that which is conceived is in the mind.

PHILONOUS: How then came you to say, you conceived a house or tree existing independent and out of all minds whatsoever?

HYLAS: That was I own an oversight; but stay, let me consider what led me into it.— It is a pleasant mistake enough. As I was thinking of a tree in a solitary place, where no one was present to see it, methought that was to conceive a tree as existing unperceived or unthought of; not considering that I myself conceived it all the while. But now I plainly see that all I can do is to frame ideas in my own mind. I may indeed conceive in my own thoughts the idea of a tree, or a house, or a mountain, but that is all. And this is far from proving that I can conceive them *existing out of the minds of all spirits.*

PHILONOUS: You acknowledge then that you cannot possibly conceive how any one corporeal sensible thing should exist otherwise than in the mind?

HYLAS: I do.

PHILONOUS: And yet you will earnestly contend for the truth of that which you cannot so much as conceive?

HYLAS I profess I know not what to think, but still there are some scruples remain with me. Is it not certain I *see* things at a distance? Do we not perceive the stars and moon, for example, to be a great way off? Is not this, say, manifest to the senses?

PHILONOUS: Do you not in a dream too perceive those or the like objects?

HYLAS: I do.

PHILONOUS: And have they not then the same appearance of being distant?

HYLAS: They have.

PHILONOUS: But you do not thence conclude the apparitions in a dream to be without the mind?

HYLAS: By no means.

PHILONOUS: You ought not therefore to conclude that sensible objects are without the mind, from their appearance, or manner wherein they are perceived.

HYLAS: I acknowledge it. But does not my sense deceive me in those cases?

PHILONOUS: By no means. The idea or thing which you immediately perceive, neither sense nor reason informs you that it actually exists without the mind. By sense you only know that you are affected with such certain sensations of light and colours, &c. And these you will not say are without the mind.

HYLAS: True: but, beside all that, do you not think the sight suggests something of *outness* or *distance?*

PHILONOUS: Upon approaching a distant object, do the visible size and figure change perpetually, or do they appear the same at all distances?

HYLAS: They are in a continual change.

PHILONOUS: Sight therefore does not suggest, or any way inform you, that the visible object you immediately perceive exists at a distance, or will be perceived when you advance farther onward; there being a continued series of visible objects succeeding each other during the whole time of your approach.

HYLAS: It does not; but still I know, upon seeing an object, what object I shall perceive after having passed over a certain distance: no matter whether it be exactly the same or no: there is still something of distance suggested in the case.

PHILONOUS: Good Hylas, do but reflect a little on the point, and then tell me whether there be any more in it than this: from the ideas you actually perceive by sight, you have by experience learned to collect what other ideas you will (according to the standing order of nature) be affected with, after such a certain succession of time and motion.

HYLAS: Upon the whole, I take it to be nothing else.

PHILONOUS: Now, is it not plain that if we suppose a man born blind was on a sudden made to see, he could at first have no experience of what may be suggested by sight?

HYLAS: It is.

PHILONOUS: He would not then, according to you, have any notion of distance annexed to the things he saw; but would take them for a new set of sensations, existing only in his mind?

HYLAS: It is undeniable.

PHILONOUS: But, to make it still more plain: is not *distance* a line turned endwise to the eye?

HYLAS: It is.

PHILONOUS: And can a line so situated be perceived by sight?

HYLAS: It cannot.

PHILONOUS: Does it not therefore follow that distance is not properly and immediately perceived by sight?

HYLAS: It should seem so.

PHILONOUS: Again, is it your opinion that colours are at a distance?

HYLAS: It must be acknowledged they are only in the mind.

PHILONOUS: But do not colours appear to the eye as coexisting in the same place with extension and figures?

HYLAS: They do.

PHILONOUS: How can you then conclude from sight that figures exist without, when you acknowledge colours do not; the sensible appearance being the very same with regard to both?

HYLAS: I know not what to answer.

PHILONOUS: But, allowing that distance was truly and immediately perceived by the mind, yet it would not thence follow it existed out of the mind. For, whatever is immediately perceived is an idea: and can any *idea* exist out of the mind?

HYLAS: To suppose that were absurd: but, inform me, Philonous, can we perceive or know nothing beside our ideas?

PHILONOUS: As for the rational deducing of causes from effects, that is beside our inquiry. And, by the senses you can best tell whether you perceive anything which is not immediately perceived. And I ask you, whether the things immediately perceived are other than your own sensations or ideas? You have indeed more than once, in the course of this conversation, declared yourself on those points; but you seem, by this last question, to have departed from what you then thought.

HYLAS: To speak the truth, Philonous, I think there are two kinds of objects:—the one perceived immediately, which are likewise called *ideas;* the other are real things or external objects, perceived by the mediation of ideas, which are their images and representations. Now, I own ideas do not exist without the mind; but the latter sort of objects do. I am sorry I did not think of this distinction sooner; it would probably have cut short your discourse.

PHILONOUS: Are those external objects perceived by sense or by some other faculty?

HYLAS: They are perceived by sense.

PHILONOUS: How! Is there any thing perceived by sense which is not immediately perceived?

HYLAS: Yes, Philonous, in some sort there is. For example when I look on a picture or statue of Julius Caesar, I may be said after a manner to perceive him (though not immediately) by my senses.

PHILONOUS: It seems then you will have our ideas, which alone are immediately perceived, to be pictures of external things: and that these also are perceived by sense, inasmuch as they have a conformity or resemblance to our ideas?

HYLAS: That is my meaning.

PHILONOUS: And, in the same way that Julius Caesar, in himself invisible, is nevertheless perceived by sight; real things, in themselves imperceptible, are perceived by sense.

HYLAS: In the very same.

PHILONOUS: Tell me, Hylas, when you behold the picture of Julius Caesar, do you see with your eyes any more than some colours and figures, with a certain symmetry and composition of the whole?

HYLAS: Nothing else.

PHILONOUS: And would not a man who had never known anything of Julius Caesar see as much?

HYLAS: He would.

PHILONOUS: Consequently he hath his sight, and the use of it, in as perfect a degree as you?

HYLAS: I agree with you.

PHILONOUS: Whence comes it then that your thoughts are directed to the Roman emperor, and his are not? This cannot proceed from the sensations or ideas of sense by you then perceived; since you acknowledge you have no advantage over him in that respect. It should seem therefore to proceed from reason and memory: should it not?

HYLAS: It should.

PHILONOUS: Consequently, it will not follow from that instance that anything is perceived by sense which is not immediately perceived. Though I grant we may, in one acceptation, be said to perceive sensible things mediately by sense: that is, when, from a frequently perceived connexion, the immediate perception of ideas by one sense suggests to the mind others, perhaps belonging to another sense, which are wont to be connected with them. For instance, when I hear a coach drive along the streets, immediately I perceive only the sound; but, from the experience I have had that such a sound is connected with a coach, I am said to hear the coach. It is nevertheless evident that, in truth and strictness, nothing can be *heard* but *sound;* and the coach is not then properly perceived by sense, but suggested from experience. So likewise when we are said to see a red-hot bar of iron; the solidity and heat of the iron are not the objects of sight, but suggested to the imagination by the colour and figure which are properly perceived by that sense. In short, those things alone are actually and strictly perceived by any sense, which would have been perceived in case that same sense had then been first conferred on us. As for other things, it is plain they are only suggested to the mind by experience, grounded on former perceptions. But, to return to your comparison of Caesar's picture, it is plain, if you keep to that, you must hold the real things, or archetypes of our ideas, are not perceived by sense, but by some internal faculty of the soul, as reason or memory. I would therefore fain know what arguments you can draw from reason for the existence of what you call real *things* or *material objects*. Or, whether you remember to have seen them formerly as they are in themselves; or, if you have heard or read of any one that did.

HYLAS: I see, Philonous, you are disposed to raillery; but that will never convince me.

PHILONOUS: My aim is only to learn from you the way to come at the knowledge of *material beings.* Whatever we perceive is perceived immediately or mediately: by sense, or by reason and reflexion. But, as you have excluded sense, pray show me what reason you have to believe their existence; or what *medium* you can possibly make use of to prove it, either to mine or your own understanding.

HYLAS: To deal ingenuously, Philonous, now I consider the point, I do not find I can give you any good reason for it. But, thus much seems pretty plain, that it is at least possible such things may really exist. And, as long as there is no absurdity in supposing them, I am resolved to believe as I did, till you bring good reasons to the contrary.

PHILONOUS: What! Is it come to this, that you only believe the existence of material objects, and that your belief is founded barely on the possibility of its being true? Then you will have me bring reasons against it: though another would think it reasonable the proof should lie on him who holds the affirmative. And, after all, this very point which you are now resolved to maintain, without any reason, is in effect what you have more than once during this discourse seen good reason to give up. But, to pass over all this; if I understand you rightly, you say our ideas do not exist without the mind, but that they are copies, images, or representations, of certain originals that do?

HYLAS: You take me right.

PHILONOUS: They are then like external things?

HYLAS: They are.

PHILONOUS: Have those things a stable and permanent nature, independent of our senses; or are they in a perpetual change, upon our producing any motions in our bodies—suspending, exerting, or altering, our faculties or organs of sense?

HYLAS: Real things, it is plain, have a fixed and real nature, which remains the same notwithstanding any change in our senses, or in the posture and motion of our bodies; which indeed may affect the ideas in our minds, but it were absurd to think they had the same effect on things existing without the mind.

PHILONOUS: How then is it possible that things perpetually fleeting and variable as our ideas should be copies or images of anything fixed and constant? Or, in other words, since all sensible qualities, as size, figure, colour, &c., that is, our ideas, are continually changing, upon every alteration in the distance, medium, or instruments of sensation; how can any determinate material objects be properly represented or painted forth by several distinct things, each of which is so different from and unlike the rest? Or, if you say it resembles some one only of our ideas, how shall we be able to distinguish the true copy from all the false ones?

HYLAS: I profess, Philonous, I am at a loss. I know not what to say to this.

PHILONOUS: But neither is this all. Which are material objects in themselves—perceptible or imperceptible?

HYLAS: Properly and immediately nothing can be perceived but ideas. All material things, therefore, are in themselves insensible, and to be perceived only by our ideas.

PHILONOUS: Ideas then are sensible, and their archetypes or originals insensible?

HYLAS: Right.

PHILONOUS: But how can that which is sensible be like that which is insensible? Can a real thing, in itself *invisible,* be like a *colour;* or a real thing, which is not *audible,* be like a *sound?* In a word, can anything be like a sensation or idea, but another sensation or idea?

HYLAS: I must own, I think not.

PHILONOUS: Is it possible there should be any doubt on the point? Do you not perfectly know your own ideas?

HYLAS: I know them perfectly; since what I do not perceive or know can be no part of my idea.

PHILONOUS: Consider, therefore, and examine them, and then tell me if there be anything in them which can exist without the mind: or if you can conceive anything like them existing without the mind.

HYLAS: Upon inquiry, I find it is impossible for me to conceive or understand how anything but an idea can be like an idea. And it is most evident that *no idea can exist without the mind.*

PHILONOUS: You are therefore, by your principles, forced to deny the reality of sensible things; since you made it to consist in an absolute existence exterior to the mind. That is to say, you are a downright *sceptic.* So I have gained my point, which was to show your principles led to scepticism.

HYLAS: For the present I am, if not entirely convinced, at least silenced.

PHILONOUS: I would fain know what more you would require in order to a perfect conviction. Have you not had the liberty of explaining yourself all manner of ways? Were any little slips in discourse laid hold and insisted on? Or were you not allowed to retract or reinforce anything you had offered, as best served your purpose? Hath not everything you could say been heard and examined with all the fairness imaginable? In a word, have you not in every point been convinced out of your own mouth? And, if you can at present discover any flaw in any of your former concessions, or think of any remaining subterfuge, any new distinction, colour, or comment whatsoever, why do you not produce it?

HYLAS: A little patience, Philonous. I am at present so amazed to see myself ensnared, and as it were imprisoned in the labyrinths you have drawn me into, that on the sudden it cannot be expected I should find my way out. You must give me time to look about me and recollect myself.

PHILONOUS: Hark; is not this the college bell?

HYLAS: It rings for prayers.

PHILONOUS: We will go in then, if you please, and meet here again tomorrow morning. In the meantime, you may employ your thoughts on this morning's discourse, and try if you can find any fallacy in it, or invent any new means to extricate yourself.

HYLAS: Agreed.

THE SECOND DIALOGUE

HYLAS: I beg your pardon, Philonous, for not meeting you sooner. All this morning my head was so filled with our late conversation that I had not leisure to think of the time of the day, or indeed of anything else.

PHILONOUS: I am glad you were so intent upon it, in hopes if there were any mistakes in your concessions, or fallacies in my reasonings from them, you will now discover them to me.

HYLAS: I assure you I have done nothing ever since I saw you but search after mistakes and fallacies, and, with that view, have minutely examined the whole series of yesterday's discourse: but all in vain, for the notions it led me into, upon review, appear still more clear and evident; and, the more I consider them, the more irresistibly do they force my assent.

PHILONOUS: And is not this, think you, a sign that they are genuine, that they proceed from nature, and are conformable to right reason? Truth and beauty are in this alike, that the strictest survey sets them both off to advantage; while the false lustre of error and disguise cannot endure being reviewed, or too nearly inspected.

HYLAS: I own there is a great deal in what you say. Nor can any one be more entirely satisfied of the truth of those odd consequences, so long as I have in view the reasonings that lead to them. But, when these are out of my thoughts, there seems, on the other hand, something so satisfactory, so natural and intelligible, in the modern way of explaining things that, I profess, I know not how to reject it.

PHILONOUS: I know not what way you mean.

HYLAS: I mean the way of accounting for our sensations or ideas.

PHILONOUS: How is that?

HYLAS: It is supposed the soul makes her residence in some part of the brain, from which the nerves take their rise, and are thence extended to all parts of the body; and that outward objects, by the different impressions they make on the organs of sense, communicate certain vibrative motions to the nerves; and these being filled with spirits propagate them to the brain or seat of the soul, which, according to the various impressions or traces thereby made in the brain, is variously affected with ideas.

PHILONOUS: And call you this an explication of the manner whereby we are affected with ideas?

HYLAS: Why not, Philonous? Have you anything to object against it?

PHILONOUS: I would first know whether I rightly understand your hypothesis. You make certain traces in the brain to be the causes or occasions of our ideas. Pray tell me whether by the brain you mean any sensible thing.

HYLAS: What else think you I could mean?

PHILONOUS: Sensible things are all immediately perceivable; and those things which are immediately perceivable are ideas; and these exist only in the mind. Thus much you have, if I mistake not, long since agreed to.

HYLAS: I do not deny it.

PHILONOUS: The brain therefore you speak of, being a sensible thing, exists only in the mind. Now, I would fain know whether you think it reasonable to suppose that one idea or thing existing in the mind occasions all other ideas. And, if you think so, pray how do you account for the origin of that primary idea or brain itself?

HYLAS: I do not explain the origin of our ideas by that brain which is perceivable to sense—this being itself only a combination of sensible ideas—but by another which I imagine.

PHILONOUS: But are not things imagined as truly *in the mind as* things perceived?

HYLAS: I must confess they are.

PHILONOUS: It comes therefore, to the same thing; and you have been all this while accounting for ideas by certain motions or impressions of the brain; that is, by some alterations in an idea, whether sensible or imaginable it matters not.

HYLAS: I begin to suspect my hypothesis.

PHILONOUS: Besides spirits, all that we know or conceive are our own ideas. When, therefore, you say all ideas are occasioned by impressions in the brain, do you conceive this brain or no? If you do, then you talk of ideas imprinted in an idea causing that same idea, which is absurd. If you do not conceive it, you talk unintelligibly, instead of forming a reasonable hypothesis.

HYLAS: I now clearly see it was a mere dream. There is nothing in it.

PHILONOUS: You need not be much concerned at it; for after all, this way of explaining things, as you called it, could never have satisfied any reasonable man. What connexion is there between a motion in the nerves, and the sensations of sound or colour in the mind? Or how is it possible these should be the effect of that?

HYLAS: But I could never think it had so little in it as now it seems to have.

PHILONOUS: Well then, are you at length satisfied that no sensible things have a real existence; and that you are in truth an arrant *sceptic?*

HYLAS: It is too plain to be denied.

PHILONOUS: Look! Are not the fields covered with a delightful verdure? Is there not something in the woods and groves, in the rivers and clear springs, that soothes, that delights, that transports the soul? At the prospect of the wide and deep ocean, or some huge mountain whose top is lost in the clouds, or of an old gloomy forest, are not our minds filled with a pleasing horror? Even in rocks and deserts is there not an agreeable wildness? How sincere a pleasure is it to behold the natural beauties of the earth! To preserve and renew our relish for them, is not the veil of night alternately drawn over her face, and does she not change her dress with the seasons? How aptly are the elements disposed! What variety and use in the meanest productions of nature! What delicacy, what beauty, what contrivance, in animal and vegetable bodies! How exquisitely are all things suited, as well to their particular ends, as to constitute opposite parts of the whole! And, while they mutually aid and support, do they not also set off and illustrate each other? Raise now your thoughts from this ball of earth to all those glorious luminaries that adorn the high arch of heaven. The motion and situation of the planets, are they not admirable for use and order? Were those (miscalled *erratic*) globes once known to stray, in their repeated journeys through the pathless void? Do they not measure areas round the sun ever proportioned to the times? So fixed, so immutable are the laws by which the unseen author of nature actuates the universe. How vivid and radiant is the lustre of the fixed stars! How magnificent and rich that negligent profusion with which they appear to be scattered throughout the whole azure vault! Yet, if you take the telescope, it brings into your sight a new host of stars that escape the naked eye. Here they seem contiguous and minute, but to a nearer view immense orbs of light at various distances, far sunk in the abyss of space. Now you must call imagination to your aid. The feeble narrow sense cannot descry innumerable worlds revolving round the central fires and in those worlds the energy of an all-perfect mind displayed in endless forms. But, neither sense nor imagination are big enough to comprehend the boundless extent, with all its glittering furniture. Though the labouring mind exert and strain each power to its utmost reach, there still stands out ungrasped a surplusage immeasurable. Yet all the vast bodies that compose this mighty frame, how distant and remote soever, are by some secret mechanism, some divine art and force, linked in a mutual dependence and intercourse with each other; even with this earth, which was almost slipt from my thoughts and lost in the crowd of worlds. Is not the whole system immense, beautiful, glorious beyond expression and beyond thought! What treatment, then, do those philosophers deserve, who would deprive these noble and delightful scenes of all reality? How should those principles be entertained that lead us to think all the visible beauty of the creation a false imaginary glare? To be plain, can you expect this scepticism of yours will not be thought extravagantly absurd by all men of sense?

HYLAS: Other men may think as they please; but for your part you have nothing to reproach me with. My comfort is, you are as much a *sceptic* as I am.

318

PHILONOUS: There, Hylas, I must beg leave to differ from you.

HYLAS: What! Have you all along agreed to the premises, and do you now deny the conclusion, and leave me to maintain those paradoxes by myself which you led me into? This surely is not fair.

PHILONOUS: I deny that I agreed with you in those notions that led to scepticism. You indeed said the *reality* of sensible things consisted in an *absolute existence* out of the minds of spirits, or distinct from their being perceived. And pursuant to this notion of reality, you are obliged to deny sensible things any real existence: that is, according to your own definition, you profess yourself a *sceptic*. But I neither said nor thought the reality of sensible things was to be defined after that manner. To me it is evident for the reasons you allow of, that sensible things cannot exist otherwise than in a mind or spirit. Whence I conclude, not that they have no real existence, but that, seeing they depend not on my thought, and have an existence distinct from being perceived by me, *there must be some other mind wherein they exist.* As sure, therefore, as the sensible world really exists, so sure is there an infinite omnipresent spirit who contains and supports it.

HYLAS: What! This is no more than I and all Christians hold; nay, and all others too who believe there is a God, and that he knows and comprehends all things.

PHILONOUS: Aye, but here lies the difference. Men commonly believe that all things are known or perceived by God, because they believe the being of a God; whereas I, on the other side, immediately and necessarily conclude the being of a God, because all sensible things must be perceived by him.

HYLAS: But, so long as we all believe the same thing, what matter is it how we come by that belief?

PHILONOUS: But neither do we agree in the same opinion. For philosophers, though they acknowledge all corporeal beings to be perceived by God, yet they attribute to them an absolute subsistence distinct from their being perceived by any mind whatever; which I do not. Besides, is there no difference between saying, *There is a God, therefore he perceives all things;* and saying, *Sensible things do really exist; and, if they really exist, they are necessarily perceived by an infinite mind: therefore there is an infinite mind or God?* This furnishes you with a direct and immediate demonstration, from a most evident principle, of the *being of a God.* Divines and philosophers had proved beyond all controversy, from the beauty and usefulness of the several parts of the creation, that it was the workmanship of God. But that—setting aside all help of astronomy and natural philosophy, all contemplation of the contrivance, order, and adjustment of things—an infinite mind should be necessarily inferred from the bare *existence* of the sensible world, is an advantage to them only who have made this easy reflexion: that the sensible world is that which we perceive by our several senses; and that nothing is perceived by the senses beside ideas; and that no idea or archetype of an idea can exist otherwise than in a mind. You may now, without any laborious search into the sciences, without any subtlety of reason, or tedious length of discourse, oppose and baffle the most strenuous advocate for Atheism. Those miserable refuges, whether in an eternal succession of unthinking causes and effects, or in a fortuitous concourse of atoms; those wild imaginations of Vanini, Hobbes, and Spinoza: in a word, the whole system of Atheism, is it not entirely overthrown, by this single reflexion on the repugnancy included in supposing the whole, or any part, even the most rude and shapeless, of the visible world, to exist without a mind? Let any one of those abettors of impiety but look into his own thoughts, and there try if he can conceive how so much as a rock, a desert, a chaos, or confused jumble of atoms; how anything at all, either sensible or imaginable, can exist independent of a mind, and he need go no farther to be convinced of his folly. Can anything be fairer than to put a dispute on such an issue, and leave it to a man himself to see if he can conceive, even in thought, what he holds to be true in fact, and from a notional to allow it a real existence?

HYLAS: It cannot be denied there is something highly serviceable to religion in what you advance. But do you not think it looks very like a notion entertained by some eminent moderns, of *seeing all things in God?*

PHILONOUS: I would gladly know that opinion: pray explain it to me.

HYLAS: They conceive that the soul, being immaterial, is incapable of being united with material things, so as to perceive them in themselves; but that she perceives them by her union with the substance of God, which, being spiritual, is therefore purely intelligible, or capable of being the immediate object of a spirit's thought. Besides the divine essence contains in it perfections correspondent to each created being; and which are, for that reason, proper to exhibit or represent them to the mind.

PHILONOUS: I do not understand how our ideas, which are things altogether passive and inert, can be the essence, or any part (or like any part) of the essence or substance of God, who is an impassive, indivisible, pure, active being. Many more difficulties and objections there are which occur at first view against this hypothesis; but I shall only add that it is liable to all the absurdities of the common hypothesis, in making a created world exist otherwise than in the mind of a spirit. Besides all which it hath this peculiar to itself; that it makes that material world serve to no purpose. And, if it pass for a good argument against other hypotheses in the sciences, that they suppose nature, or the divine wisdom, to make something in vain, or do that by tedious roundabout methods which might have been performed in a much more easy and compendious way, what shall we think of that hypothesis which supposes the whole world made in vain?

HYLAS: But what say you? Are not you too of opinion that we see all things in God? If I mistake not, what you advance comes near it.

PHILONOUS: Few men think; yet all have opinions. Hence men's opinions are superficial and confused. It is nothing strange that tenets which in themselves are ever so different, should nevertheless be confounded with each other, by those who do not consider them attentively. I shall not therefore be surprised if some men imagine that I run into the enthusiasm of Malebranche; though in truth I am very remote from it. He builds on the most abstract general ideas, which I entirely disclaim. He asserts an absolute external world, which I deny. He maintains that we are deceived by our senses, and know not the real natures or the true forms and figures of extended beings; of all which I hold the direct contrary. So that upon the whole there are no principles more fundamentally opposite than his and mine. It must be owned that I entirely agree with what the holy Scripture says, "That in God we live and move and have our being" [Acts 17:28]. But that we see things in His essence, after the manner above set forth, I am far from believing. Take here in brief my meaning:—It is evident that the things I perceive are my own ideas, and that no idea can exist unless it be in a mind: nor is it less plain that these ideas or things by me perceived, either themselves or their archetypes, exist independently of my mind, since I know myself not to be their author, it being out of my power to determine at pleasure what particular ideas I shall be affected with upon opening my eyes or ears: they must therefore exist in some other mind, whose will it is they should be exhibited to me. The things, I say, immediately perceived are ideas or sensations, call them which you will. But how can any idea or sensation exist in, or be produced by, anything but a mind or spirit? This indeed is inconceivable. And to assert that which is inconceivable is to talk nonsense: is it not?

HYLAS: Without doubt.

PHILONOUS: But, on the other hand, it is very conceivable that they should exist in and be produced by a spirit; since this is no more than I daily experience in myself, inasmuch as I perceive numberless ideas; and, by an act of my will, can form a great variety of them, and raise them up in my imagination: though, it must be confessed, these creatures of the fancy are not altogether so distinct, so strong, vivid, and permanent, as those perceived by my senses—which latter are called *real things*. From all which I conclude, *there is a mind which affects me every moment with all the sensible impressions I perceive.* And, from the variety, order, and manner of these, I conclude the author of them to be *wise, powerful, and good, beyond comprehension.* Mark it well; I do not say, I see things by perceiving that which represents them in the intelligible substance of God. This I do not understand; but I say, the things by me perceived are known by the understanding, and produced by the will of an infinite spirit. And is not all this most plain and evident? Is there any more in it than what a little observation in our own minds, and that which passes in them, not only enables us to conceive, but also obliges us to acknowledge.

HYLAS: I think I understand you very clearly; and own the proof you give of a deity seems no less evident than it is surprising. But, allowing that God is the supreme and universal cause of all things, yet, may there not be still a third nature besides spirits and ideas? May we not admit a subordinate and limited cause of our ideas? In a word, may there not for all that be *matter?*

PHILONOUS: How often must I inculcate the same thing? You allow the things immediately perceived by sense to exist nowhere without the mind; but there is nothing perceived by sense which is not perceived immediately: therefore there is nothing sensible that exists without the mind. The matter, therefore, which you still insist on is something intelligible, I suppose; something that may be discovered by reason, and not by sense.

HYLAS: You are in the right.

PHILONOUS: Pray let me know what reasoning your belief of matter is grounded on; and what this matter is, in your present sense of it.

HYLAS: I find myself affected with various ideas, whereof I know I am not the cause; neither are they the cause of themselves, or of one another, or capable of subsisting by themselves, as being altogether inactive, fleeting, dependent beings. They have therefore some cause distinct from me and them: of which I pretend to know no more than that it is *the cause of my ideas.* And this thing, whatever it be, I call matter.

PHILONOUS: Tell me, Hylas, hath every one a liberty to change the current proper signification attached to a common name in any language? For example, suppose a traveler should tell you that in a certain country men pass unhurt through the fire; and, upon explaining himself, you found he meant by the word *fire* that which others call *water.* Or, if he should assert that there are trees that walk upon two legs, meaning men by the term *trees.* Would you think this reasonable?

HYLAS: No; I should think it very absurd. Common custom is the standard of propriety in language. And for any man to affect speaking improperly is to pervert the use of speech, and can never serve to a better purpose than to protract and multiply disputes where there is no difference in opinion.

PHILONOUS: And does not *matter,* in the common current acceptation of the word, signify an extended, solid, moveable, unthinking, inactive substance?

HYLAS: It does.

PHILONOUS: And, has it not been made evident that no such substance can possibly exist? And, though it should be allowed to exist, yet how can that which is *inactive* be a cause; or that which is *unthinking* be a *cause of thought?* You may, indeed, if you please, annex to the word *matter* a contrary meaning to what is vulgarly received; and tell me you understand by it, an unextended, thinking, active being, which is the cause of our ideas. But what else is this than to play with words, and run into that very fault you just now condemned with so much reason? I do by no means find fault with your reasoning, in that you collect a cause from the *phenomena:* but I deny that the cause deducible by reason can properly be termed matter.

HYLAS: There is indeed something in what you say. But I am afraid you do not thoroughly comprehend my meaning. I would by no means be thought to deny that God, or an infinite spirit, is the supreme cause of all things. All I contend for is, that, subordinate to the supreme agent, there is a cause of a limited and inferior nature, which concurs in the production of our ideas, not by any act of will, or spiritual efficiency, but by that kind of action which belongs to matter, *viz.* motion.

PHILONOUS: I find you are at every turn relapsing into your old exploded conceit, of a moveable, and consequently an extended, substance, existing without the mind. What! Have you already forgotten you were convinced; or are you willing I should repeat what has been said on that head? In truth this is not fair dealing in you, still to suppose the being of that which you have so often acknowledged to have no being. But, not to insist farther on what has been so largely handled, I ask whether all your ideas are not perfectly passive and inert, including nothing of action in them.

HYLAS: They are.

PHILONOUS: And are sensible qualities anything else but ideas?

HYLAS: How often have I acknowledged that they are not.

PHILONOUS: But is not motion a sensible quality?

HYLAS: It is.

PHILONOUS: Consequently it is no action?

HYLAS: I agree with you. And indeed it is very plain that when I stir my finger, it remains passive; but my will which produced the motion is active.

PHILONOUS: Now, I desire to know, in the first place, whether motion being allowed to be no action, you can conceive any action besides volition: and, in the second place, whether to say something and conceive nothing be not to talk nonsense: and, lastly, whether, having considered the premises, you do not perceive that to suppose any efficient or active cause of our ideas, other than *spirit,* is highly absurd and unreasonable?

HYLAS: I give up the point entirely. But, though matter may not be a cause, yet what hinders its being an *instrument,* subservient to the supreme agent in the production of our ideas?

PHILONOUS: An instrument say you; pray what may be the figure, springs, wheels, and motions, of that instrument?

HYLAS: Those I pretend to determine nothing of, both the substance and its qualities being entirely unknown to me.

PHILONOUS: What? You are then of opinion it is made up of unknown parts, that it hath unknown motions, and an unknown shape?

HYLAS: I do not believe that it hath any figure or motion at all, being already convinced, that no sensible qualities can exist in an unperceiving substance.

PHILONOUS: But what notion is it possible to frame of an instrument void of all sensible qualities, even extension itself?

HYLAS: I do not pretend to have any notion of it.

PHILONOUS: And what reason have you to think this unknown, this inconceivable somewhat does exist? Is it that you imagine God cannot act as well without it; or that you find by experience the use of some such thing, when you form ideas in your own mind?

322

HYLAS: You are always teasing me for reasons of my belief. Pray what reasons have you not to believe it?

PHILONOUS: It is to me a sufficient reason not to believe the existence of anything, if I see no reason for believing it. But, not to insist on reasons for believing, you will not so much as let me know what it is you would have me believe; since you say you have no manner of notion of it. After all, let me entreat you to consider whether it be like a philosopher, or even like a man of common sense, to pretend to believe you know not what, and you know not why.

HYLAS: Hold, Philonous. When I tell you matter is an *instrument,* I do not mean altogether nothing. It is true I know not the particular kind of instrument; but, however, I have some notion of *instrument in general,* which I apply to it.

PHILONOUS: But what if it should prove that there is something, even in the most general notion of *instrument,* as taken in a distinct sense from *cause,* which makes the use of it inconsistent with the divine attributes?

HYLAS: Make that appear and I shall give up the point.

PHILONOUS: What mean you by the general nature or notion of instrument?

HYLAS: That which is common to all particular instruments composes the general notion.

PHILONOUS: Is it not common to all instruments, that they are applied to the doing those things only which cannot be performed by the mere act of our wills? Thus, for instance, I never use an instrument to move my finger, because it is done by a volition. But I should use one if I were to remove part of a rock, or tear up a tree by the roots. Are you of the same mind? Or, can you show any example where an instrument is made use of in producing an effect immediately depending on the will of the agent?

HYLAS: I own I cannot.

PHILONOUS: How therefore can you suppose that an all-perfect spirit, on whose will all things have an absolute and immediate dependence, should need an instrument in his operations, or, not needing it, make use of it? Thus it seems to me that you are obliged to own the use of a lifeless inactive instrument to be incompatible with the infinite perfection of God; that is, by your own confession, to give up the point.

HYLAS: It does not readily occur what I can answer you.

PHILONOUS: But, methinks you should be ready to own the truth, when it has been fairly proved to you. We indeed, who are beings of finite powers, are forced to make use of instruments. And the use of an instrument shows the agent to be limited by rules of another's prescription, and that he cannot obtain his end but in such a way, and by such conditions. Whence it seems a clear consequence, that the supreme unlimited agent uses no tool or instrument at all. The will of an omnipotent spirit is no sooner exerted than executed, without the application of means; which, if they are employed by inferior agents, it is not upon account of any real efficacy that is in them, or necessary aptitude to produce any effect, but merely in compliance with the laws of nature, or those conditions prescribed to them by the first cause, who is himself above all limitation or prescription whatsoever.

HYLAS: I will no longer maintain that matter is an instrument. However, I would not be understood to give up its existence neither; since, notwithstanding what hath been said, it may still be an *occasion.*

PHILONOUS: How many shapes is your matter to take? Or, how often must it be proved not to exist, before you are content to part with it? But, to say no more of this (though by all the laws of disputation I may justly blame you for so frequently changing the signification of the principal term)—I would fain know what you mean by affirming that matter is an occasion, having already denied it to be a cause. And, when you have shown in what sense you understand *occasion,* pray, in the next place be pleased to show me what reason induces you to believe there is such an occasion of our ideas?

HYLAS: As to the first point: by *occasion* I mean an inactive unthinking being, at the presence whereof God excites ideas in our minds.

PHILONOUS: And what may be the nature of that inactive unthinking being?

HYLAS: I know nothing of its nature.

PHILONOUS: Proceed then to the second point, and assign some reason why we should allow an existence to this inactive, unthinking, unknown thing.

HYLAS: When we see ideas produced in our minds, after an orderly and constant manner, it is natural to think they have some fixed and regular occasions, at the presence of which they are excited.

PHILONOUS: You acknowledge then God alone to be the cause of our ideas, and that he causes them at the presence of those occasions.

HYLAS: That is my opinion.

PHILONOUS: Those things which you say are present to God, without doubt he perceives.

HYLAS: Certainly; otherwise they could not be to him an occasion of acting.

PHILONOUS: Not to insist now on your making sense of this hypothesis, or answering all the puzzling questions and difficulties it is liable to: I only ask whether the order and regularity observable in the series of our ideas, or the course of nature, be not sufficiently accounted for by the wisdom and power of God; and whether it does not derogate from those attributes, to suppose he is influenced, directed, or put in mind, when and what he is to act, by an unthinking substance? And, lastly, whether, in case I granted all you contend for, it would make anything to your purpose; it not being easy to conceive how the external or absolute existence of an unthinking substance, distinct from its being perceived, can be inferred from my allowing that there are certain things perceived by the mind of God, which are to him the occasion of producing ideas in us?

HYLAS: I am perfectly at a loss what to think, this notion of occasion seeming now altogether as groundless as the rest.

PHILONOUS: Do you not at length perceive that in all these different acceptations of *matter,* you have been only supposing you know not what, for no manner of reason, and to no kind of use?

HYLAS: I freely own myself less fond of my notions since they have been so accurately examined. But still, methinks, I have some confused perception that there is such a thing as *matter.*

PHILONOUS: Either you perceive the being of matter immediately or mediately. If immediately, pray inform me by which of the senses you perceive it. If mediately, let me know by what reasoning it is inferred from those things which you perceive immediately. So much for the perception. Then for the matter itself, I ask whether it is object, *substratum,* cause, instrument, or occasion? You have already pleaded for each of these, shifting your notions, and making matter to appear sometimes in one shape, then in another. And what you have offered hath been disapproved and rejected by yourself. If you have anything new to advance I would gladly hear it.

HYLAS: I think I have already offered all I had to say on those heads. I am at a loss what more to urge.

PHILONOUS: And yet you are loath to part with your old prejudice. But, to make you quit it more easily, I desire that, beside what has been hitherto suggested, you will farther consider whether, upon supposition that matter exists, you can possibly conceive how you should be affected by it. Or, supposing it did not exist, whether it be not evident you might for all that be affected with the same ideas you now are, and consequently have the very same reasons to believe its existence that you now can have.

HYLAS: I acknowledge it is possible we might perceive all things just as we do now, though there was no matter in the world; neither can I conceive, if there be matter, how it should produce any idea in our minds. And, I do farther grant you have entirely satisfied me that it is impossible there should be such a thing as matter in any of the foregoing acceptations. But still I cannot help supposing that there is *matter* in some sense or other. What that is I do not indeed pretend to determine.

PHILONOUS: I do not expect you should define exactly the nature of that unknown being. Only be pleased to tell me whether it is a substance; and if so, whether you can suppose a substance without accidents; or, in case you suppose it to have accidents or qualities, I desire you will let me know what those qualities are, at least what is meant by matter's supporting them?

HYLAS: We have already argued on those points. I have no more to say to them. But, to prevent any farther questions, let me tell you I at present understand by *matter* neither substance nor accident, thinking nor extended being, neither cause, instrument, nor occasion, but something entirely unknown, distinct from all these.

PHILONOUS: It seems then you include in your present notion of matter nothing but the general abstract idea of *entity.*

HYLAS: Nothing else; save only that I superadd to this general idea the negation of all those particular things, qualities, or ideas, that I perceive, imagine, or in anywise apprehend.

PHILONOUS: Pray where do you suppose this unknown matter to exist?

HYLAS: Oh Philonous! Now you think you have entangled me, for, if I say it exists in place, then you will infer that it exists in the mind, since it is agreed that place or extension exists only in the mind. But I am not ashamed to own my ignorance. I know not where it exists; only I am sure it exists not in place. There is a negative answer for you. And you must expect no other to all the questions you put for the future about matter.

PHILONOUS: Since you will not tell me where it exists, be pleased to inform me after what manner you suppose it to exist, or what you mean by its *existence?*

HYLAS: It neither thinks nor acts, neither perceives nor is perceived.

PHILONOUS: But what is there positive in your abstracted notion of its existence?

HYLAS: Upon a nice observation, I do not find I have any positive notion or meaning at all. I tell you again, I am not ashamed to own my ignorance. I know not what is meant by its *existence,* or how it exists.

PHILONOUS: Continue, good Hylas, to act the same ingenuous part, and tell me sincerely whether you can frame a distinct idea of Entity in general, prescinded from and exclusive of all thinking and corporeal beings, all particular things whatsoever.

HYLAS: Hold, let me think a little—I profess, Philonous I do not find that I can. At first glance, methought I had some dilute and airy notion of pure entity in abstract; but, upon closer attention, it hath quite vanished out of sight. The more I think on it, the more am I confirmed in my prudent resolution of giving none but negative answers, and not pretending to the least degree of any positive knowledge or conception of matter, its *where,* its *how,* its *entity,* or anything belonging to it.

PHILONOUS: When, therefore, you speak of the existence of matter, you have not any notion in your mind?

HYLAS: None at all.

PHILONOUS: Pray tell me if the case stands not thus: At first, from a belief of material substance, you would have it that the immediate objects existed without the mind;

then that they are archetypes; then causes; next instruments; then occasions: lastly *something in general,* which being interpreted proves *nothing.* So matter comes to nothing. What think you, Hylas, is not this a fair summary of your whole proceeding?

HYLAS: Be that as it will, yet I still insist upon it, that our not being able to conceive a thing is no argument against its existence.

PHILONOUS: That from a cause, effect, operation, sign, or other circumstance, there may reasonably be inferred the existence of a thing not immediately perceived; and that it were absurd for any man to argue against the existence of that thing, from his having no direct and positive notion of it, I freely own. But, where there is nothing of all this; where neither reason nor revelation induces us to believe the existence of a thing; where we have not even a relative notion of it; where an abstraction is made from perceiving and being perceived, from spirit and idea: lastly, where there is not so much as the most inadequate or faint idea pretended to—I will not indeed thence conclude against the reality of any notion, or existence of anything; but my inference shall be, that you mean nothing at all; that you employ words to no manner of purpose, without any design or signification whatsoever. And I leave it to you to consider how mere jargon should be treated.

HYLAS: To deal frankly with you, Philonous, your arguments seem in themselves unanswerable; but they have not so great an effect on me as to produce that entire conviction, that hearty acquiescence, which attends demonstration. I find myself relapsing into an obscure surmise of I know not what, *matter.*

PHILONOUS: But, are you not sensible, Hylas, that two things must concur to take away all scruple, and work a plenary assent in the mind? Let a visible object be set in never so clear a light, yet, if there is any imperfection in the sight, or if the eye is not directed towards it, it will not be distinctly seen. And though a demonstration be never so well grounded and fairly proposed, yet, if there is withal a stain of prejudice, or a wrong bias on the understanding, can it be expected on a sudden to perceive clearly, and adhere firmly to the truth? No; there is need of time and pains: the attention must be awakened and detained by a frequent repetition of the same thing placed oft in the same, oft in different lights. I have said it already, and find I must still repeat and inculcate, that it is an unaccountable licence you take, in pretending to maintain you know not what, for you know not what reason, to you know not what purpose. Can this be paralleled in any art or science, any sect or profession of men? Or is there anything so barefacedly groundless and unreasonable to be met with even in the lowest of common conversation? But, perhaps you will still say, matter may exist; though at the same time you neither know what is meant by *matter,* or by its *existence.* This indeed is surprising, and the more so because it is altogether voluntary, you not being led to it by any one reason; for I challenge you to show me that thing in nature which needs matter to explain or account for it.

HYLAS: The reality of things cannot be maintained without supposing the existence of matter. And is not this, think you, a good reason why I should be earnest in its defence?

PHILONOUS: The reality of things! What things, sensible or intelligible?

HYLAS: Sensible things.

PHILONOUS: My glove for example?

HYLAS: That, or any other thing perceived by the senses.

PHILONOUS: But to fix on some particular thing. Is it not a sufficient evidence to me of the existence of this *glove,* that I see it, and feel it, and wear it? Or, if this will not do, how is it possible I should be assured of the reality of this thing, which I actually see in this place, by supposing that some unknown thing, which I never did or can see, exists after an unknown manner, in an unknown place, or in no place at all? How can the supposed reality of that which is intangible be a proof that anything tangible really exists? Or, of that which is invisible, that any visible thing, or, in general of anything which is imperceptible, that a perceptible exists? Do but explain this and I shall think nothing too hard for you.

HYLAS: Upon the whole, I am content to own the existence of matter is highly improbable, but the direct and absolute impossibility of it does not appear to me.

PHILONOUS: But granting matter to be possible, yet, upon that account merely, it can have no more claim to existence than a golden mountain, or a centaur.

HYLAS: I acknowledge it; but still you do not deny it is possible; and that which is possible, for aught you know, may actually exist.

PHILONOUS: I deny it to be possible; and have, if I mistake not, evidently proved, from your own concessions, that it is not. In the common sense of the word *matter,* is there any more implied than an extended, solid, figured, movable substance, existing without the mind? And have not you acknowledged, over and over, that you have seen evident reason for denying the possibility of such a substance?

HYLAS: True, but that is only one sense of the term matter.

PHILONOUS: But is it not the only proper genuine received sense? And, if matter, in such a sense, be proved impossible, may it not be thought with good grounds absolutely impossible? Else how could anything be proved impossible? Or, indeed, how could there be any proof at all one way or other, to a man who takes the liberty to unsettle and change the common signification of words?

HYLAS: I thought philosophers might be allowed to speak more accurately than the vulgar, and were not always confined to the common acceptation of a term.

PHILONOUS: But this now mentioned is the common received sense among philosophers themselves. But, not to insist on that, have you not been allowed to take matter in what sense you pleased? And have you not used this privilege in the utmost extent; sometimes entirely changing, at others leaving out, or putting into the definition of it whatever, for the present, best served your design, contrary to all the known rules of reason and logic? And hath not this shifting, unfair method of yours spun out our dispute to an unnecessary length; matter having been particularly examined, and by your own confession refuted in each of those senses? And can any more be required to prove the absolute impossibility of a thing, than the proving it impossible in every particular sense that either you or any one else understands it in?

HYLAS: But I am not so thoroughly satisfied that you have proved the impossibility of matter, in the last most obscure abstracted and indefinite sense.

PHILONOUS: When is a thing shown to be impossible?

HYLAS: When a repugnancy is demonstrated between the ideas comprehended in its definition

PHILONOUS: But where there are no ideas, there no repugnancy can be demonstrated between ideas?

HYLAS: I agree with you.

PHILONOUS: Now, in that which you call the obscure indefinite sense of the word matter, it is plain, by your own confession, there was included no idea at all, no sense except an unknown sense; which is the same thing as none. You are not, therefore, to expect I should prove a repugnancy between ideas, where there are no ideas; or the impossibility of matter taken in an *unknown* sense, that is, no sense at all. My business was only to show you meant *nothing;* and this you were brought to own. So that, in all your various senses, you have been showed either to mean nothing at all, or, if anything, an absurdity. And if this be not sufficient to prove the impossibility of a thing, I desire you will let me know what is.

HYLAS: I acknowledge you have proved that matter is impossible; nor do I see what more can be said in defence of it. But, at the same time that I give up this, I suspect all my other notions. For surely none could be more seemingly evident than this once was: and yet it now seems as false and absurd as ever it did true before. But I think we have discussed the point sufficiently for the present. The remaining part of the day I would willingly spend in running over in my thoughts the several heads of this morning's conversation, and tomorrow shall be glad to meet you here again about the same time.

PHILONOUS: I will not fail to attend you.

THE THIRD DIALOGUE

PHILONOUS: Tell me, Hylas, what are the fruits of yesterday's meditation? Has it confirmed you in the same mind you were in at parting? or have you since seen cause to change your opinion?

HYLAS: Truly my opinion is that all our opinions are alike vain and uncertain. What we approve today, we condemn tomorrow. We keep a stir about knowledge, and spend our lives in the pursuit of it, when, alas! we know nothing all the while: nor do I think it possible for us ever to know anything in this life. Our faculties are too narrow and too few. Nature certainly never intended us for speculation.

PHILONOUS: What! Say you we can know nothing, Hylas?

HYLAS: There is not that single thing in the world whereof we can know the real nature, or what it is in itself.

PHILONOUS: Will you tell me I do not really know what fire or water is?

HYLAS: You may indeed know that fire appears hot, and water fluid; but this is no more than knowing what sensations are produced in your own mind, upon the application of fire and water to your organs of sense. Their internal constitution, their true and real nature, you are utterly in the dark as to *that*.

PHILONOUS: Do I not know this to be a real stone that I stand on, and that which I see before my eyes to be a real tree?

HYLAS: Know? No, it is impossible you or any man alive should know it. All you know is, that you have such a certain idea or appearance in your own mind. But what is this to the real tree or stone? I tell you that colour, figure, and hardness, which you perceive, are not the real natures of those things, or in the least like them. The same may be said of all other real things, or corporeal substances, which compose the world. They have none of them anything of themselves, like those sensible qualities by us perceived. We should not therefore pretend to affirm or know anything of them, as they are in their own nature.

PHILONOUS: But surely, Hylas, I can distinguish gold, for example, from iron: and how could this be, if I knew not what either truly was?

HYLAS: Believe me, Philonous, you can only distinguish between your own ideas. That yellowness, that weight, and other sensible qualities, think you they are really in the gold? They are only relative to the senses, and have no absolute existence in nature. And in pretending to distinguish the species of real things, by the appearances in your mind, you may perhaps act as wisely as he that should conclude two men were of a different species, because their clothes were not of the same colour.

PHILONOUS: It seems, then, we are altogether put off with the appearances of things, and those false ones too. The very meat I eat, and the cloth I wear, have nothing in them like what I see and feel.

HYLAS: Even so.

PHILONOUS: But is it not strange the whole world should be thus imposed on, and so foolish as to believe their senses? And yet I know not how it is, but men eat, and drink, and sleep, and perform all the offices of life, as comfortably and conveniently as if they really knew the things they are conversant about.

HYLAS: They do so: but you know ordinary practice does not require a nicety of speculative knowledge. Hence the vulgar retain their mistakes, and for all that make a shift to bustle through the affairs of life. But philosophers know better things.

PHILONOUS: You mean, they know that they *know nothing.*

HYLAS: That is the very top and perfection of human knowledge.

PHILONOUS: But are you all this while in earnest, Hylas; and are you seriously persuaded that you know nothing real in the world? Suppose you are going to write, would you not call for pen, ink, and paper, like another man; and do you not know what it is you call for?

HYLAS: How often must I tell you, that I know not the real nature of any one thing in the universe? I may indeed upon occasion make use of pen, ink, and paper. But what any one of them is in its own true nature, I declare positively I know not. And the same is true with regard to every other corporeal thing. And, what is more, we are not only ignorant of the true and real nature of things, but even of their existence. It cannot be denied that we perceive such certain appearances or ideas; but it cannot be concluded from thence that bodies really exist. Nay, now I think on it, I must, agreeably to my former concessions, farther declare that it is impossible any real corporeal thing should exist in nature.

PHILONOUS: You amaze me. Was ever anything more wild and extravagant than the notions you now maintain: and is it not evident you are led into all these extravagances by the belief of *material substance?* This makes you dream of those unknown natures in everything. It is this occasions your distinguishing between the reality and sensible appearances of things. It is to this you are indebted for being ignorant of what everybody else knows perfectly well. Nor is this all: you are not only ignorant of the true nature of everything, but you know not whether anything really exists, or whether there are any true natures at all; forasmuch as you attribute to your material beings an absolute or external existence, wherein you suppose their reality consists. And, as you are forced in the end to acknowledge such an existence means either a direct repugnancy, or nothing at all, it follows that you are obliged to pull down your own hypothesis of material substance, and positively to deny the real existence of any part of the universe. And so you are plunged into the deepest and most deplorable *scepticism* that ever man was. Tell me, Hylas, is it not as I say?

HYLAS: I agree with you. *Material substance* was no more than an hypothesis; and a false and groundless one too. I will no longer spend my breath in defence of it. But whatever hypothesis you advance, or whatsoever scheme of things you introduce in its stead, I doubt not it will appear every whit as false: let me but be allowed to question you upon it. That is, suffer me to serve you in your own kind, and I warrant it shall conduct you through as many perplexities and contradictions, to the very same state of scepticism that I myself am in at present.

PHILONOUS: I assure you, Hylas, I do not pretend to frame any hypothesis at all. I am of a vulgar cast, simple enough to believe my senses, and leave things as I find them. To be plain, it is my opinion that the real things are those very things I see, and feel, and perceive by my senses. These I know; and, finding they answer all the necessities and purposes of life, have no reason to be solicitous about any other unknown beings. A piece of sensible bread, for instance, would stay my stomach better than ten thousand times as much of that insensible, unintelligible, real bread you speak of. It is likewise my opinion that colours and other sensible qualities are on the objects. I cannot for my life help thinking that snow is white, and fire hot. You indeed, who by *snow* and *fire* mean certain external, unperceived, unperceiving substances, are in the right to deny whiteness or heat to be affections inherent in them. But I, who understand by those words the things I see and feel, am obliged to think like other folks. And, as I am no sceptic with regard to the nature of things, so neither am I as to their existence. That a thing should be really perceived by my senses, and at the same time not really exist, is to me a plain contradiction; since I cannot prescind or abstract, even in thought, the existence of a sensible thing from its being perceived. Wood, stones, fire, water, flesh, iron, and the like things, which I name and discourse of, are things that I know. And I should not have known them but that I perceived them by my senses; and things perceived by the senses are immediately perceived; and things immediately perceived are ideas; and ideas cannot exist without the mind, their existence therefore consists in being perceived; when, therefore, they are actually perceived there can be no doubt of their existence. Away then with all that scepticism, all those ridiculous philosophical doubts. What a jest is it for a philosopher to question the existence of sensible things, till he hath it proved to him from the veracity of God; or to pretend our knowledge in this point falls short of intuition or demonstration! I might as well doubt of my own being, as of the being of those things I actually see and feel.

HYLAS: Not so fast, PHILONOUS: you say you cannot conceive how sensible things should exist without the mind. Do you not?

PHILONOUS: I do.

HYLAS: Supposing you were annihilated, cannot you conceive it possible that things perceivable by sense may still exist?

PHILONOUS: I can, but then it must be in another mind. When I deny sensible things an existence out of the mind, I do not mean my mind in particular, but all minds. Now, it is plain they have an existence exterior to my mind, since I find them by experience to be independent of it. There is therefore some other mind wherein they exist, during the intervals between the times of my perceiving them: as likewise they did before my birth, and would do after my supposed annihilation. And, as the same is true with regard to all other finite created spirits, it necessarily follows there is an *omnipresent eternal mind,* which knows and comprehends all things, and exhibits them to our view in such a manner, and according to such rules, as he himself hath ordained, and are by us termed the *laws of nature.*

HYLAS: Answer me, Philonous. Are all our ideas perfectly inert beings? Or have they any agency included in them?

PHILONOUS: They are altogether passive and inert.

HYLAS: And is not God an agent, a being purely active?

PHILONOUS: I acknowledge it.

HYLAS: No idea therefore can be like unto, or represent the nature of God?

PHILONOUS: It cannot.

HYLAS: Since therefore you have no idea of the mind of God, how can you conceive it possible that things should exist in His mind? Or, if you can conceive the mind of God, without having an idea of it, why may not I be allowed to conceive the existence of matter, notwithstanding I have no idea of it?

PHILONOUS: As to your first question: I own I have properly no idea, either of God or any other spirit; for these being active, cannot be represented by things perfectly inert, as our ideas are. I do nevertheless know that I, who am a spirit or thinking substance, exist as certainly as I know my ideas exist. Farther, I know what I mean by the terms *I* and *myself;* and I know this immediately or intuitively, though I do not perceive it as I perceive a triangle, a colour, or a sound. The mind, spirit, or soul is that indivisible unextended thing which thinks, acts, and perceives. I say *indivisible,* because *unextended;* and unextended, because extended, figured, movable things are ideas; and that which perceives ideas, which thinks and wills, is plainly itself no idea, nor like an idea. Ideas are things inactive, and perceived. And spirits a sort of beings altogether different from them. I do not therefore say my soul is an idea, or like an idea. However, taking the word *idea* in a large sense, my soul may be said to furnish me with an idea, that is, an image or likeness of God—though indeed extremely inadequate. For, all the notion I have of God is obtained by reflecting on my own soul, heightening its powers, and removing its imperfections. I have, therefore, though not an inactive idea, yet in *myself* some sort of an active thinking image of the Deity. And, though I perceive him not by sense, yet I have a notion of him, or know him by reflexion and reasoning. My own mind and my own ideas I have an immediate knowledge of; and, by the help of these, do mediately apprehend the possibility of the existence of other spirits and ideas. Farther, from my own being, and from the dependency I find in myself and my ideas, I do, by an act of reason, necessarily infer the existence of a God, and of all created things in the mind of God. So much for your first question. For the second: I suppose by this time you can answer it yourself. For you neither perceive matter objectively, as you do an inactive being or idea; nor know it, as you do yourself, by a reflex act, neither do you mediately apprehend it by similitude of the one or the other; nor yet collect it by reasoning from that which you know immediately. All which makes the case of *matter* widely different from that of the *Deity.*

HYLAS: You say your own soul supplies you with some sort of an idea or image of God. But, at the same time, you acknowledge you have, properly speaking, no idea of your own soul. You even affirm that spirits are a sort of beings altogether different from ideas. Consequently that no idea can be like a spirit. We have therefore no idea of any spirit. You admit nevertheless that there is spiritual substance, although you have no idea of it; while you deny there can be such a thing as material substance, because you have no notion or idea of it. Is this fair dealing? To act consistently, you must either admit matter or reject spirit. What say you to this?

PHILONOUS: I say, in the first place, that I do not deny the existence of material substance, merely because I have no notion of it, but because the notion of it is inconsistent; or, in other words, because it is repugnant that there should be a notion of it. Many things, for aught I know, may exist, whereof neither I nor any other man hath or can have any idea or notion whatsoever. But then those things must be possible, that is, nothing inconsistent must be included in their definition. I say, secondly, that, although we believe things to exist which we do not perceive, yet we may not believe that any particular thing exists, without some reason for such belief: but I have no reason for believing the existence of matter. I have no immediate intuition thereof: neither can I immediately from my sensations, ideas, notions, actions, or passions, infer an unthinking, unperceiving, inactive substance—either by probable deduction, or necessary consequence. Whereas the being of my Self, that is, my own soul, mind, or thinking principle, I evidently know by reflexion. You will forgive me if I repeat the same things in answer to the same objections. In the very notion or definition of *material substance,* there is included a manifest repugnance and inconsistency. But this cannot be said of the notion of spirit. That ideas should exist in what does not perceive or be produced by what does not act, is repugnant. But, it is no repugnancy to say that a perceiving thing should be the subject of ideas, or an active thing the cause of them. It is granted we have neither an immediate evidence nor a demonstrative knowledge of the existence of other finite spirits; but it will not thence follow that such spirits are on a foot with material substances: if to suppose the one be inconsistent, and it be not inconsistent to suppose the other; if the one can be inferred by no argument, and there is a probability for the other; if we see signs and effects indicating distinct finite agents like ourselves, and see no sign or symptom whatever that leads to a rational belief of matter. I say, lastly, that I have a notion of spirit, though I have not, strictly speaking, an idea of it. I do not perceive it as an idea, or by means of an idea, but know it by reflexion.

HYLAS: Notwithstanding all you have said, to me it seems that, according to your own way of thinking, and in consequence of your own principles, it should follow that you are only a system of floating ideas, without any substance to support them. Words are not to be used without a meaning. And, as there is no more meaning in *spiritual substance* than in *material substance,* the one is to be exploded as well as the other.

PHILONOUS: How often must I repeat, that I know or am conscious of my own being; and that *I myself* am not my ideas, but somewhat else, a thinking, active principle that perceives, knows, wills, and operates about ideas I know that I, one and the same self, perceive both colours and sounds: that a colour cannot perceive a sound, nor a sound a colour: that I am therefore one individual principle, distinct from colour and sound, and, for the same reason, from all other sensible things and inert ideas. But, I am not in like manner conscious either of the existence or essence of matter. On the contrary, I know that nothing inconsistent can exist, and that the existence of matter implies an inconsistency. Farther, I know what I mean when I affirm that there is a spiritual substance or support of ideas, that is, that a spirit knows and perceives ideas. But, I do not know what is meant when it is said that an unperceiving substance hath inherent in it and supports either ideas or the archetypes of ideas. There is therefore upon the whole no parity of case between spirit and matter.

HYLAS: I own myself satisfied in this point. But, do you in earnest think the real existence of sensible things consists in their being actually perceived? If so; how comes it that all mankind distinguish between them? Ask the first man you meet, and he shall tell you, *to be perceived* is one thing, and *to exist* is another.

PHILONOUS: I am content, Hylas, to appeal to the common sense of the world for the truth of my notion. Ask the gardener why he thinks yonder cherry-tree exists in the garden, and he shall tell you, because he sees and feels it; in a word, because he perceives it by his senses. Ask him why he thinks an orange-tree not to be there, and he shall tell you, because he does not perceive it. What he perceives by sense, that he terms a real being, and says it *is* or *exists;* but, that which is not perceivable, the same, he says, has no being.

HYLAS: Yes, Philonous, I grant the existence of a sensible thing consists in being perceivable, but not in being actually perceived.

PHILONOUS: And what is perceivable but an idea? And can an idea exist without being actually perceived? These are points long since agreed between us.

HYLAS: But, be your opinion never so true, yet surely you will not deny it is shocking, and contrary to the common sense of men. Ask the fellow whether yonder tree hath an existence out of his mind: what answer think you he would make?

PHILONOUS: The same that I should myself, to wit, that it does exist out of his mind. But then to a Christian it cannot surely be shocking to say, the real tree, existing without his mind, is truly known and comprehended by (that is *exists in*) the infinite mind of God. Probably he may not at first glance be aware of the direct and immediate proof there is of this; inasmuch as the very being of a tree, or any other sensible thing, implies a mind wherein it is. But the point itself he cannot deny. The question between the materialists and me is not, whether things have a real existence out of the mind of this or that person, but whether they have an absolute existence, distinct from being perceived by God, and exterior to all minds. This indeed some heathens and philosophers have affirmed, but whoever entertains notions of the Deity suitable to the Holy Scriptures will be of another opinion.

HYLAS: But, according to your notions, what difference is there between real things, and chimeras formed by the imagination, or the visions of a dream—since they are all equally in the mind?

PHILONOUS: The ideas formed by the imagination are faint and indistinct; they have, besides, an entire dependence on the will. But the ideas perceived by sense, that is, real things, are more vivid and clear; and, being imprinted on the mind by a spirit distinct from us, have not the like dependence on our will. There is therefore no danger of confounding these with the foregoing; and there is as little of confounding them with the visions of a dream, which are dim, irregular, and confused. And, though they should happen to be never so lively and natural, yet, by their not being connected, and of a piece with the preceding and subsequent transactions of our lives, they might easily be distinguished from realities. In short, by whatever method you distinguish *things* from *chimeras* on your scheme, the same, it is evident, will hold also upon mine. For, it must be, I presume, by some perceived difference; and I am not for depriving you of any one thing that you perceive.

HYLAS: But still, Philonous, you hold, there is nothing in the world but spirits and ideas. And this, you must needs acknowledge, sounds very oddly.

PHILONOUS: I own the word *idea,* not being commonly used for *thing,* sounds something out of the way. My reason for using it was, because a necessary relation to the mind is understood to be implied by that term; and it is now commonly used by philosophers to denote the immediate objects of the understanding. But, however oddly the proposition may sound in words, yet it includes nothing so very strange or shocking in its sense, which in effect amounts to no more than this, to wit, that there are only things perceiving, and things perceived; or that every unthinking being is necessarily, and from the very nature of its existence, perceived by some mind; if not by a finite created mind, yet certainly by the infinite mind of God, in whom "we live, and move, and have our being." Is this as strange as to say, the sensible qualities are not on the objects: or that we cannot be sure of the existence of things, or know any thing of their real natures—though we both see and feel them, and perceive them by all our senses?

HYLAS: And, in consequence of this, must we not think there are no such things as physical or corporeal causes; but that a spirit is the immediate cause of all the phenomena in nature? Can there be anything more extravagant than this?

PHILONOUS: Yes, it is infinitely more extravagant to say—a thing which is inert operates on the mind, and which is unperceiving is the cause of our perceptions, without any regard either to consistency, or the old known axiom: *Nothing can give to another that which it hath not itself.* Besides, that which to you, I know not for what reason, seems so extravagant is no more than the Holy Scriptures assert in a hundred places. In them God is represented as the sole and immediate author of all those effects which some heathens and philosophers are wont to ascribe to nature, matter, fate, or the like unthinking principle. This is so much the constant language of Scripture that it were needless to confirm it by citations.

HYLAS: You are not aware Philonous, that in making God the immediate author of all the motions in nature, you make him the author of murder, sacrilege, adultery, and the like heinous sins.

PHILONOUS: In answer to that, I observe, first, that the imputation of guilt is the same, whether a person commits an action with or without an instrument. In case therefore you suppose God to act by the mediation of an instrument or occasion, called *matter,* you as truly make him the author of sin as I, who think him the immediate agent in all those operations vulgarly ascribed to nature. I farther observe that sin or moral turpitude does not consist in the outward physical action or motion, but in the internal deviation of the will from the laws of reason and religion. This is plain, in that the killing an enemy in a battle, or putting a criminal legally to death, is not thought sinful; though the outward act be the very same with that in the case of murder. Since therefore, sin does not consist in the physical action, the making God an immediate cause of all such actions is not making him the author of sin. Lastly, I have nowhere said that God is the only agent who produces all the motions in bodies. It is true I have denied there are any other agents besides spirits, but this is very consistent with allowing to thinking rational beings, in the production of motions, the use of limited powers, ultimately indeed derived from God, but immediately under the direction of their own wills which is sufficient to entitle them to all the guilt of their actions.

HYLAS: But the denying matter, Philonous, or corporeal substance; there is the point. You can never persuade me that this is not repugnant to the universal sense of mankind. Were our dispute to be determined by most voices, I am confident you would give up the point, without gathering the votes.

PHILONOUS: I wish both our opinions were fairly stated and submitted to the judgment of men who had plain common sense, without the prejudices of a learned education. Let me be represented as one who trusts his senses, who thinks he knows the things he sees and feels, and entertains no doubts of their existence, and you fairly set forth with all your doubts, your paradoxes, and your scepticism about you, and I shall willingly acquiesce in the determination of any indifferent person. That there is no substance wherein ideas can exist beside spirit is to me evident. And that the objects immediately perceived are ideas, is on all hands agreed. And that sensible qualities are objects immediately perceived no one can deny. It is therefore evident there can be no *substratum* of those qualities but spirit; in which they exist, not by way of mode or property, but as a thing perceived in that which perceives it. I deny therefore that there is any unthinking *substratum* of the objects of sense, and in that acceptation that there is any material substance. But if by *material substance* is meant only sensible body— that which is seen and felt (and the unphilosophical part of the world, I dare say, mean no more)—then I am more certain of matter's existence than you or any other philosopher pretend to be. If there be anything which makes the generality of mankind averse from the notions I espouse: it is a misapprehension that I deny the reality of sensible things. But, as it is you who are guilty of that, and not I, it follows that in truth their aversion is against your notions and not mine. I do therefore assert that I am as certain as of my own being, that there are bodies or corporeal substances (meaning the things I perceive by my senses); and that, granting this, the bulk of mankind will take no thought about, nor think themselves at all concerned in the fate of those unknown natures, and philosophical quiddities, which some men are so fond of.

HYLAS: What say you to this? Since, according to you, men judge of the reality of things by their senses, how can a man be mistaken in thinking the moon a plain lucid surface, about a foot in diameter; or a square tower, seen at a distance, round; or an oar, with one end in the water, crooked?

PHILONOUS: He is not mistaken with regard to the ideas he actually perceives, but in the inference he makes from his present perceptions. Thus, in the case of the oar, what he immediately perceives by sight is certainly crooked; and so far he is in the right. But if he thence conclude that upon taking the oar out of the water he shall perceive the same crookedness; or that it would affect his touch as crooked things are wont to do: in that he is mistaken. In like manner, if he shall conclude from what he perceives in one station, that, in case he advances towards the moon or tower, he should still be affected with the like ideas, he is mistaken. But his mistake lies not in what he perceives immediately, and at present, (it being a manifest contradiction to suppose he should err in respect of that) but in the wrong judgment he makes concerning the ideas he apprehends to be connected with those immediately perceived: or, concerning the ideas that, from what he perceives at present, he imagines would be perceived in other circumstances. The case is the same with regard to the Copernican system. We do not here perceive any motion of the earth: but it were erroneous thence to conclude, that, in case we were placed at as great a distance from that as we are now from the other planets, we should not then perceive its motion.

HYLAS: I understand you; and must needs own you say things plausible enough. But, give me leave to put you in mind of one thing. Pray, Philonous, were you not formerly as positive that matter existed, as you are now that it does not?

PHILONOUS: I was. But here lies the difference. Before, my positiveness was founded, without examination, upon prejudice; but now, after inquiry, upon evidence.

HYLAS: After all, it seems our dispute is rather about words than things. We agree in the thing, but differ in the name. That we are affected with ideas from without is evident, and it is no less evident that there must be (I will not say archetypes, but) Powers without the mind, corresponding to those ideas. And, as these Powers cannot subsist by themselves, there is some subject of them necessarily to be admitted; which I call *matter*, and you call *spirit*. This is all the difference.

PHILONOUS: Pray, Hylas, is that powerful being, or subject of powers, extended?

HYLAS: It hath not extension; but it hath the power to raise in you the idea of extension.

PHILONOUS: It is therefore itself unextended?

HYLAS: I grant it.

PHILONOUS: Is it not also active?

HYLAS: Without doubt. Otherwise, how could we attribute powers to it?

PHILONOUS: Now let me ask you two questions: *First,* whether it be agreeable to the usage either of philosophers or others to give the name *matter* to an unextended active being? And, *secondly,* whether it be not ridiculously absurd to misapply names contrary to the common use of language?

HYLAS: Well then, let it not be called matter, since you will have it so, but some *third nature* distinct from matter and spirit. For what reason is there why you should call it spirit? Does not the notion of spirit imply that it is thinking, as well as active and unextended?

PHILONOUS: My reason is this: because I have a mind to have some notion of meaning in what I say: but I have no notion of any action distinct from volition, neither can I conceive volition to be anywhere but in a spirit: therefore, when I speak of an active being, I am obliged to mean a spirit. Beside, what can be plainer than that a thing which hath no ideas in itself cannot impart them to me, and, if it hath ideas, surely it must be a spirit. To make you comprehend the point still more clearly if it be possible,

I assert as well as you that, since we are affected from without, we must allow powers to be without, in a being distinct from ourselves. So far we are agreed. But then we differ as to the kind of this powerful being. I will have it to be spirit, you matter, or I know not what (I may add too, you know not what) third nature. Thus, I prove it to be spirit. From the effects I see produced, I conclude there are actions; and, because actions, volitions; and, because there are volitions, there must be a will. Again, the things I perceive must have an existence, they or their archetypes, out of my mind: but, being ideas, neither they nor their archetypes can exist otherwise than in an understanding, there is therefore an understanding. But will and understanding constitute in the strictest sense a mind or spirit. The powerful cause, therefore, of my ideas is in strict propriety of speech a *spirit*.

HYLAS: And now I warrant you think you have made the point very clear, little suspecting that what you advance leads directly to a contradiction. Is it not an absurdity to imagine any imperfection in God?

PHILONOUS: Without a doubt.

HYLAS: To suffer pain is an imperfection?

PHILONOUS: It is.

HYLAS: Are we not sometimes affected with pain and uneasiness by some other being?

PHILONOUS: We are.

HYLAS: And have you not said that being is a spirit, and is not that spirit God?

PHILONOUS: I grant it.

HYLAS: But you have asserted that whatever ideas we perceive from without are in the mind which affects us. The ideas, therefore, of pain and uneasiness are in God; or, in other words, God suffers pain: that is to say, there is an imperfection in the divine nature: which, you acknowledged, was absurd. So you are caught in a plain contradiction.

PHILONOUS: That God knows or understands all things, and that he knows, among other things, what pain is, even every sort of painful sensation, and what it is for His creatures to suffer pain, I make no question. But, that God, though he knows and sometimes causes painful sensations in us, can himself suffer pain, I positively deny. We, who are limited and dependent spirits, are liable to impressions of sense, the effects of an external agent, which, being produced against our wills, are sometimes painful and uneasy. But God, whom no external being can affect, who perceives nothing by sense as we do; whose will is absolute and independent, causing all things, and liable to be thwarted or resisted by nothing: it is evident, such a being as this can suffer nothing, nor be affected with any painful sensation, or indeed any sensation at all. We are chained to a body: that is to say, our perceptions are connected with corporeal motions. By the law of our nature, we are affected upon every alteration in the nervous parts of our sensible body; which sensible body, rightly considered, is nothing but a complexion of such qualities or ideas as have no existence distinct from being perceived by a mind. So that this connexion of sensations with corporeal motions means no more than a correspondence in the order of nature, between two sets of ideas, or things immediately perceivable. But God is a pure spirit, disengaged from all such sympathy, or natural ties. No corporeal motions are attended with the sensations of pain or pleasure in His mind. To know everything knowable, is certainly a perfection; but to endure or suffer, or feel anything by sense, is an imperfection. The former, I say, agrees to God, but not the latter. God knows, or hath ideas; but His ideas are not conveyed to him by sense, as ours are. Your not distinguishing, where there is so manifest a difference, makes you fancy you see an absurdity where there is none.

HYLAS: But, all this while you have not considered that the quantity of matter has been demonstrated to be proportioned to the gravity of bodies. And what can withstand demonstration?

PHILONOUS: Let me see how you demonstrate that point.

HYLAS: I lay it down for a principle, that the moments or quantities of motion in bodies are in a direct compounded reason of the velocities and quantities of matter contained in them. Hence, where the velocities are equal, it follows the moments are directly as the quantity of matter in each. But it is found by experience that all bodies (bating the small inequalities, arising from the resistance of the air) descend with an equal velocity; the motion therefore of descending bodies, and consequently their gravity, which is the cause or principle of that motion, is proportional to the quantity of matter; which was to be demonstrated.

PHILONOUS: You lay it down as a self-evident principle that the quantity of motion in any body is proportional to the velocity and *matter* taken together: and this is made use of to prove a proposition from whence the existence of *matter* is inferred. Pray is not this arguing in a circle?

HYLAS: In the premise I only mean that the motion is proportional to the velocity, jointly with the extension and solidity.

PHILONOUS: But, allowing this to be true, yet it will not thence follow that gravity is proportional to *matter,* in your philosophic sense of the word, except you take it for granted that unknown *substratum,* or whatever else you call it, is proportional to those sensible qualities; which to suppose is plainly begging the question. That there is magnitude and solidity, or resistance, perceived by sense, I readily grant, as likewise, that gravity may be proportional to those qualities I will not dispute. But that either these qualities as perceived by us, or the powers producing them, do exist in a *material substratum;* this is what I deny, and you indeed affirm, but, notwithstanding your demonstration, have not yet proved.

HYLAS: I shall insist no longer on that point. Do you think, however, you shall persuade me the natural philosophers have been dreaming all this while? Pray what becomes of all their hypotheses and explications of the *phenomena,* which suppose the existence of matter?

PHILONOUS: What mean you, Hylas, by the *phenomena?*

HYLAS: I mean the appearances which I perceive by my senses.

PHILONOUS: And the appearances perceived by sense, are they not ideas?

HYLAS: I have told you so a hundred times.

PHILONOUS: Therefore, to explain the phenomena, is, to show how we come to be affected with ideas, in that manner and order wherein they are imprinted on our senses. Is it not?

HYLAS: It is.

PHILONOUS: Now, if you can prove that any philosopher has explained the production of any one idea in our minds by the help of *matter,* I shall for ever acquiesce, and look on all that hath been said against it as nothing; but, if you cannot, it is vain to urge the explication of *phenomena.* That a being endowed with knowledge and will should produce or exhibit ideas is easily understood. But that a being which is utterly destitute of these faculties should be able to produce ideas, or in any sort to affect an intelligence, this I can never understand. This I say, though we had some positive conception of matter, though we knew its qualities, and could comprehend its existence, would yet be so far from explaining things, that it is itself the most inexplicable thing in the world. And yet, for all this, it will not follow that philosophers have been doing nothing; for, by observing and reasoning upon the connexion of ideas, they discover the laws and methods of nature, which is a part of knowledge both useful and entertaining.

HYLAS: After all, can it be supposed God would deceive all mankind? Do you imagine he would have induced the whole world to believe the being of matter, if there was no such thing?

PHILONOUS: That every epidemical opinion, arising from prejudice, or passion, or thoughtlessness, may be imputed to God, as the author of it, I believe you will not affirm. Whatsoever opinion we father on him, it must be either because he has discovered it to us by supernatural revelation; or because it is so evident to our natural faculties, which were framed and given us by God, that it is impossible we should withhold our assent from it. But where is the revelation? Or where is the evidence that extorts the belief of matter? Nay, how does it appear, that matter, taken for something distinct from what we perceive by our senses, is thought to exist by all mankind; or indeed, by any except a few philosophers, who do not know what they would be at? Your question supposes these points are clear; and, when you have cleared them, I shall think myself obliged to give you another answer. In the meantime, let it suffice. That I tell you, I do not suppose God has deceived mankind at all.

HYLAS: But the novelty, Philonous, the novelty! There lies the danger. New notions should always be discountenanced; they unsettle men's minds, and nobody knows where they will end.

PHILONOUS: Why the rejecting a notion that has no foundation, either in sense, or in reason, or in divine authority, should be thought to unsettle the belief of such opinions as are grounded on all or any of these, I cannot imagine. That innovations in government and religion are dangerous, and ought to be discountenanced, I freely own. But is there the like reason why they should be discouraged in philosophy? The making anything known which was unknown before is an innovation in knowledge: and, if all such innovations had been forbidden, men would have made a notable progress in the arts and sciences. But it is none of my business to plead for novelties and paradoxes. That the qualities we perceive are not on the objects: that we must not believe our senses: that we know nothing of the real nature of things, and can never be assured even of their existence: that real colours and sounds are nothing but certain unknown figures and motions: that motions are in themselves neither swift nor slow: that there are in bodies absolute extensions, without any particular magnitude or figure: that a thing stupid, thoughtless, and inactive, operates on a spirit: that the least particle of a body contains innumerable extended parts:—these are the novelties, these are the strange notions which shock the genuine uncorrupted judgment of all mankind; and being once admitted, embarrass the mind with endless doubts and difficulties. And it is against these and the like innovations I endeavour to vindicate common sense. It is true, in doing this, I may perhaps be obliged to use some *ambages,* and ways of speech not common. But, if my notions are once thoroughly understood, that which is most singular in them will, in effect, be found to amount to no more than this:—that it is absolutely impossible, and a plain contradiction, to suppose any unthinking being should exist without being perceived by a mind. And, if this notion be singular, it is a shame it should be so, at this time of day, and in a Christian country.

HYLAS: As for the difficulties other opinions may be liable to, those are out of the question. It is your business to defend your own opinion. Can anything be plainer than that you are for changing all things into ideas? You, I say, who are not ashamed to charge me with *scepticism.* This is so plain, there is no denying it.

PHILONOUS: You mistake me. I am not for changing things into ideas, but rather ideas into things; since those immediate objects of perception, which, according to you, are only appearances of things, I take to be the real things themselves.

HYLAS: Things! You may pretend what you please; but it is certain you leave us nothing but the empty forms of things, the outside only which strikes the senses.

PHILONOUS: What you call the empty forms and outside of things seem to me the very things themselves. Nor are they empty or incomplete, otherwise than upon your supposition—that matter is an essential part of all corporeal things. We both, therefore, agree in this, that we perceive only sensible forms: but herein we differ—you will have them to be empty appearances, I real beings. In short, you do not trust your senses, I do.

HYLAS: You say you believe your senses; and seem to applaud yourself that in this you agree with the vulgar. According to you, therefore, the true nature of a thing is discovered by the senses. If so, whence comes that disagreement? Why is not the same figure, and other sensible qualities, perceived all manner of ways? And why should we use a microscope the better to discover the true nature of a body, if it were discoverable to the naked eye?

PHILONOUS: Strictly speaking, Hylas, we do not see the same object that we feel; neither is the same object perceived by the microscope which was by the naked eye. But, in case every variation was thought sufficient to constitute a new kind of individual, the endless number of confusion of names would render language impracticable. Therefore, to avoid this, as well as other inconveniences which are obvious upon a little thought, men combine together several ideas, apprehended by divers senses, or by the same sense at different times, or in different circumstances, but observed, however, to have some connexion in nature, either with respect to co-existence or succession; all which they refer to one name, and consider as one thing. Hence it follows that when I examine, by my other senses, a thing I have seen, it is not in order to understand better the same object which I had perceived by sight, the object of one sense not being perceived by the other senses. And, when I look through a microscope, it is not that I may perceive more clearly what I perceived already with my bare eyes; the object perceived by the glass being quite different from the former. But, in both cases, my aim is only to know what ideas are connected together; and the more a man knows of the connexion of ideas, the more he is said to know of the nature of things. What, therefore, if our ideas are variable; what if our senses are not in all circumstances affected with the same appearances. It will not thence follow they are not to be trusted; or that they are inconsistent either with themselves or anything else: except it be with your preconceived notion of (I know not what) one single, unchanged, unperceivable, real nature, marked by each name. Which prejudice seems to have taken its rise from not rightly understanding the common language of men, speaking of several distinct ideas as united into one thing by the mind. And, indeed, there is cause to suspect several erroneous conceits of the philosophers are owing to the same original: while they began to build their schemes not so much on notions as on words, which were framed by the vulgar, merely for conveniency and dispatch in the common actions of life, without any regard to speculation.

HYLAS: Methinks I apprehend your meaning.

PHILONOUS: It is your opinion the ideas we perceive by our senses are not real things, but images or copies of them. Our knowledge, therefore, is no farther real than as our ideas are the true representations of those originals. But, as these supposed originals are in themselves unknown, it is impossible to know how far our ideas resemble them; or whether they resemble them at all. We cannot, therefore, be sure we have any real knowledge. Farther, as our ideas are perpetually varied, without any change in the supposed real things, it necessarily follows they cannot all be true copies of them: or, if some are and others are not, it is impossible to distinguish the former from the latter. And this plunges us yet deeper in uncertainty. Again, when we consider the point, we cannot conceive how any idea, or anything like an idea, should have an absolute existence out of a mind: nor consequently, according to you, how there should be any real thing in nature. The result of all which is that we are thrown into the most hopeless and abandoned *scepticism.* Now, give me leave to ask you, *first,* whether your referring ideas to certain absolutely existing unperceived substances, as their originals, be not the source of all this *scepticism? Secondly,* whether you are informed, either by sense or reason, of the existence of those unknown originals? And, in case you are not, whether it be not absurd to suppose them? *Thirdly,* whether, upon inquiry, you find there is anything distinctly conceived or meant by the *absolute or external existence of unperceiving substances? Lastly,* whether, the premises considered, it be not the wisest way to follow nature, trust your senses, and, laying aside all anxious thought about unknown natures or substances, admit with the vulgar those for real things which are perceived by the senses?

HYLAS: For the present, I have no inclination to the answering part. I would much rather see how you can get over what follows. Pray are not the objects perceived by the senses of one, likewise perceivable to others present? If there were a hundred more here, they would all see the garden, the trees, and flowers, as I see them. But they are not in the same manner affected with the ideas I frame in my imagination. Does not this make a difference between the former sort of objects and the latter?

PHILONOUS: I grant it does. Nor have I ever denied a difference between the objects of sense and those of imagination. But what would you infer from thence? You cannot say that sensible objects exist unperceived, because they are perceived by many.

HYLAS: I own I can make nothing of that objection: but it hath led me into another. Is it not your opinion that by our senses we perceive only the ideas existing in our minds?

PHILONOUS: It is.

HYLAS: But the same idea which is in my mind cannot be in yours, or in any other mind. Does it not therefore follow, from your principles, that no two can see the same thing? And is not this highly absurd?

PHILONOUS: If the term *same* be taken in the vulgar acceptation, it is certain (and not at all repugnant to the principles I maintain) that different persons may perceive the same thing; or the same thing or idea exist in different minds. Words are of arbitrary imposition, and since men are used to apply the word *same* where no distinction or variety is perceived, and I do not pretend to alter their perceptions, it follows that, as men have said before, *several saw the same thing,* so they may, upon like occasions, still continue to use the same phrase, without any deviation either from propriety of language, or the truth of things. But, if the term *same* be used in the acceptation of philosophers, who pretend to an abstracted notion of identity, then, according to their sundry definitions of this notion (for it is not yet agreed wherein that philosophic identity consists), it may or may not be possible for divers persons to perceive the same thing. But whether philosophers shall think fit to call a thing the *same* or no, is, I conceive, of small importance. Let us suppose several men together, all endued with the same faculties, and consequently affected in like sort by their senses, and who had yet never known the use of language; they would, without question, agree in their perceptions. Though perhaps, when they came to the use of speech, some regarding the uniformness of what was perceived, might call it the *same* thing: others, especially regarding the diversity of persons who perceived, might choose the denomination of *different* things. But who sees not that all the dispute is about a word? To wit, whether what is perceived by different persons may yet have the term *same* applied to it? Or, suppose a house, whose walls or outward shell remaining unaltered, the chambers are all pulled down, and new ones built in their place; and that you should call this the *same,* and I should say it was not the *same* house:—would we not, for all this, perfectly agree in our thoughts of the house, considered in itself? And would not all the difference consist in a sound? If you should say, We differed in our notions; for that you superadded to your idea of the house the simple abstracted idea of identity, whereas I did not; I would tell you, I know not what you mean by the *abstracted idea of identity;* and should desire you to look into your own thoughts, and be sure you understood yourself.—Why so silent, Hylas? Are you not yet satisfied men may dispute about identity and diversity, without any real difference in their thoughts and opinions, abstracted from names? Take this farther reflexion with you—that whether matter be allowed to exist or no, the case is exactly the same as to the point in hand. For the materialists themselves acknowledge what we immediately perceive by our senses to be our own ideas. Your difficulty, therefore, that no two see the same thing, makes equally against the materialists and me.

HYLAS: But they suppose an external archetype, to which referring their several ideas they may truly be said to perceive the same thing.

PHILONOUS: And (not to mention your having discarded those archetypes) so may you suppose an external archetype on my principles; *external,* I mean, to your own mind: though indeed it must be supposed to exist in that mind which comprehends all things; but then, this serves all the ends of identity, as well as if it existed out of a mind. And I am sure you yourself will not say it is less intelligible.

HYLAS: You have indeed clearly satisfied me—either that there is no difficulty at bottom in this point; or, if there be, that it makes equally against both opinions.

PHILONOUS: But that which makes equally against two contradictory opinions can be a proof against neither.

HYLAS: I acknowledge it. But, after all, Philonous, when I consider the substance of what you advance against *scepticism,* it amounts to no more than this:—We are sure that we really see, hear, feel; in a word, that we are affected with sensible impressions.

PHILONOUS: And how are we concerned any farther? I see this *cherry,* I feel it, I taste it: and I am sure *nothing* cannot be seen, or felt, or tasted: it is therefore *real.* Take away the sensations of softness, moisture, redness, tartness, and you take away the *cherry,* since it is not a being distinct from sensations. A *cherry,* I say, is nothing but a congeries of sensible impressions, or ideas perceived by various senses: which ideas are united into one thing (or have one name given them) by the mind, because they are observed to attend each other. Thus, when the palate is affected with such a particular taste, the sight is affected with a red colour, the touch with roundness, softness, &c. Hence, when I see, and feel, and taste, in such sundry certain manners, I am sure the *cherry* exists, or is real; its reality being in my opinion nothing abstracted from those sensations. But if by the word *cherry* you mean an unknown nature, distinct from all those sensible qualities, and by its existence something distinct from its being perceived; then, indeed, I own, neither you nor I, nor any one else, can be sure it exists.

HYLAS: But, what would you say, Philonous, if I should bring the very same reasons against the existence of sensible things in a mind, which you have offered against their existing in a material *substratum?*

PHILONOUS: When I see your reasons, you shall hear what I have to say to them.

HYLAS: Is the mind extended or unextended?

PHILONOUS: Unextended, without doubt.

HYLAS: Do you say the things you perceive are in your mind?

PHILONOUS: They are.

HYLAS: Again, have I not heard you speak of sensible impressions?

PHILONOUS: I believe you may.

HYLAS: Explain to me now, O Philonous! how it is possible there should be room for all those trees and houses to exist in your mind. Can extended things be contained in that which is unextended? Or, are we to imagine impressions made on a thing void of all solidity? You cannot say objects are in your mind, as books in your study: or that things are imprinted on it, as the figure of a seal upon wax. In what sense, therefore, are we to understand those expressions? Explain me this if you can: and I shall then be able to answer all those queries you formerly put to me about my *substratum.*

PHILONOUS: Look you, Hylas, when I speak of objects as existing in the mind, or imprinted on the senses, I would not be understood in the gross literal sense, as when bodies are said to exist in a place, or a seal to make an impression upon wax. My meaning is only that the mind comprehends or perceives them; and that it is affected from without, or by some being distinct from itself. This is my explication of your difficulty; and how it can serve to make your tenet of an unperceiving material substratum intelligible, I would fain know.

HYLAS: Nay, if that be all, I confess I do not see what use can be made of it. But are you not guilty of some abuse of language in this?

PHILONOUS: None at all. It is no more than common custom, which you know is the rule of language, hath authorised: nothing being more usual, than for philosophers to speak of the immediate objects of the understanding as things existing in the mind. Nor is there anything in this but what is conformable to the general analogy of language; most part of the mental operations being signified by words borrowed from sensible things; as is plain in the terms *comprehend, reflect, discourse,* &c., which, being applied to the mind, must not be taken in their gross, original sense.

HYLAS: You have, I own, satisfied me in this point. But there still remains one great difficulty, which I know not how you will get over. And, indeed, it is of such importance that if you could solve all others, without being able to find a solution for this, you must never expect to make me a proselyte to your principles.

PHILONOUS: Let me know this mighty difficulty.

HYLAS: The Scripture account of the creation is what appears to me utterly irreconcilable with your notions. Moses tells us of a creation: a creation of what? Of ideas? No, certainly, but of things, of real things, solid corporeal substances. Bring your principles to agree with this, and I shall perhaps agree with you.

PHILONOUS: Moses mentions the sun, moon, and stars, earth and sea, plants and animals. That all these do really exist, and were in the beginning created by God, I make no question. If by *ideas* you mean fictions and fancies of the mind, then these are no ideas. If by *ideas* you mean immediate objects of the understanding, or sensible things, which cannot exist unperceived, or out of a mind, then these things are ideas. But whether you do or do not call them *ideas,* it matters little. The difference is only about a name. And, whether that name be retained or rejected, the sense, the truth, and reality of things continues the same. In common talk, the objects of our senses are not termed *ideas,* but *things.* Call them so still: provided you do not attribute to them any absolute external existence, and I shall never quarrel with you for a word. The creation, therefore, I allow to have been a creation of things, of *real* things. Neither is this in the least inconsistent with my principles, as is evident from what I have now said; and would have been evident to you without this, if you had not forgotten what had been so often said before. But as for solid corporeal substances, I desire you to show where Moses makes any mention of them; and, if they should be mentioned by him, or any other inspired writer, it would still be incumbent on you to show those words were not taken in the vulgar acceptation, for things falling under our senses, but in the philosophic acceptation, for matter, or an unknown quiddity, with an absolute existence. When you have proved these points, then (and not till then) may you bring the authority of Moses into our dispute.

HYLAS: It is in vain to dispute about a point so clear. I am content to refer it to your own conscience. Are you not satisfied there is some peculiar repugnancy between the Mosaic account of the creation and your notions?

PHILONOUS: If all possible sense which can be put on the first chapter of Genesis may be conceived as consistently with my principles as any other, then it has no peculiar repugnancy with them. But there is no sense you may not as well conceive, believing as I do. Since, besides spirits, all you conceive are ideas; and the existence of these I do not deny. Neither do you pretend they exist without the mind.

HYLAS: Pray let me see any sense you can understand it in.

PHILONOUS: Why, I imagine that if I had been present at the creation, I should have seen things produced into being—that is become perceptible—in the order prescribed by the sacred historian. I never before believed the Mosaic account of the creation, and now find no alteration in my manner of believing it. When things are said to begin or end their existence, we do not mean this with regard to God, but His creatures. All objects are eternally known by God, or, which is the same thing, have an eternal existence in His mind: but when things, before imperceptible to creatures, are, by a decree of God, perceptible to them, then are they said to begin a relative existence, with respect to created minds. Upon reading therefore the Mosaic account of the creation, I understand that the several parts of the world became gradually perceivable to finite spirits, endowed with proper faculties; so that, whoever such were present, they were in truth perceived by them. This is the literal obvious sense suggested to me by the words of the Holy Scripture: in which is included no mention, or no thought, either of *substratum,* instrument, occasion, or absolute existence. And, upon inquiry, I doubt not it will be found that most plain honest men, who believe the creation, never think of those things any more than I. What metaphysical sense you may understand it in, you only can tell.

HYLAS: But, Philonous, you do not seem to be aware that you allow created things, in the beginning, only a relative, and consequently hypothetical being: that is to say, upon supposition there were men to perceive them; without which they have no actuality of absolute existence, wherein creation might terminate. Is it not, therefore, according to you, plainly impossible the creation of any inanimate creatures should precede that of man? And is not this directly contrary to the Mosaic account?

PHILONOUS: In answer to that, I say, *first,* created beings might begin to exist in the mind of other created intelligences, beside men. You will not therefore be able to prove any contradiction between Moses and my notions, unless you first show there was no other order of finite created spirits in being, before man. I say farther, in case we conceive the creation, as we should at this time, a parcel of plants or vegetables of all sorts produced, by an invisible Power, in a desert where nobody was present—that this way of explaining or conceiving it is consistent with my principles, since they deprive you of nothing, either sensible or imaginable; that it exactly suits with the common, natural, and undebauched notions of mankind; that it manifests the dependence of all things on God; and consequently hath all the good effect or influence, which it is possible that important article of our faith should have in making men humble, thankful, and resigned to their great creator. I say, moreover, that, in this naked conception of things, divested of words, there will not be found any notion of what you call the *actuality of absolute existence*. You may indeed raise a dust with those terms, and so lengthen our dispute to no purpose. But I entreat you calmly to look into your own thoughts, and then tell me if they are not a useless and unintelligible jargon.

HYLAS: I own I have no very clear notion annexed to them. But what say you to this? Do you not make the existence of sensible things consist in their being in a mind? And were not all things eternally in the mind of God? Did they not therefore exist from all eternity, according to you? And how could that which was eternal be created in time? Can anything be clearer or better connected than this?

PHILONOUS: And are not you too of opinion, that God knew all things from eternity?

HYLAS: I am.

PHILONOUS: Consequently they always had a being in the divine intellect.

HYLAS: This I acknowledge.

PHILONOUS: By your own confession, therefore, nothing is new, or begins to be, in respect of the mind of God. So we are agreed in that point.

HYLAS: What shall we make then of the creation?

PHILONOUS: May we not understand it to have been entirely in respect of finite spirits; so that things, with regard to us, may properly be said to begin their existence, or be created, when God decreed they should become perceptible to intelligent creatures, in that order and manner which he then established, and we now call the laws of nature? You may call this a *relative,* or *hypothetical existence* if you please. But, so long as it supplies us with the most natural, obvious, and literal sense of the Mosaic history of the creation; so long as it answers all the religious ends of that great article; in a word, so long as you can assign no other sense or meaning in its stead; why should we reject this? Is it to comply with a ridiculous sceptical humour of making everything nonsense and unintelligible? I am sure you cannot say it is for the glory of God. For, allowing it to be a thing possible and conceivable that the corporeal world should have an absolute existence extrinsical to the mind of God, as well as to the minds of all created spirits; yet how could this set forth either the immensity or omniscience of the Deity, or the necessary and immediate dependence of all things on him? Nay, would it not rather seem to derogate from those attributes?

HYLAS: Well, but as to this decree of God's, for making things perceptible, what say you, Philonous? Is it not plain, God did either execute that decree from all eternity or at some certain time began to will what he had not actually willed before, but only designed to will? If the former, then there could be no creation, or beginning of existence, in finite things. If the latter, then we must acknowledge something new to befall the Deity; which implies a sort of change: and all change argues imperfection.

PHILONOUS: Pray consider what you are doing. Is it not evident this objection concludes equally against a creation in any sense; nay, against every other act of the Deity, discoverable by the light of nature? None of which can we conceive, otherwise than as performed in time, and having a beginning. God is a being of transcendent and unlimited perfections: His nature, therefore, is incomprehensible to finite spirits. It is not, therefore, to be expected that any man, whether *materialist* or *immaterialist,* should have exactly just notions of the Deity, His attributes, and ways of operation. If then you would infer anything against me, your difficulty must not be drawn from the inadequateness of our conceptions of the divine nature, which is unavoidable on any scheme; but from the denial of matter, of which there is not one word, directly or indirectly, in what you have now objected.

HYLAS: I must acknowledge the difficulties you are concerned to clear are such only as arise from the non-existence of matter, and are peculiar to that notion. So far you are in the right. But I cannot by any means bring myself to think there is no such peculiar repugnancy between the creation and your opinion; though indeed where to fix it, I do not distinctly know.

PHILONOUS: What would you have? Do I not acknowledge a twofold state of things—the one ectypal or natural, the other archetypal and eternal? The former was created in time; the latter existed from everlasting in the mind of God. Is not this agreeable to the common notions of divines? or, is any more than this necessary in order to conceive the creation? But you suspect some peculiar repugnancy, though you know not where it lies. To take away all possibility of scruple in the case, do but consider this one point. Either you are not able to conceive the creation on any hypothesis whatsoever; and, if so, there is no ground for dislike or complaint against any particular opinion on that score: or you are able to conceive it; and, if so, why not on my principles, since thereby nothing conceivable is taken away? You have all along been allowed the full scope of sense, imagination, and reason. Whatever, therefore, you could before apprehend, either immediately or mediately by your senses, or by ratiocination from your senses; whatever you could perceive, imagine, or understand, remains still with you. If, therefore, the notion you have of the creation by other principles be intelligible, you have it still upon mine; if it be not intelligible, I conceive it to be no notion at all; and so there is no loss of it. And indeed it seems to me very plain that the supposition of matter, that is a thing perfectly unknown and inconceivable, cannot serve to make us conceive anything. And, I hope it need not be proved to you that if the existence of matter does not make the creation conceivable, the creation's being without it inconceivable can be no objection against its non-existence.

HYLAS: I confess, Philonous, you have almost satisfied me in this point of the creation.

PHILONOUS: I would fain know why you are not quite satisfied. You tell me indeed of a repugnancy between the Mosaic history and immaterialism: but you know not where it lies. Is this reasonable, Hylas? Can you expect I should solve a difficulty without knowing what it is? But, to pass by all that, would not a man think you were assured there is no repugnancy between the received notions of materialists and the inspired writings?

HYLAS: And so I am.

PHILONOUS: Ought the historical part of Scripture to be understood in a plain obvious sense, or in a sense which is metaphysical and out of the way?

HYLAS: In the plain sense, doubtless.

PHILONOUS: When Moses speaks of herbs, earth, water, &c. as having been created by God; think you not the sensible things commonly signified by those words are suggested to every unphilosophical reader?

HYLAS: I cannot help thinking so.

PHILONOUS: And are not all ideas, or things perceived by sense, to be denied a real existence by the doctrine of the materialist?

HYLAS: This I have already acknowledged.

PHILONOUS: The creation, therefore, according to them, was not the creation of things sensible, which have only a relative being, but of certain unknown natures, which have an absolute being, wherein creation might terminate?

HYLAS: True.

PHILONOUS: Is it not therefore evident the assertors of matter destroy the plain obvious sense of Moses, with which their notions are utterly inconsistent; and instead of it obtrude on us I know not what; something equally unintelligible to themselves and me?

HYLAS: I cannot contradict you.

PHILONOUS: Moses tells us of a creation. A creation of what? of unknown quiddities, of occasions, or *substratum?* No, certainly; but of things obvious to the senses. You must first reconcile this with your notions, if you expect I should be reconciled to them.

HYLAS: I see you can assault me with my own weapons.

PHILONOUS: Then as to *absolute existence;* was there ever known a more jejune notion than that? Something it is so abstracted and unintelligible that you have frankly owned you could not conceive it, much less explain anything by it. But allowing matter to exist, and the notion of absolute existence to be clear as light; yet, was this ever known to make the creation more credible? Nay, hath it not furnished the atheists and infidels of all ages with the most plausible arguments against a creation? That a corporeal substance, which hath an absolute existence without the minds of spirits, should be produced out of nothing, by the mere will of a spirit, hath been looked upon as a thing so contrary to all reason, so impossible and absurd, that not only the most celebrated among the ancients, but even divers modern and Christian philosophers have thought matter co-eternal with the Deity. Lay these things together, and then judge you whether materialism disposes men to believe the creation of things.

HYLAS: I own, Philonous, I think it does not. This of the *creation* is the last objection I can think of; and I must needs own it hath been sufficiently answered as well as the rest. Nothing now remains to be overcome but a sort of unaccountable backwardness that I find in myself towards your notions.

PHILONOUS: When a man is swayed, he knows not why, to one side of the question, can this, think you, be anything else but the effect of prejudice, which never fails to attend old and rooted notions? And indeed in this respect I cannot deny the belief of matter to have very much the advantage over the contrary opinion, with men of a learned education.

HYLAS: I confess it seems to be as you say.

PHILONOUS: As a balance, therefore, to this weight of prejudice, let us throw into the scale the great advantages that arise from the belief of immaterialism, both in regard to religion and human learning. The being of a God, and incorruptibility of the soul, those great articles of religion, are they not proved with the clearest and most immediate evidence? When I say the being of a *God,* I do not mean an obscure general cause of things, whereof we have no conception, but *God,* in the strict and proper sense of the word. A being whose spirituality, omnipresence, providence, omniscience, infinite power and goodness, are as conspicuous as the existence of sensible things, of which (nothwithstanding the fallacious pretences and affected scruples of *sceptics*) there is no more reason to doubt than of our own being. Then, with relation to human sciences. In natural philosophy, what intricacies, what obscurities, what contradictions hath the belief of matter led men into! To say nothing of the numberless disputes about its extent, continuity, homogeneity, gravity, divisibility, &c.—do they not pretend to explain all things by bodies operating on bodies, according to the laws of motion? And yet, are they able to comprehend how one body should move another? Nay, admitting there was no difficulty in reconciling the notion of an inert being with a cause, or in conceiving how an accident might pass from one body to another; yet, by all their strained thoughts and extravagant suppositions, have they been able to reach the mechanical production of any one animal or vegetable body? Can they account, by the laws of motion, for sounds, tastes, smells, or colours; or for the regular course of things? Have they accounted, by physical principles, for the aptitude and contrivance even of the most inconsiderable parts of the universe? But, laying aside matter and corporeal causes, and admitting only the efficiency of an all-perfect mind, are not all the effects of nature easy and intelligible? If the *phenomena* are nothing else but *ideas;* God is a *spirit,* but matter an unintelligent, unperceiving being. If they demonstrate an unlimited power in their cause; God is active and omnipotent, but matter an inert mass. If the order regularity, and usefulness of them can never be sufficiently admired; God is infinitely wise and provident, but matter destitute of all contrivance and design. These surely are great advantages in *physics.* Not to mention that the apprehension of a distant Deity naturally disposes men to a negligence in their *moral* actions; which they would be more cautious of, in case they thought him immediately present, and acting on their minds, without the interposition of matter, or unthinking second causes. Then in *metaphysics:* what difficulties concerning entity in abstract, substantial forms, hylarchic principles, plastic natures, substance and accident, principle of individuation, possibility of matter's thinking, origin of ideas, the manner how two independent substances so widely different as *spirit* and *matter,* should mutually operate on each other? What difficulties, I say, and endless disquisitions, concerning these and innumerable other the like points, do we escape, by supposing only spirits and ideas? Even the *mathematics* themselves, if we take away the absolute existence of extended things, become much more clear and easy; the most shocking paradoxes and intricate speculations in those sciences depending on the infinite divisibility of finite extension; which depends on that supposition. But what need is there to insist on the particular sciences? Is not that opposition to all science whatsoever, that frenzy of the ancient and modern *sceptics,* built on the same foundation? Or can you produce so much as one argument against the reality of corporeal things, or in behalf of that avowed utter ignorance of their natures, which does not suppose their reality to consist in an external absolute existence? Upon this supposition, indeed, the objections from the change of colours in a pigeon's neck, or the appearance of the broken oar in the water, must be allowed to have weight. But these and the like objections vanish, if we do not maintain the being of absolute external originals, but place the reality of things in ideas, fleeting indeed, and changeable; however, not changed at random, but according to the fixed order of nature. For, herein consists that constancy and truth of things which secures all the concerns of life, and distinguishes that which is *real* from the irregular visions of the fancy.

HYLAS: I agree to all you have now said, and must own that nothing can incline me to embrace your opinion more than the advantages I see it is attended with. I am by nature lazy; and this would be a mighty abridgment in knowledge. What doubts, what hypotheses, what labyrinths of amusement, what fields of disputation, what an ocean of false learning, may be avoided by that single notion of *immaterialism!*

PHILONOUS: After all, is there anything farther remaining to be done? You may remember you promised to embrace that opinion which upon examination should appear most agreeable to common sense and remote from *scepticism.* This, by your own confession, is that which denies matter, or the absolute existence of corporeal things. Nor is this all; the same notion has been proved several ways, viewed in different lights, pursued in its consequences, and all objections against it cleared. Can there be a greater evidence of its truth? Or is it possible it should have all the marks of a true opinion and yet be false?

HYLAS: I own myself entirely satisfied for the present in all respects. But, what security can I have that I shall still continue the same full assent to your opinion, and that no unthought-of objection or difficulty will occur hereafter?

PHILONOUS: Pray, Hylas, do you in other cases, when a point is once evidently proved, withhold your consent on account of objections or difficulties it may be liable to? Are the difficulties that attend the doctrine of incommensurable quantities, of the angle of contact, of the asymptotes to curves, or the like, sufficient to make you hold out against mathematical demonstration? Or will you disbelieve the Providence of God, because there may be some particular things which you know not how to reconcile with it? If there are difficulties attending *immaterialism,* there are at the same time direct and evident proofs of it. But for the existence of matter there is not one proof, and far more numerous and insurmountable objections lie against it. But where are those mighty difficulties you insist on? Alas! you know not where or what they are; something which may possibly occur hereafter. If this be a sufficient pretence for withholding your full assent, you should never yield it to any proposition, how free soever from exceptions, how clearly and solidly soever demonstrated.

HYLAS: You have satisfied me, Philonous.

PHILONOUS: But, to arm you against all future objections, do but consider: That which bears equally hard on two contradictory opinions can be proof against neither. Whenever, therefore, any difficulty occurs, try if you can find a solution for it on the hypothesis of the *materialists.* Be not deceived by words; but sound your own thoughts. And in case you cannot conceive it easier by the help of *materialism,* it is plain it can be no objection against *immaterialism.* Had you proceeded all along by this rule, you would probably have spared yourself abundance of trouble in objecting; since of all your difficulties I challenge you to show one that is explained by matter: nay, which is not more unintelligible with than without that supposition; and consequently makes rather *against* than *for* it. You should consider, in each particular, whether the difficulty arises from the *non-existence of matter.* If it does not, you might as well argue from the infinite divisibility of extension against the divine prescience, as from such a difficulty against *immaterialism.* And yet, upon recollection, I believe you will find this to have been often, if not always, the case. You should likewise take heed not to argue on a *petitio principii.* One is apt to say, the unknown substances ought to be esteemed real things, rather than the ideas in our minds: and who can tell but the unthinking external substance may concur, as a cause or instrument, in the productions of our ideas? But is not this proceeding on a supposition that there are such external substances? And to suppose this is it not begging the question? But, above all things, you should beware of imposing on yourself by that vulgar sophism which is called *ignoratio elenchi.* You talked often as if you thought I maintained the non-existence of Sensible Things. Whereas in truth no one can be more thoroughly assured of their existence than I am. And it is you who doubt; I should have said, positively deny it. Everything that is seen, felt, heard, or any way perceived by the senses, is, on the principles I embrace, a real being; but not on yours. Remember, the matter you contend for is an unknown somewhat (if indeed it may be termed *somewhat*), which is quite stripped of all sensible qualities, and can neither be perceived by sense, nor apprehended by the mind. Remember I say, that it is not any object which is hard or soft, hot or cold, blue or white, round or square, &c. For all these things I affirm do exist. Though indeed I deny they have an existence distinct from being perceived; or that they exist out of all minds whatsoever. Think on these points; let them be attentively considered and still kept in view. Otherwise you will not comprehend the state of the question; without which your objections will always be wide of the mark, and, instead of mine, may possibly be directed (as more than once they have been) against your own notions.

HYLAS: I must needs own, Philonous, nothing seems to have kept me from agreeing with you more than this same *mistaking the question.* In denying matter, at first glimpse I am tempted to imagine you deny the things we see and feel: but, upon reflexion, find there is no ground for it. What think you, therefore, of retaining the name *matter,* and applying it to sensible things? This may be done without any change in your sentiments: and, believe me, it would be a means of reconciling them to some persons who may be more shocked at an innovation in words than in opinion.

PHILONOUS: With all my heart: retain the word *matter,* and apply it to the objects of sense, if you please; provided you do not attribute to them any subsistence distinct from their being perceived. I shall never quarrel with you for an expression. *Matter,* or *material substance,* are terms introduced by philosophers; and, as used by them, imply a sort of independency, or a subsistence distinct from being perceived by a mind: but are never used by common people; or, if ever, it is to signify the immediate objects of sense. One would think, therefore, so long as the names of all particular things, with the terms *sensible, substance, body, stuff,* and the like, are retained, the word *matter* should be never missed in common talk. And in philosophical discourses it seems the best way to leave it quite out: since there is not, perhaps, any one thing that hath more favoured and strengthened the depraved bent of the mind towards Atheism than the use of that general confused term.

HYLAS: Well but, Philonous, since I am content to give up the notion of an unthinking substance exterior to the mind, I think you ought not to deny me the privilege of using the word *matter* as I please, and annexing it to a collection of sensible qualities subsisting only in the mind. I freely own there is no other substance, in a strict sense, than *spirit.* But I have been so long accustomed to the term *matter* that I know not how to part with it: to say, there is no matter in the world, is still shocking to me. Whereas to say, there is no *matter,* if by that term be meant an unthinking substance existing without the mind; but if by matter is meant some sensible thing, whose existence consists in being perceived, then there is matter: this distinction gives it quite another turn; and men will come into your notions with small difficulty, when they are proposed in that manner. For, after all, the controversy about *matter* in the strict acceptation of it, lies altogether between you and the philosophers: whose principles, I acknowledge, are not near so natural, or so agreeable to the common sense of mankind, and Holy Scripture, as yours. There is nothing we either desire or shun but as it makes, or is apprehended to make, some part of our happiness or misery. But what has happiness or misery, joy or grief, pleasure or pain, to do with absolute existence; or with unknown entities, abstracted from all relation to us? It is evident, things regard us only as they are pleasing or displeasing: and they can please or displease only so far forth as they are perceived. Farther, therefore, we are not concerned, and thus far you leave things as you found them. Yet still there is something new in this doctrine. It is plain, I do not now think with the philosophers; nor yet altogether with the vulgar. I would know how the case stands in that respect; precisely, what you have added to, or altered in my former notions.

PHILONOUS: I do not pretend to be a setter-up of new notions. My endeavours tend only to unite, and place in a clearer light, that truth which was before shared between the vulgar and the philosophers:—the former being of opinion, that *those things they immediately perceive are the real things;* and the latter, that *the things immediately perceived are ideas, which exist only in the mind.* Which two notions put together, do, in effect, constitute the substance of what I advance.

HYLAS: I have been a long time distrusting my senses: methought I saw things by a dim light and through false glasses. Now the glasses are removed and a new light breaks in upon my understanding. I am clearly convinced that I see things in their native forms, and am no longer in pain about their *unknown natures* or *absolute existence.* This is the state I find myself in at present; though, indeed, the course that brought me to it I do not yet thoroughly comprehend. You set out upon the same principles that Academics, Cartesians, and the like sects usually do; and for a long time it looked as if you were advancing their philosophical *scepticism:* but, in the end, your conclusions are directly opposite to theirs.

PHILONOUS: You see, Hylas, the water of yonder fountain, how it is forced upwards, in a round column, to a certain height; at which it breaks, and falls back into the basin from whence it rose: its ascent, as well as descent, proceeding from the same uniform law or principle of *gravitation.* Just so, the same principles which, at first view, lead to *scepticism,* pursued to a certain point, bring men back to common sense.